Identities
and Issues
in Literature

Identities
and Issues
in Literature

Volume 2
Emigration and immigration – *On These I Stand*

Editor
David Peck
California State University, Long Beach

Project Editor
Eric Howard

Salem Press, Inc.
Pasadena, California   Englewood Cliffs, New Jersey

Managing Editor: Christina J. Moose
Project Editor: Eric Howard   *Production Editor:* Joyce I. Buchea
Acquisitions Editor: Mark Rehn   *Proofreading Supervisor:* Yasmine A. Cordoba
Research Supervisor: Jeffry Jensen   *Page Layout and Graphics:* James Hutson
Photograph Editor: Karrie Hyatt   *Data Entry:* William Zimmerman

Library of Congress Cataloging-in-Publication Data

Identities and issues in literature / editor, David Peck; project editor, Eric Howard.
    p.   cm.
  Includes bibliographical references and index.
  ISBN 0-89356-920-8 (set : alk. paper). — ISBN 0-89356-922-4 (v. 2 : alk. paper)
  1. American literature—Minority authors—Dictionaries.   2. Literature and society—North America—Dictionaries.
3. Canadian literature—Minority authors—Dictionaries.   4. Social problems in literature—Dictionaries.   5. Group identity in literature—Dictionaries.   6. Ethnic groups in literature—Dictionaries.   7. Minorities in literature—Dictionaries.   8. North America—Literatures—Dictionaries.   I. Peck, David R.   II. Howard, Eric, 1961-
PS153.M56I34   1997
810.9'920693—dc21
                                                                    97-11951
                                                                    CIP

First Printing

Contents

CONTENTS

CONTENTS

Identities
and Issues
in Literature

Emigration and immigration

IDENTITIES: African American; European American; world

Much North American literature has been written by or about immigrants. Additionally, a significant number of North American authors have emigrated to other continents and written about their adopted homes.

Native Americans are only a small percentage of the population of North America, so it can be argued that virtually all North American literature has been written by immigrants from other continents. Chroniclers of the founding of the English colonies in the 1500's and 1600's were John White, John Smith, and William Bradford. The best collection is that of Richard Hakluyt, entitled *Divers Voyages Touching the Discovery of America* (1582). The Puritans Anne Bradstreet and Edward Taylor came in the seventeenth century from England to New England, where both wrote poetry. Another poet, Phillis Wheatley, was taken as a slave to Boston from Africa in the eighteenth century. England was denounced before the Revolutionary War by native son Thomas Paine, an immigrant to Virginia.

Immigrants

There were some voyage narratives written in French also. Jesuit missionaries to North America in the seventeenth century wrote reports in French that have come to be known as the Jesuit relations. These missionaries were great scholars and produced dictionaries and religious literature

Immigration Milestones

1582	Richard Hakluyt's *Divers Voyages Touching the Discovery of America*.	1908	The Gentlemen's Agreement restricts the immigration of Japanese laborers. Provisions of the agreement allow for picture brides.
1782	Michel-Guillaume-Jean de Crèvecœur's *Letters from an American Farmer*.	1913	Willa Cather's *O Pioneers!*
1790	Naturalization Statute establishes two-year residency for naturalization.	1915	Literacy test passed by Congress over President Wilson's veto. Period of anti-immigrant backlash.
1801	Naturalization Act changes residency for naturalization to five years.	1918	Willa Cather's *My Ántonia*.
1848	Treaty of Guadalupe Hidalgo signed after Mexican-American War, transferring about half of Mexico's territory to the United States, making a large number of Mexicans de facto immigrants.	1925	Border Patrol established.
		1927	O. E. Rölvaag's *I de dage* (1924) and *Riket grundlægges* (1925), translated together as *Giants in the Earth: A Saga of the Prairie*.
1850-1882	Chinese immigration encouraged because of labor shortages.	1942	Bracero program established; brings farmworkers into United States to work at low wages.
1864	Immigration Act encourages immigration to meet the North's need for troops in the Civil War.	1952	McCarran-Walter Immigration and Nationality Act is passed, providing for barring persons deemed subversive.
1882	Chinese Exclusion Act bars Chinese immigration after more than 100,000 Chinese, mostly men, arrive in the United States.	1964	Bracero program ends.
1885	Contract Law bars contract laborers from entry into the United States.	1965	Immigration Act allows for 170,000 persons from Old World countries and 120,000 persons from the Western Hemisphere to immigrate.
1892	Ellis Island becomes official debarkation point for immigrants.	1980	Mariel boatlift; approximately 125,000 flee Cuba.
1906	Upton Sinclair's *The Jungle*, about Polish immigrants working in Chicago's meatpacking plants.	1986	Immigration Reform and Control Act attempts to restrict illegal immigration.

in various Native American languages. In addition, the seventeenth century produced voyage narratives in Dutch and Swedish.

Michel-Guillaume-Jean de Crèvecœur left Normandy for New York, where as J. Hector St. John he wrote *Letters from an American Farmer* (1782) about the metamorphosis of a Frenchman into an American. Although Crèvecœur contrasted favorably freedom in America with oppression in Europe, he experienced that reality differed greatly from the American Dream. During the Revolutionary War, for refusing to take sides, he lost his farm, was imprisoned, and fled for

This French Canadian immigrant established a dairy farm in the United States. (Library of Congress)

Immigration to the United States

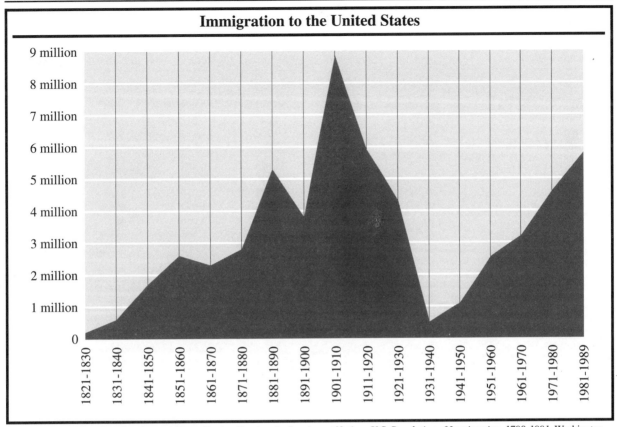

Source: Adapted from Immigration and Naturalization Service, *An Immigrant Nation: U.S. Regulation of Immigration, 1798-1991*. Washington, D.C.: U.S. Department of Justice, 1991.

England. On his return, he found that his farm was ruined, his wife dead, and his children missing. His book, however, recounts the promise of a nation in which such disturbances would not be the norm. The book remains as the tale of what America has always meant to immigrants.

Upton Sinclair wrote *The Jungle* (1906) about Polish immigrants working in Chicago's meat-packing plants. With its depiction of the immigrants' squalid living and working conditions, Sinclair's novel fits squarely into the tradition of naturalism. Willa Cather wrote about Swedish immigrants in Nebraska in *O Pioneers!* (1913) and about Bohemian immigrants to the same prairie in *My Ántonia* (1918). She also wrote about French missionaries in New Mexico in *Death Comes for the Archbishop* (1927). O. E. Rölvaag's *I de dage* (1924) and *Riket grundlægges* (1925), translated together as *Giants in the Earth: A Saga of the Prairie*, 1927) are about Norwegian immigrants to the Dakotas. Kate Chopin wrote about the Creole culture in New Orleans in her novel *The Awakening* (1899) and in her short stories.

Henry Wadsworth Longfellow's long poem *Evangeline* (1847) is about the migration of the French Canadians from Nova Scotia to Louisiana after they were expelled from their homeland, Acadia, by the British in the eighteenth century. The Harlem Renaissance was a literary and musical movement instigated by African Americans who had migrated from the Southern United States to New York to find employment during and after World War I. The Harlem Renaissance also attracted many immigrants of African heritage from the West Indies. One such immigrant was the poet Claude McKay, whose British education in his native Jamaica resulted in a formal poetic style that was distinctive from the innovative jazz rhythms of Langston Hughes, an African American poet who migrated to New York during the Harlem Renaissance.

Another Jamaican who went to New York during the Harlem Renaissance was Marcus Garvey,

Internal migrations

361

Leading States of Intended Residence for U.S. Immigrants

Country of Birth	Total [1]	California	New York	Texas	Illinois	Florida
Total [2]	1,536,483	682,979	189,589	174,132	83,858	71,603
Europe	112,401	21,417	26,392	2,828	12,358	6,021
Poland	20,537	961	4,647	212	7,776	419
Soviet Union	22,524	7,535	9,212	152	1,603	230
United Kingdom	15,928	3,761	2,062	847	459	1,841
Asia [2]	338,581	130,814	45,628	16,805	14,549	8,122
China						
Mainland	31,815	11,494	9,721	1,010	914	460
Taiwan	15,151	6,806	1,783	1,034	456	267
India	30,667	5,794	4,931	1,956	3,431	822
Iran	24,977	14,344	1,735	1,400	391	587
Korea	32,301	9,951	4,475	1,202	1,523	524
Laos	10,446	4,851	126	216	175	102
Pakistan	9,729	1,532	2,553	1,026	934	444
Philippines	63,756	31,223	5,525	1,691	3,104	1,532
Vietnam	48,792	19,675	2,254	4,343	954	1,275
North America [2]	957,558	510,106	78,610	148,302	53,472	43,395
Canada	16,812	3,249	1,709	618	370	3,329
Mexico	679,068	420,377	7,099	130,813	48,618	6,210
Caribbean	115,351	1,641	56,527	834	859	24,712
Cuba	10,645	424	401	87	97	8,519
Dominican Republic	42,195	155	26,457	95	83	1,694
Haiti	20,324	109	8,654	37	208	6,575
Jamaica	25,013	517	12,203	242	348	5,380
Central America [2]	146,202	84,812	13,264	16,023	3,623	9,136
El Salvador	80,173	51,009	5,601	12,033	751	1061
Guatemala	32,303	21,868	2,324	1,739	1,908	945
Honduras	12,024	3,483	2,794	1,263	352	1,815
Nicaragua	11,562	4,979	596	478	73	3,976
South America [2]	85,819	12,105	31,251	2,837	2,188	12,827
Colombia	24,189	2,329	8,388	1,103	668	4,820
Ecuador	12,476	1,353	6,896	193	718	721
Guyana	11,362	246	8,227	88	43	577
Peru	15,726	3,620	3,522	505	356	2,150
Africa	35,893	5,344	7,424	3,162	1,223	1,223

[1] Includes other states, Puerto Rico, and other areas not listed.
[2] Includes other countries and areas not listed separately.

Source: U.S. Department of Education.

who became leader of a movement that proposed to take all black people in North America and the West Indies back to Africa. Garvey is fictionalized in Ralph Ellison's novel *Invisible Man* (1952).

John Steinbeck's *The Grapes of Wrath* (1939) is about people who are made to feel like immigrants within their own country during the Depression. When drought results in agricultural disaster and widespread foreclosure in Oklahoma, the farmers must leave to find work as migrant workers in California. After the Civil Rights movement in the United States in the 1960's, American literature became an amalgam of books by and about immigrants from continents other than Europe. Many of the authors of these books were born in the United States, but their parents' or grandparents' tales of immigration form the basis for much of this literature. Maxine Hong

Kingston's *The Woman Warrior* (1976) and Amy Tan's *The Joy Luck Club* (1989) are classics of Asian American literature. Sandra Cisneros and Ana Castillo are notable voices of Latin American culture, as are Rudolfo Anaya and Rolando Hinojosa.

Emigrants from North America

Many North American writers have, for various reasons, felt compelled to venture abroad. Some have traveled to seek adventure and cultures different from that of North America. Many have traveled to Europe in order to experience the culture that has most influenced North American literature. Others have traveled to escape prejudice and lack of opportunity.

In the early nineteenth century, Washington Irving was the United States' first diplomatic officer stationed in Spain. *The Alhambra* (1832) is a collection of stories inspired by Irving's life in Spain. Irving also wrote *A History of New York from the Beginning of the World to the End of the Dutch Dynasty, by Diedrich Knickerbocker* (1809) about Dutch immigrants in New York. Henry Wadsworth Longfellow traveled in Europe, where his study of languages and literature was preparation for his position as the first professor of Romance languages at Harvard.

Later in the nineteenth century, Mark Twain took a tour of Europe and sent back journalistic accounts of his travels to a newspaper. Later collected as *The Innocents Abroad* (1869), these

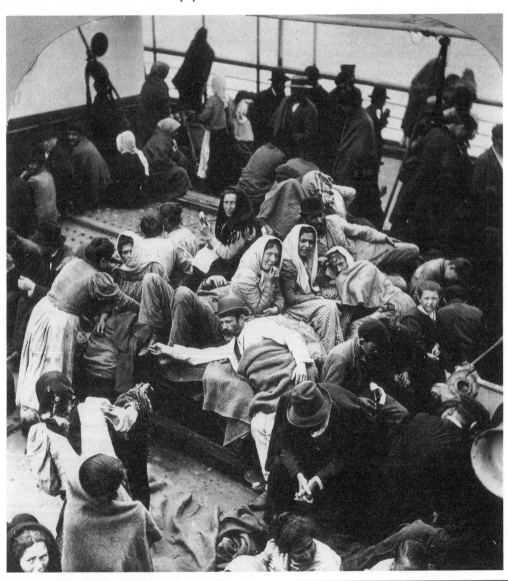

European immigrants cross the Atlantic in 1902. (Library of Congress)

363

accounts reflect Twain's opinion that Europe's artistic traditions were stifling. In the work, Twain states his preference for the artistic freedom afforded him in North America, where there is no preexisting tradition to which he must conform.

Other North American authors have differed with Twain. In the late nineteenth and early twentieth centuries, Henry James wrote many of his novels and short stories about Britain and Europe; James found the tensions of Europe's class system engrossing. Also in the early twentieth century, Ezra Pound, who was born in Idaho, found Europe a necessary aesthetic stimulus for writing poetry. Pound was particularly fond of Italian culture, especially opera, as is evident in his *Cantos* (1970). Pound aligned himself politically with Benito Mussolini, Italy's Fascist dictator, for which Pound was charged with treason at the end of World War II. T. S. Eliot was another North American poet whose attraction for the Old World was aesthetic and political. Born in St. Louis and educated at Harvard, Eliot became a British subject, as did Henry James.

Pound and Eliot were part of the lost generation, a group of American writers who, in the aftermath of World War I, found themselves emotionally and culturally adrift. The group included F. Scott Fitzgerald, Hart Crane, John Dos Passos, and Ernest Hemingway. Hemingway, for one, set most of his greatest novels in Europe, with American protagonists who find themselves unmoored in events large and small. Fitzgerald was less influenced artistically by his time abroad than the other members of the lost generation, although his novel *Tender Is the Night* (1934) has a French setting. The Canadian writer Morley Callaghan was one of the lost generation. He and Hemingway met while both wrote for the *Toronto Star*, and they were in Paris together.

Many African Americans have emigrated to Europe in order to enjoy greater personal and artistic freedom than they experienced in the United States. James Baldwin and Richard Wright are best known for their works about the oppression suffered by African Americans in the United States, but both lived in France for extended periods. Other African American writers felt thwarted artistically in their own country because, as African Americans, they were expected to write about racial issues and they could not be appreciated on strictly aesthetic grounds. Chester Himes, who had great difficulty getting published in the United States, emigrated to France to write detective novels, and Frank Yerby left for Europe to write historical novels.

SUGGESTED READINGS

Alba, Richard D. *Ethnic Identity: The Transformation of White America*. New Haven, Conn.: Yale University Press, 1990. Cites the decline of national origin as a basis for social division among European Americans and the maintenance of the line between European and non-European Americans in social division.

Boelhower, William Q. *Through a Glass Darkly: Ethnic Semiosis in American Literature*. New York: Oxford University Press, 1987. Adopts the stance that literature by minorities and immigrants should be assimilated into mainstream American literature.

Bruce-Novoa, Juan D. *Chicano Authors: Inquiry by Interview*. Austin: University of Texas Press, 1980. Contains interviews with fourteen authors.

Cheung, King-Kok, and Stan Yogi, comps. *Asian American Literature: An Annotated Bibliography*. New York: Modern Language Association of America, 1988. Focuses mostly on primary sources, which are divided into Chinese American, Japanese American, Filipino American, and so on.

Daniels, Roger. *Coming to America: A History of Immigration and Ethnicity in American Life*. New York: HarperCollins, 1990. Debunks many widely held myths about the immigrant experience. Bibliography, index.

Fabre, Michel. *From Harlem to Paris: Black American Writers in France, 1840-1980*. Urbana: University of Illinois Press, 1991. Includes discussions of many notable African American writers.

Fender, Stephen. *Sea Changes: British Emigration and American Literature*. Cambridge: Cambridge University Press, 1992. Analyzes reasons for British emigration to America from colonial times until World War II.

Kim, Elaine H. *Asian American Literature: An Introduction to the Writings and Their Social Context.* Philadelphia: Temple University Press, 1982. Distinguishes between Asian and Asian American identities, and between first and second generation immigrants.

Saldívar, Ramón. *Chicano Narrative: The Dialectics of Difference.* Madison: University of Wisconsin Press, 1990. Discusses works by José Antonio Villarreal, Anaya, Hinojosa, and others.

Simone, Roberta. *The Immigrant Experience in American Fiction: An Annotated Bibliography.* Metuchen, N.J.: Scarecrow Press, 1995. Arranges primary and secondary sources alphabetically according to immigrant group, from Armenian to Yugoslavian.

Sollors, Werner, and Maria Diedrich, eds. *The Black Columbiad: Defining Moments in African American Literature and Culture.* Cambridge, Mass.: Harvard University Press, 1994. A collection of essays, most of which focus on the diaspora as the defining moment in African American identity.

Takaki, Ronald. *Strangers from a Different Shore: A History of Asian Americans.* Boston: Little, Brown, 1989. Cites literary sources to describe the Asian immigrant experience.

Wilentz, Gay. *Binding Cultures: Black Women Writers in Africa and the Diaspora.* Bloomington: Indiana University Press, 1992. Discusses three novels by African women and three by African American women.

—Douglas Edward LaPrade

See also African American identity; Anaya, Rudolfo A.; Asian American identity: China, Japan, and Korea; Baldwin, James; Bradstreet, Anne; Caribbean American literature; Cather, Willa; Chopin, Kate; Cisneros, Sandra; Ellison, Ralph; Harlem Renaissance; Himes, Chester; Hinojosa, Rolando; Hughes, Langston; Kingston, Maxine Hong; Latino American identity; McKay, Claude; Melting pot; Multiculturalism; Pluralism versus assimilation; *So Far from God*; Steinbeck, John; Tan, Amy; Wheatley, Phillis, poetry of; Wright, Richard

Enormous Changes at the Last Minute

Author: Grace Paley (1922-   )

First published: 1974

Identities: Jewish; women

In Grace Paley's *Enormous Changes at the Last Minute*, identity is a personal and a social issue in the struggle for a peaceful world. Most of the characters in this short-story collection are middle-aged women, such as Faith Darwin, who resembles, but is not intended to be, Paley's alter ego; others are simply those about whom stories are told—the children who have died or suffered from neglect, poverty, drug abuse, and the Vietnam War.

The main characters in these stories act with defiance and hope. In "Enormous Changes at the Last Minute," Alexandra is a middle-aged social worker who accidentally becomes pregnant through a liaison with Dennis, a cabdriver, poet, and commune member. Instead of joining the commune, Alexandra invites several of her pregnant clients to come live with her, a "precedent in social work which would not be followed or even mentioned in state journals for about five years." In the story "Wants," the woman narrator meets with her ex-husband, who criticizes her, telling her that she'll "always want nothing." In answer to herself and the reader, she recites the things she has wanted in her life, including ending the war before her children grew up. In "The Long-Distance Runner," Faith Darwin takes a long run through her old neighborhood and ends up living with the black family who now occupies her childhood apartment. All three of these women examine themselves midway, finding, as Faith does, that a "woman inside the steamy energy of middle age" may learn "as though she was still a child what in the world is coming next."

The collection's most acclaimed story, "A Conversation with My Father," features Faith, who, in dialogue with her father (modeled after Paley's father, I. Goodside, M.D.), invents the story of a middle-aged woman who becomes a junkie trying to identify with her son's generation. Faith's father laments the "end of a person," but is more upset when Faith adds her characteristic openness: In the "after-story life," the junkie becomes a "receptionist in a storefront community clinic." On one hand, Faith's response is emblematic of the way in which Paley's characters will not, as Faith's father exclaims, look tragedy "in the face." On the other hand, other stories in the collection—namely, "The Little Girl," "Gloomy Tune," and "Samuel"— do precisely that. These stories study the identities of the victimized—the teenage girl who is raped and strangled by a drug addict, the neglected boy branded in violence and delinquency, the black boy dying in a freak subway accident. "Never again will a boy exactly like Samuel be known," states the narrator.

With the publication of *Enormous Changes at the Last Minute*, Paley's reputation as a writer burgeoned. Her unique blend of poetic concision and concern for women's contributions to the future makes her an important feminist voice in contemporary literature.

SUGGESTED READINGS

Gardiner, Judith Kegan. "On Female Identity and Writing by Women." In *Writing and Sexual Difference*, edited by Elizabeth Abel. Chicago: University of Chicago Press, 1982.

Isaacs, Neil. *Grace Paley: A Study of the Short Fiction*. Boston: Twayne, 1990.

Taylor, Jacqueline. *Grace Paley: Illuminating the Dark Lives*. Austin: University of Texas Press, 1990.

—Andrea J. Ivanov

See also Antiwar literature; Feminism; Jewish American identity; *Later the Same Day*; Paley, Grace; Women and identity

Environment and identity

DEFINITION: The environment is a person's surroundings; how surroundings affect a person is a common theme in literature.

Literature in North America has evolved through various movements, each of which has addressed the theme of environment. In the various genres of essay, fiction, and poetry, writers of these various movements have sought to explore in what ways the environment defines who they are, how society develops in harmony or in discord with its surroundings, and what the human potential for understanding the natural world is.

The Romantic movement Considered to span the time period from 1828 to 1865, the Romantic movement features literature that emphasizes the power of the individual in the pristine landscape of the New World. Transcendentalism, a philosophical movement within the Romantic period, brought forward a literature that focuses on the possibility of a harmonious relationship with the environment in works of nonfiction, poetry, and fiction. The poetry and prose of Ralph Waldo Emerson act as a central locus for Transcendentalism, and his work influenced a large number of his contemporaries. Emerson's essay "Nature" (1836) is considered a particularly significant piece, a beginning in North American nature writing. The most important book of the Romantic movement in affecting the tradition of nature writing was Henry David Thoreau's *Walden* (1854). Thoreau's writing foreshadowed conflicts that would emerge in later literature, as he extolled the virtues of living in the wild and attacked capitalistic urban society.

In addition to the nonfiction work of writers such as Emerson and Thoreau, the Romantic period produced poetry and fiction that centered on the land and on one's life in relation to the environment. Walt Whitman, in his many editions of *Leaves of Grass* (1855), acted as spokesman for the free individual living in concert with natural laws. The expansive themes and style of Whitman's poetry mirror the American landscape of which he spoke, moving forward from the more stylized nature poetry of John Greenleaf Whittier and Henry Wadsworth Longfellow. In fiction, the novels of Herman Melville and James Fenimore Cooper illustrate the challenges and rewards of living close to the environment, in settings far removed from the urbane pleasures of the cities. The Romantic movement characterized the optimism of a people who believed that they could control their surroundings, whether natural or societal, and ultimately rise above the forces that encumbered them.

The period from the end of the Civil War to the early twentieth century produced literature that in many ways redefined the relationship of people and the environment, often mirroring the changes that had been produced by the increasing industrialization of society. In stark opposition to the more positive tone of the literature of the Romantic movement, which generally portrayed nature—including human nature—as beneficent, the naturalistic movement produced fiction that explores the mechanistic forces that appeared to dominate the individual in all environments, whether natural or urban. Naturalism issued from a philosophical interpretation of Darwinian biology. According to such thinkers as Herbert Spencer, people are simply high-order animals whose behavior is a product of heredity and environment. Naturalistic fiction offers characters who survive or die by their individual strengths and fortunes. The characters often show animalistic drives, including sexual desire and greed. The world they inhabit is godless, dangerous, and harsh. The tone of many naturalistic works, whether set in the city or in the wild, is bleak. The intent of the naturalistic writers was to present literature with the detachment and calculation that would match that of scientific investigation.

The age of naturalism

The most significant North American naturalists include novelists Frank Norris and Theodore Dreiser, writers who often show the forces of urban life determining the success or failure of characters contending with harsh economic realities. Norris' *The Octopus* (1901) and Dreiser's trilogy, *The Financier* (1912), *The Titan* (1914), and *The Stoic* (1947), depict the ruthlessness of urban capitalism and the struggles of the classes. Jack London, through his novels and short stories, presents characters who often encounter the cruel force of nature in the wilderness, where animals had the necessary abilities to survive and where their human counterparts were often weak and inept, and who because of these frailties face annihilation. In poetry and prose, Stephen Crane offers a literature that positions people under the control of their environment. His novel about the American Civil War, *The Red Badge of Courage* (1895), brought him international acclaim, and his fiction and poetry often vividly illustrate the violence of war in the tone of a detached, objective observer. Typifying Crane's view of the human relation to the world, in his short poem, "A Man Said to the Universe," the speaker affirms his existence only to be told by the universe that "the fact has not created in me/ a sense of obligation."

The twentieth century has produced literature that incorporates the optimistic tone established by the Romantic writers without naïvely dismissing the realities addressed by the naturalists. Expressions of the relationship to the environment may also be radically different depending upon which region is described. However, a significant thread binds the best writings of the twentieth century: The particulars of place to a great extent define the lives of the inhabitants.

The modern era

Outstanding among the fiction writers whose work most poignantly illustrates identity with the environment are Ernest Hemingway and William Faulkner. Hemingway's Nick Adams stories show the idyllic surroundings of rural Michigan, where the city and the machine had yet to dominate. In Hemingway's "The Big Two-Hearted River," his main character is healed through his relationship with nature after suffering through the horror of war. Faulkner's *Go Down, Moses and Other Stories* (1942), particularly its legendary story, "The Bear," expresses the slow degradation of the wild and the spiritual loss that corresponds to that degradation. In addition, the fiction of John Steinbeck, including his novels *Tortilla Flat* (1935), *Of Mice and Men* (1937), and *The Grapes of Wrath* (1939), describes the continuing conflict between the natural world and the economic forces that shape people's lives and that often desecrate the land.

In the world of poetry, Hart Crane, Robinson Jeffers, and Theodore Roethke produced poetry that intimately describes the relationship between themselves and the environment. Crane wrote poems that attempt to re-create an American mythology. Jeffers saw people in modern society as being totally separated from the natural world, blindly pursuing a life of material wealth and consumption, a theme that would be further developed by some of the most articulate poets who came after him. Roethke articulated the presences inherent in the living things of the world and showed how identity can depend on the lives of flowers, trees, and the elements.

Postmodern literature

Contemporary writing has seen an increase in concerns about the rapidly disappearing natural world and about the loss of humanity associated with that disappearance. Postmodern nonfiction is of high rank, and not since the time of Emerson and Thoreau has so much notable writing occurred within the genre. There has been a flourishing of regional essays and nonfiction books related to place—in Barry Lopez's works detailing the environment of the Arctic and the Southwest, in the anthropologist Richard Nelson's work about Alaska, in Peter Mathiessen's writings about life on the Atlantic coast, in Gretel Ehrlich's descriptions of the West, in Farley Mowatt's observations of the lives of wolves in Canada, and in Doug Peacock's and Rick Bass's writings on grizzly bears in Montana. These books have described the human place in nature and how nature defines what is sacred. Along with the meditative qualities of the works arises an inquiry into how the actions of modern culture are destroying resources that were once taken for granted as inexhaustible and how the degradation of the environment can destroy what it means to be human. In the essay collection *Pilgrim at Tinker Creek* (1974), which won the Pulizter Prize in nonfiction, Annie Dillard examines in minute detail the environment around her home in Virginia, drawing on the tradition of close observation begun by Thoreau. Gary Snyder, basing much of his observation on principles of Zen Buddhism, expresses the sacredness of the wild in *The Practice of the Wild* (1990). Reflecting on the precarious balance between the land as a source of nourishment, literally and figuratively, and the needs of community, Wendell Berry has called for a reassessment of how the culture functions in books of essays including *Standing by Words* (1983) and *What Are People For?* (1990). The tremendous resurgence of nonfiction related to the environment indicates serious concern for the natural landscape and animal life and for the health of humanity, which is increasingly dehumanized by the machinery of culture.

Many nonfiction writers have also written fiction that addresses the same questions. Berry and Lopez have published books of short stories concerned with the environment. Mathiessen has written novels chronicling the loss of habitat, the extinction of species, and the loss of traditional ways of living. In addition, novelists such as Jim Harrison and John Nichols have charted the loss of balance between individuals and the land. The historical novels of James Welch provide a glimpse of a Native American lifestyle that draws its strength and sustenance from nature. Welch's novels also describe the decline of Native American culture with the onslaught of settlement. The contributions of Welch and other Native American authors have fueled a reexamination of the value of consumption and development.

The effects of environment on identity have been pursued and developed in poetry as well as in nonfiction and fiction. Snyder has contributed poetry that asks many of the same questions posed in his nonfiction. Poets Robert Bly, W. S. Merwin, and James Wright have created poems that attempt to position themselves outside the self and in the external world. These and other poets have sought to establish, by means of what has been called the deep image, a link between the inner world of the self and the outer one of the environment. A trend in postmodern poetry toward an entirely interior poem indicates a loss of connection to the external environment. The individual, exiled from a sense of community or place in the natural world, takes an identity that is rooted only in the activities of the mind, becoming, as the poet Galway Kinnell has written, "a corpse with a brain."

SUGGESTED READINGS

Brooks, Paul. *Speaking for Nature: How Literary Naturalists from Henry Thoreau to Rachel Carson Have Shaped America*. Boston: Houghton Mifflin, 1980. A critical survey of the most significant nature writers.

Cooley, John, ed. *Earthly Words: Essays on Contemporary Nature and Environmental Writers*. Ann Arbor: University of Michigan Press, 1994. A collection of critical essays on the foremost nature writers of the twentieth century.

Foerster, Norman. *Nature in American Literature: Studies in the Modern View of Nature*. New York: Russell & Russell, 1958. A classic text, focusing on the early nature writers of American literature.

Harrison, Jim. "Poetry as Survival." In *Just Before Dark*. Livingston, Mont.: Clark City Press, 1991. Surveys the voices, conditions, and themes related to Native American writing.

Marx, Leo. *The Machine in the Garden: Technology and the Pastoral Ideal in America*. New York: Oxford University Press, 1964. A scholarly book concerning the relationship between capitalism and nature.

—Robert Haight

See also American identity: Midwest; American identity: Northeast; American identity: South; American identity: West and the frontier; Canadian identity; Canadian identity: Quebecois

Erdrich, Louise

BORN: Little Falls, Minnesota; June 7, 1954

PRINCIPAL WORKS: *Jacklight*, 1984; *Love Medicine*, 1984 (expanded version, 1993); *The Beet Queen*, 1986; *Tracks*, 1988; *Baptism of Desire*, 1989; *The Crown of Columbus* (with Michael Dorris), 1991; *The Bingo Palace*, 1994; *Tales of Burning Love*, 1996

IDENTITIES: European American; Native American

SIGNIFICANT ACHIEVEMENT: Erdrich's poetry and novels represent some of the most creative and accessible writing by a Native American.

Louise Erdrich's identity as a mixed blood, the daughter of a Chippewa mother and a German American father, is at the heart of her writing. The oldest of seven children and the granddaughter of the tribal chair of the Turtle Mountain Reservation, she has stated that her family was typical of Native American families in its telling of stories, and that those stories became a part of her and are reflected in her own work. In her poetry and novels, she explores Native American ideas, ordeals and delights, with characters representing the European American and Native American sides of her heritage. Erdrich entered Dartmouth College in 1972, the year the Native American Studies Department was formed. The chair of that department was Michael Dorris, who later became her trusted literary collaborator and eventually her husband. Her work at Dartmouth was the beginning of a continuing exploration of her ancestry, the animating influence in her novels.

Louise Erdrich and husband Michael Dorris have written about American Indian identity.
(Jerry Bauer)

Erdrich frequently weaves stories in nonchronological patterns with multiple narrators. Her characters are multidimensional and entertaining while communicating the positives and negatives of Native American life in the twentieth century. Family relationships, community relationships, issues of assimilation, and the roles of tradition and religion are primary motifs in her novels. *Tracks*, *The Beet Queen*, *Love Medicine*, and *The Bingo Palace* form a quartet that follows four families living in North Dakota between the early 1930's and the late 1980's, exploring the relationships among themselves and within the larger cultures. The novel *Crown of Columbus*, written with coauthor Michael Dorris, explores many of the same ideas and is a literary adventure story. In these novels about the search for identity, some of her characters are hopelessly caught between worlds, but most of her characters battle the hurt caused by mixed identities with humor, tenacity, and a will to construct their own sense of identity.

The result is some of the most accomplished and popular ethnic fiction available. The excellence of her work has earned for her numerous awards, including the National Book Critics Circle Award in 1984, and each of her five novels has achieved *The New York Times* best-seller list.

SUGGESTED READINGS

Coltelli, Laura. *Winged Words: American Indian Writers Speak*. Omaha: University of Nebraska Press, 1990.

Owens, Louis. *Other Destinies: Understanding the American Indian Novel*. Norman: University of Oklahoma Press, 1992.

Rainwater, Catherine. "Reading Between Worlds: Narrativity in the Fiction of Louise Erdrich." *American Literature* 62, no. 1 (1990): 405-422.

—Jacquelyn Kilpatrick

See also Acculturation; *Beet Queen, The*; Mixed race and identity; Native American identity

Erotic identity

IDENTITIES: Gay, lesbian, and bisexual; men; women

At issue

In psychology and religion, the individual's experience of sex is of key importance in shaping the personality. Whether it be the loss of virginity, the acceptance of homosexuality, or the cultivation of a fetish, erotic experience creates a window that looks upon the writer's mind and upon the writer's culture. Eroticism in literature may unlock or loosen the bonds of guilt and shame. The erotic experience of another may allow the individual to see that he or she is not alone and that fantasies once thought to be perverse are in fact shared by many. Furthermore, the nature of fantasies, particularly if they are frowned upon by the culture, may reveal a hidden prejudice toward a group or lifestyle.

History

Historically, erotic literature has been marked by censorship. Various religious groups and community watchdogs have long sought to impose their morality on others by banning books they view as damaging. In many cases the censors' attempts at prohibition backfire, drawing attention to the book's power and even increasing its readership. Notable examples include the attempt to block the importation of James Joyce's *Ulysses* (1922) and Henry Miller's *Tropic of Capricorn* (1939), both of which were subject to seizure at the border of the United States. Regarding Miller's book, the Supreme Court ruled in 1964 that obscenity was too subjective to remain a legal matter and instead placed its definition within the hands of academics. Even so, the debate over whether particular texts should be banned continues to rage.

Particularly offensive to some, Vladimir Nabokov's *Lolita* (1955) came under fire for its treatment of pedophilia, or eroticism and children, while William S. Burroughs' *Naked Lunch* (1959) was banned for depicting homosexuality. The rise of gay rights and feminism in the 1960's and 1970's saw a decrease in censorship, with such writers as Allen Ginsberg and Erica Jong at the forefront of eroticism, but the 1980's created a conservative backlash which again called for the exclusion of certain texts from, for example, college and secondary school libraries.

The canon

Among academics, the overwritten and clichéd passages of pulp fiction are not part of the literary canon. Pulp fiction, named for the cheap quality of the paper on which it is printed, is deemed to be too obvious in its intent to be classified as literature. Its aim is only to arouse readers, leaving them comfortably stationary within their own prejudices, understanding, and views. Pulp fiction does not attempt higher levels of artistry in writing, which, although it too might arouse readers, also challenges their notions of erotic experience. Indeed, perhaps the only safe generalization that can be made about erotic experience is that it is incredibly varied. Ernest Hemingway's novel, *The Sun Also Rises* (1926), for example, explores male bonding and the competition among males for females. At the center of the novel is the narrator Jake Barnes, an alcoholic who is impotent spiritually and physically. Ironically, the courage he displays in the war, which causes his wound, creates his failure in the bedroom, becoming a commentary on men's enslavement to their own pride and to the bodies of women. Miller, on the other hand, in *Tropic of Capricorn*, sees the crippling agent as that of Puritanism, which he indicts for its demonization of sex. In Puritanism's place, Miller substitutes a manic celebration of the body, making it glorious in all its imperfection.

Another aspect of identity and eroticism in literature lies in the treatment of homosexuality. In Tennessee Williams' *Cat on a Hot Tin Roof* (1955), for example, homosexual love is seen as a threat to the male ego, challenging the athletic, macho man's sense of himself and leading to alcoholism and suicide. Burroughs' cult novel, *Naked Lunch*, however, celebrates homosexuality. The novel also examines the limits of personality as it is challenged by bondage and drug addiction. A gentler gay love is explored in Truman Capote's classic *Breakfast at Tiffany's* (1958), a novel of sexual initiation depicting a young woman's journey from her hillbilly past into the heart of New York City. "A Diamond Guitar," also by Capote, is a lyrical account of the blossoming of homosexual love in prison between an aging convict and a young man. When the young man escapes, the older man dreams of him while he strokes the diamond guitar abandoned under his bed, imagining the wide world beyond the prison walls. In *Rubyfruit Jungle* (1973), Rita Mae Brown depicts another sort of gay love: A young lesbian loses her innocence and confronts a world of prejudice and intolerance, discovering the pain and joy inherent in her sexuality.

Another woman explores a different aspect of female sexuality in Jong's *Fear of Flying* (1973). In this novel, the woman is the man's sexual equal, matching him in the lust for conquest and in the degree of her sexual pleasure. So long damned, the promiscuous woman, a childless adult who has escaped the tyranny of biology, is celebrated. In contrast, Philip Roth's *Portnoy's Complaint* (1969) presents the male as a slave to testosterone, doomed to pursue an endless quest to satisfy his insatiable libido. The darker side of lust appears in John Irving's *The World According to Garp* (1978), which depicts the average male's horror of rape—an act of sexual violence that makes him feel that his entire sex has been tainted. In Irving's novel, the Ellen James Society is so named in remembrance of a victim who had her tongue cut out so that she could not describe her attackers. Her sympathizers, members of the society, willingly undergo the same operation. Irving thus creates a symbol for the psychological mutilation of rape. In contrast to the horror that sex can bring, African American writer and Nobel Prize winner Toni Morrison creates a lushly sensual world in *Tar Baby* (1981). Set in the Caribbean, much of the action takes place inside a greenhouse where the sex life of plants mirrors that of the erotic encounters between a rural man from the American South and a fashion model from New York City. The clash of their cultures within the African American community heightens the eroticism of their liaison, as each becomes more aware of the forces that shaped the other. Finally, *Blue Movie* (1970), by Terry Southern, is considered by many critics to be one of the best erotic novels ever written. It is rife with wit and satire, and it lampoons the pornography industry.

Implications for identity

What emerges from a survey of erotic literature is, more than surprise at dissimiliarities of sexual practices, a sense of the vast likenesses: heartbreak, disappointment, happiness, and bliss. Erotic experience is a modern quest, whether it is a gay man cruising leather bars or a woman cruising upscale singles bars in search of a one-night stand. Judith Rossner's *Looking for Mr. Goodbar* (1975), an example of cruising from a woman's point of view, is a cautionary tale of casual sex. The novel tells of the sexual escapades of a woman who is seeking meaning in life through her erotic encounters. She is murdered at the close of the novel by a sexual predator who is aroused as much by the act of murder as he is by the act of sex. Like many late twentieth century writers, Rossner implies that the absence of spirituality, wrought by the skepticism of science, deprives human beings of God but not of their hunger for God. Unable to believe in an abstract protector and punisher, they seek solace in each other, their consummation and communion being the sexual act.

The fleeting nature of sexual bliss and the constant desire for renewal indicate, however, that erotic experience may be a tenuous salvation at best. The work of Jong and Roth partakes of a quest motif; that is, the protagonists will find fulfillment only if they can have sex with either the perfect partner, or, failing that, with a great many partners. As representatives of the search for meaning they are afflicted by a paradox similar to the one that haunts alcoholics or drug addicts: The more they attempt to fill the void inside them, the emptier they become. Man or woman, the erotic quester finds, cannot substitute for God; lust cannot take the place of love. The literature of the erotic seeks to engage not only the mystery of physical craving wrought by glands but also the hunger for intimacy born of the complex human heart.

SUGGESTED READINGS

Basler, Roy. *Sex, Symbolism, and Psychology in Literature*. New York: Octagon Books, 1970. Examines the psychosexual aspects of T. S. Eliot's "The Love Song of J. Alfred Prufrock" (1917).

Brooks, Peter. *Body Work: Objects of Desire in Modern Narrative*. Cambridge, Mass.: Harvard University Press, 1993. Explores the rhetoric of narration regarding sex.

Gottesman, Ronald, ed. *Critical Essays on Henry Miller*. Boston: G. K. Hall, 1992. Explores the sources for *Tropic of Cancer*, its sexual aspects, and its relation to visionary poetry.

Hapke, Laura. *Girls Who Went Wrong: Prostitutes in American Fiction*. Bowling Green, Ohio: Bowling Green State University Popular Press, 1989. Explores the treatment of prostitution in literature from a social perspective, focusing on the American heroine and on the fallen woman as reflected in the minds of men. Rehabilitation and redemption are also discussed.

Hernton, Calvin C. *The Sexual Mountain and Black Women Writers: Adventures in Sex, Literature, and Real Life*. Garden City, N.J.: Anchor Press, 1990. Explores the African American experience in literature, particularly regarding racist stereotypes. Index.

Millet, Kate. *Sexual Politics*. New York: Doubleday, 1970. Important feminist analysis of sex in fiction, particularly regarding the misogyny of male authors.

—David Johansson

See also Bisexual identity; Censorship of literature; Gay identity; Lesbian identity; Prostitution

Ethan Frome

AUTHOR: Edith Wharton (1862-1937)
FIRST PUBLISHED: 1911
IDENTITIES: Disability; European American; women

Ethan Frome depicts a nightmarish world, completely empty of the warmth and joy to be found in loving human interaction. Set in the cold and harsh landscapes of Starkfield, Massachusetts, the story is told by a narrator who attempts to discover what tragedy caused the enigmatic Ethan Frome's literal and spiritual crippling. Piecing together information, the narrator learns that years earlier Ethan married Zenobia Pierce, a distant cousin who nursed his mother during her final illness. Shortly after the wedding, Ethan realized that his was a marriage without love and that he had simply exchanged the suffocating responsibility of a sick mother for the suffocating tie of a sick wife. Ethan, once filled with aspirations, finds instead that he is lashed to a wife whom he loathes and to a near-sterile farm that he cannot sell.

With lightness and life, Mattie Silver (Zenobia's younger cousin) comes to the Frome house to help with chores. Mattie and Ethan fall in love, yet the strictures of conventional morality and Frome's own strong sense of duty and loyalty prevent him from doing any more than voicing a tender, painfully pathetic love avowal. When Mattie is forced to leave, she decides that she would rather die than be separated from Ethan. Her plan, to crash their sled into an elm at the bottom of a steep slope, is tacitly agreed to by Ethan. However, the two survive the death ride, and the lovers' suicide pact takes on a cruel twist. Mattie and Ethan, crippled and dispirited, share a living death in which their caretaker is the suddenly hardy Zenobia.

Ethan personifies the grievous waste of failed greatness. His body, a metaphor for his spirit, is described as "lame" and "warped," and his once gallant and noble head rests on once "strong shoulders" which are now "bent out of shape." In Ethan, the narrator confronts a prodigious soul grown weary, warped, and lame, and the narrator sees in Ethan's ghastly alteration the suffering of a misspent life. Ethan, believing his renunciation of Mattie was motivated by a sense of honor, fails to see that the moral significance of the situation was not as clear and definable as he believed. Centering his choice on duty, not love, Ethan failed to consider the effect of his decision on Zenobia, in a marriage with a man who found her abhorrent, or on Mattie, who apparently did love him. Frome also never understood his own fear of change and of intimate sexual expression.

Despite its apparent bleakness, *Ethan Frome* articulates Edith Wharton's most humanistic theme: The contact that people make with others can be the most meaningful thing that emerges from the stark field of human existence. The greatest tragedy is the failure to establish meaningful involvement with another.

SUGGESTED READINGS

Lewis, R. W. B. *Edith Wharton*. New York: Harper & Row, 1975.

McDowell, Margaret B. *Edith Wharton*. Boston: Twayne, 1976.

Wolff, Cynthia Griffin. *A Feast of Words: The Triumph of Edith Wharton*. New York: Oxford University Press, 1977.

—Linda Costanzo Cahir

See also *Age of Innocence, The*: Erotic identity; Wharton, Edith

Ethnic composition of universities

The countries of North America have the world's most diverse ethnic composition. During the late nineteenth and early twentieth centuries, when millions of immigrants from all over the world flocked to the continent, the dominant metaphor used to describe the process whereby these various ethnicities associated with one another in their new homeland was the melting pot. The melting pot metaphor suggested a blending process. Somehow in the middle of the heat generated by the tensions that arise from the interaction of many ethnic groups, individual ethnic elements were to lose their distinctions and merge into some new and unified culture. In the late twentieth century, as a result partly of immigration from lands which had not been represented in earlier immigration,

At issue

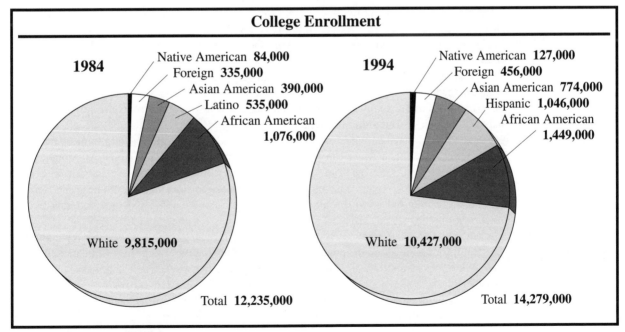

College Enrollment

1984
Native American **84,000**
Foreign **335,000**
Asian American **390,000**
Latino **535,000**
African American **1,076,000**
White **9,815,000**
Total **12,235,000**

1994
Native American **127,000**
Foreign **456,000**
Asian American **774,000**
Hispanic **1,046,000**
African American **1,449,000**
White **10,427,000**
Total **14,279,000**

Source: U.S. Department of Education.
Note: Details may not sum to totals because of rounding.

Average Scores on the Scholastic Assessment Test and the ACT Assessment, 1996			
	SAT Verbal	*SAT Mathematics*	*ACT*
Native American	483	477	18.8
Asian	496	558	21.6
African American	434	422	17.0
Mexican American	455	459	18.7
Puerto Rican	452	445	—
Other Hispanic	465	466	18.9
European American	526	523	21.6
Other	511	512	—
Men	507	527	21.0
Women	503	492	20.8
All	505	508	20.9

Sources: The College Board, American College Testing Program.

College Student Enrollment Selected States, 1994		
	Percentage of Minority Enrollment	*Percentage Share of Total U.S. Enrollment*
Hawaii	71.0	0.5
California	46.0	12.9
New Mexico	42.0	0.7
Texas	35.0	6.7
Louisiana	31.0	1.4
Mississippi	31.0	0.9
Florida	30.0	4.4
Maryland	30.0	1.9
New York	30.0	7.4
Average:	38.4	Total: 38.4

Source: U.S. Department of Education.

partly of the success of the Civil Rights movement of the 1960's, and partly of the fact that a number of ethnic groups had spent many generations on American soil while still retaining a distinct ethnic identity, the metaphor of the melting pot was replaced with that of the salad bowl, an image that suggests many different elements coexisting to make up a whole.

History

Official support of the shift from the ideal of a single national culture to the ideal of cultural pluralism appeared, in the early 1970's, with the establishment of affirmative action programs. Originally a tool to redress, through preferential hiring and promotion practices, the social and economic injustices suffered by African Americans, affirmative action soon was applied to women, Latinos, Asians, and other minorities. In order to be effective, however, affirmative action required the establishment of a new set of racial categories that would enable governments and institutions to classify people according to their ethnic origins. Until the early 1970's, official government statistics used only three categories, white, black, and other, to organize information about the population. Latinos were counted as white, while those of Asian, Pacific Island, or Native American origin were counted as other. Although the revised system of categories recognizes the fact that the population contains a variety of important ethnic groups, at least two problems arise when an attempt is made to work with such statistics. First, the categories do not accurately reflect all the ethnic identities that actually exist. American citizens whose cultural roots are Jewish, Iranian, Pakistani, Lebanese Christian, and Indian Buddhist and Hindu, for example, are all, on many statistical records, listed as white, non-Hispanic. Second, people often belong to more than one ethnic group. An African American who traces her roots to Haiti or the British West Indies, for example, has ethnic differences from African Americans whose ancestors were slaves in the South. If she marries a Chinese American, their children will belong to more than one ethnic group. Serious limitations are imposed upon discussion of the ethnic composition of North America by the inaccuracies in the official statistical records.

Ethnic groups in the university

In the mid-1970's, the government revised the racial categories it was using for gathering statistical information about the population. Instead of having two categories, white and black, or three, white, black, and other, it implemented a system that used five categories: white, non-Hispanic; black, non-Hispanic; Hispanic; Asian or Pacific Islander; Native American/Alaskan Native. Despite the limitations of these categories, they were an improvement. They did make it possible to see more clearly which groups were well represented in the country's institutions of higher learning and which were not. The Civil Rights movement of the 1960's began, by many accounts, with the struggle to enroll a black student, James Meredith, in the racially segregated

University of Mississippi. After the successful conclusion of this campaign, the nation's universities and colleges took the lead in promoting cultural pluralism and ethnic diversity. As the 1960's ended, the number of black students enrolled at public and private universities and colleges was at an all-time high. This motivated other ethnic groups to argue that they, too, had suffered from discrimination at the hands of the white European majority and so should be given preferential access to higher education. In response to pressure from these groups, the new set of statistical categories was devised and put into use in the mid-1970's.

According to figures released by the U.S. Department of Education in 1975, 84.3 percent of undergraduate students were white, 9.6 percent were black, 3.6 percent were Hispanic, 1.8 percent were Asian, and 0.7 percent Native American. This marked a clear increase in the population of African American university students, up from 7 percent in 1970. It was hard to know, however, what the figures for Hispanic, Native American, and Asian students meant. Since these ethnic categories had not been used in the previous national census in 1970, there was no way of telling whether or not these groups were represented in the country's universities in proportion to their presence in the population as a whole. The answers awaited the 1980 census.

According to the 1980 census, the population of the United States was 78.5 percent white, 12 percent black, 6 percent Hispanic, 3 percent Asian, and 0.5 percent Native American. The figures for the racial composition of the nation's universities that year were similar to those collected in

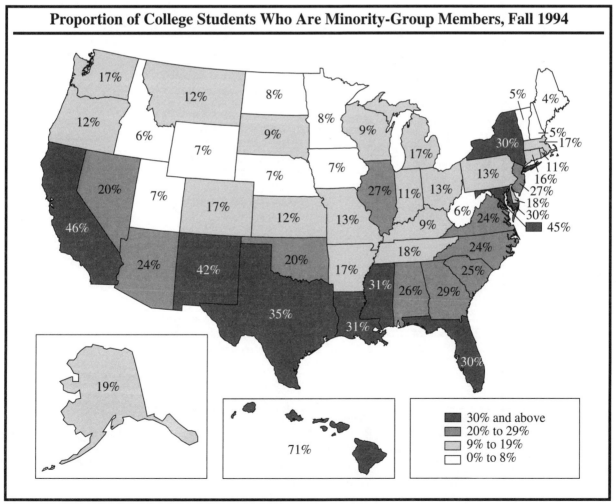

Proportion of College Students Who Are Minority-Group Members, Fall 1994

30% and above
20% to 29%
9% to 19%
0% to 8%

Source: U.S. Department of Education.

1975: white, 83.5 percent; black, 9.4 percent; Hispanic, 4.0 percent; Asian, 2.4 percent; and Native American, 0.7 percent. These results answered some questions but raised others. Whites and Native Americans enjoyed a greater presence in the university than their percentage of the population as a whole. This was what was expected for whites as the dominant political and economic group, but not what was expected for Native Americans, who remained marginalized in American society. The rest of the figures seemed to fall in line with expectations: Blacks, Hispanics, and Asians were underrepresented, though Asians seemed to be making rapid progress toward parity with their population percentage in that they were only 20 percent under it, while blacks and Hispanics were, respectively, a quarter and a third less represented in colleges than in the population as a whole.

A decade later, in 1990, a striking change was recorded. First, new waves of immigration from Mexico, South and Central America, and Asia had increased the rate of growth for these segments of the population. The 1990 census revealed that whites were on the verge of losing their status of being the absolute majority of the U.S. population. Blacks and Native Americans held steady at 12 percent and 0.5 percent respectively. Asians increased from 3 percent to 3.6 percent, while Hispanics leapt from 6 percent to 9 percent. When these data were correlated with the statistics from the nation's universities, the ethnic proportions remained virtually unchanged for every group

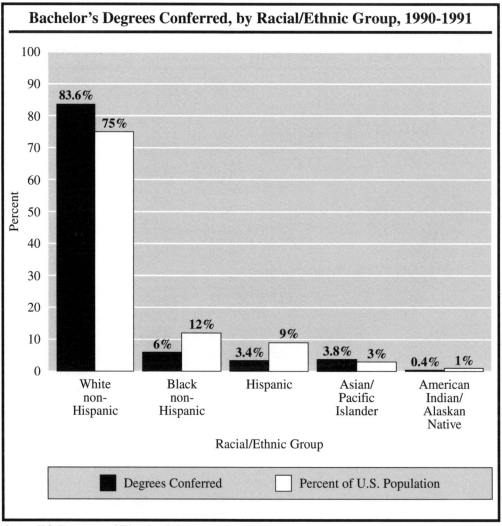

Source: U.S. Department of Education, U.S. Bureau of the Census.
Note: Population percentages are rounded figures.

Degrees Conferred, by Racial/Ethnic Group, 1993-1994

	Total	Native American	Asian American	African American	Latino	European American
Associate						
Men	220,990	1,895	8,403	17,379	13,395	174,947
Women	321,459	3,080	10,256	29,072	19,043	253,326
Total	542,449	4,975	18,659	46,451	32,438	428,273
Bachelor's						
Men	532,422	2,616	26,938	30,648	21,807	429,121
Women	636,853	3,573	28,722	52,928	28,434	507,106
Total	1,169,275	6,189	55,660	83,576	50,241	936,227
Master's						
Men	176,085	691	8,225	7,413	5,113	123,854
Women	210,985	1,006	7,042	14,524	6,800	164,434
Total	387,070	1,697	15,267	21,937	11,913	288,288
Doctorate						
Men	26,552	66	1,373	631	465	15,126
Women	16,633	68	652	762	438	12,030
Total	43,185	134	2,025	1,393	903	27,156
Professional						
Men	44,707	222	3,214	1,902	1,781	36,573
Women	30,711	149	2,678	2,542	1,353	23,567
Total	75,418	371	5,892	4,444	3,134	60,140

Source: U. S. Department of Education.

except the Asians, who amounted to 4.3 percent of the university population, despite being 3.6 percent of the country's people.

Graduate schools and university faculty

In graduate and professional schools in the academic workplace the pattern of enrollments and hirings has been much the same as that found in undergraduate programs. The most important differences are that whites have a considerably greater percentage of the available spots than they do in undergraduate institutions, that in professional schools the percentage lead that whites have is being reduced much more rapidly, and that Asian students constitute a larger percentage of the student body than their numbers in the population at large would suggest. In 1990, the official graduate school figures were white, 86.6 percent; black, 5.8 percent; Hispanic, 3.3 percent; Asian, 3.8 percent; and Native American, 0.5 percent. Not surprisingly, the same pattern that exists in the graduate and professional schools currently prevails among faculty members as well. In the early 1990's the ratios of faculty by racial group to the 1990 census ratios were white, 86.8 percent; black, 4.9 percent; Hispanic, 2.5 percent; Asian, 5.2 percent; and Native American, 0.5 percent.

Although the university was the first major institution to recruit minority students, the large gain in the 1960's in the number of African American students is an exception to the general pattern that the percentage of students in each ethnic group in the university has tended to remain constant in relation to the size of that group in the larger population. Whites consistently amount to 5 percent more of the undergraduate student body than they do of the population. Most commentators agree that without affirmative action admissions programs, the number of black and Hispanic students would fall dramatically.

Ethnicity and the curriculum

One of the most important effects of university commitment to ethnic diversity and cultural pluralism has occurred in the humanities curriculum. English and history courses, as well as core courses in Western civilization, have been modified to include larger amounts of material about Native American, African and African American, Latino, and Asian contributions to North

Differences Between White and Black College Graduates in Selected Fields of Study

In 1990 30 million white Americans and 1.9 million African Americans held college degrees. The percentages of white and black degree holders earning their degrees in many fields of study was remarkably similar. For example, 18.4 percent of white graduates and 19.3 percent of black graduates held degrees in business and management. Differences among white and black degree holders were most pronounced in the following fields:

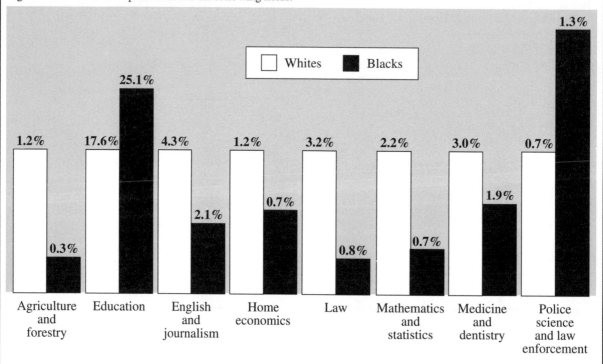

Source: U.S. Department of Education.

American history and culture. The motivation for doing this has been ideological and practical: Students who live in a multicultural society need to learn about the contributions of the various subcultures of that society, and students from each ethnic group feel more comfortable if they find their group represented in the course of study. To do this, however, parts of the traditional curriculum—especially antiquity and the Middle Ages—have been greatly reduced, while the amount of material from the twentieth century and contemporary culture has been increased. This has sparked an intense controversy about the status and quality of higher education in America. Alan Bloom's *The Closing of the American Mind* (1987) condemns the liberal cultural pluralist agenda as a form of propaganda and calls for a return to a traditional humanist curriculum. Defenders of pluralism, such as Gerald Graff, whose *Beyond the Culture Wars: How Teaching the Conflicts Can Revitalize American Education* (1992) offered a response to Bloom, have vigorously defended their projects and policies, and the university generally has continued to pursue a multicultural vision.

Suggested readings

Bergman, Barbara R. *In Defense of Affirmative Action*. New York: New Republic, 1995. An argument for affirmative action in college admissions, citing the educational and experiential benefits derived from a diverse student body.

Bloom, Allan. *The Closing of the American Mind*. New York: Simon & Schuster, 1987. The first major work criticizing the effects of cultural pluralism in the university, concerned largely with changes in the traditional curriculum and the lowering of academic standards.

Cozic, Charles P., ed. *Education in America*. San Diego, Calif.: Greenhaven Press, 1992. Presents opposing views by prominent spokespersons on various aspects of education. Chapter 4, "Should Education for Minority Students Emphasize Ethnicity?" and Chapter 6, "What Is the State of Higher Education?" examine the questions of multiculturalism.

D'Souza, Dinesh. *Illiberal Education: The Politics of Race and Sex on Campus*. New York: Macmillan, 1991. This famous study of six major American universities condemns multiculturalism and pluralism as they are currently being implemented in higher education.

Graff, Gerald. *Beyond the Culture Wars: How Teaching Conflicts Can Revitalize American Education*. New York: W. W. Norton, 1992. An important response to the attacks of Bloom and D'Souza, arguing that cultural pluralism, properly handled, can be a positive force in higher education.

Sollors, Werner, ed. *The Invention of Ethnicity*. New York: Oxford University Press, 1989. This collection of interdisciplinary essays reveals the extent to which ethnicity is a construct in American literature.

—R. A. Martin

See also Acculturation; Civil Rights movement; Melting Pot; Multiculturalism; Multiculturalism, statistics of; Racism and ethnocentrism; School

Ethnic discrimination. *See* Racism and ethnocentrism

Eurocentrism. *See* Racism and ethnocentrism

European American identity

IDENTITIES: European American

As part of the graduation ceremonies at the Ford Motor Company English school in Detroit during World War I, students climbed to the stage in native dress carrying signs that read Greece, Syria, Italy, and so on. The students entered a giant cardboard cauldron labeled Melting Pot and emerged dressed in coats and ties and carrying their diplomas and small American flags. Assimilation was dramatically complete.

This stage show is symbolic of a much larger (and usually more subtle) process that millions of immigrants to the United States in the nineteenth and twentieth centuries underwent. Between 1820 and 1990, more than fifty million immigrants entered the United States, and three-quarters of them came from Europe. Before 1890, the majority of these immigrants were—in descending numbers—German, Irish, and English. Between 1890 and 1914 fifteen million Europeans arrived in the United States, and most of them came from southern and eastern Europe: Greece, Italy, Hungary, Poland, and Russia. By 1980, individuals of European origin composed the bulk of the United States population (approximately 75 percent) and Europeans continued to make up a significant proportion of the immigrants still arriving in the United States.

In the 1980 census, 50 million Americans reported their ancestry as English, 49 million listed German, and 40 million cited Irish. African Americans numbered 21 million, French 13 million, Italian 12 million, Scottish 10 million, Polish 8 million, Mexican 8 million, American Indian 7 million, and Dutch 6 million.

Such distinctive and overwhelming national identification has often been blurred in American cultural consciousness by the peculiar assimilative process of the United States. Economic and social discrimination, on one hand, pushed immigrants into early and often involuntary assimilation. The dedication of the Statue of Liberty in 1886—where the Jewish American poet Emma Lazarus' words "Give me . . . your huddled masses yearning to breathe free" are inscribed—was not unanimously endorsed. In the press and on the streets there were attacks on immigrants from southern and eastern Europe. When not changed by Ellis Island officials, the names of many

European American Identity
Selected Dates and Works

1820-1930	More than 4.25 million Irish immigrants come to the United States; more than 4.5 million Italians arrive in the United States.
1854	Henry David Thoreau mentions in *Walden* that at the bottom of the socioeconomic ladder are Native Americans, black slaves, and the Irish.
1860-1914	Fifteen million Europeans arrive in the United States, most of them from southern and eastern Europe.
1882	*Songs of a Semite*, by Emma Lazarus.
1885	William Dean Howells' *The Rise of Silas Lapham*.
1886	One of the Jewish American poet Emma Lazarus' sonnets is used as an inscription on the base of the Statue of Liberty.
1890	Danish-born journalist Jacob Riis, in *How the Other Half Lives*, details his fight against child labor, tenement conditions, and other abuses against the poor.
1901	Jacob Riis's autobiography *The Making of an American*.
1906	Upton Sinclair's *The Jungle*.
1908	*The Melting-Pot*, by the English Jewish writer Israel Zangwill.
1912	Mary Antin's *The Promised Land* contrasts the hardships Jews find in Europe with the opportunity they find in America.
1916	*Chicago Poems* by Carl Sandburg, the son of Swedish immigrants.
1917	Literacy Test of 1917.
1917	Abraham Cahan's *The Rise of David Levinsky*.
1918	Willa Cather's *My Ántonia*.
1920	*Hungry Hearts*, stories by Anzia Yezierska (also known as Hattie Mayer, the name which she was given at Ellis Island).
1920	Ludwig Lewisohn's *The Americanization of Edward Bok*.
1925	Anzia Yezierska's novel *Bread Givers*.
1926	*Abraham Lincoln: The Prairie Years*, by Carl Sandburg.
1929	Lewisohn's *Mid-Channel* describes the problems that Jews face in America.
1930	Michael Gold's *Jews Without Money*.
1932	Louis Adamic's *Laughing in the Jungle: The Autobiography of an Immigrant in America*.
1934	William Saroyan depicts the Armenian community in works such as *The Daring Young Man on the Flying Trapeze*, *My Name Is Aram* (1940), *The Time of Your Life* (1939), and *The Human Comedy* (1943).
1934	*Call It Sleep*, by Henry Roth.
1934	John O'Hara's *Appointment in Samarra*.
1935	Isaac Bashevis Singer emigrates to the United States.
1935	James T. Farrell's *Studs Lonigan: A Trilogy*.
1936	*The People, Yes*, by Carl Sandburg.
1938	Louis Adamic's *My America*.
1938	John Fante's *Wait Until Spring, Bandini*. His continuation of that story appears in 1939 with *Ask the Dust*, which follows the hero, Arthur Bandini, to Los Angeles, and in *Dago Red* in 1940.
1939	Pietro di Donato's *Christ in Concrete*.
1941	F. Scott Fitzgerald's unfinished *The Last Tycoon*.
1943	James T. Farrell's *My Days of Anger*.
1947	*A Tree Grows in Brooklyn*, by Betty Smith.
1956	Edwin O'Connor's *The Last Hurrah*.
1956	Eugene O'Neill's *Long Day's Journey into Night*.
1957	Mary McCarthy's *Memories of a Catholic Girlhood*.
1959	John Ciardi's *How Does a Poem Mean?*
1961	Tillie Olsen's *Tell Me a Riddle*.
1965	Jerzy Kosinski's *The Painted Bird*.
1969	Mario Puzo's *The Godfather*.
1969	Philip Roth's *Portnoy's Complaint*.
1977	Philip Caputo's *A Rumor of War*.
1983	*Ironweed*, by William Kennedy.
1985	William Kennedy's The Albany Cycle, the collective title that refers to his three novels that are set in Albany, New York.
1990	*East Is East*, by T. Coraghessan Boyle.
1992	Maureen Howard's *Natural History*.
1992	Gay Talese's *Unto the Sons*.

European immigrants often quickly were changed by the immigrants themselves, who as foreigners were greeted with hostility and suspicion but who as Americans were welcome. The Polish Sciborski might become Smith; the Italian Pina, Pine; the Jewish Greenberg, simply Green.

European Americans in the late nineteenth century were drawn by the lure of the American Dream, which promised equal access to wealth and possibility to all. Supporting this dream was the dominant ideological construct of the melting pot, which, like the symbolic cauldron in the Ford Motor Company graduation ceremonies, encouraged immigrants to give up their native heritage and take on a narrower American identity. Behind the melting pot theory was the belief in homogeneity over heterogeneity, assimilation over pluralism. The term itself was first popularized in a play, *The Melting-Pot*, by the English Jewish writer Israel Zangwill in 1908. As Werner Sollors has noted in *Beyond Ethnicity: Consent and Descent in American Culture* (1986): "More than any social or political theory, the rhetoric of Zangwill's play shaped American discourse on immigration and ethnicity, including most notably the language of self-declared opponents of the melting-pot concept."

Opponents of immigration have a long history in the United States, and the objects of their attacks have kept changing. The first nativist expression was an anti-Catholic sentiment, aimed mainly at the millions of Irish who immigrated after 1820. By the end of the nineteenth century, xenophobic feelings had shifted and were aimed at Slavic, Italian, Greek, and other eastern and southern European immigrants. The height of nativist opposition to immigration came during World War I. The literacy test of 1917 marked the beginning of the end of the open-door immigration policy of the United States. Legislation in the 1920's closed the door.

The process of assimilation during the nineteenth and twentieth centuries had a profound effect not only on European American identity but also on the literature and culture that different European American ethnic groups produced. In many cases forced by discrimination, loss of language, loss or change of name, and the ideological impetus of Americanization to give up ethnic roots, many European Americans ended up torn between American and European ethnic identities. If the members of an ethnic culture did not assimilate, they faced the danger of becoming ghettoized, forced into an almost secretive, subcultural status.

Writers in the twentieth century, in common with the cultures they represented, were often afraid to exhibit their ethnic identity. As late as 1969, when Mario Puzo published *The Godfather*, for example, critics within the Italian American community argued that the work would only confirm the worst stereotypes of Italians in the United States. In another novel of the same year, Philip Roth was condemned by Jewish community leaders for his characters in *Portnoy's Complaint*. Ethnic writers were hindered by their own ethnic communities from revealing too much, which made it easier for them to make the sometimes Faustian bargain with the dominant culture to trade their ethnic consciousness for entrance into the literary mainstream.

The dominant culture of the earlier twentieth century was clearly white, Anglo-Saxon, and Protestant, and the ideology of the melting pot reinforced the dominant culture's hold on the popular mind. All writers should be American, this theory held, and ethnic cultural and literary artifacts were exotic and suspect. One perhaps could go folk-dancing as a cultural curiosity, but European American ethnic identification was discouraged on a number of ideological and institutional levels. The dominant literature and literary culture were Anglo; students in different parts of the country all read the most famous works that had been written in England and New England, but they had little knowledge of works in other languages—including their native languages. High school students from New York City to rural New Mexico, from Seattle to Maine, might know the nineteenth century English novelist George Eliot's *Silas Marner: The Weaver of Raveloe* (1861) by the time they were graduated from high school but nothing of their own ethnic literary heritage. Sociological theory supported the notion that ethnic identification was an insignificant factor in success in American life.

In the 1960's, however, this cultural history changed. Nathan Glazer and Daniel Patrick Moynihan, in *Beyond the Melting Pot: The Negroes, Puerto Ricans, Jews, Italians, and Irish of*

New York City (1963), as James A. Banks has written in *Teaching Strategies for Ethnic Studies* (1991), "presented one of the first theoretical arguments that the melting pot conception . . . was inaccurate and incomplete. They argued that ethnicity in New York was important and that it would continue to be important for both politics and culture."

Similarly, Michael Novak's *The Rise of the Unmeltable Ethnics: Politics and Culture in the 1970's* (1971) helped to fuel the growth of the "new ethnicity" and the new ethnic consciousness in the 1970's, a consciousness that used not the melting pot metaphor but rather metaphors of a patchwork quilt, a salad bowl, or a kaleidoscope to explain the pluralistic nature of ethnicity in the United States. This theoretical underpinning worked to support the massive search that members of many ethnic groups were making for their history. Alex Haley's *Roots: The Saga of an American Family* (1976), which traces his ancestors back to Africa (and which became a popular television miniseries), helped to encourage similar rediscoveries in other ethnicities—and not only in those which had experienced the most recent discrimination (African American, Asian American, Latino, and Native American) but also in those European American communities that had supposedly been dominant through the twentieth century but that actually had been downplaying their ethnicity. For although American culture was decidedly European American in essence and influence from its beginnings, the assimilative process often meant that individual European identities—Scandinavian as well as Slavic—were lost. The multicultural movement of the 1970's and 1980's helped to recover and reinvigorate a number of ethnic identities and literatures, and the last quarter of the twentieth century saw the publication of many literary works reflecting the change: ethnic autobiographies, accounts of the search for ethnic roots, studies of ethnic culture and ethnic literatures, and novels and plays about the ethnic experience. The European American experience was at the center of this ethnic renaissance.

European American identity and literature

Critics and scholars began to talk about ethnic literature only at the end of the period of unrestricted immigration, when the closed doors into the United States threw the assimilative process into a sharper, harsher focus. Probably the keystone work in this regard is Abraham Cahan's *The Rise of David Levinsky*, published in 1917. As David M. Fine has written in *The City, the Immigrant, and American Fiction, 1880-1920* (1977), the novel

> occupies a pivotal position in the history of American literature. It . . . stands at the head of a long line of twentieth-century novels which would portray modern urban America from the eyes of the city's non-Anglo component. The novel's ambitious mixture of material success and spiritual failure, its insistence on the high cost of assimilation, and its concern with the identity crisis bred by the Americanization process place it squarely in the forefront of twentieth-century "minority voice" fiction.

The themes that Fine lists permeated all immigrant literature, in nonfiction (essay, autobiography) and in fiction (short story, novel), through the twentieth century. Repeatedly after 1917, European American writers depicted in depth and detail the painful process of assimilation, the pull between native and adoptive cultures, the mixed feelings of insecurity and hope. Where does my identity come from—the protagonists of dozens of plays and novels and autobiographies asked—from which of my two selves? A whole range of replies were given, from full assimilation to marginality, but under the hegemonic hold of melting-pot theory, more often than not the replies were unclear and confused.

In 1916, the critic Randolph Bourne posed the basic problem in his essay "Trans-National America" by citing the failure of the melting pot. "We are all foreign-born or the descendants of foreign-born," the Anglo-Saxon Bourne argued, and assimilation has clearly failed. "Assimilation, in other words, instead of washing out the memories of Europe made them more and more intensely real." Bourne's call for a truly multicultural and pluralistic "Trans-National America" would not be heeded for more than half a century.

Mary Antin's *The Promised Land* (1912) is a sensitive and touching account of a young Jewish woman's journey from rural Russia to urban America, and represents one end of the assimilative continuum, since it is an autobiography arguing for total Americanization. Her vivid description of the assimilation process is told through stories like the one of her father accompanying his children to their first day of school—and following his dream: "The boasted freedom of the New World meant to him far more than the right to reside, travel, and work wherever he pleased; it meant the freedom to speak his thoughts, to throw off the shackles of superstition, to test his own fate, unhindered by political or religious tyranny."

Other autobiographers of the period were less sure of the truth of the American Dream. The Danish-born journalist Jacob Riis, who in *How the Other Half Lives* (1890) describes the terrible conditions in New York City tenements, narrates the struggles of his own life in *The Making of an American* (1901) and urged his fellow Danish Americans to remain loyal to Denmark and its traditions. Louis Adamic's *Laughing in the Jungle: The Autobiography of an Immigrant in America* (1932) and *My America* (1938) describe his journey from Slovenia to America, criticize several aspects of American democracy, and conclude that immigrants must take pride in the customs and qualities of their lands of origin. Autobiography has often been a more common and powerful literary genre than fiction, especially for ethnic writers, who could use the form to wrestle with their immigrant history and try to figure out their own identity. Ludwig Lewisohn's *Mid-Channel* (1929) and Edward Bok's *The Americanization of Edward Bok* (1920), the one German Jewish and the other Dutch, are two other examples of European American autobiography from this period.

Perhaps the most poignant and powerful literary representative of early European immigration was Anzia Yezierska, who traveled from Russian Poland to New York's Lower East Side. Writing under her European name (rather than Hattie Mayer, the name which she had been given at Ellis Island), she was the only Jewish woman from Eastern Europe of her generation to produce a real body of fiction. Her novels and short stories, including *Hungry Hearts* (stories, 1920) and *Bread Givers* (novel, 1925), depict the lives of marginalized Americans, especially immigrant women.

These histories—of immigration and assimilation, of the hope and failure of the American Dream—would be told again and again through the Great Depression of the 1930's, and in spite of the restrictions facing European American writers. Carl Sandburg (a second-generation Swede) produced some of the most powerful poetry about urban America written in the middle of the twentieth century, in addition to writing a multivolume biography of a true American hero, Abraham Lincoln. Sandburg never lost the working-class perspective of his immigrant family. Likewise, William Saroyan produced some of the most poignant descriptions of life in his Fresno, California, Armenian community (*The Daring Young Man on the Flying Trapeze*, 1934, and *My Name Is Aram*, 1940), and wrote plays, including *The Time of Your Life* (1939), and novels, such as *The Human Comedy* (1943), that capture his genial spirit.

Other European American writers were depicting the struggles of life for immigrants on the margin. Henry Roth in *Call It Sleep* (1934) follows a young Austrian Jewish immigrant through his harrowing adventures in New York City. Thomas Bell, in *Out of This Furnace* (1941), a novel of immigrant labor in America, details the hardships that faced his Slovak family in the western Pennsylvania steel mills. The two novels are comparable to a number of other Depression-era works—Roth in his implied criticism of capitalist society, and Bell in his argument that his characters should be able to retain their native heritage.

The immigrant story was told by nonimmigrant writers as well. Upton Sinclair, in *The Jungle* (1906), depicts the horrendous working conditions which his Lithuanian characters and other eastern European immigrants faced in the stockyards of Chicago. Willa Cather, in another classic of American literature, *My Ántonia* (1918), told the story of a Bohemian family struggling to make a living on the Nebraska prairie. The dying grandmother in Tillie Olsen's powerful story "Tell Me a Riddle" (1961) was once an orator in the 1905 Russian revolution.

In spite of the melting-pot theory that prevailed through the middle of the twentieth century, in other words, writers continued to tap the rich vein of their ethnic and immigrant roots. Many of the best descriptions of immigrant life—Roth's and Olsen's and Lewisohn's, or Michael Gold's *Jews Without Money* (1930)—came from Jewish American writers whose sense of community was so strong that they could more easily dip into that heritage. Saul Bellow and Bernard Malamud tapped that source after World War II, and Isaac Bashevis Singer, who was born in Poland and emigrated to the United States in 1935, and Cynthia Ozick have also explored it.

Immigration did not cease during the twentieth century for European writers. Polish American writer Jerzy Kosinski, in the secretive style that characterized so much of his life, fled his native Poland for America in an elaborate scheme in the 1950's and wrote about his childhood there during World War II in the vivid novel *The Painted Bird* (1965). Vladimir Nabokov, who was born in Russia and educated in England, lived and wrote in Germany and France. In 1940, he came to the United States and produced some of his most important novels after that date. Aleksandr Solzhenitsyn, on the other hand, who emigrated to the United States from the Soviet Union in the 1970's, never matched the literary power he had achieved when he was writing in his native Russia.

Irish American literature

Irish American literature is one of the oldest and largest collections of writing produced by a European American group. Before the Revolutionary War, the English were the majority of migrants to America. After independence, it was the Irish: Between 1820 and 1930, more than 4.25 million Irish immigrants came to the United States. For their first decades, life was hard, and they faced constant discrimination. The sign No Irish Need Apply could be seen on businesses into the twentieth century. The people Henry David Thoreau mentions in *Walden* (1854) at the bottom of the socioeconomic ladder are Native Americans, black slaves, and the Irish.

In spite of their tremendous difficulties, the Irish produced a cultural legacy in the United States second to none. A number of major nineteenth century writers—Henry James, Edgar Allan Poe, and William Dean Howells among them—had Irish ancestry that played no part in their literature, but dozens of writers used that heritage in their literary work. The first Irish American writer to gain national prominence was Peter Finley Dunne, the turn-of-the-century newspaperman whose fictional Irish bartender Mr. Dooley became the most popular figure in American journalism. Up until World War I, Mr. Dooley commented in Dunne's columns on every important American political or social event—including immigration: "As a pilgrim father that missed the first boats, I must raise me claryon voice again' the invasion iv this fair land be th' paupers an' arnychists iv effete Europe. Ye bet I must—because I'm here first." Dunne's sharp, often fatalistic humor was characteristic of much later Irish American literature.

Several of the major twentieth century American modernists were Irish. F. Scott Fitzgerald boasted of his Irish heritage, and a number of minor Irish American characters figure in his romantic novels and short stories. In Fitzgerald's unfinished *The Last Tycoon* (1941) Irish characters play major roles, and Fitzgerald seems in that book to be grappling with his own Irishness. Perhaps the most important playwright of the American stage, Eugene O'Neill, was the son of an Irishman who had come to America after the great potato famine. Some of O'Neill's masterpieces feature Irish American characters. O'Neill wrote about his family and troubled childhood late in his career in *Long Day's Journey into Night* (1956). James T. Farrell, in his *Studs Lonigan: A Trilogy* (1935) and in the later four novels centering on the character of Danny O'Neill (including *My Days of Anger*, 1943), describes Irish families struggling on Chicago's South Side to overcome economic and personal oppression, often holding on to their ethnic and religious prejudices. John O'Hara was much less sympathetic to his Irish characters, and in his novels set in the fictional Gibbsville (resembling his native Pottsville, Pennsylvania), such as the 1934 *Appointment in Samarra*, the Irish characters are usually outsiders and often contemptible.

Other writers in mid-century continued to add to the Irish American heritage. Betty Smith, who was not Irish herself but who had grown up in the Irish American Williamsburg section of Brooklyn, wrote one of the best novels about the Irish experience in America in *A Tree Grows in Brooklyn* (1947). Mary McCarthy's novels occasionally contain Irish characters, and her *Memories of a Catholic Girlhood* (1957) is a compelling account of growing up in America in the early decades of the twentieth century. The Southerner Flannery O'Connor's novels and short stories are greatly influenced by her Irish Catholic heritage.

Many Irish American writers, as might be expected, deal with the Irish in the cities. Edwin

O'Connor paints a masterful portrait of Boston Irish political bosses in *The Last Hurrah* (1956), and William Kennedy's novels about Albany, New York (including *Ironweed*, 1983) have been critical and commercial successes. Maureen Howard's *Natural History* (1992) deals with the Irish power structure in Bridgeport, Connecticut, early in the twentieth century.

Late twentieth century Irish American writers include the novelists Mary Gordon, J. F. Powers, J. P. Donleavy, and T. Coraghessan Boyle, poets from Frank O'Hara to Tess Gallagher, and journalists from the streetwise Jimmy Breslin, Pete Hamill, and Joe Flaherty to the elegant Brendan Gill of *The New Yorker*.

Italian American literature

The largest immigrant groups to arrive in the latter part of the nineteenth century were Southern and eastern Europeans. Between 1820 and 1930, more than 4.5 million Italians arrived in the United States, and, like the Irish Americans, they produced a number of writers whose work expressed particular awareness of their background.

Pietro di Donato's *Christ in Concrete* (1939) depicts the squalid world of Italian construction workers, and is the classic expression of the Italian American experience. John Fante wrote a number of novels and short stories about the Italian American experience: *Wait Until Spring, Bandini* (1938) tells of family life in his native Colorado. *Ask the Dust* (1939) follows the hero, Arturo Bandini, to Los Angeles, and *Dago Red* (1940) includes a number of family sketches. Jerre Mangione in *Monte Allegro* (1943) tells of a son who returns to Sicily and feels a mystical sense of being at home. The list of successful and popular Italian American novelists runs from Paul Gallico through Mario Puzo and Evan Hunter to Don De Lillo.

Italian American writers have in fact contributed to every literary genre. Bernard De Voto was one of the most important literary critics in the middle of the twentieth century, and John Ciardi was a preeminent American poet and translator. Lawrence Ferlinghetti and Gregory Corso were leading members of the Beat movement of the 1950's, and contemporary poets include Helen Barolini, Rose Basile Green, Diane DiPrima, and Dana Gioia. Finally, Italian Americans have become prominent journalists. Philip Caputo's *A Rumor of War* (1977) is one of the best accounts of the Vietnam War, for example, and Gay Talese has written a number of volumes of note, including *Unto the Sons* (1992), about the Italian American immigrant experience.

Immigrant literature has often dealt with the American Dream, with its promise as well as with its collapse. More than most literatures, the body of work produced by European American writers has reflected the struggles of assimilation, the loss of identity in that process, and the pain of being split between two cultures. The heroes and heroines of European American literature—David Levinsky, Studs Lonigan, and Arturo Bandini among them—are often filled with self-doubt and search blindly for their identity. In those characters and their struggles, their creators helped to expand the definition and the canon of American literature.

SUGGESTED READINGS

Banks, James A. *Teaching Strategies for Ethnic Studies*. Newton, Mass.: Allyn & Bacon, 1991. Useful for the student as well as the teacher; relates key themes and concepts to texts.

Bourne, Randolph. *The Radical Will: Selected Writings*. Edited by Olaf Hansen. Berkeley: University of California Press, 1992. An overview of Bourne's ideas.

Fine, David M. *The City, the Immigrant, and American Fiction, 1880-1920*. Metuchen, N.J.: Scarecrow Press, 1977. A starting place for study of immigrant fiction.

Fuchs, Lawrence H. *The American Kaleidoscope: Race, Ethnicity, and the Civic Culture*. Hanover, N.H.: University Press of New England, 1990. Comprehensive review of American culture, in the context of a non-melting-pot metaphor.

Glazer, Nathan, and Daniel Patrick Moynihan. *Beyond the Melting Pot: The Negroes, Puerto Ricans, Jews, Italians, and Irish of New York City*. Cambridge, Mass.: MIT Press, 1963. A landmark of ethnic studies, centered on New York City but with implications for ethnic studies in all America.

Greeley, Andrew. *Ethnicity in the United States: A Preliminary Reconnaissance*. New York: John Wiley & Sons, 1974. Ethnicity of European origin is the focus.

Novak, Michael. *The Rise of the Unmeltable Ethnics: Politics and Culture in the 1970's.* New York: Macmillan, 1971. A central work in the revival of interest in ethnicity in the 1970's and after.

Sollors, Werner. *Beyond Ethnicity: Consent and Descent in American Culture.* New York: Oxford University Press, 1986. Argues that ethnic literature is the prototypical American literature.

—David Peck

See also Acculturation; *Albany Cycle, The*; Alienation; Antin, Mary; Bellow, Saul; Boyle, T. Coraghessan; Cahan, Abraham; Cather, Willa; Emigration and immigration; Ferlinghetti, Lawrence; Jewish American identity; Kosinski, Jerzy; McCarthy, Mary; Malamud, Bernard; Melting pot; *My Days of Anger*; O'Connor, Flannery; Olsen, Tillie; O'Neill, Eugene; Ozick, Cynthia; Roth, Philip; Sandburg, Carl; Saroyan, William; Singer, Isaac Bashevis; *Studs Lonigan*

Eva's Man

AUTHOR: Gayl Jones (1949-   )
FIRST PUBLISHED: 1976
IDENTITIES: African American; women

Eva's Man, Gayl Jones's provocative second novel, is a psychological tale of repression, manipulation, and suffering. It is a gothic story of madness—Eva's madness—and the psychological effects of violence on black women. From her prison asylum room, where she has been incarcerated for five years for poisoning, then castrating, her lover, Eva Medina Canada, the psychotic title character, narrates the events which led up to her bizarre and violent act. Although she has maintained a steadfast and defiant silence in response to the grinding interrogation of the male judicial authorities—the police and psychiatrists—Eva readily tells her story to the reader. Through time and space intrusions, many flashbacks and a combination of dreams, fantasies, memories, interrogation, and exchanges between herself and her cellmate, Elvira, Eva tells everything except her motive.

In the unsequential narrative, Eva's story delineates unequivocally men's malevolence and women's natural acceptance of a destiny inevitably circumscribed by this malevolence. Eva's appropriating of and identification with the story of Queen Bee, the femme fatale whose love, like a deadly sting, kills off every man with whom she falls in love, suggests that women resign themselves to a female destiny. This horrid fatalism blames and punishes women for their sexuality. Paradoxically, since the drone is always at the service of the queen bee, it is women who have power to affirm or deny manhood. Aligning herself with the queen bee, Eva kills Davis, the drone, rather than submit to his excessive domination.

For Eva the lessons in the violent consequences of womanhood and female sexuality began early. Prepubescent Freddy, a neighbor boy, initiates her sexually with a dirty Popsicle stick. Her mother's lover, Tyrone, makes her feel him. She sees her father punish her mother's infidelity with rape. Cousin Alphonse solicits sex from her, and a thumbless man harasses her sexually. Moses Tribbs propositions her, thereby provoking her attack on him with a pocket knife. Her fifty-five-year-old husband James, out of jealousy, disallows a telephone in the house. Finally, Davis, her lover, imprisons and uses her for five days. To each of these men, Eva (like other women characters in the novel, including her mother) exists merely as an object to satisfy insatiable male sexual needs. In response to this objectification and violence by men, Eva remains steadfastly silent, choosing neither to explain her extreme action nor to defend herself.

Apart from the bizarreness of Eva's brutal act, which delineates the level of her madness, it is perhaps the exclusive use of the first-person narrative voice and the lack of authorial intrusion or questioning of Eva's viewpoint that make *Eva's Man* controversial and successful.

SUGGESTED READINGS

Davidson, C. M. "Love 'em and Lynch 'em: The Castration Motif in Gayl Jones's *Eva's Man*." *African-American Review* 29 (Fall, 1995): 393-410.

Dixon, Melvin. *Ride out the Wilderness.* Chicago: University of Illinois Press, 1987.

Evans, Mari, ed. *Black Women Writers: 1950-1980*. Garden City, N.Y.: Doubleday, 1984.
Robinson, Sally. *Engendering the Subject*. Albany: State University of New York Press, 1991.
—Pamela J. Olubunmi Smith

See also African American identity; Black English; Feminism; Jones, Gayl; Slave narratives; Violence

Exile. *See* **Expatriate identity**

Existentialism

DEFINITION: Existentialism is a way of thinking that stresses the priority of existence over essence.

The existentialist insists that, for human beings, existence precedes essence. The essence of an object is its function. For example, the essence of a chair is that it supports a seated person. As a chair is manufactured to fulfill this function, its essence precedes its existence: The manufacturer determines the function of the chair before the chair is brought into existence by being manufactured. Humans come into existence without a predetermined function, or essence, which is to say there is no manufacturer of humans. Each individual human self, or subject, must recognize that he or she exists and then determine his or her essence. Commitment to one's essence constitutes authenticity. One's essence may be whatever one chooses, within one's capacities: medical practice, criminality, aspiration to sovereignty, plumbing, teaching, meditation, aspiration to spiritual fulfillment, or whatever one may wish as a basis for meaning in life. To choose religion, as Søren Kierkegaard did, is to want something beyond existence and to commit one's self to the quest for faith in that something, faith amounting to a subjective experience of that something, which may be called God. The religious existentialist begins with existence and then posits God as, not pre-existential, but extra- or supraexistential. The atheistic existentialist seeks only to make the best of existence and to posit nothing beyond existence.

The atheistic and the religious existentialist accept responsibility for existing. Neither blames God or parents or social conditions for her or his situation. The existentialist accepts the datum that he or she has been thrown into existence. Martin Heidegger calls this having-been-thrown-into-existence *Geworfenheit* (thrownness). The existentialist is not concerned with the thrower or the whence-thrown, only with the thrownness. As an atheist, one seeks to direct one's thrownness, for which one is responsible, since it is one's own, toward one's choice of action, to which one attaches responsibility. As a religious existentialist, one responsibly directs one's thrownness "toward God" (Kierkegaard's *ad deum*), with the understanding that God is the end, not the agent, of the direction.

The criteria of authenticity are: that what one does is what one chooses to do, and not what another has chosen for one, that it is a true manifestation of one's self as one's own-most (Heidegger's *eigenst*) thing, and that one is alone responsible for it. For Heidegger authenticity is the own-ly (the *eigentlich*); for Jean-Paul Sartre it is *l'authentique*, a word which even etymologically appears to mean "guilty-self" or "responsible self."

The existentialist limitation of reality to existence is the core of ancient Greek materialism and is expressed in philosophy by the Atomists as well as in tragedy, in which the terrifying realization that there is nothing beyond existence is given dramatic form. In the Middle Ages, the philosophy of John Scotus Erigena posits existence and nothingness, along with the nonexistence, which is to say the supraexistence, of God. Like the modern religious existentialist, Erigena begins with existence and therefrom commits himself to his conceptualization of deity.

Modern existentialism begins with, and receives its name from, Kierkegaard's religious writings and his subjective view of existence. Atheistic existentialism follows in the literary work of Friedrich Nietzsche. Kierkegaard's concept of *Angst* (as discussed in his *Begrebet Angest*, 1844; *The Concept of Dread*, 1944) holds that fear without object—that is, the sense of fear unaccompanied by a knowledge of what one is afraid of—is one's fear of nothingness and the beginning

Existence and essence

Authenticity

History

of one's need for something beyond existence, which can be experienced only in religious faith. Nietzsche expressed the inability of modern people to believe in the god of primitive and medieval Judaeo-Christianity as the death of God and called upon humankind to transform itself into a higher kind of being.

In the twentieth century, existentialism developed in the philosophical school of Sartre, Simone de Beauvoir, and Maurice Merleau-Ponty. This school combined a Kierkegaardian view of existence and a Nietzschean irreligiousness with phenomenology (a subjective inquiry into the nature of the forms of consciousness). Religious thinkers who adhered to the confrontation with existence as antecedent to the determination of essence included Martin Buber and Gabriel-Honoré Marcel.

Literary existentialism

Heidegger's preoccupation with being as the reality of existence led him to find subjective reality in poetry, in illustration of which he produced a masterly critique of the poetry of Friedrich Hölderlin. In fiction and drama, Sartre, de Beauvoir, and Albert Camus present characters as exemplars of authenticity or inauthenticity. In one short story, "Le Mur" (1939; "The Wall," 1948), Sartre depicts a Spanish Loyalist whose death sentence will be revoked if he betrays a friend. At the last minute he jokingly discloses what he supposes to be the false whereabouts of his friend, and his life is spared as his fellow Loyalist is actually found there and killed. Against a reader's conventional pleasure at the character's release stands the inauthenticity of a failure either to maintain a commitment to nonbetrayal by saying absolutely nothing or to have committed the self to the betrayal. De Beauvoir has a short story in which a patently inauthentic woman blames everyone but herself for the misfortunes she has brought upon herself. Camus' *L'Étranger* (1942; *The Stranger*, 1946) is a novel about an inauthentic man who becomes authentic by learning to exercise conscious choice, although he is left only with the choice of his own execution. Outside France, writers such as Miguel de Unamuno, Franz Kafka, and Pär Lagerkvist wrote fiction involving the authentic and inauthentic reaction to the ineradicable and unsatisfiable need for religious faith.

Existentialist literature in the United States found its most practicable vehicle in the *film noir* screenplays produced between 1940 and 1958. These offered a realistic reappraisal of modern life and a very somber view of human motivations as materialistic and inauthentically centered in self, as opposed to being authentically self-determinative. Characters were developed in the context of irresponsible selfishness, like the conspiratorial Walter Neff and Phyllis Dietrichson in Raymond Chandler's screenplay *Double Indemnity* (1944). The *film noir* world is godless and psychologically existential. In the Anthony Veiller/John Huston screen adaptation of Ernest Hemingway's "The Killers," Ole Andreson is characterized as inauthentic in his inability to achieve true consciousness of his obsession with a woman whose inauthenticity, in turn, is marked by her failure to accept responsibility for her choices.

Hemingway's fiction has been appraised as existentialist by various critics, who liken Hemingway's nihilism to the nothingness of the existentialists. Existentialist despair and the exposure of inauthenticity are unmistakable in the works of T. S. Eliot, Arthur Miller, James T. Farrell, and William Faulkner. These writers, along with Henrik Ibsen and Kafka, expose a dreary world in need of spiritual orientation.

Existentialism has been found to be influential among North American writers such as John Barth, Saul Bellow, Walker Percy, and John Updike. For example, Barth's first novel, *The Floating Opera* (1955; revised, 1967), works out the theme of the question of suicide. The *Angst* in the name of Updike's character, Rabbit Angstrom, is a clue to existentialist direction. In Updike's *In the Lilies of the Field* (1966) the author traces despair consequent upon the unsatisfied need for God by, not an individual self, as would comport better with existentialism, but a family representing a collective America. In *Walker Percy: An American Search* (1978), Robert Coles examines the extent to which Kierkegaard, Heidegger, Sartre, and Camus have informed the essays and fiction of Percy. Saul Bellow introduces into his novels a small amount of German existentialism and, by contrast, Norman Mailer clearly iterates the nuances of French existentialism. North American writers tend to touch upon, use, or coincide with existentialist ideas, but not extensively to propagate existentialism, as Sartre and de Beauvoir did in their fiction, or as England's John

Fowles did in his first version of *The Magus* (1965), in which the principal character's search for authenticity and the realization of his true self exemplify existentialism. Fowles was later, however, to repudiate his own predilection for existentialism.

Mailer's portrait of Gary Gilmore, a convicted murderer executed by firing squad in Utah, in *The Executioner's Song* (1979) is, in its attention to choosing what one is, perhaps his most existentialist work. Earlier he attributed to himself an existentialist proclivity in such works as "The White Negro" and *Existentialist Errands* (1972). In "The White Negro" he claims, correctly, that "to be an existentialist, one must be able to feel oneself—one must know one's desires, one's rages, one's anguish, one must be aware of the character of one's frustration and know what would satisfy it." His insistence, however, that to be "a real existentialist . . . one must be religious" is not acceptable by atheistic existentialists, who take it as "bad faith" (self-deception) to accede to any need for anything beyond existence. Mailer's distance from Sartre can be measured in his notation of Sartre as a "perverted existentialist."

Any work of fiction that concerns itself with authentic individualism and the responsible self, whether positively or by exposure of the antitheses of either of these, is consonant with existentialism, whether or not its author claims to be existentialistic, as, in fact, few do. Minnie McInnis McMinn in William March's *The Looking Glass* (1943), J. D. Salinger's Holden Caulfield in *The Catcher in the Rye* (1945), and Charles Portis' Mattie Ross in *True Grit* (1968) are among the many North American characters who, whatever their authors' intents, incorporate the existentialist notion of a self unwilling to compromise its individuality or to blame another for its imperfections or adversities. Their authors, however, would not affirm such identification.

SUGGESTED READINGS

Barrett, William. *What Is Existentialism?* New York: Grove Press, 1964. Outlines the debt of existentialist thought to Heidegger.

Friedman, Maurice, ed. *The Worlds of Existentialism: A Critical Reader*. New York: Random House, 1964. Existentialist thought from classical antiquity to the mid-twentieth century.

Heidegger, Martin. *Poetry, Language, Thought*. Translated by Albert Hofstadter. New York: Harper & Row, 1971. Seven important essays by Heidegger on aesthetics.

Kaufmann, Walter. *Existentialism from Dostoevski to Sartre*. Rev. ed. New York: World, 1975. Readings illustrating existentialism as "not a philosophy but a label for several different revolts against traditional philosophy."

Keefe, Terry. *French Existentialist Fiction: Changing Moral Perspectives*. Totowa, N.J.: Barnes & Noble Books, 1986. Essays on the fiction of Beauvoir, Sartre, and Camus.

Santoni, Ronald E. *Bad Faith, Good Faith, and Authenticity in Sartre's Early Philosophy*. Philadelphia: Temple University Press, 1995. Helps to clarify the idea of existentialist authenticity; includes a comparison of Sartre and Heidegger on the concept.

Sartre, Jean-Paul. *What Is Literature?* Translated by Bernard Frechtman. New York: Philosophical Library, 1949. Four essays on the need for commitment in literature.

Solomon, Robert C., ed. *Existentialism*. New York: Random House, 1974. Useful survey of European existentialists, with selections from four North Americans: Mailer, Bellow, Barth, and Miller.

West, Theodora L., ed. *The Continental Short Story: An Existential Approach*. New York: Odyssey Press, 1969. Analyzes the existentialist content and direction of numerous short stories by European authors, beginning with Nikolai Gogol and Fyodor Dostoevski.

—Roy Arthur Swanson

See also Bellow, Saul; Faulkner, William; Mailer, Norman; Underground man: a literary archetype

Expatriate identity

DEFINITION: American writers have often gained personal and cultural identity by living abroad, particularly in Europe.

Definitions and background

The issues raised by the history of American literary expatriation must begin with the question of how closely writers can be associated with their country's cultural experience. Some literature seems indelibly linked to its national origin—for example, the novels of Thomas Hardy (such as *The Return of the Native*, 1878) to southwestern England, Boris Pasternak's *Doctor Zhivago* (1957) to Russia, or William Faulkner to his imaginary Yoknapatawpha County, Mississippi. Conversely, some literature seems absolutely untethered to national roots—the novels of Joseph Conrad, for example, a Polish émigré writing in English of experiences gained in sailing voyages around the world.

The question then becomes, how important is it for writers to be living in their native countries in order to produce their best work? Exiles (people who have been forced from their countries for political reasons) and expatriates (self-exiles, or those who have voluntarily left) have often produced great literature while living away from their countries of birth: The nineteenth century Russian novelist Ivan Turgenev lived much of his career in France. Isak Dinesen, the Danish short-story writer, lived from 1914 to 1931 in Kenya, Africa, although she published all of her fiction after that period. The French poet Arthur Rimbaud lived the last years of his life in Africa, while the Scottish novelist Robert Louis Stevenson died on his beloved island of Samoa.

Expatriation or self-exile can be undertaken for political reasons (for example, a disagreement with a country's government), or it can be caused by perceived cultural lacks in the native country. The artists who fled Nazi Germany to come to California, for example, were clearly political exiles or political expatriates: writers such as Thomas Mann and Bertolt Brecht, composers such as Kurt Weill, and film directors such as Billy Wilder. The cultural effect produced by this influx of talent in the 1930's is incalculable. The ideas and talents of these artists influenced American art in a number of ways, and vice versa. On the other hand, the British novelists—Evelyn Waugh and Aldous Huxley, for example—who came to Hollywood in the same period were apparently lured by what appeared to be easy living. There is no guarantee that expatriation will produce great art: The Mexican novelist Carlos Fuentes has continued to produce remarkable fiction while living in the United States; the Russian writer Aleksandr Solzhenitsyn has been less successful.

Exile and expatriation are conditions that have existed since the beginnings of literature: The famous Roman poet Ovid was exiled away from Rome. James Joyce lived most of his creative life outside Ireland, which inspired his work. Physical distance from one's native country may give writers a perspective they did not have before; travelers often comment on the fact that they see their own country more clearly from a foreign land. Certainly, some of the best descriptions of the United States have come from foreign visitors: Alexis de Tocqueville's *De la démocratie en Amérique* (1835, 1840; *Democracy in America*, 1835, 1840) and Charles Dickens' *American Notes* (1842) are two accurate depictions of the United States in the middle of the nineteenth century.

Exile and expatriation can be crucial in infusing art and literature with new ideas and spirit. Living in another culture, artists and writers are able to break free of insular, inherited habits and traditions and thus expand the possibilities of their own art. The number of American artists (the painter Mary Cassatt, for example) who lived in France at the end of the nineteenth century is proof enough of that fact.

The issue of expatriation has defined American literature. Many American writers have lived abroad at one time or another—usually, although not exclusively, in England and France—and the effects of those years of expatriation are incalculable on the development of American literature. In fact, it is easier in tracing that literary history to list those writers who did not live abroad during some important part of their career. For every Henry David Thoreau or Emily Dickinson who stuck close to home, there was a Henry Wadsworth Longfellow or a Margaret Fuller wandering Europe for long stretches. Expatriation has not only affected artists, but become a theme in their art as well: The identities of writers and the subjects of their writings often undergo significant transformations because of their expatriate experiences.

The nineteenth century

From the beginning of American literature, writers and artists have returned to Europe to renew their art. Except for Native Americans, all American writers have cultural origins somewhere else. The dominant culture of the Atlantic seaboard was British, and colonial writers showed their dependence upon English sources, imitating British literature in form and genre, if not in subject.

Two major American fiction writers, Washington Irving and James Fenimore Cooper, spent considerable time abroad, Irving for twenty-four years, and Cooper for eight. Irving in fact wrote a number of works in Europe, including a biography of Christopher Columbus, and a romantic travel book on Spain called *The Legends of the Alhambra* (1832). He is most important as the father of the American short story, and it is significant that of the thirty-two tales collected in *The Sketch Book of Geoffrey Crayon, Gent.*, of 1820, only six (including "The Legend of Sleepy Hollow" and "Rip Van Winkle") have American subjects or settings. Cooper was less influenced by European living—although his five Leatherstocking Tales (such as *The Last of the Mohicans*, 1841) certainly followed the British novel in form. His expatriation resulted in weak novels and the superior nonfiction work *Notions of the Americans* (1828). His repatriation in 1833 turned Cooper into a social satirist, and he became increasingly critical of his own country.

Nathaniel Hawthorne had published his best novels—*The Scarlet Letter* (1850) and *The House of the Seven Gables* (1851)—before he was appointed consul to Liverpool, England, in 1853. He returned to the United States in 1860, and his last novel, *The Marble Faun* (1880), reflects those years in Europe. Its setting is Italy, but its characters and themes continue to reflect Hawthorne's preoccupation with the consequences of sin and guilt.

Europe was influential on perhaps the best American novelist of the nineteenth century, Henry James, who lived most of his adult life in Europe. His major novels—from *The American* (1877) and *The Portrait of a Lady* (1881) through *The Ambassadors* (1903) and *The Golden Bowl* (1904)—are all set in Europe, and one of his central and compelling themes is the intersection of American innocence and European maturity. It is this clash that propels the plots of his major works, and which gave James his own literary identity.

The realist William Dean Howells spent the Civil War as consul in Venice, but his major novels were written later. Harold Frederic lived for many years in England, and his best novel, *The Damnation of Theron Ware* (1896), shows its influence. Edith Wharton, a disciple of James, lived in France from 1907 until her death, and, while her most important works are set in the United States, the influence of her European emigration can be seen in, for example, *The Age of Innocence* (1920). The poet T. S. Eliot emigrated to England in 1914 and became a British subject in 1927. Expatriation broadened the cultural identity of many American writers.

The major period of American expatriation occurred after World War I. A number of writers— including the poet e. e. cummings and the novelist John Dos Passos—were in Europe during World War I, and stayed. Part of the reason was that the United States in the 1920's seemed an alien place; after contact with the artistic riches of the Continent, and the devastation the war had wrought, the narrow, small-town values of the United States seemed parochial and provincial. In addition, a dollar could carry a writer much further in postwar Europe, and a number of writers—most notably Ernest Hemingway and F. Scott Fitzgerald—made the journey to Europe to live. They became what Gertrude Stein called the lost generation, but they found something of inestimable literary value in their European sojourns.

The 1920's

Stein, like the poet Ezra Pound, had actually been in Europe since before World War I, and the two became the mentors for the many younger writers who began to appear after 1920, encouraging, editing, and publishing their early efforts. Although Hemingway would later disparage Stein's influence in *A Moveable Feast* (1964), she had a great effect on the style of the younger writer. His first collection of stories, *In Our Time* (1925), was published while he was living in Paris, and reflects the early European influence. While some of the stories focus on a young Nick Adams growing up in the Midwest, at least half—including "A Very Short Story," "Cat in the Rain," and "Out of Season"—concern Americans living in Europe in the aftermath of World War I.

Hemingway's later work showed the same international dimensions. His first novel, *The Sun Also Rises* (1926), is set in Paris and Pamplona, where American characters discover their identities—or lack of them—in interaction with European citizens and geography. Likewise, *A Farewell to Arms* (1929), which takes place during World War I, concerns the protagonist's attempt to carve meaning out of a world which has seemingly lost it. Hemingway's later works—*For Whom the Bell Tolls* (1939) and *The Old Man and the Sea* (1952)—continued to reflect Hemingway's nomadic life.

Other American writers, including Katherine Anne Porter, Hart Crane, and Archibald Macleish, spent much of the 1920's and 1930's abroad. F. Scott Fitzgerald's *Tender Is the Night* (1934)—considered by many critics his best work after *The Great Gatsby* (1925)—deals with Fitzgerald's expatriate years and reflects the issues and ideas that concerned the lost generation.

After the lost generation

American writers have continued to find cultural homes in Europe. Many went abroad in disgust with American cultural policy and practice in their native country. African American writers, like their counterparts in music and art, found Europe a much more comfortable place to establish their artistic identities than their racially troubled homeland. Richard Wright spent many years in France and, while the books he wrote in expatriation never matched his earlier work (the novel *Native Son*, 1941, and the autobiography *Black Boy*, 1944), he was an important mo"tl for other African American writers such as James Baldwin, who lived in self-exile in France and Switzerland for many years and whose fiction and nonfiction often reflect Europe. The distance allowed Baldwin to see even more pointedly the limitations of his native land. Other writers found solace elsewhere—Paul Bowles and William S. Burroughs in northern African cities such as Tangiers. Katherine Anne Porter lived in Mexico. Maya Angelou spent several years in Ghana during its early years of independence. By the end of the twentieth century, in fact, as technology and travel made the world a smaller place, American writers were choosing to live in many locations, often alternating years at home and abroad. Personal and cultural identity, as writers have demonstrated, does not depend on geography. In fact, expatriation may—as in the cases of James, Hemingway, Baldwin, and Angelou—actually sharpen the artist's perspective of his or her homeland.

SUGGESTED READINGS

Cowley, Malcolm. *Exile's Return: A Literary Odyssey of the 1920's*. 1934. Reprint. New York: Viking Press, 1951. The best description of the lost generation, by a writer who participated in the expatriation of the 1920's.

Dunbar, Ernest, ed. *The Black Expatriates: A Study of American Negroes in Exile*. London: Gollancz, 1968. A collection of African American expatriate writings, with an introduction by the editor.

Earnest, Ernest. *Expatriates and Patriots: American Artists, Scholars, and Writers in Europe*. Durham, N.C.: Duke University Press, 1968. Earnest has chapters on the major writers: Irving, Cooper, Fuller, Hawthorne, James, Frederic, Wharton, and the expatriates of the 1920's.

Ross, Ishbel. *The Expatriates*. New York: Thomas Y. Crowell, 1970. A popular survey, from the diplomats of the American Revolution to the hippies of the 1960's.

—David Peck

See also Baldwin, James; Hemingway, Ernest; Wright, Richard

Face of an Angel

AUTHOR: Denise Elia Chávez (1948-   )
FIRST PUBLISHED: 1994
IDENTITIES: Latino; West and Southwest; women

Face of an Angel specifically addresses the quest for identity of Soveida Dosamantes, a hardworking waitress at El Farol Mexican Restaurant in southern New Mexico. The rich cast of characters around Soveida provides detailed portraits of the lives of Mexican, American, and Mexican American working-class men and women in the Southwest. The work describes these characters' various struggles to know themselves and to be accepted in a multicultural setting. The novel speaks compellingly of the importance of the individual self and the social attitudes that allow the individual freedom to function.

Soveida, who narrates most of the novel, has grown up in Agua Oscura, a fictional small town in the desert Southwest. Soveida explores the boundaries of her life through her interactions with her mother Dolores, her grandmother Mama Lupita, her cousin Mara, and a wide cast of other townspeople. As Denise Chávez brings this population of memorable characters to life, their actions and motivations are shown to be reflections of social attitudes about race, ethnicity, gender, and class. It is difficult for them to break through these received attitudes to wholeness and acceptance of others. Soveida, for example, seems destined to repeat the same mistakes other women in her family made in their choice of partners, and she becomes involved with a number of lazy and hurtful men, including her two husbands.

Soveida eventually writes a handbook for waitresses, called "The Book of Service," based on her thirty years of work at the El Farol. The advice she gives about service reflects her ideas about her life and her connections with other people, and it shows her growing sense of pride in herself as a Chicana. She has learned to question and reject the limited roles assigned to Mexican American women in a male-dominated society, and instead she develops a philosophy that encompasses individual strength and endurance combined with a genuine respect for others, as shown through service.

Soveida's philosophy is reinforced by the novel's unrestrained, irreverent, and hilarious scenes, by the effective use of colloquial bilingual speech, and by the in-depth exploration of such universal issues as poverty, personal relationships, illness, and death. Chávez's characters are all individuals with distinctive voices, and she draws them together in ways that show the possibilities of changing social prejudices. Her major themes focus on the rights and responsibilities of the individual and on the need for an evolving social consciousness.

SUGGESTED READINGS

Balassi, William, John F. Crawford, and Annie O. Eysturoy, eds. *This Is About Vision: Interviews with Southwestern Writers*. Albuquerque: University of New Mexico Press, 1990.

Reed, Ishmael. *Hispanic American Literature*. New York: HarperCollins, 1995.

—Lois A. Marchino

See also Chávez, Denise Elia; Erotic identity; Feminism; *Last of the Menu Girls, The*; Latino American identity

Faludi, Susan

BORN: New York, New York; April, 18, 1959

PRINCIPAL WORK: *Backlash: The Undeclared War on American Women* (1991)

IDENTITIES: Women

SIGNIFICANT ACHIEVEMENT: Faludi's *Backlash* reawakened the women's movement, putting the lie to many of society's perceptions about women and the progress of the women's movement.

Susan Faludi stepped into the spotlight in 1991 with the publication of *Backlash*, a work that became a controversial best-seller and gained her a nomination for the National Book Critics Circle award. As editor of her high school newspaper, Faludi challenged school meetings of born-again Christian students and teachers, maintaining that they violated church-state separation. Following her article's publication, the meetings were halted. At Harvard University, where she edited the student newspaper, she wrote a story about sexual harassment on campus. Despite efforts by an accused professor and a dean to stop publication, the article was printed and the professor was asked to take a leave of absence. Following graduation, Faludi served as a copy clerk for *The New York Times*. She also worked as a reporter for *The Miami Herald* and *The Atlanta Constitution*. In 1990, she began work with the *Wall Street Journal*.

Faludi gained immediate attention for her incisive investigative work, including a critique of the Reagan Administration budget for its cuts to poor children, an exposé of California's Silicone Valley corporations' dismissal of older employees in favor of younger, more cost-effective workers, and her series on the impact of the leveraged buyout of Safeway Stores, which won a Pulitzer Prize in 1991.

Although *Backlash* was favorably reviewed by many critics, some maintained that no backlash even exists. Faludi feels that many who criticized her thesis were criticizing a book she had not written. She claims emphatically that her book is not an antiman diatribe. The tremendous detail of evidence compiled by Faludi served to convince most readers. Her style is that of a reporter. Some people tried to cast her in the role of new spokeswoman for the women's movement: To such attempts, Faludi replied that she did not wish to have such a role. She expressed the desire that her accomplishment be measured by the extent that *Backlash* armed women with information and a good dose of cynicism.

In an interview in *Time* magazine, Faludi pointed out that although popular culture tries to turn women into victims, women resisted, not buying the clothes they were told they liked and that they should fit into and not rushing out to be married at eighteen.

SUGGESTED READING

Gibbs, Nancy, and Jeanne McDowell. "How to Revive a Revolution." *Time*, March 9, 1992, 56-57.

—*Patricia J. Huhn*

See also *Feminine Mystique, The*; Feminism; Friedan, Betty; Mass media stereotyping

Family. *See* Adolescent identity; Nontraditional family

Family Devotions

AUTHOR: David Henry Hwang (1957-   )

FIRST PRODUCED: 1981; first published, 1983

IDENTITIES: Chinese American; religion

Family Devotions was written when David Henry Hwang was primarily interested in writing for and about the identity of Asian Americans. The play is autobiographical in that Hwang was raised an evangelical Christian; *Family Devotions* advocates casting off the Western mythology imposed upon Asian cultures.

The play is set in an idealized house with an enclosed patio and tennis court, representing a shallow, materialistic American Dream. The extended families of Ama and Popo, first-generation Chinese Americans, are awaiting the arrival of Di-Gou, their brother whom they have not seen for thirty years and who is arriving from Communist China. As they anticipate Di-Gou's arrival, the women discuss the atrocities of the Communists, whose evil rule they are certain Di-Gou will be grateful to escape. The family descended from the great Chinese Christian evangelist See-goh-poo, and, as a boy, Di-Gou witnessed her miracles, so Ama and Popo anticipate hearing Di-Gou repeat his fervent testimony. When he arrives, however, Di-Gou quietly disavows ever being Christian. Di-Gou confides to Popo's grandson, Chester, that to establish a true American identity, he must believe the stories "written on his face," and these stories reflect many generations.

In act 2 the sisters organize a family devotional and invite Di-Gou to witness for Christ, but a family squabble erupts. Di-Gou is left with the women, who physically force him to submit before their neon cross. They implore him to remember See-goh-poo's miracles. Chester rushes in to rescue Di-Gou, and the scene transforms into a kind of Chinese opera. Di-Gou rises up speaking in tongues, the gas grill bursts into flame, and Chester interprets the revelation: Di-Gou witnessed See-goh-poo give birth out of wedlock, claiming evangelicalism to deceive her family. Di-Gou proclaims that because they now know the truth, their stories are meaningless. The old sisters collapse, dead, and Di-Gou realizes that "No one leaves America." The play ends with Chester standing where Di-Gou first stood, and the "shape of his face begins to change," a metaphor for the beginning acceptance of his Chinese heritage.

Family Devotions is an allegory depicting a cultural awakening of the individual. The world is reversed; "civilized" Christians behave as heathens, and the "heathen" Asian offers wisdom, solace, and love. Hwang calls for Asian Americans to embrace their Asian heritage.

SUGGESTED READINGS

Gerard, Jeremy. "David Hwang: Riding the Hyphen." *The New York Times Magazine*, March 13, 1988, 44, 88-89.

Hwang, David Henry. Introduction to *FOB and Other Plays*. New York: Plume, 1990.

Street, Douglas. *David Henry Hwang*. Boise, Idaho: Boise State University Press, 1989.

—Gerald S. Argetsinger

See also Acculturation; Asian American identity: China, Japan, and Korea; Hwang, David Henry; Religion

Family Installments: Memories of Growing Up Hispanic

AUTHOR: Edward Rivera (1944-   )

FIRST PUBLISHED: 1982

IDENTITIES: Adolescence and coming-of-age; Caribbean; Latino

Family Installments: Memories of Growing Up Hispanic, Edward Rivera's semifictional memoir, chronicles the lives of three generations of a Puerto Rican family. The bittersweet vignettes capture the drama of immigrant life in America and the struggle to achieve an identity within two cultures.

Santos Malánguez's paternal grandfather, Xavier F. Alegría, a schoolteacher and painter, commits suicide in 1919, heartbroken by the death of his wife Sara. Three of Xavier's children, including Gerán, Santos' father, are adopted by the maternal grandparents Josefa and Papá Santos Malánguez. During the Depression, the three brothers split up in search of work. Gerán is hired as a field hand by the tyrannical landowner Gigante Hernández, who has a son and eight daughters.

The light-skinned Gerán marries Gigante's oldest daughter Lilia, an Indian-looking young woman. The young couple, struggling through economic hardships, seek a better life in the United States for their sons Tego and Santos. Survival in the new home is difficult; the jobs are few and the pay low. Charity and welfare checks are insulting. The father is determined to pay for the education of the children and sends them to parochial school.

As a child growing up in Spanish Harlem, Santos experiences the turmoils of being a Hispanic student in an Irish Catholic school. He is ridiculed by teachers and peers because of his shyness and second-language problems. In the streets he is challenged by the neighborhood kids, who make racial remarks. He witnesses street violence and discrimination against black Puerto Rican friends. A sense of marginality and the need to achieve an identity lead Santos to focus on his studies; literature provides an escape.

Santos' brother marries and returns to the island. The parents, always homesick, join their son Tego and his family. When the father dies, Santos flies to Puerto Rico for the funeral and revisits his childhood home. The relatives ask him to remain with them, but he realizes that he needs to return home, to the United States. As did his grandfather Xavier, Santos loves learning and books. His parents inspired him to continue his studies, understanding the value of an education.

Family Installments provides a heartfelt testimonial of the Puerto Rican immigrant experience and identity in terms of family, language, and education.

SUGGESTED READINGS

Flores, Juan. *Divided Borders: Essays on Puerto Rican Identity*. Houston, Tex.: Arte Público Press, 1993.

Rivero, Eliana. "Hispanic Literature in the United States: Self-Image and Conflict." *Revista Chicano-Riqueña* 13, nos. 3-4 (1985): 173-192.

Shorris, Earl. *Latinos: A Biography of the People*. New York: W. W. Norton, 1992.

Villanueva-Collado, Alfredo. "Growing Up Hispanic: Discourse and Ideology in *Hunger of Memory* and *Family Installments*." *The Américas Review* 16, nos. 3-4 (1988): 75-90.

—*Ludmilla Kapschutschenko-Schmitt*

See also Caribbean American literature; Emigration and immigration; Latino American identity

Farm labor. *See* Migratory workers

Fatwā

IDENTITIES: Religion

DEFINITION: A fatwā is an interpretation of a religious law or doctrine delivered by a Muslim religious authority.

The fatwā and literature

The fatwā was relatively little-known in the West until the Ayatollah Ruhollah Khomeini laid his infamous fatwā (a death sentence) on the Indian author Salman Rushdie (and on his British and American publishers) in February, 1989. Rushdie incurred the wrath of the Ayatollah, and of devout Muslims across the world, for his seemingly irreverent portrayal of Muhammad and of Islam in his work *The Satanic Verses* (1988). Highly publicized, this pronouncement fueled worldwide debates about censorship, artistic privilege, and freedom of speech. Debates continued, but on a much smaller scale, in 1993, when a series of fatwās were laid on the Bangladeshi writer Taslima Nasrin by religious leaders of that country. Although fatwās have been decreed for many things other than writing, in the West (particularly the United States) they have come to be closely associated with literature.

Rushdie's case

As many critics have noted, very little of *The Satanic Verses* is actually about religion. Most of the novel's approximately 550 pages are devoted to the intertwined stories of Saladin Chamcha and Gibreel Farishta, two Indian men who miraculously survive a plane crash. Inserted somewhat uneasily into this framework are two other tales: an extended dream sequence which recounts, to a certain extent, the life of Muhammad and the tale of a holywoman who leads her followers into the Arabian Sea. The religious sequences are, at best, a subplot in a masterful tale about the postcolonial condition and the issue of migrancy in the postmodern era.

While it is clear that Rushdie's novel does not focus on Islam, and that the dream sequences do not necessarily espouse the author's belief, it cannot be denied that the title of the novel itself suggests a religious controversy. By entitling his novel *The Satanic Verses*, Rushdie revived an ancient debate about the wording of the Koran. According to some contemporary biographers of

Muhammad, the prophet made reference to three Meccan goddesses while he was inscribing the Koran, purportedly lauding their power. God, realizing that Satan had temporarily controlled Muhammad's tongue, canceled the blasphemous lines (the satanic verses). Thus the Koran retains a reference to the goddesses, yet there is no recording of their power; the subsequent lines uphold the supremacy and omnipotence of the one, true, God. While the tale of these verses troubled religious leaders for hundreds of years, it was eventually decided that the aberrant lines (which are not recorded in the Koran itself) were apocryphal and the debate was silenced.

Many readers think that Rushdie revives the contentious debate in his text. Not only did Rushdie call his book *The Satanic Verses* but also he inserts two dream sequences that can be read as denunciations of Muhammad's mission. In these sequences, the delusional Gibreel, who fancies himself the Archangel Gabriel, claims that he is controlled by Mahound's (Muhammad's) tongue. Instead of being the messenger and mouthpiece of God, as the real Archangel Gabriel was, Gibreel finds himself mouthing what Mahound wishes him to say. In Rushdie's retelling, then, the Koran is not the exact word of God; rather it is the self-serving prose of an egomaniacal man. Muhammad is even further denigrated through his appellation: "Mahound" is an obscure and very pejorative medieval Christian term for "Muhammad" and means "false prophet."

Quite a few Muslims, offended by this representation, took to the streets. There were riots, particularly in Pakistan and India, well before the Ayatollah made his famous pronouncement. This volatile issue was further exacerbated by political and cultural concerns. For example, India, unlike Great Britain or the United States, had to consider whether it should ban Rushdie's novel, and thus appease Muslim Indians, or allow the novel to be sold freely, an act which would be interpreted as a sympathetic move toward the Hindu majority. Leaders eventually decided to ban the work. The text was also banned in Pakistan, a country that was founded as a Muslim nation. In areas where ethnicity and religion were closely tied to an emerging national identity, state leaders had to carefully weigh how they would treat Rushdie's text.

The banning and rioting, along with the fatwā, made *The Satanic Verses* a best-seller. The novel had been selling sluggishly in the United States and Great Britain until the controversy began. After all the free publicity, however, the work became prized property on the black market in the countries where it was banned and found success in the West. The fatwā encouraged people to read the blasphemy it was meant to censor.

Nasrin's case

Taslima Nasrin, a Bangladeshi anesthesiologist, newspaper columnist, and writer of fiction and poetry, became a central figure in the literary community when a series of fatwās was levied against her in 1993. Bangladeshi religious leaders, ired by her frank treatment of women's sexuality as well as her open denunciation of the treatment of women under Islamic law, called for her death. Women's rights groups across the globe, as well as Bangladeshi radicals and Western literary communities, all lobbied on her behalf. The "female Rushdie," as she was described in the press, was able to escape death, but was forced, like Rushdie before her, to live in hiding.

Although there was a flurry of publicity around Nasrin as officials tried to smuggle her from Bangladesh, her story did not generate the same interest in the West as Rushdie's had. Part of this may have to do with the fact that none of Nasrin's sixteen works had been translated from their native Bengali, and the author, no matter how notorious in her native land, did not have the acclaim of Western literary critics behind her. Also, Nasrin's fatwā did not impinge upon nor involve the West in the same way Rushdie's had. The fatwā pronounced by the Ayatollah Khomeini was directed at not only Rushdie but also at his numerous publishers and translators. The Iranian leader meant to prohibit anyone, not only people in his country, from reading the text. The bomb threats, as well as the murders of some of the novel's translators in American and European cities, proved that the Ayatollah's pronouncement could affect freedom of expression well beyond Iran's borders.

Implications for identity

In many ways, the debates over Rushdie's and Nasrin's works, as well as the issuance of the fatwās, revolve around identity. In both cases, many Muslims concluded that their religious identity was being threatened by the works and writers in question. Rushdie's case in particular demonstrates this preoccupation. Indian and Pakistani Muslims felt betrayed by the writer. Not only had he written a book that questions the tenets of Islam, but also he had written the book in English for a Western audience. It seemed as if Rushdie were exposing the Muslims to the laughter of the colonial powers from which they had liberated themselves. Nasrin's case replayed this identity politics. Bangladeshi leaders concluded that her commitment to women's rights and her glorification of women's sexuality were the products of a Western culture, and thus a rejection of an indigenous cultural and religious identity.

Censorship and literature

The fatwās, especially the one laid on Salman Rushdie, created an uproar in the West. Talk shows and news programs spoke of it often. Newspapers and academic journals were filled with similar responses. Many critics, horrified by the sentences, decried the regimes of religious leaders who refuse to allow dissenting voices. In Rushdie's case in particular, critics argued, religious leaders misused their positions, propagandizing by quoting passages out of context and making sweeping generalizations about a novel they may never have read. This religious intolerance troubled many thinkers who felt that Muslims and non-Muslims alike had a right to read the novel and decide for themselves whether or not it was blasphemous.

Many liberal critics took this opportunity to decry religious Fundamentalism and to laud the freedom of the West, using Rushdie as their evidence. Not surprisingly, Rushdie has been critical of the imperialist and neocolonial abuses of Great Britain and of the United States in his fiction and nonfiction. Critics were quick to point out, however, that he found his greatest support there. The country that is arguably most vilified in *The Satanic Verses*, England, became the author's protector. Rushdie, a citizen of the United Kingdom, was placed under the protection of the British government shortly after the issuance of the fatwā.

There was much lambasting of the Third World and of Islam in particular (although not all Muslims agreed with the Ayatollah's pronouncement), but some dissenting voices did manage to make themselves heard in the West. While almost none agreed with the death sentence laid on Rushdie and later Nasrin, other critics took pains to uncover what they saw as the illusory nature of free speech, in even the West. Using the United States as an example, thinkers noted that the constitutional right to freedom of expression was constantly abridged. Sedition laws had been employed even in the home of the free. Most telling, attempts to define (and regulate) pornographic and obscene material demonstrated that America did not allow nor sanction all expression. The same was true of Great Britain. Although England's support of Rushdie seemed to validate its commitment to expression and freedom from religious Fundamentalism, it only showed, one could argue, the country's willingness to hear differing views on Islam. At the same time that England's leaders were upholding Rushdie, many of them continued to support legislation against blasphemy against the Church of England. Although neither the United States nor Great Britain went so far as to order deaths, they did use secular powers to censor expression.

Even those who sought to uncover what they saw as the ethnocentrism of the West's somewhat hypocritical fascination with Rushdie and Nasrin had to ask, however, what, if any, leader, autocrat, or pundit should be allowed to censor another's words? What happens to dialogue, expression, and literature when topics are dictated, when responses are already scripted? While the West may have made efforts to shelter and aid these renegade artists, it could not provide a sterling example on the issue of censorship of literature.

SUGGESTED READINGS

Abdallah, Anouar, et al. *For Rushdie: Essays by Arab and Muslim Writers in Defense of Free Speech*. New York: George Braziller, 1994. This work is most notable for its "Appeal of Iranian Artists and Intellectuals in Favor of Salman Rushdie," a petition which 127 Iranian intellectuals, all at peril to their lives, signed.

Appignanesi, Lisa, and Sara Maitland, eds. *The Rushdie File*. Syracuse, N.Y.: Syracuse University Press, 1990. An exhaustive compilation of the original news reports and political documents concerning the controversy over Rushdie.

Cohn-Sherbok, Dan, ed. *The Salman Rushdie Controversy in Interreligious Perspective*. Lewiston, N.Y.: Edwin Mellen Press, 1990. Offers a variety of essays, each from a different religious or cultural perspective. An invaluable tool for a scholar who wishes to explore the many facets of the controversy.

Pipes, Daniel. *The Rushdie Affair*. New York: Birch Lane, 1990. A comprehensive synthesis of the debate surrounding *The Satanic Verses*. The work presents a balanced account of the issues involved.

Rushdie, Salman. *The Satanic Verses*. New York: Viking, 1988. The novel that launched a thousand tirades. A dense but readable work that deals with issues of identity, postcolonialism, migrancy, and Islamic faith.

Weaver, Mary Anne. "Fugitive from Injustice." *The New Yorker* 70 (September 12, 1994): 48-60. The most comprehensive account in English of Taslima Nasrin's story.

—Ann Marie Adams

See also Christianity and Christian Fundamentalism; Islamic literature; Religion and identity

Faulkner, William

BORN: New Albany, Mississippi; September 25, 1897
DIED: Oxford, Mississippi; July 6, 1962
PRINCIPAL WORKS: *Sartoris*, 1929; *The Sound and the Fury*, 1929; *As I Lay Dying*, 1930; *Sanctuary*, 1931; *Light in August*, 1932; *Absalom, Absalom!*, 1936; *The Hamlet*, 1940; *Go Down, Moses*, 1942; *Intruder in the Dust*, 1948; *Collected Stories of William Faulkner*, 1950; *Requiem for a Nun*, 1951; *A Fable*, 1954; *The Town*, 1957; *The Mansion*, 1959; *The Reivers*, 1962
IDENTITIES: European American; family; South
SIGNIFICANT ACHIEVEMENT: Faulkner captured the essence of his native Mississippi, exploring racism and the legacy of the Civil War.

A white Southerner ahead of his time in many respects, William Faulkner was a product of family and region. He was named for his great-grandfather, a Confederate colonel and railroad builder, on whom he later based the character of Colonel John Sartoris of *Sartoris* and *The Unvanquished* (1938). Although he never finished high school, the young Faulkner read obsessively: the Bible, William Shakespeare, and poets such as John Keats, Algernon Charles Swinburne, and the Imagists, who were introduced to him by his lifelong friend, Phil Stone.

After publishing *The Marble Faun* (1924), a small book of poems, Faulkner traveled to New Orleans, where his life changed when author Sherwood Anderson encouraged him to write stories about his "own little postage stamp of native soil." For Faulkner, this place became his fictional Yoknapatawpha County. Jefferson, Yoknapatawpha's county seat, is based loosely on Faulkner's home town of Oxford, Mississippi. The need for money to support his wife and daughter led him through ten years of writing movie scripts, a job that he detested but that did not deter him from his real work in Oxford.

Faulkner identified with the old aristocracy, which he saw weakened by its inability to adapt to a changing South. His writing also reveals understanding of and compassion for African Americans and poor whites. In the late 1940's, he

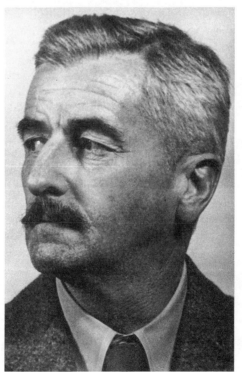

William Faulkner, winner of the Nobel Prize in Literature in 1949. (The Nobel Foundation)

began to speak out in favor of civil rights for African Americans, challenging traditional assumptions of the South. His novel *Intruder in the Dust* underscores this position.

In Faulkner's South, the past is everywhere, brooding over the present, and the present is fleeting, becoming the past. He was steeped in the history and folklore of his region, from the terrible events of the Civil War to the bitter truths of racism. In 1949, William Faulkner became the fourth American to be awarded the Nobel Prize in Literature. His Nobel Prize address is famous for its ringing defense of humanity: "I believe that man will not merely endure: he will prevail . . . because he has a soul, a spirit capable of compassion and sacrifice and endurance."

SUGGESTED READINGS

Blotner, Joseph. *Faulkner: A Biography*. New York: Random House, 1974.
Karl, Frederick R. *William Faulkner: American Writer*. New York: Weidenfeld & Nicolson, 1989.
Richardson, H. Edward. *William Faulkner: The Journey to Self-Discovery*. Columbia: University of Missouri Press, 1969.

—Joanne McCarthy

See also *Absalom, Absalom!*; American identity: South; *Intruder in the Dust*; *Light in August*; Racism and ethnocentrism; *Sound and the Fury, The*

Fauset, Jessie Redmon

BORN: Snow Hill, New Jersey; April 27, 1882
DIED: Philadelphia, Pennsylvania; April 30, 1961
PRINCIPAL WORKS: *There Is Confusion*, 1924; *Plum Bun: A Novel Without a Moral*, 1929; *The Chinaberry Tree: A Novel of American Life*, 1931; *Comedy: American Style*, 1933
IDENTITIES: African American; women
SIGNIFICANT ACHIEVEMENT: Fauset's fiction depicts an unusual perspective of middle-class African American life.

Jessie Fauset, believing that black writers could more accurately depict their race, wrote to "put the best foot of the race forward." Writing about the people she knew—the middle class—Fauset presents images different from those of other New Negro novelists of the Harlem Renaissance.

In Fauset's first novel, *There Is Confusion*, the main character, Joanna Marshall, daughter of middle-class parents, believes that African Americans "can do everything anybody else can." Only after experiencing discrimination in her attempt to become a dancer does she realize the problems posed by race. Joanna, her boyfriend Peter Bye, and a neighbor, Maggie Ellersley, overcome the difficulties of race, family, and class distinctions; Joanna's initial belief is affirmed by the novel's end. The characters, and by extension all African Americans, can triumph in spite of the hardships they have endured.

In her second novel, *Plum Bun: A Novel Without a Moral*, Fauset complicates the race issue by creating characters light enough to pass for white. The protagonist, Angela Murray, also from a middle-class family, grows up observing her mother occasionally pass. In order to realize her dreams of becoming an artist, Angela passes, which has its consequences. By denying her only sister, Virginia, Angela is isolated from family. Rejected by her boyfriend, Roger, because they are not of the same economic class, Angela learns that being white does not ensure happiness. When Rachel, a black art student, is denied a scholarship to study abroad, Angela turns down her own prize and acknowledges her race. The novel ends with a happier, wiser Angela continuing her art training in Paris. Revealing the problems facing African Americans who pass, Fauset suggests that values are more important than race.

In her final novel, *Comedy: American Style*, Fauset examines the consequences of color consciousness within the family. The color-obsessed Olivia Blanchard marries Dr. Christopher Cary because he is also light enough to pass. They have three children, Teresa, Christopher, Jr., and Oliver, whose lives are affected by their mother's obsession. Teresa marries a Frenchman she does not love. Oliver, who is too dark to pass and is therefore mistreated by his mother, commits suicide. Christopher, Jr., survives and marries a blond, blue-eyed black woman. When the novel ends, Olivia is in Europe while her family seeks to recover from her mania.

In her novels, Fauset explores the problems of identity through characters who triumph by accepting their race, class, and gender.

SUGGESTED READING

Sylvander, Carolyn. *Jessie Redmon Fauset: Black American Writer*. Troy, N.Y.: Whitston, 1981.

—Paula C. Barnes

See also African American identity; *Chinaberry Tree, The*; Harlem Renaissance

Feminine Mystique, The

AUTHOR: Betty Friedan (1921-   )
FIRST PUBLISHED: 1963
IDENTITIES: European American; family; Jewish; women

The Feminine Mystique was one of the most influential books in convincing middle-class American women during the 1960's that their personal identity as housewives and mothers had not provided them with full and meaningful lives. Herself one of the women whose plight she described, Betty Friedan examined "the problem that has no name" in a series of insightful chapters that set forth the many ways in which women felt frustrated and repressed.

The book grew out of Friedan's search for a more significant existence. A writer whose professional career had taken second place to a husband and family, she surveyed the condition of women at the end of the 1950's and then found that women's magazines for which she wrote were reluctant to publish her findings. The magazines did not want details about the anxieties and tensions of middle-class, suburban women. She decided to write a book that could explore the issue of women's identity in greater depth. *The Feminine Mystique* grew from her determination to locate the deeper causes of the frustration that she and women like her felt. As she researched how society directed women into child rearing and family to the exclusion of their own talents and abilities, she became convinced that the ideology of accepting such roles accounted for much of the problem.

The book proved to be a significant catalyst for many women in the 1960's. Friedan's powerful description of how her culture expected women to conform to certain roles within society and of the pervasive unhappiness that women felt about their predicament resonated with the public, which bought hundreds of thousands of copies. That women identified with what Friedan had said became evident in the recurring comment she received. "It changed my life," women told her.

It also changed Friedan's life; she became one of the controversial leaders of the women's liberation movement during the 1960's. For a decade her fame made her a central shaper of feminist strategy. Years after the book appeared, *The Feminine Mystique* has remained a powerful indictment of a way of identifying women in the United States that often limits their opportunity to live a full life. Stronger on analysis than on what women should do to overcome the mystique and its effects, Betty Friedan's book is still one of the classic statements of the search for women's rights and opportunities in the history of the United States.

SUGGESTED READINGS

Behm, Barbara. *Betty Friedan: Speaking Out for Women's Rights*. Milwaukee, Wis.: Gareth Stevens, 1992.

Friedan, Betty. *It Changed My Life: Writings on the Women's Movement*. New York: Random House, 1976.

Meyer, Donald. "Betty Friedan." In *Portraits of American Women: From Settlement to Present*, edited by G. J. Barker-Benfield and Catherine Clinton. New York: St. Martin's Press, 1991.

Whelehan, Imelda. *Modern Feminist Thought: From the Second Wave to "Post-Feminism."* New York: New York University Press, 1995.

—Lewis L. Gould

See also Feminism; Friedan, Betty; Identity crisis

Feminism

IDENTITIES: Women

DEFINITION: Feminism, women's struggle for social, economic, and political equality, is reflected in a number of themes in literature.

Since the rise of feminism, which began in the nineteenth century and surged again in the last decades of the twentieth, there has been an explosion of literature, in every genre, by women. Studies of women's literature have shown that there are certain common themes that tend to play out in women's writing.

Since the beginning of the women's movement, there has been a strong rise in the amount of literature that is self-consciously feminist in tone, clearly espousing the ideals of female equality. Feminists have also studied other women's writings, including those of an earlier time, probing them with renewed interest about what sets women's writings apart and what commonalities they may have.

Voice One of the primary themes of feminist writing is its insistence on expressing and valuing women's point of view about their own lives. While earlier in history, it was primarily men who wrote, from their own point of view, about women, the concern of feminist writing is to place women in the position of authority about their own lives and experiences, to hear and believe women's voices.

As feminists have become interested in hearing women's voices in literature, a number of authors from earlier times have newly been taken seriously. For example, the early Greek poet Sappho, whose work has nearly been entirely lost to the literary tradition, focuses on women's point of view and therefore was considered insignificant at best and immoral at worst. Another example is the fourteenth and fifteenth century writer Christine de Pisan, whose *Le Livre de la cité des dames* (1405; *The Book of the City of Ladies*, 1982) expresses ideas that are usually considered new: the horrors of rape and domestic abuse, arguments against the notion that women are not as intelligent as men, and arguments against the notion that women cannot handle financial matters. This work

---

Feminism Milestones

1892	Charlotte Perkins Gilman's short story "The Yellow Wallpaper" is published in *New England Magazine*.	1972	The Equal Rights Amendment (ERA) is ratified by Congress.
1898	*Women and Economics*, by Charlotte Perkins Gilman.	1973	*Roe v. Wade* affirms a woman's right to abortion.
1899	Kate Chopin's *The Awakening*.	1973	Adrienne Rich's *Diving into the Wreck*.
1917	*Summer*, a novel by Edith Wharton.	1979	*The Wanderground*, by Sally Gearhart.
1920	Nineteenth Amendment ratified.	1980-1988	The Reagan Administration's antifeminist stance causes many setbacks for the women's movement.
1924	*The Old Maid*, by Edith Wharton.		
1929	*A Room of One's Own*, by Virginia Woolf.	1980	*Stone Roots*, by Meena Alexander.
1959	Grace Paley's *The Little Disturbances of Man: Stories of Men and Women in Love*.	1982	The ERA is defeated.
		1989	Amy Tan's *The Joy Luck Club*.
1963	*The Feminine Mystique*, by Betty Friedan.	1991	The Anita Hill-Clarence Thomas hearing rekindles the women's movement.
1963	Adrienne Rich's collection of poetry *Snapshots of a Daughter-in-law*.	1991	Susan Faludi's *Backlash: The Undeclared War on American Women*.
1969	*The Left Hand of Darkness*, by Ursula K. LeGuin.	1992	*The War Against Women*, by Marilyn French.
1970	*The Female Eunuch*, by Germaine Greer.		

was lost to modern readers until it was first translated into English in 1982. It has since become a classic of feminist literature, and illustrates that women's writing, from whatever time period, expresses a clear female experience, viewpoint, and voice. The book's publication history, and the deliberate destruction of Sappho's work, are clear indications that women's voice has not been, until recently, considered significant or of literary importance.

Charlotte Perkins Gilman, a feminist writer of the late nineteenth and early twentieth centuries, wrote many works of fiction and nonfiction, including an economic analysis that focused on women's issues, *Women and Economics* (1898). However, perhaps her most well-known writing is the short story "The Yellow Wallpaper," published in *New England Magazine* in 1892, which describes a woman who is completely under the control of her husband's supposed cure for depression and who as a result goes completely mad. Although the woman, who narrates her own story, pays lip service to his superior knowledge as a man and his loving care for her, her own perception that the whole situation is being mismanaged shines subtly through her words.

Challenging the canon

In Western culture a consensus has been built about what are the primary works of literature, the works with which every educated person should be familiar. This list is called the canon. Most of these works, however, were written by white males. Furthermore, part of why these works have been considered to have universal appeal has been that literature has been judged by white male critics, who experience life in similar ways. Therefore, one of the literary concerns of feminism is to challenge these traditional assumptions and to encourage serious interest in literature by women, including women of color. A result of the feminist critique of this predominantly white male canon is that what appears to be a universal human viewpoint is exposed as, in fact, the viewpoint of only one group.

Books that are classics of women's literature, and are working their way into this new conception of the canon, include Virginia Woolf's *A Room of One's Own* (1929), the poetry of Maya Angelou and Adrienne Rich, Kate Chopin's *The Awakening* (1899), the works of Gilman and Zora Neale Hurston, and the nineteenth century works of such authors as Edith Wharton, Louisa May Alcott, Jane Austen, and the Brontë sisters. All of these works, whether or not written from a feminist perspective, illustrate a view of the world that comes from female experience and therefore provide a balance to the predominant male viewpoint of the traditional canon.

Collectivity

One difference that appears between women's writing and that of men is attention to collectivity. Rather than the individualism that is one of the hallmarks of, in particular, American male writing, women's writing tends to emphasize the importance of the community. There are, of course, notable exceptions: Ayn Rand, for example, did much to elevate, if not create, the cult of the individual (and always male) hero in mid-twentieth century America. However, the more common interest in collective authority can clearly be seen in women's utopian and science fiction. Whereas science fiction by males is often concerned with hierarchies and dominance, the imaginary worlds described by female writers are usually egalitarian, nonhierarchical, even anarchist. They are concerned with self-empowerment, and with empowerment of the group as a whole, rather than with gaining power or control over others.

The hero might be, not one person who makes it to the top, but a group of women and men who, together, are able to achieve their goals. An excellent example is in Starhawk's first novel, *The Fifth Sacred Thing* (1994), in which the people of an imagined future San Francisco are able, together, not only to repel conquest by the fascist rulers of Southern California, but even to win the army over to their nonviolent, collective lifestyle.

Nature is also considered part of this collective community, as women's science fiction shows a respect for nature that is not usually seen in male works. This is illustrated, for instance, in Sally Gearhart's *The Wanderground* (1979), in which nature has rebelled against the modern assaults against it, and refuses to allow machines to work outside cities, which are male bastions. Meanwhile, most women live in simple, natural communities out in the country. Women's science fiction also shares concerns about using technology for human needs, and imagining reproductive methods and styles of parenting that free women from carrying the brunt of bearing and rearing children. An example is Ursula Le Guin's *The Left Hand of Darkness* (1969), which takes place on a planet in which each person, randomly and periodically, changes from a neutral state and becomes either male or female.

Valuing the personal

Emphasizing community effort and heroism, women's writing also tends to value the personal. Characters are developed deeply, and their personal concerns are considered important to their own lives and to the plot of the story. Following the feminist adage that the personal is political, the concerns of individuals are seen to be integral to the community and issues in which they are involved. Jane Austen's early nineteenth century novels offer a prime example: Her protagonists, observers of community and gender roles, are the objects of their author's interest, undergoing subtle characterization and growth throughout the novels.

Another example of this theme is Louisa May Alcott's classic *Little Women: Or, Meg, Jo, Beth, and Amy* (1868-1869), in which four sisters and their mother, left alone as a community of women while their father is in Civil War, manage their lives. Each daughter's character is explored in depth, and although their personalities differ greatly, each contributes to the whole that is the family. The reader ends up caring deeply about each character and about the fate of the family as a whole as personalities and events interact.

This value given to the personal is reflected in the importance placed by feminists on biography, and particularly autobiography and autobiographical fiction. As an author looks at her own life and the lessons she has gained from it, and from her interactions with others in it, the reader can share in these lessons. Amy Tan's *The Joy Luck Club* (1989) is an example. In addition, the book gives the non-Chinese reader a glimpse of how Chinese and Chinese American women have lived out their lives, complete with glimpses of the ways they have handled the restrictions placed on them, their interactions with others, and the events of their lives. While women's autobiography at one time was considered uninteresting in any serious way, because women's lives were considered by the mainstream (white, male) critic to be uninteresting, feminists are understanding that such accounts are extremely important for understanding the breadth and depth of female experience. In fact, there is a developing interest in women's diaries, journals, and letters, and in gathering oral history of women who have not been able to write down their experiences.

The privilege of writing

One thing feminist writers have recognized at least since the days of Woolf, who writes about the issue in *A Room of One's Own*, is that writing requires a certain degree of privilege. One of the reasons, she suggests, that until the nineteenth and twentieth centuries so few women became published authors is that most women have been required to spend their whole time and energy on serving and maintaining their families, and that privacy and leisure have seldom been accorded to women. Woolf's reasoning that in order to write fiction a woman needs enough money on which to live during the process and a room of her own in which to work in solitude and without interruption, has been accepted as axiomatic, although it was not, until that time, recognized as a primary reason women and many men could not become writers.

If one main theme could be claimed for feminist literature, and for feminist evaluation of literature, it would be the importance of listening to female voices of all colors in addition to those of males, and of taking women's experiences seriously. This is done through reclaiming and valuing previously undervalued women's writings of the past, and through taking seriously the writing of women in the present.

SUGGESTED READINGS

Barrett, Ellen, and Mary Cullinan. *American Women Writers: Diverse Voices in Prose Since 1845.* New York: St. Martin's Press, 1992. Examines the work of a large number of American women writers, interpreting their work from the viewpoint of feminist literary criticism.

Baym, Nina. *Women's Fiction: A Guide to Novels by and About Women in America, 1820-1870.* Ithaca, N.Y.: Cornell University Press, 1978. Provides a feminist critique of the popular and prolific women fiction writers of the nineteenth century.

Bernikow, Louise. *Among Women.* New York: Harper & Row, 1980. Explores relationships among women, using authors such as Virginia Woolf and Louisa May Alcott as examples.

Davidson, Cathy N., and Linda Wagner-Martin, eds. *The Oxford Companion to Women's Writings in the United States*. New York: Oxford University Press, 1995. An exhaustive reference book on women writers and women's writing.

Ferguson, Mary Anne. *Images of Women in Literature*. 5th ed. Boston: Houghton Mifflin, 1991. Organizes writings, primarily of women, that shed light on various traditional and nontraditional images of women.

Pratt, Annis. *Archetypal Patterns in Women's Fiction*. Bloomington: Indiana University Press, 1981. Explores the differences in male and female perspectives on various literary themes.

Stanley, Liz. *The Auto/biographical I: The Theory and Practice of Feminist Auto/biography*. Manchester, England: Manchester University Press, 1992. Provides a feminist analysis of the value and importance of women's autobiography.

Woolf, Virginia. *A Room of One's Own*. New York: Harcourt Brace, 1929. Addresses the issue of women's need for sufficient money and privacy in order to write. Explores the question of why women have not written more by imagining the situation of William Shakespeare's equally talented hypothetical sister.

—Eleanor B. Amico

See also Angelou, Maya; Canon; Chopin, Kate; Gilman, Charlotte Perkins; Hurston, Zora Neale; Rich, Adrienne; Tan, Amy; Wharton, Edith

Fences

AUTHOR: August Wilson (1945-   )
FIRST PRODUCED: 1985; first published, 1985
IDENTITIES: African American; family

Troy Maxson, the protagonist of August Wilson's *Fences*, is the son of a frustrated sharecropper whose harshness drove off his wives and Troy. Troy has made his way north to a world where African Americans live in shacks and are unable to find work. Troy takes to stealing, kills a man, and is sent to prison, where he learns how to play baseball, which he loves and at which he excels. Segregation confines Troy, after prison, to the Negro Leagues. He is angry at the racism that frustrates his attempt at achieving the American Dream in the most American of sports, but he remains resilient. *Fences* celebrates his indomitable spirit, while acknowledging his flaws.

The play opens in 1957, when Troy is fifty-three years old. He is appealing in the zest with which he dramatizes his life. A battle with pneumonia becomes a time when he wrestles with a white-robed and hooded Death, and buying furniture on credit from a white man becomes making a deal with the devil. His friend Bono seems to acknowledge the African American tradition of these tall tales when he comments: "You got some Uncle Remus in your blood." The audience learns of Troy's admirable defiance at work in questioning the sanitation department's policy of having all the whites drive while the blacks do the lifting. Troy also has an affectionate teasing relationship with Bono and his wife Rose.

As the play continues, however, Troy erects fences between himself and those he loves. He refuses to allow his son to accept a football fellowship to college and then forces him to leave home. Troy loses contact with Bono after being promoted at work. Troy hurts his wife through an extramarital affair, and he commits his brain-damaged brother, Gabe, to a mental institution so he can collect part of Gabe's government checks.

Although Troy has tragic flaws, the ending of *Fences* is not tragic. A spirit of reconciliation is brought by Gabe, who has been allowed to leave the mental hospital to attend his brother's funeral. Gabe thinks that, when he blows his trumpet, Saint Peter will open the pearly gates and allow Troy into Heaven. Gabe's horn lacks a mouthpiece, however, and, distraught, he performs a dance, connected, presumably, to pre-Christian African ancestors. In performance, the stage is then flooded with light, indicating that the gates have opened.

SUGGESTED READINGS

Birdwell, Christine. "Death as a Fastball on the Outside Corner: *Fences*' Troy Maxson and the American Dream." *Aethlon* 8 (Fall, 1990): 16-25.

Fishman, Joan. "Developing His Song: August Wilson's *Fences*." In *August Wilson: A Casebook*, edited by Marilyn Elkins. New York: Garland, 1994.

Pereira, Kim. *August Wilson and the African-American Odyssey*. Champaign: University of Illinois Press, 1995.

Shannon, Sandra G. *The Dramatic Vision of August Wilson*. Washington, D.C.: Howard University Press, 1995.

—*Jack Vincent Barbera*

See also African American identity; American Dream; Wilson, August

Ferlinghetti, Lawrence

BORN: Yonkers, New York; March 24, 1919

PRINCIPAL WORKS: *Pictures of the Gone World*, 1955; *A Coney Island of the Mind*, 1958; *These Are My Rivers: New and Selected Poems 1955-1993*, 1993

IDENTITIES: European American

SIGNIFICANT ACHIEVEMENT: Ferlinghetti's poetry searches for a personal identity in endless conflict with the cultural and political status quo.

Lawrence Ferlinghetti's early life contributed to a lifelong search for identity. The poet grew up without a traditional family; he spent the earliest years of his life in France with an aunt who later brought him back to New York, where he attended public schools and became involved in gang activity. A later private education, however, provided the motivation that would lead to his university degrees at Columbia and the Sorbonne.

In 1953, Ferlinghetti moved to San Francisco and founded the City Lights Bookshop, which carried works of counterculture writers, such as Allen Ginsberg, not readily available elsewhere. His 1956 publication of Ginsberg's *Howl* led to a nationally publicized obscenity trial. Thereafter, Ferlinghetti became associated with the Beat movement in its efforts to expand the audience for poetry and art by removing them from the university and returning them to the people. Beat literature is thus characterized by its alienation from prevailing literary and social standards. Since the 1950's Ferlinghetti's City Lights Bookshop has been the leader in distributing radical literature to a popular audience.

Ferlinghetti's early poetry typifies the Beat search for open forms based on rhythms of colloquial speech and jazz. His work challenges the status quo of academic poetry. *Pictures of the Gone World* and *Coney Island of the Mind, A* develop an experimental form of lyrical poetry famous for unjustified left margins and an irreverent, comic tone. "The World Is a Beautiful Place" and "Constantly Risking Absurdity," two of Ferlinghetti's most famous poems, exemplify the poet's and the individual's endless search for identity, for discovering the essential self in an alien modern world. In "Christ Climbed Down" Ferlinghetti applies his theme of alienation to Christianity: Christ himself would be alienated from the modern world if he were here. Ferlinghetti's popularity was firmly established with *A Coney Island of the Mind*, often claimed to be the best-selling book of serious poetry published since 1950.

After the 1950's and 1960's, Ferlinghetti remained a prolific poet and leader in the later phases of the Beat movement. *These Are My Rivers*, a collection of his work spanning five decades, shows a steady growth of poetic voice while remaining consistent with convictions of political radicalism and the belief in the power of the poetic imagination to transform the world.

SUGGESTED READINGS

Skau, Michael. *"Constantly Risking Absurdity": The Writings of Lawrence Ferlinghetti*. Troy, N.Y.: Whitston, 1989.

Sliesky, Barry. *Ferlinghetti: The Artist in His Time*. New York: Warner, 1990.

Smith, Larry. *Lawrence Ferlinghetti: Poet-at-Large*. Carbondale: Southern Illinois University Press, 1983.

—*Paul Varner*

See also Antiwar literature; Ginsberg, Allen; *Howl*

Fertility and identity

IDENTITIES: Women

Nature

Throughout the literatures of numerous countries fertility is tied to identity, defining women and men by their reproductive capabilities. Some works celebrate fertility without question, as Willa Cather does in *My Ántonia* (1918). The narrator, Jim Burden, describes Ántonia as an Earth Mother, with a flock of children about her, tending her apple orchard and the animals of the farm, all life and goodness flowing from her. Eudora Welty too in her fiction creates images of Earth Mother characters, like the pregnant woman in "The Death of a Travelling Salesman," who is only called "the woman." Welty's allusions to the Dionysian fertility cult of ancient Greece unequivocally imply that a cyclical, natural view of the world is superior. Implicit as well is the theme that those who claim their place in nature will be self-fulfilled and those who deny it will always be alienated from themselves and the earth. Male writers do not always frame the topic in quite the same way. Eugene O'Neill, for example, depicts male characters who long for evidence of their virility, indeed pin all their hopes for the future on it, as in *Desire Under the Elms* (1924).

Culture

Several modernist writers of the early twentieth century concentrate on the metaphor of a lack of virility and fertility in the modern world. This lack of fertility is symbolic of the decline of culture and the decline of the quality of life in the urban, industrial world. T. S. Eliot's *The Waste Land* (1922) epitomizes this vision of a sterile desert in which nothing new can be produced to revitalize the world. James Joyce's *Ulysses* (1922) features as its two main characters a man who can father no son and a son who lacks a father. Without children, there is no hope for the future; without a father there is no history. D. H. Lawrence, in his novels, consistently dichotomizes life between nature and sexuality (good) and urban and industrial blight (bad). The degree to which individuals' identities suffer from this sense of sterility is apparent in the contrast between the legendary hero Ulysses and his symbolic counterpart Leopold Bloom, a henpecked, browbeaten man with little hope and no prospects.

Criticisms

In contrast to these male authors' visions of infertility, many women authors have criticized traditional metaphors of fertility. Kate Chopin's *The Awakening* (1899) questions the expectation that women are entirely fulfilled by a life of domesticity. While she bears her husband's sons, Edna Pontellier cannot embrace motherhood with the equanimity of the Creole women around her. She feels as though her identity is erased by motherhood. In Zora Neale Hurston's novel *Their Eyes Were Watching God* (1937), readers are presented with a female protagonist who takes two husbands and one lover but bears no children. These women writers assert a reality that differs from the standard literary archetype.

Three African American women writers also criticize notions of women's fertility. Toni Morrison's Baby Suggs, in *Beloved* (1987), bears six children in slavery, each by a different father, and loses all but one to the slave system. Baby asserts her right to choose the fathers of her children, but clearly her fertility is used against her. Her offspring are sold away, one after another. Morrison makes it clear that what should be a source of joy and strength is subverted and degraded. In Morrison's *Sula* (1973), the title character says that she is too busy making herself to make any children, suggesting that women have a difficult time discovering their own identities in the enveloping one of motherhood. Likewise, in Alice Walker's *Meridian* (1976), the title character bears one child but gives it up for others to rear in order to work for the Civil Rights movement. For her, fertility is an inconvenience. Gloria Naylor's novel *Mama Day* (1988) depicts a character

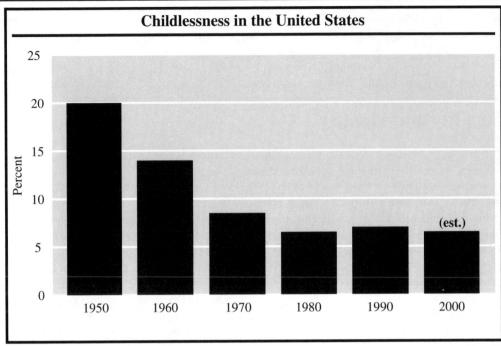

Childlessness in the United States

Percentages of women without children. The economic troubles of the 1930's, which delayed marriages, resulted in larger numbers of women remaining childless.

Source: National Center for Health Statistics.

who is so desperate to have a child that she goes to Mama Day for what she believes to be a magical fertility ritual. When the character has a baby, her entire life revolves around it. She lives to be the child's mother and when the child dies, she nearly dies.

Probably the most stunning contemporary criticism of cultural ideology about women's fertility is Nigerian Buchi Emecheta's novel *The Joys of Motherhood* (1979). In it, the main character, Nnu Ego, is bound by the thinking of her tribe, the Ibo, who believe that a woman's worth lies solely in her ability to reproduce. When she fails to conceive a child by her first husband within their first year of marriage, she is cast aside and later divorced. In disgrace, Nnu Ego's father marries her to a man in a city, far from her village, so that if she never does conceive she will not have to bear the shame in front of her kinspeople. Ironically, once the children start coming they do not stop. Nnu Ego learns that there are worse problems than infertility, namely desperate poverty and starving children. Seduced by American culture, her children one by one abandon her rather than care for her in the tradition of their native culture.

Finally, Canadian Margaret Atwood's *The Handmaid's Tale* (1985), about a future in which evangelical Christians have overtaken the United States, also depicts a world in which women are defined by their fertility or lack thereof. In the book's post-nuclear-disaster society, most people are sterile. Therefore, the women who can conceive and bear children are rounded up and given out to powerful men as broodmares. Women who are infertile are sent to work either in government-operated bordellos or in a radioactive waste site; in either case they survive about three years. Atwood deliberately subverts the image of the Earth Mother by showing women held captive and defined by their fertility rather than honored for it. Whether envisioned as a source of all life and love or as a tool of patriarchy, fertility exercises immense power over identity in this novel, as it does throughout the world.

SUGGESTED READINGS

Adams, Alice. "Out of the Womb: The Future of the Uterine Metaphor." *Feminist Studies* 19, no. 2 (Summer, 1993): 269-290.

Chester, Laura, ed. *Cradle and All: Women Writers on Pregnancy and Birth*. Winchester, Mass.: Faber & Faber, 1989.

Daly, Brenda O., and Maureen T. Reddy, eds. *Narrating Mothers: Theorizing Maternal Subjectivities*. Knoxville: University of Tennessee Press, 1991.

Lowe-Evans, Mary. *Crimes Against Fecundity: Joyce and Population Control*. Syracuse, N.Y.: Syracuse University Press, 1989.

Scarry, Elaine, ed. *Literature and the Body: Essays on Populations and Persons*. Baltimore: The Johns Hopkins University Press, 1988.

—Julie Tharp

See also Abortion and birth control; *Feminine Mystique, The*; Masculinity and the masculine mystique

Fierstein, Harvey

BORN: Brooklyn, New York; June 6, 1954

PRINCIPAL WORKS: *Torch Song Trilogy*, pb. 1979, pr. 1981; *La Cage aux Folles*, pr. 1983

IDENTITIES: Gay, lesbian, and bisexual; Jewish

SIGNIFICANT ACHIEVEMENT: Fierstein's work challenges assumptions regarding the lives of gay and bisexual Americans.

Harvey Fierstein's 1981 trio of one-act plays titled *Torch Song Trilogy* successfully introduced gay characters to the American stage without apology. The central character, Arnold Becker, is a drag queen with a desire to live a life consistent with the American Dream. He wants to secure a loving family life and sees no reason why he should be denied the opportunity of creating one simply because of his sexual orientation. The uniqueness of the play's statement lies in the fact that the work was premiered at the end of the sexual revolution of the 1970's, when gay life was viewed by many as simply a series of casual encounters. Americans seemed content with a view of gays as emotional children who lived strange, uncommitted lives. Fierstein's characters challenge this view.

The son of a handkerchief manufacturer and a librarian, Fierstein grew up in a tight family unit that accepted his gayness. His first encounters with the lifestyle were through family friends who shared long-term, committed relationships. These were his role models, who helped him develop his somewhat conservative view of gay life.

Fierstein's reworking of the popular French film *La Cage aux Folles* (1978) is another example of the playwright's ability to present fully developed gay characters for mixed audiences. Fierstein received a Tony Award for the best book for a musical in 1984. The musical enjoyed a long run in the United States and abroad. Like *Torch Song Trilogy*, the play is an old-fashioned love story espousing the virtues of family and commitment.

Fierstein's writing style is a fusion of his several identities. His work is distinguished by a mixture of Jewish and gay humor interspersed with poignant self-revelation. It is this combination that has endeared him to straight and gay audiences. Through laughter and dramatic truth, his characters are able to tap the human thread that brings all people together.

Although best known as a playwright, Fierstein is also an actor who has played various roles on stage, on national television, and in film, most notably as Frank, the gay brother in the film *Mrs. Doubtfire* (1993). In addition to his work as an artist, Fierstein is active in various gay rights organizations and devotes considerable time and energy as an activist for causes relating to the acquired immune deficiency syndrome (AIDS).

SUGGESTED READING

Kroll, Jack. "His Heart Is Young and Gay." *Newsweek*, June 13, 1983, p. 36.

—Don Evans

See also Bisexual identity; Gay identity; *Torch Song Trilogy*

Fifth Chinese Daughter

AUTHOR: Jade Snow Wong (1922-   )
FIRST PUBLISHED: 1950
IDENTITIES: Chinese American; family; women

Fifth Chinese Daughter, Jade Snow Wong's autobiography, directly and honestly relates the struggles and accomplishments of an American-born Chinese girl. Although it is an autobiography, it is written in the third person, which reflects the Chinese custom of humility. This use of the third person also reminds the reader of how difficult it is for the author to express her individual identity.

The book explains Wong's desire to prove to her parents that she was "a person, besides being a female." Even as a toddler, she was taught to obey her parents and her older brother and sisters without question. She was not allowed to express her opinions; rather, she was forced to comply with the demands of the rest of her family.

When she began school, her parents expected her to earn good grades, yet they refused to praise or even encourage her when she was recognized for her school achievements. In fact, they refused to fund her college education, although they paid her brothers' expenses, because it was not considered wise to educate a girl, who would leave the family when she married. As a result, Wong was forced to work full time throughout her teenage years in order to save the money to go to college. During this time, she was exposed to the "foreign" culture of the whites living in San Francisco, and she was surprised to learn that parents in many Anglo families listened to children and respected their opinions. Further, she learned in a college sociology class that in many families, children were afforded the right to discuss with their parents what they saw as unfair. Learning about the practices of other families caused Wong to question her parents' practices for the first time.

As a result, Wong began a slow and painful struggle to earn her parents' respect while developing her own identity. Unfortunately, her parents were not the only people who would discourage her. She also had to face prejudice and stereotyping in the white world. She refused to be discouraged by this and accepted the challenges that it brought.

Eventually, Jade Snow was able to win her parents' respect. She established her own identity and her independence by beginning a business selling handmade pottery. Although her Chinatown shop was patronized only by white customers, her ability to attract many customers was recognized by her family and by members of Wong's community. The pottery shop venture finally allowed her to find "that niche which would be hers alone."

SUGGESTED READINGS

Hong, Maria, ed. *Growing Up Asian American: An Anthology*. New York: William Morrow, 1993.
Ling, Amy. "Chinese American Women Writers: The Tradition Behind Maxine Hong Kingston."
    In *Redefining American Literary History*. New York: Modern Language Association of America,
    1990.

—Amy Beth Shollenberger

See also Asian American identity: China, Japan, and Korea; Women and identity; Wong, Jade Snow

Final Payments

AUTHOR: Mary Gordon (1949-   )
FIRST PUBLISHED: 1978
IDENTITIES: European American; religion; women

Mary Gordon's first novel, *Final Payments*, is set in the decade after the historic Second Vatican Council, which convened in 1962. The council moved toward greater liberalism in Roman Catholicism. The novel deals with Isabel Moore, a devoted daughter who spends eleven years tending to her ailing father in his decline and death.

At thirty, she has given up a good portion of her youth, not with the aim of being a good Catholic, which the church members and many acquaintances assume, but because she loves her father and is doing what she needs to do. He is, in a sense, her God incarnate.

She no longer, in truth, holds with the tenets of the church, but she is a darling of the priests, who applaud her dutiful dedication but sometimes have trouble remembering her name. She is defined in terms of her deeds rather than who she is. To the townspeople, she is a bit of an oddity, an adoring child who never puts herself first.

Her father, an arrogant conservative, is not always lovable. He is judgmental, unforgiving of human foibles, mostly uncaring. He approves of her, however, and she can make him laugh. Even after one of the final strokes leaves his face expressionless, she can feel the convulsions of laughter ripple through his body.

Her days are prescribed: Mornings are spent getting him ready for the day, lunch coming as the first event. She is comforted by the daily rituals: shaving him, singing his favorite songs, reading aloud to him while he scratches her head. Her life has direction and form. Whether neurosis or devotion drives her actions is immaterial. She cannot have it any other way.

It is when she gains her freedom and has only herself to look after that she falters, failing at first to understand that her days of presumed sainthood are over. It is then that she realizes that she rather relished the role, and so, after a period of succumbing to what she considers human weakness, she once again determines to dedicate her life to goodness, to return to ingrained ritual, to the Catholic ideal of loving the unlovable.

Isabel assigns herself the task of seeing to the needs of an elderly, despised former housekeeper. She absorbs the woman's abuse until Isabel thinks that she has made her final payments to her father, to the church, and to her guilt. Her act of forgiveness, particularly forgiveness of herself, seems quite in accord with the tenor of the period of flux in the church.

Gordon's novel speaks of a time shortly past in which some Catholic parents had no greater wish than for sons to become priests, their daughters nuns. It deals with a kind of Catholicism that is so much a part of the fabric of the church that many never lose it. Even after the easing of church rules, many Catholics understand the mindset of this novel, thus making it a timeless work. Gordon gives a new spin to an old theme.

SUGGESTED READINGS

Bloom, Harold, ed. *Twentieth-Century American Literature*. Vol. 3. New York: Chelsea House, 1986.
Howard, Maureen. "Salvation in Queens." *The New York Times Book Review*, April 16, 1978, 1.
Sheed, Wilfred. "The Defector's Secrets." *The New York Review of Books*, June 1, 1978, 14-15.

—*Gay Zieger*

See also Catholicism; Environment and identity; Religion and identity

Fisher, Rudolph

BORN: Washington, D.C.; May 9, 1897
DIED: New York, New York; December 26, 1934
PRINCIPAL WORKS: "The City of Refuge," 1925; *The Walls of Jericho*, 1928; *The Conjure-Man Dies: A Mystery Tale of Dark Harlem*, 1932
IDENTITIES: African American; Northeast
SIGNIFICANT ACHIEVEMENT: Fisher depicts the layers of Harlem life during the 1920's with humor, wit, and satirical grace.

Rudolph Fisher was educated in the arts and sciences. His first short story, "The City of Refuge," was published while Fisher was in medical school, and throughout his life he maintained careers as a doctor and as a writer of fiction and medical research.

For all his medical degrees, Fisher wanted to be known as a writer who could interpret Harlem life. Little seemed to have escaped his vision and analysis. He saw Harlem as a vast canvas upon which he painted characters from several different levels of life. There were the "rats," a Harlem term for the working class; the "dickties," which was Harlemese for upper-class aspirants to white values; Pullman porters; gangsters; barbers; pool hall owners; doctors; lawyers; misguided white liberals; and white celebrants and aspirants to Harlem culture. In the novel *The Walls of Jericho*, Fisher brings all of the economic, racial, and political strata of Harlem together at the annual costume ball. The dickties and the rats mingle with whites who are in search of what they think is black bohemia. The dance hall setting that Fisher enlivens in *The Walls of Jericho* was modeled after the Harlem cabarets and nightclubs he frequented.

Fisher achieved remarkable balance between the medical and artistic worlds. His short stories were published in national magazines in which other Harlem Renaissance writers could not publish. *The Walls of Jericho* was well received. The detective novel *The Conjure-Man Dies* was hailed as a first. From 1929 to 1934, Fisher was a hospital superintendent, a roentgenologist, a first lieutenant in the medical division of the 369th Infantry, and a lecturer at the 135th Street Branch of the New York Public Library.

Fisher seemed to know that working-class blacks in Harlem led lives that were far removed from the artistic renaissance popularized by intellectuals. In such short stories as "The City of Refuge" and "Vestiges, Harlem Sketches," he sympathetically depicts the struggles of many who have come from the South and who are disappointed or tricked by the fast, indifferent ways of the city. Characters such as Jinx Jenkins, Bubber Brown, and Joshua "Shine" Jones in *The Walls of Jericho* are subject to the competition and physical dangers of furniture moving. A maid in *The Walls of Jericho* is viewed by her white employer as slightly better than most blacks because of her light skin.

In 1934, Fisher died of cancer caused by X ray exposure. A retinue of Harlem artists, including Countée Cullen and Noble Sissle, joined Fisher's wife and son to mourn the loss of one of Harlem's visionaries.

SUGGESTED READINGS

De Jongh, James. *Vicious Modernism: Black Harlem and the Literary Imagination*. New York: Cambridge University Press, 1990.

Kramer, Victor, ed. *The Harlem Renaissance Re-examined*. New York: AMS Press, 1987.

Lewis, David Levering. *When Harlem Was in Vogue*. New York: Oxford University Press, 1989.

—*Australia Tarver*

See also *Conjure-Man Dies, The*; Du Bois, W. E. B.; Harlem Renaissance

Fixer, The

AUTHOR: Bernard Malamud (1914-1986)

FIRST PUBLISHED: 1966

IDENTITIES: Jewish

Based on the story of a Russian Jew, Mendel Beiless, who was tried and acquitted in czarist Russia for the ritual murder of a Christian child, *The Fixer* artistically re-creates that history. It also represents, in its theme, persecution in general. Bernard Malamud creates in this novel a story like a parable, similar in theme and style to his other works, that recounts the protagonist's spiritual growth and affirms personal dignity and moral integrity even in a world that seems incomprehensible. Yakov Bok, the hero, a Jew, comes to define himself, value suffering, and feel most free when most confined.

Yakov, a fixer or handyman, has had bad luck. With little work in his Jewish village and a wife first disappointing him in being childless then deserting him, he feels himself a prisoner of his circumstances. He sets off for Kiev, a city known for its anti-Semitism, in hopes of changing his life. In Kiev, Yakov, finding no work in the Jewish sector, begins looking outside the ghetto, which is illegal. Coming upon a drunken man who is lying unconscious in the street, Yakov helps the drunk, although Yakov recognizes him as an anti-Semite. To reward Yakov, the man offers him a job, which Yakov accepts with misgivings because it is outside the ghetto. One day Yakov reads in the paper of the ritual murder of a Christian child. The next day he is accused of the murder and put in prison. He is held for thirty months before being brought to trial.

The next three-quarters of the novel describes Yakov's physical agonies and spiritual growth while imprisoned. This growth is presented in his actions, dreams, hallucinations, perceptions, and memories during the daily suffering he undergoes—from deprivation of basic necessities and the torture of poisoning and chaining to the humiliation of the daily physical searches. During this time, he learns.

He discovers the strength of hate, political power, and historical events and sees that an individual is, by force, a political being. Secretly reading the Old then the New Testament, he feels connected with his people, yet fully appreciates the story of Christ. He develops compassion for the suffering of others. He acknowledges the suffering of the guard, who tells his story. Yakov forgives his wife and acknowledges his own part in their failed relationship. He accepts fatherhood, symbol of adulthood and personal identity, by declaring paternity to her illegitimate child, enabling her to return to life in her village without shame. At the same time he refuses to sign any documents that will free him by blaming other Jews. He also refuses to admit guilt. He finds, in identifying with his group and in willingly suffering for them that, despite what may happen to him, he is free.

SUGGESTED READINGS

Astro, Richard, and J. Jackson Benson, eds. *The Fiction of Bernard Malamud*. Corvallis: Oregon State University Press, 1977.

Field, Leslie, and Joyce Field, eds. *Bernard Malamud: A Collection of Critical Essays*. Englewood Cliffs, N.J.: Prentice-Hall, 1975.

Hershinow, Sheldon J. *Bernard Malamud*. New York: Frederick Ungar, 1980.

Richman, Sydney. *Bernard Malamud*. New York: Twayne, 1966.

—*Bernadette Flynn Low*

See also Anti-Semitism; *Assistant, The*; Jewish American identity

Floating World, The

AUTHOR: Cynthia Kadohata (1956-   )
FIRST PUBLISHED: 1989
IDENTITIES: Adolescence and coming-of-age; family; Japanese American

The Floating World deals with the theme of identity at two levels. The narrator, Olivia Osaka, a girl of twelve at the beginning of this episodic novel, is like all adolescents trying to understand the world around her. In her case, the problems normally associated with growing up are further complicated by the fact that her parents are of Japanese origin. Thus Olivia has to find her place not just as an adult but as an American of Japanese descent.

The experiences recounted by Olivia take place in the 1950's and 1960's. The internment camps for the Japanese Americans had been disbanded soon after World War II, but the effects of their dislocation were still discernible. The title of the novel comes from the Japanese word *ukiyo*—the floating world—the world of gas station attendants, restaurants, and temporary jobs encountered by the Osaka family. Charles Osaka is constantly on the move with his wife and four children—Olivia and three sons—to seek better opportunities.

Olivia discovers that Charlie is not her biological father and that her charming, graceful mother still mourns the loss of her first love. Olivia is baffled by her mother's unhappiness, for she cannot understand why the love of a decent man like Charlie is not enough for her mother. Like all children in families with marital tensions, Olivia wonders if she and her brothers are responsible for the unhappiness of their parents.

Obasan, Olivia's grandmother, lives with them for some years before her death. For Olivia, she becomes the link with her Japanese heritage. She is fascinated yet repelled by the seventy-three-year-old tyrant. Olivia enjoys her grandmother's fantastic tales of growing up in Japan, but she abhors her strict, Japanese ways of disciplining the children. She hates Obasan while she is alive, but Olivia realizes later that the memories of her grandmother's stories and the observations in her diaries are invaluable in helping her understand the lives of her parents and of the Japanese American community.

In Gibson, Arkansas, the family stays long enough for Olivia to finish high school. During this period, she experiences her first love, and begins to appreciate the hardships endured by the Japanese Americans. By the time she leaves for Los Angeles, she has learned certain truths about herself and her relationship to her community. She recognizes the fears and uncertainties that govern her parents' lives but has confidence in her own ability to overcome these uncertainties.

Olivia's narrative comes to an end with her decision to go to college. She has turned twenty-one and her years in Los Angeles have given her time to learn independence, to make her own mistakes, and to come to terms with the memories of Obasan and her biological father. With the acceptance of her past and her hyphenated identity, Olivia seems ready to take her place in American society.

SUGGESTED READINGS

Kakutani, Michiko. "Growing up Rootless in an Immigrant Family." *The New York Times*, June 30, 1989, C15.

Pearlman, Mickey. *Listen to Their Voices: Twenty Interviews with Women Who Write*. New York: W. W. Norton, 1993.

—Leela Kapai

See also Asian American identity: China, Japan, and Korea; *Bildungsroman* and *Künstlerroman*; Kadohata, Cynthia Lynn

Flowers for Algernon

AUTHOR: Daniel Keyes (1927-   )
FIRST PUBLISHED: 1966
IDENTITIES: Disability; European American

Flowers for Algernon by Daniel Keyes is one of the classic science fiction novels of the 1960's. It conveys a moving story about a mentally retarded man gaining genius-level intelligence, only to slowly and tragically regress to his former state. It is widely considered to be one of the most important novels ever written about the nature of human intelligence. The novel won the 1966 Nebula Award.

The novel was expanded from a novella of the same title, which itself won a Hugo Award in 1960. "Flowers for Algernon" (1959) told the story of Charlie Gordon, a thirty-year-old man with an IQ less than 70 but with an intense desire to learn. He is chosen to be the first human subject in an experiment aimed at surgically correcting his brian in a way that is hoped will triple his IQ. The same technique appeared successful on a laboratory mouse named Algernon. The entire story is told through journals written by Charlie, documenting his feelings and experiences as he increases his intelligence to genius level, then slowly and tragically returns to his former limited intellectual abilities. In 1992, science-fiction readers and professionals voted it the best science-fiction novella ever written.

In the novel, Keyes better detailed Charlie's intellectual rise and fall, adding startling details about his early life with his parents and sister, who later abandoned him. Although not as stylistically effective as the novella, the novel remains compelling as Charlie slowly uncovers hidden memories of his past life, seeks to achieve emotional maturity to match his towering intellect, and seeks to use that intellect (unsuccessfully) to stop in himself the same intellectual degeneration he has observed in Algernon. The novel was made into a successful film, *Charly* (1968), for which Cliff Robertson earned an Academy Award for best actor.

Increased human intelligence is a common theme in science fiction. *Slan* (1940) by A. E. van Vogt and *More than Human* (1953) by Theodore Sturgeon portray the hostility of the common man to his intellectual superiors. Others, such as *Brain Wave* (1954) by Poul Anderson and *Odd John: A Story Between Jest and Earnest* (1935) by Olaf Stapledon, portray intellect as cold and less human. "The Marching Morons" (1953), by Cyril Kornbluth, is set in a future in which the superintelligent few must secretly rule the moronic masses. *Flowers for Algernon*, however, provides a portrait of the nature of intelligence that differs greatly from these many previous stories. *Flowers for Algernon* portrays low intelligence in a sympathetic manner, effectively arguing that intelligence is only one of the many things that makes people human.

SUGGESTED READINGS

Clareson, Thomas D. *Understanding Contemporary American Science Fiction: The Formative Period, 1926-1970*. Columbia: University of South Carolina Press, 1990

Clute, John, and Peter Nichols. *The Encyclopedia of Science Fiction*. New York: St. Martin's Press, 1993.

Gunn, James. *The New Encyclopedia of Science Fiction*. New York: Viking Penguin, 1988.

Pringle, David. *Science Fiction: The One Hundred Best Novels*. New York: Carrol & Graf, 1985.

—*D. Douglas Fratz*

See also Intelligence; School

Fong-Torres, Ben

BORN: Alameda, California; January 7, 1945

PRINCIPAL WORKS: *The Motown Album: The Sound of Young America*, 1990; *Hickory Wind: The Life and Times of Gram Parsons*, 1991; *The Rice Room: Growing Up Chinese-American from Number Two Son to Rock 'n' Roll*, 1994

IDENTITIES: Chinese American; family

SIGNIFICANT ACHIEVEMENT: Fong-Torres chronicled the 1960's and the counterculture.

Ben Fong-Torres' beginnings, as depicted in *The Rice Room: Growing Up Chinese American from Number Two Son to Rock 'n' Roll*, had to do with his family's struggles to survive. As number two son he had to do something special in order to succeed, and, luckily, he was graduated in 1966 from San Francisco State University, where he had studied radio, television, and journalism, and was living by Golden Gate Park when rock and roll music made its historic flowering. He covered the concerts of the Grateful Dead at a time when many concerts were held in Golden Gate Park.

After working at KFOG radio station as an announcer and at Pacific Telephone's employee magazine as an editor, he joined the staff of *Rolling Stone* magazine in 1969. Somebody handed him two issues of *The New Yorker* magazine and said: "Here, make your articles upbeat like these." In his profiles, Fong-Torres employed the kind of detail and reporting for which *The New Yorker* was famous. Much as F. Scott Fitzgerald captured the Jazz Age, Fong-Torres captured the rock-and-roll essence of the 1960's.

He freelanced for many top-circulation magazines and a wide range of other national publications. His writings covered the entertainment industry, including profiles of Ray Charles, Sean Connery, and Robin Williams. Much of Fong-Torres' writing helped to create the American image of rock and roll.

He joined the *San Francisco Chronicle* in 1983 as a feature writer, but left the paper in order to write his books. In 1990, he wrote the main text for *The Motown Album: The Sound of Young America*. He next wrote a biography, *Hickory Wind: The Life and Times of Gram Parsons*. After completing his memoir *The Rice Room* in 1993, Fong-Torres joined *Gavin*, a San Francisco-based trade magazine covering the radio and music industries. While serving as managing editor of this weekly magazine, he also resumed broadcasting, hosting *Fog City Radio*, a weekly live arts program.

SUGGESTED READINGS

Chiu, Monica. Review of *The Rice Room: Growing Up Chinese-American from Number Two Son to Rock 'n' Roll*, by Ben Fong-Torres. *MELUS* 20 (Spring, 1995): 115-117.

Lis, Anthony. Review of *Hickory Wind: The Life and Times of Gram Parsons*, by Ben Fong-Torres. *Notes* 49 (March, 1993): 1078-1079.

Nicholson, David. Review of *The Rice Room: Growing Up Chinese-American from Number Two Son to Rock 'n' Roll*, by Ben Fong-Torres. *Washington Post*, April 26, 1994, e 2.

—*Donna Joyce Litherland*

See also Acculturation; Asian American identity: China, Japan, and Korea; Countercultures; *Fifth Chinese Daughter*

Food and identity

IDENTITIES: Men; women

The centrality of food to human experience and to personal and cultural identity is mirrored in the food preoccupations of literature. Without food, there is no life. Literature, the imaginative re-creation of life, often centers on food, eating, and cooking. Food practices and images help to define characters and values, enrich language, and illuminate cultures, regions, and particularly women's identity and development.

The pleasure of eating is a perennial theme in literature. Joel Barlow's mock pastoral "The Hasty-Pudding" (1796) for example, particularizes the joys of preparing and eating cornmeal. Food does more than provide sensual pleasure to the reader; it helps define character or meaning. For example, "The Hasty-Pudding," in praising cornmeal, celebrates, with some irony, the new nation and its inhabitants. Europeans would not be pleased, or admit to being pleased, to eat corn. Ichabod Crane's voracious appetite for the cooked dainties at the Van Tassel's feast in Washington Irving's "The Legend of Sleepy Hollow" (1820) underscores the humorous weaknesses of a personality torn by the opposite forces of reason, superstition, and appetite. Ernest Hemingway's narratives often identify characters as manly in their overindulgence in food and drink.

Food as metaphor So central is food to life that writers often describe seemingly unrelated experiences and events with food-related language. In Betty MacDonald's *The Egg and I* (1945), the narrator is so anxious for company that when relatives visit she "clung to them like the smell of frying"; a baby looks "as if he had been molded out of dough"; a logging victim "cracked" his "head like an egg"; and Maw's "large white breasts bobbed to the surface like dumplings in a stew." In the same book, image merges into symbol in the significance of the title. Eggs not only are food but also are the essence of productivity and fertility. MacDonald's book explores the fertility of nature, garden, orchard, and families.

Food and cultural identity Food in literature often helps to define a cultural or geographical setting. MacDonald's *Onions in the Stew* (1955) evokes the gastronomical glories of Northwestern seafood, while Marjorie Kinnan Rawlings' *Cross Creek* (1942) explores the delights of Northern Florida's rural cooking. Willa Cather's novels trace special foods identified with various cultural groups: dried mushrooms and "kolaches" with the Bohemians in *My Ántonia* (1918); the French devotion to salads, vegetables, and fine wine in *Death Comes for the Archbishop* (1927) and *Shadows on the Rock* (1931); and the pleasures of Southern meals in *Sapphira and the Slave Girl* (1940).

Women and food In most cultures women are traditionally the preparers of food, so women's identities are often bound up in food and cooking. In affluent societies particularly, the result has been a struggle for women who seek to separate themselves from overidentification with food and eating. This tension is explored in Margaret Atwood's novel *The Edible Woman* (1976), in which Marian works as a tester of consumer products, usually food, and finds herself threatened by a society that is intent on consuming her as if she, too, were food. One of the most complete fictional explorations of the relationship of women to food is found in Laura Esquivel's novel *Como agua para chocolate* (1989; *Like Water for Chocolate: A Novel in Monthly Installments with Recipes, Romances, and Home Remedies*, 1992). The novel centers on the experiences of a daughter raised on a ranch in the Rio Grande border area of Mexico, close to the United States. Tita's life centers on her relationship to cooking and food. The novel is organized around recipes appropriate to the months of the year. Throughout much of the narrative, Tita's passions are close to boiling—like water ready for chocolate beverage. In contrast to Atwood's novel, however, Esquivel's narrative depicts a mixture of positive and negative experiences inherent in the life of a woman defined by food.

Refusing to eat, or anorexia nervosa, has typically been a woman's disease, although the emphasis on thinness as an index of beauty began to affect increasing numbers of men in the last decades of the twentieth century. Anorexia goes against societal expectations, providing a mark of identity; she who refuses to eat demonstrates a degree, however self-destructive, of control over herself and her surroundings. Religious fasting and appetite control have traditionally been seen as transcendent, but when the religious symbolism is eliminated, self-starving becomes a rebellious attempt to establish identity in a society that is oblivious to women as people. One early American portrayal of intentional hunger centers on a male character searching for identity in Herman Melville's "Bartleby the Scrivener" (1853). Bartleby's rebellion against normal human expectations begins with refusals to work and ends in death from refusals to eat. Literary treatments of eating disorders typically center on women and, more often than not, on girls and young women. Young adult books that explore the dilemma of characters bent on denying themselves food and, thus, normal female development and growth, and bent on establishing an identity of thinness, include Deborah Hautzig's *Second Star to the Right* (1981), Ivy Ruckman's *The Hunger Scream* (1983), Susan Terris' *Nell's Quilt* (1987), and Margaret Willey's *The Bigger Book of Lydia* (1983).

Eating disorders

SUGGESTED READINGS

Bevan, David, ed. *Literary Gastronomy*. Amsterdam: Rodopi, 1988.

Chernin, Kim. *The Hungry Self: Women, Eating, and Identity*. New York: Harper & Row, 1985.

Hinz, Evelyn J., ed. *Mosaic* 24 (Summer-Fall, 1991), complete issue.

Restifo, Kathleen. "Portrait of Anorexia Nervosa in Young Adult Literature." *High School Journal* 71 (1988): 210-222.

Schofield, Mary Anne. *Cooking by the Book: Food in Literature and Culture*. Bowling Green, Ohio: Bowling Green State University Popular Press, 1989.

—*Delmer Davis*

See also Addiction; Atwood, Margaret; Feminism

Fool for Love

AUTHOR: Sam Shepard (Samuel Shepard Rogers, 1943-   )
FIRST PRODUCED: 1983; first published, 1983
IDENTITIES: European American; family; West and Southwest

Set in a desolate motel room on the edge of the Mojave Desert, *Fool for Love* displays an alternately tender and violent love-hate relationship. Unlike the struggle between two brothers in the playwright's *True West* (1980), the conflict in *Fool for Love* is between a woman and a man. After a long absence, Eddie has traveled 2,480 miles to reclaim May, his lover since high school. At different times during their abrupt reunion she alternately orders him to leave and begs him to stay.

Eddie boasts spurs, bucking strap, and all the other trappings of a rodeo cowboy, but his quest for glory in that arena has left him broken down and prematurely old. As if trying to hold on to his heroic Western identity, he practices roping the motel furniture. Eddie's affair with a society woman who drives a huge, black Mercedes-Benz has subverted his role as rugged cowboy. Angered by his desertion, the woman burns his pickup truck and sets his horses loose. A decrepit man trying to salvage his dream, Eddie talks of moving to Wyoming, where he can grow vegetables. Even in this fantasy, however, his residence will be a trailer, suggesting the ephemeral fragility of his dream.

May has long been confined to a trailer and to the claustrophobic motel room (against whose walls she frequently beats her head). In Shepard's first sustained development of a female character, she attempts to escape these symbolic traps and shape an identity separate from Eddie by taking a job as a cook and by dating Martin, a pleasant although somewhat bland orphan. To disparage her efforts, Eddie claims that she cannot even flip an egg and labels Martin a twerp. Eddie further asserts that he and May will "always be connected."

As in *True West*, these two characters are separate individuals and warring components of a single confused identity. May claims that she can smell Eddie's thoughts before he thinks them, and they are half-sister and half-brother. They are drawn relentlessly into an incestuous love. Their father, identified as The Old Man, sits onstage during the entire play and comments occasionally on the action. He describes his relationships with two different women (the mothers of May and Eddie) as the same love that somehow got split in two. The play's dialogue presents different versions of family history, and these debates about the past exemplify the difficulty of escaping the burden of family and forging an individual identity—a theme developed more fully in *A Lie of the Mind* (1985).

SUGGESTED READINGS

Bank, Rosemarie. "Self as Other: Sam Shepard's *Fool for Love* and *A Lie of the Mind*." In *Feminist Rereadings of Modern American Drama*, edited by June Schlueter. Madison, N.J.: Fairleigh Dickinson University Press, 1989.

Mottram, Ron. *Inner Landscapes: The Theater of Sam Shepard*. Columbia: University of Missouri Press, 1984.

Wilcox, Leonard, ed. *Rereading Shepard: Contemporary Critical Essays*. New York: St. Martin's Press, 1993.

—*Albert E. Wilhelm*

See also American identity: West and the frontier; Shepard, Sam; *True West*

Fools Crow

AUTHOR: James Welch (1940-   )
FIRST PUBLISHED: 1986
IDENTITIES: Midwest; Native American

Fools Crow dramatizes Native American life on the plains of eastern Montana toward the end of the era of the free, nonreservation tribe. This novel follows an Indian coming to manhood, his free life, his romantic marriage, his daring attack on an enemy, his struggle with the dilemma of whether to fight the white man and be slain or to submit to humiliating poverty and confinement on a reservation. James Welch inherited sympathy for Native Americans from his Gros Ventre mother and from his Blackfoot father. His mother showed Welch documents from the Indian agency where she worked. The tales of his paternal grandmother concerning the awful massacre at Marias River, Montana, provided basic material and a viewpoint from which to write. Welch's grandmother, a girl at the time of the massacre, was wounded but escaped with a few survivors. She spoke only her tribal language.

In *Fools Crow*, White Man's Dog yearns to find respect. At eighteen he has three puny horses, a musket without powder, and no wife. He joins in a raid, in which he proves himself. He woos beautiful Red Paint. His young wife fears he may be killed yet yearns for his honor as a warrior; in a war raid, he outwits and kills the renowned Crow chief, thereby winning the mature name of Fools Crow. Names such as that of his father, Rides-at-the-door, and of the medicine man, Mik-Api, suggest an Indian culture. The people pray to The Above Ones—the gods—and to Cold Maker, winter personified. These gods sometimes instruct warriors such as Fools Crow in dreams.

Fools Crow follows Raven—a sacred messenger—to free his animal helper, a wolverine, from a white man's steel trap. Later the Raven requires that Fools Crow lure to death a white man who shoots animals and leaves the flesh to rot. Smallpox ravages the teepees. Settlers push into the treaty territory, reducing buffalo, essential for food, shelter, and livelihood. Fools Crow finds a few of his people running in the northern winter away from the army slaughter of an entire village. In a vision experience, he sees his people living submissively with the powerful whites. Hope for his people resides in such children as his infant son Butterfly.

SUGGESTED READINGS

Barry, Nora. "A Myth to Be Alive: James Welch's *Fools Crow*." *Melus* 17 (Spring, 1991): 3-20.

Gish, Robert F. "Word Medicine: Storytelling and Magic Realism in James Welch's *Fools Crow*." *American Indian Quarterly* 14, no. 4 (Fall, 1990): 349-354.

McFarland, Ron. " 'The End' in James Welch's Novels." *American Indian Quarterly* 17, no. 3 (Summer, 1995): 319-327.

Murphree, Bruce. "Welch's *Fools Crow*." *The Explicator* 52, no. 3 (Spring, 1994): 186-187.

—*Emmett H. Carroll*

See also American identity: West and the frontier; Naming and identity; Native American identity; Welch, James

for colored girls who have considered suicide/when the rainbow is enuf: a choreopoem

AUTHOR: Ntozake Shange (Paulette Williams, 1948-   )
FIRST PRODUCED: 1976; first published, 1976
IDENTITIES: African American; women

For colored girls who have considered suicide/when the rainbow is enuf, Ntozake Shange's first work, tells the stories of seven women who have suffered oppression in a racist and sexist society. The choreopoem is an innovative combination of poetry, drama, music, and dance. For Shange, the combination is important. She learned about her identity as a woman through words, songs, and literature; she learned about her identity as an African through dance.

The seven women are not named; they are meant to stand for the women who make up the rainbow. They are called "lady in brown," "lady in red," and so on. Each tells her own story. The stories are interwoven together. As the women tell their stories, they reflect on what it means to be a woman of color, what chances and choices they have. These women are in pain; they are angry. They have been abused by their lovers, their rapists, their abortionists, and they have been driven to the brink of despair. What strength they have left they find in music and in each other.

Many have criticized the play for being too negative toward black men, but Shange has always attempted to direct the focus of the discussion back on the women. The play is about the women, about who they are and what they have experienced. To insist on a "balanced" view of the men in their lives is to deny these women's experiences. These women deserve a voice. The play, she insists, does not accuse all black men of being abusive. These women are not rejecting men or seeking a life without men. The women desire men and love them, and ache for that love to be returned.

Although the stories these women tell are tales of struggle, the play is ultimately uplifting. The seven women grieve, but they also celebrate their lives, their vitality, their colorfulness. As the play ends, the women recite, one at a time and then together: "i found god in myself/ & i loved her/ i loved her fiercely." These women are not entirely powerless; they have the power of their own voices. They find the courage to tell their stories and thus triumph.

SUGGESTED READINGS

Lester, Neal A. *Ntozake Shange: A Critical Study of the Plays*. New York: Garland, 1995.

Shange, Ntozake. *See No Evil: Prefaces, Essays and Accounts, 1976-1983*. San Francisco: Momo Press, 1984.

—*Cynthia A. Bily*

See also Abortion and birth control; African American identity; *Betsey Brown*; Erotic identity; Rape; Shange, Ntozake

Forché, Carolyn

BORN: Detroit, Michigan; April 28, 1950

PRINCIPAL WORKS: *Gathering the Tribes*, 1976; *The Country Between Us*, 1981; *Against Forgetting: Twentieth-Century Poetry of Witness*, 1993 (editor); *The Angel of History*, 1994

IDENTITIES: European American; women

SIGNIFICANT ACHIEVEMENT: As a poet, activist, educator, journalist, translator, and editor, Forché has sought to respond to the atrocities that have shaped the twentieth century.

Carolyn Forché's interest in responding to human oppression can be traced to her early childhood in Detroit. When she was five she discovered a series of photographs in *Life* magazine documenting the liberation of the Nazi death camps. Disturbed by these pictures of immense suffering, Forché hid them between her mattresses and returned to them throughout her childhood.

Later, she was affected even more profoundly by war. At nineteen Forché married James Turner, who, like a number of her high school classmates, fought in Vietnam and suffered from post-traumatic stress syndrome. Forché and Turner eventually divorced, but her poetry and work as an activist for Amnesty International continue to be informed by this experience with the psychic cost of war.

After being graduated from Michigan State University with a major in creative writing in 1972, Forché pursued her interest in writing at Bowling Green State University in Ohio, receiving her M.F.A. in 1975. A year later she published her first volume of poetry, *Gathering the Tribes*, which focuses on the displaced and the forgotten, including her immigrant European forebears and Native Americans.

In 1975, Forché spent several months in Mallorca, living with and translating the poetry of Claribel Alegría, a Salvadoran exile who had chronicled the oppression in her native country. After returning to the United States, a relative of Alegría invited Forché to El Salvador to observe the abuses of the United States-backed government. Beginning in 1978, she was in El Salvador for two years. Forché has described her time there as "a moral and political education" that "would change my life and work" and "propel me toward engagement." After returning from El Salvador, she spent the next four years lecturing in the United States about the injustices she observed there. Some of these experiences are documented in *The Country Between Us*, which she characterizes as poetry of confrontation and witness.

In 1984, she married Henry Mattison, a photographic correspondent for *Time* whom she had first met in El Salvador. Accompanying him on assignment in Lebanon, she became a correspondent for National Public Radio. Her most recent works continue to expose and resist human brutality. *Against Forgetting: Twentieth-Century Poetry of Witness* is an anthology of protest poetry, and *The Angel of History* is a long poem that explores, among other things, the ramifications of the Holocaust and the dropping of the atomic bomb.

SUGGESTED READINGS

Forché, Carolyn. "El Salvador: An Aide Memoire." *American Poetry Review* 10, no. 4 (July-August, 1981): 3-8.

_____. "A Lesson in Commitment." *TriQuarterly* 65 (Winter, 1986): 30-38.

—*Vincent Allan King*

See also Antiwar literature; Erotic identity; Forché, Carolyn, poetry of; Holocaust; Vietnam War

Forché, Carolyn, poetry of

AUTHOR: Carolyn Forché (1950-   )

PRINCIPAL WORKS: *Gathering the Tribes*, 1976; *The Country Between Us*, 1981; *Against Forgetting: Twentieth-Century Poetry of Witness*, 1993 (editor); *The Angel of History*, 1994

IDENTITIES: European American; women

Carolyn Forché's poetry of witness and confrontation encourages readers to cross national, geographical, and personal boundaries, boundaries that she believes serve to isolate and brutalize the less powerful. Her first volume, *Gathering the Tribes*, was published in the prestigious Yale Series of Younger Poets. These poems are about three main topics: her immigrant relatives, especially Anna, her Slavic paternal grandmother; her encounters with Native Americans in the southwestern United States; and the sexual initiation of the poet, whose search for physical fulfillment indicates her desire to escape the exile status that defines immigrants and Native Americans.

Forché's next volume, *The Country Between Us*, was a Lamont Poetry Selection of the Academy of American Poets and solidified her reputation as a writer. Despite the critical acclaim for the volume and its status as a best-seller—at least by poetry standards—some critics complained that her work was too political, even sensational. Their criticism focused almost exclusively on the eight poems titled "In Salvador, 1978-80," which deal with her experiences as a human rights activist in that country.

Yet the other two sections of the volume, "Reunion" and "Ourselves or Nothing" are set in such diverse places as the midwestern United States, Mallorca, and eastern Europe. What unites the poems in *The Country Between Us* is not geography or a specific political ideology but simply a sensitivity to the many faces of human loss. The poems document the human proclivity to hurt or maim, on a personal and a political level. Forché continues to assert, however, that the human touch is redemptive, if only temporarily.

The Angel of History is Forché's most complex work to date. Abandoning what she describes as "The first person, free-verse, lyric narrative poem of my earlier years," *The Angel of History* is, as she says, "polyphonic, broken, haunted, and in ruins, with no possibility of restoration." The five sections of this long poem, with all their different voices and locales, speak to the power of memory and confrontation. Forché suggests that by reexamining the moral failures that led to the death camps in Nazi Germany, as well as to the dropping of the atomic bomb on Hiroshima, other mass assaults on the human body and spirit can be prevented. Similarly, *Against Forgetting: Twentieth-Century Poetry of Witness* is an anthology, edited by Forché, of protest poetry that documents the curative powers of memory and engagement.

SUGGESTED READINGS

Diggory, Terrence. "Witness and Seers." *Salmagundi* 61 (Fall, 1983): 112-124.

Doubiago, Sharon. "Towards an American Criticism: A Reading of Carolyn Forché's *The Country Between Us*." *The American Poetry Review* 12, no. 1 (January-February, 1983): 35-39.

Greer, Michael. "Politicizing the Modern: Carolyn Forché in El Salvador and America." *The Centennial Review* 30, no. 2 (Spring, 1986): 160-180.

Walker, Kevin. "Inspired by War." *Detroit Free Press* (May 22, 1994): 8G.

—*Vincent Allan King*

See also Antiwar literature; Erotic identity; Forché, Carolyn; Holocaust; Vietnam War

Forcible rape. *See* **Rape**

Ford, Richard

BORN: Jackson, Mississippi; February 16, 1944

PRINCIPAL WORKS: *A Piece of My Heart*, 1976; *The Ultimate Good Luck*, 1981; *The Sportswriter*, 1986; *Rock Springs*, 1987; *Wildfire*, 1990; *Independence Day*, 1995

IDENTITIES: European American; family; men; Northeast; South; West and Southwest

SIGNIFICANT ACHIEVEMENT: Ford's much-lauded fiction expertly captures the struggle for identity faced by many American men.

Richard Ford was born in the Deep South, in the land of William Faulkner and Eudora Welty, and his first novel, *A Piece of My Heart*, is a work in the Southern gothic tradition. Ford has also written about other parts of America, paying particular attention, in the short stories in *Rock Springs* and in the short novel *Wildfire*, to the American West (especially Montana). In *The Sportswriter* and its sequel *Independence Day* Ford writes about the Northeast, where Ford lived while he taught at Princeton. Wherever his fiction is set, however, Ford shows how environment and occupation help define his characters' identities.

*Richard Ford,
author of*
The Sportswriter
(1986).
(James Hamilton)

After some teenage scrapes with the law, which, it may be said, find their expression in his stories of thieves, drifters, and losers, Ford left the South to attend college at the University of Michigan. Except for some short-term teaching positions, he has spent his adult life almost exclusively as a writer. Like his best friend, the late Raymond Carver, Ford has written extensively about lower- and lower-middle-class characters, and how they often struggle simply to get by. In his short fiction, particularly, the question of where a next paycheck (or even a next meal) will come from can define characters and can remove the element of free will that helps more affluent people define themselves.

Even for Ford's more affluent characters, the next paycheck is important. Ford's calling as a writer defines him in the same way that occupations define the identities of many of his characters. Frank Bascombe, the narrator of Ford's two best-known novels, *The Sportswriter* and *Independence Day*, allows his jobs (sportswriter and realtor, respectively) to determine not only how he spends his time but also the shape of his life, thoughts, and beliefs. Like John Updike, Ford shows how for many American men a job becomes the central focus of identity, although it is also shaped by the environment they occupy.

SUGGESTED READINGS

Hardwick, Elizabeth. "Reckless People." *The New York Review of Books*, August 10, 1995, 11-14.
Schroth, Raymond A. "America's Moral Landscape in the Fiction of Richard Ford." *The Christian Century*, March 1, 1989, 227-230.

—Greg Garrett

See also American identity: South; American identity: West and the frontier; Carver, Raymond; Faulkner, William; *Sportswriter, The*; Updike, John

Forsyte Saga, The

AUTHOR: John Galsworthy (1967-1933)

FIRST PUBLISHED: Book, 1922 (large parts were originally published as *The Man of Property*, 1906; *In Chancery*, 1920; *To Let*, 1921; "Indian Summer of a Forsyte"; and "Awakening")

IDENTITIES: Family; women; world

The Forsyte Saga, in particular *The Man of Property*, is John Galsworthy's most enduring work. It is the story of one upper middle-class family in England in the late nineteenth and early twentieth centuries.

The most important character is Soames Forsyte, the title character of *The Man of Property*. He is a successful lawyer and a collector of paintings. He is married to Irene Heron, whom he and society regard as his property. At the climax of the book, Soames rapes her. Galsworthy was horrified at the situation of a woman who is forced into the sexual act with a man she does not love. He did not agree with the prevailing attitude of the time that a husband had the right to his wife's body.

In Chancery picks up the story several years later. Soames and Irene are still legally married, but separated. Soames becomes obsessed with the need to father a son, but Irene refuses to go back to him. Soames then casts his eye on a young Frenchwoman, Annette Lamotte. The only ground on which Soames can divorce Irene, however, is adultery, but she had not taken a lover. Irene has developed a friendship with Soames' cousin, Jolyon Forsyte. They are seen together in public, but it is only after Soames confronts them that they consummate their relationship. They do not contest the divorce proceedings, so Soames marries Annette, and Jolyon and Irene legally become husband and wife.

The book ends with the birth of a son, Jon, for Jolyon and Irene and a daughter, Fleur, for Soames and Annette. Annette has a difficult birthing. Soames' doctor gives Soames the choice of saving his wife or his child. Soames chooses the child, although had he known it would be a girl he might have chosen differently. Annette survives, but she cannot have any more children.

To Let takes up the story twenty years later. Jon and Fleur meet and fall in love. Soames approves the match, but Jolyon and Irene oppose it. In a reversal of attitude, Galsworthy shows Jolyon and especially Irene as treating Jon as a possession, but shows Soames to be a loving parent. The book ends with Jolyon telling Jon the story of Soames and Irene. Jolyon dies shortly afterward, and Jon breaks off the relationship.

SUGGESTED READINGS

Barker, Dudley. *The Man of Principle: A Biography of John Galsworthy*. New York: Stein and Day, 1963.

Dupré, Catherine. *John Galsworthy: A Biography*. New York: Coward, McCann, 1976.

Kettle, Arnold. "John Galsworthy: The Man of Property." In *An Introduction to the English Novel*. Vol. 2. New York: Hutchinson's University Library, 1967.

Lawrence, D. H. "John Galsworthy." In *Selected Literary Criticism*. New York: Viking Press, 1966.

—Tom Feller

See also Class and identity; Feminism; Galsworthy, John

Fossil and Psyche

AUTHOR: Wilson Harris (1921-   )

FIRST PUBLISHED: 1974

IDENTITIES: African American; Caribbean; European American; Native American

Fossil and Psyche articulates Wilson Harris' belief that "the potentiality for dialogue, for change, for the miracle of roots, for new community is real." Using the metaphor of archery (psychic arrows and fossil targets), he situates his novels and the work of other writers within a realm of attempts to reach architectonic (mythic) realities. He argues against the opposition of the material to the spiritual and critiques the borders by means of which the real is held separate from the imaginary.

Harris asserts the potential of the imaginary to illuminate the transcendent possibilities of history and identity. Such possibilities, if realized, would result in a culturally heterogeneous world community and in an alteration of world power hierarchies.

The "idolatry of absolutes" holds readers and writers hostage to the temporal, spatial, and cultural limitations of literature when in fact those limitations are illusory. Arrows of language and imagination can reach the fossil targets of architectonic, mythic, eternal, atemporal, renewing experience. Novels by authors such as Patrick White and Malcolm Lowry, Harris claims, are dream-expeditions signaling humanity toward "a third perhaps nameless revolutionary dimension of sensibility" that evades commonly held notions of material and spiritual reality. Such an evasion is the key to enriching and understanding the value of the multiplicity of identities. Accessing these wells of timeless connection will "deepen and heighten the role of imaginative literature to wrestle with categories and to visualize the birth of community as other than the animism of fate."

Traditional oppositions lead to inadequate readings of imaginative literature and to misreadings of the processes that underlie imaginative composition. Literature, like every aspect of human experience, is lodged within a matrix of time and space. The literature Harris addresses in *Fossil and Psyche* attempts to transcend this matrix, to confound time and space, to mine the architectonic fossils of human community with present psychic projections of imagination.

Novels of expedition, then, revise history and reveal the hopeful, transformative energies of life locked away in even the most deadly and deadening acts of history. Writers who embrace such a process of revision renew the creative, psychic act of imagination. Such psychic projections of imagination join past to present and future and European to African and Native American.

SUGGESTED READINGS

Drake, Sandra E. *Wilson Harris and the Modern Tradition: A New Architecture of the World*. Westport, Conn.: Greenwood Press, 1986.

Gilkes, Michael. *Wilson Harris and the Caribbean Novel*. London: Longman, 1975.

Harris, Wilson. *Tradition, the Writer and Society: Critical Essays*. London: New Beacon, 1967.

Maes-Jelinek, Hena, ed. *Wilson Harris: The Uncompromising Imagination*. Aarhus, Denmark: Dangaroo, 1991.

Moore, Gerald. *The Chosen Tongue*. New York: Longman, 1969.

—Daniel M. Scott III

See also Colonialism; Harris, Wilson; Multiculturalism; *Womb of Space, The*

Frank, Anne

BORN: Frankfurt, Germany; June 12, 1929
DIED: Bergen-Belsen, Germany; March, 1945
PRINCIPAL WORKS: *Het Achterhuis*, 1947 (*The Diary of a Young Girl*, 1952); *Verhaaltjes en gebeurtenissen uit het Achterhuis*, 1982 (*Anne Frank's Tales from the Secret Annex*, 1983)
IDENTITIES: Adolescence and coming-of-age; Jewish; religion; world
SIGNIFICANT ACHIEVEMENT: Frank's diary provides a portrait of an ordinary girl living in extraordinary times.

Life in Germany had become difficult by 1929, when Anne Frank was born to a Jewish family. Poverty, unemployment, and dissatisfaction with the government caused increased numbers to join the National Socialist German Workers' Party, commonly known as the Nazi Party. Its leader, Adolf Hitler, believed in the superiority of the German race and blamed Jews for the country's problems. By 1933, democracy in Germany had ceased to exist and a campaign of anti-Semitism had begun. Otto Frank decided to move his family to the Netherlands, a country of religious tolerance. Germany invaded the Netherlands in May, 1940.

In June, 1942, Anne celebrated her thirteenth birthday and received a diary, the perfect outlet for her active mind. This diary eventually allowed readers an insight into the cultural and personal identity of a perceptive adolescent who recorded factual accounts, feelings, and fears. Less than a month later, the Franks were forced to go into hiding, and Anne's writings continued in the secret annex behind Otto Frank's offices.

Eventually, four more people joined the Franks in the hiding place. It was difficult, as privacy was lacking, fear of discovery constant, and nerves always on edge. Anne was still a typical adolescent; she studied, read, and struggled. The struggle involved maturing, acquiring self-confidence, and wrestling with depression. Additionally she was confused, unable to comprehend the emotional suffering of everyone in hiding. Anxiety plagued her and the sensitivity of a thirteen-year-old was sharpened. She wrote: "Sometimes I believe that God wants to try me, both now and later on; I must become good through my own efforts."

Anne's writing consoled and comforted her, recording the changing emotions of an adolescent. Trying to be positive, she states, "[S]o the radio with its miraculous voice helps us to keep our morale and to say again 'Chins up, stick it out, better times will come!'" As time progressed, she became more philosophical. Remembering her life before persecution, she felt as if another person lived it, imploring: "Oh, if only the black circle could recede and open the way for us!" Then in March, 1944: "When shall I finally untangle my thoughts, when shall I find peace and rest within myself again?"

Anne Frank was deprived of a normal life and of the opportunity to become the journalist she aspired to be. She believed that the suffering of the Jews would help them emerge stronger. The occupants of the secret annex were found by German police. In March, 1945, two months before the liberation of Holland, Anne Frank died in the concentration camp at Bergen-Belsen.

SUGGESTED READING

Van der Rol, Ruud, and Rian Verhoven. *Anne Frank Beyond the Diary*. New York: Puffin Books, 1995.

—*Doris O'Donnell Jellig*

See also Holocaust; Jewish American identity

Freeman, Mary E. Wilkins

BORN: Randolph, Massachusetts; October 31, 1852
DIED: Metuchen, New Jersey; March 13, 1930
PRINCIPAL WORKS: *A Humble Romance and Other Stories*, 1887; *A New England Nun and Other Stories*, 1891; *Pembroke*, 1894
IDENTITIES: European American; Northeast; women
SIGNIFICANT ACHIEVEMENT: Freeman portrays the life and people of a changing New England, focusing on women.

Mary E. Wilkins Freeman deals, in her best fiction (that written before her less-than-happy marriage to Dr. Charles Manning Freeman in 1902), with the rural New England mill towns and villages that are comparable to the one she knew and grew up in, Randolph, Massachusetts. From Randolph, a typical New England town that lay fourteen miles from Boston, came Freeman's sense of locale: harsh winters, raw springs, church, and school. She also experienced the security of a community in which one's neighbors shared ancestral codes of behavior. Despite the homogeneity of her community, Freeman knew as well the eccentricities and oddities of human character that result from generations of rural isolation.

From *A Humble Romance and Other Stories*, her earliest collection of short stories, to *The Winning Lady and Others* (1909), a later collection, as well as in several novels, Freeman depicts common and ordinary experiences in the lives of ordinary men and women of the New England region she knew intimately. As typical as lives and events in her fiction seem, Freeman transcends them to show readers universal truths of human character and daily living.

Her truthful treatment of a New England environment in transition as a result of post-Civil War industrialization places her in the category of regional writers. Freeman's treatment of women, their roles, their relationships with men, their children, and their status in society has also gained her increasing attention among feminist critics and women writers. In short stories such as "A New England Nun," "The Revolt of Mother," and "Gentian," Freeman explores marriage, male-female relationships, and women and their search for identity in a patriarchal world. Her characters are not only eccentric New England types but also real people struggling to cope with the problems of human existence: loneliness, frustration, self-esteem, and self-fulfillment. She presents the emerging modern woman torn between a desire for personal independence and the pressures of conforming to a patriarchal society.

SUGGESTED READINGS

Foster, Edward. *Mary E. Wilkins Freeman*. New York: Hendricks House, 1956.

Marchalonis, Shirley, ed. *Critical Essays on Mary Wilkins Freeman*. Boston: G. K. Hall, 1991.

Westbrook, Perry D. *Mary Wilkins Freeman*. Rev. ed. New York: Twayne, 1988.

Wood, Ann Douglas. "The Literature of Impoverishment: The Women Local Colorists in America 1865-1914." *Women's Studies* 1 (1972): 3-40.

—*Thomas A. Maik*

See also American identity: Northeast; Environment and identity; Feminism; Freeman, Mary E. Wilkins, short stories of; Patriarchy and matriarchy; Rural life

Freeman, Mary E. Wilkins, short stories of

AUTHOR: Mary E. Wilkins Freeman (1852-1930)

PRINCIPAL WORKS: *A Humble Romance and Other Stories*, 1887; *A New England Nun and Other Stories*, 1891; *Silence and Other Stories*, 1898; *Edgewater People*, 1918; *Best Stories*, 1927

IDENTITIES: European American; Northeast; women

In a literary career than spanned almost fifty years, Mary E. Wilkins Freeman wrote fifteen collections of short stories, sixteen novels, one play, and eight volumes of prose and poetry for children. Of the various genres she attempted, her best writing occurs in the genre of short fiction during the 1880's and 1890's. She rejected a career in teaching to concentrate on her goal of becoming a writer.

Freeman is recognized for two fine collections of short stories: *A Humble Romance and Other Stories* and *A New England Nun and Other Stories*. The two elderly sisters of "A Mistaken Charity" represent the typical Freeman female protagonists of these short-story collections: fiercely independent, a product of their New England environment, capable, determined, and nonconformist. The title of "A Mistaken Charity" typifies the well-meaning but misplaced intentions of social do-gooders in a New England community who believe that two elderly sisters who live alone would be better off in the "old ladies home" and who make such arrangements. Harriet and Charlotte, the two sisters in question, disagree, make their escape, and return to their dilapidated but perfectly suitable cottage.

Freeman continues themes of independence, determination, and female capabilities in short stories included in *A New England Nun and Other Stories*. Louisa Ellis of "The New England Nun" discovers, on her suitor's return after fourteen years from seeking adventure and fortune in Australia, that the quiet life of spinsterhood is preferable to marriage. In rejecting marriage, Louisa's actions are dramatic, feisty, and most unusual for the time. That same feistiness, will, and determination are characteristic of "The Revolt of Mother," perhaps Freeman's most famous story. After waiting patiently through forty years of marriage for a new home, which her husband promised her before they were married, Sarah Penn has had enough and revolts. Determined to live at least as well as her husband's livestock do, she and her two children take up residence in a new barn that her husband has built. The barn was built to hold livestock that he neither needs nor owns and occupies the site designated for Sarah's future home. This story's characteristics are vintage Freeman: independent and strong-willed women, a stifling and oppressive New England environment, and universal truths from everyday experiences of ordinary men and women.

SUGGESTED READINGS

Donovan, Josephine. *New England Local Color Literature: A Women's Tradition*. New York: Frederick Ungar, 1983.

Marchalonis, Shirley, ed. *Critical Essays on Mary Wilkins Freeman*. Boston: G. K. Hall, 1991.

Westbrook, Perry D. *Mary Wilkins Freeman*. Rev. ed. New York: Twayne, 1988.

Wood, Ann Douglas. "The Literature of Impoverishment: The Women Local Colorists in America 1865-1914." *Women's Studies* 1 (1972): 3-40.

—*Thomas A. Maik*

See also American identity: Northeast; Environment and identity; Feminism; Freeman, Mary E. Wilkins; Patriarchy and matriarchy; Women and identity

French, Marilyn

BORN: Brooklyn, New York; November 21, 1929

PRINCIPAL WORKS: *The Women's Room*, 1977; *The Bleeding Heart*, 1980; *Beyond Power: On Women, Men, and Morals*, 1986; *Her Mother's Daughter*, 1987; *The War Against Women*, 1992

IDENTITIES: European American; women

SIGNIFICANT ACHIEVEMENT: French's novels illustrate the concepts and conflicts of the feminist movement by using believable characters and a straightforward writing style.

Marilyn French lived through the women's movement as it was happening and is one of the premier chroniclers of its evolution. As a writer of fiction and nonfiction works about women's place in society, she uses invention and research to describe women's thoughts and reactions to their situations and to trace the societal causes that lead to these reactions.

French began publishing relatively late in life, although she began writing at the age of ten. French grew up in Long Island, New York. A precocious child, she read works by the German philosophers Friedrich Nietzsche and Arthur Schopenhauer in her early teens. In 1950, she married shortly before receiving her B.A. degree. She gave up intellectual pursuits to cope with the time-consuming tasks of working to put her husband through law school, taking care of the house, and having children.

The next years were spent as a suburban housewife, listening to the stories of the other suburban housewives, and writing stories that were never published and that her husband criticized. In the early 1960's, she returned to university to earn an M.A., then taught English. In 1967, she was divorced and went to Harvard to earn a Ph.D. Her thesis on James Joyce launched her into the field of literary criticism. This experience in writing nonfiction began her later alternation between fiction and nonfiction. She has written nonfiction on William Shakespeare's view of women, on the history of women in patriarchal culture, and on the evils done to women throughout history in the name of cultural institutions. While the tone toward men in these works may be considered vindictive, and the conclusions she draws are open to argument, her scholarship is extensive and the works impressive in scope and concept.

French's more well-known contributions to feminist literature, however, have been her works of fiction. She focuses on the themes of the relationships between mothers and daughters, how motherhood affects a woman's life, and how men are perceived by women as impediments to be stepped around. Although her writing style is often criticized for lack of plot, for its two-dimensional male figures, and for its relentlessly bleak outlook on relations between the sexes, the stories of the female characters offer an insight and clarity of experience with which many women identify.

SUGGESTED READINGS

Dworkin, Susan. "Straight from the Heart." *Ms.* 14 (July, 1985): 20-25.

Green, Carol Hurd, and Mary Grimley Mason, eds. *American Women Writers*. New York: Continuum, 1994.

—*Konny Thompson*

See also Feminism; *Women's Room, The*

French Canadians. *See* Canadian identity: Quebecois

Fresh Girls, and Other Stories

AUTHOR: Evelyn Lau (1971-   )
FIRST PUBLISHED: 1993
IDENTITIES: Canada; Chinese American; women

Fresh Girls, and Other Stories, Evelyn Lau's collection of short stories, centers around young women who seek love and human affection in a netherworld of prostitution and bizarre, alternative sexual lifestyles. Many of the stories' protagonists live on two or more levels. They often wear a mask during the sex work they perform, but have retained a different identity in which they long for a more conventional life and for loving acceptance.

Lau's stories are told from the perspective of the young women, who chase after a dream which continues to elude them. The reader is made to share, for example, the sadness of the drug-addicted teenage narrator of the title story. Looking around the massage parlor where she works, she suddenly recognizes that, although many of her friends still look nice in regular clothes and outside their work, they have lost that special youthful freshness after which their clients lust with such depravity.

The astonishing ease with which men and women cross from an arcane subculture of sadomasochism to a mainstream life that is officially unaware and innocent of the other world is described with brilliant sharpness in "The Session" and "Fetish Night." Alternate identities are taken on quickly, and discarded just as easily, as young women agree to perform strange sexual acts on men who want to live out their secret fantasies and change from a position of power into that of helpless submission.

A core of stories explores the unhappy relationships of young women in love with older, married men who refuse to commit to their new lovers. In these stories, a man's wedding band takes on the identity of a weapon "branding" the narrator's skin. Fiercely subjective in her view, the protagonist of "Mercy" feels that "we are victims of each other," as she sexually tortures her lover on his wife's birthday.

The pain of the experience sometimes proves too much for the young women to bear. Out of a feeling of self-hatred and despair, "Glass" implies, a dejected girl cuts her wrists while she smashes her window, ready to follow the falling glass onto the street below. What gives artistic shape to Lau's collection is her unflinching, sympathetic look at a world that is alien to most readers. Her young, often nameless narrators are allowed to speak for themselves and scrutinize their tortured identities. In Lau's stories, the literary perspective is not that of a prurient voyeur who looks in but that of young souls who look out. Lau's stories challenge readers to examine the abyss of their own lives.

SUGGESTED READINGS

Canadian Literature. Review of *Fresh Girls*, by Evelyn Lau. Summer, 1995, 147.
Hungry Mind Review. Review of *Fresh Girls*, by Evelyn Lau. Summer, 1995, 25.
Kirkus Review. Review of *Fresh Girls*, by Evelyn Lau. 63 (January 1, 1995): 13.
Los Angeles Times Book Review. Review of *Fresh Girls*, by Evelyn Lau. September 3, 1995, 6.

—*R. C. Lutz*

See also Adultery; Asian American identity: China, Japan, and Korea; Erotic identity; Lau, Evelyn; Mental disorders; Prostitution; *Runaway*; Violence

Freud, Sigmund

BORN: Frieberg, Moravia, Austrian Empire (now Příbor, Czech Republic); May 6, 1856
DIED: London, England; September 23, 1939
PRINCIPAL WORKS: *Die Traumdeutung*, 1900 (*The Interpretation of Dreams*, 1913); *Zur Psychopathologie des Alltagslebens*, 1904 (*The Psychopathology of Everyday Life*, 1914); *Drei*

Sigmund Freud, the father of psychoanalysis. (Library of Congress)

Abhandlungen zur Sexualtheorie, 1905 (*Three Essays on the Theory of Sexuality*, 1910); *Totem und Tabu*, 1913 (*Totem and Taboo*, 1918); *Vorlesungen zur Einführung in die Psychoanalyse*, 1917 (*A General Introduction to Psychoanalysis*, 1920); *Jenseits des Lustprinzips*, 1920 (*Beyond the Pleasure Principle*, 1922); *Das Ich und das Es*, 1923 (*The Ego and the Id*, 1926); *Das Unbehagen in der Kultur*, 1930 (*Civilization and Its Discontents*, 1930); *Der Mann Moses und die monotheistische Religion*, 1938 (*Moses and Monotheism*, 1939); *Abriss der Psychoanalyse*, 1940 (*An Outline of Psychoanalysis*, 1949)

IDENTITIES: Jewish; world

SIGNIFICANT ACHIEVEMENT: Freud explained the unconscious and changed the way people think about themselves.

Sigmund Freud had three public personas. There was Freud the scientist, a neurologist who predicted the development of drugs to treat mental illness. There was Freud the founder of psychoanalysis—he coined the term—who developed the talking cure for patients he could not treat with traditional medicine. Finally, there was Freud the writer, whose brilliant prose turned case histories into compelling detective stories.

Freud first influenced writers and readers of literature as a theorist of the psyche, who offered insight into the meaning of dreams, the association of ideas, and the conflicts within the family and the self. Freud offered these insights at a time when writers questioned the older sense of character as a self-contained actor in the moral conflict. By suggesting that personality is a compound of superego, ego, and id, Freud gave writers a way to explore new understandings of self and identity. By describing childhood trauma and interpreting the story of Oedipus, who killed his father and married his mother, Freud put an end to the myth of family bliss. Readers of novels such as D. H. Lawrence's *Sons and Lovers* (1913) recognized Freud's influence in the novel's depiction of the Oedipal struggle.

Like many writers, Lawrence denied Freud's influence but read his books. The works of many twentieth century writers were deeply influenced by Freud's ideas. Freud has also been debunked. For example, few people believe his idea of penis envy. Others complained that a Freudian would make every straight object into a phallic symbol and every round one into a symbol of the womb.

Freud's greatest influence may be as a writer. He described the eternal struggle of Eros and Thanatos, of love and death. He wrote about the universal parent, adult, and child, which he termed the Superego, ego, and id. A character in J. D. Salinger's *Franny and Zooey* (1961) calls Freud a great epic poet. Protagonists in works by Sylvia Plath and Philip Roth voice anxieties in ways that Freud made possible.

Suggested readings

Gay, Peter. *Freud: A Life for Our Time*. New York: W. W. Norton, 1988.

Mahoney, Patrick J. *Freud as a Writer*. New Haven, Conn.: Yale University Press, 1987.

Osborne, Richard. *Freud for Beginners*. New York: Writers and Readers Publishing, 1993.

—Thomas Willard

See also Alienation; Anti-Semitism; Jung, Carl Gustav; Mental disorders; Patriarchy and matriarchy; Plath, Sylvia; Psychological theories of identity; Roth, Philip; Salinger, J. D.

Fried Green Tomatoes at the Whistle-Stop Cafe

Author: Fannie Flagg (1944-   )

First published: 1987

Identities: African American; European American; family; gay, lesbian, and bisexual; South; women

Fried Green Tomatoes at the Whistle-Stop Cafe is a novel that discusses several different topics. The story is about two women who meet in a nursing home. They strike up a friendship and the older woman tells the story of her family, particularly the lives of two other women, Ruth and Idgie.

Whistle Stop is the name of a very small town in rural Alabama on one of the main trunks of several railroads. Ruth and Idgie's story takes place in the early 1900's in and around the cafe that they own. Using flashbacks, Flagg re-creates these women's lives and experiences from the flapper era of the 1920's to the women's movement of the 1960's and 1970's.

Big George and his mother Sipsey are the African Americans who have the responsibility of taking care of Idgie's family. They are the household help that are part of the family. As the story continues readers learn about Big George's family and their relation with Ruth's son Buddy, named after a favorite brother of Idgie who was killed in a train accident. Young Buddy is called Stump because he lost one arm in another train accident.

One of the earmarks of the novel is the rural slang used to make the story more credible, the appearance of the Ku Klux Klan at various times to remind readers of the culture of racism of the South at that time, and the predominance of the theme that all people have a responsibility to care for all who are in need. The train brings homeless men to the cafe for a meal—the black men are given food out the back door, the white men are fed inside the cafe at the table.

Love of family is the thread that appears throughout the novel. Love of birth family members, love of women for each other, love of people who are of different races, love of all, regardless of race or gender, who make up a family. The novel argues that family is based on love, not biology. Idgie is female, yet wears men's clothing, drinks liquor "like a man," tells tall stories, and loves Ruth and her baby with all her soul. As a result Idgie is loved, protected, and defended by all who know her.

SUGGESTED READING

Steinberg, Sybil. Review of *Fried Green Tomatoes at the Whistle-Stop Cafe*, by Fannie Flagg. *Publishers Weekly* 232 (August 28, 1987): 64.

—*Sandra J. Parsons*

See also American identity: South; Feminism; Lesbian identity

Friedan, Betty

BORN: Peoria, Illinois; February 4, 1921

PRINCIPAL WORKS: *The Feminine Mystique*, 1963; *It Changed My Life*, 1976; *The Second Stage*, 1981; *The Fountain of Age*, 1993

IDENTITIES: European American; family; Jewish; women

SIGNIFICANT ACHIEVEMENT: Friedan's book *The Feminine Mystique* was a major force in launching the women's liberation movement during the 1960's and made her a leader in the cause of women's rights.

A dominant theme of Betty Friedan's life has been her persistent endeavor to establish her own identity as a woman and feminist. Born Betty Naomi Goldstein in 1921, she started a writing career in New York after her graduation from Smith College in 1942 and graduate work at the University of California at Berkeley. From the outset she encountered experiences that drove home her standing as a woman in a male-dominated society. Employed by a labor newspaper during World War II, her job disappeared when the soldiers returned. She married Carl Friedan in 1947 and had three children. Trying to remain active professionally, she found work as a writer. When she became pregnant with her second child, she sought maternity leave and was fired instead. Plunging into the life of a suburban housewife, Friedan became restive at the shallowness of a housewife's daily routine. She began to explore the situation of women such as herself in magazine articles, but the editors were unreceptive. Instead, she wrote *The Feminine Mystique*, which became a best-seller and made Friedan a famous leader of the women's liberation movement.

For the next decade, she functioned as a spokeswoman for the cause of women's rights. She founded the National Organization for Women in 1966 and organized the Women's Strike for Equality in 1970. Her role as an activist slowed in the early 1970's, and she became more of a teacher and writer throughout the remainder of the decade. In *The Second Stage* she argued that men and women needed to work more closely together, a position that impaired her standing as a feminist for some of her critics. By the early 1990's, she was writing about growing older in *The Fountain of Age*, and she saw herself as going through the universal condition of men and women rather than simply as an older woman who was a feminist. At each stage of her life, Betty Friedan has tried to explain her own situation in terms that tap into the lives and experiences of women generally, and she has seen herself as the advocate of an inclusive and humanistic feminism. Her moderate posture has made her controversial and much-criticized within the women's movement that she did so much to create.

SUGGESTED READINGS

Behm, Barbara. *Betty Friedan: Speaking Out for Women's Rights*. Milwaukee, Wis.: Gareth Stevens, 1992.

Meyer, Donald. "Betty Friedan." In *Portraits of American Women from Settlement to the Present*, edited by G. J. Barker-Benfield and Catherine Clinton. New York: St. Martin's Press, 1981.

—*Lewis L. Gould*

See also *Feminine Mystique, The*; Feminism

Friends, Religious Society of. *See* **Religious minorities**

Frontier, the. *See* **American identity: West and the frontier**

Fuentes, Carlos

BORN: Panama City, Panama; November 11, 1928

PRINCIPAL WORKS: *La región más transparente*, 1958 (*Where the Air Is Clear*, 1960); *La muerte de Artemio Cruz*, 1962 (*The Death of Artemio Cruz*, 1964); *Cambio de piel*, 1967 (*A Change of Skin*, 1968); *Terra nostra*, 1975 (*Terra Nostra*, 1976); *Una familia lejana*, 1980 (*Distant Relations*, 1982); *Gringo viejo*, 1985 (*The Old Gringo*, 1985); *Cristóbal nonato*, 1987 (*Christopher Unborn*, 1989)

IDENTITIES: Latino; world

SIGNIFICANT ACHIEVEMENT: Fuentes has attained recognition for writings that articulate a viable and independent Mexican identity.

Carlos Fuentes is one of a small number of writers from Latin America whose works are recognized throughout the world. His life and work are truly international. His father was a diplomat, so Fuentes' early life was influenced by his schooling and experiences in such capitals as Washington, D.C., Santiago, Buenos Aires, and Mexico City. He is equally fluent in Spanish and English and is familiar with the cultural life of most American and European countries. As one of Mexico's most distinguished citizens, he has held important diplomatic positions in Europe, has lectured at major universities throughout the Western world, and has been awarded prestigious literary awards. *The Old Gringo* was made into a successful film and became the first novel by a Mexican writer to be included on *The New York Times* best-seller list.

Carlos Fuentes, author of The Old Gringo *(1985).*

All of his writings deal with the complexity of identifying what it means to be a Mexican. He seeks the identity of his people in the myth, legend, and history of the Aztec culture, in the traditions of the Catholic faith that the Spanish brought to the New World in the fifteenth century, and in the failed hopes of the Mexican Revolution. All these elements are included in his novel *Terra Nostra*.

Fuentes is also concerned with articulating Mexico's relationship with the rest of the world. In *Distant Relations*, he examines the often troubled interaction between Mexican and European cultures. His most famous novel, *The Old Gringo*, is a study of Mexican-American relations. *Christopher Unborn*, his Christopher Columbus novel, is a penetrating investigation and satire of contemporary Mexico approaching the five hundredth anniversary of Columbus' arrival in the Americas. Fuentes warns of a certain fall to ruin if a reformation and a redefinition of Mexico's basic values—as found in its myth, legend, and history—do not take place immediately.

SUGGESTED READINGS

Brody, Robert, and Charles Rossman, eds. *Carlos Fuentes: A Critical View*. Austin: University of Texas Press, 1982.

Brushwood, John S. *Mexico in Its Novel: A Nation's Search for Identity*. Austin: University of Texas Press, 1966.

Faris, Wendy B. *Carlos Fuentes*. New York: Frederick Ungar, 1983.

—Thomas H. Falk

See also Columbus, Christopher, literature about; Latino American identity

Fuller, Charles

BORN: Philadelphia, Pennsylvania; March 5, 1939

PRINCIPAL WORKS: *The Village: A Party*, pr. 1968; *An Untitled Play*, pr. 1970; *In My Many Names and Days*, pr. 1972; *The Candidate*, pr. 1974; *First Love*, pr. 1974; *In the Deepest Part of Sleep*, pr. 1974; *The Lay Out Letter*, pr. 1975; *The Brownsville Raid*, pr. 1976; *Sparrow in Flight*, pr. 1978; *Zooman and the Sign*, pr. 1980, pb. 1982; *A Soldier's Play*, pr. 1981, pb. 1982; *Sally*, pr. 1988; *Prince*, pr. 1988 (*Sally* and *Prince* performed together as *We*, 1989); *Jonquil*, pr. 1990

IDENTITIES: African American; men

SIGNIFICANT ACHIEVEMENT: Fuller has helped break a long tradition of stereotyping blacks, especially black men, in literature.

Charles Fuller wrote and produced his first play, *The Village: A Party*, in 1968. His place as a significant and talented playwright in contemporary African American theater is marked by an impressive number of dramas, among them *Zooman and the Sign*, for which he received two Obie Awards for best play and best playwright in 1980, and *A Soldier's Play*, which received the New York Drama Critics Circle Award for best American play, the 1982 Pulitzer Prize for Drama, and a film contract in 1984.

Fuller was reared in comfortable circumstances in an extended family of many foster children in North Philadelphia. He attended a Roman Catholic high school with his lifelong friend, Larry Neal, and attended Villanova University from 1956 to 1958. After a four-year hiatus in the U.S. Army in Japan and Korea, he returned to complete his undergraduate studies at LaSalle College from 1965 to 1968. Fuller began writing short stories, poetry, and essays in the 1960's in Philadelphia mostly at night after working various daytime jobs. His interest in literature, largely a result of assuming the responsibility of proofreading his father's print jobs, began early and served as the fertile source for a formal writing career, which developed from his short stories long after he began writing.

In addition to his Pulitzer Prize-winning *A Soldier's Play*, a number of his best-known plays have been produced by the Negro Ensemble Company, notably *The Brownsville Raid*, *Zooman and the Sign*, and the *We* plays.

As a social reformer, Fuller is concerned with brushing away deeply rooted stereotypes and uprooting preconceptions in order to explore the complexities of human relationships—particularly black-white relationships in America—and rectify the portrayals that distort African Americans, especially the black male. Critical of black hatred for and treatment of other blacks, Fuller is just as critical of the negative portrayal of the black male by the white media. Convinced that the stage is a powerful medium that can effectively rectify the stereotyped image of blacks shaped by white media, Fuller combined the mystery genre with his knowledge of the military structure of the U.S. Army to expose some of the real conflicts of white and black, and of black and black in America.

SUGGESTED READINGS

Carter, Steven R. "The Detective as Solution: Charles Fuller's *A Soldier's Play*." *Clues* 12, no. 1 (Spring-Summer, 1991): 33-42.

Demastes, William W. *Beyond Naturalism: A New Realism in American Theater*. Westport, Conn.: Greenwood Press, 1988.

Harriot, Esther. *American Voices: Contemporary Playwrights in Essays and Interviews*. Jefferson, N.C.: McFarland, 1988.

Hughes, Linda, and Howard Faulkner. "The Roles of Detection in *A Soldier's Play*. *Clues* 7, no. 2 (Fall-Winter, 1986): 83-97.

—*Pamela J. Olubunmi Smith*

See also African American identity; Racism and ethnocentrism; *Soldier's Play, A*

Fundamentalism. *See* Christianity and Christian Fundamentalism; Fatwā

G

Gaines, Ernest J.

Born: Oscar, Louisiana; January 15, 1933

Principal works: *Catherine Carmier*, 1964; *Of Love and Dust*, 1967; *Bloodline*, 1968; *The Autobiography of Miss Jane Pittman*, 1971; *In My Father's House*, 1978; *A Gathering of Old Men*, 1983; *A Lesson Before Dying*, 1993

Identities: African American; South

Significant achievement: Gaines's regionalist short stories and novels are distinguished contributions to modern African American fiction.

Born on a southern Louisiana plantation, Ernest J. Gaines was raised by a disabled aunt who became the model for the strong women in his works, including Miss Jane Pittman. There was no high school for Gaines to attend, so he left Louisiana in 1948 to live with relatives in California, where he suffered from the effects of his displacement. Displacement—caused by racism, by Cajuns' acquisition of land, or by loss of community ties—is a major theme for Gaines.

Young Gaines discovered works by John Steinbeck, William Faulkner, and Anton Chekhov, who wrote about the land. Not finding acceptable literary depictions of African Americans, Gaines resolved to write stories illuminating the lives and identities of his people. After completing military service, he earned a degree in English, published his first short stories, and received a creative writing fellowship at Stanford University.

Gaines rejected California as a subject for fiction, chose southern Louisiana as his major setting, and, like the Southern literary giant Faulkner, invented his own county. *Catherine Carmier*, an uneven apprentice novel, is the first of Gaines's works revealing Louisiana's physical beauty and folk speech.

Receiving a grant from the National Endowment for the Arts, Gaines published *Of Love and Dust*, inspired by a blues song about an African American who escapes prison by doing hard labor on a Louisiana plantation. This and other works by Gaines are not protest fiction, but they are concerned with human rights, justice, and equality.

Years of listening to the conversations of plantation folk led Gaines to employ multiple narrators in "Just Like a Tree" in *Bloodline*, a short-story collection. He also employs the technique in *A Gathering of Old Men*, which gives new form to another favorite theme, the achievement of manhood. Twelve elderly African American men, after a lifetime of passivity, stand up against ruthless Cajuns and rednecks who have mistreated them, taken over their farmland, and threatened to de-

Ernest J. Gaines, author of A Lesson Before Dying *(1993).* (© Jerry Bauer)

stroy their past, represented by family homes and graveyards. In Gaines's somber moral drama, *A Lesson Before Dying*, an African American teacher who has difficulty being a man in his segregated society learns to love. He helps to humanize an illiterate teenager wrongly condemned for murder and to convince the boy to die courageously. With a firmer personal and racial identity, the teacher becomes dedicated to educating young African Americans.

Gaines has served as a teacher in his position as writer-in-residence at a Louisiana university. His honors include a Guggenheim Fellowship and awards from the American Academy and Institute of Arts and Letters and the MacArthur Foundation.

SUGGESTED READINGS

Babb, Valerie. *Ernest Gaines*. Boston: Twayne, 1991.

Bryant, Jerry H. "Ernest J. Gaines: Change, Growth, and History." *Southern Review* 10 (October, 1984): 851-864.

Simpson, Anne. *A Gathering of Gaines*. Lafayette: University of Southwestern Louisiana, 1991.

—Philip A. Tapley

See also African American identity; American identity: South; *Autobiography of Miss Jane Pittman, The*

Gallant, Mavis

BORN: Montreal, Quebec, Canada; August 11, 1922

PRINCIPAL WORKS: *The Other Paris*, 1956; *Green Water, Green Sky*, 1959; *A Fairly Good Time*, 1970; *The Affair of Gabrielle Russier*, 1971; *The Pegnitz Junction: A Novella and Five Short Stories*, 1973; *From the Fifteenth District: A Novella and Eight Short Stories*, 1979; *Home Truths: Selected Canadian Stories*, 1981; *In Transit: Twenty Stories*, 1988; *Across the Bridge: Stories*, 1993

IDENTITIES: Canada; women

SIGNIFICANT ACHIEVEMENT: Gallant has probed into the question of Canadian identity.

The distinguishing feature in the life of Mavis Gallant, an Anglo-Canadian born Mavis de Trafford Young in French-speaking Montreal, is that her artist father died while she was away at school. Her mother promptly remarried, leaving the child with strangers. This was the beginning of a solitary and unsettled existence for the girl who, starting at a French-speaking convent in her native city (Gallant was not a Catholic), attended seventeen different schools in Canada and the United States. By her own admission, the isolation and transiency she experienced when young have influenced her writing.

This problem of belonging (or not belonging) was not improved by her brief, failed marriage to John Gallant of Canada. Except for a short residence in English-speaking Ontario Province, Gallant has been part of a minority most of her life, despite her fluency in French.

After her return from New York with a high school diploma and following a stint as a reporter at the anglophone *Montreal Standard* from 1944 to 1950, Gallant became a voluntary expatriate, ultimately settling in Paris. Despite her cosmopolitan tendencies—a Canadian abroad writing primarily for an American magazine, *The New Yorker*—Gallant has retained her original citizenship and her Canadian identity. This is especially evident in her collection *Home Truths*. Another central theme in her writings reflects her concern, initially for displaced persons and refugees in Canada and later for the rootless and orphans of all kinds—physical and spiritual exiles.

Gallant's sensitivity to the collision of cultures in Canadian and various European settings surfaces in *A Fairly Good Time*, one of her few novels. *The Pegnitz Junction* is a collection of stories about postwar Germans who live in interior exile in a world that resembles only superficially the one they knew.

SUGGESTED READINGS

Besner, Neil K. *The Light of Imagination: Mavis Gallant's Fiction*. Vancouver: University of British Columbia Press, 1988.

Davies, Robertson. "The Novels of Mavis Gallant." *Canadian Fiction Magazine* 28, no. 3 (1978): 68-73.

Hatch, Ronald. "Mavis Gallant and the Creation of Consciousness." In *Present Tense*, edited by John Moss. Toronto: NC Press, 1985.

Keefer, Janice Kulyk. *Reading Mavis Gallant*. New York: Oxford University Press, 1989.

—*Peter B. Heller*

See also Canadian identity; Class and identity; *Home Truths*; Identity crisis

Galsworthy, John

BORN: Kingston Hill, Surrey, England; August 14, 1867
DIED: London, England; January 31, 1933
PRINCIPAL WORKS: *The Man of Property*, 1906; *In Chancery*, 1920; *To Let*, 1921; *The Forsyte Saga*, 1922 (containing the three previous novels plus "Indian Summer of a Forsyte" and "Awakening")
IDENTITIES: Family; women; world
SIGNIFICANT ACHIEVEMENT: Galsworthy's novels are among the finest portrayals of the English upper-middle-class of the late nineteenth and early twentieth centuries.

John Galsworthy was born into a wealthy family. His father was a lawyer and director of many companies. The elder Galsworthy provided the model for the elder Jolyon Forsyte in *The Man of Property* and "Indian Summer of a Forsyte." Galsworthy attended Harrow, where he excelled at sports but not academics. He then studied law at Oxford. He was to practice little. At neither place did John show any literary talents or ambitions. His wealth allowed him to travel extensively as a young man.

The turning point in his life occurred when he met Ada Galsworthy, the wife of a cousin. It is not known why Ada married her first husband, but it was a loveless marriage. Learning her plight, John fell in love with Ada, who came to reciprocate his feelings. They carried on a relationship for several years until the death of John's father. After they lived together openly in Dartmoor, Ada's husband finally sued for divorce. Eventually, John and Ada married and remained together until his death. She provided the model for Irene Heron in *The Forsyte Saga*. At the heart of *The Forsyte Saga* is the plight of women as the property of men. The situation of the woman who became his wife made him sensitive to the second-class status of women in his society. Some critics have even argued that Galsworthy's prowoman bias is excessive.

Before meeting Ada, Galsworthy made some attempts at writing. With her encouragement, he became more earnest and prolific, writing books and plays for nearly forty years. His best book is perhaps *The Man of Property*, a superb characterization of the new, prosperous class that arose from industrialization. The many characters are drawn from people in his family and others he knew.

SUGGESTED READINGS

Barker, Dudley. *The Man of Principle: A Biography of John Galsworthy*. Briarcliff Manor, N.Y.: Stein & Day, 1963.

Kettle, Arnold. "John Galsworthy: The Man of Property." In *An Introduction to the English Novel*. 2 vols. London: Hutchinson University Library, 1967.

—*Tom Feller*

See also Class and identity; *Forsyte Saga, The*

Gay identity

IDENTITIES: Gay, lesbian, and bisexual

Considerable scholarship has been dedicated to homosexuality in history and culture. One of the main controversies in gay studies has centered on two schools of thought, essentialist and social constructionist. The essentialist position maintains that the characteristics of gay identity have

Historical context

remained constant, so that, for example, same-sex behavior in ancient Greece and in the United States in the 1990's would have some fundamental similarities. The social constructionist view, on the other hand, argues that particular practices are historically specific; therefore, their meanings change according to the time and place in which they occur. Most of the scholarship exploring gay identity in American literature has emerged out of the constructionist school, and the standard position has been that homosexuality was repressed until at least the end of World War II, when it began to be more in the public consciousness, culminating in the Stonewall riots, an uprising of gay people against a police raid on a gay bar, the Stonewall Inn, in New York in June, 1969.

Historian George Chauncey has expanded and complicated the constructionist reading of gay American history. In *Gay New York: Gender, Urban Culture, and the Making of the Gay Male World, 1890-1940* (1994), Chauncey argues that a sharp dichotomy between the homosexual and the heterosexual emerged in the twentieth century, suggesting that same-sex relationships in earlier times should not be thought of in a context that came later. Thus, "homoerotic" texts of the nineteenth century do not necessarily imply that their writers were expressing homosexual identity or that they themselves were what would come to be known as gay. Perhaps the most important implication of Chauncey's work is that critics should not be making the claim that such "homo-erotic" writers were heterosexual, since that identity, like its counterpart, is a twentieth century phenomenon, and since the meanings of both identities are interdependent.

The nineteenth century

What can be learned from representations of same-sex eroticism and desire in pre-twentieth century texts? Clearly, some prominent writers placed tremendous importance on same-sex love. Literary critics, beginning with Leslie Fiedler (*Love and Death in the American Novel*, 1960), have found a tradition of male homoerotic bonding in American literature. Fiedler located that tradition in James Fenimore Cooper's Leatherstocking Tales (1823-1841) and especially in Queequeg's "marriage" to Ishmael in Herman Melville's *Moby Dick* (1851). This kind of study, because it tends to desexualize the homosexual into the homoerotic, cannot be considered affirmative of a gay tradition in American literature.

Other scholars have suggested that Henry James, Henry David Thoreau, and Horatio Alger, among many others, should be included in any discussion of gay American literature. Although the sexual identity of these writers is not certainly homosexual, what is clear is that male

---

Gay Identity Milestones

1855   Walt Whitman's *Leaves of Grass*.

1870's   The Hamilton Lodge in New York City holds drag balls.

1920's   The Harlem Renaissance. Richard Bruce Nugent's short story "Smoke, Lillies, and Jade" is published in *Fire!!*, a periodical, in 1926.

1944   Poet Robert Duncan publicly acknowledges his homosexuality in the periodical *Politics*.

1948   Gore Vidal's *The City and the Pillar*, often thought of as the first openly gay novel published in America.

1954   Christopher Isherwood publishes *The World in the Evening*, which presents a gay couple and a bisexual protagonist.

1956   Allen Ginsberg's *Howl* treats homosexuality openly, for example, in "Supermarket in California," Ginsberg addresses Whitman and invokes the gay Spanish poet Federico García Lorca.

1956   James Baldwin's *Giovanni's Room*, a novel of anger and self-loathing, is published to hostile reviews.

1963   John Rechy, a gay Chicano writer, publishes *City of Night*.

1969   The Stonewall Inn Riots, an uprising against a police raid on a gay bar, the Stonewall Inn, in New York in June.

1979   Harvey Fierstein has critical and commercial success with his *Torch Song Trilogy*.

1980's   The AIDS epidemic hits the gay community and the general population; a new literature about the crisis arises.

attachments structured their lives and writing in significant ways. Critics may therefore argue that such facts should not be "explained" by critics invested in "protecting" these figures.

Walt Whitman

The central figure in gay American literature is Walt Whitman. More than half of Robert K. Martin's *The Homosexual Tradition in American Poetry* (1979) is focused on Whitman. Martin argues persuasively that many poets and other writers who followed Whitman consciously looked to him as a father-figure, spiritual and sexual mentor, and even as a kind of lover.

Much of Whitman's poetry, especially *Leaves of Grass* (1855), stresses the importance of a highly sexualized and eroticized body and the centrality of "adhesiveness," Whitman's term for male same-sex behavior. Whitman's vision, which affirmed the values of America and democracy, placed its faith in the love of men for each other. He celebrated that dynamic in his writing, even in his impassioned Civil War writing, which contains elements of love and physical contact with the soldiers on both sides.

British writers John Addington Symonds and Oscar Wilde identified closely with the sentiments they found in Whitman's work. Wilde visited Whitman in the 1880's, and Symonds corresponded with him, trying to tease admissions out of him. One may argue that the chief aspect of Whitman's sexual identity in terms of gay American literature is that readers and writers alike identify with him and with the importance he placed on the love between men.

The early twentieth century

In Chauncey's account, New York City, which he takes as prototypical rather than typical, had a thriving gay subculture in the late nineteenth and early twentieth centuries. The Hamilton Lodge held drag balls as early as the 1870's. Times Square, Harlem, and Greenwich Village were known gay hangouts, where "fairies" were flamboyantly visible. This view is rather different from the typical understanding that homosexuality was closeted until the 1960's.

The literature of this period depicts gay identity. The poetry of Hart Crane, especially "Voyages" (1926) and *The Bridge* (1930), reflects the visibility and the growing public presence of gay people and gay concerns. Crane's poetry exhibits a conflicted position regarding homosexuality; he maintains a spiritual view of love and its redemptive power, but sees himself as exiled as a gay artist. Whitman served as a helpful forefather, however, whose vision of brotherhood partly relieved some of Crane's anxieties. "Cape Hatteras" (1930), which Crane referred to as his "ode to Whitman," took its epigraph from Whitman's "Passage to India," suggesting the value of Whitman to Crane's work.

A different gay tradition and identity in American writing of this period can be found in the work of some of the key figures in the Harlem Renaissance. Flourishing in the 1920's, black writers reflected the sexual and cultural diversity of their milieu. Langston Hughes, Countée Cullen, Alain Locke, Wallace Thurman, Richard Bruce Nugent, and the white novelist Carl Van Vechten have all been identified as writers for whom homoerotic attraction and homosexuality were crucial. Nugent's impressionistic short story, "Smoke, Lillies, and Jade"—concerning the seduction of a Latin lover—was first published in *Fire!!*, a periodical edited by Thurman, in 1926. An autobiographical work, Nugent's story owes debts to Oscar Wilde's *The Picture of Dorian Gray* (1891) and has been included in the controversial film *Looking for Langston* (1989), in which gay black filmmaker Isaac Julien uses Hughes as a symbol of the secrecy associated with homosexuality in the Harlem Renaissance.

Gay identities at midcentury

The 1930's, it may be argued, began a more repressive time for gay people in America. It certainly seems that gay representations in literature and film disappeared during this time, though Allan Berube has suggested, in *Coming Out Under Fire: The History of Gay Men and Women in World War II* (1990), that military paranoia about gay and lesbian soldiers actually helped solidify that identity in American culture. Likewise, increased mobility and urbanization lead to the development of gay communities and organizations, such as the Mattachine Society, in the early 1950's.

The most important and visible gay writer of the midcentury was Allen Ginsberg. His epic poem *Howl* (1956) uses homosexuality as a catalyst for social protest and as a scathing critique of the reactionary politics of McCarthyite America. While the position of exile was troubling for Crane,

Ginsberg and his fellow Beat writers embraced outsider status. In "Supermarket in California," Ginsberg addresses Whitman directly, and also invokes the Spanish gay poet Federico García Lorca. *Howl* was involved in an obscenity trial, a landmark case in which the poem was found to have literary value. William S. Burroughs, one of Ginsberg's fellow Beats, wrote disturbing portraits of gay sexuality and drug use in his novels *Queer* (written, 1952; published, 1985) and *Naked Lunch* (1959).

Many recognizable American writers of this period were gay, but their work does not necessarily contribute to an understanding of gay identity, except possibly through a reading of repression and denial in what they have written. Tennessee Williams and Truman Capote wrote highly coded works in which homosexuality is sometimes present. Gore Vidal's *The City and the Pillar* (1948) was published the same year as the Kinsey report on sexual behavior in the human male, which suggests in overt terms that American men had much more experience with gay sex than had previously been thought. Vidal's novel, which ends tragically, is often thought of as the first openly gay novel published in America. James Baldwin's *Giovanni's Room* (1956), a novel of anger and self-loathing, was published to hostile reviews. British expatriate and new American citizen Christopher Isherwood published *The World in the Evening* in 1954, which presents a gay couple and a bisexual protagonist and which is highly critical of the military's antigay policy.

Other important gay writers to emerge in the 1960's include John Rechy, a gay Chicano writer whose *City of Night* (1963), *Numbers* (1967), and *Sexual Outlaw* (1977) portray the highly sexualized world of hustlers and dangerous sex; Richard Howard, a poet and translator whose relationship to the gay tradition of Wilde, Whitman, and Crane is central to his work and identity as a writer; Thom Gunn, a highly formal poet who embraces various forms of pleasure in a Whitmanesque way; John Ashberry, an expressionist poet concerned with the creative process and identity, for whom the body is a source of knowledge and absence; James Merrill, a master of poetic form who wrote autobiographical, epic poetry and who embraced his homosexuality as a source of creativity; and Robert Duncan, a highly erotic poet who publicly acknowledged his homosexuality in the periodical *Politics* in 1944 and called for honesty and strength in the face of homophobia.

Stonewall and after

The Stonewall Inn riots, which began on the evening of gay icon Judy Garland's funeral, mark the beginning of the Gay Pride movement. Increased visibility and public activism reverberated in gay literature. Gay presses began to emerge, as did magazines catering to gay audiences. Important writers in the 1970's and early 1980's include Edmund White, Felice Picano, and Robert Ferro, who comprised the Violet Quill writers' group in New York. Playwright Harvey Fierstein had critical and commerical success with his *Torch Song Trilogy* (1979) and *La Cage aux folles* (1983).

This boon in the decade after Stonewall was a time of great achievement. Writers such as Larry Kramer and Paul Monette began to emerge as important figures, but their work, like the lives of most gay men in the 1980's and after, has become centered on AIDS, the pandemic that has changed the face of gay identity in literature and culture as much as any other phenomenon.

Suggested readings

Bergman, David. *Gaiety Transfigured: Gay Self-Representation in American Literature*. Madison: University of Wisconsin Press, 1991. A clearly written, accessible survey of nineteenth and twentieth century gay writers and critics. Chapters on race, AIDS, and families.

Clum, John. *Acting Gay: Male Homosexuality in Modern Drama*. New York: Columbia University Press, 1992. A thorough study of gay issues in drama, including the codes in which homosexuality was represented during more repressive times.

Katz, Jonathan Ned. *Gay American History: Lesbians and Gay Men in the U.S.A., a Documentary*. 1976. New York: Harper & Row, 1985. Attempts to recover the buried history of lesbians and gays in America.

Martin, Robert K. *The Homosexual Tradition in American Poetry*. Austin: University of Texas Press, 1979. A careful and thoughtful early work on American poetry and poets. Especially good on Whitman, Crane, Duncan, and Merrill. Traces the importance of Whitman on writers of the twentieth century.

Summers, Claude J. *Gay Fictions, Wilde to Stonewall: Studies in a Male Homosexual Literary Tradition*. New York: Continuum, 1990. Concerned with the critical and historical debates about a gay "tradition." Important figures include Vidal, Capote, Williams, Baldwin, and Isherwood.

Yingling, Thomas E. *Hart Crane and the Homosexual Text: New Thresholds, New Anatomies*. Chicago: University of Chicago Press, 1990. Successor to Martin's study; focuses on Crane, but also has insights into the gay critic F. O. Matthiessen and his book *American Renaissance* (1941).

—Chris Freeman

See also AIDS; Baldwin, James; Bisexual identity; Delaney, Samuel R.; Fierstein, Harvey; Ginsberg, Allen; Harlem Renaissance; Lesbian identity; Maupin, Armistead; Rechy, John; *Song of Myself*; Williams, Tennessee

Gemini

Author: Nikki Giovanni (1943-   )
First published: 1971
Identities: African American; women

Nikki Giovanni identifies her first work of prose, *Gemini*, in its subtitle as "an extended autobiographical statement on my first twenty-five years of being a black poet." *Gemini* is in a sense neither an autobiography nor an extended statement; rather, it is a collection of thirteen essays, about half of which discuss aspects of Giovanni's life. Readers learn something of Giovanni's life, but *Gemini* reveals more of her ideas. All of the essays involve personal observations mingled with political concerns, as the final lines of the essay "400 Mulvaney Street" illustrate: "They had come to say Welcome Home. And I thought Tommy, my son, must know about this. He must know we come from somewhere. That we belong." These lines are a capsule of Giovanni's major themes: family and belonging, identity, and one's relationship to the world. As the people of Knoxville come to hear her, Giovanni realizes her connection to a place and people. Sharing this with her son underscores the importance of family and passing on legacies, a lesson for not only him but also all blacks. To know that they come from somewhere and therefore belong is part of the message in this work.

The central message in *Gemini* is love. Giovanni claims, "If you don't love your mama and papa then you don't love yourself." This includes racial love; Giovanni provides tributes to black writer Charles Waddell Chesnutt and to black musicians Lena Horne and Aretha Franklin. Giovanni states that black people "must become the critics and protectors" of black music and literature. Love of oneself leads to a sense of identity: This is Giovanni's second message.

Giovanni cautions blacks against carelessly adopting "white philosophies." Her advice is to "know who's playing the music before you dance." Giovanni discusses respect as an outgrowth of love and identity, particularly for blacks of other nationalities and for the elderly. In Giovanni's discussion of the black revolution, she emphasizes the need to change the world. She addresses what one should be willing to live for: hope to change the world or some aspect of it. The essays of *Gemini* combine to give readers a sense of Giovanni, her world, and their world.

Suggested readings

Fowler, Virginia. *Nikki Giovanni*. New York: Twayne, 1992.

Jordan, June. Review of *Gemini*, by Nikki Giovanni. *The New York Times Book Review*, February 13, 1972, 6, 26.

Mitchell, Carolyn. "Nikki Giovanni." In *Black Women in America: An Historical Encyclopedia*, edited by Darlene Clark Hine. New York: Carlson, 1993, 487-490.

—Paula C. Barnes

See also African American identity; *Black Feeling, Black Talk*; Feminism; Giovanni, Nikki

Geography III

Author: Elizabeth Bishop (1911-1979)
First published: 1976
Identities: European American; women

Geography III, Elizabeth Bishop's last book of poetry and most autobiographical, is considered by many critics to be her strongest work. The title is derived from a nineteenth century geography primer. Its epigraph, taken from that same text, consists of a series of catechism-like questions designed to teach children basic lessons in geography. The simple questions and answers frame a collection of ten poems in which Bishop explores the nature of nostalgia in shaping the realities of past, present, and future.

Loss and survival is a major theme in Bishop's work. The ironic "One Art" establishes Bishop as a survivor of losses, using an archaic formal French poetic form, the villanelle. In the dramatic monologue "Crusoe in England," Bishop empathizes with Daniel Defoe's shipwrecked hero and survivor, now in England but displaced, bored, lonely, and nostalgic.

"In the Waiting Room" revisits Bishop's childhood and a frightening moment of female definition. In a dentist's waiting room, the nearly seven-year-old Elizabeth reads the *National Geographic* while her aunt is being treated. A photograph of bare-breasted African women shocks her into a cry of astonishment which coincides with Aunt Conseulo's cry of pain from inside the office. Unable to distinguish her own voice from her aunt's, she has a critical moment of perception about the social constructs of race and female identity and the ways in which they both separate and connect her to a world outside her provincial life.

Similarly, "The Moose," with its numerous female images, elucidates how an unexpected discovery of something larger than one's self contributes to identity. A passenger on a bus leaving Nova Scotia, her early childhood home, Bishop is in a reverie of nostalgia and memory as she listens to the idle conversation of the other passengers. When the bus stops suddenly at the sight of a large female moose in the middle of the road, the passengers and the moose contemplate each other. A collective sense of joy and awe coalesces the group as they regard the moose, an archetype of otherworldliness, a creature that exists outside of human experience.

Bishop speaks to the collaboration between artist and observer as a process of self-discovery. In "Poem" she relives moments of childhood joy when she recognizes scenes from childhood in a small landscape painting. The restless search for self is not easy, however. In "The End of March" she imagines a "dream house" that is typical and mysterious, a place where she can retire from her quest. The house is boarded up and too cold to reach; she has no home.

By asking more questions than she answers, Bishop suggests in *Geography III* that identity is fluid and often contradictory. Exterior and interior landscapes which shape the sense of self, change with time and memory. Bishop shows us that the "home" of self-discovery is elusive, but survival depends on the constant search.

Suggested readings

Lombardi, Marilyn May, ed. *Elizabeth Bishop: The Geography of Gender*. Charlottesville: University Press of Virginia, 1993.

Parker, Robert Dale. *The Unbeliever*. Chicago: University of Illinois Press, 1988.

Travisano, Thomas J. *Elizabeth Bishop: Her Artistic Development*. Charlottesville: University Press of Virginia, 1988.

—*Susan Chainey*

See also Bishop, Elizabeth

Gilbert, Sandra M., and Susan Gubar

Born: Sandra M. Gilbert, New York, New York; December 27, 1936
Born: Susan Gubar, New York, New York; November 30, 1944

PRINCIPAL WORKS: *The Madwoman in the Attic*, 1979; *Shakespeare's Sisters: Feminist Essays on Women Poets*, 1979 (editors); *The Norton Anthology of Literature by Women*, 1985 (editors); *The Female Imagination and the Modernist Aesthetic*, 1986 (editors); *No Man's Land: The Place of the Woman Writer in the Twentieth Century*, 3 vols., 1988-1994; *The War of the Words*, 1988; *Sexchanges*, 1989; *Letters from the Front*, 1994; *Masterpiece Theatre: An Academic Melodrama*, 1995

IDENTITIES: European American; women

SIGNIFICANT ACHIEVEMENT: The leading feminist literary critics of their generation, Gilbert and Gubar establish, in their collaborative works, the central importance of women writers in the nineteenth and twentieth centuries.

Sandra Gilbert, a poet and literary critic, was educated at Cornell University, New York University, and Columbia University. She has taught at numerous colleges and universities, including Indiana University, Princeton University, and the University of California, Davis. Susan Gubar studied at City College of New York, the University of Michigan, and the University of Iowa. She has taught at Indiana University at Bloomington since 1973.

Gilbert and Gubar began collaborating on literary criticism in the mid-1970's while both taught at Indiana University. Each had previously published extensively, but their discussions led them to new discoveries about literature. The excitement generated by their joint exploration of the subject matter is evident throughout the volumes they have produced as a team. After Sandra Gilbert left Indiana in 1975, she and Susan Gubar continued working together through phone calls and extensive travel. The focus in their writing on women writers' sense of identity reflects the women's movement's attempts to redefine women's place in society. Gilbert and Gubar's persuasive arguments that literary works reflect the time and culture in which they are written, as well as the gender of the author, helped to revolutionize literary criticism. Many previous critical schools treated works of literature as timeless monuments to human greatness. Gilbert and Gubar's collaborative method embodies the ideal of solidarity between women, which is central to the women's movement.

SUGGESTED READINGS

Cain, William E., ed. *Making Feminist History: The Literary Scholarship of Sandra M. Gilbert and Susan Gubar*. New York: Garland, 1994.

Cofresi, Lina L. "Sandra M. Gilbert and Susan Gubar." In *Critical Survey of Literary Theory*, edited by Frank N. Magill. Pasadena, Calif.: Salem Press, 1987.

—Joan Hope

See also Canon; Feminism; Literary standards; *Madwoman in the Attic, The*; *No Man's Land*; Women and identity

Gilman, Charlotte Perkins

BORN: Hartford, Connecticut; July 3, 1860

DIED: Pasadena, California; August 17, 1935

PRINCIPAL WORKS: *The Yellow Wallpaper*, 1892; *Women and Economics*, 1898; *Herland*, serial, 1915, book, 1979

IDENTITIES: European American; women

SIGNIFICANT ACHIEVEMENT: Gilman's pioneering works are about the personal and cultural identities of women.

Charlotte Perkins Gilman's childhood experiences prepared her for a life of solitude and discipline, which is often essential to the life of an author. Abandoned by her husband, Charlotte's mother decided to prepare her daughter for hardships by denying affection. Not only did she withhold from Gilman natural physical contact, but she also saw to it that Gilman had no intimate friends. Gilman turned to books for solace. When she was seventeen, her father sent her nonfiction books that prompted her to see her life's work as a mission to help society.

From her teenage years, she seemed destined to pursue the arts in one form or another. She attended the Rhode Island School of Design and gave drawing lessons to children. Her formal education took place during eight years in seven different schools; at age fifteen, her formal education was finished. For the remainder of her life she was self-taught.

Gilman had social awareness, and she soon realized the role of women in her time was changing. They were becoming more educated and some were working outside the home. By the age of twenty-one she was eager to go out alone, much to her mother's displeasure. In 1882, she met Charles Walter Stetson, who was also a painter, and in 1884 they were married. A daughter was born to them in 1885, but serious bouts of depression followed the birth of her child. Gilman's illness became so acute that Doctor Mitchell of Philadelphia recommended a rest cure and the chronicle of that treatment became the inspiration for her famous work, *The Yellow Wallpaper*.

In 1887, Charlotte left her husband and daughter and rented a small cottage in Pasadena, California, where by 1890 she claimed to have produced some of her best work. To earn money, she took in boarders, taught art, and wrote short stories, plays, and books. Influenced by Darwinism and the social climate of the times, Gilman published one of her most famous works, *Women and Economics*, in 1898. In 1915, *Herland* was published serially. Many of the oppressive conditions for women in Gilman's society are remedied in this humorous piece about a utopian land without men. Gilman was sought as a lecturer, and she traveled extensively throughout Europe and the United States, spreading her message about the necessity of concentrating on the humanness of the individual rather than on the male or female identity.

After the divorce from her first husband, she married George Houghton Gilman, who provided her with support and companionship during her later years. In her last illness, she returned to Pasadena with her daughter. In an effort to spare her family the pain of seeing her die of cancer, Gilman ended her life.

SUGGESTED READING

Hill, Mary A. *Charlotte Perkins Gilman: The Making of a Radical Feminist*. Philadelphia: Temple University Press, 1980.

—*Mary Dunn*

See also Class and identity; Economics of identity; Feminism; *Herland*; *Women and Economics*; Women and identity

Gimpel the Fool

AUTHOR: Isaac Bashevis Singer (1904-1991)
FIRST PUBLISHED: "Gimpel Tam," 1945 (English translation, 1953)
IDENTITIES: European American; Jewish; religion

The publication of "Gimpel the Fool," in a translation from the Yiddish by Saul Bellow, launched Isaac Bashevis Singer's career. During the 1950's and thereafter, his work appeared widely in English, and throughout the history of Singer studies, "Gimpel the Fool" has held a place of honor. Gimpel belongs to a brotherhood of literary characters—that of the schlemiels. In this work, Singer explores the nature of belief, which, in the modern, secular world, is often considered foolish.

Gimpel believes whatever he is told: that his parents have risen from the dead, that his pregnant fiancée is a virgin, that her children are his children, that the man jumping out of her bed is a figment of his imagination. Gimpel extends his willingness to believe to every aspect of his life, because, he explains: "Everything is possible, as it is written in the Wisdom of the Fathers, I've forgotten just how."

When, on her deathbed, his wife of twenty years confesses that none of her six children are his, Gimpel is tempted to disbelieve all that he has been told and to enact revenge against those who have participated in his humiliation. His temptation is a central crisis of faith. His faith in others, who have betrayed him, is challenged, as is his faith in himself and in God, because among the stories he has believed are those pertaining to the existence of God. Gimpel's belief has always been riddled with doubt; only after he concretizes his spiritual exile by becoming a wanderer does he resolve his faith.

In Singer's fictional worlds, God is the first storyteller who, through words, spoke or wrote the world into being. Belief in God is linked to belief in stories. Thus, when Gimpel is tempted to disbelieve in God, he responds by becoming a wandering storyteller. In so doing Gimpel links himself with the great storyteller and transforms what was once simple gullibility into an act of the greatest faith. As a storyteller, Gimpel opens himself fully to the infinite possibilities of the divine word as it is transformed into the world. At the end, Gimpel still yearns for a world where even he cannot be deceived. He never finds this world. Despite the void he may face, he chooses to believe, and he finds, in his final great act of suspending disbelief, a faith to which he can firmly adhere.

SUGGESTED READINGS

Farrell, Grace. "Suspending Disbelief: Faith and Fiction in I. B. Singer." *Boulevard* 9, no. 3 (Fall, 1994): 111-117.

Pinsker, Sanford. *The Schlemiel as Metaphor*. Carbondale: Southern Illinois University Press, 1991.

Wisse, Ruth R. *The Schlemiel as Modern Hero*. Chicago: University of Chicago Press, 1971.

—Grace Farrell

See also Bellow, Saul; *Crown of Feathers, A*; Jewish American identity; Singer, Isaac Bashevis

Ginsberg, Allen

BORN: Newark, New Jersey; June 3, 1926
DIED: New York, New York; April 5, 1997
PRINCIPAL WORKS: *Howl*, 1956; *Kaddish and Other Poems*, 1961; *The Fall of America: Poems of These States, 1965-1971*, 1972
IDENTITIES: Family; gay, lesbian, and bisexual; Jewish; religion
SIGNIFICANT ACHIEVEMENT: Ginsberg helped inaugurate major literary, social, and cultural changes in the post-World War II United States through his role as one of the members of the Beat generation.

Allen Ginsberg's earliest literary influences were his childhood experiences among the politically disenfranchised: Socialists, Communists, the working class, Russians, and Jews. His mother, Naomi, a teacher, was a Russian Jewish immigrant whose family was active in the Communist Party. Louis, his father, a teacher and poet, was a child of Russian Jewish immigrants and was active in the Socialist Party.

Ginsberg's earliest ambition was to become a labor lawyer. As Ginsberg grew older, his concerns for class inequities continued, even when he decided to give up law school for literary ambitions. In college he became less inclined to hide his homosexuality, and in his writing he increasingly sought to legitimize gay and bisexual experience. These identities—Socialist, Communist, gay, bisexual—are most fully realized in *Howl*, a major poem that broke the hegemony of the impersonal, academic poetry that had dominated much of the century. The poem eulogizes "the best minds" of the era, those imprisoned or driven mad by their resistance to the sexual and political uniformity of postwar American capitalist culture. In 1957, *Howl* was seized by San Francisco authorities and declared obscene.

Ginsberg won the subsequent trial, the first of his many encounters with political and legal establishments. In 1965 he was expelled from Cuba and Czechoslovakia because of his adamant support for gay civil rights in those countries. His later poetry, including *The Fall of America* and *Plutonian Ode* (1982), is influenced by his work in the United States in support of gay rights, the peace movement, freedom of speech, and drug decriminalization.

Ginsberg's career was marked by the convergence of Western and Eastern religious practices. He took vows as a Tibetan Buddhist in 1972. In 1974, he co-founded the Jack Kerouac School of

Disembodied Poetics at the Naropa Institute, in Boulder, Colorado, the first accredited Buddhist college in the Western world.

SUGGESTED READINGS

Hyde, Lewis, ed. *On the Poetry of Allen Ginsberg*. Ann Arbor: University of Michigan Press, 1984.

Miles, Barry. *Ginsberg: A Biography*. New York: Simon & Schuster, 1989.

Schumacher, Michael. *Dharma Lion: A Critical Biography of Allen Ginsberg*. New York: St. Martin's Press, 1992.

Tonkinson, Carol, ed. *Big Sky Mind: Buddhism and the Beat Generation*. New York: Riverhead Books, 1995.

Tytell, John. *Naked Angels: The Lives and Literature of the Beat Generation*. New York: McGraw-Hill, 1976.

—*Tony Trigilio*

See also Antiwar literature; Censorship of literature; Drugs; Eastern religion and philosophy; Erotic identity; Gay identity; *Howl*; Jewish American identity; *Kaddish and Other Poems*; Kerouac, Jack

Giovanni, Nikki (Yolande Cornelia Giovanni, Jr.)

BORN: Knoxville, Tennessee; June 7, 1943

PRINCIPAL WORKS: *Black Feeling, Black Talk, Black Judgement*, 1970; *Re:Creation*, 1970; *Gemini*, 1971; *Spin a Soft Black Song: Poems for Children*, 1971; *My House*, 1972; *Ego-Tripping and Other Poems for Young People*, 1973; *The Women and the Men*, 1975; *Cotton Candy on a Rainy Day*, 1978; *Vacation Time: Poems for Children*, 1980; *Those Who Ride the Night Winds*, 1983; *Sacred Cows and Other Edibles*, 1988; *Racism 101: A Collection of Essays*, 1994; *Selected Poems of Nikki Giovanni*, 1996

Nikki Giovanni
(Jill Krementz)

IDENTITIES: African American; women

SIGNIFICANT ACHIEVEMENT: Giovanni's works have earned critical acclaim and have remained in print in an era when poetry typically does not sell.

When Nikki Giovanni began, in journal publications and readings, to appear on the literary scene in the late 1960's, she was hailed as one of its most noted black poets. Critics praised her work for its themes of militancy, black pride, and revolution. The majority of poems in her volumes, however, address themes such as love, family, and friendship. Her militant poems received more attention, however, and they reflected Giovanni's own activism. It is then, arguably, not accurate when critics argue that Giovanni abandoned the cause of black militancy when, in the 1970's, her poems became more personal. The change was not as marked as some believed.

Giovanni's work took on a different perspective in 1970, when she became a mother. That year she published *Re:Creation*, whose themes are black female identity and motherhood. In *My House*, Giovanni more clearly addresses issues of family, love, and a twofold perspective on life, which is revealed in the two divisions of the book. With poems about the "inside" and "outside," Giovanni acknowledges the importance of not only the personal but also the world at large. Another dimension of this two-part unity is seen in *The Women and the Men*. Giovanni's poetry, over time, also seems to have undergone another change—an increased awareness of the outside world. Giovanni's poetry since 1978 reflects her interest in the human condition. The poems become more meditative, more introspective, and eventually more hopeful as they focus upon life's realities. Examined as a whole, Giovanni's work reveals concerns for identity, self-exploration, and self-realization. These concerns also appear in her works of other genres: recorded poetry, read to music; children's poetry, which she wrote to present positive images to black children; and essays. Giovanni's most consistent theme is the continual, evolving exploration of personal identity and individualism amid familial, social, and political realities.

SUGGESTED READING

Fowler, Virginia. *Nikki Giovanni*. New York: Twayne, 1992.

—Paula C. Barnes

See also African American identity; *Black Feeling, Black Talk*; *Gemini*; Racism and ethnocentrism

Giovanni's Room

AUTHOR: James Baldwin (1924-1987)

FIRST PUBLISHED: 1956

IDENTITIES: African American; European American; gay, lesbian, and bisexual

Giovanni's Room was James Baldwin's second novel, after *Go Tell It on the Mountain* (1953). It was a risky book for Baldwin because it openly explored male homosexuality at a time when few writers discussed gay themes. It almost went unpublished. Knopf had taken Baldwin's first novel, but rejected *Giovanni's Room* and may even have suggested that Baldwin burn the manuscript to protect his reputation. Other rejections followed before Dial Press accepted the book for publication.

Baldwin, who was gay, had touched on homosexual love in "The Outing" (1951) and toward the end of *Go Tell It on the Mountain*, but *Giovanni's Room* was a frank portrayal of a gay man's feelings and torments. The book involves white rather than black characters, which added to the book's commercial and critical risk. *Giovanni's Room* focuses on David, an American expatriate living in Paris, France. Other characters include Hella, an American woman and David's lover, and Giovanni, an Italian who becomes David's gay partner. The story is narrated in first person by David.

Part 1 begins with Hella having left for America and Giovanni about to be executed. The rest is told primarily in flashbacks. In the flashbacks, David comes to Paris after a homosexual affair and attaches himself to Hella. He asks her to marry him, and she goes to Spain to think about it. During Hella's absence, David meets Giovanni, who works in a bar owned by a gay man. David and Giovanni are immediately drawn together and become lovers. David moves into Giovanni's room and the two are happy for a time. David cannot fully accept his gay identity, however, and reminds himself that Hella will return. In part 2, Giovanni and David's relationship sours, mainly because David begins to despise his own feelings and to resent Giovanni's affection. The tension increases when Giovanni loses his job.

Hella comes back and David returns to her without even telling Giovanni. He pretends to be purely heterosexual, and finally breaks off his relationship with Giovanni, who is devastated emotionally. David and Hella plan to get married, but then hear that Giovanni has murdered the owner of the bar where he once worked. Giovanni is sentenced to death. David stays with Hella during Giovanni's trial, but finally gives in to his feelings and goes to the gay quarter. Hella sees him with a man and realizes David will never love her fully. She leaves for America, and David is left to think of Giovanni and to feel empty. David can neither accept his nature nor escape it.

SUGGESTED READINGS

Goldstein, Richard. "Go the Way Your Blood Beats." In *James Baldwin: The Legacy*, edited by Quincy Troupe. New York: Simon & Schuster, 1989.

Kenan, Randall. *James Baldwin*. New York: Chelsea House, 1994.

Weatherby, W. J. *James Baldwin: Artist on Fire*. New York: Donald I. Fine, 1989

—Charles A. Gramlich

See also Baldwin, James; Bisexual identity; Erotic identity; Gay identity

Glaspell, Susan

BORN: Davenport, Iowa; July 1, 1876

DIED: Provincetown, Massachusetts; July 27, 1948

PRINCIPAL WORKS: *The Visioning*, 1911; *Trifles*, pr. 1916; *Plays*, pb. 1920 (includes *Trifles*); *Inheritors*, pr., pb. 1921; *The Verge*, pr., 1921; *Allison's House*, pr., pb. 1930; *Ambrose Holt and Family*, 1931; *Norma Ashe*, 1942; *Judd Rankin's Daughter*, 1945

IDENTITIES: European American; family; Midwest; Northeast

SIGNIFICANT ACHIEVEMENT: Glaspell was instrumental in advancing twentieth century drama in the United States through her work with the Provincetown Players; she was also a novelist.

The regional elements in Susan Glaspell's fiction derive from her midwestern roots. She was born in Davenport, Iowa, and was graduated from Drake University in Des Moines. She began her career as a journalist for local newspapers and later published short stories in popular women's magazines. Her first novel, *The Glory of the Conquered*, was published in 1909.

In 1911, she left Iowa for Greenwich Village, New York, and in 1913, she married George Cram Cook. The move and the marriage transformed her life and writing. Under Cook's influence, she began to experiment with new ideas and literary forms. Glaspell and Cook formed a theater group known as the Provincetown Players. This group provided impetus for Glaspell, along with Eugene O'Neill and other playwrights, to write and direct original dramas.

Glaspell's themes concern society and the individual; her characters sometimes face isolation. Often her protagonists are women in conflict with the established moral code of their community. Her most successful work, the one-act play *Trifles* and the short-story version of the same tale, "A Jury of Her Peers," portrays the plight of Minnie Wright, a woman accused of murdering her husband. While the sheriff and county attorney search for evidence and motive, the sheriff's wife, Mrs. Peters, and a neighbor, Mrs. Hale, come to gather "trifles," articles Mrs. Wright will need in jail. The drama focuses on the women's ability to identify with the isolation and loneliness that might drive a woman like Minnie to murder her cold, domineering husband. While the lawmen sent to investigate the crime dismiss the women as little more than domestic help, Mrs. Peters and Mrs. Hale manage to discover and purloin evidence that the men overlook.

Glaspell's plays and novels combine the search for individual identity with the hope that society will advance and evolve. Her humanitarian vision is described in the novel *Judd Rankin's Daughter*. The characters envision an altruistic world in which one willingly gives the "shirt off his back" to clothe a needy friend.

Glaspell's literary works include forty-three short stories, thirteen plays, and ten novels. Glaspell succeeded as a novelist, but her greatest contribution lies in her promotion of the Provincetown Players, which advanced the career of Eugene O'Neill and spurred the development of American drama.

SUGGESTED READINGS

Alkalay-Gut, Karen. "Jury of Her Peers: The Importance of Trifles." *Studies in Short Fiction* 21 (Winter, 1984): 1-9.

McGovern, Edythe M. "Susan Glaspell." In *American Women Writers*, edited by Lina Mainierto. 2 vols. New York: Frederick Ungar, 1980.

Waterman, Arthur E. *Susan Glaspell*. New York: Twayne, 1966.

—Paula M. Miller

See also American identity: Midwest; *Judd Rankin's Daughter*; O'Neill, Eugene; Rural life

Glass Menagerie, The

AUTHOR: Tennessee Williams (Thomas Lanier Williams, 1911-1983)
FIRST PRODUCED: 1944; first published, 1945
IDENTITIES: Disability; European American; family; South; women

The Glass Menagerie, Tennessee Williams' first major play to appear on Broadway, is an autobiographical work. In it he delineates several personal and societal problems: the isolation of those who are outsiders for one reason or another, the hardships faced by single mothers, the difficulties a disability may create for a family, and the struggle of a young artist to begin his career.

The play has four characters. Amanda Wingfield is a woman from Mississippi whose husband moved the family to St. Louis and abandoned her and her two children. Laura has been left disabled by disease, and Tom is a would-be poet. Amanda yearns for her youth, when she was a Southern belle in plantation society in the Mississippi Delta. Her life is a mixture of reality and fantasy; she has struggled to support her children, who are now grown, but she refuses to acknowledge Laura's disability and dreams of a happy married life for her.

Laura, however, still dependent on her mother, seems destined to remain a prisoner in her own little world. Tom, working at a shoe factory to support the three of them, yearns to flee the stifling environment of their apartment and make a life for himself. The fourth character, Jim O'Connor, the Gentleman Caller, is an "emissary from a world of reality." He has no true grasp of the harshness of reality, so he is better equipped to survive in society than the other three characters.

One predominant symbol in the novel is that of the dead-end alleyway, in which cats are trapped and killed by dogs. Amanda, Tom, and Laura are all trapped, although in different ways, and each escapes into some kind of illusion. Laura, painfully shy because of her limp, spends much of her time with her glass animals (the menagerie of the title) and old phonograph records. Tom goes to the cinema and writes late into the night. Amanda, at a moment's notice, can escape into the past, forgetting in her reveries the brutal facts of her existence. In this play as in others, Williams sees illusion as a sustaining element in troubled human lives. Even the Gentleman Caller, connected as he is to reality, has impossible dreams of rising beyond his present station through attending night school.

The play ends unhappily, for the Gentleman Caller is already engaged, so Amanda's hopes for a husband for Laura are smashed. Tom runs away to join the merchant marine but is unable to escape the memory of his sister. The burden of the past remains with Tom, wherever he is, just as for the author: Williams' sister Rose and her mental problems were a constant, painful memory as well as a source of inspiration.

SUGGESTED READINGS

Bigsby, C. W. E. *A Critical Introduction to Twentieth Century American Drama*. 3 vols. New York: Cambridge University Press, 1982-1985.

Devlin, Albert J., ed. *Conversations with Tennessee Williams*. Jackson: University Press of Mississippi, 1986.

Leavitt, Richard Freeman, ed. *The World of Tennessee Williams*. New York: Putnam, 1978.

Leverich, Lyle. *Tom: The Unknown Tennessee Williams*. New York: Crown, 1995.

—*W. Kenneth Holditch*

See also American identity: South; Williams, Tennessee

God Made Alaska for the Indians

AUTHOR: Ishmael Reed (1938-   )

FIRST PUBLISHED: 1982

IDENTITIES: African American; Native American

God Made Alaska for the Indians, a collection of essays by Ishmael Reed, is a short book, but it manages to pack into its 130 pages many of the widely varied interests of one of the most interesting multicultural figures on the American literary scene. Reed is primarily thought of as an African American writer, but he is also much aware of his Native American ancestry. This dual viewpoint informs the title essay, a lengthy account of political and legal conflicts over the use of Alaskan lands. Reed sympathizes with the Sitka Tlingit Indians, but he realizes that the question is complicated, with other tribes opposing them.

Reed is, as always, critical of the white establishment, and he demonstrates that supposedly benign conservationist forces such as the Sierra Club can be as uncaring of the interests and customs of the indigenous population as any profit-maddened capitalist corporation. An afterword informs the reader that the Sitka Tlingits finally won.

"The Fourth Ali" covers the second fight between Muhammad Ali and Leon Spinks, late in Ali's career. There is little description of the actual fight, and one learns little more than that Ali won. Reed emphasizes the fight as spectacle, describing the followers, the hangers-on, and Ali's near-mythic role.

In the brief "How Not to Get the Infidel to Talk the King's Talk," Reed demolishes the theory that the supposed linguistic flaws of Black English keep African Americans from social advancement by pointing to the success of such verbally challenged European Americans as Gerald R. Ford and Nelson A. Rockefeller.

"Black Macho, White Macho" attacks some of the male-supremacist views Reed has been accused of holding, pointing out that such views are particularly dangerous in those with access to atomic weapons. "Race War in America?" makes some strong points about racial attitudes in the United States, in the then-pressing context of worry about the minority government in South Africa. In "Black Irishman" Reed, who has always refused to consider himself anything but an African American, looks at his Irish ancestry.

Perhaps the most interesting essay in the book is the last, "American Poetry: Is There a Center?" Reed recounts the controversies over a poetry center set up in Colorado by an Asian religious leader. The center's supporters made claims that it represented a focal point of all that is good in American poetry. Reed replies with his uncompromising view that the genius of American art can be found in the works of all races and cultures.

SUGGESTED READINGS

Clark, Tom. *The Great Naropa Poetry Wars*. Santa Barbara, Calif.: Cadmus, 1980.

Martin, Reginald. *Ishmael Reed and the New Black Critics*. New York: St. Martin's Press, 1988.

—*Arthur D. Hlavaty*

See also African American identity; Native American identity; Reed, Ishmael

Gone with the Wind

AUTHOR: Margaret Mitchell (1900-1949)

FIRST PUBLISHED: 1936

IDENTITIES: African American; European American; South; women

Gone with the Wind, perhaps the most famous American novel of the twentieth century, tells the story of Scarlett O'Hara, a Southern woman trying to maintain her identity as her world is torn apart by the United States Civil War. Upon publication, the novel attained instant popularity, and the premiere of the film version in 1939 met with equal enthusiasm.

The story begins when Scarlett, at age sixteen, experiences the first real disappointment of her pampered life. Ashley Wilkes, the man she loves, marries Melanie Hamilton, a soft-spoken and gentle woman whom Scarlett despises. Scarlett irrationally marries Melanie's brother, but he dies a few months later, leaving Scarlett to discover that widowhood is the most restrictive of all female roles in her Southern society. The upheaval caused by the war, however, gives Scarlett some opportunities for independence. She eventually marries Frank Kennedy and manages a successful lumber business, but is widowed once again. Scarlett then marries an unprecedented third time, to the dashing but socially unrespectable Rhett Butler. Unwilling to admit her sexual attraction for Rhett, Scarlett convinces herself she is marrying him for his money. She continues to pursue Ashley, until she finally realizes, perhaps too late, that she loves Rhett.

Gone with the Wind is a long, sweeping tale and as such encompasses a variety of issues. The views on slavery held by most Southerners at the time are effectively portrayed by the novel's detailed setting. The plantation owners believe they have the right to own slaves, yet paradoxically treat some of the house slaves as members of their families. In turn, many slaves develop tremendous loyalty to their owners, remaining in their service even after the war has made them free. The novel also reflects the Southerners' views of themselves. Even after the war has reduced most of them to poverty, they consider themselves superior to the newly rich Northerners who seek their fortunes in the South.

More overt themes are expressed through Scarlett's vividly drawn character. Naturally willful, Scarlett is nonetheless bound by society's restrictions; only when the war alters those rules can she openly rebel against the standard of passive, helpless womanhood. In addition, Scarlett's courage and personal development are effectively traced throughout the novel. Although born and bred to be a decorative companion to men, Scarlett's tumultuous life teaches her that her resolve is as strong as any man's. She has many flaws, but her determination at the end of the novel to win back Rhett's love has endeared her to countless readers.

SUGGESTED READINGS:

Harwell, Richard, ed. *Margaret Mitchell's "Gone with the Wind" Letters, 1936-1949.* New York: Macmillan, 1976.

Pyron, Darden Asbury. *Southern Daughter: The Life of Margaret Mitchell.* New York: Oxford University Press, 1991.

Sweeney, Patricia E. *Women in Southern Literature.* Westport, Conn.: Greenwood Press, 1986.

—Amy Sisson

See also African American identity; American identity: South; European American identity; Feminism; Slavery

Good Country People

AUTHOR: Flannery O'Connor (1925-1964)

FIRST PUBLISHED: 1955

IDENTITIES: European American; religion; South

In addition to representing the Christian and Southern American identities seen in most of Flannery O'Connor's fiction, "Good Country People" touches on the roles of the intellect and intellectualism, as well as physical challenges in developing the individual identity. The central character is emotionally scarred by a hunting accident that has left her with one leg. This disfigurement causes her to retreat from the physical world into the world of the intellect. She was named Joy by her appropriately named mother, Mrs. Hopewell, a rather simplistic optimist who confronts adversity simply by hoping for the best. This philosophy of cheer irritates Joy, who retaliates by legally changing her name to the ugliest one she can think of: Hulga.

While the story does hint at the way various people react to the physically challenged, O'Connor's interest in Hulga/Joy's identity seems to lie in a different direction. The deliberate ugliness in her choice of a name mirrors the deliberate ugliness of her personality. Hulga is deliberately as rude as possible to her mother because of Hulga's disgust for her mother's sweetness-and-light simplicity. O'Connor reveals Mrs. Hopewell's insensitivity to Hulga's bitterness at her maiming, but greater thematic importance is placed on the disfigurement as an analogue for a spiritual leglessness. Moral ugliness, O'Connor's Catholic belief instructs, is always the result of the brokenness of human nature. Humanity was crippled in the Fall, Adam and Eve's first sin.

This Christian orthodoxy is not Hulga's belief at all. Her self-made identity is of an elite intellectual, rising above such superstition. Christian morality, in the story, seems at first to be represented in the story by a travelling Bible salesman named Manley Pointer. To some extent, the plot he engenders is an old joke: He is a traveling salesman trying to seduce the daughter. Seduce her he does, but not by appealing to her emotions—Hulga denies that she has any. Rather, he sees her true weakness: intellectual pride. Hulga's self-created identity is that of the great intellect (she holds a Ph.D. in philosophy) among country bumpkins, and by pretending to succumb to Manley's bumbling professions of love, she can prove that there is no such thing. She intends to demonstrate that what is called "love" is simply a hypocritical disguise for lust. Love, she thinks, is as illusory as Christianity, the other myth in which Manley seems to believe.

Yet the joke is on her. Manley, it turns out, is not the Christian he claims to be: He is a con artist who uses Hulga's pride to attempt to win from her not only sexual favors but also her prosthetic leg. Her reactions to his attentions reveal her hypocrisy: She is outraged, like a traditional belle whom Hulga would hold in contempt, at his frank sexual proposition. She also is mentally bested by the young man. The story ends with Manley disappearing in the distance with Hulga's prosthetic leg, leaving her to question her presuppositions about her own identity while she awaits an embarrassing rescue in a hay loft.

SUGGESTED READINGS

Bloom, Harold. *Flannery O'Connor*. New York: Chelsea House, 1986.

Brinkmeyer, Robert H. *The Art and Vision of Flannery O'Connor*. Baton Rouge: Louisiana State University Press, 1989.

Shloss, Carol. *Flannery O'Connor's Dark Comedies: The Limits of Inference*. Baton Rouge: Louisiana State University Press, 1980.

Walters, Dorothy. *Flannery O'Connor*. Boston: Twayne, 1973.

—John R. Holmes

See also American identity: South; Catholicism; "Good Man Is Hard to Find, A"; O'Connor, Flannery; "Revelation"

Good Man Is Hard to Find, A

AUTHOR: Flannery O'Connor (1925-1964)
FIRST PUBLISHED: 1953
IDENTITIES: European American; religion; South

"A Good Man Is Hard to Find," the title story of Flannery O'Connor's first collection of short stories, is one of her most anthologized stories. As in most of her stories, the theme of identity in this story involves O'Connor's Christian conviction about the role of sin, particularly the sin of pride, in distorting one's true identity. The focal character in the story, who is identified only as the grandmother, convinces herself and, she thinks, her family, that she is a good judge of human nature.

In fact, she assumes that she is the best judge on any matter. The story opens with her son, Bailey, planning a family vacation to Florida. The grandmother opposes the idea, because an escaped killer known in the papers as the Misfit is supposedly headed toward Florida. She has very clear ideas of the flaws in character and the influence of class that go to making a criminal such as the Misfit. The grandmother's false sense of self-importance, which she sees as separating herself from vulgarity, which is represented by the Misfit, is a motif typical of O'Connor's fiction, and the plot hinges on the revelation of the falseness of the grandmother's self-image.

From the beginning, O'Connor is careful to distance the narration from the grandmother's delusions, with judicious use of irony. After describing the physical details of the grandmother's extravagant traveling clothes, the narration offers a reflection that is apparently intended to represent the grandmother's thoughts: "In case of an accident, anyone seeing her dead on the highway would know at once that she was a lady." Being "a lady" is an important part of the grandmother's self-identity, yet it is defined externally, by clothing, and seems dependent on other people's opinions. A further irony is that the grandmother is reflecting on her appearance and class in death, a time when neither matters much. The same irony reappears a few pages later when the grandmother tells her grandchildren, John Wesley and June Star, that she would have done well to marry a certain Mr. Teagarden because he was "a gentleman" and had died a very wealthy man. Again the insistence on wealth and status appears in the context of death, which renders them meaningless.

The grandmother's own death at the end of the story provides the final irony. After lamenting with a restaurant owner on the decline of gentility—the scarcity of "good men" suggested by the title—the family encounters the only character in the story with the sort of manners and external refinement that the grandmother values, and he turns out to be the Misfit. She can tell by looking at him, the grandmother tells the Misfit, that he has no "common blood" in him, and the Misfit agrees. Then he and his henchmen shoot the entire family dead.

SUGGESTED READINGS

Asals, Frederick. *Flannery O'Connor: The Imagination of Extremity*. Athens: University of Georgia Press, 1982.

Bloom, Harold. *Flannery O'Connor*. New York: Chelsea House, 1986.

Shloss, Carol. *Flannery O'Connor's Dark Comedies: The Limits of Inference*. Baton Rouge: Louisiana State University Press, 1980.

Walters, Dorothy. *Flannery O'Connor*. Boston: Twayne, 1973.

—*John R. Holmes*

See also American identity: South; Catholicism; "Good Country People"; O'Connor, Flannery; "Revelation"

Good Morning, Midnight

AUTHOR: Jean Rhys (Ella Gwendolen Rees Williams, 1894-1979)

FIRST PUBLISHED: 1939

IDENTITIES: Disease; women

Good Morning, Midnight tells the story of a middle-aged woman's return to Paris. Sasha Jensen was there first in the 1920's, as a newlywed with little money. In October, 1938, after several years in England and no longer married, she returns and confronts her past. The familiar streets, shops, hotels, and cafés all haunt her. They remind her she is no longer young, and they tempt her with new adventures.

The novel's four-part structure reflects Sasha's state of mind. The story begins and ends in her room in a cheap hotel. " 'Quite like old times,' the room says, 'Yes? No?' " When she ventures out, she avoids certain cafés, but does not feel much better in others. She thinks everyone is staring at and talking about her. She often breaks down and cries. The past overwhelms her, and the present does little to calm her. Her reliance on alcohol only makes things worse.

In the second part, she has an encouraging triumph. She accompanies a Russian man to the studio of a painter. Though she cries in their presence, they are kind and sympathetic. She buys a painting of a banjo player with a sad expression sitting on a curb. Her exultation fades when she returns to her room, and, despite her best resolves, dwells upon the past. "It's all the rooms I've ever slept in, all the streets I've ever walked in. Now the whole thing moves in an ordered, undulating procession past my eyes. Rooms, streets, streets, rooms."

The third part focuses on her early years in Paris, how she and her husband struggled to get by. Despite their lack of money and the death of a baby son, she thinks of that time as her golden days. "After all, those were still the days when I went into a café to drink coffee, when I could feel gay on half a bottle of wine, when this happened and that happened." The chapter ends with her resolve to buy new gloves, perfume, cosmetics, jewelry—and to try to blur temporal distinctions. "When I have had a couple of drinks I shan't know whether it's yesterday, today, or tomorrow."

In the fourth part, she spends an evening with a gigolo. She buys him dinner, and he follows her back to her room. "Now everything is in my arms on this dark landing—love, youth, spring, happiness, everything I thought I had lost. I was a fool, wasn't I? to think all that was finished for me." What follows is chilling—her distrust of the gigolo turns out to be founded, and her distrust of her own resolve equally so.

As in her other novels, Jean Rhys brilliantly re-creates the thoughts of a woman in psychological distress. Sasha Jensen typifies her heroines who refuse to give up, whatever the odds against them—and who struggle with their desires, as much as with unsympathetic societies.

SUGGESTED READINGS

Naipaul, V. S. "Without a Dog's Chance." *New York Review of Books*, May 18, 1972, 29-31.

Rose, Phyllis. *Writing of Women: Essays in a Renaissance*. Middletown, Conn.: Wesleyan University Press, 1985.

Wyndham, Francis, and Diana Melly, eds. *Jean Rhys: Letters 1931-66*. London: Andre Deutsch, 1984.

—*Alan Ziskin*

See also Caribbean American literature; Expatriate identity; *Wide Sargasso Sea*

Goodbye, Columbus

AUTHOR: Philip Roth (1933-   )
FIRST PUBLISHED: 1959
IDENTITIES: Jewish

Philip Roth's first published volume, *Goodbye, Columbus*, won for the young writer not only the National Book Award in 1960 but also accusations, as a result of the book's comically piercing portraits of middle-class American Jews, of Roth's harboring self-hatred. The ambivalent exploration of Jewish American life in *Goodbye, Columbus*, and its mixed reception among Jewish readers who were sensitive to the public image of Jews established two of the central themes of Roth's fiction: a frank and often ironic look at Jewish American identity, and an intense but playful examination of the relationship between art and life.

In the novella "Goodbye, Columbus," Neil Klugman's confrontation with his Jewish American identity is represented by his love affair with Brenda Patimkin. Brenda signifies the American Dream, her parents' suburban prosperity symbolized by a refrigerator in the basement overflowing with fresh fruit. Neil's ambivalence toward the Patimkins' conspicuous consumption and their eager assimilation into American culture is expressed by the guilt he feels when he helps himself to fruit from the refrigerator. Although Neil finally rejects Brenda, the novella closes without offering Neil a clear sense of where he might belong.

Roth poses other choices in the book's subsequent stories. Ozzie Freedman in "The Conversion of the Jews" believes he must choose between Jewish authority and the American notion of personal freedom. In outrage at his rabbi's denial that an omnipotent God could indeed have caused Mary to conceive without intercourse, Ozzie threatens to leap from the roof of the synagogue, and demands that the rabbi, his mother, and the assembled crowd kneel and affirm belief that God can do anything he wants, with the clear implication that God could have created Jesus in the manner that Christians believe. When Ozzie experiences the power of self-definition at this ironic climax, Roth suggests that Judaism, personified by the rabbi, must confront the shaping forces of the American context if it is not to lose its adherents.

In "Defender of the Faith," Sergeant Nathan Marx questions whether Jews are obligated to define themselves in relation to other Jews. After a Jewish recruit repeatedly manipulates Nathan for favors during basic training, he realizes that his greater responsibility to his fellow Jews lies in refusing to let them be different, despite the dangers that assimilation poses. As if Roth is in dialogue with himself, however, the final story in the collection reverses Nathan's decision. Eli of "Eli, the Fanatic" dons, as a challenge to his "progressive suburban community," the stale black clothes of a recent Jewish immigrant, and, with them, an identity that refuses assimilation into American life. *Goodbye, Columbus*, then, represents Roth's first and notable attempt to explore the problem of Jewish American identity from a variety of angles and without resolution.

Suggested readings

Baumgarten, Murray, and Barbara Gottfried. *Understanding Philip Roth*. Columbia: University of South Carolina Press, 1990.

Halio, Jay L. *Philip Roth Revisited*. New York: Twayne, 1992.

Milbauer, Asher Z., and Donald G. Watson, eds. *Reading Philip Roth*. New York: St. Martin's Press, 1988.

—Debra Shostak

See also Acculturation; Jewish American identity; *Portnoy's Complaint*; Roth, Philip

Gorilla, My Love

Author: Toni Cade Bambara (1939-1995)

First published: 1972

Identities: African American; women

Published in 1972, *Gorilla, My Love* is a collection of short stories written between 1959 and 1971. The book is an upbeat, positive work that redefines the black experience in America. It affirms the fact that inner-city children can grow into strong, healthy adults. It indicates clearly that black men are not always the weak, predatory element in the family but can be a strong, protective force. It intimates that African Americans are not the socially alienated, dysfunctional people that the mainstream society sometimes suggests. Instead, the stories project an image of a people who love themselves, who understand themselves, and who need no validation.

The fifteen short stories that compose the text are set in urban areas, and the narrative voices are usually streetwise, preadolescent girls who are extremely aware of their environment. The titular story, "Gorilla, My Love" is centered in the misunderstanding between a child and an adult. Jefferson Vale announces that he is getting married, but he has promised his preadolescent niece, Hazel, to marry her. Hazel sees her "Hunca" Bubba as a "lyin dawg." Although her uncle and her grandfather attempt to console her, Hazel believes adults "mess over kids, just cause they little and can't take em to court."

All of the stories are informative and entertaining. A story that typifies the anthology is "Playin with Ponjob," which details how a white social worker, Miss Violet, underestimates the influence of a local thug and is forced to leave the community. "Talkin Bout Sunny" explores the effects of the mainstream on the black male by pointing out how pressures from the larger community cause Sunny to kill his wife. "The Lesson" points out the disparity between the rich and the poor by telling of children window-shopping on Fifth Avenue. "Blues Ain't No Mockin Bird" details how one man protects his family from prying photographers employed by the welfare system.

What is significant in "Playin with Ponjob" is that Toni Cade Bambara does not depict Ponjob as being predatory. He is male, "jammed-up by the white man's nightmare." To the community, he is "the only kind of leader we can think of." In "Talkin Bout Sunny" Bambara indicates that the larger community is partly responsible for Sunny's actions, but she also indicates that the community of Sunny's friends is also responsible because they know of his distemper, but do nothing. "The Lesson" teaches children that what one wealthy person spends on one toy can feed eight of them for a year. "Blues Ain't No Mockin Bird" indicates that the patriarch of an extended family can protect his own. The collection depicts African Americans as a strong, progressive people.

SUGGESTED READINGS

Evans, Marre, ed. *Black Women Writers (1950-1980): A Critical Evaluation.* Garden City, N.J.: Anchor Press, 1984.

Hargrave, Nancy D. "Youth in Bambara's *Gorilla, My Love.*" In *Women Writers of the Contemporary South*, edited by Peggy Whitman Prenshow. Jackson: University of Mississippi Press, 1984.

—Ralph Reckley, Sr.

See also Adolescent identity; Bambara, Toni Cade

Grace Notes

AUTHOR: Rita Dove (1952-   )
FIRST PUBLISHED: 1989
IDENTITIES: African American; women

In *Grace Notes*, Rita Dove explores the implications of being an African American who is prepared to step forward into a world broader than any limiting labels would suggest. Many poems focus on the relationship between her biracial child and herself, revealing how the child discovers and accepts these differences. Others show the daughter learning what it means to become a woman. Still other poems question the effect that the development of identity can have on the artist.

Dove sets the stage with the first poem, "Summit Beach, 1921," which examines the risk of being at the edge of development. A girl watches her friends dance as she rests her broken leg. She had climbed to the top of her father's shed, then stepped off. Dove shows that the girl wants to date but that her father had discouraged her. This poem suggests that the search for identity does not occur without risks because the search involves making choices.

Married to a German, Dove's daughter learns to belong in both worlds. "Genetic Expedition" contains images which delve into the physical differences between the black mother and her biracial child. Beginning with images of her own body, Dove mentions that she resembles pictures of natives in the *National Geographic* more than she does her own daughter. Because of the *National Geographic*'s sensual, naked women, her father had not allowed the children to read the magazine. While Dove identifies physically with the bodies of these women, she acknowledges that her daughter's features and hair reflect her biracial heritage. Thus the poem exemplifies Dove's rootedness in her own culture while being open to other cultures.

Other poems that feature Dove's daughter show the child as she discovers her mother's body, the source of her life and future. "After Reading *Mickey in the Night Kitchen* for the Third Time Before Bed" describes a tender moment between mother and daughter as the daughter compares her budding body with her mother's mature body. Dove emphasizes the daughter's innocent curiosity and her delight at realizing what her future holds.

Several poems discuss artists searching for ways to express who they have come to be through their art. "Canary" looks at the difficulty of such inquiry. Focusing on Billie Holiday, the poem describes the downward spiral of her life. Whether it was more difficult for her to be black or to be female is the question of identity that Dove explores, suggesting that circumstances conspired to take away Holiday's power to carve out her own identity. Dove's poems allow the questions and implications of a search for identity to take shape as an ongoing process.

SUGGESTED READINGS

McDowell, Robert. "The Assembling Vision of Rita Dove." *Callaloo* 25 (Winter, 1985): 61-70.

Steinman, Lisa M. "Dialogues Between History and Dream." *Michigan Quarterly Review* 26 (Spring, 1987): 428-438.

—Martha Modena Vertreace

See also Appearance and identity; Dove, Rita; Feminism; Mixed race and identity; Multiculturalism

Grapes of Wrath, The

AUTHOR: John Steinbeck (1902-1968)
FIRST PUBLISHED: 1939
IDENTITIES: European American; family; Midwest; West and Southwest; women

The Grapes of Wrath, John Steinbeck's masterpiece, is a starkly realistic rendition of the Depression-era struggle of an Oklahoma farm family forced to move to California in order to find employment. The family's dilemma represents that of all rural, working-class households in the Midwest and West during an age of increasing mechanization for upper-class, capitalistic profit. In addition, Steinbeck's female characters, especially, convey his message of working-class unity.

The Joads are typical 1930's tenant farmers, forced from home because "one man on a tractor can take the place of twelve or fourteen families." Reading advertisements of work available in California, the Joads buy an old truck for the journey. The trip quickly kills lifelong Oklahoman Grandpa Joad, and Grandma Joad dies in the Nevada desert. Throughout, the impoverished Joads are victimized repeatedly, microcosmically representative of the entire capital exploitation system underlying the Great Depression.

Ma Joad's determination, however, helps the Joads reach California. They then learn of their further victimization by machines. The work advertisements were mass-produced and deliberately overdisseminated to entice excess workers, thereby depressing wages even further and creating widespread unemployment in California. Fortunately, the family finds shelter in a government-operated, socialist-style cooperative camp, where a central committee makes management decisions and tenants work and share equally. The Joads begin to realize that only by working-class unity can they hope to combat the crop owners and their police. As Ma Joad states, "If you're in trouble or hurt or need—go to poor people. They're the only ones that'll help—the only ones."

The Joads then show they can reciprocate as class-conscious members of the struggle for economic survival in an America dominated by the capitalist "monster." After Rose of Sharon's baby is predictably stillborn, given the family's deprivation, the Joads are forced from home by a flood. Struggling to higher ground, they take refuge in an old barn, where they discover a starving man and his son. Proving their newfound dedication to their class and ability to adjust, endure, and eventually conquer, Ma and Rose of Sharon look at each other, Rose of Sharon saying "Yes." Ma responds, "I knowed you would. I knowed!" as Rose of Sharon kneels beside the starving man to feed him from her breast. The Joad women thus demonstrate that all of the suffering poor are their family, to be nurtured and sustained in the unending struggle for economic justice in an economically unjust America.

SUGGESTED READINGS

Davis, Robert Con, ed. *Twentieth Century Interpretations of "The Grapes of Wrath."* Englewood Cliffs, N.J.: Prentice-Hall, 1982.
Ditsky, John, ed. *Critical Essays on Steinbeck's "The Grapes of Wrath."* Boston: G. K. Hall, 1989.
Donohue, Agnes McNeill. *A Casebook on "The Grapes of Wrath."* New York: Thomas Y. Crowell, 1968.

—John L. Grigsby

See also *Cannery Row*; Steinbeck, John; *Tortilla Flat*

Great Gatsby, The

AUTHOR: F. Scott Fitzgerald (1896-1940)
FIRST PUBLISHED: 1925
IDENTITIES: European American; Northeast

In a sense, *The Great Gatsby* is a novel about identities, as each of its major characters struggles to find or create himself or herself as an independent figure in twentieth century American life. In these efforts the characters reveal themselves either as fully rounded, authentic individuals, or as hollow shells, devoid of personality and reality. Taken together, the group portrait Fitzgerald paints in his novel is a fitting representation of the false prosperity of post-World War I America and, more important, is perhaps the most perfectly constructed fiction of its time.

Nick Carraway, the narrator, comes from the Midwest to New York to work as a stockbroker. Taking a home in the Long Island community of West Egg, he makes the acquaintance of his rich neighbor Jay Gatsby, who is the subject of myriad rumors. Gatsby is reputed to have dubious connections, to have been a German spy during the war, and perhaps to have killed a man. While some of this is true (Gatsby has connections with the criminal world, and he served in the war, but was a hero for the Allies), the most salient fact is that Gatsby remains, after many years, in love with Daisy Buchanan, Nick's cousin, who lives across the bay. Through Nick, Gatsby reestablishes a relationship with her and seeks to rekindle the long-dead flame. The attempt fails and, in the end, Gatsby is dead, Daisy left in her loveless marriage, and Nick wiser and less hopeful.

Much hope is lost as identity is gained or revealed, and Nick is honest in his chronicle of those events. Daisy and Tom Buchanan are like the Bourbons of French history, for they forget nothing and learn nothing. They enter the novel as self-centered, essentially uncaring persons, obsessed with their own concerns and indifferent to the feelings and the existence of other people. Tom is having an affair with Myrtle Wilson, wife of a garage owner on Long Island. Daisy rather easily decides to renew her connection with Gatsby, begun years ago while he was in army training on a military base in her home town in the South. When Myrtle Wilson's death places their world in jeopardy, husband and wife quickly abandon their "loves" and retreat into the safety of money and privilege. The identities of the Buchanans are shaped, Fitzgerald clearly indicates, by social status, not personal worth.

Nick is a more difficult identity to define, and, much as the seed his name implies, he is constantly changing and emerging. Throughout the novel he is a figure in transition. During one critical passage—as he, Gatsby, and the Buchanans motor into town on the drive that will lead to Myrtle Wilson's death—Nick suddenly realizes that it is his birthday, and that he has just turned thirty. "Before me stretched the portentous, menacing road of a new decade." In a sense, there is no single narrator for this novel, for the Nick who begins the book is clearly not the same man who ends it after a summer of carnivals and carnage.

Yet Nick's change is more than one of experience; it is one of understanding. At the novel's beginning, fresh from the experience of the war, he says he is ready for the world to stand "at moral attention." Clearly, this is not the sort of person who would accept, much less become a friend with, a questionable character such as Gatsby. However, by the end of the novel, Nick is able to tell Gatsby: "You're worth the whole damn bunch put together." Gatsby's romanticism is, in the end, innocent, despite his criminal connections. Compared to the hypocrisy that the Buchanans and the various partygoers represent, Gatsby is admirable.

Gatsby is not Gatsby but Jimmy Gatz, a poor boy from the Midwest—like Nick Carraway—who happened upon a chance that took him away from his life and gave him the opportunity to move into a different world. That world included Daisy, whom Gatsby romanced while he was a military officer in training. Later, on Long Island, after he has re-created himself, Gatsby tries to win her, and all she represents, again. Gatsby fails, and Nick is the sole honest witness to Gatsby's heroic effort.

In the end, identity is the central message of *The Great Gatsby*. Is Gatsby a war hero or a gangster? Is he Jimmy Gatz or Jay Gatsby? Is Daisy Buchanan a happily married woman or one enamored with a love from her past? Is Nick Carraway really the honest narrator or a special advocate for his friend, who might be either a romantic hero or a successful, but common, thug? The answer, Fitzgerald implies, lies in human memory. People are not what they are but what they think they used to be.

SUGGESTED READINGS
Bruccoli, Matthew. *Some Sort of Epic Grandeur*. New York: Harcourt Brace Jovanovich, 1981.
Kenner, Hugh. *A Homemade World*. New York: Morrow, 1975.
Kuehl, John. *F. Scott Fitzgerald*. Boston: Twayne, 1991.
Stern, Milton. *The Golden Moment: The Novels of F. Scott Fitzgerald*. Champaign: University of Illinois Press, 1970.
Way, Brian. *F. Scott Fitzgerald and the Art of Social Fiction*. London: Edward Arnold, 1980.

—*Michael Witkoski*

See also American Dream; American identity: Midwest; Class and identity

Great Slave Narratives

EDITOR: Arna Wendell Bontemps (1903-1972)
FIRST PUBLISHED: 1969
IDENTITIES: African American

Great Slave Narratives, Arna Bontemps' 1960's revival of a once-popular American literary genre, is a compilation of three book-length narratives written by former slaves. During much of the nineteenth century, slave narratives were best-sellers for American publishers. The reintroduction of this literary form was inspired by the Black Power movement of the 1960's and 1970's and the resurgent interest in black culture and the African American experience. Readers were again curious about how it felt to be black and a slave; they wanted to know how the world looked through the eyes of one who had achieved a measure of freedom by effort and suffering. Who, readers wanted to know, were the people who had passed through the ordeal, and how had they expressed their thoughts and feelings?

Bontemps chose for this book three outstanding examples of the genre. The first, *The Interesting Narrative of the Life of Olaudah Equiano, or Gustavus Vassa, the African* (1789), by Olaudah Equiano, who was given the name Gustavus Vassa, gained wide attention, and is particularly interesting for the author's vivid recall of his African background. In 1794, it went into its eighth edition, with many more to follow in America and Europe.

The second book, *The Fugitive Blacksmith; Or, Events in the History of James W. C. Pennington, Pastor of a Presbyterian Church, New York, Formerly a Slave in the State of Maryland, United States* (1850), is the colorful tale of a full-blooded African who was honored with the degree of Doctor of Divinity by the University of Heidelberg, Germany. Yale University denied him admission as a regular student but did not interfere when he stood outside the doors of classrooms in order to hear professors lecture. Pennington also was the first black to write a history of his people in America: *A Text Book of the Origin and History of the Colored People* (1841).

The final narrative in the trilogy, *Running a Thousand Miles for Freedom: Or, The Escape of William and Ellen Craft from Slavery* (1860), an exciting story of a courageous slave couple's escape, is perhaps the high point in the development of the slave narrative genre. Apparently no two slaves in their flight from subjugation to freedom ever thrilled the world so much as did this handsome young couple. Not everyone was pleased, however. President James Polk was so infuriated by their success that he threatened to use the Fugitive Slave Law and the military in their recapture. By then the Crafts were in England.

Bontemps, in his introduction to *Great Slave Narratives*, explained the importance of this "half-forgotten history," placing it in the context of American literature: "Hindsight," he wrote, "may yet disclose the extent to which this writing, this impulse, has been influential on subsequent American writing, if not indeed on America's view of itself. . . . The standard literary sources and the classics of modern fiction pale in comparison as a source of strength."

SUGGESTED READINGS
Aptheker, Herbert. *A Documentary History of the Negro People*. Secaucus, N.J.: Citadel Press, 1973.
Blackett, R. J. M. *Building an Antislavery Wall*. Baton Rouge: Louisiana State University Press, 1983.

Blockson, Charles L. *The Underground Railroad: First Person Narratives of Escapes to Freedom in the North*. New York: Prentice Hall, 1987.

—Barbara Day

See also African American identity; Bontemps, Arna Wendell; Slave narratives; Slavery

Greed

Author: Ai (1947-   )
First published: 1993
Identities: African American; European American; multiracial; religion

Greed is a collection of poems about the identity of America in the late twentieth century. In dramatic monologues spoken by famous or obscure Americans, Ai exposes amorality in the institutions of society, business, and private life. For most of the speakers, America has not kept its promises. Truth and justice are illusions in a society made more vicious, because of greed, than the Darwinian struggle for survival among animals. Money, power, drugs, sex—these are the gods of late twentieth century America.

To the African American speakers, slavery is still alive in the "big house" of white America. Violence is the result. In "Riot Act, April 29, 1992," a black man, going to get something on the day the wealth "finally trickled down," threatens to "set your world on fire." In "Self Defense," Marion Barry, mayor of Washington, D.C., trapped using crack cocaine by the FBI, warns: "The good ole days of slaves out pickin' cotton/ ain't coming back no more." In "Endangered Species," a black university professor, perceived as "a race instead of a man," is stopped by police while driving through his own neighborhood.

In "Hoover, Edgar J.," Ai indicts the director of the FBI for abuse of power. Hoover admits he has "files on everybody who counts" and "the will to use them." Deceptions by government are implicated in poems concerning the assassination of President John F. Kennedy. In "Jack Ruby on Ice," Ruby is refused sanctuary, in exchange for his testimony, by the Chief Justice of the United States. In "Oswald Incognito and Astral Travels," Oswald finds himself "trapped/ in the palace of lies,/ where I'm clothed in illusion/ and fed confusion with a spoon."

Other poems explore domestic violence and sexual abuse of children. In "Finished," a woman kills her husband after repeated episodes of physical abuse. In "Respect, 1967," such a man expresses rage "against the paycheck that must be saved for diapers/ and milk." The speaker in "Life Story" is a priest who sexually abuses young boys. As a child, he was abused by his uncle, also a priest. In "The Ice Cream Man," the speaker lures a little girl inside his truck to sexually molest her. He tells of his own abuse by his stepfather and his mother.

Ai offers little hope for the promise of America in *Greed*. She closes the book with the title poem, about the savings and loan scandal of the 1980's. The responsible working man in "Family Portrait, 1960" has little chance to succeed. Even so, he takes care of his sick wife, cooks dinner, oversees the baths of his young daughters, then dozes—"chaos kept at bay" for one more day.

Suggested readings

Ai. "An Interview with Ai." Interview by Catherine French, Rebecca Ross, and Gary Short. *Hayden's Ferry Review* 5 (Fall, 1989): 11-31.

Wilson, Rob. "The Will to Transcendence in Contemporary American Poet Ai." *Canadian Review of American Studies* 17, no. 4 (Winter, 1986): 437-448.

—James Green

See also African American identity; Ai; *Cruelty*; Mixed race and identity

Green Grow the Lilacs

Author: Lynn Riggs (1899-1954)
First produced: 1931; first published, 1931
Identities: European American; Midwest

Lynn Riggs's play *Green Grow the Lilacs* tells a folktale of young love in the Indian Territory in 1900, seven years before it became the state of Oklahoma. Breaking with the theatrical tradition of acts, his experimental play is constructed in six related scenes. Its old songs and cowboy ballads charmed Broadway audiences.

When cowboy Curly McClain comes courting Laurey on a June morning, her Aunt Eller welcomes him and his boast of a fancy surrey and white horses to take them to the party. When Laurey prefers to go with Jeeter, the "bullet-colored" hired hand, Curly sings a ballad of a disappointed lover who changes the green lilacs of home "for the red, white, and blue" of the army.

The rivalry between Curly and Jeeter over Laurey's affections starts in Jeeter's smokehouse and peaks at the party, where Laurey flees to Curly for protection. Curly's marriage proposal, which is accepted, makes him realize that he must change his cowboy life for a farmer's plow, saying, "the ranches are breakin' up fast. They're puttin' in barbed w'ar, and plowing up the sod fer wheat and corn."

The lovers' marriage night is interrupted by a shivaree, a raucous wedding celebration by the townspeople. The shivaree is an Oklahoma custom. The townspeople put the couple on a haystack and toss straw dolls, representing children, to them. When Jeeter sets fire to the couple's haystack, Curly defends Laurey and, when the two men fight, Jeeter falls on his own knife and dies. Three days later, as Aunt Eller is consoling Laurey over her thwarted marriage night, Curly escapes from jail before his hearing and returns to the farmhouse. Aunt Eller convinces pursuing townsmen to let Curly stay for his wedding night by insisting that "if a law's a good law—it can stand a little breakin'." She assures the posse that Curly will return in the morning for the hearing and that he will be found not guilty.

Rather than showing a glamorized Western setting, Riggs emphasizes the strength of character needed to exist in the harsh land. The women in particular comment on the rigors of Oklahoma life, which robs them of youth and health. Riggs was deliberately preserving the dialect and rhythms of Oklahoma speech and the songs and ballads he loved. When Richard Rodgers and Oscar Hammerstein molded the play into the musical *Oklahoma!* (1943), they did so by incorporating Riggs's rhythms and regional dialects directly into their lyrics without much change.

SUGGESTED READINGS

Braunlich, Phyllis Cole. *Haunted by Home: The Life and Letters of Lynn Riggs*. Norman: University of Oklahoma Press, 1988.
Wilk, M. *The Story of "Oklahoma!"* New York: Grove Press, 1993.

—Anne K. Kaler

See also American identity: Midwest; Riggs, Lynn

Group, The

AUTHOR: Mary McCarthy (1912-1989)
FIRST PUBLISHED: 1963
IDENTITIES: European American; Northeast; women

Mary McCarthy's *The Group* traces eight Vassar students from 1933, the year of their graduation, to 1940, as each struggles to find her identity in society. It opens at the wedding of Kay Leiland Strong, one of the most vibrant and daring members of the group. At Vassar, the eight had shared a dorm and had been considered members of the student body's elite. They were all attractive, intellectual, envied, and members of privileged, monied classes.

After graduation, each felt a need to distinguish herself, to attain an identity separate from college and from parents. They believed themselves, McCarthy tells the reader, a different breed. Each planned to work, in a time when the more common expectation for such women was marriage, and to contribute to society.

The story is told in the third person, using a variety of voices. Each character assumes the central role at some point during the novel, exposing her personal values and attitudes, many of which are conventional, even stereotypical. As a result, some critics describe the novel as full of clichés, yet McCarthy has brilliantly mimicked the problems and worries of the different characters, revealing flaws, excuses, self-delusions. The novel's irony lies in the difference between the characters' perceptions and desires and reality, which is clear to the reader.

For example, Dottie loses her virginity in an attempt to be modern and adult. She spends much of that fateful evening in a fantasy conversation with her mother. Later on, the reader discovers that her mother is not only equally modern but also possibly wiser as well. Dottie soon settles for marriage to an older man in spite of her continued fascination for her first lover. She is afraid to find an identity on her own. In fact, in spite of the idealistic goals the group sets forth at Kay's wedding, most settle for marriage and family. They find themselves trapped by the expectations of family and society. Priss eventually quits the job she loves to become a full-time mother. She and her son even become an experiment in child rearing for her husband, a pediatrician with theories.

The novel ends as the group gathers again, this time at Kay's funeral. McCarthy makes it clear that it is not easy for a woman to find her identity in the society of this period, no matter how privileged and bright she may be. *The Group* received much advance publicity and went almost immediately to the top of the best-seller list. Its frank portrayals of sex and sexuality, virginity, and birth control contributed to its initial appeal. Women's roles were changing, both in literature and society, and *The Group* provided an intriguing portrait of the problems relating to this emerging independence and sexuality.

SUGGESTED READINGS

Brightman, Carol. *Writing Dangerously: Mary McCarthy and Her World*. New York: Clarkston Potter, 1992.

Gelderman, Carol. *Mary McCarthy: A Life*. New York: St. Martin's Press, 1988.

Hardy, Willene. *Mary McCarthy*. New York: Frederick Ungar, 1981.

McKenzie, Barbara. *Mary McCarthy*. New York: Twayne, 1967.

—Mary Mahony

See also American identity: Northeast; Feminism; McCarthy, Mary; *Memories of a Catholic Girlhood*

Growing Up in Minnesota: Ten Writers Remember Their Childhoods

EDITOR: Chester G. Anderson (1923-   )
FIRST PUBLISHED: 1976
IDENTITIES: Midwest; Native American

Growing Up in Minnesota: Ten Writers Remember Their Childhoods is a collection of regional autobiographical stories, including contributions by Meridel Le Sueur, Harrison E. Salisbury, Keith Gunderson, Robert Bly, and others. Native American author Gerald Vizenor's story, "I Know What You Mean, Erdupps MacChurbbs: Autobiographical Myths and Metaphors," roughly outlines this prominent writer's life, beginning with his father's brutal murder, at age twenty-six, in a downtown Minneapolis alley in 1936. Vizenor is a mixed-blood Ojibwa-Chippewa.

Vizenor's story progresses through a series of vignettes that describe how powerful people take advantage of the weak. As a boy, he tangles with Mean Nettles, the local bully, gets caught shoplifting, is the victim of a demeaning practical joke, visits a house of prostitution for the first time, and goes squirrel hunting. After his mother leaves his stepfather, Vizenor is beaten by the abusive man. Vizenor leaves home and only returns after careful negotiations that establish him as his stepfather's equal.

The title character of the story, Erdupps MacChurbbs, is a little woodland person the young Vizenor conjures in his imagination. Vizenor imagines this person in order to escape the violence of powerful people who are dominated by one vision of the world. Erdupps appears at key moments in Vizenor's life. A trickster from Native American lore, Erdupps uses humor and stories to balance good and evil energies and reinvent the world. At a militant American Indian Movement protest, Erdupps encourages Vizenor to act more like a trickster: "You have given too much thought in your life to the violence of terminal believers! Show more humor and give yourself more time for the little people and compassionate trickery." Terminal believers are victimizers who dominate others and believe in their own natural superiority.

Through the various pieces of Vizenor's autobiography, the ironic spirit of the woodland sprite floats between words and dreams in its mission to subvert the logic of terminal believers. For Vizenor, who accepts Erdupps' advice to act like a trickster, tricksters signal an end to the domination of terminal creeds, which cannot endure humor and play. The trickster imagination becomes a means of survival and control. Vizenor's trickster autobiography is a way to evade victimization.

SUGGESTED READINGS

Coltelli, Laura, ed. *Winged Words: American Indian Writers Speak*. Lincoln: University of Nebraska Press, 1990.

McCaffery, Larry, and Tom Marshall. "Head Water: An Interview with Gerald Vizenor." *Chicago Review* 39, nos. 3-4 (Summer-Fall, 1993): 50-54.

Ruoff, A. LaVonne Brown. "Gerald Vizenor: Compassionate Trickster." *Studies in American Indian Literature* 9 (1986): 52-63.

Vizenor, Gerald, ed. *Narrative Chance: Postmodern Discourses on Native American Indian Literatures*. Norman: University of Oklahoma Press, 1993.

—*Trey Strecker*

See also *Interior Landscapes*; Native American identity; Vizenor, Gerald; *Wordarrows*

H

H. D. (Hilda Doolittle)

BORN: Bethlehem, Pennsylvania; September 10, 1886
DIED: Zurich, Switzerland; September 27, 1961
PRINCIPAL WORKS: *Sea Garden*, 1916; *Hymen*, 1921; *Heliodora and Other Poems*, 1924; *Collected Poems of H. D.*, 1925; *Palimpsest*, 1926; *Red Roses for Bronze*, 1929; *The Walls Do Not Fall*, 1944; *Tribute to the Angels*, 1945; *The Flowering of the Rod*, 1946; *Tribute to Freud*, 1956; *Helen in Egypt*, 1961; *Trilogy*, 1973; *End to Torment: A Memoir of Ezra Pound*, 1979; *HERmione*, 1981 (*Her*, 1984); *Collected Poems, 1912-1944*, 1983; *Selected Poems*, 1988
IDENTITIES: European American; family; gay, lesbian, and bisexual; women
SIGNIFICANT ACHIEVEMENT: H. D.'s poems, fiction, and nonfiction are noteworthy for their exploration of feminine identity.

From her early childhood onward, H. D. was aware of others' expectations of her. Her mother, a devoutly religious woman, was a highly conventional wife, and her father, an astronomer at the University of Pennsylvania, hoped his daughter would be an important scientist. After her study at Bryn Mawr College, however, H. D. began pursuing poetic goals. In 1911, she went to Europe and decided to remain there among the many other expatriate American writers.

In 1913, Hilda Doolittle submitted some of her poems for publication under the pen name H. D., a name that was given to her by her onetime fiancé, the poet Ezra Pound. Pound and other male poets and thinkers always influenced H. D.'s life and writing; however, she made deliberate efforts to find a name and a voice for herself as a woman author among these strong male influences. She would remain close to Pound for years to come, but in 1913 H. D. married another poet, Richard Aldington. Her first collection of poems, *Sea Garden*, appeared in 1916, and she published a number of additional volumes within a decade, including *Hymen* (1921), *Heliodora and Other Poems*, and *Collected Poems of H. D.*

Near the end of her marriage to Aldington, in 1918, H. D. met the woman who would be her lifelong companion—Bryher (Annie Winifred Ellerman MacPherson). That year and the following one would bring a number of dramatic events for her, including the deaths of her father and brother, the birth of her daughter, Frances Perdita, and a life-threatening case of pneumonia. In 1920, Bryher took H. D. to Greece to recuperate physically and emotionally.

Known during her lifetime as a poet, H. D. also wrote a number of autobiographical and semiautobiographical novels. Two of the most significant, written in the 1920's, are *Palimpsest* and *HERmione*. In addition, she composed a number of essays on film and acted in several experimental films, including *Borderline* (1930), produced by her friend Kenneth MacPherson. Two additional experiences influenced much of her later work: psychoanalysis with Sigmund Freud in the 1930's and living in London during the German air raids of World War II. The war produced the three collections of poems that became *Trilogy* (1942-1944), and Freud's influence on her writing is clear in *Helen in Egypt* (1961). *Helen in Egypt*, a reconsideration of the story of Helen, was the last of her works to be published during her lifetime.

SUGGESTED READINGS

Guest, Barbara. *Herself Defined: The Poet H. D. and Her World*. Garden City, N.Y.: Doubleday, 1984.
Robinson, Janice S. *H. D.: The Life and Work of an American Poet*. Boston: Houghton Mifflin, 1982.

—*Amy Carolyn Fuqua*

See also *Bildungsroman* and *Künstlerroman*; Bisexual identity; Expatriate identity; Freud, Sigmund

H. D., poetry of

AUTHOR: H. D. (Hilda Doolittle, 1886-1961)

PRINCIPAL WORKS: *Sea Garden*, 1916; *Hymen*, 1921; *Heliodora and Other Poems*, 1924; *Collected Poems of H. D.*, 1925; *Red Roses for Bronze*, 1929; *The Walls Do Not Fall*, 1944; *Tribute to the Angels*, 1945; *The Flowering of the Rod*, 1946; *Helen in Egypt*, 1961; *Trilogy*, 1973; *Collected Poems, 1912-1944*, 1983; *Selected Poems*, 1988

IDENTITIES: European American; gay, lesbian, and bisexual; women

The first poems published by Hilda Doolittle—whose pen name was H. D.—were what she and her contemporaries called Imagist. Imagist poems emphasize one powerful image, natural rhythm, and a careful economy of words. Imagism dominates the poems of her first book, *Sea Garden*, and traces of it continue throughout her work. The titles of her next major volumes—*Hymen* and *Heliodora and Other Poems*—reveal her lifelong interest in Greek literature and in particular female figures from mythology, with whom she often identified herself.

Nearly all H. D.'s poetry is about woman's identity. In some poems, she reconstructs myths of women who are trying to understand their own experiences. In other poems, the subject of womanhood is less obvious. Particularly in the early poems, H. D. endows objects from nature with subtle feminine qualities. Most of H. D.'s writer friends were male, but she described her beliefs about her writing as a specifically womanly activity. In her 1919 notebooks, she describes her inspiration as a "vision of the womb and vision of the brain."

From about 1925 until World War II, H. D. published only one volume of poetry, *Red Roses for Bronze*, which contains many of her usual subjects but written in a new style dominated by the repetition of words and phrases. With the advent of World War II and because of her traumatic experiences then in London, she found her voice and wrote what many believe are her best works—*The Walls Do Not Fall*, *Tribute to the Angels*, and *The Flowering of the Rod*. At the beginning of these poems, published later as *Trilogy* (1973), H. D. directly addresses the woman poet's struggle to find a voice in the modern age. She creates that voice, in part, by resurrecting lost pagan myths of women, which she believes have been overshadowed by the male-oriented stories of Christianity.

H. D.'s last major works of poetry include *Helen in Egypt*, which, like many of her earlier, shorter poems, is a retelling of a classic myth from a woman's perspective. As in *Trilogy*, themes of historical and religious continuity compose a part of a female speaker's quest for identity. H. D.'s interest in Freudian psychology is especially clear in this work. Her *Collected Poems: 1912-1944* contains all her poems up to those in *Trilogy*, including many pre-World War II poems not published during her lifetime.

SUGGESTED READINGS

DuPlessis, Rachel Blau. *H. D.: The Career of That Struggle*. Brighton, England: Harvester, 1986.

Friedman, Susan Stanford, and Rachel Blau DuPlessis, eds. *Signets: Reading H. D.* Madison: University of Wisconsin Press, 1990.

Fritz, Angela DiPace. *Thought and Vision: A Critical Reading of H. D.'s Poetry*. Washington, D.C.: Catholic University of America Press, 1988.

—*Amy Carolyn Fuqua*

See also Bisexual identity; Feminism; Freud, Sigmund; Religion and identity

Hagedorn, Jessica Tarahata

BORN: Manila, Philippines; 1949

PRINCIPAL WORKS: *Dangerous Music*, 1975; *Pet Food and Tropical Apparitions*, 1981; *Dogeaters*, 1990; *Danger and Beauty*, 1993; *Charlie Chan Is Dead: An Anthology of Contemporary Asian American Fiction*, 1993 (editor)

IDENTITIES: Pacific Islander; women

SIGNIFICANT ACHIEVEMENT: Hagedorn expresses the "tough and noble" lives of Asian immigrants who feel only partially assimilated.

Born and raised in the Philippines, Jessica Hagedorn experienced the United States through the eyes of her mother and through images provided by American textbooks and movies. "The colonization of our imagination was relentless," she has said. Only when she started living in California in 1963 did she begin to appreciate what was precious in the Filipino extended family, a cultural feature partially left behind. In California, she began to feel allied with persons of various national origins who challenged American myths. Kenneth Rexroth, who had been patron of the Beat generation in San Francisco during the 1950's, introduced her to the poets who gathered at the City Lights bookstore. In 1973, Rexroth helped her publish her first poems, later collectively titled "The Death of Anna May Wong." Her principal concern was the exploitation of Filipino workers.

Her poetry became more and more influenced by the rhythms of popular street music. In 1975, she gathered together a volume of prose and poetry called *Dangerous Music*. That same year Hagedorn formed her band, The West Coast Gangster Choir, and sang lyrics of her own invention with them. In 1978, she left San Francisco without her band and established herself in New York City. There, along with Ntozake Shange and Thulani Davis, she performed her poetry at Joseph Papp's Public Theater. In 1981, Hagedorn published her second collection of mixed prose and poetry. During the 1980's she worked on her first novel, *Dogeaters*, which exposes corruption in her homeland as a result of Ferdinand Marcos' years of "constitutional authoritarianism." *Dogeaters* is also a novel that she has described as a love letter to her motherland. The characters in her novel for the most part are trapped by consumerism; this plight is caused by the Filipinos' long history as a colony and by their dreams of success, which too often come from American soap operas. Hagedorn's work is devoted to substituting for such stereotypes the complexities visible among people in Metro Manila and the urban reaches of the American coasts. Her anthology, *Charlie Chan Is Dead*, signifies a new image for Asians.

SUGGESTED READINGS

Casper, Leonard. *Sunsurfers Seen from Afar: Critical Essays 1991-1996*. Metro Manila, Philippines: Anvil, 1996.

Kim, Elaine H. *Asian American Literature*. Philadelphia: Temple University Press, 1982.

Zapanta Manlapaz, Edna. *Songs of Ourselves*. Metro Manila, Philippines: Anvil, 1994.

—Leonard Casper

See also *Aiiieeeee!*; Asian American identity: Pacific Islands; Brainard, Cecilia Manguerra; Rosca, Ninotchka

Handmaid's Tale, The

AUTHOR: Margaret Atwood (1939-   )
FIRST PUBLISHED: 1985
IDENTITIES: Religion; women

Dire explorations of future societies, dystopias, have usually been written by and about men. What future hell awaits women? Margaret Atwood asked, after surveying major news stories of the early 1980's: industrial pollution, surrogate parenthood, AIDS, conservative backlash, televangelism, and oppressive regimes in Argentina and Iran. *The Handmaid's Tale* is her imaginative answer. In this bleak narrative, the government of the United States has been overthrown by the Republic of Gilead, a theocracy based on total conformity and reactionary Christianity. With human fertility reduced, by toxic pollution, to crisis point, the fecund womb is now Gilead's most valuable resource. Consequently, it has been nationalized. A Puritan polygamy, inspired by the Old Testament and by Mormon pioneers in Utah, has been imposed as the norm.

Offred, who tells her story, is an official womb, a red-clad handmaid. Once she had a family identity, but now even her personal name is unknown. She is simply "of-Fred," bearing the name of the Commander to whom she is assigned. Her chief duty is regular participation in the

"Ceremony," during which Fred, in the presence of his wife and servants, must attempt to impregnate Offred. If he should succeed, her offspring, like those of handmaids of old, will become the possession of his wife, Serena Joy, once a televangelist known for her tears and songs.

Daily life in the Republic of Gilead is detailed. Handmaids purchase necessities from shops called All Flesh, Loaves and Fishes, and Milk and Honey; there are no luxuries. Women are forced to attend brutal ceremonies in which wrongdoers are punished. Routinely, handmaids visit the wall—once apparently a part of Harvard campus—where criminals are impaled on hooks as examples for all.

Offred's passive acceptance of her lot is only temporary. Eventually she communicates with the underground, indulges in an illicit affair of passion, and even visits a forbidden brothel with the Commander. Then the account of her increasingly dangerous life abruptly ends. Why was she silenced? Was she whisked away to Canadian sanctuary or was she betrayed?

Like captives before her, this handmaid has managed to leave behind her narrative, which is scrutinized by the Twelfth Symposium of Gileadean Studies, meeting in 2195. Atwood records conference proceedings, noting satirically how the chilling records of the defunct theocracy are now the primary sources for academic study far removed from the pain of those who lived in Gilead.

Like Aldous Huxley's *Brave New World* (1932), Atwood's novel combines dire prediction with considerable satire. Atwood's skill at character development, atmospheric description, and narrative structure give her book a virtue other dystopic novels rarely possess.

SUGGESTED READINGS

Hite, Molly. *The Other Side of the Story: Structures and Strategies of Contemporary Feminist Narrative*. Ithaca, N.Y.: Cornell University Press, 1989.

St. Andrews, Bonnie. *Forbidden Fruit: On the Relationship Between Women and Knowledge in Doris Lessing, Selma Lagerlof, Kate Chopin, Margaret Atwood*. Troy, N.Y.: Whitston, 1986.

Wilson, Sharon Rose. *Margaret Atwood's Fairy-Tale Sexual Politics*. Jackson: University Press of Mississippi, 1993.

—*Allene Phy-Olsen*

See also Christianity and Christian Fundamentalism; Patriarchy and matriarchy; Slave narratives

Hansberry, Lorraine

BORN: Chicago, Illinois; May 19, 1930

DIED: New York, New York; January 12, 1965

PRINCIPAL WORKS: *A Raisin in the Sun*, pr., pb. 1959; *The Sign in Sidney Brustein's Window*, pr. 1964, pb. 1965; *To Be Young, Gifted and Black*, pr. 1969, pb. 1971

IDENTITIES: African American; gay, lesbian, and bisexual; women

SIGNIFICANT ACHIEVEMENT: Hansberry is credited with being the first African American woman playwright to have a play produced on Broadway.

With the successful Broadway opening in 1959 of *A Raisin in the Sun*, Lorraine Hansberry became a major voice in behalf of racial, sexual, economic, and class justice. During Hansberry's childhood, her father, a well-to-do real estate broker, and her mother, a schoolteacher, were involved in politics and were active supporters of the National Association for the Advancement of Colored People (NAACP) and its causes. Hansberry grew up in a Chicago household where racial issues, oppression, African American identity, and the struggle against discrimination were major concerns. Her early intellectual development was influenced by her uncle, William Leo Hansberry, a professor and scholar at Howard University and writer of African history. He put Hansberry in contact with her African roots and introduced her to a world of articulate black artists and thinkers who personified the struggle to overcome discrimination in American society.

Hansberry was a student in the segregated Chicago public school system. She proceeded to the University of Wisconsin, where she became the first African American woman to live in her dormitory. At the university she was active in politics and developed an interest in the theater and its power.

Dropping out of school, Hansberry moved to New York and became a writer and associate editor for the progressive newspaper *Freedom*. She championed civil rights causes, writing not only on behalf of blacks but also on behalf of other socially repressed groups, including women and gays. With encouragement and inspiration from such luminaries as W. E. B. Du Bois, Langston Hughes, and Paul Robeson, her active professional and intellectual life in Harlem soon blossomed into stories, poems, and plays.

After marrying Robert Nemiroff in 1953, Hansberry left *Freedom* to devote all her attention to writing. Drawing upon her Chicago experiences, she completed *A Raisin in the Sun*, a play that explores the tensions that arise as a black family in Chicago tries to escape the ghetto. The family faces white hostility as it plans to move into a white neighborhood. The play was a phenomenal success.

Hansberry's second Broadway production, *The Sign in Sidney Brustein's Window*, explores such topics as prostitution, marriage, homosexuality, and anti-Semitism. The play's depictions of the plight of those oppressed and discriminated against and of the nature of society's reaction to injustice and prejudice are vivid and thoughtful. Hansberry died from cancer at the age of only thirty-four. Her call for justice and human sympathy continues to reverberate in the work she left behind.

SUGGESTED READINGS

Carter, Steven R. *Hansberry's Drama: Commitment and Complexity*. Champaign: University of Illinois Press, 1991.

Cheney, Anne. *Lorraine Hansberry*. Boston: G. K. Hall, 1984.

Wilkerson, Margaret B. "The Dark Vision of Lorraine Hansberry: Excerpts from a Literary Biography." *Massachusetts Review* 28 (Winter, 1987): 642-650.

—Richard M. Leeson

See also African American identity; American identity: Northeast; *Raisin in the Sun, A*

Harjo, Joy

BORN: Tulsa, Oklahoma; May 9, 1951

PRINCIPAL WORKS: *She Had Some Horses*, 1983; *In Mad Love and War*, 1990; *The Woman Who Fell from the Sky*, 1994

IDENTITIES: Native American; women

SIGNIFICANT ACHIEVEMENT: Harjo's poetry has won acclaim for its substance, style, and themes combining many elements of Native American and mainstream American experience.

Joy Harjo's collections of poetry express a close relationship to the environment and the particularities of the Native American and white cultures from which she is descended. She is an enrolled member of the Creek tribe, the mother of two children (a son, Phil and a daughter, Rainy Dawn), and a grandmother. Various forms of art were always a part of her life, even in childhood. Her grandmother and aunt were painters. In high school, she trained as a dancer and toured as a dancer and actress with one of the first Indian dance troupes in the country. When her tour ended, she returned to Oklahoma, where her son was born when she was seventeen years old. She left her son's father to move to New Mexico, enrolling at the university as a pre-med student. After one semester, she decided that her interest in art was compelling enough to engage in its formal study.

Educated at the Institute of American Indian Arts in Santa Fe, New Mexico, where she later worked as an instructor, she received a bachelor's degree from the University of New Mexico and a master's degree in fine arts from the University of Iowa. She was a professor of English at both the University of Arizona and the University of New Mexico.

Harjo has received numerous awards for her writing, including the William Carlos Williams award from the Poetry Society of America, the Delmore Schwartz Award, the American Indian Distinguished Achievement in the Arts Award, and two creative writing fellowships from the National Endowment for the Arts. Harjo's poetry has been increasingly influenced by her interest

*Native American
author Joy Harjo.*

in music, especially jazz. She plays the saxophone in a band, Poetic Justice, that combines the musical influences of jazz and reggae with her poetry. Many of her poems are tributes to the various musicians that have influenced her work, including saxophonists John Coltrane and Jim Pepper.

The history and mythology of her people and the current state of their oppression also are prominent themes in her work. As she states in the explanation of her poem "Witness," "The Indian wars never ended in this country . . . we were hated for our difference by our enemies."

SUGGESTED READINGS

Leen, Mary. "An Art of Saying." *American Indian Quarterly* 19, no. 1 (Winter, 1995): 1-16.
Smith, Stephanie. "Joy Harjo." *Poets and Writers* 21, no. 4 (July/August, 1993): 23-27.

—Robert Haight

See also Feminism; *In Mad Love and War*; Native American identity; *Woman Who Fell from the Sky, The*; Women and identity

Harlem Renaissance

IDENTITIES: African American

DEFINITION: The Harlem Renaissance was the era during the 1920's and early 1930's that marked the prolific and innovative production of African American literary, artistic, and musical works.

The Harlem Renaissance had social and historical causes, among them the arrival to Harlem of many rural, Southern, African Americans who were migrating to the urban North in search of better economic and social conditions. World War I and the generally improving economy of the 1920's

Origins

inspired hope of finding jobs and a better life in New York City. Most of the writers, artists, and musicians of the Harlem Renaissance were born elsewhere. Their creations did not always center on Harlem, either, but the acknowledged focal point of African American culture during the 1920's and 1930's was Harlem.

Redefining African American identity

Harlem Renaissance writers boldly rejected prevalent stereotypes that portrayed African Americans as nothing more than pitiable societal problems. Harlem Renaissance writers blended awareness of their racial heritage and progress with their considerable literary talents in efforts to present realistic images of black life. Harlem Renaissance authors built upon the rich tradition of strong, persevering, African American characters established in nineteenth century slave narratives and autobiographies by Frederick Douglass, Harriet Jacobs, and others. Writers of the Harlem Renaissance also could discredit literary stereotypes by recalling fiction by William Wells Brown, Harriet Wilson, and Charles Chesnutt, among others.

Unlike earlier African American writers, Harlem Renaissance authors found that their works received greater exposure; during the 1920's and early 1930's, major publishers produced books by African Americans with an unprecedented frequency. Black writers had improved opportunities to accomplish two major goals: to portray African American life accurately and to promote African American culture. Collectively, works of the Harlem Renaissance provide a panorama of early twentieth century black life. Characters vary from ones whose deeds are virtuous to those whose actions are questionable, although in general, Harlem Renaissance literature presents more upright characters. They represent all levels of society, socially and economically. For the first time in American literature, there are consistent attempts to portray African Americans in urban locations. The works of Harlem Renaissance writers proudly display the great variety in African American life and assert that regardless of their status, African Americans are worthy of respect.

Harlem Renaissance writers wrote considerably about the double identity of being black and American. This dual identity could be cause for rejoicing, as in James Weldon Johnson and John Rosamond Johnson's "Lift Every Voice and Sing" (1900), known as the black national anthem. Other times being black and American could be cause for despair, as many African American World War I veterans discovered upon their return to the United States. The veterans hoped that their service to their country would result in better employment and housing opportunities. Instead, the veterans were still treated as second-class citizens. Harlem Renaissance writers recorded the pleasures and pains resulting from dual identity.

Mentors

Four prominent visionaries articulated the need for an African American awakening, created influential works, and promoted the works of new and younger authors. The most influential mentor was W. E. B. Du Bois, who was a prolific writer and a civil rights leader. Du Bois, who called for an African American literary renaissance as early as 1920, served as editor of *Crisis*, one of the two major black periodicals that included Harlem Renaissance fiction and poetry. The second periodical, *Opportunity*, was edited by Charles S. Johnson, who was also instrumental in promoting Harlem Renaissance writers. Du Bois' novel *Dark Princess: A Romance* (1928), published during the Harlem Renaissance, presents an African American protagonist who realizes that racism extends beyond America and that Third World people should unite to end racial oppression.

Another architect of the movement was Jessie Redmon Fauset, who believed that portrayals of African Americans must be written by African Americans. As literary editor for *Crisis* from 1919 to 1926, Fauset promoted the talents of Langston Hughes, Countée Cullen, and others. As author of four novels, Fauset shows the impact of race and gender limitations on African American women. Her novels, often about middle-class blacks (a first), have such themes as racial discrimination in the North, racial identity, heritage, miscegenation, and blacks passing for white. Fauset's *There Is Confusion* (1924) was the first novel by a woman to be published during the Harlem Renaissance. Her other novels are *Plum Bun: A Novel Without a Moral* (1929), *The Chinaberry Tree: A Novel of American Life* (1931), and *Comedy: American Style* (1933). University professor and literary critic Alain Locke played a pivotal role in the Harlem Renaissance. He edited a special issue of *Survey Graphic* (March, 1925), a magazine that until then had ignored black culture. It became the magazine's most widely read issue. Among the authors included were Cullen, Du Bois, Angelina Grimké, Hughes, James Weldon Johnson, Claude McKay, Anne Spencer, Jean Toomer, and Walter White. Building upon the success of the *Survey Graphic* issue, Locke edited an anthology, *The New Negro* (1925), an expanded version of the magazine issue that includes additional Harlem Renaissance writers such as Arna Bontemps, Fauset, Zora Neale Hurston, Georgia Douglas Johnson, Helene Johnson, Willis Richardson, and Eric Walrond. *The New Negro* remains the Harlem Renaissance's landmark publication.

The fourth inspirer of the Harlem Renaissance was James Weldon Johnson. Originally published anonymously, *The Autobiography of an Ex-Coloured Man* (1912) was reprinted in 1927 with Johnson's name. The novel involves a character's regretting his decision to pass for white after witnessing a lynching, yet he is afraid to reveal his true identity. Johnson's greatest Harlem Renaissance contributions were poetic. *The Book of American Negro Poetry* (1922) is the first major collection of black poetry. *God's Trombones* (1927) transforms seven folk sermons into poetry. Included in this volume is Johnson's well-known "The Creation."

Poetry

The era's poets included Sterling Brown, Grimké, Georgia Douglas Johnson, Helene Johnson, and Spencer. Major poets included Cullen, McKay, and Hughes. Cullen published three volumes of poetry during the era: *Color* (1925), *Copper Sun* (1927), and *The Black Christ and Other Poems* (1929). Poems such as "From the Dark Tower," "Heritage," and "Yet Do I Marvel" reflect Cullen's concerns about racial identity and his role as a poet. McKay's two volumes of poetry published during the time of the Harlem Renaissance are *Spring in New Hampshire and Other Poems* (1920) and *Harlem Shadows* (1922), which has been heralded as one of the era's finest works. Much of McKay's and Cullen's poetry focuses on the dual-identity issue and the notion that blacks are aliens in America. The militant "If We Must Die" remains McKay's most widely known poem. The most famous Harlem Renaissance writer, who was also called the poet laureate of Harlem, was Hughes. A prolific writer, Hughes published two volumes of poetry during the era: *The Weary Blues* (1926) and *Fine Clothes to the Jew* (1927). His poems such as "The Negro Speaks of Rivers" show racial pride and perseverance; poems such as "Prayer Meeting" provide glimpses into everyday Harlem life.

Novels

In addition to Fauset and Johnson, many other novelists published during the Harlem Renaissance, such as Nella Larsen, who wrote *Quicksand* (1928) and *Passing* (1929), and White, author of *The Fire in the Flint* (1924) and *Flight* (1926). Fauset, Johnson, Larsen, and White's works often represent the African American middle class. Fauset and Larsen's novels also reveal the lives of African American women. Other novels satirize whites' and blacks' obsession with color. Illustrating this category are Wallace Thurman's *The Blacker the Berry* (1929) and George Schulyer's *Black No More: Being an Account of the Strange and Wonderful Workings of Science in the Land of the Free* (1931).

In addition to satire, there are realistic novels of place. Examples include Cullen's *One Way to Heaven* (1932), Hurston's *Jonah's Gourd Vine* (1934), Thurman's *Infants of the Spring* (1932), and Jean Toomer's *Cane* (1923). African Americans in foreign locales are represented by Du Bois' *Dark Princess* (1928), Claude McKay's *Banjo: A Story Without a Plot* (1929) and *Banana Bottom* (1933). The coming-of-age novel is represented by Hughes' *Not Without Laughter* (1930). Rudolph Fisher's *The Conjure-Man Dies: A Mystery Tale of Dark Harlem* (1932) is the first African American detective novel. In addition to poetry and novels, writers of the Harlem Renaissance created short stories, essays, biographies, and autobiographies. The Harlem Renaissance lives on in its writings.

SUGGESTED READINGS

Andrews, William L., ed. *Classic Fiction of the Harlem Renaissance.* New York: Oxford University Press, 1994. Introduces seven of the era's most famous authors.

Huggins, Nathan Irvin. *Harlem Renaissance.* New York: Oxford University Press, 1971. A pioneering historical study of the era.

_____, ed. *Voices from the Harlem Renaissance.* New York: Oxford University Press, 1995. Anthologizes 120 works according to theme.

Kellner, Bruce, ed. *The Harlem Renaissance: A Historical Dictionary for the Era.* New York: Methuen, 1987. Presents information in an easy-to-find format.

Knopf, Marcy, ed. *The Sleeper Wakes: Harlem Renaissance Stories by Women.* New Brunswick, N.J.: Rutgers University Press, 1993. Acknowledges the important but traditionally overlooked contributions of Harlem Renaissance women writers.

Lewis, David Levering, ed. *The Portable Harlem Renaissance Reader.* New York: Viking, 1994. Anthologizes forty-five writers of the era and is a valuable resource for any student of the Harlem Renaissance.

_____. *When Harlem Was in Vogue.* New York: Oxford University Press, 1989. Is regarded as a classic study of the Harlem Renaissance; this historical overview is an excellent introduction to the era.

Locke, Alain, ed. *The New Negro.* New York: Atheneum, 1968. A reprint of the Harlem Renaissance's first anthology.

Turner, Darwin T. *In a Minor Chord: Three Afro-American Writers and Their Search for Identity.* Carbondale: Southern Illinois University Press, 1971. Discusses Toomer, Cullen, and Hurston.

Watson, Steven. *The Harlem Renaissance: Hub of African American Culture, 1920-1930.* New York: Pantheon Books, 1995. Provides a historical and entertaining introduction to the era.

—Linda M. Carter

See also African American identity; Bontemps, Arna Wendell; Cullen, Countée; Du Bois, W. E. B.; Fauset, Jessie Redmon; Fisher, Rudolph; Hughes, Langston; Hurston, Zora Neale; Larsen, Nella

Harper, Michael S.

BORN: Brooklyn, New York; March 18, 1938

PRINCIPAL WORKS: *Dear John, Dear Coltrane*, 1970; *History Is Your Own Heartbeat*, 1971; *Song: I Want a Witness*, 1972; *Debridement*, 1973; *Nightmare Begins Responsibility*, 1974; *Images of Kin: New and Selected Poems*, 1977; *Rhode Island: Eight Poems*, 1981; *Healing Songs for the Inner Ear*, 1985

IDENTITIES: African American; European American

SIGNIFICANT ACHIEVEMENT: Harper's poetry synthesizes diverse ethnic, racial, and historic components to create an inclusive perspective on American culture.

The first son in his middle-class African American family, Michael S. Harper was encouraged to follow the career path of his grandfather and great-grandfather: medicine. An intense interest in the rhythms of language and in exploring the apparent schisms in American society, however, led Harper to his dual vocations of writer and scholar.

In the Harper home, music and poetry were important parts of family life. Poems by Langston Hughes were a familiar presence in Harper's childhood home. Harper's parents also owned an extensive collection of contemporary jazz recordings. The poet recalled spending many happy hours listening to, among others, Bessie Smith, Billie Holiday, Charlie Parker, and John Coltrane.

As an adolescent, Harper was forced into an awareness of racism in America. The family moved from New York to West Los Angeles, where African Americans were the targets of racial violence. During high school, Harper began experimenting with creative writing. In college, he continued writing in addition to working full time for the post office. He later attended the famous Iowa Writers Workshop at the University of Iowa in Iowa City.

As the only African American student in the poetry and fiction workshop classes, Harper endured misunderstanding and prejudice. These experiences motivated him to confront the dualism inherent in being an African American writer. Harper refused exclusive containment in either the

African American or in the American category. Rather, he affirmed his identity in both groups.

Harper interrupted his studies at Iowa to enter the student teacher program at Pasadena City College in 1962. He became the first African American to complete the program, and after finishing his courses at Iowa, he accepted an instructorship at Contra Costa College in San Pablo, California. This was the beginning of an extensive and distinguished teaching career, including professorships at Colgate University, Brown University, and Harvard University. In addition to eight volumes of poetry, Harper has contributed to numerous journals and anthologies and has edited several anthologies of poetry.

SUGGESTED READINGS

Harper, Michael S. "My Poetic Technique and the Humanization of the American Audience." In *Black American Literature and Humanism*, edited by Miller R. Baxter. Lexington: University Press of Kentucky, 1981.

Stepto, Robert B. "Let's Call Your Mama and Other Lies About Michael S. Harper." *Callaloo* 13, no. 4 (Fall, 1990): 801-804.

Young, Al, Larry Kart, and Michael S. Harper. "Jazz and Letters: A Colloquy." *TriQuarterly* 68 (Winter, 1987): 118-158.

—*Anne B. Mangum*

See also African American identity; Harper, Michael S., poetry of; Hughes, Langston

Harper, Michael S., poetry of

AUTHOR: Michael S. Harper (1938-   )

PRINCIPAL WORKS: *Dear John, Dear Coltrane*, 1970; *History Is Your Own Heartbeat*, 1971; *Song: I Want a Witness*, 1972; *Debridement*, 1973; *Nightmare Begins Responsibility*, 1974; *Images of Kin: New and Selected Poems*, 1977; *Healing Song for the Inner Ear*, 1985

IDENTITIES: African American; European American

Michael S. Harper is a poet with a strong individual style. His poetry is notable for the variable rhythm of its lines. Harper's poems echo a variety of human speech patterns and rhythms. This characteristic distinguishes his rhythm from the more traditionally metric patterns of many poets. Harper's looser rhythms work along with such techniques as repetition, internal rhyme, and enjambment (lines flowing together without pause at the end) to modulate sound in the poem. Sound is important in Harper's poems; they are most effective when read aloud.

The content of Harper's poetry reflects a concern with unification. Harper's poetic speakers explore connections. For Harper, the poem evidences the connections between the poet's individual utterances and universal concerns that transcend time and place. A major theme through all of Harper's books is that of connections among racial and ethnic groups. Other major themes include the importance of an awareness of history, the relationship between the individual and the group, and the connections between one geographic location and another.

Harper's development of these major themes begins in *Dear John, Dear Coltrane*. The poems in this book pay homage to the greats of jazz and the blues. The musicians also represent individual and collective human achievement, achievement attained and achievement still possible.

The exploration of the individual's connection to history and possibility continues in *History Is Your Own Heartbeat*. This second book won the Poetry Award of the Black Academy of Arts and Letters. The idea that an awareness of individual and collective history is essential is further developed in *Song: I Want a Witness*. In the preface, Harper writes: "Where there is no history/ there is no metaphor." In other words, an individual ignorant of history has no basis for comparison (metaphors are comparisons), for testing feelings and attitudes.

In *Debridement* Harper narrows the theme of the importance of history to explore the historical relationships between black and white Americans. The poems collectively suggest that understanding of history is necessary for the individual's moving beyond misunderstanding and hatred. "Debridement" means surgically removing dead flesh from old wounds so that healing can begin.

In *Nightmare Begins Responsibility*, Harper metaphorically reviews his own personal history. In his two later books, *Images of Kin: New and Selected Poems* and *Healing Song for the Inner Ear*, Harper steps back somewhat from personal history to consider the universal traditions of black and white poets.

In addition to his books of thematically linked poetry, Harper has published in many journals and anthologies. His poems testify in the voice of the American trying to reconcile the past, present, and future of the individual's relationship with the nation.

SUGGESTED READINGS

Brown, Joseph A. "Their Long Scars Touch Ours: A Reflection on the Poetry of Michael Harper." *Callaloo* 9, no. 1 (Winter, 1986): 209-220.

Harper, Michael S. "It Is the Man/Woman Outside Who Judges: The Minority Writer's Perspective on Literature." *TriQuarterly* 65 (Winter, 1986): 57-65.

Lloyd, David. "Interview with Michael S. Harper." *TriQuarterly* 65 (Winter, 1986): 119-128.

—*Anne B. Mangum*

See also African American identity; Harper, Michael S.

Harris, Wilson

BORN: New Amsterdam, British Guiana (now Guyana); March 24, 1921

PRINCIPAL WORKS: *Palace of the Peacock*, 1960; *The Secret Ladder*, 1963; *Tradition, the Writer, and Society: Critical Essays*, 1967; *Fossil and Psyche*, 1974; *The Tree of the Sun*, 1978; *The Womb of Space*, 1983; *Carnival*, 1985

IDENTITIES: African American; Caribbean; European American; Native American

SIGNIFICANT ACHIEVEMENT: As philosopher, novelist, and critic, Harris imagines recent world history and colonialism in order to present a vision of a possible human community that celebrates multiple, mixed, and interrelating identities.

Wilson Harris is an extremely eclectic and expansive writer. In *The Womb of Space*, he writes that "literature is still constrained by regional and other conventional suffocating categories." Harris has spent his career attempting to transcend notions of genre, tradition, and discipline, constructing texts founded on philosophical speculation. Harris attempts, in his writing, to promote new models for civilization and for creative art.

Influenced by Carl Gustav Jung, Martin Buber, Elizabethan poetry, William Blake, Native American folklore, and nineteenth century expedition literature, Harris investigates the ambiguities of life and death, of history and innovation, of self and other, and of reality and illusion. Harris questions received concepts of origin, history, and reality. It is Harris' hope that such inquisitions of the self may prove crucial in the development of a radical revision of history, origin, and identity.

Opening with a series of nightmare vignettes that awaken into each other, the narrator of Harris' *Palace of the Peacock* declares: "I dreamt I awoke with one dead eye seeing and one living each closed." The novel hovers between reality and illusion, death and life, insight and blindness. It chronicles an expeditionary party's journey into the interior of Guyana. In this expedition into the territory of the self, each member of the party embodies a part of Guyanese identity. A European, an African, and a Native American set out together in a quest to retrieve renegade farmworkers but find along the way that they are, perhaps, the ghostly repetitions of a party that perished on the same river in the early days of European conquest. The allegorical and existential significances of the quest give Harris the opportunity to delve into the nature of narration, of time, of space, and of being. He asserts that humanity can alter fate through recognition of connections and by articulating and celebrating commonly held identities.

The themes *Palace of the Peacock* raises are also found in the novels that succeed it. In subsequent novels, Harris returns to elaborate and examine the psychological and existential structures by way of which identity ossifies and resists participation in change. By carefully constructing contradictory narrative puzzles, Harris leads his readers into ambiguous regions of understanding where opposites (life and death, reality and illusion, self and other) meet. It is his hope that such expeditions of the imagination will result in greater understanding of identity and community.

SUGGESTED READINGS

Drake, Sandra E. *Wilson Harris and the Modern Tradition: A New Architecture of the World.* Westport, Conn.: Greenwood Press, 1986.

Gilkes, Michael. *Wilson Harris and the Caribbean Novel.* New York: Longman, 1975.

Maes-Jelinek, Hena, ed. *Wilson Harris: The Uncompromising Imagination.* Aarhus, Denmark: Dangaroo, 1991.

Moore, Gerald. *The Chosen Tongue.* New York: Longman, 1969.

—Daniel M. Scott III

See also Colonialism; *Fossil and Psyche*; Multiculturalism; *Womb of Space, The*

Hawthorne, Nathaniel

BORN: Salem, Massachusetts; July 4, 1804

DIED: Plymouth, New Hampshire; May 19, 1864

PRINCIPAL WORKS: *Twice-Told Tales*, 1837 (expanded, 1842); *Mosses from an Old Manse*, 1846; *The Scarlet Letter*, 1850; *The House of the Seven Gables*, 1851; *The Blithedale Romance*, 1852; *The Marble Faun*, 1860

IDENTITIES: European American; Northeast; religion

SIGNIFICANT ACHIEVEMENT: Hawthorne's short stories and novels are among the best examples of American psychological fiction.

Born in Salem, Massachusetts, Nathaniel Hawthorne grew up surrounded by reminders of the town's infamous past and his own family's role in the Quaker persecutions and witch trials of the seventeenth century. By the time he was graduated from Bowdoin College in 1825, he had resolved to return to Salem, become a writer, and investigate the influence of the Puritan past on nineteenth century New England.

Hawthorne was a fundamentally reclusive person who avoided revealing himself to others except through the masks of his fiction. His persistent brooding over the historical sins of New England and his fascination with guilt and secrecy dominate his work as early as *Twice-Told Tales*, his first short-story collection. Including such early masterpieces as "The Minister's Black Veil" and "Wakefield," the volume reveals his continued interest in the ways characters confront their secrets or create new ways to conceal themselves from others.

After a stint in the Boston Custom House and a brief stay at the transcendentalist community Brook Farm, he married Sophia Peabody in 1842 and moved to Concord, Massachusetts. Life at the idyllic Old Manse, a house rented from Ralph Waldo Emerson, inspired him to happier celebrations of nature, but his persistent concern with the darker aspects of humanity soon reasserted itself. "Rappaccini's Daughter," written during this period, concerns a beautiful woman made poisonous by her father as part of a scientific experiment. She falls in love with a student, Giovanni, but the handsome young man is unable to distinguish between Beatrice's poisonous body and her innocent soul.

In 1846, financial difficulties forced Hawthorne back into government service, this time at the Salem Custom House, but in three years he was removed from office after a change in administration. His continued study of local history and his new understanding of community politics helped shape *The Scarlet Letter*, his first novel. In a similar vein, his second novel, *The House of the Seven Gables*, explores the effects of a family secret on the lives of nineteenth century descendants living in Salem. Many of Hawthorne's own questions about his background and the deeper character of his hometown are the foundation for the book's plot.

Still shy of public appearances, despite his duties as American consul in Liverpool, Hawthorne spent the bulk of his later years journalizing on life abroad and the effects of exile on personal and national character. His desire to question the secrets of individual personality never waned, and in later works he continued to search for what he had once called "the truth of the human heart."

SUGGESTED READINGS

Martin, Terence. *Nathaniel Hawthorne*. Boston: Twayne, 1983.
Mellow, James R. *Nathaniel Hawthorne in His Times*. Boston: Houghton Mifflin, 1980.
Turner, Arlin. *Nathaniel Hawthorne: A Biography*. New York: Oxford University Press, 1980.

—Clark Davis

See also *Marble Faun, The*; Puritan and Protestant tradition; *Scarlet Letter, The*

Hayden, Robert

BORN: Detroit, Michigan; August 4, 1913
DIED: Ann Arbor, Michigan; February 25, 1980
PRINCIPAL WORKS: *Heart-Shape in the Dust*, 1940; *The Lion and the Archer*, 1948; *Figure of Time*, 1955; *A Ballad of Remembrance*, 1962; *Selected Poems*, 1966; *Words in the Mourning Time*, 1970; *The Night-Blooming Cereus*, 1972; *Angle of Ascent: New and Selected Poems*, 1975; *American Journal*, 1978, 1982; *Collected Prose*, 1984; *Collected Poems*, 1985
IDENTITIES: African American
SIGNIFICANT ACHIEVEMENT: Hayden's poetry provides a learned, kind observer's view of major events and figures in American and African American history.

Robert Hayden's childhood independence was instrumental to his becoming a scholar and poet. He was reared in a poor Detroit neighborhood, where such distinctions were rare. Soon after he was born Asa Bundy Sheffey, Hayden was adopted by the Haydens, neighbors of his birth parents. A sufferer of extreme myopia as a child, Hayden was separated from his peers into a "sight conservation" class; although his handicap kept him from participating in most sports, the resulting time alone allowed him to read (especially poetry, which demanded less of his vision), write, and play the violin, thereby developing rhythmical and tonal sensitivities that would well serve his eventual vocation.

Several fortuitous events and encounters in Robert Hayden's life supported his choosing texts in African American history, especially the narratives of rebellious slaves, as fruitful subjects for his verse. After attending Detroit City College (which later became Wayne State University), Hayden, in 1936, began working for the Federal Writers' Project of the Works Progress Administration; he was assigned to research "Negro folklore." Two major figures encouraged his ensuing interest in African American history. The first, Erma Inez Morris, a pianist and a teacher in Detroit's public schools, became Hayden's wife and, for a time, his financial support. She also introduced her new husband to Countée Cullen, the Harlem Renaissance poet who admired Hayden's first book, *Heart-Shape in the Dust*, and who motivated Hayden to keep writing. Hayden also found inspiration from the British poet W. H. Auden, also a folklorist, who instructed Hayden at the University of Michigan when the younger poet began graduate work there.

In 1946, Hayden began a twenty-three-year tenure as a professor at Fisk College in segregated Nashville. During this time Hayden wrote steadily, despite being hampered by a heavy teaching load. The quality of Hayden's work was recognized internationally—it was broadcast by the British Broadcasting Company, and his 1962 book *A Ballad of Remembrance* won the Grand Prize for Poetry at the First World Festival of Negro Arts in Dakar, Senegal—before he was discovered in the United States. Eventual recognition included invitations to teach at several universities and to edit anthologies of work by his poetic heroes and contemporaries. The year that *Angle of Ascent* was published, 1975, Hayden was elected fellow of the Academy of American Poets and Appointed Consultant in Poetry to the Library of Congress.

Hayden's greatest personal successes, however, occurred in the last few months of his life. The poet was publicly celebrated both by President Jimmy Carter, at "A White House Salute to

American Poetry," and by his peers at the University of Michigan with "A Tribute to Robert Hayden," the latter occurring the day before Hayden died of a respiratory embolism at age sixty-six. Popular appreciation of Hayden's sensitive lyrics, dramatic monologues, and poignant remembrances has grown since his death.

Suggested readings

Fetrow, Fred M. *Robert Hayden*. Boston: Twayne, 1984.

Hatcher, John. *From the Auroral Darkness: The Life and Poetry of Robert Hayden*. Oxford, England: G. Ronald, 1984.

Nicholas, Xavier. "Robert Hayden: Some Introductory Notes." *Michigan Quarterly Review* 31, no. 3 (Summer, 1992): 8.

—Andrew O. Jones

See also African American identity; Hayden, Robert, poetry of

Hayden, Robert, poetry of

Author: Robert Hayden (1913-1980)

Principal works: *Heart-Shape in the Dust*, 1940; *The Lion and the Archer*, 1948; *Figure of Time*, 1955; *A Ballad of Remembrance*, 1962; *Selected Poems*, 1966; *Words in the Mourning Time*, 1970; *The Night-Blooming Cereus*, 1972; *Angle of Ascent: New and Selected Poems*, 1975; *American Journal*, 1978, 1982; *Collected Poems*, 1985

Identities: African American

Much of Robert Hayden's poetry reflects one man's wrestling with the sway of poetic influence. His early verse echoes the themes and styles of many of his immediate forebears: Harlem Renaissance poets such as Langston Hughes and Countée Cullen, and American modernists such as Edna St. Vincent Millay and Hart Crane. The subjects of Hayden's later poetry reflect his belief that African American poets need not focus exclusively on sociological study or on protest. Early mentors such as Hughes and Cullen guided Hayden through his years of apprenticeship and obscurity, and defended Hayden during his later successful years, when he was often upbraided by some black poets for being insufficiently political. Hayden's persevering confidence in his poetic voice and learning inured him against such criticism.

Throughout most of his career as a poet, from the publication of *Heart-Shape in the Dust* to that of his breakthrough book, *Selected Poems*, Hayden was sustained by academic work—heavy teaching loads and an occasionally funded research project—more than he was by popular acclaim. Working in the 1930's and 1940's as a researcher for the Federal Writers' Project, and in various university libraries, Hayden found the historical material for some of his most celebrated poems. Interested especially in the motivations of rebellious slaves, Hayden in "The Ballad of Nat Turner" imagines Turner's almost sympathetic understanding of his captors as the educated slave "Beheld the conqueror faces and, lo,/ they were like mine." In "Runagate Runagate" Hayden celebrates Harriet Tubman as "woman of earth, whipscarred," who has "a shining/ Mean to be free." The culmination of Hayden's study of his political heroes can be found in the perfectly crafted sonnet titled "Frederick Douglass," a poignant paean to "this man, this Douglass, this former slave, this Negro/ beaten to his knees, exiled, visioning a world/ where none is lonely, none hunted, alien."

Throughout his middle years Hayden himself might have felt like an alien, teaching at Fisk University in segregated Nashville. He was composing often formal, often disinterested poetry in a time when confessional poetry was fashionable. As was the case with Frederick Douglass a century earlier, Robert Hayden did not let his dissimilarity from those around him keep him from speaking his mind. An inherently peaceful person, Hayden was most upset by the violence of the 1960's; the title poem of his 1970 book *Words in the Mourning Time* mourns "for King for Kennedy . . . / And for America, self-destructive, self-betrayed." Himself feeling betrayed by America's policies in Vietnam, Hayden asks: "Killing people to save, to free them?/ With napalm lighting routes to the future?" Despite this expressed skepticism toward American nationalism, in the 1960's and 1970's Hayden was welcomed by the poetic and political establishment. Named poetry consultant at the Library of Congress and invited to read at the Carter White House, Hayden felt particularly gratified regarding his late ascendancy. His successes corroborated Hayden's belief that literature composed by African Americans should be judged objectively and should meet the same high standards as the best literature written in English.

SUGGESTED READINGS

Fetrow, Fred M. *Robert Hayden*. Boston: Twayne, 1984.

Williams, Pontheolla. *Robert Hayden: A Critical Analysis of His Poetry*. Champaign: University of Illinois Press, 1987.

—Andrew O. Jones

See also African American identity; Civil Rights movement; Cullen, Countée; Hayden, Robert; Hughes, Langston

Hayslip, Le Ly (Phung Thi Le Ly)

BORN: Ly La, Vietnam; December 19, 1949

PRINCIPAL WORKS: *When Heaven and Earth Changed Places: A Vietnamese Woman's Journey from War to Peace*, 1989 (with Jay Wurts); *Child of War, Woman of Peace*, 1993 (with James Hayslip)

IDENTITIES: Vietnamese American; women

SIGNIFICANT ACHIEVEMENT: Hayslip's memoirs chronicle a largely successful merger of her Vietnamese ancestry with her acquired American identity.

Born Phung Thi Le Ly in 1949 to Buddhist peasants living under Vietnam's French colonial rule, Le Ly Hayslip ardently supported her nation's struggle for independence. Years later, when Viet Cong soldiers of the North wrongly accused her of treason, she fled her village in central Vietnam to live in Danang and, later, Saigon. After giving birth to her wealthy employer's son and witnessing the cruelty of Communist rebels against the peasants they purported to defend, she shifted her allegiance to the republican-backed American forces. She supported herself and her child through black marketeering and other illegal activity and entered into a series of unhappy love affairs with United States servicemen before marrying Ed Munro, an American contractor more than forty years her senior. In 1970, without notifying her family, she left Vietnam for the United States as Munro's bride and the mother of his infant son.

The pattern of being caught in the middle—between the North and the South or between allies and enemies—continued in her new home in suburban San Diego, where Hayslip experienced culture shock, homesickness, and racial antagonism. Soon after Munro's death in 1973, she married Dennis Hayslip, a mentally unstable man by whom she had her third son before he committed suicide. The resilient Hayslip supported herself in the United States as a maid, nurse's aide, and factory worker; with money from her late husband's insurance settlement and trust fund, she purchased stock options, real estate, and a share in a successful restaurant. Combining investment revenues with the proceeds from her memoir about her life in Vietnam (*When Heaven and Earth Changed Places*), Hayslip founded the nonprofit East Meets West Foundation, a humanitarian relief organization that delivers medical and relief supplies to the Vietnamese.

Child of War, Woman of Peace, the sequel to her first memoir and the account of her American acculturation and subsequent return trips to Vietnam, attests Hayslip's ability to endure and heal, which she attributes to her potential to forgive. That second memoir, cowritten with her eldest son, James Hayslip, reveals her ability to embrace America while reconnecting to her Vietnamese past. She explains that her philanthropy, financing her mission in Vietnam through resources acquired in the United States, is the means to bind her old country to her new one, "to sponsor a healing handshake across time and space." The two autobiographies form the basis for Oliver Stone's 1993 film, *Heaven and Earth*, about Hayslip's life in Vietnam and America.

SUGGESTED READING
Rose, Phyllis, ed. *The Norton Book of Women's Lives*. New York: W. W. Norton, 1993.
—Theresa M. Kanoza

See also Acculturation; Asian American identity: Vietnam; Emigration and immigration; Vietnam War; *When Heaven and Earth Changed Places*

Hearn, Lafcadio

BORN: Levkás, Ionian Islands, Greece; June 27, 1850
DIED: Tokyo, Japan; September 26, 1904
PRINCIPAL WORKS: *Chita: A Memory of Last Island*, 1889; *Glimpses of Unfamiliar Japan*, 1894; *Kwaidan*, 1904
IDENTITIES: Caribbean; world
SIGNIFICANT ACHIEVEMENT: Hearn's stories of the Caribbean and Japanese cultures are among the earliest and best in English.

Lafcadio Hearn, a man long without family and cultural ties of his own, displayed a keen sensitivity to other cultures and peoples. He was born on the Greek island of Levkás. His father, a British army surgeon on assignment, and his mother, a local Greek woman, separated when he was four years old. As a result of his parents' separation, he was reared by a wealthy, elderly relative in Ireland. Always identifying with his Greek mother, Hearn later described his painful feelings of the loss of her. His attraction to faraway cultures and peoples is possibly due to his interest in his own Greek heritage, which was unfamiliar to him.

As a child and youth, Hearn attended elite, religious boarding schools in France and England. During those years he acquired a fluency in the French language and knowledge of French culture, such that in later years he translated French literary works into English. A bright eighteen-year-old student, he expected to go to a university and inherit sufficient money to live comfortably. Instead, his guardian unexpectedly lost the family fortune and, in 1869, sent him alone to America to find work and make a life for himself.

Arriving in a strange new country without funds or friends, young Hearn faced serious obstacles. He was nearly blind, as a result of a childhood sports accident, and felt haunted by feelings of painful alienation. These problems continued to plague him throughout his life. He eventually found work as a journalist, restlessly changing jobs. His literary talents and vision problems led Hearn to write newspaper stories of local color, describing the history and flavor of neighborhoods and local places. By 1887, he had arrived in the French-speaking Caribbean island of Martinique, where his fluent French allowed him to write about the life around him, in, for example, *Youma* (1890), as few other American journalists could.

In 1890, feeling restless and unsatisfied, Hearn accepted an invitation to teach in a small school in Japan. There he married the daughter of a samauri and began collecting Japanese folktales for publication. He was especially drawn to the magical tales of the Shinto and Buddhist religions.

Finally Hearn earned a position teaching English literature at the Imperial University of Tokyo. He also began a series of popular works describing and interpreting Japanese culture for Westerners. During this period, he was adopted into his wife's samauri family, a rare honor for a foreigner. Although a well-established, happily married professor, Hearn continued to feel unsettled and anxious. At fifty-four, he died of heart disease.

SUGGESTED READINGS
Cott, Jonathan. *Wandering Ghost*. Tokyo: Kodansha, 1990.
Kunst, Arthur E. *Lafcadio Hearn*. New York: Twayne, 1969.
Stevenson, Elizabeth. *Lafcadio Hearn*. New York: Macmillan, 1961.
Yu, Beongcheon. *An Ape of Gods*. Detroit: Wayne State University Press, 1964.
—Patricia H. Fulbright

See also Asian American identity: China, Japan, and Korea; Caribbean American literature; *Youma*

Heart of Aztlán

AUTHOR: Rudolfo A. Anaya (1937-   )
FIRST PUBLISHED: 1976
IDENTITIES: Latino; West and Southwest

Heart of Aztlán is Rudolfo Anaya's second novel of a trilogy that includes *Bless Me, Ultima* (1972) and *Tortuga* (1979). It is a psychological portrait of a quest for Chicano identity and empowerment. It is the story of the Chávez family, who leave the country to search for a better life in the city only to discover that their destiny lies in a past thought abandoned and lost.

The story is carried by two major characters, Clemente Chávez, the father, and Jason, one of the sons. Jason depicts the adjustments the family has to make to everyday life in the city. Clemente undergoes a magical rebirth that brings a new awareness of destiny to the community and a new will to fight for their birthright.

The novel begins with the Chávez family selling the last of their land and leaving the small town of Guadalupe for a new life in Albuquerque. They go to live in Barelas, a barrio on the west side of the city that is full of other immigrants from the country.

The Chávezes soon learn, as the other people of the barrio already know, that their lives do not belong to them. They are controlled by industrial interests represented by the railroad and a union that has sold out the workers. They are controlled by politicians through Mannie García, "el super," who delivers the community vote.

In Barelas, Clemente also begins to lose the battle of maintaining control of the family, especially his daughters, who no longer believe in his insistence on the tradition of respect and obedience to the head of the family. The situation gets worse when Clemente loses his job in the railroad yard during a futile strike.

Clemente becomes a drunk and in his despair attempts to commit suicide. Crespín, a magical character who represents eternal wisdom, comes to his assistance and points the way to a new life. With Crespín's help, Clemente solves the riddle of a magical power stone in the possession of "la India," a sorceress who symbolically guards the entryway to the heart of Aztlán, the source of empowerment for the Chicano.

Clemente's rebirth takes the form of a journey to the magical mountain lake that is at the center of Aztlán and Chicano being. Reborn, Clemente returns to his community to lead the movement for social and economic justice. It is a redeeming and unifying struggle for life and the destiny of a people.

The novel ends with Clemente physically taking a hammer to the Santa Fe water tower in the railroad yard, a symbol of industrial might, before coming home to lead a powerful march on his former employers.

SUGGESTED READING

González-T, César A., ed. *Rudolfo A. Anaya: Focus on Criticism*. La Jolla, Calif.: Lalo Press, 1990.

—David Conde

See also Anaya, Rudolfo A.; *Bless Me, Ultima*; Chicano identity; Chicano Renaissance; *Tortuga*

Hector Quesadilla Story, The

AUTHOR: T. Coraghessan Boyle (Thomas John Boyle, 1948-   )
FIRST PUBLISHED: 1984
IDENTITIES: Latino

"The Hector Quesadilla Story" is one of several tales in T. Coraghessan Boyle's second collection of short fiction, *Greasy Lake and Other Stories* (1985), in which identity and experience are so closely intertwined that they achieve a magic fusion. The title character is an aging baseball player whose profession has consumed his life. A "saint of the stick" during his teenage years in the Mexican League, he enjoyed a respectable career as a utility infielder with several major-league teams. Hector serves as a last-resort pinch hitter for the Los Angeles Dodgers. He refuses to acknowledge his forty—possibly fifty—years, although "he hasn't played regularly for nearly ten years and can barely trot to first after drawing a walk."

Hector's long-suffering wife, Asunción, pleads with him to give up the game and accept his age gracefully, but Hector—who is a father of two and grandfather of four—is intoxicated by the timelessness of the national pastime: "How can he get old? The grass is always green, the lights always shining, no clocks or periods or halves or quarters, no punch-in or punch-out; this is the game that never ends." Each year, Hector promises Asunción that the next will be his last.

On his birthday, with his family in attendance at a game with the Atlanta Braves, Hector finally senses his "moment of catharsis. The moment to take it out." It is the bottom of the ninth inning, and the game is tied with two men out and a relief pitcher who has struck out Hector twice before that year on the mound. Another pinch hitter is summoned, and when he strikes out the game goes into extra innings.

Hector stays benched while the game continues for a record-setting twenty-two more innings. Although the fans have left and the players are collapsing from exhaustion, his manager knows that putting Hector in the batting lineup means he will have to play him on the field if the game does not end. Hector finally gets his chance to bat in the bottom of the thirty-first inning but fails to bring in the winning run and is asked to substitute as pitcher, a position he has not played since the Mexican League.

As Hector's past and present merge, the ball game becomes more universal and symbolic. With its ethnically diverse teams, repetitive tasks, and undetermined endpoint, the game becomes a metaphor for life. The aging Hector, who has lived from one year to the next on the promise of what tomorrow will bring, realizes that for him this game will never end.

SUGGESTED READINGS

Boyle, T. Coraghessan. "T. Coraghessan Boyle." Interview by Alexander Neubauer. In *Conversations on Writing Fiction: Interviews with Thirteen Distinguished Teachers of Fiction Writing in America*. New York: HarperCollins, 1994.

Dee, Jonathan. Review of *Greasy Lake and Other Stories*, by T. Coraghessan Boyle. *Village Voice*, July 30, 1985, 49-50.

McCaffery, Larry. Review of *Greasy Lake and Other Stories*, by T. Coraghessan Boyle. *The New York Times Book Review*, June 9, 1985, 15-16.

Walker, Michael. "Boyle's 'Greasy Lake' and the Moral Failure of Postmodernism." *Studies in Short Fiction* 31 (Spring, 1994): 247-255.

—*Stefan Dziemianowicz*

See also Aging; Boyle, T. Coraghessan; Chicano identity; Latino American identity

Heidi Chronicles, The

AUTHOR: Wendy Wasserstein (1950-   )
FIRST PRODUCED: 1988; first published, 1988
IDENTITIES: European American; gay, lesbian, and bisexual; women

The Heidi Chronicles, which won the Pulitzer Prize in drama in 1989, focuses on the women's movement of the late twentieth century from the point of view of Heidi Holland, feminist art historian. The two acts each open with a prologue about overlooked women painters. The action of the play begins at a dance in 1965 where Heidi meets Peter Patrone, who charms her with his wit. They promise to know each other all their lives.

Several years later during a Eugene McCarthy rally, Heidi encounters Scoop Rosenbaum. Scoop is obnoxious and extremely arrogant, and he has a tendency to grade everything, yet Heidi leaves the party to go to bed with him. At a consciousness-raising session a lesbian explains to Heidi that in feminism, "you either shave your legs or you don't." Heidi considers body hair in the range of the personal, but she participates in the group, detailing her pathetic attachment to Scoop. Distraught, she begs the women to tell her that all their daughters will feel more worthwhile than they do.

Next, Heidi attends a rally at the Chicago Art Institute, protesting the opening of a major retrospective containing no women artists. Peter arrives and confesses his homosexuality. Act 1 closes with Scoop's wedding to another woman. Although he claims to love Heidi, Scoop does not promise her equality. At the wedding he knowingly marries a woman he considers his lesser. By act 2 Heidi has written her book, *And the Light Floods in from the Left*. She attends Scoop's wife's baby shower, which is held on the same day as the memorial service for John Lennon. In 1982, Heidi appears with Peter, now a popular pediatrician, and Scoop, owner of *Boomer* magazine on a talk show. The men continually interrupt her. Later, when Heidi tries to tell an old friend, Susan Johnston, now a television producer, how unhappy she is, Susan is too involved with her own career to care.

In 1986, Heidi gives an address to the alumni of her alma mater, divulging how sad she is. She feels stranded, and she thought the whole point of the feminist movement was that they were all in it together. In 1987, Peter explains that her kind of sadness is a luxury after all the memorial services for those who have died of acquired immune deficiency syndrome (AIDS). The play's final scene occurs in 1989, when Scoop comes to meet Heidi's adopted child. He has sold *Boomer* and is planning to run for Congress. Heidi hopes that Scoop's son and her daughter will someday find a truer equality. The final image of the play is Heidi and child in front of a banner displaying a major Georgia O'Keeffe retrospective.

By turns heartwrenching and hilarious, the play captures the angst, admittedly sometimes whiny, of a generation of women who could not understand why the world would not accept them as they were and as they wanted to be.

SUGGESTED READINGS

Arthur, Helen. "Wendy Wasserstein's *The Heidi Chronicles*." Review of *The Heidi Chronicles*, by Wendy Wasserstein. *The Nation* 261, no. 12 (October 16, 1995): 443-445.

Finn, William. "Sister Act." *Vogue*, September, 1992, 360.

Hoban, Phoebe. "The Family Wasserstein." *New York* 26 (January 4, 1993): 32-37.

Shapiro, Walter. "Chronicler of Frayed Feminism." *Time*, March 27, 1989, 90-92.

—Shira Daemon

See also *Sisters Rosensweig, The*; Wasserstein, Wendy

Heirs of Columbus, The

AUTHOR: Gerald R. Vizenor (1934-   )
FIRST PUBLISHED: 1991
IDENTITIES: Native American

Published shortly before the quincentennial of Christopher Columbus' 1492 voyage, Vizenor's *The Heirs of Columbus* proclaims: "I am not a victim of Columbus!" The novel tells of the nine tribal descendants of Christopher Columbus, including Stone Columbus, a late-night talk radio personality, and Felipa Flowers, a liberator of cultural artifacts. For the heirs, tribal identity rests in tribal stories, and they are consummate storytellers. "We are created in stories," the heirs say, and "language is our trick of discovery." Their trickster storytelling rewrites and renews the history of white and tribal peoples. Stone tells a story, central to the novel, asserting Columbus' Mayan, not Italian, ancestry. The Mayans brought their civilization to the Old World savages long ago, Stone argues. Columbus escaped Europe's "culture of death" and brought his "tribal genes" back to his homeland in the New World. Columbus did not discover the New World; he returned to it.

For some readers, *The Heirs of Columbus* might recall African American novelist Ishmael Reed's *Mumbo Jumbo* (1972). Both works have a fragmented style and are concerned with the theft and repatriation of tribal property. Felipa Flowers undertakes a mission to recapture sacred medicine pouches and the remains of her ancestor Christopher Columbus from the Brotherhood of American Explorers. After Felipa's successful raid, the heirs are taken to court to tell their story. They win their court case, but Felipa is later kidnapped and murdered in London when she tries to recapture the remains of Pocahontas.

After Felipa's death, the heirs create a sovereign nation at Point Assinika, "the wild estate of tribal memories and the genes of survivance in the New World." Theirs is a natural nation, where tricksters heal with their stories and where humor rules. Stone plans "to make the world tribal, a universal identity" dedicated to healing, not stealing, tribal cultures. To this end, the heirs gather genetic material from their tribal ancestors. They devise genetic therapies that use these healing genes to combat the destructive war herbs, which have the power to erase people from memory and history. Soon, Point Assinika becomes a place to heal abandoned and abused children with the humor of their ancestors.

Stories and genes in *The Heirs of Columbus* operate according to trickster logic, which subverts the "terminal creeds" of cultural domination and signals the reinvention of the world.

SUGGESTED READINGS

Coltelli, Laura, ed. *Winged Words: American Indian Writers Speak*. Lincoln: University of Nebraska Press, 1990.

Laga, Barry E. "Gerald Vizenor and His *Heirs of Columbus*: A Postmodern Quest for More Discourse." *American Indian Quarterly* 18, no. 1 (Winter, 1994): 71-86.

McCaffery, Larry, and Tom Marshall. "Head Water: An Interview with Gerald Vizenor." *Chicago Review* 39, nos. 3-4 (Summer-Fall, 1993): 50-54.

Vizenor, Gerald, ed. *Narrative Chance: Postmodern Discourses on Native American Indian Literatures*. Norman: University of Oklahoma Press, 1993.

—Trey Strecker

See also Columbus, Christopher, literature about; *Interior Landscapes*; Native American identity; Vizenor, Gerald; *Wordarrows*

Heller, Joseph

BORN: Brooklyn, New York; May 1, 1923

PRINCIPAL WORKS: *Catch-22*, 1961; *We Bombed in New Haven*, pr. 1967; *Something Happened*, 1974; *Good as Gold*, 1979; *God Knows*, 1984; *No Laughing Matter*, 1986 (with Speed Vogel); *Picture This*, 1988; *Closing Time*, 1994

IDENTITIES: Jewish; Northeast

SIGNIFICANT ACHIEVEMENT: Heller's first novel, *Catch-22*, put into words the antiwar and antibureaucracy sentiments of Vietnam War protesters.

Joseph Heller was born into a family consisting of Russian Jewish immigrant parents and two children from Heller's father's first marriage. Heller's father died when Heller was five, and although he claims not to have known of the significance of this event, critics speculate that this early trauma colors much of Heller's work.

Although both of Heller's parents were Jewish, there was little religion in the Heller household. His mother required him to wear his best clothes on Sunday, but Heller neither attended services regularly nor had a Bar Mitzvah. Despite living in a neighborhood populated mainly by Jewish and Italian immigrants, Heller enjoyed a child-

Joseph Heller, author of the best-selling and critically acclaimed Catch-22 *(1961).* (Mariana Cook)

hood relatively free of religious or ethnic conflicts. He spent many hours among crowds near the boardwalk section of Coney Island, an environment that heightened his awareness of the fine line between the real and the illusory. Although he admits that his Coney Island experiences made him cynical, Heller describes his childhood environment as idyllic.

Heller's career as a writer began in 1945, when he returned from World War II and began submitting short stories to magazines such as *Story*, *Esquire*, and the *Atlantic*. Heller obtained a bachelor's degree from New York University, then earned a master's degree from Columbia University, and finally studied on a Fulbright scholarship at Oxford University. Like the crafty, amoral Milo Minderbinder in *Catch-22*, Heller profited from his war experiences; they provided the material for his novel, and he was able to go to college as a result of the G.I. Bill.

The most-repeated themes in Heller's work are the stories of people who try to maintain their human and humane perspective in an inhuman and inhumane world. Sometimes this struggle leaves his characters teetering on the brink of madness. This happens to Yossarian in *Catch-22*, to Slocum, Martha, and Holloway in *Something Happened*, and to nearly everyone in *Good as Gold*. Often, the protagonists are also beset with questions about mortality, particularly when they find themselves facing death. Another common concern is illness, which may relate to Heller's own brush with Guillain-Barré syndrome, which inspired him to write *Picture This*. Fans of Heller point out that although his novels are often dark, harsh, critical, and pessimistic, they also feature Heller's famous sense of humor. That irreverent humor, as well as the criticism, has enabled him to sell more than twenty-five million copies of *Catch-22* alone.

SUGGESTED READINGS

Saurian, Adam J. *Conversations with Joseph Heller*. Jackson: University Press of Mississippi, 1993.
Seed, David. *The Fiction of Joseph Heller*. New York: St. Martin's Press, 1989.

—*T. A. Fishman*

See also Antiwar literature; *Catch-22*; Jewish American identity; World War II

Hellman, Lillian

BORN: New Orleans, Louisiana; June 20, 1905
DIED: Martha's Vineyard, Massachusetts; June 30, 1984
PRINCIPAL WORKS: *The Children's Hour*, pr., pb. 1934; *The Little Foxes*, pr., pb. 1939; *Another Part of the Forest*, pr. 1946, pb. 1947; *The Autumn Garden*, pr., pb. 1951; *Toys in the Attic*, pr., pb. 1960; *Three*, 1979 (includes *An Unfinished Woman*, *Pentimento*, *Scoundrel Time*)
IDENTITIES: Family; gay, lesbian, and bisexual; Jewish; South; women
SIGNIFICANT ACHIEVEMENT: Hellman's problem plays are the most successful American dramas written by a woman.

Lillian Hellman spent her life attempting to establish a singular identity apart from any one cultural or political group. Reared in a Southern Jewish American family, she was educated in New Orleans and New York City. She was married for relatively few years (1925-1932) to author Arthur Kober and bore no children. She took a succession of male lovers, generally on her own terms, although her long relationship (1930-1961) with author Dashiell Hammett was an exception in that she usually followed his advice and accepted his criticism.

Although lesbianism figures in her first successful play, *The Children's Hour*, Hellman refused to be called a feminist and was never active in women's groups. She also charted an independent role in her career. All of her best plays, however, include strong-willed women characters whose independence and self-reliance thwart the males with whom they interact. Experiences from her upbringing in New Orleans formed the basis for her picture of the South in transition in *The Little Foxes* and *Another Part of the Forest*. She was fascinated by the business successes of her relatives, yet repelled by their selfishness and lack of interest in social issues. In contrast, she was an outspoken defender of liberal causes, including labor unions, anti-Franco efforts in the Spanish Civil War, civil rights, freedom of speech, and protests against the Vietnam War.

Although Jewish American, Hellman seemingly cared little about the Jewish religion and traditions. She was never a supporter of Zionism and identified most closely with Jewish culture during the 1930's and 1940's, when it was attacked by the Nazis. Her antifascist plays *Watch on the Rhine* (1941) and *The Searching Wind* (1944) do not, however, center directly on the mistreatment of Jews but rather emphasize the shortcomings of American liberals in combatting the fascist threat to American freedoms. Hellman's staunch antifascism was somewhat based on her attraction to socialism and communism, a flirtation that led to her famous and largely successful confrontation with the House Committee on Un-American Activities in 1952.

Hellman became a living legend, admired by many for her outspoken independence and social commitment. Ironically, her last years were spent in bitter disputes over the reliability of her memoirs. The evidence suggests that Hellman's very flattering self-portrait was largely fictional in the famous "Julia" section from *Pentimento: A Book of Portraits* (1973), upon which a highly successful motion picture was based.

SUGGESTED READINGS

Estrin, Mark, ed. *Critical Essays on Lillian Hellman*. Boston: G. K. Hall, 1989.

Falk, Doris. *Lillian Hellman*. New York: Frederick Ungar, 1978.

Lederer, Katherine. *Lillian Hellman*. Boston: Twayne, 1979.

Rollyson, Carl. *Lillian Hellman: Her Legend and Her Legacy*. New York: St. Martin's Press, 1988.

—*Delmer Davis*

See also American identity: South; *Children's Hour, The*; Feminism; Jewish American identity; *Little Foxes, The*

Hemingway, Ernest

BORN: Oak Park, Illinois; July 21, 1899
DIED: Ketchum, Idaho; July 2, 1961
PRINCIPAL WORKS: *The Sun Also Rises*, 1926; *A Farewell to Arms*, 1929; *For Whom the Bell Tolls*, 1940; *The Old Man and the Sea*, 1952; *A Moveable Feast*, 1964; *The Nick Adams Stories*, 1972
IDENTITIES: European American
SIGNIFICANT ACHIEVEMENT: Hemingway won a Nobel Prize in Literature for his mastery of the art of narration.

The son of a Midwest doctor, Ernest Hemingway began his writing career as a reporter for the Kansas City *Star*. In 1918, he went to Italy, where he drove a Red Cross ambulance in World War I and was wounded by machine gun fire. After recuperation, he returned to Europe as a war correspondent, but he soon gave up journalism to write fiction.

His first major novel, *The Sun Also Rises*, portrays the lost generation of expatriates who wandered Europe in the wake of World War I. *A Farewell to Arms* tells the story of an American lieutenant in the Italian army. In 1936 and 1937, Hemingway covered the Spanish Civil War for an American newspaper syndicate. From his experiences came the novel *For Whom the Bell Tolls*. In 1942, he returned to Europe as a war correspondent. He flew with the British Royal Air Force and crossed the English Channel on D day. In 1952, he published *The Old Man and the Sea*, a sentimental tale of quiet courage in the face of adversity. Hemingway was awarded a Pulitzer Prize for the novel.

Hemingway married four times and fathered three children. Depressed in later life, he died from a self-inflicted gunshot wound in 1961. It is impossible to separate the much-publicized persona of Hemingway from the autobiographical projection that emerges from his work. Like his heroes, he was an adventurer: boxer, hunter, fisherman, bullfighter, soldier, war correspondent, expatriate. The Hemingway hero is—perhaps like his creator—a reluctant hero. He is ravaged by inexplicable forces of violence and suffering that he cannot alter. He is a man of few words and few regrets; he accepts pain, injustice, and anguish with stoic dignity.

Hemingway's bare-bones style earned praise from some critics for arousing emotion through omission and restraint. Others judged his simple declarative sentences and spare descriptions as limited, superficial, and unevocative. Hemingway earned a place among the greats of twentieth century literature. In 1954, he received the Nobel Prize in Literature. The citation lauded "his natural admiration for every individual who fights the good fight in a world of reality overshadowed by violence and death."

SUGGESTED READINGS

Baker, Carlos. *Ernest Hemingway: A Life Story.* New York: Charles Scribner's Sons, 1969.

Brian, Denis. *The True Gen: An Intimate Portrait of Hemingway by Those Who Knew Him.* New York: Dell Books, 1989.

Burgess, Anthony. *Ernest Hemingway and His World.* New York: Macmillan, 1985.

Hardy, Richard E., and John G. Cull. *Hemingway: A Psychological Portrait.* New York: Irvington, 1987.

Meyers, Jeffrey. *Hemingway: A Biography.* New York: Harper & Row, 1985.

—*Faith Hickman Brynie*

See also Expatriate identity; *Moveable Feast, A*; *Nick Adams Stories, The*; Spanish Civil War; Violence; World War I; World War II

Herland

AUTHOR: Charlotte Perkins Gilman (1860-1935)
FIRST PUBLISHED: serial, 1915; book, 1979
IDENTITIES: European American; men; women

Herland, by Charlotte Perkins Gilman, is a humorous Utopian novel about an ideal world in which women are free to demonstrate their personal and cultural identities. The three main characters are Terry Nicholson, a misogynist explorer; Jeff Margrave, a doctor who idolizes women; and Vandyck Jennings, a sociologist whose views on women are more empirical, if no more informed, than those of his comrades. The men, clearly, represent different types of male perspectives about women. Jeff idealizes females as Southern belles. Terry is concerned only with their physical appeal. Vandyck has a scientific outlook and regards them as objects of study.

The three discover the women's Utopia. In their first encounter with the young native women, the explorers describe the inhabitants as tree dwellers who are skittish and defy capture. Lured by curiosity about the creatures, who are described in neuter terms, the men venture into the town. Not long after their arrival, they are surrounded by the elders of the settlement, who treat them hospitably but with much caution and who define for the three men the areas they may see within the new culture. Jeff, Terry, and Vandyck, however, seek more information than that provided by their polite captivity, and they escape their quarters and venture out on their own. During what proves to be an awakening for the three men, they are introduced to an ancient culture of women who have lived successfully for centuries without male influence. The women have built roads, a town, and a system of government; they have borne and reared children and flourished in the arts and sciences. The inhabitants of this Utopia become acquainted with their male captives, and the two groups enter into a dialogue about their separate worlds. Gilman uses conversation between the representatives of the sexes to compare the men's culture with that of the entirely feminine culture. In this exchange, she illustrates the striking contrasts between the two sexes as they grapple to understand their histories, their beliefs about love, the maternal instinct, and the importance of child rearing, education, and work outside the home. Since courtship, sex, and marriage are unheard of social relations in the women's culture, the men have difficulties explaining these practices and later trying to initiate them into the new culture. Through the comparison, Charlotte Gilman stresses the humanity that people share rather than the differences between the sexes.

Gilman's purpose for writing *Herland* is inescapable. The book has many humorous examples of women's independence and resourcefulness, but its purpose is serious; she points accusingly at the social flaws of her male-dominated culture. The inadequacies of her culture stand out in sharp relief against the Utopian world of the women.

SUGGESTED READINGS

Donaldson, Laura E. "The Eve of De-Struction: Charlotte Perkins Gilman and the Feminist Re-Creation of Paradise." *An Interdisciplinary Journal* 16 (1989): 373-387.

Keyser, Elizabeth. "Looking Backward: From *Herland* to *Gulliver's Travels*." In *Critical Essays on American Literature*, edited by Joanne B. Karpinski. Boston: G. K. Hall, 1992.

Peyser, Thomas Galt. "Reproducing Utopia: Charlotte Perkins Gilman and *Herland*." *Studies in American Fiction* 20, no. 1 (1992): 1-16.

—Mary Dunn

See also Feminism; Gilman, Charlotte Perkins; *Women and Economics*

Hijuelos, Oscar

BORN: New York, New York; August 24, 1951

PRINCIPAL WORKS: *Our House in the Last World*, 1983; *The Mambo Kings Play Songs of Love*, 1989; *The Fourteen Sisters of Emilio Montez O'Brien*, 1993; *Mr. Ives' Christmas*, 1995

IDENTITIES: Family; Latino

SIGNIFICANT ACHIEVEMENT: Hijuelos, a Latino writer, was awarded the 1990 Pulitzer Prize in fiction for *The Mambo Kings Play Songs of Love*.

Oscar Hijuelos' family came from the Oriente province of Cuba. Hijuelos was reared amid two divergent worlds: that of Columbia University, teeming with scholars, and that of Morningside Park, overflowing with drug addicts and muggers. At age four, Hijuelos and his mother visited Cuba, and upon his return, he succumbed to nephritis. Bedridden, Hijuelos lingered in a hospital for two years. The theme of separation and isolation, especially from family, saturates Hijuelos' novels. After receiving his master's degree in 1976 from the City University of New York, Hijuelos moved to within a few blocks of his childhood home to begin his author's life, supported by a menial job in an advertising agency.

Our House in the Last World is a portrait of his family's exodus from Cuba. The work recalls Hijuelos' family relationships; he hated and loved his alcoholic father, and he misunderstood and miscommunicated with his mother. *The Mambo Kings Play Songs of Love* also recalls Hijuelos' family life. One of Hijuelos' uncles had been a musician with Xavier Cougat. The elevator operator in Hijuelos' building played music. Hijuelos jumbled these two characters into Cesar Castillo.

Cuban American author Oscar Hijuelos. (Roberto Koch)

Cesar and his brother Nestor reach the highest point in their lives when the Mambo Kings appear on the *I Love Lucy* television show. Later, the brothers are separated.

In *The Fourteen Sisters of Emilio Montez O'Brien*, Hijuelos addresses issues of cross-cultural identity with the connection of Cuban and Irish families in a marriage. In *Mr. Ives' Christmas*, Hijuelos examines father-son relationships from the father's perspective. Mr. Ives seeks penance and peace after the disaster of his son's murder.

SUGGESTED READINGS

Barbato, Joseph. "Latino Writers in the American Market." *Publishers Weekly*, February 1, 1991, 17-21.

Chávez, Lydia. "Cuban Riffs: Songs of Love." *Los Angeles Times Magazine*, April 18, 1993, 22-28.

Coffey, Michael. "Oscar Hijuelos." *Publishers Weekly*, July 21, 1989, 42-44.

—*Craig Gilbert*

See also Caribbean American literature; Latino American identity; *Mambo Kings Play Songs of Love, The*; *Mr. Ives' Christmas*

Himes, Chester

BORN: Jefferson City, Missouri; July 29, 1909

DIED: Moraira, Spain; November 12, 1984

PRINCIPAL WORKS: *If He Hollers, Let Him Go*, 1945; *Lonely Crusade*, 1947; *Third Generation*, 1954; *The Quality of Hurt*, 1972; *My Life of Absurdity*, 1976

IDENTITIES: African American

SIGNIFICANT ACHIEVEMENT: Himes's work evokes the social and psychological burden of being a black man in a white society.

Chester Himes wrote nearly twenty novels, two volumes of autobiography, and a series of popular crime thrillers. Whatever form his writing took, the dominant theme was usually racism: the pain it causes and the hateful legacy it creates. In *If He Hollers, Let Him Go*, Himes uses a wartime West Coast shipyard to set the central confrontation between an educated Northern black man and his poor Southern white coworkers. The results are violent. In spare, functional prose that highlights the psychological paths the novel charts, Himes describes what has been called the American dilemma, or the contrast between a black man believing in democracy and the realities that bruise his dreams. Critics, while not always enamored with the novel, praised Himes for his relentless honesty.

Lonely Crusade, Himes's second novel, treats the betrayal, dislocation, and terror at the nexus of race and sex in United States society. The book makes a laudable effort to understand the relationship between the oppressed and the oppressor.

Third Generation, thought by many critics to be thinly veiled autobiography, dramatizes three generations in a family, from slavery to the middle of the twentieth century. It tellingly captures the fear and hatred that can fester in a troubled family, making it perhaps Himes's most ambitious and moving novel.

Himes left the United States in 1954 for Europe, where he received greater literary recognition than he had ever achieved at home. In France, Himes published ten sophisticated, fast-paced crime novels. The protagonists, a pair of cynical street-smart black detectives, were hailed by French critics. When, years later, the novels were finally printed in the United States, the series achieved wide success. Himes's two-volume autobiography, *The Quality of Hurt* and *My Life of Absurdity*, was written in Spain.

SUGGESTED READING

Fabre, Michael, Robert E. Skinner, and Lester Sullivan, comps. *Chester Himes: An Annotated Primary and Secondary Bibliography*. Westport, Conn.: Greenwood Press, 1992.

—*Barbara Day*

See also African American identity; Autobiographies of Chester Himes; Racism and ethnocentrism

Hinojosa, Rolando

BORN: Mercedes, Texas; January 21, 1929

PRINCIPAL WORKS: *Estampas del valle y otras obras-Sketches of the Valley and Other Works*, 1973; *Generaciones y semblanzas*, 1977; *Korean Love Songs from Klail City*, 1978; *Mi querido Rafa*, 1981; *Rites and Witnesses: A Comedy*, pb. 1982; *The Valley*, 1983; *Partners in Crime*, 1985; *Klail City*, 1987; *Becky and Her Friends*, 1990; *The Useless Servants*, 1993

IDENTITIES: Latino; West and Southwest

SIGNIFICANT ACHIEVEMENT: Hinojosa's fiction gives a view of Mexican American life in the Rio Grande Valley of Texas in the twentieth century.

Rolando Hinojosa began writing book-length works of fiction in the 1970's when he was in his forties and after he had established a successful academic career. He attended the University of Texas at Austin, but he left to serve in Korea before returning to complete his degree in Spanish in 1953.

In the 1950's, he taught at Brownsville High School. He next took a master's degree in Spanish from New Mexico Highlands University (1962) and a Ph.D. in Spanish from the University of Illinois (1969). From 1968 to the present, he has taught and held administrative posts at various universities in Texas.

Korean Love Songs from Klail City, which is poetry, and his novels form the Klail City Death Trip series, which deals with ethnic identity, the perils and rewards of cultural assimilation, and the importance of education. Hinojosa's major characters undergo epic struggles with the issues of identity, moving from a discrete, self-contained Mexican American community of the 1930's into a world in which young Mexican American men fight and die for the institutions that have relegated them to second-class citizenry.

Hinojosa shows that life in the Rio Grande Valley must change. The Klail City Death Trip series in particular shows the subtle mid-century changes in the social and economic landscape of the small towns of the valley and the ways in which Mexican Americans began to demand equality.

Because many of Hinojosa's characters believe in the American Dream, they become more Americanized and less Chicano as the twentieth century moves forward. By the time of *Partners in Crime* and *Becky and Her Friends*, the main characters have achieved status within the Anglo community and appear to thrive within it.

SUGGESTED READINGS

Calderón, Héctor. "Texas Border Literature: Cultural Transformation and Historical Reflection in the Works of Américo Paredes, Rolando Hinojosa, and Gloria Anzaldua." *Disposito* 16, no. 41 (1991): 13-27.

Penzenstadler, Joan. "La frontera, Aztlán, el barrio: Frontiers in Chicano Literature." In *The Frontier Experience and the American Dream*, edited by David Mogen, Mark Busby, and Paul Bryant. College Station: Texas A&M Press, 1989.

Saldívar, José David. "Chicano Border Narratives as Cultural Critique." In *Criticism in the Borderlands: Studies in Chicano Literature, Culture, and Ideology*, edited by Héctor Calderón and José David Saldívar. Durham, N.C.: Duke University Press, 1991.

—Joyce J. Glover

See also American Dream; American identity: West and the frontier; Chicano identity; *Klail City*; Stereotypes and identity

Hispanics. *See* Latino American identity

Hmong Means Free: Life in Laos and America

EDITOR: Sucheng Chan (1941-   )

FIRST PUBLISHED: 1994

IDENTITIES: Hmong American

Hmong Means Free: Life in Laos and America is an extraordinary collection of the life stories of four Hmong families who were able to escape from Laos when the Communists took over the Asian country in 1975. The book is the result of the work of four Hmong students, Lee Fang, Vu Pao Tcha, Maijue Xiong, and Thek Moua, and their professor, editor Sucheng Chan, of the University of California at Santa Barbara. Each student asked immediate family members to tell the stories of their lives; Professor Chan provides a cogent introduction to history and culture of the Hmong people of Laos.

As a result of this teamwork, voice is given, for the first time in print, to many first-person accounts of Hmong who came to live in California. The tales older family members—such as Boua Neng Moua—tell about their lives back in Laos become safeguards of their memories. Most Hmong were slash-and-burn farmers living a life far removed from that of American farmers in the twentieth century. Women worked very hard in the fields and at home, and children were taught to be obedient, hardworking, and chaste until marriage.

Change came when the war in Vietnam began to spill over to Laos in the 1960's. Many Hmong joined the American war effort and fought under General Vang Pao against their mutual Communist enemies. Thus, one of the many photographs that illustrate *Hmong Means Free* shows Xia Shoua Fang in his military uniform, flanked by his wife and their three oldest children.

The Communist victory caused many Hmong to try to flee Laos, and Xang Mao Xiong tells of Communist massacres of Hmong refugees who never made it to safe camps in Thailand. The camp experience often occupies the middle part of the Hmong narratives told in the book. Almost everybody was hoping to leave for America, even though some, like the Tcha family, arrived via France. Life in America brought with it a tremendous culture shock. Industrialized, urbanized, English-speaking America is often experienced as a promised land full of mind-boggling differences and dangers. Older Hmong are united in bemoaning the decay of family life and loss of cultural tradition among their young, Americanized offspring who seem to adopt American food and American violence with equal speed. Across the generations, most Hmong are startled by their experience of racism in America; coming from a relatively homogeneous country, they are saddened that so often, the different races and ethnicities cannot seem to get along in America.

Overall, *Hmong Means Free* offers a fascinating inside view of identity, culture, and traditions of a people whose alliance with America has caused about 100,000 of them to start over in the country of their old ally. With American culture all around them, this book may also help young Hmong to keep a sense of their specific cultural heritage.

SUGGESTED READINGS

Downing, Bruce, et al., eds. *The Hmong in the West*. Minneapolis: University of Minnesota Press, 1982.

Hendricks, Glenn, et al., eds. *The Hmong in Transition*. Staten Island: Center for Migration Studies, 1986.

Mitchell, Roger. *Tradition, Change, and Hmong Refugees*. Logan: Utah State University Press, 1992.

Roberts, A. E. Review of *Hmong Means Free*, edited by Sucheng Chan. *Choice* 32 (January, 1995): 878.

Wu, Jennifer L. Review of *Hmong Means Free*, edited by Sucheng Chan. *Multicultural Review* 3 (December, 1994): 82.

—*R. C. Lutz*

See also Asian American identity: Vietnam; Emigration and immigration; Multiculturalism

Holocaust

DEFINITION: The Holocaust was Nazi Germany's systematic murder, during World War II (1939-1945), of approximately ten million civilians, six million of whom were Jews.

IDENTITIES: Jewish

The Holocaust stands as the twentieth century's most hideous outburst of evil. Since then, civilization's challenge is to remember the tragedy, to keep it from becoming clichéd, and to recount specifics of the act. Literature has been one of the primary means of attempting to meet this challenge. North Americans have made a significant contribution to the literature of the Holocaust.

Works by survivors

Many of the survivors of the Holocaust have written memoirs and works of fiction dealing with their experiences. The works of Nobel Prize winner Isaac Bashevis Singer—of which *Enemies, a Love Story* (1972) is the most relevant and representative—are infused with an abiding faith in the value of humanity and being human, but tempered by his knowledge of the fragility and potential transience of experience and memory. Elie Wiesel's *Night* (1960) is a slim, evocative history of his experience in the camps. Wiesel's most successful fictional account of that time is *The Gates of the Forest* (1966), a novel about the Jews who survived either by hiding out or by becoming partisans, living and fighting in the woods. Many other concentration camp memoirs, notably *Survival in Auschwitz* (1960), by Primo Levi, who settled in Italy, deal directly with the experience of the Holocaust. Possibly the most interesting hybrid of fact and fiction is Jerzy Kosinski's *The Painted Bird* (1965), a hyperrealistic work of fiction that its author maintained was autobiographical long after the evidence that it was not was beyond debate. Additionally, there are noteworthy nonfiction works such as Terrence Des Pres's *The Survivor: An Anatomy of Life in the Death Camps* (1976) and essay collections such as *Holocaust Testimonies: The Ruins of Memory* (1991) that

The twentieth century witnessed probably the worst episode in history of planned, deliberate mass murder in the Holocaust. (National Archives)

provide the reader with painful, evocative looks at life in the death camps.

Several writers write of the time but did not have a direct experience of the Holocaust. Kurt Vonnegut, as a prisoner of war, experienced the American firebombing of Dresden. Vonnegut's *Mother Night* (1966) is the tale of Howard W. Campbell, Jr., "an American by birth, a Nazi by reputation, and a nationless person by inclination." Campbell stands convicted of having written and broadcast radio propaganda (which one of his guards, a Jew who joined the Hungarian S.S. to survive, describes as "weak"); in reality, he was working for U.S. counterintelligence. Like Oskar Matzerath in noted German author Günter Grass's *Die Blechtrommel* (1959; *The Tin Drum*, 1961), Campbell accepts his fate because it seems the right thing to do. *Mother Night* notes the need to teach the next generation about the Holocaust.

The next generation

The works of the descendants of Holocaust victims and survivors reveal the tension between those who teach their memories and those who are taught to remember. The nature of the Holocaust as a literary rather than as a personal experience is exemplified by Art Spiegelman's *Maus, a Survivor's Tale: My Father Bleeds History* (1986) and *Maus, a Survivor's Tale: And Here My Troubles Began* (1991). Originally published serially in the pages of *Raw* magazine, Spiegelman's work deals with his relationship with his father but centers upon the latter's experiences as a Polish Jew, including his internment in the concentration camp in Auschwitz, Poland. Spiegelman, a graphic artist, relates the tale in comic-book style, with the Jews pictured as mice and the German soldiers as cats. While many readers approached the books as fictional, Spiegelman argued—successfully—that *Maus* is a memoir, and the Library of Congress duly classifies *Maus* as such.

The books use the experiences of Spiegelman's parents, Vladek and his wife Anja, to reveal the gradual societal decay that permitted the Holocaust to occur. The first volume opens by quoting Adolf Hitler's declaration, "The Jews are undoubtedly a race, but they are not human." The first chapter tells of how Vladek broke off a long-standing sexual relationship to marry his wife, closing with Vladek telling Spiegelman that he should not use the story because "such *private* things, I don't want you should mention."

Spiegelman makes no attempt to sanitize his father's character, knowing that it is through such "private things" that the horrors are revealed. Vladek tells of the increasing cruelties directed against Jews, and Spiegelman's images—such as the German troops taking Anja's bedridden mother's bed in "The Noose Tightens"—emphasize the situation. The first volume, concluding with Vladek and Anja's arrival at Auschwitz, truly "bleeds history."

The second volume is more personal. Interspersed among tales of Vladek's relationship with another concentration camp survivor, Mala, and Spiegelman's own travails dealing with the success of the first volume is Vladek's tale of how he survived in Auschwitz. His abiding love for Anja is shown to be what sustained both of them through the camp. By the end of *Maus*, the reader understands Vladek and his actions. The interaction across the generations makes Vladek's Holocaust survival tale quite accessible.

The Holocaust in popular literature

One of the best-known works about the Holocaust is *Schindler's List* (1982), by Australian author Thomas Keneally. The fact-based story of a gentile businessman who risks his life to protect his Jewish employees was made into a feature film, which debuted in 1993, by Steven Spielberg. Keneally's work is realistic; unfortunately, much popular literature reduces the Holocaust to a caricature of evil. Such work does nothing to strengthen the memory of the Holocaust as it actually happened. In Ira Levin's *The Boys from Brazil* (1976), Josef Mengele survives in Brazil, producing young clones of Adolf Hitler and rearing the boys in a manner intended to produce new Hitlers. Mengele hopes to renew Hitler's "cleansing" efforts. The plan is foiled by a Jewish Nazi hunter (loosely based on Simon Wiesenthal). Levin's work, undermined by authorial moralizing, is one of the better popular tales whose abrogation of memory trivializes history.

Stephen King's "Apt Pupil," which appears in *Different Seasons* (1982), features Todd Bowden, who discovers that his quiet, unassuming neighbor was "Kurt Dussander, the Blood-Fiend of Patin." He forces Dussander to tell him tales of the atrocities committed. King's work is part of a subgenre of Holocaust tales: stories in which non-Jewish protagonists become fascinated with and sympathetic to the suffering. Most interesting among these is Emily Prager's *Eve's Tattoo* (1991), the story of a woman who, for her fortieth birthday, gets the identification number of a death camp victim stenciled onto her arm "to give the victim life." Eve also tells tales not only about life under the Nazis but also about the deliberate and inadvertent complicities among women that allowed the regime to enact its brutal tortures.

Jane Yolen's *Briar Rose* (1992) is the story of Rebecca ("Becca") Berlin, who tries to discover the truth of her grandmother's assertion that she—known to the family only as "Gemma"—was the Briar Rose of fairy tale, resuscitated from death by a Prince Charming. Becca follows the few clues she can find about Gemma's life—photographs, immigration documents, apartment leases—to Poland. Becca learns much about the attitude in the United States toward the Jewish refugees (all of whom were sent to a barbed-wired Relocation Camp in Oswego, New York). After meeting a survivor of the camps, she discovers that Gemma was sent to an extermination camp from which no woman ever survived.

Fantasies of remembrance

Becca's search leads her in the second half of the book to Poland, where a guide named Magda Bronski aids her in her search and shows her Polish society. When Becca and Magda ask the residents around Chelmno about the concentration camp in which Gemma was interred, the reply of one of the residents is "that nothing happened here and that we should take our Jew questions away or that the nothing would happen again."

Yolen's young adult novel *The Devil's Arithmetic* (1988) also deals with the persistence of memory. Thirteen-year-old Hannah "is tired of remembering" as she approaches her grandparents' house for the first night of Passover. As she opens the door for Elijah, she finds herself being called Chaya (her Hebrew name, meaning "life") in a small Jewish village in Nazi-occupied Poland. Matters soon go from bad to worse as she finds herself taken in a cattle car to a concentration camp, where survival is dependent on whim and life, especially Jewish life, is expendable.

British author Martin Amis' *Time's Arrow* (1991) features a man living his life backwards, becoming progressively more terrifying to the reader as he finds himself becoming the camp doctor at Auschwitz. Amis manages the novel, and the disingenuous tone, with a grace that is at times almost too precious, but still manages to plumb some of the depths of the horror. William Styron's *Sophie's Choice* (1979) is the tale of a Polish refugee, Sophie Zawatowska, who becomes involved with an aspiring writer. She is a survivor of the Holocaust and suffers from guilt about having survived and about her choice: A Nazi forced her to decide which of her two children was to die.

SUGGESTED READINGS

Burrin, Philippe. *Hitler and the Jews: The Genesis of the Holocaust.* Translated by Patty Southgate. London: Edward Arnold, 1994.

Dawidowicz, Lucy S. *The War Against the Jews, 1933-1945.* New York: Holt, Rinehart and Winston, 1975.

Friedlander, Saul. *Memory, History, and the Extermination of the Jews of Europe.* Bloomington: Indiana University Press, 1993.

Helmreich, William B. *Against All Odds: Holocaust Survivors and the Successful Lives They Made in America.* New York: Simon & Schuster, 1982.

—Kenneth L. Houghton

See also Anti-Semitism; Frank, Anne; Jewish American identity; Kosinski, Jerzy; Singer, Isaac Bashevis; Vonnegut, Kurt; Wiesel, Elie

Home Truths

AUTHOR: Mavis Gallant (1922-   )
FIRST PUBLISHED: 1981
IDENTITIES: Canada; family; women

In this collection of sixteen short stories written over an approximately twenty-five-year period, all deal with Canadians at home or abroad; all the stories are autobiographical. Mavis Gallant speaks through the voice of Linnet (also the name of a bird, like Mavis) Muir. Paralleling the author's life, Linnet, on being graduated from high school in New York, returns to wartime Montreal, marries a Canadian, and eventually finds a job as a reporter. During her stint, Linnet overhears derogatory remarks about the need to hire women because the men are away.

Gallant's alter ego is not above more direct criticism of Canadians. As Gallant had in an article she had written as a reporter in *The Standard Magazine* of Montreal of March 30, 1946, in this collection Linnet finds them cautious, dull, passive, noncommittal, given to conform in dress and mindset, and distrustful of the imagination. Commenting on her return to Montreal, Linnet narrates: "I was entering a poorer and a curiously empty country, where the faces of the people gave nothing away." The target is primarily English-speaking Canadians, the group to which Gallant nominally belongs.

The three sections of the collection—"At Home," "Canadians Abroad," and "Linnet Muir"—elaborate on this theme of Canadian identity. For example, in "The Ice Wagon Going Down the Street," Peter Frazier and Agnes Brusen discover that for different reasons, they do not belong to their Canadian-peopled milieu abroad. In "Virus X" referring to a mysterious sickness that shook post-World War II Europe and was used as a symbol of Europe's spiritual malaise, Lottie Benz, whose parents have come from Germany, is contrasted with Vera Rodna, a Ukrainian classmate from Winnipeg. The Linnet Muir cycle of six stories in particular affirms many of the home truths about time, memory, history, imagination, and last but not least, the meaning of being Canadian. As Gallant writes in an introduction to the Canadian edition of the collection: "A Canadian who did not know what it was to be Canadian would not know anything else: he would have to be told his own name." Through Linnet Muir, Gallant describes her own spiritual and emotional journey from exile into identity. Although on the face of it these short stories are about Canadian home truths, Gallant may also be writing about a nameless country of the imagination and about the fact that feeling exiled or alienated is not merely a Canadian condition.

SUGGESTED READINGS

Grady, Wayne. "The Other Canada." *Books in Canada* October 10, 1981, 18-19.
Grosskurth, Phyllis. "Close to Home." *Saturday Night* 96, no. 10 (November, 1981): 68.
Martens, Debra. "An Interview with Mavis Gallant." *Rubicon* 4 (Winter, 1984-1985): 151-182.
Ryval, Michael. "Profile." *Quill and Quire* 47, no. 12 (December, 1981): 27.
Thorpe, Michael. "A National Sense of Self." *Canadian Forum* 61 (February, 1982): 40.

—*Peter B. Heller*

See also Canadian identity; Gallant, Mavis; Identity crisis; Naming and identity

Homelessness

Homeless people are without many of the possessions that give identity. Without permanent residence, they have no fixed regional identity; they are everywhere and anywhere. Most have also left their families and professions; they are therefore without those networks by which the majority of people define themselves. Homeless people leave the world of public identity to enter what amounts to another world. Authors who portray the homeless in their works set about to depict and to understand this world apart from houses, jobs, and material possessions.

First-person realism

One of the first writers to explore the world of the homeless was George Orwell, whose *Down and Out in Paris and London* appeared in 1933. In this book, Orwell describes his own experiences living as a homeless man. Orwell wants people to drop their prejudices and accept the homeless as fellow humans. He claims that begging is a job like any other—a difficult and very low-paying job, but a job. Orwell addresses the accusation that the homeless are drifters, always on the move, and answers that there are laws that prohibit vagrants from staying in any one shelter longer than a few days. Such laws are still common.

With much wit, Orwell shows that the charities that help the homeless do so by demanding that vagrants pay for their supper by listening to a sermon. He asks why, when people drop below a

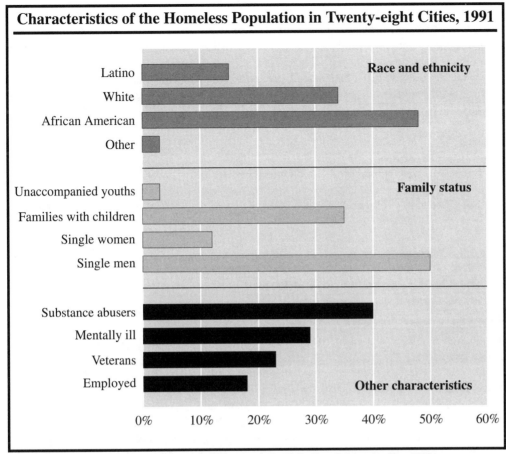

Characteristics of the Homeless Population in Twenty-eight Cities, 1991

Source: Data are from Carol Foster, ed., *Women's Changing Role*. Wylie, Tex.: Information Plus, 1992.
Note: Bars total more than 100% because most people fit into several categories.

certain level of income, others believe they have the right to preach to them. In one absurd sequence, he shows vagrants who have marched for miles to get a charity meal. They are forced to spend a half hour on their knees in prayer to pay for that meal. Orwell's account is written in the first person. It is highly realistic; he tries to overwhelm the reader with the gritty details of homeless life.

In John Steinbeck's *Cannery Row* (1945), a small group of homeless men are central characters. Mack and the boys live in Monterey, where the book is set, in an abandoned warehouse, which they have converted into a flophouse and which they call the Palace. Mack and the boys provide comic relief throughout the book with their bumbling misadventures. Their best plans go awry: They decide to give a party for a man who has befriended them. It is to be a surprise party, so they give it in the man's own home when he is away, expected back any moment. By the time he returns home, his house is a shambles. His favorite possessions are broken. The wonderful party backfires completely. Mack and the boys, however, recover from this as from every disaster to try again.

Comic romanticism

Steinbeck romanticizes this group of tramps. They are brave and lovable figures, akin to Charlie Chaplin. Because they are without ambition, he sees them as healthier than "normal" competitive people. They are true philosophers.

Laurie King, in her novel *To Play the Fool* (1995), makes a homeless man her central hero. She creates a character who was once a famous scholar and who gave up his former life to become a vagrant. Her main character speaks only in quotations from the Bible, even when ordering food at a restaurant. Her novel is set in Berkeley and San Francisco, and the students at the University of California, Berkeley, have turned the man into a popular prophet.

Homeless as heroic

King's book is fascinating in that she brings in much material pertaining to the literary tradition of the fool. This figure dresses in motley and, through mime and other modes, acts the fool in order to expose foolishness in society. King's implication is that her central character has given up the comfortable trappings of being socially acceptable. He has made a sacrifice of his former life. He has done so in order to reach more people on a common level and is, therefore, heroic.

It is a tradition in fiction to satirize and to question the customs and conventions of society. Homeless people are living outside of those customs that make up "normal life" for the majority. Therefore, they make good material for authors who wish to reflect upon the human condition from a perspective that is outside of the norm.

SUGGESTED READINGS

Blau, Joel. *The Visible Poor*. New York: Oxford University Press, 1992.
Brandenburg, Franz, and Michael Rosen, eds. *Home*. New York: HarperCollins, 1992.
Nelson, Theresa. *The Beggars' Ride*. New York: Orchard Books, 1992.
Neufeld, John. *Almost a Hero*. London: Macmillan, 1995.
Spohn, Kate. *Broken Umbrellas*. New York: Viking, 1994.
Torrey, E. Fuller. *Nowhere to Go*. New York: Harper & Row, 1988.

—*Denise Blue*

See also Addiction; Alcoholism; Steinbeck, John

Homewood Trilogy, The

AUTHOR: John Edgar Wideman (1941-   )

FIRST PUBLISHED: *Damballah*, 1981; *Hiding Place*, 1981; *Sent for You Yesterday*, 1983; *The Homewood Trilogy*, 1985

IDENTITIES: African American; Northeast

In *The Homewood Trilogy*, which comprises the short-story collection *Damballah* and the novels *Hiding Place* and *Sent for You Yesterday*, John Edgar Wideman re-creates Homewood, the black section of Pittsburgh, and describes the myriad relationships among ancestors and a living African American family in the hundred years since slavery. *Damballah* is an African voodoo god, "the good serpent of the sky." The hero of the trilogy is John French, who specializes in a kind of benevolent fatherhood. Wideman's return to Homewood through these novels convinces readers of his determination to find and understand his identity through tracing his roots as deep as he can. In *Damballah* and *Hiding Place*, Wideman furnishes a family tree. Readers are told of his great-great-great grandmother, who fled through the Underground Railroad with a white man to safety in Pittsburgh. Biological roots traced, the job of understanding begins.

One sour apple on the family tree is Tommy. The character Tommy is actually Robby, Wideman's brother. Tommy and Wideman are complex dimensions in finding the identity that Wideman seeks. The main character in *Hiding Place*, Tommy, is a fugitive from history as well as the law. He is taken in by Mama Bess, who is family and who represents what family does. Family tries to put together the "scars" and the "stories" that give young people their identities. Essentially, *Hiding Place* is the story of two lost souls, Mama Bess and Tommy. Mama Bess is lost because she has lost her husband and her son; she becomes a recluse, a fugitive living on a hill overlooking Pittsburgh, away from the family. Tommy is lost because he is too headstrong to listen and finds himself on the run after a scheme to rob a ghetto hoodlum ends in murder. Tommy does not want to hear the stories and learn about the scars; he is too absorbed in preservation.

Sent for You Yesterday, through the characters of Doot and Albert Wilkes, the outspoken blues pianist, suggests that creativity and imagination are important means of transcending despair. Creativity also strengthens the common bonds of race, culture, and class. *Homewood Trilogy* is a monumental work of investigating and understanding the origins of self and identity.

SUGGESTED READINGS

Marcus, James. "The Pain of Being Two." *The Nation*, October 4, 1986, 321-322.

Rushdy, Ashraf H. A. "Fraternal Blues: John Edgar Wideman's *Homewood Trilogy*." *Contemporary Literature* 32 (Fall, 1991): 312-343.
Wilson, Matthew. "The Circles of History in John Edgar Wideman's *The Homewood Trilogy*." *College Language Association* 33 (March, 1990): 239-259.

—*Barbara Cecelia Rhodes*

See also African American identity; American identity: Northeast; Black English; Class and identity

Homosexuality. *See* Bisexual identity; Gay identity; Lesbian identity

Hongo, Garrett Kaoru

Born: Volcano, Hawaii; May 30, 1951

Principal works: *Yellow Light*, 1982; *The River of Heaven*, 1988; *Volcano: A Memoir of Hawai'i*, 1995
Identities: Japanese American; multiracial; Pacific Islander
Significant achievement: Hongo writes lyrically and evocatively about personal history, place of origin, and ethnicity.

Garrett Hongo was born in the shadow of the Kilauea volcano but reared near Los Angeles. When he comes to terms with his origins during his first sojourn to Hawaii at middle age, he liberates his spirit with a moving insight that solidifies his sense of self. His poetry and prose are reverent, precise, and evocative, celebrating male ancestors, early Japanese poets, family, birthplace, and home.

Estranged from his past, his Japanese family hiding the bitter truths of the World War II internment from him, Hongo has continually lived a racially mixed life. Gardena, California, the town where he grew up, boasting the largest community of Japanese Americans on the mainland United States at the time, was bordered on the north by the black towns of Watts and Compton and on the southwest by Torrance and Redondo Beach, white towns. Hongo was sensitized to issues of uneasy race relations and urban street life.

Hongo studied in Japan for a year following graduation from Pomona College, then earned a master's degree in fine arts from the University of California at Irvine. As a poet in residence in Seattle, he founded and directed a local theater group called The Asian Exclusion Act. Hongo identifies largely with the West Coast, a mecca for many Asian American writers, and early became a friend and collaborator with Lawson Fusao Inada, a pioneer Japanese American poet. His marriage to white violinist Cynthia Thiessen and their rearing of two sons, Alexander and Hudson, have given Hongo particular sensitivity to the cultural terrain he calls "the borderlands."

The only Asian member of the faculty at the University of Oregon, Eugene, Hongo has di-

Garrett Hongo has traced his identity as an Asian American back to his family's Hawaiian beginnings. (Ellen Foscue Johnson)

rected the creative writing program there since 1989 and has received several extended leaves that allowed time in Hawaii to work on his prose memoirs, published in 1995 as *Volcano*. Among the most important influences he identifies is Wakako Yamauchi, a widely anthologized Japanese American short-story and play writer, whose works Hongo collected and edited under the title *Songs My Mother Taught Me*, which was published in 1994.

SUGGESTED READINGS

Chock, Eric, and Darrell H. Y. Lum, eds. *The Best of Bamboo Ridge: The Hawaii Writer's Quarterly*. Honolulu: Bamboo Ridge Press, 1986.

Hongo, Garrett. "A Vicious Kind of Tenderness: An Interview with Garrett Hongo." Interview by Alice Evans. *Poets and Writers* 20, no. 5 (September/October, 1992): 36-46.

Jarman, Mark. "The Volcano Inside." *The Southern Review* 32, no. 2 (Spring, 1996): 337-343.

—Jill B. Gidmark

See also Asian American identity: China, Japan, and Korea; Emigration and immigration; Japanese American internment; Mixed race and identity; *Volcano*

House Made of Dawn

AUTHOR: N. Scott Momaday (1934-   )

FIRST PUBLISHED: 1968

IDENTITIES: Native American

House Made of Dawn, N. Scott Momaday's first novel, is the story of an outcast who learns that his being is bound up in his culture. The novel, which relates the experiences of a mixed-race World War II veteran, was a signal achievement, winning the Pulitzer Prize in fiction for Momaday in 1969 and paving a way for other Native American novelists.

It begins with Abel's return to his ancestral village. Although he is so drunk that he does not recognize his grandfather, Abel's troubles run much deeper. He feels cut off from the Tanoan tribe yet unwilling to live in white America. Even more disturbing to Abel is his inability to "say the things he wanted" to anyone. His inability to express himself hampers his achieving a true identity. Wrapped up in his own problems, Abel is jealous and violent toward those who do participate in Tanoan culture. While at Walatowa, Abel loses a competition to an albino Indian and murders him.

After his release from prison, Abel tries to build a new life in California, where he comes in contact with a small community of Indians, who are also alienated from their cultures. The leader of this exile community is John Tosamah, a self-proclaimed priest of the sun, who sermonizes on the failure of white society to recognize the sacredness of the American landscape and of language. Tosamah victimizes Abel, however. Eventually, Abel is cast out of this group and is savagely beaten by a sadistic police officer, Martinez.

After the beating, Abel is physically what he was once only psychologically: an invalid. He returns to Walatowa, where his grandfather is dying. Aware that he must embrace his Tanoan heritage, if only to perform the burial rites for his grandfather, Abel begins to heal psychologically. At the novel's end, Abel participates in another ceremony, this time a race between the young men of the tribe, which his grandfather had won years before. Abel finds "a sort of peace of mind" through participation, but is certainly not healed by it. Unable to keep pace with the others, Abel keeps stumbling and falls behind. Abel's position in the tribe likewise remains unsettled. On the threshold between the world of his grandfather and that of modern America, on the threshold between spiritual values and lack of faith, Abel can do little but keep running, which becomes a gesture of hope and healing.

SUGGESTED READINGS

Momaday, N. Scott. "The Man Made of Words." In *The Remembered Earth: An Anthology of Contemporary Native American Literature*, edited by Geary Hobson. Albuquerque: University of New Mexico Press, 1980.

Trimble, Martha Scott. "N. Scott Momaday." *Fifty Western Writers: A Bio-Bibliographical Source-book*, edited by Fred Erisman and Richard W. Etulain. Westport, Conn.: Greenwood Press, 1982.
Velie, Alan R. *Four American Indian Literary Masters*. Norman: University of Oklahoma Press, 1982.

—*Michael R. Meyers*

See also American identity: West and the frontier; *Ancient Child, The*; Momaday, N. Scott

House of a Thousand Doors: Poems and Prose Pieces

AUTHOR: Meena Alexander (1951-   )
FIRST PUBLISHED: 1988
IDENTITIES: Family; South Asian; women

House of a Thousand Doors: Poems and Prose Pieces is a collection of fifty-nine poems and prose pieces. Meena Alexander's poetry reflects her multicultural heritage and the tension it creates. The book is organized into three sections, the first and third sections serving as a synthesis for the wide variety of subject and theme treated in the body of the work. Many of the poems reflect the writer's subjective response to her experience; many also project or create new experiences that underscore the importance of imagination as a lens through which to focus the inner life into poetry.

The title poem of *House of a Thousand Doors* uses the title metaphor to describe the variety of forces that operate on the persona: gender, heritage, language, experience, ideology, and the search for meaning. A complex array of images embody these forces in the book, reflecting the author's sensitivity to their influence. Alexander uses her writing to integrate the diversity of her experience.

Dominating the persona's early life is the figure of her grandmother, a powerful member of the family who learned to exercise some control over the many lines of force that affected her life. The mature awareness of the persona is imposed on the re-created memory of herself as a girl watching the figure of the grandmother kneel in turn before each of the thousand doors on a never-ending pilgrimage, "a poor forked thing" praying for the favor of her ancestors. The grandmother becomes a figure of myth and a symbol of tradition serving as the focus of many of the poems in the collection. Conciliation and unity with the culture and solidity of the past are central to *House of a Thousand Doors*.

The three major sources of imagery in the book are family, culture, and nature. Family images, though literal, have a universal quality—she describes finding her grandmother's letters "in an old biscuit box" and wonders if her grandmother was, like herself, "inventing a great deal." Other images reflect the diminution of women at the behest of a patriarchal society; a cell door closing on a woman raped by the police clangs "like an old bell left over by the British," while a portrait of the pacifist leader Mohandas Gandhi looks down from the wall. A third class of imagery, the imagery of nature, reflects the persona's romantic theory of art; she laments, "My body/ part water/ part rock/ is searching for heaven." This searching brings her back to her past, real and mythical, and ultimately back to herself and her need for meaning.

SUGGESTED READINGS

Perry, John Oliver. Review of *House of a Thousand Doors*, by Meena Alexander. *World Literature Today* 63 (Winter, 1989): 163.
Rao, Susheela N. Review of *Fault Lines*, by Meena Alexander. *World Literature Today* 68 (Autumn, 1994): 883.

—*Andrew B. Preslar*

See also Alexander, Meena; Asian American identity: India; Women and identity

House of the Spirits, The

AUTHOR: Isabel Allende (1942-   )
FIRST PUBLISHED: *La casa de los espíritus*, 1982 (English translation, 1985)
IDENTITIES: Family; Latino; women

The House of the Spirits, Isabel Allende's first novel, established the Chilean writer's international reputation and remains her best-known work. Drawing on the Latin American literary style known as Magical Realism, the book tells the story of the Trueba family over several generations. Set in an unidentified South American country that resembles Allende's homeland, the novel chronicles the social and political forces that affect the family's fate.

The story begins with Esteban Trueba and his marriage to Clara del Valle, a young woman who possesses clairvoyant gifts and communicates easily with the spirit world. Their marriage produces a daughter, Blanca, and twin sons. Esteban also fathers a son by one of the peasant women on his family estate; years later his illegitimate grandson, a member of the secret police, will torture his legitimate granddaughter, Alba, a political prisoner. Esteban's political ambitions take him to the country's senate, where he opposes left-wing reform efforts, while Blanca's affair with an idealistic peasant boy results in Alba's birth. The boy becomes a populist songwriter and a leading figure in the Socialist movement. A subsequent leftist victory is short-lived, however, and the elected government is deposed in a military coup. Alba, who has married one of the leftist leaders, is arrested and tortured before her grandfather can secure her release. In an effort to come to terms with all that has happened to her and to her family, she sets about writing the book that will become *The House of the Spirits*.

Allende's novel has been compared to Gabriel García Márquez's masterpiece *Cien años de soledad* (1967; *One Hundred Years of Solitude*, 1970) in style and structure and in the use of Magical Realism, a technique that combines ordinary events with the fantastic and miraculous, giving rise to startling and vivid imagery. Allende herself maintains that much that seems incredible in the book is drawn from memories of her childhood. The characters of Esteban and Clara Trueba are based on her own maternal grandparents, and she began the book not as a novel but as a letter to her aging grandfather meant to reassure him that the family stories would live on through her. The book's political themes are also taken in part from Allende's family history; her uncle was Salvador Allende, the Socialist president slain in Chile's 1973 military coup.

The House of the Spirits brings a strong female voice to the forefront of Latin American literature and offers a collection of vital female characters who embody the book's spirit of endurance, resilience, and courage.

SUGGESTED READINGS

Meyer, Doris, and Margarite Fernandez Olmos, eds. *Contemporary Women Authors of Latin America*. New York: Brooklyn College Press, 1983.

Zinsser, William, ed. *Paths of Resistance: The Art and Craft of the Political Novel*. Boston: Houghton Mifflin, 1989.

—Janet E. Lorenz

See also Allende, Isabel; Feminism; *Infinite Plan, The*; Latino American identity; Patriarchy and matriarchy

House on Mango Street, The

AUTHOR: Sandra Cisneros (1954-   )

FIRST PUBLISHED: 1984

IDENTITIES: Adolescence and coming-of-age; family; Latino; Midwest; women

The House on Mango Street, by Sandra Cisneros, speaks in an adolescent Chicana's voice of coming-of-age in a poor Chicago neighborhood in the mid-twentieth century. Cisneros' first book of fiction received immediate acclaim, becoming a widely studied text in schools and universities.

The novella consists of sketches, each exploring some aspect of the experiences of the narrator, Esperanza Cordero, after her family moves into a house of their own. These sketches are drawn from Cisneros' own life; her family moved into a Puerto Rican neighborhood on Chicago's north side during her twelfth year. Cisneros discovered this voice and subject in resistance against the pressure to conform to what she felt was, at the University of Iowa Writers' Workshop, a "terrible

East-coast pretentiousness." She realized that growing up Chicana in Chicago set her apart from most other writers. Esperanza's story also is one of resistance, especially against the expectations for women in her culture. She and her family have dreamed of having an even grander home, but she discovers strongly ambivalent feelings about home once they have one. On one hand, it is a place to be and to become. On the other, it is a sort of prison, especially for women.

In "The Family of Little Feet," Esperanza and two girlfriends get high-heeled shoes and wander playfully into the neighborhood, imagining themselves adults. At first, when men notice them and women seem jealous, they enjoy the attention, but when a drunk demands a kiss from Esperanza in exchange for a dollar, she and her friends flee and get rid of the shoes. Every other specifically feminine artifact and feature becomes a potential trap: hips, cooking, dresses, physical beauty, and most of all houses. Repeatedly, wives and daughters are locked in houses, where they serve men.

Finally, Esperanza dreams of a house of her own, one that is not her husband's or her father's but hers. At the end of the novella, Esperanza begins the story again, revealing that her book has become her house on Mango Street, the home in her heart that her best female mentors have told her to find. By writing, she gets hold of it, and in this way she can have a home and still resist becoming a man's property.

SUGGESTED READINGS

Carter, Nancy C. "Claiming the Bittersweet Matrix: Alice Walker, Sandra Cisneros, and Adrienne Rich." *Critique* 35, no. 4 (Summer, 1994): 195-205.

Cisneros, Sandra. "On the Solitary Fate of Being Mexican, Female, Wicked, and Thirty-Three: An Interview with Writer Sandra Cisneros." Interview by Pilar E. Rodríguez Aranda. *The Americas Review* 18, no. 1 (Spring, 1990): 64-80.

—Terry Heller

See also Cisneros, Sandra; Feminism; Urban life; *Woman Hollering Creek and Other Stories*; Women and identity

How the García Girls Lost Their Accents

AUTHOR: Julia Alvarez (1950-   )
FIRST PUBLISHED: 1991
IDENTITIES: Latino; women

Set in New York City and the Dominican Republic, Julia Alvarez's novel traces the lives of the four García sisters—Carla, Sandra, Yolanda, and Sofia—as they struggle to understand themselves and their cross-cultural identities. The novel is structured in three parts, focusing on the time spans of 1989-1972, 1970-1960, and 1960-1956. Throughout these years the García girls mature and face various cultural, familial, and individual crises. The sisters' mother, Laura, comes from the well-known, wealthy de la Torres family, who live in the Dominican Republic. The third part of the novel narrates the Garcías' flight from their homeland due to political problems within the country.

The Garcías emigrate to the United States, planning to stay only until the situation in their homeland improves. Once arriving in America, the sisters struggle to acclimate themselves to their new environment. The second part of the novel traces the sisters' formative years in the United States. Included among the numerous stories told are Yolanda's struggle to write an acceptable speech for a school event, Carla's trial of attending a new public school where she is bombarded by racial slurs, and Sandra's hatred of an American woman who flirts with her father during a family night out. In addition, part 2 narrates the García girls' summer trips to the Dominican Republic—their parents' way to keep them from becoming too Americanized. During these trips the García sisters realize that although they face great struggles as immigrants in the United States, they have much more freedom as young women in the United States than they do in the Dominican Republic.

Part 1 of the novel begins with Yolanda, who is known as the family poet, returning to the Dominican Republic as an adult. She discovers that the situation in her country has not changed.

When she wants to travel to the coast alone, her relatives warn her against it. This early chapter sets Yolanda up as the primary narrator and introduces the tension between the traditions of the island and the new and different culture of America. In this first part readers learn about the girls' young adult lives, primarily about their sexual awareness, relationships, and marriages. Virginity is a primary issue, for the sisters' traditions and customs haunt them as they negotiate their sexual awakenings throughout their college years in the United States. In short, it is in this first part in which readers learn precisely how Americanized the García girls have become, and throughout the rest of the novel readers learn how the girls have lost their "accents" gradually, throughout the years.

SUGGESTED READINGS

Alvarez, Julia. "An American Childhood in the Dominican Republic." *The American Scholar* 56 (Winter, 1987): 71-85.

Garcia-Johnson, Ronie-Richele. "Julia Alvarez." In *Notable Hispanic American Women*, edited by Diane Telgen and Jim Kamp. Detroit: Gale Research, 1993.

—Angela Athy

See also Acculturation; Adolescent identity; Alvarez, Julia; Class and identity; Emigration and immigration; Feminism; Latino identity

Howl

AUTHOR: Allen Ginsberg (1926-1997)

FIRST PUBLISHED: 1956

IDENTITIES: Gay, lesbian, and bisexual; Jewish

The protagonists of *Howl*, Allen Ginsberg's best-known book, are marginalized because of their rejection of, or failure to measure up to, the social, religious, and sexual values of American capitalism. The poem "Howl," central to the book, is divided into three sections. Part 1 eulogizes "the best minds of my generation," whose individual battles with social, religious, and sexual uniformity leave them "destroyed by madness, starving hysterical naked." Ginsberg said that his use of the long line in *Howl*, inspired by Walt Whitman, is an attempt to "free speech for emotional expression." The poem is structured to give voice to those otherwise silenced by the dominant culture, to produce from their silence a "cry that shivers the cities down to the last radio."

Part 2 focuses on Moloch, the god for whom parents burned their children in sacrifice. Moloch symbolizes the physical and psychological effects of American capitalism. From America's "mind" of "pure machinery" emerges Moloch's military-industrial complex, whose bomb threatens to destroy the world.

Part 3 is structured as a call-and-response litany, specifically directed to Carl Solomon, whom Ginsberg met in 1949 when both were committed to the Columbia Presbyterian Psychiatric Institute. Solomon, to whom the poem is dedicated, represents the postwar counterculture, all of those whose "madness basically is rebellion against Moloch." The addendum to the poem, "Footnote to Howl," celebrates the holy cleansing that follows the apocalyptic confrontation dramatized in the poem.

Ginsberg termed crucial those elements of the poem that specifically describe the gay and bisexual practices of his protagonists as "saintly" and "ecstatic." Drawing from Ginsberg's experiences as a gay man in the sexually conformist 1940's and 1950's, the poem affirms gay eroticism as a natural form of sexual expression, replacing, as he said, "vulgar stereotype with a statement of act." The sexual explicitness of the poem prompted the San Francisco police to seize *Howl* and to charge Ginsberg's publisher, Lawrence Ferlinghetti, with obscenity. The judge in the case found the book to be "not obscene" because of its "redeeming social importance." The *Howl* case remains a landmark victory for freedom of expression in the twentieth century.

SUGGESTED READINGS

Hyde, Lewis, ed. *On the Poetry of Allen Ginsberg*. Ann Arbor: University of Michigan Press, 1984.

Miles, Barry. *Ginsberg: A Biography*. New York: Simon & Schuster, 1989.

Portuges, Paul. *The Visionary Poetics of Allen Ginsberg*. Santa Barbara, Calif.: Ross-Erikson, 1978.

Schumacher, Michael. *Dharma Lion: A Critical Biography of Allen Ginsberg*. New York: St. Martin's Press, 1992.

—*Tony Trigilio*

See also Bisexual identity; Censorship of literature; Drugs; Erotic identity; Ferlinghetti, Lawrence; Gay identity; Ginsberg, Allen; Jewish American identity

Hughes, Langston

BORN: Joplin, Missouri; February 1, 1902
DIED: New York, New York; May 22, 1967
PRINCIPAL WORKS: *The Ways of White Folks*, 1934; *The Big Sea*, 1940; *I Wonder as I Wander: An Autobiographical Journey*, 1956; *Poetry: Selected Poems*, 1959; *The Best of Simple*, 1961; *The Panther and the Lash: Or, Poems of Our Times*, 1967
IDENTITIES: African American
SIGNIFICANT ACHIEVEMENT: Hughes's writings reflect on the struggles and triumphs of African American people in the idiom of black America.

A prominent African American writer, Langston Hughes led an active literary life. His writings extend from the Harlem Renaissance of the 1920's to the Black Arts movement of the 1960's. Hughes's father abandoned his wife and infant son in 1903 to seek wealth in Mexico. His mother, unable to find menial labor in Joplin, moved frequently to look for work. In his youth, Hughes lived predominantly with his maternal grandmother in Lawrence, Kansas. Hughes understood poverty, dejection, and loneliness, but from his grandmother he learned the valuable lessons of perseverance and laughter. Her resilience and ingenuity made a lasting impression upon Hughes's imagination, and she seems the prototype of his self-assured female characters.

After his grandmother's death, Hughes reunited with his mother in Lincoln, Illinois, but for a time was placed with his Auntie Reed and her husband, religious people who pressured Hughes into joining their church. Hughes marked this unsuccessful attempt at conversion as the beginning

Langston Hughes, author of The Ways of White Folks *(1934). (Library of Congress)*

of his religious disbelief, as illustrated in the story "Salvation."

Hughes later moved to Cleveland, where his intellectual growth began in earnest. His earliest poems were influenced by Paul Laurence Dunbar and Carl Sandburg. He read the German philosophers Arthur Schopenhauer and Friedrich Nietzsche and was introduced to socialist ideas. When Hughes's father, having become prosperous, asked Hughes to join him in Mexico in 1920, Hughes rode a train across the Mississippi River at St. Louis and penned the famous "The Negro Speaks of Rivers" on the back of an envelope.

In Mexico, Hughes became dissatisfied with his father's materialism and his plans to send him to a European university. Hughes escaped and attended bullfights and studied Mexican culture. He wrote little of these experiences, although a few pieces were published in *The Brownies' Book*, founded by W. E. B. Du Bois' staff at *Crisis*, the official journal of the National Association for the Advancement of Colored People (NAACP).

In 1921, Hughes enrolled at Columbia University. He was quickly disillusioned with Columbia's coldness and spent more time in Harlem and at Broadway productions. Consequently, Hughes failed most of his classes and dropped out. He worked odd jobs while devoting his free time to the shaping forces of the Harlem Renaissance. Hughes led a nomadic life for two years as a cabin boy on freighters that took him to Europe and Africa. On his initial voyage, he threw away his books because they reminded him of past hardships. He discovered how cities such as Venice had poor people too. These voyages and observations became the genesis of his first autobiography, *The Big Sea*. Hughes made many influential friends, among them Countée Cullen, James Weldon Johnson, Carl Van Vechten, and Arna Bontemps. Van Vechten helped Hughes find a publisher for his work. Bontemps and Hughes later collaborated on numerous children's books and anthologies.

Hughes matriculated at Lincoln University in Pennsylvania in 1926, the year that his first book, *The Weary Blues*, was published. This book was soon followed by many others. During the 1930's, Hughes made trips to Haiti and to the Soviet Union. In 1937, he was a correspondent in Spain during that country's civil war. He wrote about these excursions in his second autobiography, *I Wonder as I Wander*. During the 1940's, he wrote columns for the *Chicago Defender*, formulating the humorous persona Jesse B. Semple, or "Simple," who would later become the basis of the "Simple" stories. In the 1950's, his politically edged writings made Hughes a brief target of Senator Joseph McCarthy's hunt for communists. In the last years of his life, Hughes continued to produce volumes of edited and creative work. Hughes died following prostate surgery at Polyclinic Hospital in New York City.

SUGGESTED READING

Rampersad, Arnold. *The Life of Langston Hughes*. 2 vols. New York: Oxford University Press, 1986, 1988.

—Mark Sanders

See also African American identity; American identity: Northeast; Autobiographies of Langston Hughes; Bontemps, Arna; Cullen, Countée; Du Bois, W. E. B.; Harlem Renaissance; Johnson, James Weldon; *Selected Poems of Langston Hughes*; *Ways of White Folks, The*

Hundred Secret Senses, The

AUTHOR: Amy Tan (1952-   )
FIRST PUBLISHED: 1995
IDENTITIES: Chinese American; family; women

The Hundred Secret Senses, Amy Tan's third novel, continues her interest in Chinese and Chinese American culture, especially the strife between family members who are traditionally Chinese and those who are more Americanized. Half-Caucasian, half-Chinese Olivia meets, at age six, her eighteen-year-old Chinese half sister, Kwan, the daughter of her father's first marriage. Kwan instigates Olivia's struggle with her Chinese identity. Olivia is alternately embarrassed, annoyed, and mystified by this sister who claims that she has daily communication with "yin people"—

helpful ghosts—many of whom are the spirits of friends from Kwan's past lives. Despite her ambivalence, however, Olivia gains most of her awareness about her Chinese background from Kwan. The sisters' Chinese father has died, and Olivia is being raised in the United States by a Caucasian mother and an Italian American stepfather. After Kwan's arrival from China, the older girl is largely responsible for her sister's care. Thus, Olivia resentfully learns Chinese and learns about her Chinese heritage, including knowledge about the ghosts who populate her sister's world. Olivia is understandably skeptical about the presence of these yin people. In Olivia's culture, such ghosts are the stuff of scary movies, while for Kwan, they are a part of everyday life. The title, then, refers to the hundred secret senses that, Kwan asserts, enable one to perceive the yin people. Kwan's stories about a past life are the fairy tales with which Olivia grows up.

Later, Olivia marries a half-Hawaiian, half-Caucasian man, Simon, and as the novel opens, they are beginning divorce proceedings after a long marriage. Olivia begins these proceedings in part because she believes that Simon is still in love with a former girlfriend, who died shortly before Simon and Olivia met. Olivia must develop her own sense of personal and ethnic identity in order to release this ghost from her past. She must begin to believe that she is worthy of Simon's love, and in order to discover her self-worth, she must travel to the tiny Chinese village where her sister grew up.

Although Olivia believes herself to be very American, once she, Simon, and Kwan arrive in China, she begins to feel much closer to her Chinese heritage, and in the storytelling tradition of all Tan's novels, Olivia learns about her family's past while talking to residents of the village in which Kwan grew up. Olivia also is able to confront her difficulties with Simon as a result of the trip.

SUGGESTED READINGS

Kakutani, Michiko. Review of *The Hundred Secret Senses*, by Amy Tan. *The New York Times*, November 17, 1995, p. C29.

Messud, Claire. Review of *The Hundred Secret Senses*, by Amy Tan. *The New York Times Book Review*, October 29, 1995, 11.

Shapiro, Laura. Review of *The Hundred Secret Senses*, by Amy Tan. *Newsweek*, November 6, 1995: 91-92.

Wilkinson, Joanne. Review of *The Hundred Secret Senses*, by Amy Tan. *Booklist*, September 15, 1992, 116.

—J. Robin Coffelt

See also Asian American identity: China, Japan, and Korea; Eastern religion and philosophy; Mixed race and identity; Tan, Amy

Hunger of Memory: The Education of Richard Rodriguez

AUTHOR: Richard Rodriguez (1944-   )
FIRST PUBLISHED: 1981
IDENTITIES: Adolescence and coming-of-age; Latino; religion

Hunger of Memory: The Education of Richard Rodriguez is a memoir that explores Richard Rodriguez's coming-of-age in an America that challenges him to understand what it is to be a Mexican American and what it is to be a Catholic in America. At the heart of this autobiography is Rodriguez's recognition that his is a position of alienation, a position that he accepts with resignation and regret. As the title of this collection of autobiographical pieces suggests, he remembers his early childhood with nostalgia, while acknowledging that his coming-of-age has resulted in his displacement from that simple, secure life.

The most critical aspect of his education and his development of an adult self is language. He explores his first recollection of language in the opening essay, which describes his hearing his name spoken in English for the first time when he attends a Catholic elementary school in Sacramento, California. He is startled by the recognition that the impersonality and public quality of this announcement herald his own adoption of public language—English—at the expense of his private language—Spanish. Rodriguez has begun to be educated as a public person with a public language.

This education, as he recalls it, occurred before the advent of bilingual education, an event that Rodriguez soundly criticizes. In his view bilingual education prevents children from learning the public language that will be their passport to success in the public world, and he uses his own experience—being a bilingual child who was educated without bilingual education as it was introduced into the American school system in the 1960's—as an example.

Rodriguez offers himself as another example in criticizing affirmative action programs. Turning down offers to teach at various postsecondary educational institutions that he believed wanted to hire him simply because he was Latino, Rodriguez began what has been his persistent criticism of affirmative action policies in America.

Still another object of his criticism in *Hunger of Memory* is the Roman Catholic church and its changed liturgy, language, and rituals. Recalling the religious institution that had shaped his identity, he regrets the changes that he believes have simplified and therefore diminished the mystery and majesty that he associates with the traditional Catholic church. He is nostalgic about what has been lost while accepting the reality of the present.

In providing an account of his education, Rodriguez also provides an account of his profession: writing. From his early choice of a public language to his later choice to write about this decision, he paints a self-portrait of a man whose love of words and ideas compels him to explore his past. Rodriguez accepts the adult who writes in English and who writes about the person whose identity is defined by his struggle to find his own voice.

SUGGESTED READINGS

Rodriguez, Richard. "Mexico's Children." *The American Scholar* 55, no. 2 (Spring, 1986): 161-177.

Zwieg, Paul. *"Hunger of Memory: The Education of Richard Rodriguez." The New York Times Book Review*, February 28, 1982, 1.

—*Marjorie Smelstor*

See also Chicano identity; Latino identity; *Reflections of an Affirmative Action Baby*; Rodriguez, Richard

Hurston, Zora Neale

BORN: Eatonville, Florida; January 7, 1891
DIED: Fort Pierce, Florida; January 28, 1960
PRINCIPAL WORKS: *Jonah's Gourd Vine*, 1934; *Mules and Men*, 1935; *Their Eyes Were Watching God*, 1937; *Dust Tracks on a Road*, 1942
IDENTITIES: African American; South; women
SIGNIFICANT ACHIEVEMENT: Hurston depicts the plight and records the language of her people.

Zora Neale Hurston was born in the first incorporated all-black town in America; her father was one of its influential citizens. Her identity was formed in Eatonville; her works clearly show her attachments to that community. When Hurston was nine, her mother died. Hurston was moved among relatives, deprived of a stable home.

She worked to support herself from an early age; at only fourteen she worked as a maid with a touring Gilbert and Sullivan troupe. She later went to night school in Baltimore to catch up on her schooling, to Howard University, and to Barnard College as a scholarship student. She loved learning. Settled in New York in the early 1920's, Hurston filled her life with people who encouraged her work and gave her advice. Some of the most important of these were white: novelist Fanny Hurst and anthropologist Franz Boas, for example. Yet her identity comes from her own people: African American folklore was the focus of her research, and black women's experience informs her best work.

Novelist and folklorist Zora Neale Hurston. (Library of Congress)

Hurston was influenced by the Harlem Renaissance of the 1920's and is considered one of its stars, but she was not readily accepted in the movement at the time. Protest writers such as Richard Wright and Ralph Ellison found her writing "quaint" and "romantic." She speaks in a clear feminine voice that, if not full of protest, affirms the black woman's identity. Hurston was equally at home with upper-class whites and poor blacks, but she never forgot her heritage.

Hurston's most important works were published during the 1930's: her collection of folklore, *Mules and Men*, in 1935; her novels *Jonah's Gourd Vine* and her masterpiece *Their Eyes Were Watching God* in 1934 and 1937 respectively. An autobiography, *Dust Tracks on a Road*, was published in 1942. She was married and divorced twice.

Throughout her life Hurston was compelled to discover and translate the Southern black, often female, existence. In her collections of folklore, her fiction, her articles, and her life, she presented her people honestly and sympathetically, faithfully recording their language and their beliefs. Not until after her death was the significance of her work fully appreciated. She died in a welfare home in 1960 and was buried in an unmarked grave. In 1973, acclaimed black writer Alice Walker found Hurston's grave and led a revival of interest in her work.

SUGGESTED READINGS

Hemenway, Robert. *Zora Neale Hurston: A Literary Biography*. Champaign: University of Illinois Press, 1977.

Howard, Lillie. *Zora Neale Hurston*. Boston: Twayne, 1980.

Lyons, Mary E. *Sorrow's Kitchen: The Life and Folklore of Zora Neale Hurston*. New York: Collier Books, 1990.

Witcover, Paul. *Zora Neale Hurston*. New York: Chelsea House, 1991.

Yanuzzi, Della. *Zora Neale Hurston: Southern Storyteller*. Springfield, N.J.: Enslow, 1996.

—*Janine Rider*

See also African American identity; American identity: South; *Dust Tracks on a Road*; Harlem Renaissance; *Their Eyes Were Watching God*; Walker, Alice; Women and identity

Hwang, David Henry

BORN: Los Angeles, California; August 11, 1957

PRINCIPAL WORKS: *F. O. B.*, pr. 1978, pb. 1983; *The Dance and the Railroad*, pr. 1981, pb. 1983; *Family Devotions*, pr. 1981, pb. 1983; *M. Butterfly*, pr., pb. 1988; *Bondage*, pr. 1992, pb. 1993

IDENTITIES: Chinese American; family; gay, lesbian, and bisexual; religion

SIGNIFICANT ACHIEVEMENT: Hwang is the first playwright to depict the identity, culture, and history of Chinese Americans in mainstream American theater.

David Henry Hwang is a second-generation Chinese American. From his earliest plays, Hwang has been concerned with the Chinese American experience. Hwang has identified three developmental phases in his early work. His "assimilationist" phase was motivated by the overwhelming desire to be accepted by white American culture. Hwang's first play, *F.O.B.*, exemplifies this first period. Dave, a Chinese American, reacts negatively to a "fresh-off-the-boat" Chinese, Steve, because Steve exhibits all the stereotypic mannerisms that Dave has tried to suppress his entire life.

In college, Hwang lived in an all-Asian dormitory and was caught up in an "isolationist-nationalist" phase. During this phase, Hwang was primarily concerned with writing for a Chinese American audience. This resulted in *The Dance and the Railroad*, which recaptures the history of

Chinese American playwright David Henry Hwang.

the Chinese American railroad strike of 1867, and *Family Devotions*, which encourages Chinese Americans to reject negative Western perceptions and remember their Chinese heritage.

After the isolationist phase, Hwang next became interested in the love story. He adapted two classic Japanese love stories and wrote a play without identified Asian characters. Although not successful, this last experiment led directly to Hwang's masterpiece, *M. Butterfly*, in which a French diplomat carries on an affair with a Chinese actress for years, only to discover that "she" is really a man. Identity is explored as Hwang shows how the Frenchman Gallimard falls in love with an Asian stereotype. Gallimard commits suicide at the loss of his lover, a role-reversal of Giacomo Puccini's *Madama Butterfly* (1904). Wanting to advocate a broader forum against sexism and racism in literature, Hwang created *Bondage*, an allegory of love that challenges a variety of prejudices. *Bondage* takes place in a fantasy bondage parlor where domination is subverted when stereotypes are rejected by masked participants.

The historical and cultural identity of Chinese Americans is at the heart of Hwang's plays, which present a significant exploration of the evolving identity of Asians in a pluralistic society.

SUGGESTED READINGS

DiGaetani, John Lewis. "*M. Butterfly*: An Interview with David Henry Hwang." *The Drama Review: A Journal of Performance Studies* 33, no. 3 (Fall, 1989): 141-153.

Skloot, Robert. "Breaking the Butterfly: The Politics of David Henry Hwang." *Modern Drama* 33, no. 1 (March, 1990): 59-66.

Street, Douglas. *David Henry Hwang*. Boise, Idaho: Boise State University Press, 1989.

—Gerald S. Argetsinger

See also Asian American identity: China, Japan, and Korea; Bisexual identity; *Bondage*; *Dance and the Railroad, The*; Emigration and immigration; Erotic identity; *Family Devotions*; *M. Butterfly*

I

"I Am Who I Am": Speaking Out About Multiracial Identity

AUTHOR: Kathlyn R. Gay (1930-   )
FIRST PUBLISHED: 1995
IDENTITIES: Multiracial

"I Am Who I Am" is a nonfiction account of biracial or multiracial teenagers who are struggling with identity. Adolescence is a trying time of learning about self for those who have mixed ancestry. They struggle as their peers and society demand that they choose one race with which to identify. As the number of multiracial people increases, their voices become more powerful as agents of change.

Kathlyn Gay begins the work with a discussion about prejudice and how it is based on stereotypes. She defines racism and the power of racism. She concludes that racism is based solely on stereotypes and myths, not on any conclusive scientific evidence. Gay next addresses the fondly-held view that the United States is a country that is a melting pot in which all are valuable as Americans. The reality, according to the author, is that the common cultural demand for a single homogenous identity wipes away important parts of the self. The culture talks about a melting pot and demands that all identify as a single race, which is impossible for some. The teenagers in the book believe that picking one of the cultures in their ancestry eliminates all of the others. They believe such a choice eliminates parts of themselves.

Gay states that U.S. society does in fact believe that, when a child is born to parents who are of different ethnic backgrounds, the multiracial child somehow "dilutes" the bloodline. She cites apartheid in South Africa, the abandoned biracial children (fathered by American soldiers) in Vietnam, and the inability of American multiracial children to mark an appropriate box on any school or employment application as the defense of this argument.

The book ends with a call for all multiracial people to come together to demand change. Gay states that close to five million multiracial people live in the United States. Gay believes that some form of the Canadian system of population identification would be ideal for U.S. culture. In the Canadian form there are classifications for all races, and each applicant can mark as many as apply. The racist legacy of the U.S. system suggests that categories are based on the notion of skin color. The new manner of identification will eliminate the focus on skin color and celebrate cultures. All Americans, regardless of their color, are a mixture of various and probably numerous cultures.

SUGGESTED READINGS

Allison, Lynn. Review of "*I Am Who I Am,*" by Kathlyn Gay. *Book Report* 14, no. 2 (September-October, 1995): 58.

Flynn, Kellie. Review of "*I Am Who I Am,*" by Kathlyn Gay. *School Library Journal* 4, no. 8 (August, 1995): 160.

—Sandra J. Parsons

See also Ethnic composition of universities; Identity crisis; Mixed race and identity; Multiculturalism; Racism and ethnocentrism

I Know Why the Caged Bird Sings

Author: Maya Angelou (Marguerite Johnson, 1928-   )

First published: 1970

Identities: Adolescence and coming-of-age; African American; South; women

Maya Angelou begins her autobiographical *I Know Why the Caged Bird Sings* with reflections about growing up black and female during the Great Depression in the small, segregated town of Stamps, Arkansas.

Following their parents' divorce, Angelou, then three years old, moved to Stamps with her brother Bailey to live with their paternal grandmother and uncle Willie. Their home was the general store, which served as the secular center of the African American community in Stamps. Angelou's memories of this store include weary farmworkers, the euphoria of Joe Louis' successful prizefight, and a terrifying nocturnal Ku Klux Klan hunt.

Angelou also recollects lively African American church services, unpleasant interracial encounters, and childhood sexual experimentation. An avid love of reading led the young Angelou to African American writers, including the poet Paul Laurence Dunbar, from whose verse Angelou borrows the title for her narrative.

Singing is heard in Angelou's memories of her segregated Arkansas school. At their grade-school graduation ceremony, Angelou and her classmates counter the racism of a condescending white politician with a defiant singing of James Weldon Johnson's "Lift Every Voice and Sing." For Angelou this song becomes a celebration of the resistance of African Americans to the white establishment and a key to her identity as an African American poet.

Angelou spends portions of the narrative with her mother in St. Louis and in California. She has a wild visit to Mexico with her father and is even a homeless runaway for a time. As a girl in St. Louis, Angelou is sexually abused by her mother's boyfriend. Following his trial and mysterious death, Angelou suffers a period of trauma and muteness. Later, an adolescent Angelou struggles with her sexual identity, fears that she is a lesbian, and eventually initiates an unsatisfactory heterosexual encounter, from which she becomes pregnant.

Angelou matures into a self-assured and proud young woman. During World War II, she overcomes racial barriers to become one of the first African American female streetcar conductors in San Francisco. Surviving the uncertainties of an unwanted pregnancy, Angelou optimistically faces her future as an unwed mother and as an African American woman.

Suggested readings

Elliot, Jeffrey M., ed. *Conversations with Maya Angelou*. Jackson: University Press of Mississippi, 1989.

McPherson, Dolly A. *Order out of Chaos*. London: Virago, 1990.

Shuker, Nancy. *Maya Angelou*. Englewood Cliffs, N.J.: Silver Burdett Press, 1990.

Spain, Valerie. *Meet Maya Angelou*. New York: Random House, 1994.

Walker, Pierre A. "Racial Protest, Identity, Words and Form in Maya Angelou's *I Know Why the Caged Bird Sings*." *College Literature* 22 (1995): 91-108.

—*Thomas J. Sienkewicz*

See also Adolescent identity; African American identity; *All God's Children Need Traveling Shoes*; American identity: South; Angelou, Maya; Angelou, Maya, poetry of; Black church; Identity crisis; Lesbian identity; Rape

Identity crisis

Definition: An identity crisis is a state of psychological distress during which a person seeks a sense of self.

Literary criticism concerns itself not so much with the reconstruction of plot as with the study of themes, characters, and the use of techniques. From Greek playwright Sophocles' *Oidipous Tryanos* (c. 429 B.C.; *Oedipus Tyrannus*, 1729) to African American writer Alice Walker's *The*

Significance

Color Purple (1982), the identity crisis has demonstrated its power as one of the main thematic concerns in literature. Tragedy becomes ineluctable when characters are unable to extricate themselves from the conflict between who they are and who they are supposed to be. Conversely, characters' awareness of their true selves is essential to the eventual achievement of self-actualization. In American literature, especially contemporary American literature, an identity crisis is frequently occasioned by conflict. Conflict between a person or group and another person, group, or natural force is what drives one into change.

Society and the identity crisis

Literature is often born in protest, in rebellion. The previous generation, the other continent, the other race seeks to impose upon the new generation an outdated set of rules; the new culture, to exist, must overturn the old culture that can no longer serve. Being fully aware of the dialectical relationship between individual and society, many contemporary American writers are antithetical to society's propensity for materialism and commercialization and are suspicious of tradition's valetudinarian impact. In their works, characters' sense of self and their acceptable role in society constitutes a major conflict, which possesses the potential for tragedy.

J. D. Salinger's *The Catcher in the Rye* (1951) concerns the narrator Holden Caulfield's struggle to identify his relationship with society. Holden, a teenager, is well read and perceptive. He has been kicked out of four private prep schools, partly because he does not want to "play the game according to the rules." It is true that Holden's self-righteousness blinds him to his own weaknesses and limitations. His negative feelings about society eliminate any possibility of compromise. Social pressure that is directed toward molding him into who he does not want to be equally contributes to the emotional stress he has to endure. An identity crisis takes its toll; Holden suffers a nervous breakdown and is sent to a mental hospital.

In Walker's *The Color Purple*, a group of characters suffer confusion about their true identity and their designated roles in society. Their confusion precipitates the creation of not only personal but also social tragedy. Harpo and Sofia are a happy couple. Harpo is not as physically and emotionally strong as Sofia. Given a choice, he would be happy to be who he is, but Harpo's father tells him to be the man of the house and take control. Harpo and Sofia's resultant conflict eventually leads to the separation of the two. The reader learns that Harpo's father, Albert, had a similar experience. Listening to his father turned Albert into a victim of moribund traditions.

Culture and the identity crisis

To celebrate the diversity of American society is to recognize literary voices whose power is generated by writers' deep identification with their race and gender. Such voices call readers' attention to the uniqueness of experience. In an attempt to democratize American literary voices, many contemporary American writers of color want to reclaim their sense of history and identity by exploring what has been lost in scholars' subjective reconstruction of history. Their works portray characters' struggle in search of their ontological as well as cultural identity.

Japanese American writer John Okada's *No-No Boy* (1957) describes a person's struggle to balance two cultures. Ichiro Yamada is a Nisei, a second-generation Japanese American. His confusion about his identity is revealed in his imaginary conversation with his mother in which he laments that there was a time in which he believed he was the peach boy, born to an old woman and a Japanese warrior. There was also a time in which he was only half Japanese because "one is not born in America and raised in America and taught in America and one does not speak and swear and drink and smoke and play and fight and see and hear in America among Americans in American streets and houses without becoming American and loving it." Ichiro refuses to join the military during World War II, partly because of his loyalty to his parents and partly because of his resentment of the mistreatment Japanese Americans have experienced. After he is released from prison, his search for his identity leads him to the conclusion that he is just as Japanese as he is American.

In Chinese American writer Amy Tan's critically acclaimed *The Joy Luck Club* (1989), the author portrays a group of second-generation Chinese Americans' search for their ontological connection with their ethnic cultural heritage. After Suyuan Woo passes away, Jing-mei Woo is asked by members of the Joy Luck Club to replace her mother at the mah-jongg table. At first, she is reluctant.

Although she half-heartedly accepts her Chinese name and tells her "aunties" that it is "becoming fashionable for American-born Chinese to use their Chinese names," she is not aware of the fact that it is impossible for her to find her identity without reclaiming her relationship with her ethnic cultural heritage. After joining the Joy Luck Club, Jing-mei starts to understand her mother. She finally realizes that "Once you are born Chinese, you cannot help but feel and think Chinese." Her trip to China enables her to see that together with her sisters, they look just like their mother, her "same eyes, her same mouth, open in surprise to see, at last, her long-cherished wish." *The Joy Luck Club* also deals with issues related to gender identity. Ying-ying St. Clair has been struggling with her identity throughout her life. As a little girl in China, she is told by people around her that a "girl can never ask, only listen," a "boy can run and chase dragonflies, because that is his nature," but "a girl should stand still." She is also told that woman is "yin, the darkness within where untempered passions" lie and man is "yang, bright truth lighting our minds." After she and Clifford St. Clair are married, Clifford starts to tell people that he has "saved her from a terrible life" in China. He also replaces her Chinese name (Gu Ying-ying) with an American name, Betty St. Clair, and puts down the wrong birth year when they first come to the United States. The "sweep" of Clifford's pen not only changes Ying-ying's name and birth year, it also threatens to obliterate her identity by cutting her off from her culture and her past. Ying-ying's insistence on using her Chinese first name, therefore, takes on a thematic significance.

Conflict has always been an important subject in literature. It has a direct bearing on writers' thematic concerns. In much American literature, tragedy is closely tied to characters' confusion about their identity. Their emotional sufferings are frequently occasioned by their inability to overcome the crisis. T. S. Eliot's poem "The Love Song of J. Alfred Prufrock" uses the dramatic monologue form to depict a person's wavering between wanting to be himself and the familiar comforts of an emotionally closed, drawing-room life. Prufrock is a middle-aged man who feels attracted and repulsed by a room symbolic of highbrow society. He oscillates between a reality filled with "sawdust restaurants with oyster-shells" and a room in which "women come and go/ Talking of Michelangelo." The narrator's problem is not that he does not know who he is, but that he lacks the courage to be who he is. The conflict between his true and false identities vividly portrays a modern tragedy: not one in which the hero dies but one in which the hero lives an unheroic life. The poem ends with the narrator's capitulation: "Till human voices wake us, and we drown." Arthur Miller's *Death of a Salesman* (1949) is another modern tragedy. The main character Willy Loman has been unable to resolve his identity crisis throughout his life. Willy's sometimes contradictory behavior underlines the intensity of the war within himself. It reveals the conflict between Willy the innocent and Willy the imposter. Publicly, Willy teaches his sons received and accepted values. When he is by himself, Willy wonders if he is teaching his children the right kind of values. The Willy in public is all business. He warns his children about the importance of appearance and speech: "And don't say 'Gee'. 'Gee' is a boy's word. A man walking in for fifteen thousand dollars does not say 'Gee'!" Willy in private displays his aesthetic sense: "Gee, look at the moon moving between the buildings." Willy the salesman makes a living, or fails to, with his appearance and mouth. The true Willy enjoys working with his hands. After Willy commits suicide, his son Biff suggests that Willy's problem is not only that "he had the wrong dreams," but also that "he never knew who he was."

Tragedy and identity crisis

Together with love and death, the identity crisis has consistently demonstrated its thematic power in literature. Its portrayal challenges readers to think about their own relationship with society, to elevate their self-awareness to a higher level, and to pursue and achieve self-realization.

SUGGESTED READINGS

Barrow, Craig. *Gender, Race, and Identity*. Chattanooga, Tenn.: Southern Humanities Press, 1993.
  Ties together the study of gender and race identity.
Dixon, Melvin. *Ride out the Wilderness: Geography and Identity in Afro-American Literature*.
  Champaign: University of Illinois Press, 1987. A unique study of the connection between culture and individual identity.

Frosh, Stephen. *Identity Crisis: Modernity, Psychoanalysis, and the Self*. London: Routledge & Kegan Paul, 1991. A perceptive analysis of the dialectical connections among the individual, culture, and society.

Massey, Irving. *Identity and Community: Reflections on English, Yiddish, and French Literature in Canada*. Detroit: Wayne State University Press, 1994. A comprehensive study of identity related issues in Canadian literature.

Schier, Helga. *Going Beyond: The Crisis of Identity and Identity Models in Contemporary American, English, and German Fiction*. Tubingen, Germany: Niemeyer, 1993. One of few works that focuses on the study of identity crisis and provides a global perspective on the issue.

Singh, Amritjit, Joseph T. Skerrett, and Robert E. Hogan. *Memory, Narrative, and Identity: New Essays in Ethnic American Literatures*. Boston: Northeastern University Press, 1994. A collection of essays that examine identity issues in African American, Asian American, Hispanic, and Native American literature and cultures. Includes bibliographical references and index.

Wright, Lee Alfred. *Identity, Family, and Folklore in African American Literature*. New York: Garland, 1995. Takes a historical look at how African American writers use folklore and literature to deal with identity crisis.

Zeineddine, Nada. *Because It Is My Name: Problems of Identity Experienced by Women, Artists, and Breadwinners in the Plays of Henrik Ibsen, Tennessee Williams, and Arthur Miller*. Braunton, Devon, England: Merlin Books, 1991. A study of identity crisis in drama, especially in contemporary American theater.

—*Qun Wang*

See also Acculturation; Adolescent identity; Alienation; Psychological theories of identity; Women and identity

Illness as Metaphor

AUTHOR: Susan Sontag (1933-   )
FIRST PUBLISHED: 1978
IDENTITIES: Disease; women

Illness as Metaphor, a groundbreaking book, grew out of Susan Sontag's own struggle with disease. She was diagnosed with breast cancer and was given only a slim chance of surviving. Her first reaction was fear and self-blame. Perhaps her repressed personality had contributed to her sickness, she surmised. Then she began to take charge of her own therapy—not only deciding on a radical mastectomy but also on a rigorous two-and-a-half-year course of chemotherapy—against the advice of doctors who doubted the efficacy of the experimental drugs she was taking. She attributed her aggressive response to her illness a key factor in her recovery.

Sontag's experience and her research into the history of disease convinced her to reject psychological explanations of disease. *Illness as Metaphor*, as she later noted, is against interpretation, in the sense that the book counsels people to treat illness as illness—not as some judgment on their character or as a product of bad behavior. To bolster her case, she presents the history of diseases such as tuberculosis, which were thought to be connected with certain kinds of artistic and sensitive personalities. When the true, physical cause of the disease was discovered, and a treatment with antibiotics was developed, such psychological explanations were abandoned, she concludes. So it will be with the many different manifestations of cancer, Sontag contends.

Illness as Metaphor is also a work of literary criticism in the sense that Sontag attacks writers, including herself, who have used cancer as a metaphor. To compare a country's actions to the spread of cancer—as she did in her attack on U.S. policy in the Vietnam War—is to demean people who have the real disease and to use language not to reveal reality but to distort it. Such exaggerations, Sontag points out, further neither an understanding of cancer nor of the issues to which cancer is compared.

Thus Sontag cautions against using disease to define personality and to establish identity. To suppose that a certain personality type is susceptible to cancer or other diseases is to take away from the individual his or her ability to fight that disease. Sontag is against fatalistic interpretations and believes that with most diseases people can intelligently use medical advice to ameliorate if not always to cure their illnesses.

Sontag acknowledges that people cannot do without metaphors; they are the staple of language, and they establish human identity. To use metaphors without due caution and understanding of their consequences, however, can actually inhibit, rather than extend, the individual's control over his or her life.

SUGGESTED READINGS

Bruss, Elizabeth. *Beautiful Theories: The Spectacle of Discourse in Contemporary Criticism.* Baltimore: The Johns Hopkins University Press, 1982.

Kennedy, Liam. *Susan Sontag: Mind as Passion.* Manchester, England: Manchester University Press, 1995.

Sayres, Sohnya. *Susan Sontag: The Elegiac Modernist.* New York: Routledge & Kegan Paul, 1990.

—Carl Rollyson

See also *Against Interpretation*; Sontag, Susan

Immigration. *See* Emigration and immigration

Imperialist, The

AUTHOR: Sara Jeannette Duncan (1861-1922)
FIRST PUBLISHED: 1904
IDENTITIES: Canada; women

The Imperialist is the only one of Sara Jeannette Duncan's novels set in her native Canada. Although in her lifetime her other works, many of which are set in India, were well-known, her reputation rests primarily on *The Imperialist*. The novel chronicles life in the town of Elgin, Ontario, in the first decade of the twentieth century. Its central theme is the issue of whether Canada should have its own national identity or be part of a federation with Great Britain.

Lorne Murchison is a young man whose family has emigrated from Scotland to Elgin, where they have made their wealth and reputation over a period of thirty years. Lorne is talented and ambitious, and he becomes known as someone destined for great things in the future. He proposes marriage to a woman of inherited wealth, Dora Milburn, but their engagement must be kept secret because of Lorne's background. Lorne's sister Advena falls in love with Hugh Finlay, the recently installed assistant to the town's longtime Presbyterian clergyman, Mr. Drummond. Finlay reveals he is engaged to another woman in his original home of Scotland.

A visit to England has made Lorne convinced of the necessity of imperial ties between Britain and its former colony, Canada. The novel uses the word "imperialist" in a special, limited sense: to refer to close relations between Canada and Great Britain. Lorne attempts to run for Parliament as a Liberal. Although he is a Canadian patriot, he believes Canada's national interest is best served by forging closer trade ties with Britain. This policy threatens Canadian manufacturers, who want protected markets for their goods, and British traders, who see no reason why former colonies should receive special economic consideration. Lorne's position also is at odds with the growing sense of national pride among Canadians, who scoff at a British friend of Lorne. Lorne loses the election, is spurned by Dora and, disillusioned, moves south to the United States—the great enemy of all he had formerly represented. He eventually moves back to Canada, and a bright future is predicted for Lorne and his nation.

Meanwhile, Advena and Finlay marry when Mr. Drummond unexpectedly proposes to Christie Campbell, Finlay's fiancée. The interaction between these two generations of Scottish migrants to Canada highlights the novel's primary concern: Canadian national identity as established through and in spite of traditional ties with Great Britain. In dealing with the contrast between Europe and the New World, Duncan mirrors a theme of her contemporary Henry James. She adds a distinctly regional and Canadian emphasis.

SUGGESTED READINGS

Dean, Misao. *A Different Point of View: Sara Jeannette Duncan.* Montreal: McGill-Queen's University Press, 1991.

Keith, W. J. *Canadian Literature in English.* New York: Longman, 1985.

Tausky, Thomas. *Sara Jeannette Duncan: Novelist of Empire.* Port Credit, Ontario, Canada: P. D. Meany, 1980.

—*Margaret Boe Birns*

See also Canadian identity; James, Henry

In Dreams Begin Responsibilities

AUTHOR: Delmore Schwartz (1913-1966)

FIRST PUBLISHED: 1938

IDENTITIES: Jewish; Northeast

The short story "In Dreams Begin Responsibilities," which lends its title to the title of this collection of prose, poetry, and drama, was apparently written over a weekend in July, 1935. Vladimir Nabokov recognized its merit and recommended it as the lead piece in the *Partisan Review.* Schwartz's literary career was launched. The enigmatic title suggests that destiny is located in dreams, what Schwartz would later call in his fictional autobiography *Genesis* (1943) "a fixed hallucination." The attempt to realize dreams in poetry and to acknowledge the past as prologue to the future draws its inspiration from the artistic context established by William Butler Yeats and T. S. Eliot—perhaps the most powerful forces to influence Schwartz's writing.

The narrator witnesses the events leading up to his father's marriage proposal. The narrator watches a series of six film episodes depicting Sunday afternoon, June 12, 1909, in Coney Island, New York. The climactic moment when his mother accepts proves unbearable to the eventual offspring of this union and, in the darkened, womblike theater, he screams in protest against his future birth. An authoritative usher, representing the narrator's superego, reminds him that he has no control over his birth, and hence the outburst is futile. The scene closes when a fortune-teller predicts an unhappy marriage, ending in divorce.

The theme of the anguished child continues in the five-act long poem "Coriolanus and His Mother," in which the protagonist shifts his allegiance from Rome to a barbarian cause. Based on William Shakespeare's play, the drama unfolds before a boy, the poet's alter ego, and five ghosts: Karl Marx, Sigmund Freud, Ludwig von Beethoven, Aristotle, and a small anonymous presence, perhaps Franz Kafka, chronicler of the absurd. This "dream of knowledge" play is a parable about self-destructive tendencies—anger, insolence, pride.

The management of identity is a theme carried through many of the thirty-five poems collected under the heading "Experimentation and Imitation." For example, rebel spirits such as Hart Crane, Robinson Crusoe, Wolfgang Amadeus Mozart, and Charlie Chaplin inhabit the vaudevillian circus atmosphere of the poetry, captured in the phrases "the octopus in love with God" ("Prothalamion"), "Now I float will-less in despair's dead sea ("Faust in Old Age"), and "the radiant soda of the seashore fashions" ("Far Rockaway").

"Dr. Bergen's Belief," a short play, is a lamentation on the death by suicide of the doctor's daughter. After meditating on the promise of an afterlife and God's providence—"the dream behind the dream, the Santa Claus of the obsessed obscene heart," the doctor and a second daughter leap to their deaths. Schwartz's lurid inventiveness and capricious style conjure a world of comic shame and imminent dread. *In Dreams Begin Responsibilities* represents an attempt to mold commonplace happenings into mystical shapes.

SUGGESTED READINGS

Atlas, James. *Delmore Schwartz: The Life of an American Poet.* New York: Farrar, Straus & Giroux, 1977.

Breslin, Paul. "Delmore Schwartz." In *American Writers*, edited by A. Walton Litz. New York: Charles Scribner's Sons, 1981.

Kloss, Robert J. "An Ancient and Famous Capital: Delmore Schwartz's Dream." *Psychoanalytic Review* 65, no. 3 (1978): 475-490.

McDougall, Richard. *Delmore Schwartz.* New York: Twayne, 1974.

—Robert Frail

See also Eliot, T. S.; Jewish American identity; Urban life

In Mad Love and War

AUTHOR: Joy Harjo (1951-   )
FIRST PUBLISHED: 1990
IDENTITIES: Native American; women

In Mad Love and War comprises two sections of poems expressing the conflicts and joys of Joy Harjo's experiences as a Native American woman living in contemporary American culture. The poems draw on a wealth of experiences, including those relating to tribal tradition and sacredness of the land. Such positive experiences are compared to the sometimes grim realities inherent in the modern society in which Harjo lives.

The first section, titled "The Wars," offers poetry that imagistically develops themes relating to oppression and to survival in the face of daunting problems of poverty, alcoholism, and deferred dreams. In her notable poem "Deer Dancer," Harjo retells a traditional myth in the contemporary setting of "a bar of broken survivors, the club of shotgun, knife wound, of poison by culture." Through the dance, the deer dancer becomes "the myth slipped down through dreamtime. The promise of feast we all knew was coming." Like many of Harjo's poems, "The Deer Dancer" ends with beauty being experienced amid lost hope and despair.

Many of the other poems in "The Wars" are political in nature, containing stark images of violence and deprivation, most notably her poem dedicated to Anna Mae Pictou Aquash, a member of the American Indian Movement whose murdered body was found on the Pine Ridge Reservation, and the poems "We Must Call a Meeting," "Autobiography," "The Real Revolution Is Love," and "Resurrection."

The poems of the second section, "Mad Love," are more personal in their treatment of subject, more lyrical in their voice, and quieter in their tone. In a poem titled with the name of Harjo's daughter, "Rainy Dawn," Harjo concludes by expressing the joy of Rainy Dawn's birth.

> And when you were born I held you wet and unfolding, like a butterfly newly born from the chrysalis of my body. And breathed with you as you breathed your first breath. Then was your promise to take it on like the rest of us, the immense journey, for love, for rain.

In Mad Love and War encompasses a variety of styles, from narrative poems written in expansive lines to tightly chiseled lyrics. Many of the poems in the "Mad Love" section are prose poems, whose unlined stanzas create a notable incongruity with respect to the increasingly personal, softer mood of the pieces. The book offers a journey from the ruins of dislocation to the joys of membership and love. In the final masterful poem of the collection, "The Eagle," Harjo writes, "That we must take the utmost care/ And kindness in all things. . . . We pray that it will be done/ In beauty/ In beauty."

SUGGESTED READINGS

Leen, Mary. "An Art of Saying." *American Indian Quarterly* 19, no. 1 (Winter, 1995): 1-16.

Smith, Stephanie. "Joy Harjo." *Poets and Writers* 21, no. 4 (July/August, 1993): 23-27.

—Robert Haight

See also Feminism; Harjo, Joy; Native American identity; *Woman Who Fell from the Sky, The*

In the Heart of the Valley of Love

AUTHOR: Cynthia Kadohata (1956-   )
FIRST PUBLISHED: 1992
IDENTITIES: Multiracial; West and Southwest

In the Heart of the Valley of Love is a futuristic novel depicting life in Los Angeles in the 2050's. Narrated by Francie, who comes to stay with her aunt in Los Angeles after she loses her African American father and Japanese mother to cancer, the novel portrays the decline of the once-prosperous city.

The picture that Francie draws of Los Angeles in the 2050's is clearly based on the demographical changes in California and the widening chasm between the rich and the poor in the 1990's. Kadohata envisions a bleak city where the nonwhites and poor whites make up 64 percent of the population and where extreme pollution causes unusual and unheard-of diseases. Shortages of all essential commodities have led to rationing of water and gas; corruption and lawlessness among officials is widespread. The city is clearly divided into the areas of haves and have-nots, and rioting by unhappy citizens is commonplace.

It is no surprise then that this city of despair is inhabited by "expressionless people." Young people lead undisciplined lives in the absence of responsible adults in their lives. They tatoo their faces and their bodies—a way of "obliterating themselves," according to the narrator.

Francie, too, is affected by the times. Her adoptive family is disintegrated after Rohn, her aunt's boyfriend, disappears. It is suspected that he has been arrested by the authorities. As her aunt risks her life and devotes all her time to tracing him, Francie drifts, like her young peers. She joins a community college where there are several other men and women in their twenties and thirties keeping themselves occupied in aimless activities. Eventually, she overcomes her cynical approach to love and life in general, for amid the ruins she sees signs of renewal of the land.

Francie observes at the end of the novel: "I didn't know whether, a hundred years from now, this would be called The Dark Century or The Century of Light. Though others had already declared it the former, I hoped it would turn out to be the latter." Her comment does little to diminish the chilling picture of a possible future for Los Angeles.

SUGGESTED READINGS

Pearlman, Mickey. *Listen to Their Voices: Twenty Interviews with Women Who Write*. New York: W. W. Norton, 1993.

See, Lisa. "Cynthia Kadohata." *Publishers Weekly* 239 (August 3, 1992): 48-49.

—Leela Kapai

See also Asian American identity: China, Japan, and Korea; *Floating World, The*; Kadohata, Cynthia Lynn; Multiculturalism

Inada, Lawson Fusao

BORN: Fresno, California; May 26, 1938

PRINCIPAL WORKS: *Before the War: Poems as They Happened*, 1971; *The Big Aiiieeeee! An Anthology of Chinese American and Japanese American Literature*, 1991 (edited with Jeffery Paul Chan, Frank Chin, and Shawn Wong); *Legends from Camp*, 1992
IDENTITIES: Japanese American; religion
SIGNIFICANT ACHIEVEMENT: Inada is the first Japanese American poet to achieve a nationwide readership.

Educated at the University of California at Berkeley, the University of Oregon, and the University of Iowa's famed writer's workshop, Lawson Fusao Inada published his first major collection, *Before the War: Poems as They Happened*, in 1971. Another collection, *Legends from Camp* (1992) includes recollections of Inada's early childhood, part of which was spent with his parents in the World War II internment camp at Amache, Colorado.

Although designated "Relocation Camps," the sites where 120,000 Japanese Americans were housed were in fact military prisons, with barracks surrounded by barbed wire fences and armed sentries. In a section of the long poem "Legends from Camp," Inada ironically recalls: "The people were passive/ Even when a train paused/ in the Great Plains, even/ When soldiers were eating,/ they didn't try to escape." These poems, and some in *Before the War*, explore being Asian in a hostile environment. Inada's Japanese American identity was also complicated by the fact that his parents were Christians, not Buddhists, and thus had felt themselves isolated in the tight-knit and traditional Japanese community of Fresno. Other poems about childhood focus on Fresno, growing up in a multicultural environment with Hispanic and African American schoolmates. The poem "Rayford's Song" poignantly depicts how a teacher's insensitivity can unwittingly damage the child's pride in his ethnic heritage.

Inada's study of jazz is reflected in his performances of poetry recitations with jazz and in poems celebrating artists such as Louis Armstrong, Lester Young, John Coltrane, Miles Davis, and Mal Waldron. The collective ethos of jazz also influences Inada's view of himself as "a community poet with a responsible role in society." His work embraces American culture's multiethnic roots—as exemplified by jazz music—and an attempt to understand his Asian cultural background. "Tradition is a place to start," he has written and, in "On Being Asian American," he writes: *"Distinctions are earned,/ and deserve dedication."* Inada's own distinctions have included the American Book Award in 1988 and appointment as Oregon State Poet in 1991. As a professor at Southern Oregon State College and an expert in multiethnic American literature, Inada also helped to direct multicultural projects for the National Council of Teachers of English.

SUGGESTED READINGS

Baker, Houston A., Jr., ed. *Three American Literatures*. New York: Modern Language Association of America, 1982.

Kim, Elaine H. *Asian American Literature: An Introduction to the Writings and Their Social Context*. Philadelphia: Temple University Press, 1982.

Reed, Ishmael. *Shrovetide in Old New Orleans*. New York: Avon Books, 1978.

—Lorenzo Thomas

See also Asian American identity: China, Japan, and Korea; *Aiiieeeee!*; Japanese American internment

Incest

DEFINITION: Incest is the sexual union between family members, long considered taboo in most societies.

IDENTITIES: Family; men; women

In literature, incest has been associated with the desire to do evil (incest being evil in most cultures), with a wish to revolt against taboo or law, or with a desire to achieve the most intimate of all possible connections with another being (incest between twins being an example). Many literary works, beginning with mythology and the Bible, depict incestuous relationships, and not always with censure; however, in general incest has been regarded with horror.

History

Historically, the incest theme in literature has varied less in its depiction than in its moral subtexts. Incestuous marriages were commonplace in writings describing the lives of the gods of ancient peoples. Isis and Osiris, gods of the Egyptians, were brother and sister before they were husband and wife—a situation duplicated by the Grecian gods' incestuous couplings. Further, the literary actions of the gods set a standard for human actions; the Oedipus myth is based on the desire for incestuous union. In the Old Testament, various of God's chosen become involved in incestuous unions; Lot with his daughters and Abraham with his half sister, among others.

Sophocles' tragedy *Oedipus Tyrannus* (c. 429 B.C.) has been central in incest literature. Oedipus kills his father and marries Jocasta, his mother—each act having been predicted by an oracle and performed without knowledge or suspicion of kinship. In the literature of the medieval period and during the Renaissance, the incest theme is occasionally present, but it was not until John Ford's drama *'Tis Pity She's a Whore* (1629?) was performed that it was treated by a serious writer in the English language.

In the seventeenth and eighteenth centuries, the theme of incest was uncommon, although the Marquis de Sade did mention it briefly among many other vices. It was primarily the nineteenth century that drew upon incest themes in serious literature. Nathaniel Hawthorne's "Alice Doane's Appeal" and Herman Melville's *Pierre: Or, The Ambiguities* (1852) return to familial horror, depicting the grotesque and the macabre. What constitutes incest has varied over time. In Jane Austen's *Mansfield Park* (1814), a family disapproves when a daughter elopes, disowns a daughter who leaves her idiotic husband for a man she loves, and rejoices when a son marries a sickly first cousin. A family in the late twentieth century would probably react differently.

The twentieth century brought fervor to the depiction of incest, as seen in Somerset Maugham's "The Book-Bag" (1932), in which separated siblings relate to each other as man and woman rather than brother and sister. This work also portrays the conflict in which one character wishes to continue the relationship while the other does not. Virginia Cleo Andrews has written numerous works solely concerned with the erotic in family ties: *Flowers in the Attic* (1979), *My Sweet Audrina* (1982), and *Heaven* (1985) are examples.

Playwright Eugene O'Neill's *Mourning Becomes Electra* (1931) depicts frustrated incestuous passions that result in tragedy. Erskine Caldwell's novel *God's Little Acre* (1933) tells of incestuous passions in a family of Southern farmers, which lead to violence. William Faulkner, another Southern writer, also presents the hateful complexities arising from incest, including interracial incest, in his novels about the fictional Yoknapatawpha County, Mississippi. An example is the McCaslin family, which includes a son resulting from the union of cousins, one white and one black.

Implications for identity

Since ancient times in the West, incest has generally been regarded as an abhorrence to be avoided and severely punished. Taboos are compelling themes for literature ancient and modern. For Sophocles, people's lives were rigidly determined by fate; even warnings of what may lie ahead cannot divert one from the path along which one is doomed to travel. In Ford's *'Tis Pity She's a Whore*, love between a brother and a sister is presented as an example of the helplessness of humans before fate. The siblings' reverie is fatal and irresistible. The Renaissance play is as fatalistic as Sophocles' drama about Oedipus.

Unlike Oedipus, the brother and sister in *Pierre* are aware of their familial ties, although they have been separated from each other since early childhood. In Melville, there is familial awareness, with all the associated guilt that such awareness implies. In Sophocles, fate punishes the knowing and the unknowing equally. In literature that depicts couples who know of their family ties, there is often a theme of disorganization and social degeneration. Faulkner's *The Sound and the Fury* (1929), for example, tells of Quentin Compson's repressed sexual passion for his sister, Caddy; the self-destructive guilt that his passion produces is a symbol for the general self-destructiveness of the culture of which Quentin is a part.

Incest Ten Key Works			
c. 429 B.C.	Sophocles' *Oedipus Tyrannus*.	1970	Maya Angelou's *I Know Why the Caged Bird Sings*.
1852	Herman Melville's *Pierre: Or, The Ambiguities*.	1979	V. C. Andrews' *Flowers in the Attic*.
1931	Eugene O'Neill's *Mourning Becomes Electra*.	1982	Alice Walker's *The Color Purple*.
1933	Erskine Caldwell's *God's Little Acre*.	1983	Sam Shepard's *Fool for Love*.
1968	Cormac McCarthy's *Outer Dark*.	1992	Dorothy Allison's *Bastard out of Carolina*.

Often, then, incest may be seen as a symptom or a specific example of a general social ill. Oedipus learns of his incest as a result of an investigation into the decline of his kingdom; incest in Faulkner's novels may be said to be indicative of the moral failures of the American South. Other works, such as Alice Walker's *The Color Purple* (1982), depict incest as an example of the moral failure of patriarchy.

SUGGESTED READINGS

Arens, W. *The Original Sin: Incest and Its Meaning*. New York: Oxford University Press, 1986.

Cory, Donald Webster. *Violation of Taboo: Incest in Great Literature of the Past and Present*. New York: Julian Press, 1963.

Hall, Constance. *Incest in Faulkner: A Metaphor for the Fall*. Ann Arbor: University of Michigan Press, 1986.

Masters, R. E. L. *Patterns of Incest*. New York: Julian Press, 1963.

Rank, Otto. *Language and Literature: The Incest Theme in Literature and Legend*. Translated by Gregory C. Richter. Baltimore: The Johns Hopkins University Press, 1992.

—Julia M. Meyers

See also Erotic identity; Faulkner, William; Freud, Sigmund

Independence Day

AUTHOR: Richard Ford (1944-   )
FIRST PUBLISHED: 1995
IDENTITIES: European American; family; Northeast

Independence Day is the sequel to the widely admired *The Sportswriter* (1986) and is a highly acclaimed example of contemporary realistic fiction. In returning to the life of Frank Bascombe, a sort of suburban Everyman, some years after the events chronicled in *The Sportswriter*, Richard Ford (as has John Updike in a similar series of novels) further explores the ways in which occupation, environment, and relationships define American men to others and to themselves. *Independence Day* is an ultimately hopeful depiction of the search for meaning and identity at the end of the twentieth century.

After his careers as budding novelist and as sportswriter prove, respectively, impossible to consummate or insufficient to give his life meaning, Frank Bascombe becomes a realtor in the New Jersey suburb of Haddam (modeled after Princeton, where Ford once taught), scene of the action in both novels. He still loves his former wife Ann, who has remarried and carried their children away to Connecticut (he has purchased and moved into their old home in a vain attempt to maintain his former roles), making it necessary to finally acknowledge the end of his marriage and his identity as a former husband. The divorce complicates his identity as father so considerably that there are times he considers giving it up entirely. The novel is built around Bascombe's Fourth of July weekend journey with his troubled adolescent son Paul, a trip that begins to seem like his last opportunity to make a difference in his son's life and thus to reclaim his role as father.

As in *The Sportswriter*, however, Frank Bascombe is most clearly defined by his occupation. Bascombe finds something worthwhile about selling people homes. He considers himself to be a useful member of society, to be of service, which is his new way of trying to make a worthwhile identity for himself. His assumed role as solid businessman and community booster lacks closure, however—he has, for example, shown dozens of houses to one troublesome couple in the novel without success—and in any case, selling homes to others does not make him any less alone in the home he occupies.

As the title of the novel suggests, Frank Bascombe finally faces head-on his problems in an effort to gain some independence from them, and *Independence Day* ends on a note of hope. Ironically, Frank's independence may finally come by allowing himself to forge strong connections to others—especially his children and his girlfriend Sally. In the future, Frank Bascombe may again define himself as husband, father, and friend if he carries through on the convictions working in him as the novel ends.

SUGGESTED READINGS
Gray, Paul. "Return of the Sportswriter." *Time*, June 19, 1995, 60.
Hardwick, Elizabeth. "Reckless People." *The New York Review of Books*, August 10, 1995, 11-14.
—Greg Garrett

See also Ford, Richard; *Sportswriter, The*; Updike, John

Indian Americans. *See* Asian American identity: India

Indians, American. *See* Native American identity

Infinite Plan, The

AUTHOR: Isabel Allende (1942-   )
FIRST PUBLISHED: *El plan infinito*, 1991 (English translation, 1993)
IDENTITIES: Adolescence and coming-of-age; family; Latino; West and Southwest; women

The Infinite Plan was Chilean writer Isabel Allende's first novel following her move to the United States. Although it was written in Spanish, the book is set in California and chronicles the life of a European American man. Allende uses her character's experiences to examine the factors that shaped the United States' social history in the decades following World War II. Her focus is the Latino culture in California, in which the main character comes of age.

As the book opens, young Gregory Reeves and his family are living a nomadic life as his father preaches a spiritual doctrine he calls the Infinite Plan. When the elder Reeves falls ill in Los Angeles, the family settles in the barrio (although they are not Latino). Gregory grows up experiencing life as a member of a minority group within the community. His closest friend is Carmen Morales, whose family comes to regard him as an honorary son. Following high school, Gregory leaves home for Berkeley and college while Carmen remains in the barrio until an unwanted pregnancy and near-fatal abortion make her an outcast.

Gregory leaves an unhappy marriage to serve a harrowing tour of duty in Vietnam, while Carmen lives abroad and begins designing jewelry. Both meet again in Berkeley, where Gregory embarks on an ambitious quest for success that leads him away from his youthful idealism and into a second failed marriage and problems with alcoholism. Carmen adopts her dead brother's half-Vietnamese son and discovers a strong sense of herself, marrying an old friend and settling in Italy. Gregory begins at last to take stock of his life and to see the pattern—the infinite plan—that has shaped it.

Allende's first novel set in her adopted country reflects her perspective on the United States as an immigrant. Her delight in tolerance and openness—matters of great importance to a writer whose life was marred by the repressive military coup in Chile in 1973—is apparent in her affectionate portrait of the freewheeling Berkeley of the 1960's. Her cultural identity as a Latina also comes into play in her portrayal of life in the barrio and the effect that religion and a patriarchal society have on Carmen.

Allende makes use in the novel of some aspects of the Latin American literary style known as Magical Realism, bringing a kind of heightened realism to the story, which blends realistic events with exaggerated or improbable ones. The result is a book filled with memorable characters that brings a fresh perspective to the post-World War II history and culture of the United States.

SUGGESTED READING
Bly, Robert. Review of *The Infinite Plan*, by Isabel Allende. *The New York Times Book Review*, May 16, 1993, 13.

—Janet E. Lorenz

See also Chicano identity; Class and identity; Feminism; Latino American identity; Nontraditional family; Patriarchy and matriarchy; Vietnam War

Insanity. *See* Mental disorders

Intelligence

DEFINITION: Intelligence, the assessment of an individual's learning ability, problem-solving capacity, and adaptability, is often used to characterize individual or group identity.

It is no accident that the philosophic school of pragmatism was developed in the United States. Americans have always prided themselves on having practical ability. It should be no surprise, therefore, that there is a strong trend in North American culture that is anti-intellectual but that does not devalue practical intellectual accomplishment. North America's cultural heroes may not always be educated or socially polished, but they usually display a genius for something which large numbers of people appreciate. There is tradition in American literature of the character who appears to be slow-witted but who actually is outmaneuvering his or her adversaries. Joel Chandler Harris' Brer Rabbit outsmarts Brer Fox, and Mark Twain's Tom Sawyer tricks others into painting a fence for him. Cunning has always been part of the identity of Americans.

Cunning seems to be a characteristic not only of the extremely intelligent but also of those who might be regarded as mentally deficient. The fool who is gifted with special insights is an ancient literary character; such fools are also found in American literature, in which the mentally disabled are frequently not without resources. The triumph of the less-than-bright individual is a recurring literary motif. Winston Groom's *Forrest Gump* (1992), Ring Lardner's "Haircut," and plays such as Tom Griffin's *The Boys Next Door* (1988) are examples. Forrest Gump, the title character of Groom's novel, serves as a mirror of mid-twentieth century America. Born in a small Southern town, he participates in almost everything that has defined American identity since the 1950's. He plays football, fights in Vietnam, visits John Kennedy at the White House, breaks racial barriers, and operates a highly successful business. He also barely surpasses intellectual dysfunctionality. Gump manages more or less on his own, but the four retarded men of Griffin's play live in a state-supported residence supervised by a social worker. They only function some of the time, and it seems that their chief purpose in life is to drive their well-meaning social worker supervisor—who stands as a symbol of sensible authority—into intellectual exhaustion.

The difference between Groom's Gump and Griffin's boys is that Gump is usually involved in something grand, such as visiting the White House. What happens more often than not is that the grand event is made commonplace by Gump's refreshing simplicity. For example, he asks the president if he may use the toilet. Conversely, Griffin's characters stand the universe on its head by making every trivial problem into something momentous. Lucien Smith, for example, has the mind of a five-year-old, but imagines that he is able to read and understand the weighty books he is always lugging about. No amount of patient but increasingly exasperated dissuasion from Jack, the social worker, changes Lucien's opinion.

Writers are always searching for a device that will shift traditional points of view in order to illuminate. Using the mentally deficient as a means of turning the world upside down is one such device. It is not always used with the zany touches of joy and comedy typical of Groom and Griffin.

John Steinbeck's *Of Mice and Men* (1935), for example, is dark and morose. Lennie is a man of great physical strength, but he is so mentally deficient that he must be looked after by his friend George. Together they are a fine example of how caring and companionship can overcome many obstacles. They have managed for years as itinerant farmhands, and they dream of owning a ranch of their own. Lennie, who is sexually innocent, is overwhelmed by anxiety when his employer's wife initiates, then tries to stop, a sexual encounter with him. In a panic, he kills her. Then, on the run with Lennie and facing being a witness to Lennie's lynching, George has to kill his friend.

That sex and love are great problems for the mentally retarded is not surprising. Sex and love are great problems for everyone. Forrest Gump is redeemed by love: the love of his mother, the love of his African American friend and comrade in arms, and the love of his school sweetheart, who finally leaves him with a child of his own to love. Love and sex are also present in *The Boys*

Next Door and bring a deep poignancy to the play. They bring terrible outcomes in Mary McCarry Morris' *A Dangerous Woman* (1991).

Morris begins her novel with a sexual assault on Martha Horgan, the novel's simple-minded heroine, by a group of high school classmates. The boys stop short of rape, but Martha never fully recovers. The community and her own family blame her for the event. She drops out of school, leaves her rural home, and takes a job in town. She lives in a rented room, lonely and isolated. She is a dedicated worker at the local dry cleaners because she is just bright enough to love her routine job and because she is befriended by Birdy, a fellow worker. Martha, unfortunately, is not bright enough to handle the subtle moral twists required in the everyday affairs of her simple social milieu. She reports a theft perpetrated by Birdy's lover. Birdy stands by her lover, and Martha loses her job and her friend. Bereft and emotionally devastated, Martha allows herself to be seduced by the cynical Colin Mackey; she mistakes sex for love. The result is disastrous and proves that low intelligence can make people dangerous because they are ill-equipped to distinguish ethical complexities, thus leading themselves and others into danger.

Similar problems are explored in *Flowers for Algernon* (novella, 1959; novel, 1966) by Daniel Keyes. In the work, Charlie Gordon is thirty-two and has an IQ of seventy. He works in a bakery for eleven dollars a week and "bred." He attends the local college's Center for Retarded Adults, where he is being taught to write. He also is a subject at the college psychology laboratory, where he is pitted against Algernon, a very smart mouse who has been taught to run a labyrinth effectively. Algernon is placed in his mouse labyrinth and Charlie in a similar maze built to human scale. Every time they compete, Algernon wins.

Charlie's life is changed by an operation, similar to one performed on Algernon, that implants some new technology into his brain. As a result, Charlie grows brighter. The novel is presented in the first person, being Charlie's daily reports, which he does as a school assignment. Readers thus become aware of his growth in intelligence because his spelling, syntax, and logic continually improve. Soon he displays not only high intelligence but advanced intellectual activity. What he at first reports only as simple sensory experience he begins to comment on and uses for complex philosophic observations.

Charlie, having been rescued, rescues Algernon, and takes him to his home. Charlie is therefore in a position to notice that Algernon begins to decline. Charlie, who falls in love with his writing teacher, also begins to degenerate. Slowly, he reverts to his original state. His loss of intelligence is apparent in his reports. In a poignant moment, Charlie realizes that he must reject his new love, because he is becoming unsuitable for her. Having seen Algernon's degeneration and death, Charlie studies the procedure done on him and realizes that the same fate awaits him.

Keyes's study of retardation is an allegory of all human life, which begins with the intellectual limitations of infancy, achieves a peak in youth and young adulthood, and suffers a fatal decline. Readers begin with a person of greatly limited intelligence, see him mature to the point of being philosophical, and then see him languish into senility.

A common use of characters of extremely high or extremely low intelligence is as allegories or as metaphors for a more general condition. *Flowers for Algernon* is an example, as is William Faulkner's novel *The Sound and the Fury* (1929), the first section of which is told by the "idiot" Benjy. Benjy is a metaphor for the degeneration of the Compson family and similar families throughout the South.

Implications for identity

It is extremely difficult to define intelligence. It is also difficult to separate intelligence from cultural knowledge, a situation which accounts for the attacks on standardized intelligence tests by those who claim that the tests are culturally biased. Psychologists and sociologists have wrestled with the problem of defining intelligence and its implications for identity. David Hovey Calhoun's *The Intelligence of a People* (1973) is a landmark investigation into the issues of group identity and group intelligence. Studying the citizens of New York State between 1750 and 1870, Calhoun assesses their group intellectual level as a function of the ways in which they expressed their cultural identity. He studies their schools, their notions, their approach to learning problems, their expressions of moral conditions in sermons, and their use of shared space in ships and bridges. A more general consideration of group and individual issues of intelligence and identity in America is Jack Fincher's *Human Intelligence* (1976). Rebecca Norton, in *An Exposure of the Heart* (1989), is concerned with the identity of each person she encounters in New York's Wassack Developmental Center. With carefully drawn detail, she argues for the uniqueness of those whom society is likely to dismiss generally as the retarded.

SUGGESTED READINGS

Butcher, H. J., and D. E. Lomax. *Readings in Human Intelligence.* New York: Methuen, 1972. Collection of essays on aspects of human intelligence, including problem-solving, mental growth, organizational abilities, IQ, and learning.

Cunningham, Michael. *Intelligence: Its Organization and Development.* New York: Academic Press, 1996. Review of the principal theories and issues of intelligence.

Furth, Hans G. *Piaget and Knowledge.* Englewood Cliffs, N. J.: Prentice-Hall, 1969. Good general presentation of the fundamental theories of intelligence as proposed by the very influential Jean Piaget.

Heim, Alice Winnifred. *Intelligence and Personality.* New York: Penguin Books, 1970. A study of the complex interrelationship between personality traits and intelligence.

Hunt, Joseph McVicker. *Intelligence and Experience.* New York: Roland Press, 1961. A basic work examining the effect typical life experiences have on intelligence.

Vernon, Philip E. *Intelligence and Cultural Environment.* New York: Methuen, 1969. A consideration of how the expectations of a culture influence the identity and the intelligence level of individuals within the culture.

Wiseman, Stephen, ed. *Intelligence and Ability: Selected Readings.* New York: Penguin Books, 1967. Collection of lively essays on the nature of intelligence and its relation to various human capabilities.

—August W. Staub

See also Class and identity; Elitism; Mental disorders; Poverty; Stereotypes and identity

Intercourse

AUTHOR: Andrea Dworkin (1946-   )
FIRST PUBLISHED: 1987
IDENTITIES: Women

Intercourse, one of Andrea Dworkin's most powerful books on sexuality in a repressive culture, is about self-disgust and self-hatred. Dworkin's "Amerika" is the modern world, or rather, the world that lives within the modern American. In "Amerika," sex is good and liking it is morally right. In "Amerika," sex is defined solely as vaginal penetration. In "Amerika," women are happy to be passive and accepting while their men are aggressive and demanding. *Intercourse* attempts to question the rigid sexual roles that define the male as literally and figuratively on top of the woman and the symbolic implications of sexual contact—entry, penetration, and occupation.

Intercourse, documenting a series of literary excerpts and comments by and for women, develops Dworkin's theory that sexual congress is an act in which, typically, men rape women. The book's theory is that because the penis of a man goes inside a woman during the sexual act, intercourse is a hostile act of occupation, ready to degenerate into gynocide and cannibalism. Dworkin describes a woman's individuality as being surrounded by her body and bordered by her skin. The privacy of the inner self is essential to understanding exactly who one is. Thus, having no boundaries between one's own body and the body of another makes one feel invaded and skinless. The experience of being skinless is the primary force behind "Amerika's" sexuality, since "Amerikan" sexuality relies so heavy on the man being superior or on top of the woman.

Strictly speaking, however, it is not only the act of heterosexual penetration that causes one to lose one's sense of individuality. In *Intercourse*, even lesbianism seems to be no answer to the repressive society that Dworkin describes. The "real privacy" of the body can be as violated by another woman's objectification of her lover as it can be by a heterosexual rape. So long as women can stay outside each other's skins, metaphorically speaking, then and only then will they escape sexual domination of one another. One of Dworkin's earlier books, *Woman Hating: A Radical Look at Sexuality* (1974), describes heterosexual contact as being acceptable so long as men do not insist on the superiority of an erect penis. In *Intercourse*, even a flaccid member does not negate female suppression in the sexual act. Dworkin's preoccupation is the obscenity of the ordinary; one finds oneself closely examining what one had originally thought to be harmless, even trivial.

SUGGESTED READINGS

Glastonbury, Marion. "Unsisterly." *New Statesmen* 106, no. 2732 (July 29, 1983): 57-64.

Heller, Zoe. "Mercy." *The Times Literary Supplement*, October 5, 1990, 1072.

O'Driscoll, Sally. "Andrea Dworkin: Guilt Without Sex." *The Village Voice*, July 15-21, 1981, 26.

Rosenthal, Carole. "Rejecting Equality." *Ms.* 5, no. 8 (February, 1977): 86-90, 114.

Sage, Lorna. "Staying Outside the Skin." *The Times Literary Supplement*, October 16, 1987, 49-54.

—*Julia M. Meyers*

See also Dworkin, Andrea; Erotic identity; Feminism

Interior Landscapes: Autobiographical Myths and Metaphors

AUTHOR: Gerald R. Vizenor (1934-   )

FIRST PUBLISHED: 1990

IDENTITIES: Adolescence and coming-of-age; Native American

Mixed-blood Native American novelist, poet, essayist, and critic Gerald Vizenor's imaginative autobiography *Interior Landscapes: Autobiographical Myths and Metaphors* (winner of the 1990 Josephine Miles PEN Award), recounts the author's triumphs, tragedies, and confrontations with racism. Throughout his autobiography, Vizenor adopts the mythic identity of the Native American trickster, who uses humor and stories to reinvent his world. "My stories are interior landscapes," Vizenor writes, and, as trickster autobiography, these stories about Vizenor's life enable him to mold his experience of his own life.

Vizenor had a rough childhood by any standard. After his father was stabbed to death, his mother left him with foster families while she vanished for years at a time. Later, she returned and married an alcoholic who beat him. When he was eighteen, Vizenor escaped into the Army. In the Army, Vizenor traveled to Japan, one of the most important experiences of his life. Views of Mount Fuji, a romance with a Japanese woman, and his first visit to a brothel inspired him to write haiku. After his discharge from the Army, Vizenor stayed in Japan. He later returned to the United States to study at New York University and the University of Minnesota, where he discovered writers such as Lafcadio Hearn, Jack London, and Thomas Wolfe. He also studied haiku in translation. Vizenor calls his discovery of Japanese literature his "second liberation." His haikus won for him his first college teaching job, and his continuing fascination with the haiku form is demonstrated in the collections *Two Wings the Butterfly* (1962), *Raising the Moon Vines* (1964), *Seventeen Chirps* (1964), *Empty Swings* (1967), and *Matsushima: Pine Island* (1984).

Vizenor relates his experience as a community activist. As a *Minneapolis Tribune* reporter Vizenor organized civil rights protests and exposed illegal domestic operations by the Central Intelligence Agency. He wrote key articles about the funeral of Dane Michael White and the trial of Thomas James White Hawk. As a founding director of the American Indian Employment and Guidance Center, he combated the "new urban fur traders" and worked to get services for urban Indians who chose to leave the reservation.

Interior Landscapes ends in a haunted house in Santa Fe, New Mexico, where Vizenor's dreams are invaded by skinwalkers, lost souls from the world of the dead. This dream begins a meditation on the rights of remains that informs Vizenor's writing of his autobiography, a "crossblood remembrance," motivated by a trickster's desire to weave the myths and metaphors of his own life.

SUGGESTED READINGS

Coltelli, Laura, ed. *Winged Words: American Indian Writers Speak*. Lincoln: University of Nebraska Press, 1990.

Vizenor, Gerald. "Head Water: An Interview with Gerald Vizenor." Interview by Larry McCaffery and Tom Marshall. *Chicago Review* 39, nos. 3-4 (Summer-Fall, 1993): 50-54.

_____, ed. *Narrative Chance: Postmodern Discourse on Native American Indian Literatures*. Norman: University of Oklahoma Press, 1993.

—*Trey Strecker*

See also *Growing Up in Minnesota*; *Heirs of Columbus, The*; Native American identity; Vizenor, Gerald; *Wordarrows*

Internal migration

DEFINITION: Internal migration is a move, especially a mass movement, from one part of a country to another.

Two patterns for the movement of people emerge from American history. One or the other pattern, or some combination, characterizes most internal migration. The first pattern is immigration, a voluntary move; the second pattern is dislocation, a forced move. North America is often called a land of immigrants, populated by people who came from other countries or whose ancestors did. Immigrants come seeking the American Dream: freedom, success, prosperity, a home. Some soon found what they were seeking, but many others did not, so they moved on, generally westward. From the beginning, then, Americans have been restless seekers, on the move, pursuing their dreams. This spirit takes its purest form in road stories, prominent in American literature, whether the "road" is the Mississippi River in Mark Twain's *Adventures of Huckleberry Finn* (1884) or the Beat generation's highways in Jack Kerouac's *On the Road* (1957) or the cheap motels in Vladimir Nabokov's *Lolita* (1955). Paradoxically, the Beat generation's pursuit of drugs and sex and the pursuit of perversity in *Lolita* are, in one sense, continuations of the ancestral Puritan quest for salvation depicted in John Bunyan's *The Pilgrim's Progress* (1678). In stories of internal migration, people are seeking something good, whether or not they know exactly what it is.

Foreign critics tend to see this restlessness as a source of energy and as an ominous flaw in the American character. To them, Americans seem unsettled, shallow, maybe empty. For example, D. H. Lawrence bluntly called "Amerika" the "Death Continent." Variations on this theme appear in Evelyn Waugh's satirical *The Loved One* (1948), whose opening paragraph characterizes Americans as savages, and in Milan Kundera's *The Unbearable Lightness of Being* (1984), in which the character Sabina escapes Communism only to succumb to American "lightness."

Perhaps a more substantial criticism of the immigrant pattern is implied by its opposite, the dislocation pattern. The dislocation model is represented by the Native Americans whose homelands were snatched from them, and by African Americans, who were snatched from their homelands. This model is full not of promise but of loss—loss of land, family, language, culture,

Net Migration—Top Gaining States	
Gain in net migration from 1980 to 1989.	
1. Nevada	29.1%
2. Florida	26.2%
3. Arizona	19.5%
4. New Hampshire	13.2%
5. California	12.4%

Source: U.S. Bureau of the Census.

527

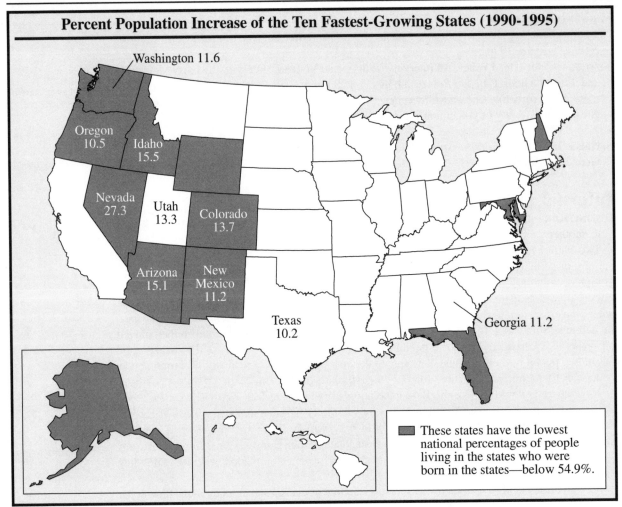

Percent Population Increase of the Ten Fastest-Growing States (1990-1995)

Washington 11.6

Oregon 10.5

Idaho 15.5

Nevada 27.3

Utah 13.3

Colorado 13.7

Arizona 15.1

New Mexico 11.2

Texas 10.2

Georgia 11.2

These states have the lowest national percentages of people living in the states who were born in the states—below 54.9%.

Source: U.S. Bureau of the Census.

identity, freedom, life. Stories of internal migration often reflect the same sense of loss as are told in stories of dislocation. People miss something good in both stories, whether or not they can remember exactly what it was.

In practice, the same literary work may reflect both patterns, even if one predominates. Older characters may see internal migration as uprooting and loss, whereas younger characters may see it as escape and promise. Immediate feelings about internal migration might also be modified by what eventually happens in the new place: The older generation might adjust and be unable to go home again, whereas for the younger generation the new place is home. One of the paradoxes of American mobility is that an Appalachian can have a grandson who speaks with a Boston accent. For these reasons, internal migration makes an interesting subject for literary works: It offers insights about American identity.

History   Internal migration in literary works set during the nineteenth century and earlier is generally westward, part of the settlement movement. Written almost always from the point of view of the settlers, the works emphasize frontier conditions, pioneer challenges, and relations with Native Americans. Typical of such works, except that he considers the Native American point of view, are James Fenimore Cooper's Leatherstocking Tales (1823-1841), such as *The Pioneers* (1823) and *The Last of the Mohicans* (1826). Much later representative works are those by Willa Cather, such as *O Pioneers!* (1913), *My Ántonia* (1918), and *Death Comes for the Archbishop* (1927). Few individual chroniclers of the westward migration stand out. Instead, such literature consists primarily of factual accounts of travel and exploration, of works by minor authors, and of popular literature. This literature contributed to a composite national myth for which no epic has yet been written, but which led to the creation of the Western and children's classics such as Laura Ingalls Wilder's *Little House on the Prairie* (1935).

Based on the immigrant model, the literature of westward migration tends to celebrate an aggressive, acquisitive American identity. It culminates in tales of the gold rush (to California or Alaska) written by such authors as Mark Twain, Bret Harte, and Jack London. An exception to the immigrant model is Henry Wadsworth Longfellow's *Evangeline* (1847), about the forced removal of Acadians to Louisiana. Other exceptions, usually written in the twentieth century, include stories of Indian removals, such as the long march of the Cherokees from the Great Smokies to Oklahoma. In Twain's satirical edge and in London's embrace of Darwinism, a seamier, uglier side of the immigrant model appears. Significantly, the immigrant pattern died as inspiring literature only after the western limits of the continent had been reached and historian Frederick Jackson Turner announced the end of the frontier.

In the twentieth century, literature of internal migration leaned toward a sense of disillusion. After the United States became settled, this trend was perhaps inevitable. This more complex trend has also produced the greatest literature about internal migration. John Steinbeck's *The Grapes of Wrath* (1939) is about the flight of Okies in the 1930's to California. Following the Joad family, *The Grapes of Wrath* in many ways typifies literature of internal migration in the twentieth century.

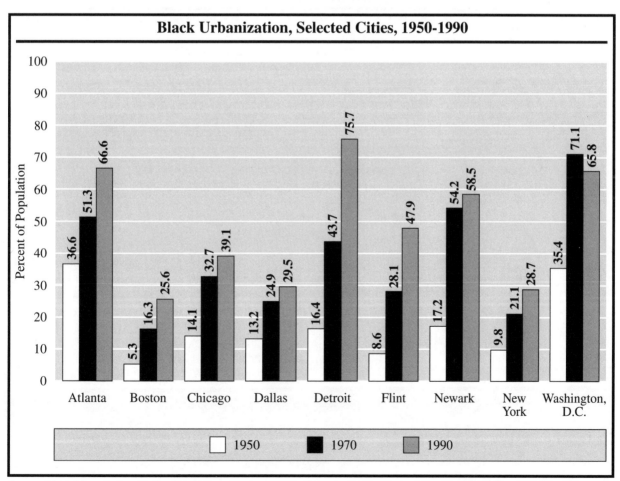

Black Urbanization, Selected Cities, 1950-1990

Source: Adapted from Andrew Hacker, *Two Nations: Black and White, Separate, Hostile, Unequal.* New York: Ballantine, 1992. Page 265.

When Oklahoma tenant farmers are pushed off the land, the Joads invest all their pitiful resources on a troubled but hopeful trek west, only to arrive in California and be exploited as migrant laborers. The novel mixes elements of forced and of voluntary migration. The novel's end, in which the character Rose of Sharon breast feeds a starving man, holds out symbolic hope.

The South moves North

The most common direction of internal migration in twentieth century literature has been from the South to the North. During the first half of the century, there was a massive migration of African Americans north. Around the middle of the century and a bit later, there was also a steady stream of Appalachians moving north. To a great extent, both migrations were from a rural to an urban environment, from the Deep South and the Southern mountains to Northern cities of all sizes.

During the 1920's and 1930's the congregation of African American writers in uptown Manhattan, or Harlem, produced the Harlem Renaissance, an outpouring of literary creativity by such writers as Jean Toomer, Claude McKay, Countée Cullen, Langston Hughes, Zora Neale Hurston, and Arna Bontemps. These writers tended to write about where they came from rather than their trip; it remained for the next two generations of African American writers to say more about the great migration itself.

Among African American writers the great migration evokes the immigrant pattern of seeking the American Dream. Crossing the Mason-Dixon line was like a personal declaration of inde-

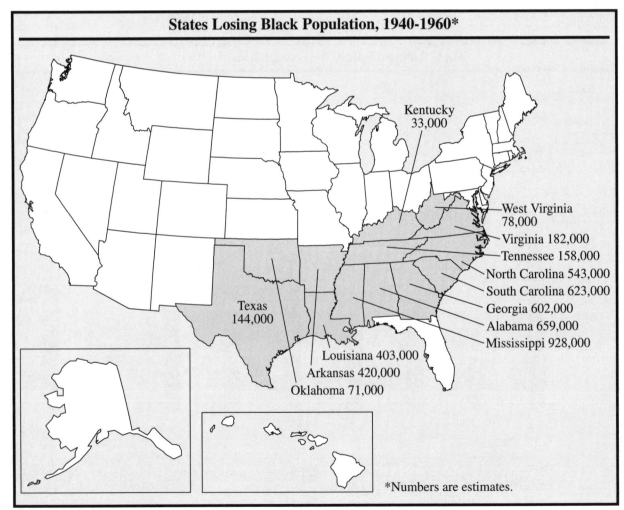

States Losing Black Population, 1940-1960*

Kentucky 33,000

West Virginia 78,000

Virginia 182,000

Tennessee 158,000

North Carolina 543,000

South Carolina 623,000

Georgia 602,000

Alabama 659,000

Mississippi 928,000

Texas 144,000

Louisiana 403,000

Arkansas 420,000

Oklahoma 71,000

*Numbers are estimates.

Source: U.S. Bureau of the Census.

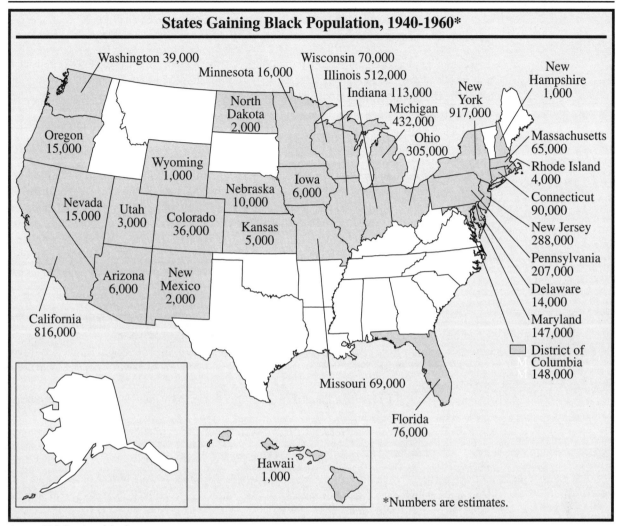

States Gaining Black Population, 1940-1960*

Washington 39,000
Minnesota 16,000
Wisconsin 70,000
Illinois 512,000
Indiana 113,000
Michigan 432,000
Ohio 305,000
New York 917,000
New Hampshire 1,000
Oregon 15,000
Wyoming 1,000
North Dakota 2,000
Iowa 6,000
Massachusetts 65,000
Rhode Island 4,000
Nevada 15,000
Utah 3,000
Colorado 36,000
Nebraska 10,000
Kansas 5,000
Connecticut 90,000
New Jersey 288,000
Pennsylvania 207,000
Arizona 6,000
New Mexico 2,000
Delaware 14,000
Maryland 147,000
California 816,000
District of Columbia 148,000
Missouri 69,000
Florida 76,000
Hawaii 1,000

*Numbers are estimates.

Source: U.S. Bureau of the Census.

pendence. The North was the promised land, and Harlem was heaven. Toni Morrison's *Jazz* (1992), set in 1926 Harlem, captures this mood:

> At last, everything's ahead. The smart ones say so and people listening to them and reading what they write down agree: Here comes the new. Look out. There goes the sad stuff. The bad stuff. The things-nobody-could-help stuff. The way everybody was then and there. Forget that. History is over, you all, and everything's ahead at last.

The ironic voice here—"History is over, you all"—suggests that the euphoric mood could not be sustained. It seemed to be based as much on escaping the South as on finding anything in the North.

What African American migrants found in the North was much like what they had left behind, except in a colder climate. Ralph Ellison's protagonist migrates to the North only to discover that he is an invisible man (in the novel *Invisible Man*, 1952). Gloria Naylor documents the ghetto conditions that migrants found in *The Women of Brewster Place* (1982):

> Mattie saw that . . . the northern light would be blocked from her plants. All the beautiful plants that once had an entire sun porch for themselves in the home she had exchanged thirty years of her life to

531

pay for would now have to fight for life on a crowded windowsill. . . . She pitied them because she refused to pity herself.

In a comment preceding his play *Fences* (1985), August Wilson contrasts the fates of European immigrants and African American migrants: The European immigrants "won" their dream, but when African American immigrants came north "strong, eager, searching . . . the city rejected them." Still, as Darryl Pinckney shows in *High Cotton* (1992), African Americans succeeded in establishing a remarkably vibrant culture in Harlem, even if the pull of the "Old Country" (as Pinckney's protagonist refers to the South) continues.

If disillusion often sets in for African American migrants in literature, Appalachian migrants are frequently overcome by loss. As are Steinbeck's Okies, the Appalachians are usually forced off their land by economic conditions and attracted by the lure of jobs in the North. In exchange, they leave behind a traditional culture and small communities in which each person has a place. They lose their identity and, as do the Okies and African Americans, come face to face with stereotypes of themselves. Appalachian poet Jim Wayne Miller compares the experience to being in a house of mirrors. The classic novel of Appalachian migration is Harriette Arnow's *The Dollmaker* (1954). Miller explores the Appalachian house of mirrors in *The Mountains Have Come Closer* (1980).

SUGGESTED READINGS

Coles, Robert. *The South Goes North*. Vol. 3 in *Children of Crisis*. Boston: Little, Brown, 1971. Examines the effects of migration on African Americans and poor whites.

Kirby, Jack Temple. *Rural Worlds Lost: The American South, 1920-1960*. Baton Rouge: Louisiana State University Press, 1987. Studies migration in the context of change from a rural to an urban society.

Lemann, Nicholas. *The Promised Land: The Great Black Migration and How It Changed America*. New York: Alfred A. Knopf, 1991. One of several books on the African American migration.

Moore, Deborah Dash. *To the Golden Cities: Pursuing the American Jewish Dream in Miami and L.A.* New York: Free Press, 1994. Focuses on one migration during the last half of the twentieth century.

Philliber, William W., and Clyde B. McCoy, eds. *The Invisible Minority: Urban Appalachians*. Lexington: University Press of Kentucky, 1981. An excellent collection of essays on Appalachian migrants. Bibliography.

—Harold Branam

See also African American identity; American Dream; Emigration and immigration; Harlem Renaissance; Rural life; Stereotypes and identity

Internment. *See* Japanese American internment

Intruder in the Dust

AUTHOR: William Faulkner (1897-1962)

FIRST PUBLISHED: 1948

IDENTITIES: African American; European American; family; South

Intruder in the Dust proved to be one of William Faulkner's most popular novels when it was first published. Set in the late 1940's, it addresses the issue of civil rights for African Americans. In 1949, the novel was made into a film in Oxford, Mississippi.

Lucas Beauchamp, black descendant of the old slaveowner Carothers McCaslin, refuses to fit into the social pattern of race and position in Jefferson, Mississippi. This proud man of mixed blood, accused of murdering a white man, maintains his dignity by refusing to defend himself. Considered the noblest of Faulkner's black male characters, Lucas also appears in *Go Down, Moses* (1942), which details the intertwining lives of the black and the white McCaslins.

Distantly related to Lucas through McCaslin is Chick Mallison, a sixteen-year-old white youth who views the old man with awe and respect. When Lucas sends for lawyer Gavin Stevens, Chick's uncle, Chick goes with him. Initially Stevens believes that Lucas is guilty. Chick, however, does not. He becomes engaged by Lucas' refusal to clear himself; he cannot let this man be lynched.

Chick determines to dig up the victim's body to prove that Lucas is innocent. Miss Eunice Habersham's participation in this scheme makes it possible. Miss Habersham, who grew up with Lucas Beauchamp's wife Molly, seems utterly fearless. One of Faulkner's grand old ladies, she knows who she is: descendant of a respected white family and unafraid to take risks for what she knows is right. She puts herself in jeopardy of the lynch mob because she, like Chick, refuses to stand by and allow Lucas to be taken. Only Chick and Miss Habersham have the courage to act at first. Lawyer Stevens is slower but is finally convinced by his nephew.

In this novel of conscience, Chick discovers what it means to be a man. He must choose between conforming to his society and his moral responsibility to the white and the black inhabitants of Jefferson. The loquacious Stevens is given a number of speeches representing Faulkner's position on the civil rights issue in the South, namely, that the South must take responsibility for and solve by itself the racial problems that it has created and inherited. Stevens tells Chick: "Some things you must never stop refusing to bear. Injustice and outrage and dishonor and shame."

SUGGESTED READINGS

Karl, Frederick R. *William Faulkner: American Writer*. New York: Weidenfeld & Nicolson, 1989.

Lytle, Andrew. "Regeneration for the Man." In *Faulkner: A Collection of Critical Essays*, edited by Robert Penn Warren. Englewood Cliffs, N.J.: Prentice-Hall, 1966.

Vickery, Olga W. "Initiation and Identity: *Go Down, Moses* and *Intruder in the Dust*." In *The Novels of William Faulkner: A Critical Interpretation*. Baton Rouge: Louisiana State University Press, 1964.

Wilson, Edmund. "William Faulkner's Reply to the Civil-Rights Program." In *Classics and Commercials: A Literary Chronicle of the Forties*. New York: Farrar, Straus & Giroux, 1950.

—*Joanne McCarthy*

See also *Absalom, Absalom!*; American identity: South; Faulkner, William; *Light in August*; Racism and ethnocentrism; *Sound and the Fury, The*

Invisible Man

AUTHOR: Ralph Ellison (1914-1994)

FIRST PUBLISHED: 1952

IDENTITIES: African American

Frequently discussed as a novel addressing racial identity in modern, urban America, *Invisible Man* is also discussed regarding the larger issue of personal identity, especially self-assertion and personal expression in a metaphorically blind world. In the novel, the unnamed young black narrator is invisible within the larger culture because of his race. Race itself, in turn, is a metaphor for the individual's anonymity in modern life. The novel is scathing, angry, and humorous, incorporating a wide range of African American experiences and using a variety of styles, settings, characters, and images. Ralph Ellison uses jazz as a metaphor, especially that of the role of a soloist who is bound within the traditions and forms of a group performance.

The novel describes a series of incidents that show how racism has warped the American psyche. As a boy, the nameless narrator hears his grandfather say: "Undermine 'em with grins, agree 'em to death and destruction." Later, the youth sees a social function degenerate into a surrealistic and barbarous paroxysm of racism. Next, the narrator is expelled from a black college and heads north. After a job in a paint factory ends in shock treatment, the narrator heads to the big city and falls in with the Brotherhood, a group of political radicals. After realizing that the Brotherhood is just as power-hungry and manipulative as the other organizations and institutions that have victimized him, the narrator leaves the Brotherhood. He comes to understand that racism denies personal identity: As long as he is seen by others as a sample of a group rather than as an individual, he is invisible. The narrator finally becomes an urban hermit, living anonymously in a cellar and using pirated electricity.

The novel's narrator is typically viewed as representing a generation of intelligent African Americans born and raised in the rural South before World War II who moved to large cities such as New York to widen their opportunities. Such historical context aside, readers also see him as a black Everyman, whose story symbolically recapitulates black history. Attending a Southern black college, the narrator's idealism is built on black educator Booker T. Washington's teaching that racial uplift will occur by way of humility, accommodation, and hard work. The narrator's ideals erode, however, in a series of encounters with white and black leaders. The narrator learns of hypocrisy, blindness, and the need to play roles even when each pose leads to violence. The larger, white culture does not accept the narrator's independent nature. Accidents, and betrayals by educators, Communists, and fellow African Americans, among others, show him that life is largely chaotic, with no clear pattern of order to follow. The narrator's complexity shatters white culture's predetermined, stereotyped notions of what role he should play. He finds himself obliged as a result to move from role to role, providing the reader a wide spectrum of personalities that reflect the range of the black community.

In the end the narrator rejects cynicism and hatred and advocates a philosophy of hope, a rejection mirroring Ellison's desire to write a novel that transcended protest novels, emphasizing rage and hopelessness, of the period. The narrator decides to look within himself for self-definition, and the act of telling his story provides meaning to his existence, an affirmation and celebration preceding his return to the world. He has learned first of his invisibility, second of his manhood.

In his later years, Ellison realized that his novel expands the meaning of the word "invisible." He observed that invisibility "touches anyone who lives in a big metropolis." A winner of numerous awards, including the National Book Award in 1953, *Invisible Man* has continually been regarded as one of the most important novels in twentieth century American literature.

SUGGESTED READINGS

Hersey, John, ed. *Ralph Ellison: A Collection of Critical Essays*. Englewood Cliffs, N.J.: Prentice-Hall, 1974.

Margolis, Edward. "History as Blues: Ralph Ellison's *Invisible Man*." In *Native Sons: A Critical Study of Twentieth Century Black American Writers*. Philadelphia: J. B. Lippincott, 1966.

Reilly, John. M. *Twentieth Century Interpretations of "Invisible Man": A Collection of Critical Essays*. Englewood Cliffs, N.J.: Prentice-Hall, 1970.

—*Wesley Britton*

See also African American identity; Ellison, Ralph; Underground Man: a literary archetype

Islamic literature

IDENTITIES: African American; religion

The prophet Muhammad's teaching is the foundation of the Islamic religion, the religion with the second largest number of adherents in the world. Muslims, or followers of Islam, adhere to the Koran, often referred to as the foremost example of literature in Arabic.

Early Islamic literature

Early Islamic literature, including prose and poetry, was intended to be read aloud. Written and oral folk literature illustrates Islamic civilization and is often based on religious considerations. Scholars of the time frowned on folk literature, including the masterpiece *Alf layla wa-layla* (fifteenth century A.D.; *The Arabian Nights' Entertainments*, 1706-1708), because such narratives do not observe the established literary style. The literary style established by the Koran has had overwhelming influence on Islamic literature. Much Islamic literature has come to the West through Spain, which Arab peoples occupied from 711 to 1492. Islamic scholars and philosophers such as Avicenna and Averroës were widely influential in the West as well as in Arabic-speaking regions.

Nineteenth and twentieth centuries

In the United States, interest in Islamic literature began to emerge in the late 1800's and again after World War I and World War II. A small group of scholars knew of Muslim literature, but the general public did not. Scholars concluded that familiarity in the West and in the United States with Islamic literature could build an intellectual bridge between the East and West. During the mid-1800's, libraries initiated collections of Islamic literature from the Middle Ages forward. Living poets and writers gained an audience in translation; for example, the author and critic Taha Hussein established a reputation in the West. After World War II, interest in the Islamic world grew as a result of the desire for political and commercial paternership. American studies of Islamic literature are geared toward providing greater understanding of and tolerance for what has often been viewed as religious and cultural systems that are at odds with the West and with America.

Nonfiction

Adult and juvenile nonfiction Islamic literature of North America includes several biographical books on Malcolm X and on Elijah Muhammad, a religious leader of a Muslim sect. Informational books on Muslims and Islam are widely available. Nonfiction books on the Koran, the role of women, political difficulties, subgroups within Islam, and the differences between Fundamentalist Muslims and non-Fundamentalist Muslims abound. One example is *Guests of the Sheik: An Ethnography of an Iraqi Village* (1965) by Elizabeth Fernea, which depicts differences in the lives of men and women in Iraq. Najmeh Najafi's *Persia Is My Heart* (1953) describes holiday traditions, festivals, and rules binding courtship and marriage.

Fiction

Diana Abu-Jaber's novel *Arabian Jazz* (1993) recounts the interplay of many identities. It employs Magical Realism to tell the story of Jemorah and Melvina Ramound, Arab Americans who live in a poor white community. Their aunt continues to try to arrange for a marriage between Jemorah, who does not want to be thus married, and a cousin in Jordan. Abu-Jaber's father was a pilot in the Royal Jordanian Air Force, her mother a European American Catholic. Her family, she has stated, comprised "a great jumble of cultures and religions . . . each segment fairly insistent on its unique identity." *Arabian Jazz* was praised by critics and won an Oregon Book Award in 1994.

The Islamic version of Adam and Eve's banishment from Paradise was initiated by the clever Iblis; a children's version of this story is enhanced by Ed Young's illustrations in *Iblis* (1994), as retold by Shulamith Levey Oppenheim. *The Tales from the Land of the Sufis* (1994; translated by Mojdeh Bayat and Mohammed Ali Jamnia) deals with relationship to self, relationship to society, and relationship to God. The stories often have sad endings and have a didactic purpose. The classic *Twilight in Delhi* (1940) by Ahmed Ali (a story writer, poet, translator, and critic) incorporates many important aspects of Islam in daily life.

The encounter of traditional Islam with Western secular modernism is represented in many works by Turkish woman writer Resat Nuri Guntekin. Other works on this topic include *Zuqaq al-Midaqq* (1947; *Midaq Alley*, 1966, 1975), by the Egyptian Nobel Prize-winner Naguib Mahfouz,

Islam **Eight Selected Dates**		
650	Official version of the Koran is established.	1940	Ahmed Ali's classic *Twilight in Delhi*, about the decline of Islam in India.
c. 1179	Islamic philosopher Averroës' *Manāhij*, a work on logic and reason.	1978	Islamic Fundamentalist revolution in Iran.
1400's	*Alf layla wa-layla* (*The Arabian Nights' Entertainments*, 1706-1708).	1988	Naguib Mahfouz, an Egyptian, is awarded the Nobel Prize in Literature.
1899	Qasim Amin advocates the emancipation of women.	1993	Jordanian American Diana Abu-Jaber's novel *Arabian Jazz*.

which depicts daily life in Egypt, and his *Bayna al-qasrayn* (1956; *Palace Walk*, 1990), which describes the decline of traditional Islamic social values in the years 1917-1919.

Sadly, a substantial amount of Islamic literature has not been translated into English. Perhaps the most widely read book written in English that may be said to reflect Islamic mysticism is *The Prophet* (1923), by Lebanese American Kahlil Gibran.

SUGGESTED READINGS

Allen, Roger. *The Arabic Novel: An Historical and Critical Introduction*. Syracuse, N.Y.: Syracuse University Press, 1982.

Mikhail, Mona N. *Studies in the Short Fiction of Mahfouz and Idris*. New York: New York University Press, 1992.

Young, Barbara. *This Man from Lebanon: A Study of Kahlil Gibran*. New York: Alfred A. Knopf, 1945.

—Sharon Mikkelson

See also Eastern religion and philosophy; Nation of Islam

I've Been a Woman: New and Selected Poems

AUTHOR: Sonia Sanchez (1934-   )
FIRST PUBLISHED: 1978
IDENTITIES: African American; women

I've Been a Woman: New and Selected Poems is a compilation of selections from Sonia Sanchez's major works up to 1978. This collection offers a cross section of the themes that characterize Sonia Sanchez's poetic vision. Sanchez's work balances the private and the public. The private, or introspective poems, are intensely personal. The public poems cover a number of concerns. Selections from *Homecoming* (1969), *We a Badd DDD People* (1970), *Love Poems* (1973), *A Blues Book for Blue Black Magical Women* (1974), and *Generations: Selected Poetry 1969-1985* (1986) make up *I've Been a Woman*.

Themes include issues of identity among African Americans. Sanchez's work is characterized by her ability to offer clear-eyed commentary on African American conditions while offering poetry of destiny and self-determination. For example, one of Sanchez's ongoing concerns is drug addiction among African Americans. In works such as *Wounded in the House of a Friend* (1995), she focuses this concern on the devastating effects of addiction to crack cocaine.

This intermingling of themes is found in poems such as "Summary." This poem represents an example of Sanchez's technique. She combines personal and public concerns. Within this poem, Sanchez does not allow the narrator to move inward and remain there. She seems to assume an introspective position as a momentary restful pose. In this energizing space, the narrator is renewed and arrives at a political solution to problems noted in the poems.

The poems included in these sections are examples of Sanchez's virtuosity as a poet. Section 5 is devoted exclusively to Sanchez's "Haikus/Tankas & Other Love Syllables." Use of forms offers an example of the poet's technique.

This collection offers an excellent example of Sanchez's range as an artist. In the various sections of *I've Been a Woman*, the speaker of Sanchez's poetry is revealed as a quester for identity and resolution. Distinguished from male quest epics, Sanchez's quest focuses on the desire to embark on a quest not only for herself but also for other women as well. The knowledge that the quester seeks is assumed to be available in the person of an Earth Mother who can help the quester understand the relationship between past and present. Such a figure can also help the quester learn to have faith in the future.

SUGGESTED READINGS

Gabbin, Joanne Veal. "The Southern Imagination of Sonia Sanchez." In *Southern Women Writers: The New Generation*, edited by Tonnette Bond Inge. Tuscaloosa: University of Alabama Press, 1990.

Jennings, Regina B. "The Blue/Black Poetics of Sonia Sanchez." In *Language and Literature in the African American Imagination*, edited by Carol Aisha Blackshire-Belay. Westport, Conn.: Greenwood Press, 1992.

Joyce, Joyce Ann. "The Development of Sonia Sanchez: A Continuing Journey." *Indian Journal of American Studies* 13 (July, 1983): 37-71.

—*Frenzella Elaine De Lancey*

See also African American identity; Black English; Sanchez, Sonia

J

Jackson, Helen Hunt

BORN: Amherst, Massachusetts; October 15, 1830
DIED: San Francisco, California; August 12, 1885
PRINCIPAL WORKS: *A Century of Dishonor*, 1881; *Ramona*, 1884
IDENTITIES: Native American; West and Southwest; women
SIGNIFICANT ACHIEVEMENT: Jackson's protest literature drew public attention to the plight of North American tribes.

After the death of her first husband in 1863, Helen Hunt began writing as an outlet for her creative energies and to earn a living. She wrote travel articles, poems, short stories, and novels, publishing in many periodicals, including *Century, Harper's,* and *The Atlantic Monthly.* Her work appeared under a variety of pseudonyms, most notably H. H., Saxe Holm, and as part of the No Name series of novels. Having suffered from respiratory illnesses, she went to Colorado Springs, Colorado, for her health. There she met and married, in 1875, William Jackson. She lived in Colorado the rest of her life, for several years continuing to write travel articles about the American West.

During the nineteenth century, publishers brought out several collections of her popular early work, but it was her later work, which championed the cause of Native American peoples, that earned more lasting acclaim.

On a trip to Boston in 1879, Jackson attended a lecture by two Ponca Indians, Standing Bear and Bright Eyes. Although she had never gone in for causes, she became interested in the plight of these Indians and spent many hours researching the United States government's treaty relations with various North American tribes. The results of her study appeared in *A Century of Dishonor,* a history of the making and breaking of treaties by the government in its dealings with several tribes from 1776 to 1876. A strong denunciation of government practices, the book documents the successive removal of native Americans from their lands. It drew some official attention; Jackson was appointed to a federal Indian Commission to study the mission Indians of California.

Disappointed that *Century of Dishonor* did not excite more public response, Jackson wrote a novel, *Ramona,* in hopes of appealing to a wider audience. *Ramona* is one of the few works of its time to present a picture of whites moving into a West that already had two established cultures, the mission Indian and the Spanish American. The novel recounts the story of the California Indians, who were repeatedly dispossessed of their lands, their homes, and their cultures by land-grabbing Americans, who had the support of their government.

A Century of Dishonor and *Ramona* were Jackson's protest literature, presenting a side of the debate on the government's treatment of the tribes that was generally obscured. It was not until the 1960's that other authors echoed her protests.

SUGGESTED READINGS

Mathes, Valerie Sherer. *Helen Hunt Jackson and Her Indian Reform Legacy.* Austin: University of Texas Press, 1990.

O'Dell, Ruth. *Helen Hunt Jackson.* East Norwalk, Conn.: Appleton-Century-Crofts, 1939.

—Arlene Larson

See also American identity: West and the frontier; *Ramona*

Jackson decried mistreatment of American Indians; her Ramona *(1884) portrays a California native woman who is victimized by land-hungry settlers. Her popular novel has often been dramatized with emphasis on its romantic elements.* (Ramona Pageant Association)

Jackson, Shirley

BORN: San Francisco, California; December 14, 1919

DIED: North Bennington, Vermont; August 8, 1965

PRINCIPAL WORKS: *The Lottery: Or, The Adventures of James Harris*, 1949; *The Haunting of Hill House*, 1959; *We Have Always Lived in the Castle*, 1962

IDENTITIES: European American; family; women

SIGNIFICANT ACHIEVEMENT: Jackson's best-known fiction depicts the turmoil of women characters in a context of social, psychological, and supernatural horror.

Shirley Jackson's horrific fiction belies the biographical facts of her life. Her women characters in particular are often neurotic, alienated, or outcasts from their families and communities. Jackson herself, however, was by all accounts a happily married mother of four who balanced her literary career with activities ranging from school bake sales to entertaining friends, such as fellow author Ralph Ellison, in her family's home in Vermont. Biographical material by her husband—the writer, teacher, and critic Stanley Edgar Hyman—stresses the disjuncture between her personal life and the content of her most famous fiction, which she viewed as a craft and profession, as opposed to a forum for self-revelation.

The mother, hostess, and lecturer at writers' conferences who was thoroughly integrated into the life of her family and community created the character of Tessie Hutchinson, whose neighbors, friends, husband, and children stone her to death in the ritual sacrifice that climaxes her most famous and influential work, "The Lottery." The short story's impact cannot be underestimated; its terrifying picture of alienation and violence prompted subscription cancellations when *The New Yorker* published it in 1948. The story was banned in South Africa, which pleased Jackson because she felt that those who had banned the story understood it.

The Haunting of Hill House and *We Have Always Lived in the Castle* places lonely, sensitive women—the psychic Eleanor Vance and troubled teenager Mary Katherine Blackwood, respectively—in gothic settings. The books feature houses haunted by ghosts of unrealized dreams, frustrated desires, and mysterious deaths. These novels, Jackson's most successful, gave further impetus to critics who viewed her work as the product of a warped personality. Sensitive to such criticism, Jackson downplayed the single real-life parallel to her fiction—her personal study and practice of witchcraft.

Largely forgotten but closer to Jackson's personal experience are her humorous accounts of family life, *Life Among the Savages* (1953) and *Raising Demons* (1957), whose titles reflect the disparity between appearance and reality so evident in her life and work. Jackson, who condemned her characters to terrible fates, died quietly in her sleep of heart failure at age forty-six.

SUGGESTED READINGS

Cervo, Nathan. "Jackson's 'The Lottery.' " *The Explicator* 50, no. 3 (Spring, 1992): 183-185.

Hall, Joan Wylie. *Shirley Jackson: A Study of the Short Fiction.* New York: Twayne, 1993.

Oppenheimer, Judy. *Private Demons: The Life of Shirley Jackson.* New York: G. P. Putnam's Sons, 1988.

—Charles Avinger

See also Adolescent identity; American identity: Northeast; Women and identity

James, Henry

BORN: New York, New York; April 15, 1843

DIED: London, England; February 28, 1916

PRINCIPAL WORKS: *A Passionate Pilgrim and Other Tales*, 1875; *Roderick Hudson*, 1876; *The American*, 1876-1877; *Watch and Ward*, serial, 1871, book, 1878; *The Europeans*, 1878; *Daisy Miller: A Study*, 1878; *An International Episode*, 1879; *Washington Square*, 1881; *The Portrait of a Lady*, 1882; *The Bostonians*, 1886; *The Princess Casamassima*, 1886; *The Spoils of Poynton*, 1897; *What Maisie Knew*, 1897; *The Awkward Age*, 1899; *The Sacred Fount*, 1901;

The Wings of the Dove, 1902; *The Ambassadors*, 1903; *The Golden Bowl*, 1905; *The Finer Grain*, 1910; *Master Eustace*, 1920

IDENTITIES: European American

SIGNIFICANT ACHIEVEMENT: Expatriate author James depicts American identity from the vantage point of one detached from America while remaining spiritually identified with it.

Born to affluent parents who reveled in not putting down roots, Henry James had crossed the Atlantic six times before he was eighteen. His family enjoyed extended stays in Germany, France, Switzerland, and England, returning to the United States in 1860 when the eldest son, William, reached an age that required educational opportunities not available to him abroad. The family took up residence in Newport, Rhode Island, where Henry, exempted from military service in the Civil War because of an injury, spent his time reading voraciously and sketching.

James entered Harvard Law School, but during his first year there realized that he did not want a career in law. He spent most of his time reading in the library or attending the literary lectures of James Russell Lowell. He also cultivated a substantial coterie of artistic and literary friends. By 1869, when James first returned to Europe on his own, he had published numerous reviews and over a dozen stories. His trip began in England, progressing to France and Italy, the country he loved most throughout his life. Many of his stories have Italian settings, often focusing on rootless Americans spending extended periods abroad.

Never quite feeling American but certainly not feeling European either, James was abroad from 1872 until 1874, and returned to Paris in 1875, there falling in with writers Ivan Turgenev, Émile Zola, and Gustave Flaubert. By December, 1876, he had moved to England, which, from that time on, was essentially his home, although he returned to the United States periodically for extended stays. During World War I, for practical reasons, James took British citizenship.

Much of James's writing is set in Europe, but it usually concerns Americans living or visiting abroad. His output of imaginative fiction includes more than a hundred short stories, twelve long short stories, eleven short novels, and eleven longer novels. In addition, James published penetrating works of literary theory and criticism, including the first full-length critical biography of Nathaniel Hawthorne. His travel books also gained renown.

SUGGESTED READINGS

Edel, Leon. *Henry James: A Life*. New York: Harper & Row, 1987.

Moore, Harry T. *Henry James*. New York: Viking, 1974.

Rowe, John Carlos. *The Theoretical Dimensions of Henry James*. Madison: University of Wisconsin Press, 1984.

Wagenknecht, Edward. *The Tales of Henry James*. New York: Frederick Ungar, 1984.

—R. Baird Shuman

See also *Ambassadors, The*; American identity: Northeast; *Bostonians, The*; Expatriate identity; *Portrait of a Lady, The*

Japanese American internment

IDENTITIES: Japanese American; West and Southwest

DEFINITION: During World War II approximately 120,000 Japanese Americans, two-thirds of whom were American born and thus American citizens, were evacuated from their homes on the Pacific coast and incarcerated into ten "relocation centers" located in remote areas of seven Western states.

Within hours after Japan's bombing attack of the United States naval station at Pearl Harbor, Hawaii, on December 7, 1941, the Federal Bureau of Investigation (FBI) began arresting community leaders, teachers at Japanese schools, and anyone who had business ties to Japan. Most of the two thousand men arrested were Issei (born in Japan, immigrants to the United States). Their status as resident aliens was changed to that of enemy aliens. The two-week period of arrests along the

Identifying Issei and Nisei

World War II Internment Camps

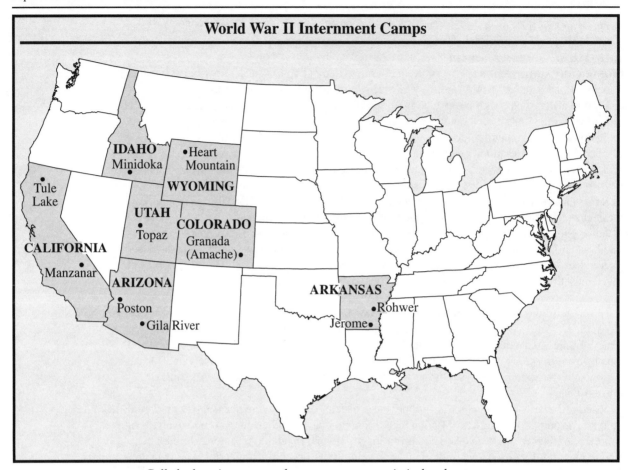

Called relocation centers, these camps were set in isolated areas.

Pacific coast was also a time of search and seizure of Japanese American households. Homes, businesses, and personal property were lost.

For the Nisei (born in the United States) the wartime hysteria and subsequent actions on the part of fellow American citizens were simply not believable. This is evident in Monica Sone's fictionalized autobiography *Nisei Daughter* (1953). In *Nisei Daughter*, Sone recalls the FBI raids on ordinary citizens, confiscating radios, cameras, firearms, knives, and anything Japanese that could be construed as subversive. For the shocked Nisei, their identities as citizens were erased along with their constitutional rights. Having one's identity suddenly become a number on a cardboard tag is an issue universal to internment narratives. Mine Okubo even titled her memoirs by her family number, *Citizen 13660* (1946). The loss of their names is yet another example of the assault on Japanese American identity. In Janice Mirikitani's poem "Crazy Alice" Alice remembers that before the war she had a name.

Evacuation   In reaction to pressure from special interest groups, Congress, and the military, President Franklin Roosevelt signed Executive Order 9066 on February 19, 1942, which authorized the removal of certain people from military areas. It was Lieutenant General John DeWitt, commander of the Western Defense Command, who issued civilian exclusion orders to all persons of Japanese ancestry, alien and nonalien. Evacuation zones included the western half of Washington and Oregon, all of California, and the southern third of Arizona. Prior to actual mass evacuations, which began at the end of March, 1942, a designated responsible person, representing a family unit, was required to register with the wartime civil control agency. *Station J: An American Epic* (1979) reveals the harsh scrutinizing of two Japanese American brothers during processing at a civil control station. Based on facts, this play by Richard France follows the changing identities of a typical Japanese American family from the time of the attack on Pearl Harbor to the dedication of the Japanese Cultural Center in San Francisco in 1968. *Station J* is an artistic testament to the humiliation experienced by Nisei Japanese American men as they learned that their draft status had been changed from 1-A to 4-C. Suddenly enemy aliens, they were forced to assume an unwanted new identity.

Evacuees were held from two to six months in temporary assembly centers. Twelve centers were in California and one each in Washington, Oregon, and Arizona. These holding centers were typically fairgrounds and race tracks. Living in horse stables and livestock pavilions with spiders and rats caused many Japanese Americans to question their basic identity. Okubo's poignant prose in *Citizen 13660* takes the reader inside the Tanforan assembly center in California. Typical of all the assembly centers, it was surrounded by military police and barbed-wire fences. *Citizen 13660* depicts the inadequate sanitary facilities and complete lack of privacy as being particularly devastating to one's personal dignity. Forced to live in the hastily whitewashed stalls with linoleum floors laid over manure-covered boards, eating boiled potatoes and canned sausage in mess halls with thousands of people, the people in the internment camps faced the beginning of the devastating way of life Japanese Americans and their alien parents were forced to endure during World War II. **Assembly centers**

The first literature published about camp life was a collection of Japanese poetry titled *Nararebashi* (shooting star) mimeographed in 1945 at the Crystal City, Texas, internment camp. The poems in the collection and others written by Issei men were translated by Jiro Nakano and Kay Nakano for the anthology *Poets Behind Barbed Wire* (1983), illustrated by internee George Hoshida. These poems illuminate the irony of their internees' identity as prisoners of war of the United States while their sons were United States soldiers. **Camp life**

One of the most damaging effects of camp life was its tearing apart of family identity. Mothers could no longer run a household, fathers could no longer be breadwinners, high school and college students no longer had a campus life, and no one had any privacy. The full-length narrative *Farewell to Manzanar: A True Story of Japanese American Experience During and After the World War II Internment* (1973), written by Jeanne Wakatsuki Houston and James D. Houston, tells the story of a changing family through the eyes of a girl. *Long Road from White River* (1983), a novel written by Lois Morioka, gives readers a picture of camp life through the eyes of a Caucasian woman married to a Nisei farmer. The heroine Lisa represents the 219 voluntary residents of the camps, who were primarily spouses. *Long Road from White River*, along with other literature, calls the internment centers American concentration camps. Joy Kogawa's novel *Obasan* (1984) describes the Japanese Canadian experience of evacuation and relocation.

Despite their internment and loss of rights, most Japanese in the camps tried to maintain their identity as Americans. Janice Mirikitani edited a Japanese American literary anthology entitled *Ayumi: The Japanese American Anthology* (1980) containing several of her own poems about the internment. Many of the poems illustrate the ironies of concentration camp life: In one poem, the speaker's mother makes paper flowers for the American Legion for two cents a dozen.

The issue of loyalty played a major role in the identity of Japanese Americans. *Farewell to Manzanar* highlights the devastating effect on Japanese American families of the infamous loyalty questions twenty-seven and twenty-eight, which are reprinted verbatim at the opening of chapter eleven. Answers to the questions were required of all internees over the age of seventeen. Question twenty-seven asked if one would be willing to serve in the armed forces. Question twenty-eight asked if one would swear unqualified allegiance to the United States and forswear allegiance to any foreign power. The effects of these questions are the subject of the first novel published about the internment, John Okada's *No-No Boy* (1957). Approximately 10,000 "disloyals," or those who did not answer yes to both questions, were segregated at the Tule Lake center in northern California. Eventually about 4,700 people repatriated to Japan, many as part of prisoner-of-war exchanges. Of those repatriated, 65 percent were American born. **Loyalty**

Long Road from White River includes the loyalty theme of Japanese American identity by telling about the young men who served in the 442nd Regimental Combat Team of the United States Army. In January, 1944, the federal government reversed the 4-C (enemy alien) status of draft-age men and created a segregated Nisei unit of the United States Army. Fighting on the front lines in Italy and France, the 442nd became the most decorated unit in the entire American Army. The men of the 442nd participated in the liberation of the Nazi concentration camp at Dachau while their families remained behind barbed wire in America.

Relocation and resettlement

Nisei Daughter relates two positive experiences with "relocation," the War Relocation Authority's program that was instituted after the "disloyals" were segregated to Tule Lake. The first is the experience of the young people who received seasonal work releases to harvest potatoes and sugar beets in agricultural areas of the West. The second is college student Monica's relocating to the Midwest. The autobiography concludes with Monica securing a position in a church-sponsored home and leaving camp to attend college, as did 4,600 students. On the other hand, *Long Road from White River* describes the difficulties of resettlement for a family whose collective identity had been severely altered during the war. Like the family in this novel, many Japanese American families lost elder members and babies in the camps and their young men in battles overseas. Facing strong racial prejudice, Japanese American families were not welcome on the West Coast and many relocated to midwestern urban areas.

Hisaye Yamamoto's short story "Las Vegas Charley" explores the life of Charley as a young man in Japan, his coming to America, his family's removal to a concentration camp, and his

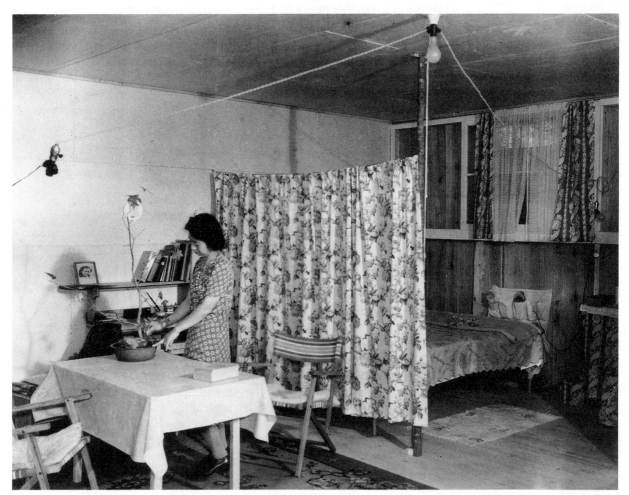

After being forcibly evacuated from her home, a woman tends a plant at an internment camp. (National Archives)

resettlement in Las Vegas. A dishwasher in a Chinese restaurant with long-standing gambling and drinking habits, Charley still maintains the identity he assumed while incarcerated during World War II. Typical of many Japanese families during internment, Charley lost two sons: one who repatriated to Japan after renouncing his American citizenship and another who was killed in action while fighting for the Allies.

Internment's effect on the family is also the focus of the film *Come See the Paradise* (1990). Based on historical facts and events, this film, with an Irish American hero, tells the internment stories narrated by a Nisei heroine, his wife. *Come See the Paradise* incorporates major incidents occurring at the Santa Anita assembly center, Manzanar relocation center, and Tule Lake segregation camp. Lawson Fusao Inada's poem "Amanche Gate" reveals the identities of teens in the 1950's who were children in the camps.

SUGGESTED READINGS

Chan, Sucheng. *Asian Americans: An Interpretive History*. Boston: Twayne, 1991. Provides a chronology dating from 1600; the chapter "Changing Fortunes, 1941 to 1965" covers Japanese American internment.

Chang, Gordon H. " 'Superman Is About to Visit the Relocation Centers' and the Limits of Wartime Liberalism." *Amerasia Journal* 19, no. 1 (1993): 37-60. Commentary and reproduction of a daily Superman series that ran in national newspapers the summer of 1943; Superman suppresses an insurrection in one of the camps.

Kikuchi, Charles. *The Kikuchi Diary Chronicle from an American Concentration Camp*. Champaign: University of Illinois Press, 1973. This college student's diary explores the changing identities of his family members in the Manzanar camp.

Kitagawa, Daisuke. *Issei and Nisei: The Internment Years*. New York: Seabury Press, 1967. This autobiography begun in 1956 examines the identities of first-and second-generation Japanese Americans during World War II.

Kitano, Harry. *The Japanese Americans*. New York: Chelsea House, 1988. This photo essay explores Japanese immigration to America, culture and religion, survival in the internment camps, and adjustment to postwar America.

Nishimoto, Richard S. *Inside an American Concentration Camp: Japanese American Resistance at Poston, Arizona*. Edited by Lane Ryo Hirabayashi. Tuscon: University of Arizona Press, 1995. This portrait of daily life within the camps contains an autobiography, reports on gambling, and a discussion of labor. This work sheds new light on Japanese American identity.

Takaki, Ronald. *Strangers from a Different Shore: A History of Asian Americans*. Boston: Little, Brown, 1989. The chapter "Hyphenated Americans: The Nisei Generation" examines the American-born Japanese who remained loyal to the United States even after being stripped of their constitutional rights.

Weglen, Michi. *Years of Infamy: The Untold Story of America's Concentration Camps*. New York: William Morrow, 1976. Contains photographs smuggled from the camps.

—*Susan R. Dominguez*

See also Asian American identity: China, Japan, and Korea; *Camp Notes and Other Poems*; Inada, Lawson Fusao; Kogawa, Joy; *No-No Boy*; *Obasan*; Okada, John; World War II; Yamada, Mitsuye Yasutake

Japanese Americans. *See* Asian American identity: China, Japan, and Korea

Japanese internment. *See* Japanese American internment

Jeffers, Robinson

Born: Pittsburgh, Pennsylvania; January 10, 1887
Died: Carmel, California; January 20, 1962
Principal works: *Flagons and Apples*, 1912; *Californians*, 1916; *Tamar and Other Poems*, 1924; *Roan Stallion, Tamar, and Other Poems*, 1925; *The Women at Point Sur*, 1927; *Cawdor and Other Poems*, 1928; *Dear Judas and Other Poems*, 1929; *Give Your Heart to the Hawks and Other Poems*, 1933; *The Selected Poetry of Robinson Jeffers*, 1938; *The Double Axe and Other Poems*, 1948; *Hungerfield and Other Poems*, 1954; *The Beginning and the End*, 1963; *Selected Poems*, 1965
Identities: European American; family; West and Southwest
Significant achievement: Jeffers wrote long narrative poems of violence and conflict set in the natural splendor of the Northern California coastline.

Robinson Jeffers was a child prodigy who could read Greek at age five and who was graduated from Occidental College at the age of seventeen. He rejected the Calvinistic teachings of his minister father, but Calvinistic notions of the depravity of human nature characterize much of his later writings. In the decade preceding World War I, Jeffers pursued graduate studies in medicine, foreign languages, and forestry at the University of Southern California (USC), briefly at the University of Zurich, and at the University of Washington. He did not earn a degree in any of his graduate school endeavors. In a German class at USC, Jeffers met Una Call Kuster, a wealthy, married socialite, who married Jeffers in 1913 after a divorce that was reported in West Coast newspapers.

Jeffers and his wife moved to Carmel, California, in 1914, and Jeffers began building Tor House in 1919. Tor House was a stone house and tower with woodwork and finish details that Jeffers slowly built by his own hand and with the occasional aid of hired craftsmen. He purposely never finished the tower and relished the stone house and unfinished tower both as a domicile for his family and as a metaphor in his poetry. Jeffers lived in Tor House until his death in 1962, raising twin sons with his wife, who predeceased him in 1950.

Jeffers' first two works of poetry were conventional collections, celebrating the beauty of nature in a romantic vein. With the publication of *Tamar and Other Poems*, however, Jeffers forged his identity as a writer of long narrative poems that describe futile and violent interactions between people who live in the hills and valleys of the Carmel Peninsula in California.

Robinson Jeffers described the wild beauty of the California coast. (Library of Congress)

Jeffers was extremely popular throughout the 1920's, but his popularity declined in the 1930's and never recovered in his lifetime. The characteristics which made his poetry popular in the 1920's—unique style, colorful and at times profane diction, his eccentric personal philosophy of Inhumanism—contributed to the decline of his popularity and critical acclaim during the Depression of the 1930's. Inhumanism was the name of Jeffers' personal philosophy, which held that all human civilizations inevitably decline, becoming narcissistic and self-consuming (symbolized in the incest in many of the novel-length narrative poems). Inhumanism places the locus of meaning in a pantheistic God who is revealed through the beauty of the natural landscape. All human endeavor is transitory and ultimately insignificant.

Although Jeffers is known principally for his narrative poems, several of his shorter, lyric poems, especially "Shine, Perishing Republic," are frequently anthologized. Jeffers' most significant experiment in drama was his 1946 translation of ancient Greek playwright Euripides' *Medea*, which is one of the most compelling interpretations of Greek drama done in North America.

SUGGESTED READINGS

Everson, William. *Robinson Jeffers: Fragments of an Older Fury*. Berkeley, Calif.: Oyez, 1968.

Powell, Lawrence Clark. *Robinson Jeffers: The Man and His Work*. 3d ed. New York: Gordon, 1973.

Squires, Radcliffe. *The Loyalties of Robinson Jeffers*. Ann Arbor: University of Michigan Press, 1956.

Zaller, Robert. *The Cliffs of Solitude: A Reading of Robinson Jeffers*. Cambridge, England: Cambridge University Press, 1983.

—Richard Sax

See also American identity: West and the frontier; Incest; Violence

Jewett, Sarah Orne

BORN: South Berwick, Maine; September 3, 1849

DIED: South Berwick, Maine; June 24, 1909

PRINCIPAL WORKS: *Deephaven*, 1877; *Old Friends and New*, 1879; *Country By-ways*, 1881; *A Country Doctor*, 1884; *The Mate of the Daylight, and Friends Ashore*, 1884; *A Marsh Island*, 1885; *A White Heron and Other Stories*, 1886; *The King of Folly Island, and Other People*, 1888; *Strangers and Wayfarers*, 1890; *Tales of New England*, 1890; *A Native of Winby and Other Tales*, 1893; *The Country of the Pointed Firs*, 1896; *The Queen's Twin and Other Stories*, 1899; *The Tory Lover*, 1901; *An Empty Purse: A Christmas Story*, 1905; *Verses*, 1916; *The Uncollected Stories of Sarah Orne Jewett*, 1971

IDENTITIES: European American; Northeast; women

SIGNIFICANT ACHIEVEMENT: The stark and controlled realism of Jewett's writing records indelibly a New England identity.

Living at a time when women were overshadowed by the men in their lives, Sarah Orne Jewett as a girl began to establish her identity as an individual by observing closely and recording her observations in writing. As a child, she often accompanied her father, a physician, on his house calls, thereby coming into contact with the total community of South Berwick, with which she always strongly identified.

Jewett began publishing (as A. C. Eliot) when she was eighteen. Her first melodramatic story, "Jenny Garrow's Lovers," is set in England and is preposterous in its details although stylistically impressive. Jewett did not come into her own as a writer, however, until she focused on her New England surroundings in *Deephaven*, a series of thirteen interconnected sketches about life in a small Maine town as it is observed by two twenty-four-year-old women. Recent critics have detected veiled suggestions of lesbianism in this book and in elements of Jewett's life.

Jewett published prolifically until a carriage accident in 1902 left her badly injured. She had published more than 150 sketches as well as two dozen children's stories. She wrote three episodic novels, two novels for girls, and a children's history. Her most celebrated works are *Deephaven* and *The Country of the Pointed Firs*.

Earlier dismissed as a marginal writer, Jewett has recently received renewed critical interest as a local colorist—in which category her stature is secure—and as a woman writer publishing at a time when the male publishing establishment was wary of female writers. Henry James's reference to Jewett's achievement did little to enhance Jewett's reputation in her own time.

SUGGESTED READINGS

Cary, Richard. *Sarah Orne Jewett*. New York: Twayne, 1962.

Donovan, Josephine. *Sarah Orne Jewett*. New York: Frederick Ungar, 1980.

Nagel, Gwen L. *Critical Essays on Sarah Orne Jewett*. Boston: G. K. Hall, 1984.

Roman, Margaret. *Sarah Orne Jewett: Reconstructing Gender*. Tuscaloosa: University of Alabama Press, 1992.

—*R. Baird Shuman*

See also American identity: Northeast; *Country of the Pointed Firs, The*; *Deephaven*; Feminism

Jewish American identity

IDENTITIES: European American; family; Jewish; religion

Jews immigrated to the United States as early as 1654. By the eighteenth century, substantial Jewish communities existed in New England, New York, the middle states, and parts of the South, most notably in Charleston, South Carolina. It was not until the late nineteenth century, however, that Jewish immigration swelled. Between 1882 and 1903, 1,300,000 Eastern European Jews, subjected to persecution in their homes, mostly in czarist Russia and Poland, sought a new life in the United States.

Jewish immigrants came to the United States from many parts of the world, and the literary traditions and languages they brought with them were quite diverse. Jewish immigrants shared a common religious heritage, but they usually brought with them the ways of life that characterized the countries in which they had previously lived. Yiddish was a unifying language of these immigrants, although in many cases it was not their native tongue.

Most of the new arrivals settled in large cities, of which New York, being the city in which most immigrants landed, was the most convenient and had the largest Jewish population. Impoverished, often unable to speak English, large numbers of these Jews managed a life of bare subsistence on New York's Lower East Side, clustering around Hester Street and other such Jewish enclaves, where Yiddish was the common language. By the early 1920's, New York City, with some two million Jewish residents, was the largest Jewish community in the world.

Immigrant Jews found themselves in an ambiguous situation. On one hand, it was difficult for them to abandon the religious and cultural heritages they had left behind. On the other hand, they soon realized that it was to their great advantage to be assimilated as quickly as possible into an American society that was not entirely hospitable to outsiders of any stripe. The new arrivals pushed their children to learn English and to excel in school.

New York City became a national model for providing free or inexpensive education for all of its citizens from elementary through graduate school. These immigrants, seeking to establish a new American identity as quickly as possible, made every possible sacrifice to enable their children to obtain as much education as they could. Many of the leading intellectuals in the United States sprang from these immigrant roots. Part of the immigrants' gaining an American identity involved a relationship of rejection of but not escape from the Eastern European identities they had brought with them to the United States.

The Yiddish theater
Jewish American theater has figured prominently in the development of drama in the United States. Such theater draws directly and heavily upon the Yiddish theater that helped Jewish immigrants from Eastern Europe deal with homesickness. The Jewish immigrants enjoyed theater in a language they could understand and about situations to which they could relate. The Yiddish theater became a haven and a preserver of culture.

Early Yiddish theater, along with providing classical drama in translation, also offered original melodramas and comedies. Joseph Lateiner, a Yiddish playwright, turned out as much as a play a week for eager audiences during the late 1880's and early 1890's. Immigrant Jews took theater seriously. It was their major release from the frustrations of adapting to an alien society. The theater became a major topic of conversation and, at times, animated controversy, among Jews. It became a spawning ground, directly or indirectly, for Jewish actors and actresses as well as for such future Jewish American dramatists as Albert Maltz, S. N. Behrman, Elmer Rice, Clifford Odets, Paddy Chayefsky, Arthur Miller, Lillian Hellman, and Neil Simon.

A Yiddish theater was established as early as 1882 in New York City's Bowery and, by 1915, twenty Yiddish theaters were flourishing in the city, along with music halls and vaudeville theaters that alternated between English and Yiddish in their presentations. Yiddish theater companies, professional and amateur, existed in most of America's large cities, where clusters of Jewish American immigrants had settled.

Along with presenting plays by William Shakespeare and other classical playwrights in Yiddish translation, the Yiddish theater brought new plays from Europe to the New York stage, where they were performed in Yiddish. Among the plays whose New York debuts occurred not on Broadway but in Yiddish theaters in Yiddish translation were Anton Chekhov's *Dyadya Vanya* (1897; *Uncle Vanya*, 1914), Johan August Strindberg's *Fadren* (1887; *The Father*, 1899), and Arthur Schnitzler's *Professor Bernhardi* (1912; English translation, 1913).

Religious Jews sought drama that would revive their own faith and help bolster the faith of their children. Members of the cultural elite hankered after a theater that would elevate them ideologically. Those with more political leanings looked to the theater as a vehicle for effecting political and social reform. What many Jewish immigrants wanted, indeed demanded, from theater, however, were plays that projected models of behavior, ways of adapting to the new culture with which they were trying to identify.

Ironically, one of the most successful and popular Jewish American plays of the transitional period between Yiddish theater and Broadway was *Abie's Irish Rose* (1922), a comedy by Anne Nichols, who was not Jewish. The play is about assimilation: intermarriage between a Jew and his Irish sweetheart. In *Riverside Drive* (1928), Leon Kobrin deals with yet another aspect of assimilation, that of grandparents who speak only Yiddish and are thereby cut off from their grandchildren, who speak only English.

The melting pot

In 1908, Israel Zangwill, an English Jew who wrote unmemorable plays about a variety of social causes, produced a melodramatic play about a Russian Jew, David Quixano, who lives in New York. This play, *The Melting Pot*, which was dedicated to Theodore Roosevelt and was unconvincing in many respects, gained a substantial following and introduced into the American consciousness and vocabulary the concept of the melting pot.

David's lines in this play have to do with his plan to write an American symphony about an "America that is God's Crucible, the great Melting-Pot where all the races of Europe are melting and reforming! . . . Germans and Frenchmen, Irishmen and Englishmen, Jews and Russians—into the Crucible with you all! God is making the American."

David, a musician who can no longer play his violin because his shoulder has been injured in a pogrom, reminds one of Joe Bonaparte in Odets' *Golden Boy* (1937), a violinist turned prizefighter whose success in the ring marks the end of his career as a musician. There are also suggestions of *The Melting Pot* in Odets' *Till the Day I Die* (1935), in which the hand of violinist Ernst Tausig is smashed by Nazis. In all these instances, the play projects an image of thwarted dreams, certainly a part of the early American experience of many immigrants, Jewish and otherwise.

Later Jewish American drama

The second and third generations of immigrant families assimilated into American society. Many altered their original identities by changing their names to ones that sounded more Western European or American than the names of their forebears. Yiddish theater, which flourished throughout the 1920's, began to decline toward the end of the decade and into the 1930's. It was being replaced by companies like the mainstream Theatre Guild and the experimental Group Theatre. These two major companies drew their talent heavily from actors and actresses, playwrights and directors who had been associated in one way or another with Yiddish theater and knew its traditions firsthand. Among the more notable performers who moved from Yiddish theater to mainstream theater were Jacob Adler and Stella Adler, Paul Muni, and Molly Picon.

Some of the playwrights who emerged from this period remained Jewish in the topics they addressed as well as in the dialogue they wrote, capturing the speech cadences of Yinglish, as the combination of Yiddish and English has been called. Religion diminished in thematic importance; the cultural aspects of being Jewish received greater emphasis. Perhaps the most notable Jewish

American play of the Depression era is Odets' *Awake and Sing!* (1935), whose title alludes to the book of Isaiah. This play addresses questions of the importance, in rank order, of money, class, and family loyalty. The middle-class Berger household is threatened with extinction as the economic noose of the Depression tightens around it. The family matriarch struggles valiantly, not nicely, to hold the family together, but fails.

In Jacob, the grandfather, Odets presents the ideological Jew who espouses Marxism as the cure-all for the social ills of the world. Bessie Berger, Jacob's middle-aged daughter, rules her house with a determination born of terror about what might happen to her family in a collapsing

Jewish American Identity Milestones

1654	Jews begin to immigrate to the United States and settle in what was then Dutch New Amsterdam (New York).
1700's	Substantial Jewish communities exist in New England, New York, the middle states, and parts of the South, most notably in Charleston, South Carolina.
1812	Mordecai Manuel Noah's *Paul and Alexis*, a play.
1821	Noah's retitled melodrama, *The Wandering Boys*.
1825-1850	The population of American Jews doubles during this time frame, reaching nearly 18,000 by 1850.
1859	Sholom Aleichem, who is credited with the virtual creation of modern Yiddish literature, is born in Pereyaslav, Russia.
1876	The beginnings of professional Yiddish theater.
1882	The first Yiddish theater opens in New York City's Bowery.
1882	Emma Lazarus' "The New Colossus," in *Songs of a Semite*.
1882-1903	The increased immigration of Jews creates an audience for the "great Jewish novel." Jewish writers began to depict American Jewish life in memoirs and novels, such as Mary Antin's *The Promised Land* (1912) and Ludwig Lewisohn's *Upstream* (1922).
1885-1914	There are more than 150 Yiddish publications available, twenty of them daily newspapers. The *Jewish Daily Forward* becomes the largest Yiddish newspaper in the world. Isaac Bashevis Singer is a frequent contributor to the newspaper.
1894-1914	Aleichem's *Tevye der Milkhiger* (*Tevye's Daughters*, 1949; also translated as *Tevye the Dairyman*, 1987), a group of nine short stories.
1908	Israel Zangwill, an English Jew, publishes *The Melting Pot*, which introduces into the American consciousness and vocabulary the concept of the melting pot.
1912	Arthur Schnitzler's *Professor Bernhardi* (English translation, 1913).
1914-1918	World War I. More Jews immigrate, fleeing the destruction of the war in their homelands.
1915	Twenty Yiddish theaters flourishing in New York City.
1917	Abraham Cahan's *The Rise of David Levinsky*, a title that recalls William Dean Howells' *The Rise of Silas Lapham* (1885).
1920	Sholem Asch's *Kiddush Hashem* (English translation, 1926).
1922	*Abie's Irish Rose*, a comedy by Anne Nichols, who is not Jewish. The play is about intermarriage between a Jew and his Irish sweetheart.
1923	Elmer Rice's *The Adding Machine*, a play.
1928	Leon Kobrin's *Riverside Drive*.
1929	The Depression begins and Jewish immigration slows considerably.
1930	Michael Gold's *Jews Without Money*.
1933	Nathanael West's *Miss Lonelyhearts*, a satire about a newspaper columnist obsessed with the lives of his readers, who write to him seeking advice.
1934	*Call It Sleep*, by Henry Roth. The novel is recognized as the best in the American Jewish ghetto style.
1935	Clifford Odets' *Awake and Sing!*, about a Jewish family torn apart by poverty.
1935	Clifford Odets' *Till the Day I Die*.
1937	Clifford Odets' *Golden Boy*.
1937	*The Old Bunch*, by Meyer Levin, is the story of the children of Russian-Jewish immigrants in Chicago.
1939-1945	World War II. Six million European Jews are killed in the Holocaust.

economy. She expresses her most terrifying image in the lines, "They threw out a family on Dawson Street today. All the furniture on the sidewalk. A fine old woman with gray hair."

Hellman, who was emerging as a dramatist of note during the 1930's, was quite different from Odets and other essentially Jewish writers. Hellman's opinion was that anything Jewish in the arts would place its creator at an artistic disadvantage, so she scrupulously avoided Jewish themes and did not employ Yinglish in her dialogue. She did not feel comfortable with Jewish themes until late in her career, when she wrote *My Mother, My Father, and Me* (1963), a play that focuses on a Jewish family but that emphasizes its hypocrisy and philistinism. Her earlier World War II plays,

---

Jewish American Identity Milestones — CONTINUED

1941	*Watch on the Rhine*, a play by Lillian Hellman.
1943	Delmore Schwartz's *Genesis*, a story about an American Jew's identity.
1945	Arthur Miller's *Focus*, a novel about anti-Semitism.
1946	Elmer Rice's *Dream Girl*, a play.
1947	Laura Z. Hobson's *Gentleman's Agreement*.
1948	Irwin Shaw's *The Young Lions* follows the path of two American soldiers, a Jew and a Gentile. The Jew is killed by a Nazi, who is in turn killed by the Gentile character.
1950	Isaac Bashevis Singer's *The Family Moskat*.
1953	Saul Bellow's *The Adventures of Augie March*.
1957	*The Assistant*, Bernard Malamud's second novel.
1961	Bernard Malamud's *The Fixer*.
1958	Karl Shapiro's *Poems of a Jew*.
1958	Anthony Hecht's *The Seven Deadly Sins*, a collection of poems.
1959	*Inscriptions*, by Charles Reznikoff, whose work is steeped in Jewish tradition.
1960	Philip Roth's *Goodbye, Columbus and Five Short Stories* presents Jewish life in the United States.
1960	Arthur Miller focuses on Jewish themes in *The Price*.
1960	*The Tenth Man*, by Paddy Chayefsky, attracts a large Jewish following.
1961	*Come Blow Your Horn*, by Neil Simon. Simon deals obliquely with Jews and Jewish culture in this play and others.
1961	*The Pawnbroker*, by Edward Lewis Wallant.
1962	Paddy Chayefsky's *Gideon* appeals to Jewish audiences.
1962	Philip Roth's *Letting Go* centers on young

	Jewish scholars in Chicago, New York, and elsewhere.
1963	Edward Lewis Wallant's *The Tenants of Moonbloom*.
1963	Lillian Hellman's *My Mother, My Father, and Me*.
1964	Meyer Levin's *The Fanatic*.
1964	Saul Bellow's *Herzog*.
1964	Jewish themes are recurrent in Arthur Miller's *Incident at Vichy*.
1964	Karl Shapiro's *The Bourgeois Poet*.
1966	*Trust*, a novel by Cynthia Ozick.
1967	Chaim Potok's *The Chosen* focuses on the son of a Hasidic rabbi.
1969	Philip Roth's *Portnoy's Complaint*.
1971	Cynthia Ozick's *The Pagan Rabbi and Other Stories* centers on immigrant, scholarly Jews in America.
1972	Chaim Potok's *My Name Is Asher Lev*, a novel.
1973	Arthur Cohen's *In the Days of Simon Stern*.
1975	Charles Reznikoff's *Holocaust*, poems based on the Nuremberg trials.
1976	Saul Bellow is awarded the Nobel Prize in Literature.
1978	Isaac Bashevis Singer is awarded the Nobel Prize in Literature.
1979	Leslie Epstein's *King of the Jews*.
1980	Arthur Miller's television drama, *Playing for Time*, about Fania Fenelon's experience in Auschwitz.
1982	*Levitation: Five Fictions*, by Cynthia Ozick, focuses on American Jews and the Holocaust.
1987	Isaac Bashevis Singer's *Enemies: A Love Story*.
1989	Ben Hecht's *The Transparent Man*, a collection of poems.
1989	Cynthia Ozick's *The Shawl*.

Watch on the Rhine (1941) and *The Searching Wind* (1944), are anti-Fascist plays rather than notably Jewish ones.

Miller also writes of American experience generally rather than of clearly and specifically Jewish themes. Two of his earliest plays, however, *No Villain* (1936) and *Honors at Dawn* (1937), are social protest plays about middle-class Jews. After his graduation from the University of Michigan, he moved away from dramas with a specific ethnicity. The protagonists in *All My Sons* (1947) and *Death of a Salesman* (1949) are likely Jewish, but the fact is never revealed nor does ethnicity become an issue in these plays. Rather, the plays deal with the American identity of people caught in the grips of situations that are largely economic. Only later in his career does Miller focus on Jewish themes in *The Price* (1960) and *Incident at Vichy* (1964). His television drama, *Playing for Time* (1980), also focuses on a Jewish topic, that of Fania Fenelon's experience in Auschwitz. His drama *The American Clock* (1980) has Jewish characters, but the play is not overwhelmingly a Jewish play.

Chayefsky wrote two notably Jewish plays, *The Tenth Man* (1960) and *Gideon* (1962), which attracted large Jewish followings. Simon deals obliquely with Jews and Jewish culture in plays such as *Come Blow Your Horn* (1961), *The Odd Couple* (1965), *The Sunshine Boys* (1973), *God's Favorite* (1975), and *Fools* (1981), but in these plays the ethnic Jewish American provides a comic backdrop rather than posing issues such as those found in the more cerebral dramas of Rice, Odets, Maltz, Chayefsky, and Miller.

Jewish American fiction

The most notable fiction produced by Jewish writers in America did not begin to appear until World War I. Those who produced it do not agree among themselves about whether one can legitimately speak of Jewish American fiction. Among those most often associated with such fiction are the writers Abraham Cahan, Michael Gold, Nathanael West, Isaac Bashevis Singer, Henry Roth, Delmore Schwartz, Bernard Malamud, Saul Bellow, Norman Mailer, Edward Lewis Wallant, Stanley Elkin, and Cynthia Ozick. Two of the authors on this list, Bellow and Singer, have been awarded Nobel Prizes in Literature.

In a sense, these two Nobel laureates represent two different camps in their attitudes about whether one can say that there is such a thing as Jewish American literature. Singer, born in Lithuania, has produced writing in Yiddish and English. He has clung to his Jewish and Eastern European identity and uses it as a basis for much of his prolific writing.

Bellow, on the other hand, born in Quebec and associated for most of his adult life with Chicago, draws only to a limited extent on his Jewish background. Bellow objects to being called a Jewish writer much as Georgia O'Keeffe objected to being called a woman artist. She, like Bellow, saw no need for the qualifying adjective before the noun. Bellow's identity and outlook are American generally.

Early Jewish American fiction

Cahan's *The Rise of David Levinsky* (1917), a title that recalls William Dean Howells' *The Rise of Silas Lapham* (1885), is among the earliest examples of Jewish American fiction. Cahan, born in Lithuania, was a dedicated socialist who immigrated to the United States and, in 1897, became the first editor of the *Jewish Daily Forward*, a newspaper whose mission he conceived as being to help as broad a segment of the immigrant populace as possible to learn about their Yiddish culture while, ironically, working at the same time to separate them from it, to make them Americans.

In *The Rise of David Levinsky*, Cahan has captured the complexity of an eastern European immigrant whose ambitions are great but whose accomplishment, in his own eyes at least, always falls short. Levinsky forever strives to be better because he never feels fulfillment, even though by any objective standard, he has done quite well.

In this character, Cahan depicts the conflicts with which many first-generation Jewish immigrants were wrestling: the inner struggles that make them feel forever that they have not quite achieved real fulfillment and self-satisfaction. This novel, in which quest is central, represents an important milestone in Jewish American fiction because it presents the themes with which much of such fiction was to deal in the decades ahead.

As Jewish American fiction developed, its creators became identified with various factions whose religious, social, and economic differences were reflected in a literature about which it is difficult to generalize. Zionism is reflected in the writings of such Jewish American writers as Emma Lazarus, Mordecai Manuel Noah, and Henrietta Szold, all of whose work has strong religious overtones and an affinity to Hebrew rather than Yiddish.

American Jews were urged to become better Americans by becoming better Jews. Zionism was touted as the road to achieving this end. The Jewish and Yiddish press, which flourished during the first third of the twentieth century, published literature that might be termed Zionist. Voluminous short fiction found its way into the newspapers these presses produced. Much early Jewish American fiction was short fiction of the sort with which Mendele Mocher Sforim, Singer, and Sholom Aleichem are most frequently identified. The Zionist movement was one of stalwart religious faith and singular idealism.

Perhaps the greatest Jewish American novel of this early period was Sholem Asch's *Kiddush Hashem* (1920; English translation, 1926). Asch, however, like his contemporaries Abraham Weissen, Solomon Libin, Aleichem, and Jonah Rosefeld, tended to write short fiction for the Yiddish press.

Another camp developed among the Jews of North America, many of whom were experiencing anti-Semitic discrimination in the workplace and in other areas of their lives. They tried to find leadership in the labor unions that would protect them as well as in the more left-leaning Yiddish press. This movement led to a literature of social protest.

Assimilation

To many Jewish Americans, the safest course to follow was that of assimilation, which is inherent in the melting-pot theory. Jews who espoused this solution worked to minimize national differences, often supporting an internationalism that was too idealistic ever to succeed or a cosmopolitanism that was equally unattainable.

The writing that proceeded from writers in the assimilationist camp is, understandably, like the fiction of non-Jewish American writers of the time. Novels like Laura Z. Hobson's *Gentleman's Agreement* (1947), Miller's *Focus* (1945), and Irwin Shaw's *The Young Lions* (1948) blur the distinctions between gentiles and Jews in mid-century America. Many of the writers who reflect assimilation have been castigated for their seeming detachment from the Jewish community.

Bellow and Mailer

Some of America's most renowned post-World War II fiction was written by Bellow and Mailer, both Jewish. Understanding what was going on in a rapidly changing United States, they wrote about it with vigor in books such as Bellow's *Dangling Man* (1944), *The Victim* (1947), and, much later, *Seize the Day* (1956). Mailer's fame began with his much-celebrated *The Naked and the Dead* (1947). Most of their work, despite the presence of Jewish characters in it, is not so notably Jewish as that of Philip Roth, Malamud, Chaim Potok, Leslie Epstein, Arthur Cohen, Ozick, or a host of other Jewish American writers.

Jewish American self-hate

Among the significant psychological themes reflected in Jewish American writing after the mid-twentieth century was self-hate. Meyer Levin's *Compulsion* (1956) explores the psychological underpinnings of the murder of Bobby Frank by Nathan Leopold and Richard Loeb, attributing it to Jewish self-hate. Unlike his novel, *The Old Bunch* (1937), which traces the lives of twenty neighborhood Jewish youths from Chicago after they leave their families to begin their independent existences, *Compulsion* focuses upon the motivation for a single, seemingly irrational act. Levin goes on in *The Fanatic* (1964) to suggest that when Jews commit themselves to Communism, the basic reason is self-hate.

Philip Roth's parody on self-hate, his onanistic novel *Portnoy's Complaint* (1969), resulted in part from his being reviled as a purveyor of the self-hate doctrine in such early works as *Goodbye, Columbus and Five Short Stories* (1960) and *Letting Go* (1962). He was denounced in synagogues and chided by his publisher to move from this stance. His reaction was to write *Portnoy's Complaint*, a novel that was exuberantly politically incorrect before the term "politically incorrect" existed.

Malamud and Ozick

Malamud was close to his Jewish roots and made little attempt to write fiction that did not have Jewish themes. Books such as *The Assistant* (1957), *The Fixer* (1961), and *The Tenant* (1971) are notably Jewish, as is his collection of stories, *The Magic Barrel* (1958). Malamud, however, deviated from his roots in such works as his academic novel, *The New Life* (1961).

Ozick also remains close to her roots in *Trust* (1966), *The Pagan Rabbi and Other Stories* (1971), and *Levitation: Five Fictions* (1982). Ozick criticized the gentile writer John Updike for his attempts to present Jewish characters authentically in his Bech stories, which did not ring true to Jewish ears.

The Holocaust

Many Jewish American writers have avoided writing about the Holocaust. Some Jewish writers suffered from survivor guilt, having escaped Europe before Hitler's annihilation of six million Jews. Ozick's *The Shawl* (1989) addresses the Holocaust and attracted favorable notice. Prior to the publication of Ozick's work, Cohen's *In the Days of Simon Stern* (1973) and Leslie Epstein's *King of the Jews* (1979) broached the subject, as did Singer's *Enemies: A Love Story* (1987).

Poetry

The Jewish American poet best known to early immigrants was Emma Lazarus, whose sonnet "The New Colossus" expressed what the Statue of Liberty means to the "huddled masses yearning to breathe free." Lazarus, the daughter of an affluent, assimilated family, showed few Jewish influences in her early writing; her volume *Songs of a Semite* (1882) marks the beginning of Jewish American poetry in the United States.

The early objectivist poets were almost exclusively Jewish. Objectivism grew out of an earlier poetic movement, Imagism. Imagism, as its name implies, makes a visual image central to a poem; Objectivism seeks to make the poem an object, with historic and cultural particulars in a unifying context. The typical Objectivist lyric poem is spare and brief; longer poems also incorporate the style of referring to specific objects and events and of being terse. Poets belonging to the Objectivist school include Charles Reznikoff, George Oppen, Louis Zukovsky, and Carl Rakosi. Reznikoff was thoroughly Jewish in his literary approach, writing poems with titles such as "Kaddish," "The Fifth Book of Macabees," and "A Short History of Israel" in his *Collected Poems* (1978). Paul Goodman is notable among Jewish poets for writing unabashedly about homosexual topics. Allen Ginsberg, in his Beat poetry, sometimes deals with the topic.

Karl Shapiro's *Poems of a Jew* (1958) and *The Bourgeois Poet* (1964) have helped to assure his sterling literary reputation. Noteworthy also are Muriel Rukeyser, Stanley Kunitz, and Louis Untermeyer, the last as a poet and as an anthologist.

Other important Jewish American poets include Delmore Schwartz, Laurence Lieberman, Howard Nemerov, Irving Feldman, Anthony Hecht, and John Hollander, all of whom have incorporated considerable Jewish ethnicity, as well as scholarship, into their writing.

SUGGESTED READINGS

Cohen, Sarah Blacher, ed. *From Hester Street to Hollywood: The Jewish American Stage and Screen.* Bloomington: Indiana University Press, 1983. The eighteen essays in this valuable collection deal with playwrights, actors, actresses, and Yiddish theater.

_____, ed. *Jewish Wry: Essays on Jewish Humor.* Detroit: Wayne State University Press, 1990. This solid presentation of Jewish humor delves into many aspects of Jewish American literary production.

Erens, Patricia. *The Jew in American Cinema.* Bloomington: Indiana University Press, 1984. Erens' book remains the preeminent treatment of the Jewish presence in Hollywood.

Gitenstein, R. Barbara. *Apocalyptic Messianism and Contemporary Jewish American Poetry.* Albany: State University of New York Press, 1983. Although limited in scope, this thin volume supports its main thesis well and provides ample coverage of the major Jewish American poets.

Guttmann, Allen. *The Jewish Writer in America: Assimilation and the Crisis of Identity.* New York: Oxford University Press, 1971. Provides valuable historical background and is remarkably inclusive in its coverage.

Hertzberg, Arthur. *The Jew in America: Four Centuries of an Uneasy Encounter, a History.* New York: Simon & Schuster, 1989. Among the best historical presentations of the Jewish presence in the United States, this book offers invaluable background material for understanding Jewish American literature in its cultural and ethnic context.

Klingenstein, Susanne. *Jews in the American Academy, 1900-1940: The Dynamics of Intellectual Assimilation.* New Haven, Conn.: Yale University Press, 1991. Shows how the exclusion of Jews from many academic situations discouraged the serious academic study of Jewish American writing.

Malin, Irving, ed. *Contemporary American-Jewish Literature: Critical Essays*. Bloomington: Indiana University Press, 1973. The four overview essays are especially helpful, as is Jackson Bryer's bibliographical essay at the end of the book.

Pinsker, Sanford. *Jewish American Fiction, 1917-1987*. New York: Twayne, 1992. So useful that one wishes similar volumes existed for Jewish American drama and poetry.

—*R. Baird Shuman*

See also Acculturation; Anti-Semitism; Bellow, Saul; Elkin, Stanley; Emigration and immigration; Ginsberg, Allen; Hellman, Lillian; Holocaust; Mailer, Norman; Malamud, Bernard; Melting pot; Miller, Arthur; Ozick, Cynthia; Pluralism versus assimilation; Religion and identity; Roth, Philip; Rukeyser, Muriel; Schwartz, Delmore; Singer, Isaac Bashevis; West, Nathanael

Johnson, Charles

BORN: Evanston, Illinois; April 23, 1948

PRINCIPAL WORKS: *Faith and the Good Thing*, 1974; *Oxherding Tale*, 1982; *The Sorcerer's Apprentice*, 1986; *Middle Passage*, 1990

IDENTITIES: African American

SIGNIFICANT ACHIEVEMENT: Johnson's philosophical fiction continues an African American literary tradition.

Reared in a tight-knit Midwestern black community, Charles Johnson remembers his childhood environment as loving and secure. An only child, he often read to fill up his time. Johnson especially loved comic books and spent hours practicing drawing in hopes of becoming a professional cartoonist. To this end he took a two-year correspondence course and was publishing cartoons and illustrations by the time he completed high school.

At the last minute Johnson decided to attend Southern Illinois University rather than art school. There he became passionately drawn to the study of philosophy and to writing. During his first summer vacation he began to pursue another lifelong interest, the martial arts. Before his undergraduate college days were over he had published a book of his own cartoons, *Black Humor* (1970), had hosted a television series on drawing, and had worked as a reporter for the *Chicago Tribune*. In 1970, he married Joan New, whom he had met two years earlier.

After graduation, Johnson began working as a reporter for the *Illinoisan*; already, however, he had decided to become a novelist. Over the next two years, with John Gardner as his mentor, he wrote six "apprentice novels." Finally, in 1974, he published *Faith and the Good Thing*, which he had extensively researched while completing his master's degree in philosophy and writing a thesis on Marxism.

Johnson continued his studies in philosophy at the State University of New York at Stony Brook, this time concentrating on phenomenology. *Oxherding Tale* is a work he intended, he wrote, to be a reply to German novelist Hermann Hesse's *Siddartha* (1922; English translation, 1951). Johnson fashioned *Oxherding* into a "neo-slave narrative for the second half of the twentieth century." A melding of Eastern thought, the American slave experience, and a sharp, witty twentieth-century consciousness, *Oxherding Tale* traces the misadventures of Andrew Hawkins, a privileged slave given the finest education because of his status as the child of the plantation's black butler and the white mistress. Eventually, Andrew leaves home and begins to experience a variety of identities and to test various philosophical stances toward life. His tale culminates with his marriage, his reconciliation with his past, and his final encounter with Soulcatcher, the fugitive slave hunter long on his trail.

By the time *Oxherding Tale* was published, Johnson had accepted an invitation to teach creative writing at the University of Washington. There, he continued to write; in addition to numerous essays, book reviews, and works for television, his credits include a collection of short stories, *The Sorcerer's Apprentice*, *Being and Race: Black Writing Since 1970* (1988), and his most acclaimed success *Middle Passage*, winner of the National Book Award. Another neo-slave narrative in the style of *Oxherding Tale*, *Middle Passage* continues Johnson's quest to produce entertaining yet seriously philosophical black literature. Johnson also continues his commitment to the martial arts and to Eastern philosophy, especially Buddhism.

SUGGESTED READINGS

Coleman, J. W. "Charles Johnson's Quest for Black Freedom in *Oxherding Tale*." *African American Review* 29, no. 4 (Winter, 1995): 631-644.

Scott, D. M. "Interrogating Identity: Appropriation and Transformation in *Middle Passage*." *African American Review* 29, no. 4 (Winter, 1995): 645-655.

Travis, M. A. "*Beloved* and *Middle Passage*: Race, Narrative, and the Critics' Essentialism." *Narrative* 2, no. 3 (October, 1994): 179-200.

—*Grace McEntee*

See also African American identity; Eastern religion and philosophy; *Middle Passage*; Slavery

Johnson, James Weldon

BORN: Jacksonville, Florida; June 17, 1871

DIED: Wiscasset, Maine; June 26, 1938

PRINCIPAL WORKS: *The Autobiography of an Ex-Coloured Man*, 1912; *The Book of American Negro Poetry*, 1922 (editor); *The Book of American Negro Spirituals*, 1925 (editor); *God's Trombones: Seven Sermons in Verse*, 1927; *Along This Way*, 1933; *Saint Peter Relates an Incident: Selected Poems*, 1935

IDENTITIES: African American

SIGNIFICANT ACHIEVEMENT: One of the first to celebrate African American art forms, Johnson was a major figure in the Harlem Renaissance.

James Weldon Johnson was born in Jacksonville, was graduated from Atlanta University in 1894, and went on to become one of the most versatile artists of his time. In addition to expressing his artistic talents, he led a successful professional life and was an influential civil rights advocate. After his graduation in 1894, Johnson became principal of Stanton School and edited a newspaper, the *Daily American*. He advocated civil rights in his articles in a time that saw a dramatic rise in the number of lynchings. He thus assumed a public role in the African American community. Encouraged by his brother Rosamond, Johnson and his brother went to New York in 1899 to work

James Weldon Johnson, a key figure of the Harlem Renaissance. (Library of Congress)

on a musical career. Their most lasting achievement of that period is the song "Lift Every Voice and Sing," also known as the African American national anthem. After having been appointed consul in Venezuela and Nicaragua, Johnson, after publication of *The Autobiography of an Ex-Coloured Man*, decided to attempt to support himself through literary work. He returned to New York to begin writing an influential column for the *New York Age*, commenting on literary matters and encouraging black literary activity. He published *The Book of American Negro Poetry* three years before Alain Locke's anthology *The New Negro* (1925) officially ushered in the Harlem Renaissance.

Beginning in 1916, Johnson was field secretary for the National Association for the Advancement of Colored People (NAACP), organizing new branches and looking into matters of racial injustice nationwide. In 1920, he became the first African American secretary of the NAACP, a post he would hold until 1930. Johnson saw his civil rights work and his artistic activity as complementary, believing that the production of great works of art would improve African Americans' position in society. Johnson contributed major work to that effort with the publication of *God's Trombones*, bringing the language of the African American church into the realm of literature. Weldon also collected two volumes of African American spirituals, which made clear that this expression of African American folk spirit belonged to the world of art. His death in a car accident in 1938 interrupted Johnson in his wide-ranging efforts.

SUGGESTED READINGS

Fleming, Robert E. *James Weldon Johnson*. Boston: Twayne, 1987.

Levy, Eugene. *James Weldon Johnson: Black Leader, Black Voice*. Chicago: University of Chicago Press, 1973.

Phylon 32 (Winter, 1971): 330-402.

—Martin Japtok

See also African American identity; *Along This Way*; *Autobiography of an Ex-Coloured Man, The*; Black church; Black English; Harlem Renaissance; *Saint Peter Relates an Incident*

Jones, Gayl

BORN: Lexington, Kentucky; November 23, 1949

PRINCIPAL WORKS: *Chile Woman*, 1974; *Corregidora*, 1975; *Eva's Man*, 1976; *White Rat*, 1977; *Song of Anninho*, 1981; *The Hermit-Woman*, 1983; *Xarque and Other Poems*, 1985; *Liberating Voices: Oral Tradition in African American Literature*, 1991

IDENTITIES: African American; women

SIGNIFICANT ACHIEVEMENT: Jones's conventional gothic novels and short stories are among the most intense psychological portrayals of black female characters in African American literature.

Poet, novelist, essayist, short-story writer, and teacher, Gayl Jones is best known for the intensity and probing nature of her gothic tales, which mix the conventions of the gothic with radically unconventional worlds of madness, sexuality, and violence. Jones began writing seriously at age seven under the encouraging and guiding influence of her grandmother, her mother, and her high school Spanish teacher, Anna Dodd. Later, her mentors would be Michael Harper and William Meredith at Brown University, where she earned two degrees in creative writing. She published her first and best-known novel, *Corregidora*, while still at Brown.

No stranger to the art of writing and storytelling, Jones grew up in a household of female creative writers: Her grandmother wrote plays for church production. Jones's mother, Lucille, started writing in fifth grade and read stories she had written to Jones and her brother. It is therefore not surprising that stories, storytelling, and family history are the source of most of the material for her fiction.

In addition to her distinction as teller of intense stories about insanity and the psychological effects of violence on black women, another characteristic of Jones's art is her consistent use of the first person for her protagonists. Claiming neither "political compulsions nor moral compulsions," Jones is first and foremost interested in the "psychology of characters" and therefore seeks to examine their "puzzles," as she states, by simply letting her characters "tell their stories." Her interest in the character as storyteller permits her to evoke oral history and engage the African American tradition of storytelling, which she accomplishes in her novels *Corregidora* and *Eva's Man*.

Corregidora, a historical novel, is what Jones calls a blues narrative. The novel examines the psychological effects of slavery and sexual abuse on three generations of women, particularly Ursa, a professional blues singer. *Eva's Man*, Jones's more provocative and controversial second novel, explores the psychological effects of violence. Eva Medina Canada, the protagonist-narrator, tells in confusing but gripping detail the story of her violent reaction to her victimization in a male-dominated society. Jones continues her thematic concerns with *White Rat*, a volume of twelve short stories, and *Song of Anninho*, a long narrative poem. In addition to her fiction and essay writing, Jones teaches full-time, writes poetry, and conducts research.

SUGGESTED READINGS

Coser, Stelamaris. *Bridging the Americas: The Literatures of Paule Marshall, Toni Morrison and Gayl Jones*. Philadelphia: Temple University Press, 1994.

Dixon, Melvin. *Ride out the Wilderness*. Chicago: University of Illinois Press, 1987.

Evans, Mari, ed. *Black Women Writers: 1950-1980*. New York: Doubleday, 1984.

—*Pamela J. Olubunmi Smith*

See also African American identity; Black English; *Eva's Man*

Jones, LeRoi. *See* Baraka, Amiri

Joy Luck Club, The

AUTHOR: Amy Tan (1952-   )

FIRST PUBLISHED: 1989

IDENTITIES: Chinese American; family; women

The Joy Luck Club, Amy Tan's first novel, debuted to critical acclaim. It takes its place alongside Maxine Hong Kingston's *The Woman Warrior* (1976) as a chronicle of a Chinese American woman's search for and exploration of her ethnic identity. *The Joy Luck Club* is the best-selling, accessible account of four Chinese-born mothers and their four American-born daughters. One of the women, Suyuan Woo, has died before the story opens, but the other seven women tell their own stories from their individual points of view. Critics have noted that this approach is an unusually ambitious one. Nevertheless, the novel has reached a wide audience, especially since it was made into a feature film in 1992.

At the center of the story is Jing-mei "June" Woo, who has been asked to replace her dead mother as a member of the Joy Luck Club, a group of four women who meet for food and mah-jongg. Although Americanized and non-Chinese-speaking June is initially uncertain whether she wishes to join her mother's friends, she discovers that these women know things about her mother's past that she had never imagined. Her decision to become part of the Joy Luck Club culminates in a visit to China, where she meets the half sisters whom her mother was forced to abandon before she fled to the United States. The other Chinese-born women have similarly tragic stories, involving abandonment, renunciation, and sorrow in their native country. June says of her mother's decision to begin the club: "My mother could sense that the women of these families also had unspeakable tragedies they had left behind in China and hopes they couldn't begin to express in their fragile English." Each of these women's hopes includes hopes for her daughter. Each American daughter feels that she has in some way disappointed her mother. Waverly Jong fulfills her mother's ambitions by becoming a chess prodigy, then quits suddenly, to her mother's sorrow. June can never live up to her mother's expectations, and rebels by refusing to learn the piano. Rose Hsu turns away for a moment, and her youngest brother drowns. Lena St. Clair makes a marriage based on false ideals of equality, and only her mother understands its basic injustice. These American-born daughters insist that they are not Chinese; as June says, she has no "Chinese whatsoever below my skin." By the end of the novel, they find themselves realizing how truly Chinese they are.

SUGGESTED READINGS

Schell, Orville. Review of *The Joy Luck Club*, by Amy Tan. *The New York Times Book Review*, March 19, 1989, 3.

Skow, John. "Tiger Ladies." Review of *The Joy Luck Club*, by Amy Tan. *Time*, March 27, 1989, 98.

Wang, Dorothy. "A Game of Show Not Tell." *Newsweek*, April 17, 1989, 69.

—*J. Robin Coffelt*

See also Asian American identity: China Japan, and Korea; Emigration and immigration; Tan, Amy

Judaism. *See* Jewish American identity

Judd Rankin's Daughter
AUTHOR: Susan Glaspell (1882-1948)
FIRST PUBLISHED: 1945
IDENTITIES: European American; family; Midwest; Northeast

Susan Glaspell's last novel, *Judd Rankin's Daughter*, is concerned with social advancement and humankind's potential for greater awareness. Glaspell, who was born and educated in Iowa, illustrates the regional conflict of midwestern conservatism and the more radical political philosophies of New England, particularly Provincetown, Massachusetts, where Glaspell lived and where the novel is set.

The work contains four character sketches that feature people in conflict with societal or ideological values. The central figure, Francis Rankin Mitchell, is not the focal character of each section, but often her perceptions are vital to the reader's understanding. The story is set in 1944. Part 1 introduces Cousin Adah, a free spirit and nonconformist from Iowa, who dies before she relays her worldly wisdom to a young soldier headed to World War II. In part 2, Glaspell presents Judd Rankin, Francis' father, a seventy-six-year-old gentleman farmer who publishes a local paper, *Out Here*.

Part 3 occupies the major portion of the novel. Francis lives in Provincetown with her family. Her husband Len, a writer for a leftist magazine, advocates socialist causes. The children, Madeleine and Judson, are abandoning adolescence for adulthood. Judson, disturbed by his war experience, returns home confused and withdrawn.

In part 4, Francis returns to Iowa. She seeks the same wisdom that the young soldier of part 1 desired from Cousin Adah. Francis is troubled by her son Judson's emotional breakdown, so she appeals to her father for help; he complies by writing Judson a letter. Judson, as is his mother Francis, is searching for truth—a way to view the world. After reading his grandfather's letter, Judson no longer feels alone; his grandfather explains life in a manner that Judson can understand.

Judd Rankin's Daughter expresses the hope that Americans can develop a philosophy of life that will transcend social and national boundaries. The family dreams of a world where "fine fellows" give the shirts off their backs to clothe others. The family pictures what "life could be like," as Judson states in the closing chapter.

In 1945, the novel received positive reviews as the work of a polished writer and observer of human nature. Its ambiguities were also noted. Glaspell leaves some issues open to interpretation; for example, the wisdom in Judd Rankin's letter that brings self-revelation to Judson is never revealed, just as Cousin Adah dies before dispensing her advice. Thus, Glaspell only hints at solutions for social advancement. Her novel suggests that progressive idealism and freedom can improve society and the individual.

SUGGESTED READINGS

Carpentier, Martha C. "Susan Glaspell's Fiction: Fidelity as American Romance." *Twentieth Century Literature* 40 (Spring, 1994): 92-113.

Levin, Milton. "Susan Glaspell." In *American Writers*, edited by Lea Beachler and A. Walton Litz. New York: Charles Scribner's Sons, 1991.

McGovern, Edythe M. "Susan Glaspell." In *American Women Writers*, edited by Lina Mainierto. New York: Frederick Ungar, 1980.

—*Paula M. Miller*

See also American identity: Northeast; Glaspell, Susan; Rural life; World War II

Jung, Carl Gustav
BORN: Kesswil, Switzerland; July 26, 1875
DIED: Küsnacht, Switzerland; June 6, 1961

PRINCIPAL WORKS: *Wandlungen und Symbole der Libido*, 1912 (*The Psychology of the Unconscious*, 1915); *Psychologische Typen*, 1921 (*Psychological Types*, 1923); *Die Archetypen und das Kollektiven Unbewussten*, 1934 (*The Archetypes and the Collective Unconscious*, 1959); *Psychologie und Alchemie*, 1944 (*Psychology and Alchemy*, 1953); *Aion*, 1951; *Antwort auf Hiob*, 1952 (*Answer to Job*, 1954); *Mysterium Coniunctionis*, 1955; *Erinnerungen, Träume, Gedanken*, 1961 (with Aniela Jaffé; *Memories, Dreams, Reflections*, 1963)

IDENTITIES: Religion; world

SIGNIFICANT ACHIEVEMENT: Jung expanded the horizons of psychology to include spiritual concerns.

Carl Gustav Jung's influence on literature transcends brief summary. Even before a 1913 break from Sigmund Freud (who had chosen Jung as the next leader of the psychoanalytical movement), Jung began publishing original theories in his *The Psychology of the Unconscious*. In English translation, the work influenced Jack London's *The Red One* (1918) and *On the Makaloa Mat* (1919) as well as Eugene O'Neill's *The Emperor Jones* (1920) and *The Great God Brown* (1926).

Jung's theories have joined the modern intellectual milieu, and numerous writers have undergone Jungian therapy (including Doris Lessing) or had a family member analyzed (such as James Joyce's daughter) or gained interest in Jung through some other personal contact (as with Thomas Mann via Karl Kerenyi, a collaborator of Jung). Illustrative of the variety of writers whom Jung influenced is Hermann Hesse, who received treatment from one of Jung's students and from Jung himself. Figures resembling therapists appear in Hesse's subsequent novels. *Demian* (1919; English translation, 1923) employs terms from the ancient religions collectively called Gnosticism, which Hesse encountered in Jung's works. Hesse's fascination with Buddhism, Hinduism, and Taoism may have been augmented by Jung's praising their psychological insights.

Among influential Jungian ideas are the distinction between "extroversion" and "introversion"; the doctrine that unconscious personality traits are the opposite of conscious ones, acting as a balance to them; belief in "synchronicity" (meaningful coincidence between internal and external events); and the collective unconscious, which contains physical instincts and archetypes (spiritual patterns shared by all). Jung most often discussed the following archetypes: anima (a man's unconscious femininity), animus (a woman's unconscious masculinity), shadow (the sum of repressed traits), and self (the totality of a personality unified through a process Jung called "individuation"). Particularly through such popularizers as Joseph Campbell, Jung's ideas have influenced modern authors and the way writers of all ages are interpreted.

SUGGESTED READINGS

Barnaby, Karin, and Pellegino D'Acierno, eds. *C. G. Jung and the Humanities: Toward a Hermeneutics of Culture*. Princeton, N.J.: Princeton University Press, 1990.

Meurs, Jos van, and John Kidd. *Jungian Literary Criticism, 1920–1980*. Metuchen, N.J.: Scarecrow Press, 1988.

Whitlark, James. *Behind the Great Wall: A Post-Jungian Approach to Kafkaesque Literature*. Rutherford, N.J.: Fairleigh Dickinson University Press, 1991.

—*James S. Whitlark*

See also Freud, Sigmund; London, Jack; O'Neill, Eugene; Psychological theories of identity

Kaddish

AUTHOR: Allen Ginsberg (1926-1997)

FIRST PUBLISHED: 1961

IDENTITIES: Disease; family; gay, lesbian, and bisexual; Jewish; religion

Kaddish is Allen Ginsberg's elegy for his mother, Naomi. In *Kaddish* Ginsberg portrays the course of Naomi's mental illness and its effect on the extended Ginsberg family. The perceptions of Ginsberg, the narrator, are crucial to understanding how sexual and religious themes of identity work in the poem. Naomi's worsening condition coincides with Ginsberg's realization as a young boy that he is gay, and with his emerging discomfort with traditional American religious institutions.

Invoking both "prophesy as in the Hebrew Anthem" and "the Buddhist Book of Answers," section 1 remembers Naomi's childhood. Naomi passes through major American cultural institutions—school, work, marriage—all of which contribute to her illness. Section 2 details her descent into madness and its harrowing effects on the family. Throughout the poem, Ginsberg seeks rescue from Naomi's madness, yet recognizes that her condition also inspires his own critique of the United States. "Naomi's mad idealism" frightens him; it also helps him understand the sinister qualities of middle-class American institutions. As he admits Naomi's condition caused him sexual confusion, he also confers imaginative inspiration to her. She is the "glorious muse that bore me from the womb, gave suck/ first mystic life"; and it was from her "pained/ head I first took vision." Unlike Naomi, the truly mad in *Kaddish* are those incapable of compassion, such as the psychiatric authorities who brutalize Naomi with electroshock treatments, leaving her "tortured and beaten in the skull."

By the end of *Kaddish*, Ginsberg seeks to redeem Naomi's life according to the Eastern and Western religious traditions which inform the poem. The final sections of *Kaddish* seek to transform the trauma of Naomi's illness into sacred poetry. The key to this transformation is Ginsberg's revision of the Kaddish, the Jewish prayer for the dead. The Kaddish was not said at Naomi's grave because the required minimum of ten Jewish men—a *minyan*, in traditional Judaism—was not present, as required by Jewish law. Therefore, the poem accomplishes what Naomi's original mourners could not: Ginsberg eulogizes Naomi with his Kaddish, and by doing so he offers his own revision of traditional Judaic law.

SUGGESTED READINGS

Hyde, Lewis, ed. *On the Poetry of Allen Ginsberg*. Ann Arbor: University of Michigan Press, 1984.

Miles, Barry. *Ginsberg: A Biography*. New York: Simon & Schuster, 1989.

Portugés, Paul. *The Visionary Poetics of Allen Ginsberg*. Santa Barbara, Calif.: Ross-Erikson, 1978.

Rosenthal, M. L. *The New Poets: American and British Poetry Since World War II*. New York: Oxford University Press, 1967.

Schumacher, Michael. *Dharma Lion: A Critical Biography of Allen Ginsberg*. New York: St. Martin's Press, 1992.

—*Tony Trigilio*

See also Eastern religion and philosophy; Emigration and immigration; Erotic identity; Gay identity; Ginsberg, Allen; *Howl*; Jewish American identity; Mental disorders

Kadohata, Cynthia Lynn

BORN: Chicago, Illinois; July 2, 1956

PRINCIPAL WORKS: *The Floating World*, 1989; *In the Heart of the Valley of Love*, 1992
IDENTITIES: Japanese American; women
SIGNIFICANT ACHIEVEMENT: Kadohata is best known for her portrayal of a Japanese American family in her first novel, *The Floating World.*

Cynthia Lynn Kadohata aspired to be a journalist after she was graduated from college, believing that only nonfiction can express the truth. Her parents, as were other Japanese Americans, were uprooted during World War II and traveled extensively across the country in search of work. Kadohata's keen observation of landscape and people during these long drives prepared her for her later career.

Kadohata changed her plans for the future after she was seriously injured in an automobile accident. While recuperating, she read extensively and discovered the power of fiction, its ability to say what could not be said otherwise. She tried her hand at writing short stories, and, after several rejections, one of her stories was accepted by *The New Yorker*. She felt encouraged to devote her life to writing fiction.

Kadohata's two attempts at obtaining formal instruction in creative writing were of little use to her. She found her own observations and travels to be more useful than any theoretical discussions. In her first novel, *The Floating World*, Kadohata drew upon her own experiences of moving with her family from various cities on the Pacific coast to Arkansas. The protagonist and narrator, Olivia Osaka, is a third-generation Japanese American whose years of growing up are typical of all adolescents. The novel was well received and commended for its portrayal of a Japanese American migrant family. The success of the novel enabled her to win awards from the Whiting Foundation and the National Endowment for the Arts.

In the Heart of the Valley of Love, Kadohata's second novel, depicts Los Angeles in the 1950's. Her picture of grim and bleak life in the years to come is based on the implications of the changing demographics in California in the 1990's. Living in a period when a widening chasm between the classes breeds discontent and lawlessness, the protagonist, Francie, a young woman of Asian-African American ancestry, undergoes traumatic experiences. She loses her parents and then her surrogate parents, but eventually finds love, hope, and the possibility of renewal. She expresses Kadohata's optimism about the survival of a multicultural society in the future.

Kadohata is clearly influenced by writers such as Maxine Hong Kingston and Amy Tan, who draw upon their Chinese heritage. She adds another dimension to the multicultural experience by adding the Japanese American perspective.

SUGGESTED READINGS

Pearlman, Mickey. *Listen to Their Voices: Twenty Interviews with Women Who Write*. New York: W. W. Norton, 1993.
See, Lisa. "Cynthia Kadohata." *Publishers Weekly*, August 3, 1992, 48-49.

—Leela Kapai

See also Asian American identity: China, Japan, and Korea; *Floating World, The*; *In the Heart of the Valley of Love*

Keller, Helen

BORN: Tuscumbia, Alabama; June 27, 1880
DIED: Westport, Connecticut; June 1, 1968
PRINCIPAL WORKS: *The Story of My Life*, 1902; *The World I Live In*, 1908; *Out of the Dark*, 1913; *My Religion*, 1927; *Midstream: My Later Life*, 1929; *Teacher*, 1955
IDENTITIES: Disability; European American; women

SIGNIFICANT ACHIEVEMENT: Keller, deaf and blind from an early age, went on to lead a successful and highly influential career as a writer, speaker, and activist.

Helen Keller was born in 1880 in Alabama, the daughter of Arthur Keller, a former captain in the Confederate Army. At the age of nineteen months, Keller was stricken with a disease which has never been clearly identified. It left her blind and deaf. Her education began when Anne Sullivan became her teacher in 1887, after young Helen's situation had come to the attention of many celebrities of the time.

Keller was a rapid learner, and her earliest letters and school assignments proclaimed her love for literature and her desire to become a professional writer. Her first book, *The Story of My Life*, was written while she was a student at Radcliffe College, from which she was graduated, with honors, in 1904. The autobiographical work describes in great detail Keller's education by Anne Sullivan.

Most of Keller's works have been largely autobiographical; the author often complained that nobody seemed interested in her views about the world at large. When she wrote of politics, religion, and other outside matters, many critics dismissed her writings as the works of others who were merely trying to use Keller's celebrity status to further their own ends. Those who actually knew the woman, however, have always denied this.

In 1909, Keller joined the Socialist Party, and in 1913, published *Out of the Dark*, a compilation of essays on her political views. In 1917, she joined the Industrial Workers of the World (IWW), a labor organization that advocated radical, often socialist solutions to world problems. Along with her IWW colleagues, Keller opposed United States entry into World War I. During and after the war, she became involved in a series of lecture tours, almost always accompanied by Anne Sullivan.

At one point in her life, her pacifism, based on a religious belief that killing was evil, came into direct conflict with her more general humanitarian impulses. When the Nazis came into power, Keller for the first time advocated war, because she felt that the Nazis must be stopped, at whatever cost. In connection with this, she spoke and wrote widely about the horrors of Fascism.

Keller's last book, *Teacher*, a biography of Anne Sullivan, was published in 1955, after a long delay. In 1961, Keller suffered a mild stroke and decided to retire from public life. She died in 1968, in Connecticut.

SUGGESTED READING

Lash, Joseph P. *Helen and Teacher: The Story of Helen Keller and Anne Sullivan Macy*. New York: Delacorte Press, 1980.

—Marc Goldstein

See also *Miracle Worker, The*; School; *Story of My Life, The*

Kennedy, Adrienne

BORN: Pittsburgh, Pennsylvania; September 13, 1931

PRINCIPAL WORKS: *A Rat's Mass*, pr. 1966; *Cities in Bezique*, pb. 1969; *Funnyhouse of a Negro*, pr. 1962, pb. 1969; *The Lennon Play: In His Own Write*, pr. 1967, pb. 1969 (with John Lennon and Victor Spinetti); *A Lesson in a Dead Language*, pr., pb. 1968; *Sun: A Poem for Malcolm X Inspired by His Murder*, pr. 1968, pb. 1971; *A Beast's Story*, pr., pb. 1969; *Boats*, pr. 1969; *An Evening with Dead Essex*, pr. 1973; *A Movie Star Has to Star in Black and White*, pr. 1976; *A Lancashire Lad*, pr. 1980; *Orestes and Electra*, pr. 1980; *Black Children's Day*, pr. 1980; *People Who Led to My Plays*, 1987; *Adrienne Kennedy in One Act*, 1988; *Deadly Triplets: A Theatre Mystery and Journal*, 1990; *The Alexander Plays*, pb. 1992

IDENTITIES: African American; women

SIGNIFICANT ACHIEVEMENT: Kennedy's surrealist plays are leading examples of African American drama.

*African American
playwright
Adrienne Kennedy.*

Adrienne Kennedy's plays baffle and entice theater critics. In Kennedy, critics recognize a singularly able writer whose surrealism surpasses that of Tom Stoppard and Amiri Baraka. Edward Albee's early recognition of Kennedy's ability encouraged the yet-unpublished playwright to persist in her writing and led to the production of her *Funnyhouse of a Negro*.

Raised in a multiethnic neighborhood in Cleveland, Ohio, where her father, Cornell Wallace Hawkins, was an executive secretary for the Young Men's Christian Association and her mother, Etta Haugabook Hawkins, was a teacher, Kennedy was secure in her identity. She grew up associating with her neighbors: blacks, Jews, Italians, eastern Europeans. Where she lived, these people existed harmoniously, so Adrienne was not exposed to a racially motivated identity crisis until she entered Ohio State University in Columbus in 1949. There Kennedy felt isolated and inferior. Columbus' restaurants were still segregated, and there was little interaction between blacks and whites. By the time she was graduated in 1953, her racial anger and her detestation of prejudice had eaten away at her in ways that would shape her future writing career.

Kennedy married Joseph Kennedy shortly after graduation and followed him to New York City, where they both attended Columbia University. She studied creative writing there from 1954 until 1956. In 1958, she studied at the American Theatre Wing, then at the New School of Social Research, and finally at Edward Albee's Circle-in-the-Square School in 1962, where she was the only black student. Albee's encouragement led to Kennedy's continuing her writing career.

Her drama examines the inner struggles people encounter as they cope with their identities in relation to the outside forces that confront them. Kennedy's plays are essentially without plot. Her leading characters have multiple personalities, reflecting aspects of their identities. She relies heavily on the use of masks, each reflecting the different identities of her characters and suggesting elements of African art and culture as well.

SUGGESTED READINGS

Betsko, Kathleen, and Rachel Konig. *Interviews with Contemporary Women Playwrights*. New York: William Morrow, 1987.

Bryant-Jackson, Paul K., and Lois More Overbeck, eds. *Intersecting Boundaries: The Theatre of Adrienne Kennedy*. Minneapolis: University of Minnesota Press, 1992.

Cohn, Ruby. *New American Dramatists: 1960-1990*. New York: Grove, 1982.

—*R. Baird Shuman*

See also African American identity; Class and identity; Feminism

Kerouac, Jack

BORN: Lowell, Massachusetts; March 12, 1922

DIED: St. Petersburg, Florida; October 21, 1969

PRINCIPAL WORKS: *On the Road*, 1957; *The Dharma Bums*, 1958; *The Subterraneans*, 1958; *Mexico City Blues*, 1959; *Big Sur*, 1962

IDENTITIES: Canada; men

SIGNIFICANT ACHIEVEMENT: An unwilling folk hero of the Beat generation, Kerouac reflected his visionary life in his lyrical, often spontaneous works, revived American nonconformism, and broke new ground in fictive technique.

It is likely that as a very young boy Jack Kerouac spoke only French, and certainly he was immersed in his French Canadian heritage. His father died in his arms in 1946 and he adored his mother, but rebelled against his Catholic upbringing. The death in 1926 of his revered older brother, Gerard, may have heightened an early sense of disconnection. The twin brothers in Kerouac's first novel, *The Town and the City* (1950), are fictional alter egos. His nonfiction *Book of Dreams* (1961) reveals his awareness of his own divided personality. Thematically and stylistically, identity informs Kerouac's adolescent and adult writing and shaped his experiences and expressions; in Kerouac, the latter pair are barely distinguishable.

Impulsive and energetic, Kerouac produced huge amounts of material during marathon spontaneous writing sessions. He savored experiences and had a remarkable memory. His fiction comes from accurate remembrances. He was known as an adept typist and was chided by Truman Capote as being nothing else. He surrounded himself with music, specifically jazz. Such talents and inclinations resulted in his signature use of stream-of-consciousness and embedded blues phrasings in prose and poetry. He is often compared to Thomas Wolfe and to Walt Whitman (both writers were masters of a style that is, or appears to be, spontaneous and free-flowing). Kerouac traces his artistic self-discovery in the allegorical novel *Doctor Sax: Faust Part Three* (1959).

Kerouac's affinity for literature, philosophy, common folk, and music fostered associations with some of the most active, innovative minds of his generation. A close friendship with the spirited Neal Cassady (Dean Moriarty in *On the Road*) fueled Kerouac's lust for road experience. Kerouac and his companions' experimental approach to life and art often shocked America's prim post-World War II society.

Indifferent politically and hedonistic practically, Kerouac nevertheless claimed conservative views. For a time he embraced Buddhism; *The Dharma Bums* is a product of that interval. *Big Sur* chronicles his nervous breakdown of 1960. His death resulted from alcoholism. Curiosity, his and others', stemming from his reclusion, sexuality, and personae has enhanced the minor mythos around him. Kerouac's 1952 coining of the special meaning of the word "beat" eventually led to his defining it on *The Steve Allen Show* in 1960 as "sympathetic," an apt vision of Kerouac at his best.

SUGGESTED READINGS

Charters, Ann. *Kerouac: A Biography*. San Francisco: Straight Arrow Books, 1973.

Duffey, B. L. "The Three Worlds of Jack Kerouac." In *Recent American Fiction: Some Critical Reviews*, edited by Joseph Waldmeir. Boston: Houghton Mifflin, 1963.

Gifford, Barry, and Lawrence Lee. *Jack's Book: An Oral Biography of Jack Kerouac*. New York: St. Martin's Press, 1978.

Nicosia, Gerald. *Memory Babe: A Critical Biography of Jack Kerouac*. New York: Grove Press, 1983.

Walsh, Joy. "Jack Kerouac: An American Alien in America." *Moody Street Irregulars* 1, no. 1 (1978): 31-33.

—*Mary L. Otto Lang*

See also Alcoholism; Bilingualism; Bisexual identity; Canadian identity: Quebecois; Countercultures; *Dharma Bums, The*; Ferlinghetti, Lawrence; Ginsberg, Allen; *On the Road*

Kesey, Ken

BORN: La Junta, Colorado; September 17, 1935

PRINCIPAL WORKS: *One Flew over the Cuckoo's Nest*, 1962; *Sometimes a Great Notion*, 1964; *Kesey's Garage Sale*, 1973; *Demon Box*, 1986; *The Sea Lion: A Story of the Sea Cliff People*, 1991; *Sailor Song*, 1992

IDENTITIES: European American

SIGNIFICANT ACHIEVEMENT: A hero of the 1960's counterculture, Kesey is best known for his widely read and adapted *One Flew over the Cuckoo's Nest*.

Ken Kesey created a bridge between the 1950's Beat generation and the 1960's hippie movement. He wrote other works of fiction and nonfiction, but none rivaled the success of *One Flew over the Cuckoo's Nest*. Few contemporary works have been so influential. Kesey attended creative writing classes while working nights as a psychiatric attendant at a Veterans Administration hospital, where he volunteered as a research subject to take such drugs as LSD-25, psilocybin, and mescaline. These experiences influenced his writing of *One Flew over the Cuckoo's Nest* and his legendary bus trip with the Merry Pranksters.

In San Francisco, the bohemian lifestyle of the Beat generation was giving way to a more powerful counterculture revolution. Kesey influenced the transition, initiating mixed-media presentations with exotic costumes, strobe lights, sexual experimentation, freakouts, and Eastern mysticism.

One Flew over the Cuckoo's Nest, an indictment of American society and not only specifically of mental institutions, deals with conformity, authority, and social ills. It uses a colloquial style, myth, parables, and ironic commentaries to describe freedom, authenticity, cultural hegemony, and conformity. Kesey's rugged American individualism, frontiersmanship, and self-sufficiency are imbued in his writings and activities. He was a descendant of two lines of farm families. His later novel, *Sometimes a Great Notion*, reflects his agrarian heritage.

After the financial success of *One Flew over the Cuckoo's Nest*, Kesey arranged a psychedelic version of Jack Kerouac's trips as described in Kerouac's *On the Road* (1957). In fact, some of the people involved in Kerouac's trips also played major roles in Kesey's Merry Pranksters bus trip, memorialized in Tom Wolfe's *The Electric Kool-Aid Acid Test* (1968).

In high school and college, Kesey dabbled with magic, ventriloquism, costumes, theater, and athletic pageantry. This explains the exotic nature of the bus painting and the Prankster's outrageous costumes, which became imitated around the world. Kesey's experiments with drugs and the writing of *One Flew over the Cuckoo's Nest* may seem unrelated. In both, however, he was searching for spiritual or social transcendence, affirmation, or resolution. His investigations can be compared with the nineteenth century American Transcendentalism derived from Emanuel Swedenborg and modified by Ralph Waldo Emerson, Henry David Thoreau, and Walt Whitman. Emerson and Thoreau sought transcendence in the woods and mountains; Kesey and his Pranksters in day-glo paint, amplifiers, and the music of the Grateful Dead. All, however, loved nature, abhorred and resisted organized authorities, and relied on intuition as the mystical source from which all things found expression and meaning.

SUGGESTED READINGS

Leeds, Barry H. *Ken Kesey*. New York: Frederick Ungar, 1981.

Perry, Paul. *On the Bus: The Complete Guide to the Legendary Trip of Ken Kesey and the Merry Pranksters and the Birth of the Counter Culture*. New York: Thunder Mouth Press, 1990.

Tanner, Stephen. *Ken Kesey*. Boston: Twayne, 1983.

Wolfe, Tom. *The Electric Kool-Aid Acid Test*. New York: Farrar, Straus & Giroux, 1968.

—*Chogollah Maroufi*

See also Antiwar literature; Drugs; Eastern religion and philosophy; Kerouac, Jack; Wolfe, Tom

Keyes, Daniel

BORN: Brooklyn, New York; August 9, 1927

PRINCIPAL WORKS: "Flowers for Algernon," 1959 (short fiction); *Flowers for Algernon*, 1966 (novel)

IDENTITIES: Disability; European American; family

SIGNIFICANT ACHIEVEMENT: *Flowers for Algernon* is one of the world's best stories about human intelligence.

Daniel Keyes began writing science-fiction stories in 1952, during a brief career as an editorial associate with a fiction magazine. He began to write soon after receiving his college degree at the age of thirty-three. None of his stories gained critical notice, however, until his short-fiction piece "Flowers for Algernon" was published in 1959.

"Flowers for Algernon" tells the story of Charlie Gordon, a thirty-year-old man with an IQ less than seventy. Charlie has, however, an intense desire to learn and to become more intelligent. He is chosen to be the first human subject in an experiment aimed at surgically correcting the brain in a way that is hoped will triple Charlie's IQ. The same technique appears to have been successful on a white laboratory mouse named Algernon. The entire story is told through the journal written by Charlie, documenting his feelings and experiences as he increases in intelligence to genius level, then slowly and tragically returns to his former intellectual abilities.

The story brought immediate attention to Keyes, earning a Hugo Award as the best short science fiction in 1960. The story was innovative in style and content. The challenging technique of telling the story entirely in Charlie's words is extremely effective. In addition, Keyes's portrait of the nature of intelligence differs greatly from those in numerous previous science-fiction stories. Keyes portrays low intelligence in a sympathetic manner, effectively arguing that intelligence is only one of the things that makes people human.

Keyes wrote "Flowers for Algernon" while working as an English teacher, where his experiences with educationally challenged students may have formed much of the basis for the story. In 1961, Keyes earned his Master of Arts degree and became an instructor in English at Wayne State University. After moving to Ohio University, Athens, he attained his professorship in 1972.

In 1966, Keyes published an expanded version of his story, detailing Charlie's intellectual rise and fall and adding startling details about Charlie's tragic early life with his parents and sister, who abandon him. The novel *Flowers for Algernon* was also very well received, earning Keyes the Nebula Award for the best science-fiction novel in 1967. In 1968, a film titled *Charly* was made, with Charlie played by Cliff Robertson, who won an Oscar for best actor for his performance.

Keyes later wrote two other novels, *The Touch* (1968), about psychological stress after an industrial accident, and *The Fifth Sally* (1980), based on a true case of a woman with multiple personalities. None of his other fiction, however, achieved the success and critical notice of his stories about Charlie Gordon. Keyes's moving and effective "Flowers for Algernon" remains, perhaps, the best story on the nature of human intelligence and what it means to be human.

SUGGESTED READINGS

Clute, John, and Peter Nichols. *The Encyclopedia of Science Fiction*. New York: St. Martin's Press, 1993.

Gunn, James. *The New Encyclopedia of Science Fiction*. New York: Viking Penguin, 1988.

Pederson, Jay P. *St. James Guide to Science Fiction Writers*. Detroit: St. James Press, 1996.

—D. Douglas Fratz

See also Intelligence

Kincaid, Jamaica (Elaine Potter Richardson)

BORN: St. Johns, Antigua, West Indies; May 25, 1949

PRINCIPAL WORKS: *At the Bottom of the River*, 1983; *Annie John*, 1985; *A Small Place*, 1988; *Lucy*, 1990; *The Autobiography of My Mother*, 1994

IDENTITIES: Caribbean; family; women

SIGNIFICANT ACHIEVEMENT: Kincaid's short stories and novels are admired for their lyricism and for their insights into feminist and racial issues.

Jamaica Kincaid was born Elaine Potter Richardson on the tiny Caribbean island of Antigua. The family was poor, but she recalls her early years as idyllic. As does the protagonist of *Annie John*, Kincaid felt secure as the focus of her mother's attention. With the births of three younger brothers, however, Kincaid became increasingly alienated from her mother, and with adolescence, her alienation turned to bitter resentment.

*Jamaica Kincaid,
author of
Lucy (1990).
(© Sigrid Estrada)*

In addition to her antipathy toward her mother, there were other reasons for Kincaid to leave her Caribbean home as soon as she was old enough to do so. As she points out in *A Small Place*, on Antigua blacks were still relegated to the bottom tiers of the social structure, just as they had been in the colonial past. Black women were even more repressed than black men. In her short story "Girl," which appears in the collection *At the Bottom of the River*, the mother makes it clear to her daughter that a woman's sole purpose in life is to wait on a man and to keep him happy.

Determined to find her way in the world, in 1966, the seventeen-year-old young woman left Antigua for the United States. Her impressions of the different country are reflected in her second semiautobiographical novel, *Lucy*. In common with the title character, Kincaid first supported herself by working as a live-in baby-sitter in New York City. Although Kincaid took high school and college courses, in the main she educated herself by reading. Eventually she found a job on a magazine, turned out articles, and tried her hand at short stories. She was finding a new identity as a writer; in 1973, she took the name Jamaica Kincaid, in a sense inventing herself as a person. In 1978, "Girl" was published in *The New Yorker*, the first of many stories to appear there. Shortly thereafter, Kincaid married and moved to Vermont.

After an absence of nearly two decades, Kincaid returned to Antigua. Having found herself, Kincaid was now free, and in the years which followed she often took her children to visit her early home. By leaving her native island, Kincaid learned not only to understand herself but also to empathize with women who, like the protagonist in *Autobiography of My Mother* and like her own mother, were assigned their identities in a society that permitted them no options.

SUGGESTED READINGS

Kreilkamp, Ivan. "Jamaica Kincaid: Daring to Discomfort." *Publishers Weekly* 243 (January 1, 1996): 54-55.
Lee, Felicia R. "Dark Words, Light Being." *The New York Times*, January 25, 1996, C1, C10.
Weather, Diane. "Jamaica Kincaid: Her Small Place." *Essence* 26 (March, 1996): 98-99.

—*Rosemary M. Canfield Reisman*

See also *Annie John*; *At the Bottom of the River*; Caribbean American literature; Colonialism; Feminism

Kinflicks

AUTHOR: Lisa Alther (1944-   )
FIRST PUBLISHED: 1976
IDENTITIES: European American; family; gay, lesbian, and bisexual

Kinflicks, Lisa Alther's first published novel, is a funny, realistic account of a young woman growing up in the 1960's and of her struggle to come to terms with her mother's approaching death. Virginia (Ginny) Babcock's story is told in chapters which alternate between her own narrative of her growing up and third-person narrations of the present (about 1974) in which she returns to her Tennessee home to be with her desperately ill mother. In both story lines, the emphasis is on Ginny's attempts to define herself sexually and as a member of a family. Neither struggle concludes with any final definition.

Ginny rejects her parents when she is a teenager. She is repelled by her father's rigidity and her mother's fascination with death, and she is not close to either of her brothers. Her rebellion takes different forms, but once she is in high school her search for definition is largely in terms of her sexual behavior. Her mother tries to ignore Ginny's activities, while the father is enraged by what he learns.

Ginny's early efforts to find a sexual definition are based on her popularity in high school. She is the flag twirler with the marching band and the girlfriend of the school's athletic hero. In a series of very funny scenes, they experiment with a variety of sexual activities, always stopping short of intercourse, but one side of Ginny's nature rejects conventionality, and she loses her virginity with a half-crippled boy who is an outcast. None of this activity is very satisfying.

Ginny finds sexual fulfillment with a lesbian lover named Eddy, whom she encounters at the New England college to which she is sent by her father. When Eddy convinces Ginny that they are being socially irresponsible by remaining in school, they leave and join a small female commune in rural Vermont. When this episode ends in Eddy's violent death, Ginny tries marriage to one of the townsmen, and has a daughter named Wendy. She loves her daughter, but in other ways she is unsatisfied.

Ginny's husband eventually rejects her, and she returns to Tennessee to be with her dying mother. The two disagree about almost everything, including the events of their past, and Ginny is unable to provide much comfort for her mother. When the mother's death leaves their family disagreements unresolved, Ginny tries several times to commit suicide. None of these attempts is successful, and in the end she decides to live, although she has already decided not to return to her husband and daughter. Her search for definition has not succeeded, but she will keep trying.

Suggested readings

Brown, Laurie L. "Interviews with Seven Contemporary Writers." In *Women Writers of the Contemporary South*, edited by Peggy Whitman Prenshaw. Jackson: University Press of Mississippi, 1984.

Ferguson, Mary Anne. "Lisa Alther." In *Contemporary Fiction Writers of the South: A Bio-Bibliographical Sourcebook*, edited by Joseph M. Flora and Robert Bain. Westport, Conn.: Greenwood Press, 1993.

_____. "Lisa Alther: The Irony of Return." *The Southern Quarterly* 21 (Summer, 1983): 103-115.

Hall, Joan Lord. "Symbiosis and Separation in Lisa Alther's *Kinflicks*." *Arizona Quarterly* 38 (Winter, 1982): 336-346.

Peel, Ellen. "Subject, Object, and the Alternation of First- and Third-Person Narration in Novels by Alther, Atwood and Drabble." *Critique* (Summer, 1989): 107-122.

—John M. Muste

See also Alther, Lisa; Bisexual identity; Identity crisis; Lesbian identity; *Other Women*

King, Martin Luther, Jr.

Born: Atlanta, Georgia; January 15, 1929

Died: Memphis, Tennessee; April 4, 1968

Principal works: *Stride Toward Freedom*, 1958; *Strength to Love*, 1963, "I Have a Dream," 1963; *Why We Can't Wait*, 1964; *Where Do We Go from Here: Chaos or Community?*, 1967; "I've Been to the Mountaintop," 1968

Identities: African American; religion; South

Significant achievement: King's speeches and essays united, motivated, and mobilized people of all colors during the civil rights struggles of the 1950's and 1960's.

Martin Luther King, Jr., was formally ordained at the age of nineteen, in the church over which his father presided, thus officially beginning his public-speaking career. Within ten years, he had secured a position as pastor of a Montgomery, Alabama, church and had established himself as a civil rights leader by leading a boycott against the Montgomery public transportation system. After the successful conclusion of the boycott, King founded the Southern Christian Leadership Council,

Civil rights leader and author Martin Luther King, Jr., winner of the Nobel Peace Prize in 1964. (The Nobel Foundation)

in the hope of harnessing the momentum of the movement to further the cause of racial equality.

Supported by a network of churches and civil rights organizations, King became the most vocal opponent to segregation, and thus became a lightning rod for criticism and accolades. On August 28, 1963, King led a march on Washington, D.C., at which he delivered his best-known speech, "I Have a Dream." The following year, he was awarded the Nobel Peace Prize. Also during 1963 and 1964, King was arrested four times on charges such as parading without a permit, trespassing, and contempt of court. One of King's most powerful works, "Letter from the Birmingham Jail," was composed while he was incarcerated during this time, and several other pieces were occasioned by the arrests and subsequent confinements.

The focus of most of King's writings was upon the necessity for all citizens to effect necessary social changes by using a system of passive resistance and economic empowerment. The tenets of his strategy were outlined in such speeches as "The Power of Nonviolence" (1957) and "Love, Law, and Civil Disobedience" (1961). In addresses such as "A Time to Break Silence" (1967), he spoke of the need for Americans to examine their beliefs about race and culture, with respect not only to conflicts within the United States but also in international relations, such as those with Vietnam.

King's later works, such as *Where Do We Go from Here: Chaos or Community?*, show King's reluctant recognition that the struggle for racial equality would be a long-term battle. Although he believed that civil rights would eventually be equally afforded to all Americans, he warned of the dangers of complacency and backsliding. In his final address ("I've Been to the Mountaintop"), given on April 3, 1968, he urged supporters of civil rights to continue the struggle in his absence. The next day, he was shot to death.

SUGGESTED READINGS

Branch, Taylor. *Parting the Waters: America in the King Years, 1954-63*. New York: Simon & Schuster, 1988.

Fairclough, Adam. *Martin Luther King, Jr.* Athens: University of Georgia Press, 1995.

Oates, Stephen B. *Let the Trumpet Sound: The Life of Martin Luther King, Jr.* New York: Harper & Row, 1982.

—*T. A. Fishman*

See also African American identity; Civil Rights movement; Class and identity; *Testament of Hope, A*

Kingsolver, Barbara

BORN: Annapolis, Maryland; April 8, 1955

PRINCIPAL WORKS: *The Bean Trees*, 1988; *Holding the Line: Women in the Great Arizona Mine Strike of 1983*, 1989; *Homeland and Other Stories*, 1989; *Animal Dreams*, 1990; *Another America-(Otra America)*, 1991; *Pigs in Heaven*, 1993; *High Tide in Tucson: Essays from Now or Never*, 1995

IDENTITIES: Latino; Native American; West and Southwest; women

SIGNIFICANT ACHIEVEMENT: Kingsolver's fiction portrays working-class Americans maintaining families, friendships, and communities with honesty, humor, and hard work.

Barbara Kingsolver grew up in a family of three children in Eastern Kentucky. Her family background of a two-parent home differs from much of her fiction. All three novels to some degree explore the impact of a missing parent.

Kingsolver describes her father as a doctor with a social conscience, often accepting payment in garden vegetables. Her father's social conscience apparently influences her fiction and nonfiction, for example, her study of women's roles in the Arizona mine strike of 1983.

Kingsolver's personal participation in campus activism and antiwar demonstrations matches a motif in her fiction: commitment to social responsibility and change. Hallie Noline in *Animal Dreams* follows her conscience to farming communities in Nicaragua, "where farmers were getting ambushed while they walked home with their minds on dinner" and where Hallie is kidnapped and murdered. Issues such as environmental degradation and immigration injustices play significant roles in her fiction as well.

An especially strong autobiographical

Barbara Kingsolver, author of Pigs in Heaven *(1993)* (Seth Kantner)

influence is the Western setting of her novels. Having headed west for doctoral study in biology at the University of Arizona, Kingsolver settled in Tucson, fascinated by the landscape, animal life, and indigenous cultures of the desert. Her close observation of nature and deep respect for Native American culture are evident in her fiction. Kingsolver chose not to finish her dissertation, instead taking a job as a technical writer with the University of Arizona. She was married and gave birth to a daughter, Camille. An insomniac during pregnancy, she began writing at night, typing in a closet to keep the light from disturbing her husband. She thus produced the manuscript of *The Bean Trees*, which she sent to its publisher prior to her daughter's birth. Publication of the novel led her to write fiction full time.

In interviews, Kingsolver says that all of her characters contain a part of her. Codi Noline in *Animal Dreams*, for example, teaches high school biology, spurring the students and community to fight against industrial pollution of the river. Kingsolver's hobbies and interests—gardening, environmental and human rights activism, piano, hand drums, and rock and roll keyboards—enrich her fiction. Her childhood, her parents, and her daughter have apparently provided her insight for many of her voices and characters. Her focus on relationship as central to identity echoes in a line from the preface to *High Tide in Tucson: Essays from Now or Never*: "Maybe I could have done it alone. But I sure wouldn't want to."

SUGGESTED READINGS

Cincotti, Joseph A. "Intimate Revelations." *The New York Times Book Review*, September 2, 1990, 2.

Perry, Donna. *Backtalk: Women Writers Speak Out*. New Brunswick, N.J.: Rutgers University Press, 1993.

—*Janet Taylor Palmer*

See also American identity: West and the frontier; *Bean Trees, The*; Class and identity; Latino identity; Native American identity; *Pigs in Heaven*

Kingston, Maxine Hong

BORN: Stockton, California; October 27, 1940

PRINCIPAL WORKS: *The Woman Warrior: Memoirs of a Girlhood Among Ghosts*, 1976; *China Men*, 1980; *Tripmaster Monkey: His Fake Book*, 1989

IDENTITIES: Chinese American; women

SIGNIFICANT ACHIEVEMENT: Kingston's autobiographical books and her novel, brilliantly interweaving imagination and fact, convey Chinese American immigrant experience to a wide readership.

Born Maxine Ting Ting Hong, Kingston's first language was Say Up, a Cantonese dialect spoken by her immigrant parents, who made their living in California by running a laundry. They struggled to retain their Chinese identity and values in a new world peopled by ominous aliens: immigration officials, teachers, non-Chinese. Kingston's mother admonished and inspired her six children, particularly her daughters, with talks of the disasters that befell women who broke men's rules and of legendary heroines who dared battle for justice.

Silent and wordless among "white ghosts," Kingston was also threatened in childhood and adolescence by the specter of traditional Chinese prejudices against women. "Better to raise geese than girls," was a family motto. Kingston nevertheless became an *A* student and entered the

Maxine Hong Kingston, author of Tripmaster Monkey: His Fake Book *(1989)* (Franco Salmoiraghi)

University of California at Berkeley, where she drank in all the idealism of the Civil Rights and anti-Vietnam War movements of the 1960's.

Kingston married classmate and actor, Earll Kingston, and for many years pursued a career as a teacher, first in California and then in Hawaii. Meanwhile, finding her voice and experimenting with the linguistic means by which she could express the rich imagery and rhythms of Chinese American speech in her writing, she began working on two autobiographical books simultaneously. Enthusiastic critical acclaim accompanied the publication of the best-selling *The Woman Warrior* and *China Men*. Often called novels, these autobiographies combine imaginative flights and her memories of Chinese myths with the facts of Chinese immigrant history. In these works, Kingston claims full citizenship for Chinese Americans. "We Chinese belong here. This is our country, this is our history, we are a part of America. If it weren't for us, America would be a different place." Kingston says that, in telling the story of the Chinese in America, a major influence was William Carlos Williams' *In the American Grain* (1925).

Besides asserting the justice of the struggle against racism, Kingston also affirms the right of women of all races to full equality. Her writings make important contributions to feminist literature and women's studies. She stands as the most widely read and influential interpreter of the Chinese American experience.

SUGGESTED READINGS

Cheung, King-Kok, and Hiraye Yamamoto. *Articulate Silences*. Ithaca, N.Y.: Cornell University Press, 1993.

Islas, Arturo. "Maxine Hong Kingston." In *Women Writers of the West Coast: Speaking of Their Lives and Careers*, edited by Marilyn Yalom. Santa Barbara, Calif.: Capra Press, 1983.

Juhasz, Suzanne. "Maxine Hong Kingston." In *Contemporary American Women Writers: Narrative Strategies*, edited by Catharine Rainwater and William J. Scheick. Lexington: University Press of Kentucky, 1985.

—Joseleyne Ashford Slade

See also Asian American identity: China, Japan, and Korea; *China Men*; *Woman Warrior, The*

Kinsella, W. P.

BORN: Edmonton, Alberta, Canada; May 25, 1935

PRINCIPAL WORKS: *Dance Me Outside*, 1977; *Scars*, 1978; *Born Indian*, 1981; *Shoeless Joe*, 1982; *The Moccasin Telegraph and Other Indian Tales*, 1983; *The Thrill of the Grass*, 1985; *The Iowa Baseball Confederacy*, 1986; *The Fencepost Chronicles*, 1986; *Red Wolf, Red Wolf*, 1987; *The Further Adventures of Slugger McBatt*, 1988; *Box Socials*, 1990; *The Winter Helen Dropped By*, 1995

IDENTITIES: Canada; Native American

SIGNIFICANT ACHIEVEMENT: Kinsella's fiction explores the Native American experience and the American fascination with baseball.

After various jobs as a young adult, W. P. Kinsella returned to college, earned a degree in and taught creative writing, and became a full-time writer. Born in Canada, Kinsella has lived in the United States and regularly travels across the country watching baseball games. His innumerable stories and occasional novels often involve either the Native American residents of the Ermineskin Reserve in Alberta, Canada, or the game of baseball.

Kinsella's Ermineskin stories—in *Dance Me Outside*, *Scars*, *Born Indian*, *The Moccasin Telegraph and Other Indian Tales*, *The Fencepost Chronicles*, and elsewhere—artfully convey the wisdom and stoic humor of their Native American characters. The Indians frequently have to confront ignorant, arrogant, and sometimes oppressive white officials and visitors. Narrator Silas Ermineskin is a complex character known to friends as someone who writes and publishes stories; the series becomes a meditation on writing as a way to develop and express personal identity.

The Indian stories are noteworthy, but Kinsella's baseball fiction made him famous. For Kinsella, baseball, with its fixed traditions, pastoral setting, and leisurely pace, embodies everything admirable in the American character, and baseball enables troubled people to achieve fulfillment. In *Shoeless Joe*, when a voice tells a farmer to build a baseball diamond, dead players return to play their favorite game, the farmer reconciles with his dead father, and a bitter recluse, writer J. D. Salinger, finds happiness when he departs with the players. Other baseball stories feature magically gifted players, divine intervention, or people transformed by a devotion to baseball.

Kinsella's interests combine in *The Iowa Baseball Confederacy*, in which two men travel back in time to a 1906 baseball game, while a Native American spirit watches and hopes for an Iowa victory that will return his lost lover. In this work, Native Americans and baseball embody the essential American identity, which is fragile, since the game's end breaks the spell and erases the event from history. Kinsella's love for baseball is unalloyed, and the popularity of these stories proves that other Americans share his attitude.

SUGGESTED READINGS

Aitken, Brian. "Baseball as Sacred Doorway in the Writing of W. P. Kinsella." *Aethlon: The Journal of Sports Literature* 8, no. 1 (Fall, 1990): 61-75.

Feddersen, R. C. "Interview with W. P. Kinsella." *Short Story* 1, no. 2 (Fall, 1993): 81-88.

Murray, Don. *The Fiction of W. P. Kinsella: Tall Tales in Various Voices*. Fredericton, New Brunswick, Canada: York, 1987.

—*Gary Westfahl*

See also Canadian identity; *Moccasin Telegraph and Other Indian Tales, The*; Native American identity

Kitchen God's Wife, The

AUTHOR: Amy Tan (1952-   )
FIRST PUBLISHED: 1991
IDENTITIES: Chinese American; family; women

The Kitchen God's Wife, Amy Tan's second novel, is concerned with a young, Americanized Chinese American woman's quest to accept her heritage, and in so doing accept her family, especially her mother. The first section of the novel, told from the daughter Pearl's point of view, concerns Pearl's difficult relationship with her mother, Winnie. Pearl perceives Winnie only as an old, unfashionable woman with trivial concerns. Pearl is troubled by a secret that she believes she cannot tell her mother. Pearl has been diagnosed with multiple sclerosis, but dreads her mother's reaction, her reproaches, her list of ways Pearl could have prevented her disease.

Pearl comes to recognize that her mother has secrets of her own, which Winnie finally decides to share with her daughter. Most of the novel, which is also the part that has received the most critical praise, is Winnie's first-person account of her childhood. The reader discovers along with Pearl that her mother has not always been the penny-pinching part-owner of a dingy, outdated florist's shop. Instead, Winnie has had a life of tragedy and adventure before immigrating to the United States. She lived another life in China, complete with another husband and three long-dead children. Winnie's mother disappeared when Winnie was a child, leaving her with her father and his other wives, who promptly sent her to live with an uncle. That uncle married her to Wen Fu, a sadistic, adulterous pilot, and Winnie soon began the nomadic life of a soldier's wife during wartime. By the end of the war, Winnie found love with the man Pearl knows as her father, the Chinese American serviceman Jimmie Louie. Wen Fu had Winnie imprisoned for adultery when she tried to divorce him, then raped her upon her release. Pearl learns the secret her mother has been hiding—Jimmie Louie, who died when Pearl was fourteen, is not her biological father after all. When Pearl learns these secrets about her mother's past, she is finally able to reveal the secret of her illness.

The title refers to an altar that Pearl inherits from a woman Winnie had known in China, and it symbolizes the growing closeness that Winnie and Pearl develop after sharing their secrets. The final scene shows Winnie buying her daughter a deity for the altar. This statue, whom Winnie names Lady Sorrowfree, the kitchen god's wife, represents Winnie and her care for her daughter. By the end of the novel, Pearl achieves a greater understanding of her mother and of their often trying relationship.

SUGGESTED READINGS

Dew, Robb Forman. Review of *The Kitchen God's Wife*, by Amy Tan. *The New York Times Book Review*, June 16, 1991, 9.

Iyer, Pico. Review of *The Kitchen God's Wife*, by Amy Tan. *Time*, June 3, 1991, 67.

Shapiro, Laura. Review of *The Kitchen God's Wife*, by Amy Tan. *Newsweek*, June 24, 1991, 63-64.

—*J. Robin Coffelt*

See also Asian American identity: China, Japan, and Korea; Emigration and immigration; Tan, Amy

Klail City

AUTHOR: Rolando Hinojosa (Rolando Hinojosa-Smith, 1929-   )
FIRST PUBLISHED: *Klail City y sus alrededores*, 1976 (English translation, 1987)
IDENTITIES: Latino; West and Southwest

Klail City is part of the Klail City Death Trip, a chronicle of the Texas Rio Grande Valley. This novel moves between past and present so that the past and the present often appear to be the same. Like most of Rolando Hinojosa's novels, *Klail City* lacks linear plot development. A series of vignettes create a sense of place and ultimately present a picture of a changing world. Several narrators, including the main characters of the series, Rafe Buenrostro ("Buenrostro" means "good face") and Jehú Malacara ("Malacara" means "bad face") tell the stories.

P. Galindo, Esteban Echevarría (a kind of wise man throughout the series), Rafe, and Jehú recount a variety of tales ranging from the story of a hastily arranged marriage between the pregnant Jovita de Anda and Joaquín Tamez to tales of the Texas Rangers' abuse of Mexican Americans to the story of how Alejandro Leguizamón planned the murder of Rafe's father, Jesús, and the revenge exacted by Jesús' brother, don Julián. There is also a kind of interior monologue by Jehú as he and Rafe attend their twenty-second high school class reunion.

The past is interwoven with the present, particularly in the scenes that occur in the bars, where the old men, the *viejitos*, sit drinking and talking until don Manuel Guzmán, Klail City's only Mexican American police officer, comes to take them home.

The sections entitled "The Searchers," tell the stories of migrant workers as they leave their homes in the valley to travel north to pick produce. The narrator P. Galindo is introduced, and he reveals himself to be a kind of surrogate author for Hinojosa as he explains his interest in preserving a history of these people.

In addition, Rafe gives a personal account of what it was like in the 1940's for Mexican American students in the American high school, and Jehú recounts some of his experiences as an orphan, an acolyte, and a traveling evangelist with Brother Imás. Brother Imás' life story is told, as is Viola Barragán's (Hinojosa's prototype of the liberated woman), along with an account of how the whites used "bought" Mexicans to get their hand-picked candidates elected. This eclectic collection of vignettes makes up a book that, in 1976, won Latin America's most prestigious literary award, the Casa de las Américas prize.

SUGGESTED READINGS

Broyles, Yolanda Julia. "*Klail City y sus alrededores*: Oral Culture and Print Culture." In *The Rolando Hinojosa Reader*, edited by José David Saldívar. Houston, Tex.: Arte Público Press, 1985.

Calderón, Héctor. "On the Uses of Chronicle, Biography and Sketch in Rolando Hinojosa's *Generaciones y semblanzas*. In *The Rolando Hinojosa Reader*, edited by José David Saldívar. Houston, Tex.: Arte Público Press, 1985.

Hinojosa, Rolando. "The Texas-Mexico Border: This Writer's Sense of Place." In *Open Spaces, City Places: Contemporary American Writers on the Changing Southwest*, edited by Judy Nolte Temple. Tucson: University of Arizona Press, 1994.

—*Joyce J. Glover*

See also American identity: West and the frontier; Chicano identity; Hinojosa, Rolando

Kogawa, Joy (Joy Nozomi Goichi)

BORN: Vancouver, British Columbia, Canada; June 6, 1935

PRINCIPAL WORKS: *A Choice of Dreams*, 1974; *Jericho Road*, 1977; *Obasan*, 1981; *Woman in the Woods*, 1985; *Itsuka*, 1992

IDENTITIES: Canada; Japanese American; women

SIGNIFICANT ACHIEVEMENT: Kogawa's novel *Obasan* brings literature of the World War II internment camp experience to a new level of psychological depth and lyrical brilliance.

Joy Kogawa grew up in the relatively sheltered environment provided by her minister father in Vancouver. That security was shattered with World War II relocation policies, which sent Japanese Canadians to internment camps in the inhospitable interior lands of Canada. The atomic bombs dropped on Hiroshima and Nagasaki by the United States also profoundly affected her.

As a young woman Kogawa attended the University of Alberta, the Anglican Women's Training College, and the Conservatory of Music. She married David Kogawa on May 2, 1957; they had

Asian Canadian novelist Joy Kogawa.

two children, Gordon and Deirdre. The years 1967 to 1968 seem to have been a transitional period in Kogawa's life, since her first book of poems (*The Splintered Moon*, 1968) was published, she divorced David Kogawa, and she returned to college, attending the University of Saskatchewan, in those two years.

The next ten years of Kogawa's life became increasingly productive. Her second collection of poems, *A Choice of Dreams*, was published in 1974. Kogawa worked in the Office of the Prime Minister in Ottawa, Ontario, as a staff writer from 1974 to 1976. A third collection of poetry, *Jericho Road*, was published in 1977. During this time Kogawa worked primarily as a freelance writer. Kogawa contributed poems to magazines and journals in Canada and the United States.

In 1981, *Obasan* was published. Widely acclaimed as one of the most psychologically complex and lyrically beautiful novels on the topic of Japanese Canadians' wartime experiences, *Obasan* continues to intrigue readers and critics alike with its powerful story of a silent, reserved woman, Megumi Naomi Nakane, learning of the fate of her family in Japan many years after the fact. Naomi's experience of dispossession, relocation, and internment, as well as the loss of her parents, has made her ethnicity, her self-image, and her relationships with others deeply problematic. Published in 1986, *Naomi's Road* retells the tale of *Obasan* in a manner intended for child readers.

Itsuka is Kogawa's sequel to *Obasan*. *Itsuka* follows Naomi's political awakening and the healing of her wounds from the past.

SUGGESTED READINGS

Cheung, King-Kok. *Articulate Silences: Hisaye Yamamoto, Maxine Hong Kingston, Joy Kogawa*. Ithaca, N.Y: Cornell University Press, 1993.

Davidson, Arnold E. *Writing Against the Silence: Joy Kogawa's "Obasan."* Toronto: ECW Press, 1993.

—*Julie Tharp*

See also Asian American identity: China, Japan, and Korea; Canadian identity; *Obasan*

Korean Americans. *See* Asian American identity: China, Japan, and Korea

Korean War

In contrast to most of the major wars that have occurred in the twentieth century, the Korean War resists attempts to render it in literature. Most of the literature that exists about the Korean War was written long after the war was over. Some of the best literature about the Korean conflict has been written by American soldiers who were introduced to the country by tours of duty as peacekeepers. These soldiers saw Korea after the fighting ceased. The Korean War is the subject of a crop of Hollywood films, but writers have been largely silent.

One theory regarding this silence is James Jones's idea that although he was able to write about World War II, a popular and patriotic war, almost at will, those who served in Korea, and many of those in the United States and in Britain, were not certain what the war was about. Finally, with a shaky peace in place, it was necessary to maintain a military presence to enforce peace. The Korean

A machine-gun crew takes aim at the enemy during the Korean War, which was the first war fought by integrated U.S. forces. (National Archives)

War, in a sense, did not end. Some may even consider it to be the first war that America lost. Writers were loathe to present such a possibility in the 1950's, which were years of prosperity and contentment for many Americans. The Korean War was not hugely unpopular, as the Vietnam War was; the Korean War sparked little protest. It neither generated a strong national prowar feeling, as World War II did, nor an antiwar feeling, as the Vietnam War did. The Korean War was also relatively short (1950-1953).

There are good novels about the Korean War, and many personal memoirs. Some were written as early as 1956. The only collection of poetry about the Korean War appears to be *The Hermit Kingdom: Poems of the Korean War*, published in 1995 by the Center for the Study of the Korean War. One poet to discuss Korea in his poetry is William Wantling, whose book *The Source* (1966) talks about the war, his morphine addiction after being wounded, the extreme cold of Korea, the ironies of fighting with South Koreans against North Koreans, and the taking of meaningless hills only to surrender them the next day, at the cost of lives. Wantling's is one of the first openly critical literary reflections on the war from someone who was there in the trenches.

Another useful anthology is *The Field of Crosses*, published in 1988 by the British Korean Veterans Association. The literature it presents is a combination of the patriotic and the disaffected, and the anthology is wide-ranging in subjects and attitudes. An important novel, published at the war's end, is Duane Thorin's *A Ride to Panmunjom* (1956).

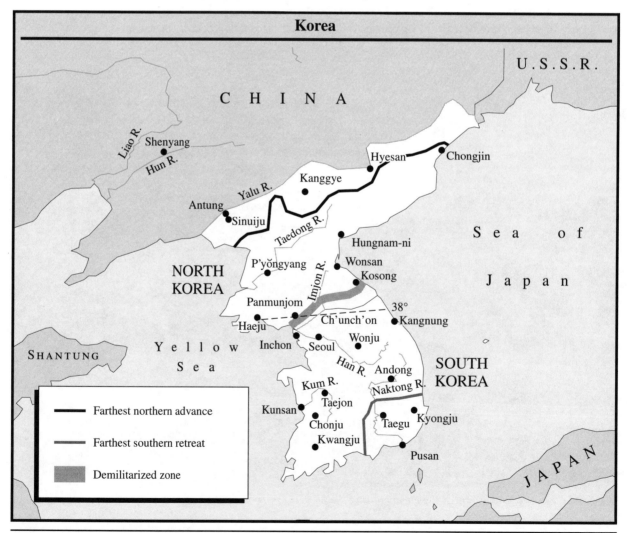

Korean War Milestones

1950	June 25, North Korean Communist army invades South Korea.
1950	June 27, President Harry S Truman orders armed forces into Korea.
1950	June 28, North Koreans capture Seoul.
1950	Armed forces of the United Nations (U.N.) and the United States form a unified force against the Communists.
1950	July-October, U.N. forces capture Seoul and P'yŏngyang, the North Korean capital. Douglas MacArthur, head of the U.N. forces, threatens to continue to push his army into China, seeking retaliation. President Truman asks for MacArthur's
	resignation; the replenished Communist forces push back the U.N. forces to the thirty-ninth parallel.
1951	Armistice negotiations begin.
1953	Armistice negotiations end, with Korea divided at roughly the thirty-eighth parallel between the Communist North and the non-Communist South.
1956	Duane Thorin's *A Ride to Panmunjom*.
1966	*The Source*, by William Wantling.
1980	*The Field of Crosses*, an anthology of British Korean War veterans.
1995	*The Hermit Kingdom: Poems of the Korean War*, an anthology.

The war in Korea presented Americans with a conflict that was unclear in its results and purpose. Many Americans objected to being peacekeepers of the world, and when they came back, most Korean War veterans kept quiet about their experiences.

SUGGESTED READINGS

Axelsson, Arne. *Restrained Response: American Novels of the Cold War and Korea, 1945-1962*. Westport, Conn.: Greenwood Press, 1990.

Coon, Gene L. *Meanwhile, Back at the Front*. New York: Crown, 1961.

Pollini, Francis. *Night*. Paris: Olympia Press, 1960.

Thorin, Duane. *A Ride to Panmunjom*. Chicago: Regnery, 1956.

Walker, Wilbert L. *Stalemate at Panmunjom*. Baltimore: Heritage Press, 1980.

Wantling, William. *The Source*. Paradise, Calif.: Dustbooks, 1966.

Woods, Denis J. *British Forces in the Korean War*. United Kingdom: The British Koreans Veterans Association, 1988.

—John Jacob

See also Antiwar literature; Vietnam War; World War II

Koreans. *See* Asian American identity: China, Japan, and Korea

Kosinski, Jerzy

BORN: Lodz, Poland; June 14, 1933

DIED: Manhattan, New York; May 3, 1991

PRINCIPAL WORKS: *The Painted Bird*, 1965; *Steps*, 1968; *Being There*, 1971; *The Devil Tree*, 1973; *Cockpit*, 1975; *Blind Date*, 1977; *Passion Play*, 1979; *Pinball*, 1982; *The Hermit of Sixty-ninth Street: The Working Papers of Norbert Kosky*, 1988

IDENTITIES: Jewish; world

SIGNIFICANT ACHIEVEMENT: Kosinski is best known for his depiction of the Holocaust in *The Painted Bird* and for his creation of characters who grapple with the absurdity and cruelty of contemporary life.

Jerzy Kosinski achieved immediate success with his first novel, *The Painted Bird*, which Kosinski claimed was an autobiographical account of his childhood experiences during the

German occupation of Poland. The author spent the rest of his life defending those experiences, and the autobiographical content of his other books, against his critics and supporters.

There are two central questions raised by Kosinski's work. First, were his novels merely records of his extraordinary life—and his life was without question extraordinary—as many have claimed, or are the novels a creative refashioning of his experience? Kosinski experienced enormous popularity as a novelist; his books sold in the tens of millions of copies. As one critic has noted: Can a writer who pandered to the crassest commercial standards of popular fiction by employing graphic sex and violence, conventional fictional types, and sensational contemporary events really have anything seriously significant to say to his readers? The search for answers to such questions has dominated the writing about Kosinski's life and art.

There is no question that Kosinski's life had a profound effect on his writing. The search for identity, with all that implies, is the primary focus of his fiction and began with his own quest occasioned by his profoundly unsettling experiences as a child. Most of his protagonists try on a series of personas, creating roles with which to attempt to cope with the perplexity of contemporary life. The most obvious of these is Chance, the central character in *Being There*, whose whole life is formed by his television watching. Chance is not unique in reflecting Kosinski's fascination with popular culture and its effect in determining identity.

The implications Kosinski pursued regarding personality-shaping events make him, along with Albert Camus, one of the primary writers to deal with important postwar existentialist questions. His search for personal definition in a hostile and alienating world earned for him a prominent place among writers of the late twentieth century.

SUGGESTED READINGS

Everman, Welch D. *Jerzy Kosinski: The Literature of Violation.* San Bernardino, Calif.: Borgo Press, 1991.

Lavers, Norman. *Jerzy Kosinski.* Boston: Twayne, 1982.

Lilly, Paul R., Jr. *Words in Search of a Victim: The Achievement of Jerzy Kosinski.* Kent, Ohio: Kent State University Press, 1988.

Lupack, Barbara Tepa. *Plays of Passion, Games of Chance: Jerzy Kosinski and His Fiction.* Bristol, Ind.: Wyndham Hall Press, 1988.

Sloan, James Park. *Jerzy Kosinski.* New York: E. P. Dutton, 1996.

—Charles L. P. Silet

See also Anti-Semitism; Appearance and identity; Erotic identity; Existentialism; Holocaust; Popular culture; Violence

Kramer, Larry

BORN: Bridgeport, Connecticut; June 25, 1935

PRINCIPAL WORKS: *Women in Love*, 1969 (screenplay); *Faggots*, 1978; *The Normal Heart*, pr., pb. 1985; *Reports from the Holocaust: The Making of an AIDS Activist*, 1989; *The Destiny of Me*, 1993

IDENTITIES: Disease; European American; gay, lesbian, and bisexual

SIGNIFICANT ACHIEVEMENT: Kramer's plays and essays are among the earliest and most powerful works dealing with the acquired immune deficiency syndrome (AIDS) epidemic.

After his 1957 graduation from Yale, Larry Kramer moved quickly into the world of filmmaking. For more than a decade, he wrote and produced films, winning an Academy Award nomination for his screenplay for the film version of the D. H. Lawrence novel *Women in Love* (1920).

Supported by money from his career, and lessons learned from years of psychological therapy, begun after a suicide attempt during his freshman year in college, Kramer determined to explore artistic ways to respond to being gay. After his 1972 play, *Sissies' Scrapbook*, failed to please critics or attract audiences, Kramer published a controversial but wildly successful novel, *Faggots*, which characterizes gay men as obsessed with sex but longing for love. Friends expressed their anger at Kramer for what they felt was the novel's negative portrayal of gay men. In the early 1980's, an alarming number of gay men were becoming ill with a strange new disease. Kramer gathered eighty men together in August, 1981, to talk about what was happening. From that meeting was born Gay Men's Health Crisis (GMHC), one of the first AIDS advocacy and service organizations.

Kramer quickly found his niche as a spokesman for gay men with AIDS. His anger was fueled by meager research funds, by what he saw as the Reagan Administration's failure to act, and by what seemed like blindness to the seriousness of the crisis on the part of New York officials. Many gay men directed their anger at Kramer, who urged them to rein in their sexual activity until the cause of the disease was found.

In Kramer's incendiary—and highly influential—1983 essay for the *New York Native*, "1,112 and Counting," he affirmed anger as the appropriate emotion for contemporary gay men, claiming that "continued existence depends on how angry you can get." Soon GMHC removed Kramer from its board of directors.

Kramer dramatized the early years of the AIDS crisis, including his role in the formation of GMHC, in his play *The Normal Heart*. In the late 1980's, Kramer discovered that he, too, was infected with the AIDS virus. That knowledge spurred him to publish a collection of essays, *Reports from the Holocaust: The Making of an AIDS Activist*, and to form a new, radical organization: AIDS Coalition to Unleash Power, or ACT-UP.

In *The Destiny of Me*, his 1993 sequel to *The Normal Heart*, Kramer's alter ego, Ned Weeks, reappears, still venting his rage at institutions that he thinks are ignoring or making worse the AIDS epidemic. At the same time, Ned confronts his family demons and his tortured childhood.

Suggested readings

Shilts, Randy. *And the Band Played On*. New York: St. Martin's Press, 1987.
Shnayerson, Michael. "Kramer vs. Kramer." *Vanity Fair*, October, 1992, 228-297.

—*James B. Graves*

See also AIDS; Coming out; Gay identity; Kushner, Tony; Monette, Paul; *Normal Heart, The*

Kunitz, Stanley

Born: Worcester, Massachusetts; July 29, 1905

Principal works: *Intellectual Things*, 1930; *Passport to the War: A Selection of Poems*, 1944; *Selected Poems, 1928-1958*, 1958; *The Testing-Tree: Poems*, 1971; *The Terrible Threshold: Selected Poems, 1940-1970*, 1974; *Next-to-Last Things: New Poems and Essays*, 1985

Identities: Jewish

Significant achievement: Kunitz achieves a complexity and coherence unique in lyric poetry.

While a scholarship student at Harvard University, Stanley Kunitz won a prize for a poem anticipating his acknowledged themes of time and mutability. Critics speculate that Kunitz's thematic preoccupations stem from an event that occurred weeks before his birth: his father's suicide. Kunitz suffered a further blow at the age of fourteen when his beloved stepfather died.

Significantly, the dramatized "I"—the protagonist throughout Kunitz's poetry—is the ever-questing self, determined to survive against the odds "the hurt/ Which is unanswerable [and] fill[s] the brow/ with early death." The basis of Kunitz's work is personal, but he is not a poet of the confessional school. He intends his poetry to be a vehicle that transforms private themes and events into legend. That is, the poetry is meant to give the particular and the personal a universal dimension. "All the essential details of the poem are true as dreams are," Kunitz explains in his commentary on "Father and Son."

The "I" in "Father and Son" pursues his ghostly father across a dreamscape. His face a "white ignorant hollow," the figure remains to the end wordless, incapable of imparting knowledge. Kunitz characteristically sounds the note of bitterness against family and tradition in his early poetry. "Let sons learn from their lipless fathers how/ Man enters hell," he declares in "For the World Is Flesh."

With World War II, during which, as a conscientious objector, he took a noncombatant role, Kunitz appears to have reforged links with his Jewish immigrant heritage. In "Reflection by a Mailbox," then-current horrors in Adolf Hitler's Europe precipitate an imaginative journey backward through time to the pogroms that brought his parents from Russia to America. The discovery of Russian poetry, which he began to translate, also revived ancestral ties. "Journal for My Daughter," occasioned by Kunitz's divorce in 1958, marks a major development toward reconciliation in his work, as he confronts his own parental responsibility for a child's suffering.

Kunitz's love of the natural world, traced to his boyhood solace in exploring the woods and fields surrounding his home, has remained a source of renewal, evident particularly in the expansive perspective of his later poetry. Recognition has included the Pulitzer Prize in poetry in 1959 for *Selected Poems, 1928-1958*, designations as Library of Congress consultant on poetry from 1974 to 1976 and, in 1987, State Poet of New York.

SUGGESTED READINGS

Hagstrum, Jean H. "The Poetry of Stanley Kunitz: An Introductory Essay." In *Poets in Progress*, edited by Edward Hungerford. Evanston, Ill.: Northwestern University Press, 1962.

Hénault, Marie. *Stanley Kunitz*. Boston: Twayne, 1980.

Orr, Gregory. *Stanley Kunitz: An Introduction to the Poetry*. New York: Columbia University Press, 1985.

Rodman, Seldon. *Tongues of Fallen Angels*. New York: New Directions, 1974.

—*Amy Allison*

See also Jewish American identity

Kushner, Tony

BORN: New York, New York; July 16, 1956

PRINCIPAL WORKS: *A Bright Room Called Day*, pr. 1985, pb. 1991; *Angels in America: A Gay Fantasia on National Themes*, part 1, *Millennium Approaches*, pr. 1990, pb. 1993, part 2, *Perestroika*, pr. 1991, pb. 1994; *Thinking About the Longstanding Problems of Virtue and Happiness*, 1995 (including the play *Slavs!*, pr. 1994)

IDENTITIES: Disease; gay, lesbian, and bisexual; Jewish

SIGNIFICANT ACHIEVEMENT: Kushner's work brings together issues of national politics, sexuality, and community.

Tony Kushner grew up in Lake Charles, Louisiana. His parents, musicians, immersed him in culture, leftist politics, and the arts. He returned to New York City, his birthplace, to attend Columbia University, where he studied medieval history, developed an interest in Marxist thought, and began to come to terms with his homosexuality. He underwent psychoanalysis during his early years in New York, attempting to "cure" himself of being gay. After being graduated from Columbia in 1978, Kushner earned a Master in Fine Arts degree in directing from New York University in 1984.

Kushner is best known for *Angels in America: A Gay Fantasia on National Themes*, a play about life in Ronald Reagan's America and the pandemic of acquired immune deficiency syndrome (AIDS). Much of *Angels in America*—and of Kushner's other work—focuses on political thought, especially the connections between world history and contemporary politics. Kushner's first major play, *A Bright Room Called Day*, uses an artistic character to draw explicit links between the rise of Nazism in Germany in the 1930's and what Kushner saw as the smothering conservatism of the 1980's. *Slavs!*, Kushner's sequel to *Angels in America*, opens with a character from *Perestroika*, Aleksii Antedilluvianovich Perlapsarianov, the world's oldest Bolshevik. The play focuses on a postsocialist world in which leftist politics has lost out to its more conservative counterparts. Kushner sees the loss of the left to be a loss of hope and a foreboding of a dangerous, heartless future. These themes are also developed in *Angels in America*, but in *Slavs!* Kushner does not use sexuality as a major symbol, although two main characters of *Slavs!* are a lesbian couple.

Kushner writes what he has referred to as Theater of the Fabulous. His plots examine the close relationship between the public, political world and the private lives of people. An activist who has been arrested more than once at demonstrations against government inaction in the face of the AIDS crisis, Kushner sees himself as an inheritor of Bertolt Brecht's explicitly political theater. In order for theater to be socially relevant, moving, and artistically successful, Kushner believes that theater must be confrontational, that it must not leave its audience comfortable or satisfied with the status quo. Theater, for Kushner, is an art of engagement, with politics, with issues, and with audiences—and theater is always political.

SUGGESTED READINGS

Felman, Jyl Lynn. "Lost Jewish (Male) Souls: A Midrash on *Angels in America*." *Tikkun* 10, no. 3 (May, 1995): 27-30.

Kushner, Tony. Interview by David Savran. In *Speaking on Stage: Interviews with Contemporary American Playwrights*, edited by Philip C. Kolin and Colby H. Kullman. Tuscaloosa: University of Alabama Press, 1995.

—Chris Freeman

See also AIDS; *Angels in America*; Gay identity; Jewish American identity

L

Lakota Woman

AUTHORS: Mary Crow Dog (Mary Brave Bird, 1953-   ) and Richard Erdoes (1912-   )
FIRST PUBLISHED: 1990
IDENTITIES: Native American; religion; women

Lakota Woman describes Mary Crow Dog's life from her birth in 1953 to the early 1970's. Daughter of a full-blooded Lakota mother and a white father, Crow Dog was reared by her mother on the Rosebud Sioux Reservation in tiny He Dog, South Dakota. She is a member of the Brule (Burned Thigh) or Sichangu Tribe, one of seven that constitute the Lakota (also known as Sioux) Nation. Before identifying herself with the American Indian Movement (AIM), she attended a grim and repressive Catholic school and lived a marginal existence as a shoplifter. The central events in her biography described in *Lakota Woman* are her participation in the AIM Trail of Broken Treaties March on Washington in 1972; her participation in the siege of Wounded Knee in 1973, where she gave birth to her son Pedro in April; and her involvement with the Native American church.

Lakota Woman interweaves Mary's public story as an AIM Indian and her private story as a half-Native American woman whose troubled life exemplifies the lives of many Native Americans. As a historical account *Lakota Woman* is cheerfully biased and unsupported by documentation, but the drama of Mary's story and her confident voice make the book a convincing portrait of her identity as a Native American woman.

Richard Erdoes, Mary Crow Dog's collaborator, pieced together *Lakota Woman* and its sequel, *Ohitika Woman* (1993), out of audiotaped conversations and dialogue. The book therefore has the flavor and the rambling organization of talk, but it also is carefully constructed so that each chapter coalesces around the chapter title and epigraph. Thus, for example, the chapter titled "Aimlessness," describing Mary's wild youth and the problems of reservation life, comes right before the chapter titled "We AIM Not to Please," which outlines the development of the American Indian Movement.

In *Lakota Woman*, Mary Crow Dog describes the conflict of Indian and European values, a conflict that has escalated into a clash between modern materialistic consumerism and the spiritual values of the Lakota. The spiritual side is represented by her then-husband Leonard Crow Dog. In another sense, the book is about change and assimilation. A main thrust of AIM's efforts has been to secure for Native Americans the civil rights they are guaranteed under United States law. Mary Crow Dog's story reveals a woman in the process of helping a new cultural identity emerge out of synthesis of ancient Lakota values and modern society.

SUGGESTED READINGS

Brave Bird, Mary, and Richard Erdoes. *Ohitika Woman*. New York: Grove Press, 1993.

Fire, John, and Richard Erdoes. *Lame Deer: Seeker of Visions*. New York: Simon & Schuster, 1972.

Matthiessen, Peter. *In the Spirit of Crazy Horse*. New York: Viking, 1991.

Means, Russell. *Where White Men Fear to Tread: The Autobiography of Russell Means*. New York: St. Martin's Press, 1995.

Wexler, Rex. *Blood of the Land: The Government and Corporate War Against First Nations*. Philadelphia: New Society Publishers, 1992.

—Thomas Lisk

See also Erotic identity; Native American identity

Larsen, Nella

BORN: Chicago, Illinois; April 13, 1891
DIED: New York, New York; March 30, 1964
PRINCIPAL WORKS: *Quicksand*, 1928; *Passing*, 1929
IDENTITIES: African American; women
SIGNIFICANT ACHIEVEMENT: Larsen's novels are among the first to portray realistically the dilemma of identity for biracial women.

In common with her protagonists—Helga Crane in *Quicksand* and Clare Kendry in *Passing*—Nella Larsen, throughout her life, never thoroughly resolved the crisis of her identity. Larsen often invented details about her life to suit her audience and the effect she wanted to have on it; it may be said that she learned this habit of invention from her parents. Mystery surrounds her identity because she wanted it that way.

Even in such matters as her birth certificate, school records, and early childhood whereabouts, it is possible that no absolutely definitive history will arise. Thadious M. Davis, in the biography *Nella Larsen, Novelist of the Harlem Renaissance: A Woman's Life Unveiled*, makes a thorough summary of the information available on the basics of Larsen's identity. Nella Larsen was born Nellie Walker, child of a Danish woman and a cook designated as "colored." The baby was designated, therefore, as "colored." When the girl entered school, she did so under the name Nellie Larson. It is possible that her supposed stepfather, Peter Larson, was in fact the same person as her "colored" father, Peter Walker, and that Peter Walker had begun to pass for white. Nellie Larson also attended school as Nelleye Larson. In 1907, she began to use the surname Larsen. The 1910 census of her household does not include her (her officially white sister, Anna, is mentioned), perhaps because her birth certificate, with the word "colored," was being disassociated from the family. Later, she adopted the first name Nella; with marriage, she became Nella Larsen Imes. Larsen thus had considerable experience in her life with such issues as passing and identity.

After completing a nursing degree at Lincoln Hospital, Larsen worked as a nurse at Tuskegee Institute in Alabama. As does her character Helga, Larsen quickly tired of the uplifting philosophy at Tuskegee and headed north. Larsen worked for the New York City Department of Health and married Elmer S. Imes.

Between 1921 and 1926, Larsen worked for the New York City Public Library in Harlem. There, Larsen became involved with Harlem Renaissance writers, capturing her own following with the publication of several critically acclaimed short stories. Shortly afterward, Larsen wrote *Quicksand*, a novel for which she was awarded a Harmon Award in literature. Following the success of this book and her next novel, *Passing*, Larsen became the first African American woman to receive the prestigious Guggenheim Fellowship.

Her popularity ended, however, with the public embarrassment of being accused in 1930 of plagiarizing one of her short stories, "Sanctuary," and a messy divorce from her husband, whose unfaithfulness was the talk of the town. Her readership abandoned her, and she retreated to nursing at New York City's Gouverneur Hospital, transferring to Metropolitan Hospital in 1961. In 1963, she went through a period of depression that may have been because her white sister (or perhaps half-sister) had shunned Larsen for the last of many times. In 1964, her absence from work being noted, Larsen was found dead in her apartment.

Larsen enjoyed literary success only briefly during her lifetime. Her literary talents and achievements went largely unrecognized until reappraisal of women's literature elevated her works as contributing a distinctive voice to American literature.

SUGGESTED READINGS

Bone, Robert A. *The Negro Novel in America*. Rev. ed. New Haven, Conn.: Yale University Press, 1965.

Davis, Thadious M. *Nella Larsen, Novelist of the Harlem Renaissance: A Woman's Life Unveiled*. Baton Rouge: Louisiana State University Press, 1994.

Gayle, Addison, Jr. *The Way of the World: The Black Novel in America*. Garden City, N.J.: Anchor Press, 1975.

—*Betty L. Hart*

See also African American identity; Harlem Renaissance; Mixed race and identity; *Quicksand*

Last of the Menu Girls, The

AUTHOR: Denise Elia Chávez (1948-   )
FIRST PUBLISHED: 1986
IDENTITIES: Latino; West and Southwest; women

Denise Elia Chávez's *The Last of the Menu Girls* is a collection of seven interrelated stories about Rocío Esquibel, a young Mexican American woman in southern New Mexico who seeks to understand herself, her family, and her community. Rocío's development from girl to woman gives unity to the collage of stories. Rocío observes those around her she provides a portrait of a culturally diverse community and a clear insight into the human condition.

The title story introduces Rocío at age seventeen beginning her first job as an aide in a hospital in her home town. It is the summer of 1966. One of her tasks is to take menus to patients and get their requests for meals. Rocío studies the patients with great attention. She sees them as individuals with differing needs, and her heart reaches out to them so fully that she suspects she is too emotional for the job. Her emotional investment, however, helps Rocío understand others and makes her better able to understand herself. By the end of the summer Rocío has been promoted to other duties in the hospital and the system has changed; she is literally the last of the menu girls. Her compassion for others continues to serve her well as a way of understanding herself and her relationship to the world.

In the other stories Rocío increasingly looks to the past, to her personal history and to that of her Mexican American culture. She also tries to envision the future, to create the woman she hopes to be. By the end of the stories Rocío has found her mission. As her mother says, it would take a lifetime to write even the story of their home; there are stories all around. Rocío dedicates herself to writing the lives of the ordinary people she knows, people who often cannot speak for themselves. In the process of telling their stories, Rocío will speak for herself and for her culture.

Chávez's talents as a playwright and a poet give a distinctive quality to her fiction. She captures the small gestures and the precise voice of her characters and shows rather than tells their actions. Her work is filled with humor and the hope of the heart that makes her characters enduring.

SUGGESTED READINGS

Balassi, William, John F. Crawford, and Annie O. Eysturoy, eds. *This Is About Vision: Interviews with Southwestern Writers*. Albuquerque: University of New Mexico Press, 1990.

Herrera-Sobek, María, and Helena Maria Viramontes, eds. *Chicana Creativity and Criticism: Charting New Frontiers in American Literature*. Houston, Tex.: Arte Público Press, 1988.

Reed, Ishmael. *Hispanic American Literature*. New York: HarperCollins, 1995.

—*Lois A. Marchino*

See also Chávez, Denise Elia; *Face of an Angel*; Feminism; Latino American identity

Last Picture Show, The

AUTHOR: Larry McMurtry (1936-   )
FIRST PUBLISHED: 1966
IDENTITIES: Adolescence and coming-of-age; European American; family; religion; South

The Last Picture Show, Larry McMurtry's third novel, treats the struggle to come of age in a society that has lost traditional moorings. In the small fictional town of Thalia, Texas, Sonny Crawford, from whose point of view the story is told, has no real family. In his senior year in high school in 1954, Sonny lives in a rooming house with his friend Duane.

Their football coach, Herman Popper, is a poor coach, but he is even worse as a classroom teacher. Unfortunately, most of the other teachers are no better, and Sonny and Duane sleep through most of their classes. The only outlets for youth in the town besides athletics are Fundamentalist religious activities, sexual experimentation, and the movies at the town's one "picture show."

The title of the book suggests small-town monotony and emptiness: The best Thalia can offer is the escape of movies, a way out of facing drab realities. The "picture show," however, is about to close. Television—a social change that does not seem to be an improvement—has made the movie house unprofitable.

Sonny and Duane and the others have no family to guide them, no school that offers positive challenges, no meaningful religious grounding. Their sexual experimentation brings no real intimacy, no lasting relationships. What once was an agricultural ranching economy is now dominated by oil. Newly rich men drive fast cars, exploit the land's natural resources, and callously use and discard young women.

There are some positive role models, however. Sam the Lion, who owns the pool hall, looks out for Sonny and Duane and the helpless mentally retarded Billy. As a father figure, Sam represents the old ways of integrity and compassion. Genevieve, the waitress at the all-night café, also offers wholesome support and guidance. Sam, however, dies; Duane goes off to the Korean War after fighting with Sonny; Genevieve prepares to leave the café since her husband is well again; and the retarded Billy is run over by a passing cattle truck. Sonny's life seems governed by loss. He gets into his pickup truck and heads out of town. He soon realizes that he has no place to go and nothing to seek, so he turns around and heads back into Thalia.

The Last Picture Show has been favorably compared to other coming-of-age books such as *Adventures of Huckleberry Finn* (1884) and *The Catcher in the Rye* (1951). It presents a sometimes harsh but always insightful picture of small town life in the rural Southwest in the 1950's.

SUGGESTED READINGS

Busby, Mark. *Larry McMurtry and the West: An Ambivalent Relationship*. Denton: University of North Texas Press, 1995.

Degenfelder, E. Pauline. "McMurtry and the Movies: *Hud* and *The Last Picture Show*." *Western Humanities Review* 29 (Winter, 1975): 81-91.

Peavy, Charles D. *Larry McMurtry*. Boston: Twayne, 1977.

Reynolds, Clay, ed. *Taking Stock: A Larry McMurtry Casebook*. Dallas: Southern Methodist University Press, 1989.

—Jeff H. Campbell

See also Adolescent identity; McMurtry, Larry; Rural life; School

Later the Same Day

AUTHOR: Grace Paley (1922-   )
FIRST PUBLISHED: 1985
IDENTITIES: Jewish; women

Grace Paley's *Later the Same Day* contains the stories of people speaking in the varied dialects of New York City. In these stories, identity is formed through people's acts and through their unique stories. As in Paley's earlier collection, *Enormous Changes at the Last Minute*, Faith Darwin is a recurring character, but here she is the mature woman, looking back at her life. In "The Story Hearer," for instance, Faith is asked to tell her lover, Jack, the story of her day. Despite her effort to "curb [her] cultivated individualism," she ends up sidetracking, watering her "brains with time spent in order to grow smart private thoughts." Jokingly, Faith comments on men's love of beginnings, and thus suggests that women move through stories and time quite differently, tempted by the private, rather than the "public accounting" of life. Similarly, in "Zagrowsky Tells," "Lavinia: An Old Story," and "In This Country, but in Another Language, My Aunt Refuses to Marry the Men Everyone Wants Her To," identity is a matter of individual stories told in first-person narratives and ethnic dialects.

To a lesser degree than in *Enormous Changes at the Last Minute*, identity is also a matter of one's relationship to history and community. In "The Story Hearer," Faith wants to rise above her time and name, but finds herself "always slipping and falling down into them, speaking their narrow language." In "The Expensive Moment," Faith's friends and families respond to the aftereffects of China's Cultural Revolution, relating their experiences to America's "revolutions" of the 1960's. A visiting Chinese woman quickly identifies herself as still a Communist, but later in the story, another Chinese woman asks about children and "how to raise them." Like Faith and other mothers in Paley's fiction, these women "don't know the best way." In a world and country divided by different voices, different genders, and different politics, there is still possibility for community and for common identities. "Friends" pays tribute to Faith's dying friend Selena, and the circle of women who go to visit her. Dying sets her apart from the others, but Selena is a mother, as are they, of a child in a generation "murdered by cars, lost to war, to drugs, to madness."

Later the Same Day was highly acclaimed by critics for its sensitivity to human and ethnic identity and for its experiments with storytelling. It continues to be significant in light of feminist concern with world peace, relationships among women, theories of women's language, and the importance of finding one's own voice.

SUGGESTED READINGS

Baba, Minako. "Faith Darwin as Writer-Heroine: A Study of Grace Paley's Short Stories." *Studies in American Jewish Literature* 7 (Spring, 1988): 40-54.

Isaacs, Neil. *Grace Paley: A Study of the Short Fiction*. Boston: Twayne, 1990.

Taylor, Jacqueline. *Grace Paley: Illuminating the Dark Lives*. Austin: University of Texas Press, 1990.

—*Andrea J. Ivanov*

See also *Enormous Changes at the Last Minute*; Feminism; Jewish American identity; Paley, Grace; Women and identity

Latino American identity

IDENTITIES: Latino

At issue
In the last decades of the twentieth century, a new generation of Latino writers in North America established a strong literary reputation, enriching mainstream literature. This development reflects demographic changes. Latino literature, characterized by impressive versatility, provides critical insights into the problematic issues of identity in terms of language, family, religion, education, acculturation, and artistic expression. Latino literature is in essence a literature of uprootedness, self-search, and recovery. The American experience constitutes a collective cultural heritage, and the readership of an ethnic literature is not confined to one minority.

Historical context
Latinos do not represent a homogeneous group. The term "Latino" includes a diversity of ethnic, racial, national, and cultural groups, with historic, economic, and social differences. The diaspora from Central and South America is also being included in what is becoming a transnational culture, with a greatly varied collective identity that has at root the use of the Spanish language. The most heterogeneous of the Latino American groups are those of Caribbean origins, residing mostly on the Eastern coast of the United States.

The beginnings of the presence of Spanish-speaking groups in North America can be found in the mid-sixteenth century, when Spaniards arrived in what became the United States. Since then, Latinos have been documenting their life experiences in writings that combine autobiographical and imaginative modes, expressing feelings of rupture and displacement, and a need to recapture the past in order to find the "true" self. A most active period of literary production emerged in the late 1960's, generated by cultural and political awakening, with each writer often excelling in several genres.

Two literary groups have been recognized: the native Hispanic, and the migrated Hispanic. There are problems of definition for "migrated" and "native"—for example, with Puerto Ricans—but in

Latino American Identity
Milestones

1492- Historical accounts by explorers, missionaries
onward (for example, the works collectively known as
the *Jesuit Relations*), and conquerors make a deeply
influential contribution to the literature of the New
World. Florida, the Southwest, and California are
first colonized by Spanish-speaking people, whose
language, architecture, customs, music, ranching,
mining, and irrigation practices are of permanent
influence and are reflected in the literature of
English- and Spanish-speaking Americans. From
the Spanish instrument—the guitar—that the
cowboy strums, to the place names and to the
language of legal documents and historical
accounts before 1848, Spanish influence
predominates in many regions of North America.

1850- The Mexican folk ballad known as the *corrido*
onward begins to flourish, continuing into the late twentieth
century.

1892 Eusebio Chacon's *El hijo de la tempestad* (the son
of the storm) is published in Santa Fe, New Mexico.

1942 James Branch Cabell's *The First Gentlemen of
America*.

1959 *Pocho*, by José Antonio Villarreal, follows a family
from the Mexican Revolution to World War II.

1961 Jesús Colón's *A Puerto Rican in New York and
Other Sketches*.

1967 Rudolfo Gonzales' *I Am Joaquín*, the epic poem of
the Chicano Renaissance.

1967 Piri Thomas' *Down These Mean Streets*.

1970 Ricardo Sánchez's book of poetry *Canto y grito mi
liberación*.

1970 Luis Omar Salinas' *Crazy Gypsy*.

1971 Luis Valdez publishes a collection of short plays,
Actos, which were written and performed for César
Chávez's farmworkers' movement in California.

1971 Alurista publishes *Floricanto en Aztlán*, a classic
book of poetry.

1971 Tomás Rivera's *. . . y no se lo tragó la tierra-And
the Earth Did Not Part*.

1972 Rudolfo Anaya publishes his first novel, *Bless Me,
Ultima*.

1973 Rolando Hinojosa's *Estampas del valle y otras
obras-Sketches of the Valley and Other Works*, a
humorous novel that presents a series of sketches
about the Spanish-speaking communities along
the Rio Grande River in Southern Texas.

1974 José Antonio Villarreal's *The Fifth Horseman*.

1975 *El Bronx Remembered*, by Nicholasa Mohr.

1976 Rudolfo Anaya's *Heart of Aztlán*.

1979 José Antonio Villarreal's *Clemente Chacón*.

1979 Rudolfo Anaya's *Tortuga* completes the trilogy
begun with *Bless Me, Ultima*.

1982 *Family Installments: Memories of Growing Up
Hispanic*, by Edward Rivera.

1983 Sandra Cisneros' *The House on Mango Street*.

1986 Denise Elia Chávez's first novel, *The Last of
the Menu Girls*.

1986 Ana Castillo's novel, *The Mixquiahuala
Letters*.

1987 Mary Helen Ponce's *Taking Control*.

1989 *The Mambo Kings Play Songs of Love*, by Oscar
Hijuelos.

1989 Mary Helen Ponce's *The Wedding*.

1990 Denise Elia Chávez's long novel *Face of an Angel*.

1990 Ana Castillo's *Sapogonia*.

1990 Judith Ortiz Cofer's *Silent Dancing: A Partial
Remembrance of a Puerto Rican Childhood*.

1991 *How the García Girls Lost Their Accents*, by Julia
Alvarez.

1992 Editor Rodolfo Cortina's *Cuban-American Theater*,
an anthology.

1992 Cristina García's *Dreaming in Cuban*.

1993 Ana Castillo's *So Far from God*.

1995 Rudolfo Anaya's *Zia Summer*.

1995 Ana Castillo's collection of feminist-oriented
poetry, *My Father Was a Toltec*.

1996 Rudolfo Anaya's *Jalamanta*, a novel.

terms of literary records, these problems are moot. Both groups—those who were born in the United States and those who left their countries as emigrants or exiles—come to feel that their home is "neither here nor there," exemplifying a polarized identity and a common sense of marginality. Through nostalgic remembrances and memories of their ancestors or their own countries, writers create an idealized homeland as a key source of reference. They write in Spanish,

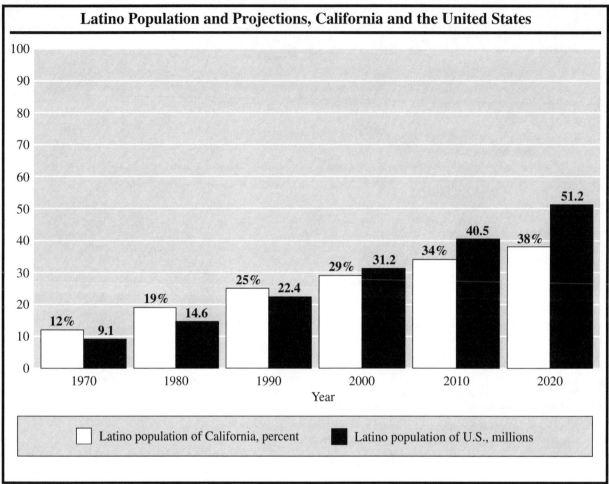

Latino Population and Projections, California and the United States

Latino population of California, percent

Latino population of U.S., millions

Source: U.S. Bureau of the Census.

English, or in both, according to personal experiences and objectives. For example, Rosario Ferré, a leading Puerto Rican writer, wrote *The House on the Lagoon* (1995) in English; the migrated Puerto Rican Esmeralda Santiago translated her novel *When I Was Puerto Rican* (1993) into Spanish to reach more Latino readers.

Regardless of their status as native or migrated Latinos, writers often indicate sociocultural hybridism and a need to preserve roots by including Spanish words and expressions in English text. Such switching from one language to another reflects the recognition of a double identity, Hispanic and Anglo, in New York-born Puerto Rican Nicholasa Mohr's *Nilda* (1973), New York-born Cuban Oscar Hijuelos' *Our House in the Last World* (1983), Puerto Rican Judith Ortiz Cofer's *Silent Dancing* (1990), Dominican Julia Alvarez's *How the García Girls Lost Their Accents* (1991), and Cuban Cristina Garcia's *Dreaming in Cuban* (1992). In these works, the rendering of growing up Latino in America includes self-exploration through writing as an act of artistic survival.

Puerto Ricans have migrated to the United States in search of a better life. Those settled in New York became known as Nuyoricans. *A Puerto Rican in New York and Other Sketches* (1961), the landmark work of essays and reminiscences by the Puerto Rican activist Jesús Colón, marks the birth of Nuyorican literature. Written in English with the inclusion of colloquial Puerto Rican Spanish, Colón's book depicts the brutal existence of young immigrants in the barrio. Piri Thomas, born in New York, documents dehumanizing life in urban streets and prison in the autobiographical classic *Down These Mean Streets* (1967) and in *Seven Long Times* (1994), as Miguel Piñero does in his play *Short Eyes* (1975).

Pedro Pietri's *Puerto Rican Obituary* (1973), Mohr's *El Bronx Remembered* (1975), *In Nueva York* (1977), and *Rituals of Survival: A Woman's Portfolio* (1985), Edward Rivera's *Family Installments: Memories of Growing Up Hispanic* (1982), Santiago's *When I Was Puerto Rican*, and Alba Ambert's *A Perfect Silence* (1995) portray survival strategies and the courage needed by underprivileged youth.

Ed Vega's novel *The Comeback* (1985) and short fiction *Mendoza's Dreams* (1987) offer a Puerto Rican interpretation of the American Dream. Vega's *Casualty Report* (1991) chronicles the death of dreams in the face of racism, poverty, and crime. Victor Rodriguez's novel *Eldorado in East Harlem* (1992) depicts nostalgia for the island and dreams of making it on the mainland. Nuyorican poetry, inspired by Caribbean rhythms of African origin, exhibits pride in Victor Hernández Cruz's *Mainland* (1973), *Tropicalization* (1976), and *By Lingual Wholes* (1982). Miguel Algarín's *On Call* (1980), Miguel Piñero's *La Bodega Sold Dreams* (1985), and Tato Laviera's *La Carreta Made a U-Turn* (1979), *Enclave* (1981), *AmeRícan* (1985), and *Mainstream Ethics* (1988) affirm that Latinos must lay claim to territory in the literary and cultural mainstream because Latinos are transforming the national American identity. Mohr and Laviera also write about discrimination in Puerto Rico against Nuyoricans, who are marginalized as gringos.

The major Cuban wave of immigration to the United States occurred after the 1959 Cuban Revolution. Typically middle-class political refugees, hoping to return home soon, older Cuban writers distanced themselves from the U.S. mainstream experience and wrote in Spanish. Most often settled in Miami, Cuban writers focused on the exile experience. Younger writers who arrived

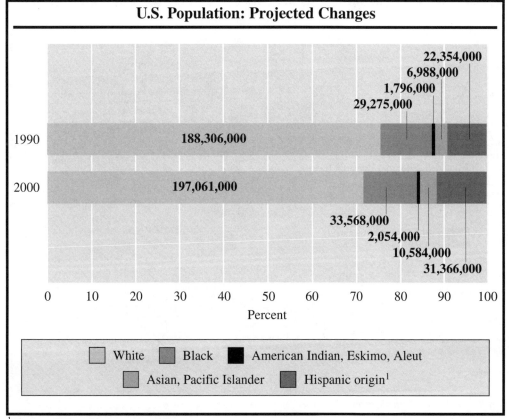

[1] Persons of Hispanic origin may be of any race.
Source: U.S. Bureau of the Census.

in their teens or early twenties, such as Eliana Rivero, Achy Obejas, Rafael Catalá, and Dolores Prida identified with the social struggles of minority groups. Spanish remained the primary language, and bilingual discourse captured their sense of a divided self, questioning the values of both cultures—the ancestral and the adopted one. Many of those who came on the 1980 Mariel boatlift focused on political and sexual persecution in Fidel Castro's Cuba and exile experiences, as exemplified in Reinaldo Arenas' works.

Virgil Suárez, the author of two novels, *Latin Jazz* (1989) and *The Cutter* (1991), and the short fiction collection *Welcome to the Oasis and Other Stories* (1992), which shows the United States through the eyes of a recent arrival from the Mariel boatlift, explores generational change in *Havana Thursdays: A Documentary Novel* (1995), noting that sorrow and joys transcend ethnicity. Suárez has also edited *Paper Dance: Fifty-Five Latino Poets* (1995). Roberto Fernández portrays the Cuban American experience in the satirical *Raining Backwards* (1988) and *Holy Radishes* (1995). Elías Miguel Muñoz's musical theater adaptation of the novel *Crazy Love* (1988) had a successful run in 1990. Muñoz's poetic novel *The Greatest Performance* (1991) reflects cultural and sexual alienation.

Hijuelos, born in New York, recalls the rich Afro-Cuban musical tradition in *The Mambo Kings Play Songs of Love* (1989). This novel, a 1990 Pulitzer Prize winner, was made into a film. Hijuelos reflects on exile in *The Fourteen Sisters of Emilio Montez O'Brien* and depicts goodwill in ethnically divided urban America in *Mr. Ives' Christmas* (1995). Pablo Medina shares personal recollections in *Exiled Memories: A Cuban Childhood* (1990) and examines the spiritual and material effects of exile in his novel *The Marks of Birth* (1994). Gustavo Pérez Firmat, poet and

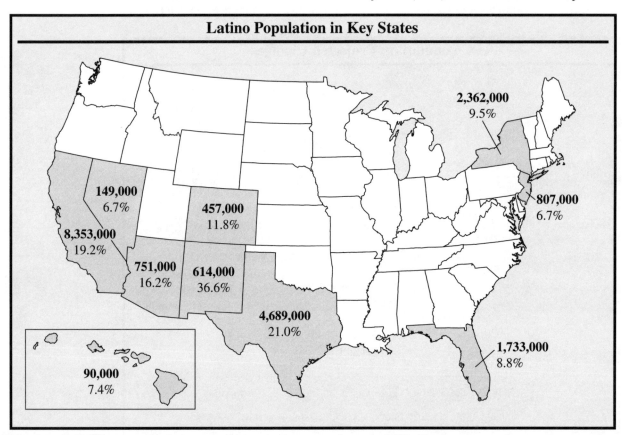

Latino Population in Key States

Numbers in **boldface** are the Latino population in the states shown in 1992. Numbers in regular typeface are the percentages of Latinos in the total population of the states shown.
Source: U.S. Bureau of the Census.

Latino American Population Distribution

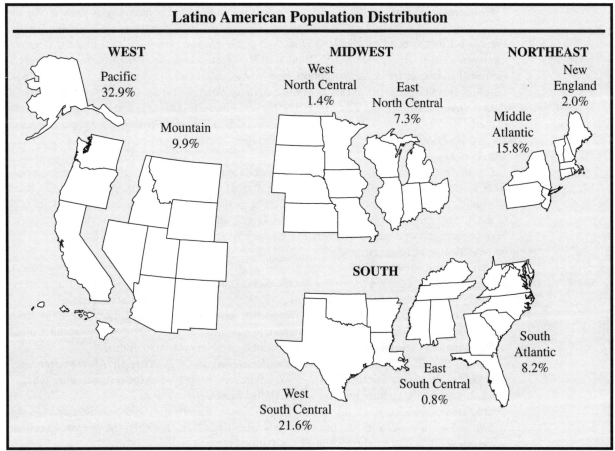

WEST

Pacific
32.9%

Mountain
9.9%

MIDWEST

West
North Central
1.4%

East
North Central
7.3%

NORTHEAST

New
England
2.0%

Middle
Atlantic
15.8%

SOUTH

West
South Central
21.6%

East
South Central
0.8%

South
Atlantic
8.2%

Source: U.S. Bureau of the Census.

fiction writer, reveals exposure to cultural differences in his memoir *Next Year in Cuba: A Cubano's Coming of Age in America* (1995). Editor Rodolfo Cortina's *Cuban-American Theater* (1992) includes works by leading playwrights concerned about exile, culture clash, the generational gap, and discrimination.

Latina writers combine the Hispanic experience with a feminist overview of women's lives in American society. Doubly marginalized as women and as Latinas, Latina writers approach myths of religion and marriage with a critical look at Catholicism. Prida, a Cuban American journalist, poet, playwright, actress, and director, addresses ethnic identity, assimilation, and women's sexuality with feminist satire—American style—in her musical *Beautiful Señoritas* (1977) and in *Coser y Cantar: A One-Act Bilingual Fantasy for Two Women* (1981). Sandra María Esteves, a Nuyorican poet, painter, and actress, who shows women's poetic militancy in *Yerba Buena* (1981), blends the realities of the urban poor with spiritual, blues, and women's poetics in *Bluestown Mockingbird Mambo* (1990). The novel *In the Time of the Butterflies* (1994) by Alvarez describes the horrors lived by four sisters under Rafáel Trujillo's dictatorship; as in her family saga *How the García Girls Lost Their Accents* she explores life in exile and return to the homeland in the poems of *The Other Side-El Otro Lado* (1995).

An important development since the early 1980's has been a growing interest by mainstream media and academic scholarship in Latino literary discourse. Critical and historical studies have been describing the evolving Latino culture. Readings in anthologies edited by Latinos, representing a whole spectrum of race, class, gender, ethnicity, and political experiences, are often organized around central themes, such as family, religion, immigration, language, and the arts.

593

Historical overviews, contexts, and approaches are to be found in anthologies such as Miguel Algarín and Piñero's *Nuyorican Poetry: An Anthology of Puerto Rican Words and Feelings* (1975), Francisco Jiménez and Gary Keller's *Hispanics in the United States: An Anthology of Creative Literature* (1979), Evangelina Vigil's *Woman of Her Word: Hispanic Women Write* (1983), Alma Gómez, Mariana Romo-Carmona, and Cherríe Moraga's *Cuentos: Stories by Latinas* (1983), Carolina Hospital's *Los Atrevidos: Cuban American Writers* (1988), Delia Poey and Suárez's *Iguana Dreams: New Latino Fiction* (1992), Nicolás Kanellos' *Short Fiction by Hispanic Writers of the United States* (1993), Harold Augenbraum and Ilan Stavans' *Growing Up Latino: Memoirs and Stories* (1993), and Roberta Fernández's *In Other Words: Literature by Latinas of the United States* (1994).

Impact   Latino writers chronicling the Hispanic experience in America have taken center stage, receiving recognition through prizes and awards. The nature of the bilingual texts, giving voice to lives attempting to come to terms with intertwined cultures, has led to the consideration of a redefinition of the literary canon. Latino American writings, with differences of voice, style, and expression, have become part of American literary life, making it more representative and contributing to the cultural identity of North America.

SUGGESTED READINGS

Abalos, David T. *Latinos in the United States*. Notre Dame, Ind.: University of Notre Dame Press, 1986. Discusses literature as a means of politicizing and empowering Latino people.

Fabre, Genevieve, ed. *European Perspectives on Hispanic Literature of the United States*. Houston, Tex.: Arte Público Press, 1988. American and European scholars compare visions of United States majority and minority cultures and identities, as reflected in literature.

Gutiérrez, Ramón, and Genaro Padilla, eds. *Recovering the U.S. Hispanic Literary Heritage*. Houston, Tex.: Arte Público Press, 1993. Addresses the potential for reconstituting what is significant for the cultural heritage of the United States.

Heyck, Denis Lynn Daly, ed. *Barrios and Borderlands: Cultures of Latinos and Latinas in the United States*. New York: Routledge, 1994. Readings from a variety of genres. Excellent overview of the historical development of Latino literature.

Horno-Delgado, Asunción, Eliana Ortega, Nina M. Scott, and Nancy Saporta Sternbach, eds. *Breaking Boundaries: Latina Writings and Critical Readings*. Amherst: University of Massachusetts Press, 1989. A collection of literary criticism by Latinas.

Kanellos, Nicolás, ed. *Hispanic Theater in the United States*. Houston, Tex.: Arte Público Press, 1984. Studies on the popular theater of diverse Hispanic groups.

Rivero, Eliana. "Hispanic Literature in the United States: Self-Image and Conflict." *Revista Chicano-Riqueña* 13, nos. 3-4 (1985): 173-192. Focuses on linguistic expressiveness as the most poignant form of identity conflict.

Shorris, Earl. *Latinos: A Biography of the People*. New York: W. W. Norton, 1992. The chapter "Neither Here Nor There" discusses the vitality of Latino culture as expressed in literature, art, and music.

—*Ludmila Kapschutschenko-Schmitt*

See also Acculturation; Alvarez, Julia; Arenas, Reinaldo; Bilingualism; Caribbean American literature; Ortiz Cofer, Judith; *Dreaming in Cuban*; Emigration and immigration; Hijuelos, Oscar; Mohr, Nicholassa

Lau, Evelyn

BORN: Vancouver, Canada; July 2, 1971

PRINCIPAL WORKS: *Runaway: Diary of a Street Kid*, 1989, 1995; *You Are Not Who You Claim*, 1990; *Oedipal Dreams*, 1992; *Fresh Girls*, 1993; *In the House of Slaves*, 1994; *Other Women*, 1996

IDENTITIES: Canada; Chinese American; women

SIGNIFICANT ACHIEVEMENT: Lau's writing features young women, often entangled in prostitution, drug abuse, and bizarre sexual subcultures, who are in search of love and acceptance.

Evelyn Lau started to write when she was six years old in 1977; at fourteen, her self-described obsession with writing led her to run away from her Chinese Canadian family, who did not permit her to pursue this passion. Keeping journals and penning poetry kept Lau's spirit alive while she descended into a nightmare world of juvenile prostitution, rampant drug abuse, and homelessness.

Lau left the streets at sixteen, and wrote *Runaway: Diary of a Street Kid* (1989, 1995) about her experience. She also published her first collection of poetry, *You Are Not Who You Claim*, in which her harrowing ordeals find artistic expression. The persona of Lau's poetry is often a woman who resembles Lau, and her voice hauntingly evokes the mostly futile search for human warmth and genuine affection in a nightmare adult world.

In Lau's poetry and fiction, lovemaking can end sadly. Thus, "Two Smokers" ends on a note of complete alienation: While the sleeping lover of the persona "gropes at the wall" and "finds flesh in his dreams," the woman "watches the trail of smoke" from her cigarette "drift towards the ceiling,/ hesitate, fall apart."

The haunting lucidity, freshness of imagination, and stunning power of Lau's writings have earned for her important literary prizes. Her first poetry collection won the Milton Acorn People's Poetry award, and her second collection, *Oedipal Dreams*, which contains many interrelated poems reflecting on a young woman's relationship with her married psychiatrist and lover, was nominated for the Governor-General's Award, Canada's highest literary honor. Perhaps most important, Lau's youth has given her writing a sharp awareness of the startling coexistence of mainstream and alternative lifestyles. Her poems and stories feature many a professional man who shows pictures of his children to the teenage sex worker whom he has hired to be his dominatrix. Similarly, the persona of *In the House of Slaves* watches a squirrel as a customer drips hot wax on her body. As has the author, the main character of *In the House of Slaves* has lived simultaneously in the world of pop culture adolescence and in hell.

SUGGESTED READINGS

Dieckmann, Katherina. Review of *In the House of Slaves*, by Evelyn Lau. *Village Voice Literary Supplement*, April, 1994, 32.

Halim, Nadia. Review of *In the House of Slaves*, by Evelyn Lau. *The Canadian Forum* 73 (October, 1994): 41.

James, Darlene. Review of *Runaway: Diary of a Street Kid*, by Evelyn Lau. *Maclean's*, November 13, 1989, 81.

—*R. C. Lutz*

See also Asian American identity: China, Japan, and Korea; Drugs; Erotic identity; *Fresh Girls and Other Stories*; Mental disorders; Prostitution; *Runaway*; Violence

Laughing Boy

AUTHOR: Oliver La Farge (1901-1963)
FIRST PUBLISHED: 1929
IDENTITIES: Native American; West and Southwest

Oliver La Farge's *Laughing Boy* is a moving novel about Navajo culture in the early twentieth century. An anthropologist, La Farge gathered much of his Navajo material during an expedition to the Southwest. Consequently, *Laughing Boy* is more factually accurate than many works on Indians that preceded it. Its plot resembles a traditional romantic tragedy, but the novel evidences the concern of a white writer for embattled native cultures that American society tended to overlook and to overwhelm.

The novel tells of the love affair between Laughing Boy (a Navajo raised on the reservation with little influence from the outside world) and Slim Girl (a beautiful Navajo woman reared in white society near the reservation). Despite familial objections Laughing Boy marries Slim Girl, and the couple moves into her hut near Los Palos, a town. There Laughing Boy continues his traditional way of life, tending animals and making jewelry, while Slim Girl devotes herself to learning Navajo culture so that she and her husband can eventually move back onto the reservation.

Their plans are disrupted when Laughing Boy learns of his wife's affair with an American rancher. He shoots several arrows at the adulterous couple, wounding them. Later, Slim Girl explains that she stayed with the rancher only to make enough money to allow herself and her husband to move back onto the reservation. Laughing Boy accepts this explanation—especially after he sees how hard Slim Girl has worked toward adopting a traditional Navajo lifestyle—and the two of them set out for the reservation site where they plan to live. On the way, however, they are ambushed by Red Man, a Navajo who earlier vied for Slim Girl's affections. In his jealousy, Red Man tries to kill Laughing Boy but shoots Slim Girl instead. Before his wife dies, Laughing Boy promises not to seek revenge. He gives Slim Girl a Navajo funeral, then returns forever to the reservation.

Certain dissatisfied critics have claimed that *Laughing Boy* only manages to fit native characters into a European story. La Farge's well-researched observations of the Navajo, however, are far more genuine than the stereotypical depictions of Indians that abounded at the time. For its time, then, *Laughing Boy* offered an honest and sympathetic depiction of native life that although not perfect anticipates many similar stories by writers yet to come.

SUGGESTED READINGS

Dennis, Philip A. "Oliver La Farge: Writer and Anthropologist." In *Literature and Anthropology*, edited by Philip Dennis. Lubbock: Texas Tech University Press, 1989.

McNickle, D'Arcy. *Indian Man: A Life of Oliver La Farge*. Bloomington: Indiana University Press, 1971.

Pearce, T. M. *Oliver La Farge*. New York: Twayne, 1972.

—David Stevens

See also Acculturation; American identity: West and the frontier; Native American identity

Laurence, Margaret

BORN: Neepawa, Manitoba, Canada; July 18, 1926
DIED: Lakefield, Ontario, Canada; January 5, 1987
PRINCIPAL WORKS: *A Tree of Poverty: Somali Poetry and Prose*, 1954 (editor); *This Side Jordan*, 1960; *The Prophet's Camel Bell*, 1963; *The Tomorrow-Tamer*, 1963; *The Stone Angel*, 1964; *A Jest of God*, 1966; *The Fire-Dwellers*, 1969; *A Bird in the House*, 1970; *Jason's Quest*, 1970; *The Diviners*, 1974; *Heart of a Stranger*, 1976; *The Christmas Birthday Story*, 1980; *Dance on the Earth: A Memoir*, 1989
IDENTITIES: Canada; family; women
SIGNIFICANT ACHIEVEMENT: Laurence's works dramatize the isolation and pain of the Métis in a multicultural but European-dominated society in Canada.

A few events shaped Margaret Laurence's life and affected her highly autobiographical writings: her birth as Jean Margaret Wemyss and early years in the Canadian prairie environment; her time in Africa with her civil-engineer husband on assignments; and her separation and ultimate divorce. Her African experience led her to an understanding of language, culture, and folktales; poetry; and a nomadic way of life. Her African experience also taught her of the need for myths that define human lives and bind communities. Finally, it gave her greater appreciation for home and self.

Laurence's adolescence in a predominantly Scot-Irish Canadian but also Métis cultural environment pervaded her mental landscape and made her agonize over the latter's plight. The result was the Manawaka cycle of novels and an interconnected set of short stories that Laurence described as "fictionalized autobiography." This work records the saga of an Indian French Canadian Métis family over generations. The story is told from the perspective of Vanessa

MacLeod, Laurence's alter ego. The dichotomy that Laurence discovered between Africans living by faith and Canadians living by logic she finds replicated between Indians and whites in Canada.

Laurence's broken marriage, which left her with the care of two children, led to *A Jest of God*, a pioneering work on the subject of a woman's sexual awakening and single parenthood. Despite the centrality of Laurence's feminist vision, her view is that men can play a crucial role by assisting women in their search for self-discovery. Laurence's compassion in drawing her characters' failures takes her beyond the genre of social realism. Thus, her Canadian-focused novels and short stories also trace the intellectual and psychological development of female protagonists, such as Hagar Shipley in *The Stone Angel*. Through narrators, Laurence observes how characters would like to be heroic or at least survive with some dignity and set of values, but also how life denies them the romantic grandeur that they desire. Thus, growing up as a woman and securing female identity are precarious. Some of the women, such as Morag Gunn in *The Diviners*, by summoning up all their past, manage to understand their present and their place in it. Others, like the Métis Piquette Tonnerre in the Manawaka cycle, never do.

SUGGESTED READINGS

Coger, Greta M. K., ed. *New Perspectives on Margaret Laurence: Poetic Narrative, Multiculturalism, and Feminism*. Westport, Conn.: Greenwood Press, 1996.

Morley, Patricia. *Margaret Laurence: The Long Journey Home*. Rev. ed. Montreal: McGill-Queen's University Press, 1991.

Stovel, Norma. *Rachel's Children: Margaret Laurence's "A Jest of God."* Toronto: ECW Press, 1992.

Woodcock, George. *Introducing Margaret Laurence's "The Stone Angel."* Toronto: ECW Press, 1989.

—*Peter B. Heller*

See also Canadian identity; Erotic identity; Feminism; Mixed race and identity

Law-Yone, Wendy

BORN: Mandalay, Burma; April 1, 1947

PRINCIPAL WORKS: *The Coffin Tree*, 1983; *Irrawaddy Tango*, 1993

IDENTITIES: Asian American; women

SIGNIFICANT ACHIEVEMENT: Law-Yone's novels describe the alienation caused by harsh upbringings, political turmoil, and immigration.

Wendy Law-Yone's novels reflect the events in her turbulent life. In 1962, while a teenager in Burma, she watched her country become a military dictatorship and imprison her father, a newspaper publisher and political activist. In 1967, attempting to leave the country, she was captured and held for two weeks before being released. After living in Southeast Asia, she immigrated to America in 1973. She was graduated from college two years later and worked as a writer, publishing in the *Washington Post Magazine* and researching and writing *Company Information: A Model Investigation* (1983).

Her first novel, *The Coffin Tree*, portrays an Asian American immigrant in a different situation than that of many other novels. In many books, protagonists need to choose between, or reconcile, their native culture and American culture. Law-Yone's heroine, however, lacks connections to both cultures. Growing up with no mother and a distant father, she develops no attachment to Burma and is never nostalgic. When she and her brother immigrate, however, she remains detached from and unenthusiastic about America. Unable to express or follow her own desires, she obeys her tyrannical father and grandmother in Burma and her deranged brother in America. When brother and father die, twisted logic leads her to attempt suicide to fulfill her newly "uncovered . . . identity." Although she survives, institutional treatment engenders only a mild affirmation of life: "Living things prefer to go on living."

Irrawaddy Tango also describes a woman living more for others than herself: In a fictionalized Burma, a friend inspires her to love dancing. She marries an officer who becomes the country's dictator; when kidnapped by rebels, she agrees to be their spokeswoman. After her rescue, she helps other refugees before drifting into homelessness in America; she then returns to publicly reconcile with the dictator. Despite her political activities, she evidences no commitment to any cause and also can express herself only by violence, finally murdering her husband.

Law-Yone does not fully account for her heroines' alienation and lack of self-esteem, though possible factors include unhappy childhoods—with cold fathers and absent mothers. Politics is also corrosive in Law-Yone's fiction, leading parents and spouses to neglect personal relationships. Finally, fate forces some to lead unrewarding lives. The absence of easy answers in her fiction demonstrates her maturity as a writer.

SUGGESTED READINGS

Law-Yone, Wendy. "Life in the Hills." *The Atlantic Monthly*, December, 1989, 24-36.

Ling, Amy. "Wendy Law-Yone." In *The Oxford Companion to Women's Writing in the United States*, edited by Cathy N. Davidson and Linda Wagner-Martin. New York: Oxford University Press, 1995.

—*Gary Westfahl*

See also Asian American identity: Vietnam; Mental disorders

Lee, Gus (Augustus Samuel Jian-Sun Lee)

BORN: San Francisco, California; August 8, 1946

PRINCIPAL WORKS: *China Boy*, 1991; *Honor and Duty*, 1994

IDENTITIES: Adolescence and coming-of-age; Chinese American; West and Southwest

SIGNIFICANT ACHIEVEMENT: Lee's novels capture the dilemma of an Asian American youth who tries to please the demands of two opposing cultures.

Gus Lee came to writing late in life, at age forty-five, after careers in the military and as a lawyer. In 1989, his daughter asked him a question about his mother, and that simple question led to his first book, *China Boy*, in 1991. Born in San Francisco in a tough black neighborhood, the Panhandle, Lee found his childhood full of danger on the streets. At home he felt divided. His father and mother had come from mainland China in the early 1940's and were wealthy and educated. His father had a military background and had fought for the Nationalist army. His mother had been educated by American Christian missionaries. Lee's mother died when he was five years old, and his new stepmother had new ideas about the traditional Chinese ways. Lee had to fight in the streets, with the help of boxing courses he took at the Young Men's Christian Association (YMCA). He also had to battle at home with his stepmother, who wanted him to become more American.

His first novel, *China Boy*, uses many autobiographical events to tell the story of a young boy, Kai Ting, who is growing up in San Francisco. Skinny, weak, and timid, Kai Ting finds a friend at the neighborhood YMCA, learns self-defense, and returns to the streets with more confidence.

Lee describes the early days as being very stifled by rules at home. Lee rebelled against his controlling stepmother, reading his homework but refusing to concentrate. He got good grades but was not involved. Lee's father also attempted to direct him, objecting to the Christianity that the stepmother taught her stepson and projecting an atheistic approach that Lee felt was not right. Lee kept his mind focussed on one goal: He wanted to become a West Point cadet. When he was appointed, he felt great relief, even though his life away from home as a plebe would be hellish. Lee actually found the horrible harassment as a plebe at West Point to be easier than living at home.

His second novel, *Honor and Duty*, also uses Kai Ting as his fictional hero and takes this character through many tough days at West Point. Kai Ting must obey the older cadets, he must study mathematics, and he must obey the West Point honor code. Coming upon a group of cadets who are cheating, Kai Ting agonizes about reporting them to the authorities, knowing that they will be removed from West Point if he informs on them.

In Lee's life, after a long tenure as an Army Command Judge Advocate and later as senior Deputy District Attorney in Sacramento, Lee found himself unfulfilled. Then his daughter's question provoked Lee to write about an Asian American adjusting to life in the United States.

SUGGESTED READING

Olson, K. Review of *China Boy*, by Gus Lee. *The New York Times Book Review*, July 21, 1991.

—*Larry Rochelle*

See also Acculturation; American identity: West and the frontier; Asian American identity: China, Japan, and Korea

Lee, Harper

BORN: Monroeville, Alabama; April 28, 1926

PRINCIPAL WORK: *To Kill a Mockingbird*, 1960

IDENTITIES: European American; family; South; women

SIGNIFICANT ACHIEVEMENT: In one brilliant novel, Lee showed how prejudice can be defeated by kindness, courage, and decency.

Harper Lee is known for a single book. Her first novel, *To Kill a Mockingbird*, was published when the author was thirty-four. It won the Pulitzer Prize in fiction in 1961 and was made into a film for which Gregory Peck won an Academy Award for Best Actor. For decades, the novel has been considered a classic text in the study of prejudice. For years, Lee described herself as working on a second novel, but it did not appear. Perhaps Lee felt that in *To Kill a Mockingbird* she had explored so completely the problems of prejudice and identity that she could not better her effort.

Ironically, from the time of her birth Harper Lee had the best that such a society could offer. Her parents, Amasa Coleman Lee and Frances Finch Lee, were both members of old, highly respected Southern families. After settling in Monroeville, Alabama, Amasa Coleman Lee became a community leader, a state legislator, and a newspaper editor. As a practicing attorney, he was no stranger to controversy. Watching him from her vantage point in the courthouse balcony, Lee learned to think for herself and to stand up for what she believed.

Although she was a female member of a patriarchal society, Lee did not assume the role of wife and mother, like most girls of her generation, or become a lawyer, as her father intended. It was not Harper, but her sister Alice, who was to become their father's law partner. Six months short of graduation, Harper Lee left law school at the University of Alabama and went to New York to be a writer. At first she worked as an airline reservations clerk, but when a literary agent said that one of her short stories could be made into a novel, Lee quit her job and devoted all of her time to the project. The result was *To Kill a Mockingbird*.

In the book, Lee questions gender roles, as she did in her life. Thus the young protagonist, Scout, insists on being herself, rather than acting like a little lady. Scout's father, Atticus Finch, supports her, because he believes that people are individuals, not members of a gender, a race, or a social class. Modelled on Lee's father, Finch represents the liberal-minded Southerners who choose to live in the South, respecting its traditions but working to make it better. In her own way, Lee followed the family pattern. After writing a book which pointed out the defects of her society, as well as its virtues, the author returned to Monroeville to live.

SUGGESTED READINGS

Betts, Doris. Introduction to *Southern Women Writers: The New Generation*, edited by Tonette Bond Inge. Tuscaloosa: University of Alabama Press, 1990.

Going, William T. "*Store* and *Mockingbird*: Two Pulitzer Novels About Alabama." In *Essays on Alabama Literature*. Tuscaloosa: University of Alabama Press, 1975.

Johnson, Claudia. "The Secret Courts of Men's Hearts: Code and Law in Harper Lee's *To Kill a Mockingbird.*" *Studies in American Fiction* 19, no. 2 (Autumn, 1991): 129-139.

—Rosemary M. Canfield Reisman

See also American identity: South; Racism and ethnocentrism; *To Kill a Mockingbird*

Lee, Li-Young

BORN: Jakarta, Indonesia; 1957

PRINCIPAL WORKS: *Rose*, 1986; *The City in Which I Love You*, 1990; *The Winged Seed: A Remembrance*, 1995

IDENTITIES: Chinese American; family

SIGNIFICANT ACHIEVEMENT: Lee's writing is inspired by his relation to his father and his family.

When Li-Young Lee's first collection of poetry, *Rose*, was published, its Chinese American author had lived in America for twenty-two of his twenty-nine years. The poet's immigrant experience, his strong sense of family life, and his recollections of a boyhood spent in Asia have provided a background to his writing.

Lee was born in Jakarta; his Chinese parents were exiles from Communist China. They traveled until their arrival in Pittsburgh in 1964. The sense of being an alien, not a native to the place where one lives, strongly permeates Lee's poetry and gives an edge to his carefully crafted lines. There is also a touch of sadness to his poetry: The abyss lurks everywhere, and his personae have to be circumspect in their words and actions, since they, unlike a native, can take nothing for granted in their host culture. Looking at his sister, the speaker in "My Sleeping Loved Ones" warns "And don't mistake my stillness/ for awe./ It's just that I don't want to waken her."

Faced with a new language after his arrival in America, Lee became fascinated with the sound of words, an experience related in "Persimmons." Here, a teacher slaps the boy "for not knowing the difference/ between persimmon and precision." After college work at three American universities, Lee focused on his writing. Before the publication of his second collection, *The City in Which I Love You*, he received numerous awards.

Lee has always insisted that his writing searches for universal themes, and the close connection of his work to his life cannot be discounted. His father, for example, appears in many poems. Lee offers, in *The Winged Seed*, a factual yet poetic account of his young life. Lee's poetry and his prose reveal a writer who appreciates his close family and strives to put into words the grief and the joy of a life always lived in an alien place.

SUGGESTED READINGS

Berk, L. Review of *The City in Which I Love You*, by Li-Young Lee. *Choice* 28 (June, 1991): 1640.

Greenbaum, Jessica. Review of *Rose*, by Li-Young Lee. *The Nation*, October 7, 1991, 416.

Muske, Carol. Review of *The City in Which I Love You*, by Li-Young Lee. *The New York Times Book Review*, January 27, 1991, 20.

Waniek, Marylin. Review of *The City in Which I Love You*, by Li-Young Lee. *Kenyon Review* 13 (Fall, 1991): 214.

—R. C. Lutz

See also Asian American identity: China, Japan, and Korea; Emigration and immigration

Lesbian identity

IDENTITIES: Gay, lesbian, and bisexual; women

Literature has identified lesbians in many different ways; most male authors have taken great license with their description of women who were or were suspected of having sexual interest in other women. The power of literature to define and describe the common terms and ideas of a society can keep groups of people invisible. It is possible that the literary description of lesbians and their lives have had a great impact on the lives of women who read the literature in anticipation of learning more about themselves. Thus, one may argue that life may have imitated art; women who read about certain—often stereotypical—aspects of lesbianism may have found themselves accepting what they read.

Sappho, a poet of ancient Greece, has been identified as the first woman in literature who wrote about her attraction to and her love of women. With the arrival of Christianity, her works were systematically destroyed by scandalized leaders of the church. As a result, only fragments of her poetry survive and very little about her life is known. Literary scholars continue to debate the identity of this woman; they even debate her sexuality and attraction to women. Some critics believe that Sappho was primarily a teacher of young women who were preparing themselves for marriage. From the time of Sappho until the mid-nineteenth century, there was very little, if any, direct mention of lesbians in North American literature. What was mentioned in various ways were those women who were different from other women in lifestyle, in physical attributes, or in not having to rely on a male for financial security. These women were typically identified as mannish. Such women appear in Isabel Miller's *Patience and Sarah* (1969), for example.

During the late eighteenth century, romantic friendship between women was not a societal taboo, and in fact was encouraged so that men's and women's lives could be largely separate and yet able to maintain gender roles and expectations. In *Life with the Ladies of Llangollen* (1984), Eleanor Butler tells of her life with Sarah Ponsonby; the two women, members of a sewing circle, fell in love, moved away from their families, and lived together as a couple for more than fifty years.

During the Victorian era (Queen Victoria ruled from 1837 to 1901), women were still encouraged to develop close relationships with other women (although sex between women was, officially at least, unthinkable), often with the tacit assumption that their husbands could thereby continue their liaisons with mistresses or prostitutes.

As women became more self-sufficient in the twentieth century, literature began to present mixed versions of lesbians. Radclyff Hall published *The Well of Loneliness* in 1928. Although it was not the first book by and about lesbians, the fact of its publication is a milestone. The book is the first modern lesbian novel. Hall tells a sad and horrifying tale of a woman who must dress like and act like a man in order to love another woman. As a result of the *Well of Loneliness*, many women who believed that they might be homosexual used the book's characters as identities for themselves. As a result lesbians became identified as butch if they appeared more masculine than feminine, and as femme if they appeared feminine. Another dramatic advance in the acknowledgement and literary portrayal of lesbians resulted from the artistic ferment of Paris early in the twentieth century. The writer Gertrude Stein was greatly influential; Sylvia Beach, a bookseller and publisher, was another lesbian of the time whose influence in the literary world was wide and lasting. Lesbians began to be portrayed in literature with regularity, although often not favorably. Lillian Faderman, in *Surpassing the Love of Men: Romantic Friendship and Love Between Women from the Renaissance to the Present* (1981), argues that the work of French fiction writer Collette contains the beginnings of the idea that lesbians are a productive and positive part of the literary world.

During the late 1940's and the 1950's there was, in comparison with the drought of previous centuries, a deluge of lesbian fiction on the market. Many of the works of this time were inexpensive paperbacks with lurid covers and equally colorful prose within. Some titles include *The Girl with the Golden Yo-Yo* (1955), by Edmund Schiddel, *The Naked Storm* (1952), by Simon Fisher, and J. C. Priest's *Private School* (1959), the cover of which warns: "Every parent should read this shocking novel of adolescent girls who first tolerated vice, then embraced it, then could not live without it." Lesbian identity in literature was at that time criminal and something away from which young women were warned. The books sold well to a public eager for knowledge of that from which young women needed protection and of what the embracing of vice wrought.

By the mid-twentieth century, women were beginning to make great strides in exhibiting their athletic and academic abilities. Faderman states in *Surpassing the Love of Men* that "the association of brilliance and talent with a masculine, evil, invariably neurotic or psychotic woman is common in antilesbian and antifeminist literature. It appeared in fiction at the beginning of the century and continued for decades." History, however, was progressing and a new form of literature entered the market that began to describe self-actualizing women in a positive light.

In the 1960's North America became embroiled in several major cultural events. First was the Civil Rights movement; aligned with that was the women's movement. These events irrevocably challenged long-standing cultural assumptions. Women began to study, and therefore question, gender roles and the portrayal of women in history. Included in the massive cultural reevaluation of the 1960's was literature about lesbians. Women studied lesbian history, fiction, poetry, drama, and theory.

Rita Mae Brown published *Rubyfruit Jungle* in 1973; it is one of the first novels to portray lesbians as normal girls and women, finally demolishing the enduring literary stereotype of the psychologically twisted lesbian. *Rubyfruit Jungle* is one of the first books to portray a lesbian as being proud of who she is and as one who does not care if the world knows that she is lesbian. Katherine V. Forrest is another leading name in lesbian fiction. Her *An Emergence of Green* (1987) is one of the most popular lesbian novels. *The Color Purple* (1982), by Alice Walker, is a novel that portrays the difference between the abusive relationship that Celie, the main character, has with a man and the fulfilling relationship that she has with a woman. Fannie Flagg's lesbian novel *Fried Green Tomatoes at the Whistle-Stop Cafe* (1987) uses flashbacks to an earlier time to tell the story of women in a small Southern town. Love between the women is strong and positive, not obsessive or unhealthy as is typical in novels from earlier in the twentieth century and before. The female characters of the novels by Brown, Walker, and Flagg fit the entire range of human behavior. These women are feminine, mannish, athletic, academic, and motherly, filling any number of occupations. Concomitant with the rise of positive, realistic literary portrayals of lesbians, lesbians have become more visible in the public sphere.

Implications for identity

Lesbians were almost invisible in literature; they have become almost abundant. Literature is known as one of the major forms of recording history. In the early literature lesbians and their lifestyle were not discussed in any positive manner if they were discussed at all. They were portrayed as perverse, almost psychotic, even in the days when romantic friendships between women were so acceptable that society encouraged young women to live together until they found a husband.

Analysis of literature for what it reveals about social history shows that women were expected to live within a particular boundary according to their class. If any woman, regardless of her social or economic class, deviated in any manner, she was labeled sick, an old maid, or a spinster. So as society perceived lesbianism, so its literature reflected, and created, these perceptions. A woman who knew that she was attracted to other women had, before the twentieth century, nothing in the library to encourage her in seeking a positive self-image or in seeking a fulfilling relationship.

The Naiad Press of Tallahassee, Florida, opened its doors in 1973 as a publisher of works written by and written for lesbians. Since that time the view of lesbians in literature and the view of lesbians in the world have become much more positive and ordinary. Lesbians in literature will continue to be identified in negative ways by some authors, but lesbian writers continue to produce literature that is positive about their lives. Society has a greater chance of identifying lesbians positively.

SUGGESTED READINGS

Donohue, Emma. *Passions Between Women: British Lesbian Culture 1668-1801*. London: Scarlet Press, 1992. An excellent resource for the period discussed.

Faderman, Lillian, ed. *Chloe Plus Olivia: An Anthology of Lesbian Literature from the Seventeenth Century to the Present*. London: Scarlet Press, 1993. Challenges assumptions about the invisibility of lesbians in literature since the seventeenth century.

_____. *Odd Girls and Twilight Lovers: A History of Lesbian Life in Twentieth-Century America*. New York: Viking Penguin, 1991. This work brings lesbian lives out of the closet and into mainstream America with no shame or guilt.

_____. *Surpassing the Love of Men: Romantic Friendship and Love Between Women from the Renaissance to the Present*. New York: William Morrow, 1981.

Martin, Del, and Phyllis Lyon. *Lesbian Woman*. New York: Bantam Books, 1972. The authors have been a married couple for more than twenty years and the book is a written record of their lives.

Martin, Jane Roland. *Reclaiming the Conversation: The Ideal of the Educated Woman*. New Haven, Conn.: Yale University Press, 1985. An imaginary conversation between a woman and great philosophers of the past examines women's education.

Nicholson, Nigel. *Portrait of a Marriage*. New York: Bantam Books, 1973. The son of Vita-Sackville-West writes an autobiographical analysis of a mother's life.

—*Sandra J. Parsons*

See also Bisexual identity; Coming out; Erotic identity; Feminism; Gay identity; Patriarchy and matriarchy; Stereotypes and identity; Women and identity

Let Us Now Praise Famous Men
AUTHOR: James Agee (1909-1955)
FIRST PUBLISHED: 1941
IDENTITIES: Family; religion; South

Let Us Now Praise Famous Men, the Depression-era photodocumentary masterpiece, originated in 1936 when James Agee, a writer, and Walker Evans, a photographer on leave from the Farm Security Administration, were commissioned by *Fortune* magazine to do an article on cotton tenantry that would be a photographic and verbal record of "the daily living of three representative white tenant families." In the summer of 1936, Agee lived with a sharecropping family, intimately experiencing their daily routine, while Evans carried out his photographic assignment with detachment but comparable integrity.

Having familial ties to the South and sympathy for the plight of the tenant farmers, Agee felt a tremendous sense of responsibility for this project. He was aware of various ethical and political conflicts inherent in documentary work. The reporter-photographer team was determined not to put the tenants on display for a curious audience; nor did they want their work to be seen as politically motivated. Agee and Evans were conscious, moreover, of the social and educational differences that separated them from the members of the Gudger, Wood, and Rickett families and understood the suspicion with which the tenants initially regarded them. These issues are woven into the text.

When the article prepared for publication in *Fortune* was turned down, Agee and Evans envisioned *Let Us Now Praise Famous Men*, complete in itself, as part of a larger whole to be called *Three Tenant Families*. The other volumes were never completed. The book's structure is nonlinear and fragmented. Book 1 is composed of sixty-two captionless, black and white photographs of the tenants and their surroundings. Book 2 has three sections: Section 1 includes three vignettes that recall encounters with local citizens, as well as meditational prose pieces ("On the Porch: 1," "A Country Letter," and "Colon"). Section 2 contains, among other items, chapters on "Money," "Shelter," "Clothing," "Education," and "Work." Part 3 opens with "Inductions," a description of Agee and Evans' awkward initial encounters with the tenant families, includes "Notes and Appendices," and closes with another lyrical reflection ("On the Porch: 3").

In this intensely personal book, Agee intends that the sharecroppers be represented "with the whole of consciousness." *Let Us Now Praise Famous Men* is a hybrid work—a narrative of fact, a regional study, a moving moral document, a lyric meditation on life and art, and an exercise in style.

SUGGESTED READINGS

Kramer, Victor A. *Agee and Actuality: Artistic Vision in His Work*. Troy, N.Y.: Whitston, 1991.

Lofaro, Michael, ed. *James Agee: Reconsiderations*. Knoxville: University of Tennessee Press, 1992.

Moreau, Genevieve. *The Restless Journey of James Agee*. New York: William Morrow, 1977.

Rathbone, Belinda. *Walker Evans: A Biography*. Boston: Houghton Mifflin, 1995.

Stott, William. *Documentary Expression and Thirties America*. Chicago: University of Chicago Press, 1986.

—*Michelle A. Balée*

See also Agee, James; American identity: South; *Death in the Family, A*; Education and identity; Migratory workers; Poverty

Lewis, Sinclair

BORN: Sauk Centre, Minnesota; February 7, 1885
DIED: Rome, Italy; January 10, 1951
PRINCIPAL WORKS: *Main Street: The Story of Carol Kennicott*, 1920; *Babbitt*, 1922; *Arrowsmith*, 1925; *Elmer Gantry*, 1927; *Dodsworth*, 1929
IDENTITIES: European American; Midwest
SIGNIFICANT ACHIEVEMENT: Lewis' novels attack the narrow provincialism of American small towns and give voice to the rebellious modernity that was sweeping the country in the 1920's.

Sinclair Lewis was the son of a conservative, highly respected physician in the small town of Sauk Centre, Minnesota. His birthplace had not too long before been wild prairie populated by pioneers and native American tribes and retained the wooden sidewalks and hitching posts of that era. The heroic individualism of the pioneers would always be a standard by which he would judge the small-minded conformity into which he felt his town and the country had descended.

An imaginative child, Lewis was also influenced by tales of medieval Camelot and the Holy Grail, which offered another vantage point by which to judge the staid Sauk Centre. Lewis felt like an outsider in a town that valued the sports and popularity over intellectual and artistic gifts. This sense of alienation and isolation would follow him the rest of his life. His admission to Yale University liberated him from Sauk Centre but did nothing to assuage his sense of dissatisfaction. Demonstrating a restless need for movement and change, during his college years Lewis worked his way to England on a cattle boat two separate summers, went to Panama to work on the Canal, and left school for a time to join an experimental commune run by crusading novelist Upton Sinclair. It was with his first major novel in 1920, a derisive satire of Sauk Centre titled *Main Street*, that Lewis became a prominent voice for the decade's new, defiant spirit. His identity as a serious satirist was consolidated with subsequent novels written during the 1920's, all of which questioned the myth of small-town America as the ideal place to lead the good life. Instead, American small towns are depicted as promulgating narrowness, conformity, and mediocrity.

Lewis capped the most creative period of his life when, in 1930, he became the first American to win the Nobel Prize in Literature. In his address to the Swedish Academy he suggested that the serious writer in America would always be an outsider, as Lewis had been for his entire life. Lewis was, indeed, an isolated man. His two marriages ended in divorce, and he died alone in Rome of heart disease. His ashes, however, were returned for burial in Sauk Centre, a town that gave him not only his great subject but also his identity as a social critic.

SUGGESTED READINGS

Bucco, Martin, ed. *Critical Essays on Sinclair Lewis*. Boston: G. K. Hall, 1986.
Grebstein, Sheldon Norman. *Sinclair Lewis*. New York: Twayne, 1962.
Lundquist, James. *Sinclair Lewis*. New York: Frederick Ungar, 1973.
O'Connor, Richard. *Sinclair Lewis*. New York: McGraw-Hill, 1971.

—*Margaret Boe Birns*

See also American identity: Midwest; *Babbitt*; *Main Street*

Light in August

AUTHOR: William Faulkner (1897-1962)
FIRST PUBLISHED: 1932
IDENTITIES: African American; European American; South

Light in August, one of William Faulkner's great novels, centers on Joe Christmas, whom the critic Alfred Kazin called "the most solitary character in American fiction." His father, a swarthy man who may have been Mexican or black, is murdered by Christmas' fanatical white grandfather, Doc Hines, who abandons the baby at an orphanage. Christmas grows to manhood in Mississippi, where race necessarily defines who he is. Unsure of his racial identity and divided within himself, Christmas discovers that he belongs neither to the white world nor the black. His tortured figure is always halved, clothed symbolically in dark pants and white shirt, seen alternately in light and shadow. Arrogant and proud, he learns to answer every insult with violence.

Christmas is discovered by Joanna Burden in her kitchen, where he has come to steal food, and he becomes her lover. Daughter of a Yankee abolitionist and a philanthropist and supporter of African American colleges, Joanna quickly slides into a terrifying corruption, consumed by sexual desire for Christmas in the autumn of her life. She finds her Puritan and Calvinist identity perverted into cruelty like that of mad Doc Hines and Christmas' harsh adoptive father. Eventually she urges Christmas to study law at a black college so that he can take over her work. By doing so, Joanna tries to make him admit that he is a black man. When he refuses to pray with her, she draws a pistol, and he is forced to kill her.

Hunted down for Joanna's murder, Christmas attempts to escape a white mob by fleeing to the home of the Reverend Gail Hightower, a failed Presbyterian minister who has been expelled by his congregation. Hightower has been rendered ineffectual by guilt and grief since the death of his wife, but he redeems himself by attempting to save Christmas from his attackers, even though this act brings about his own death.

Christmas in turn is shot and castrated by white supremacist Percy Grimm, but he dies "with peaceful and unfathomable and unbearable eyes," a sacrifice to the unreasoning hatred between men. Christmas' name and initials, his birthdate, his dual nature, and his acceptance of death suggest that he may represent a Christlike figure, offering himself in atonement for the sins of others.

SUGGESTED READINGS

Brooks, Cleanth. "The Community and the Pariah." *William Faulkner: The Yoknapatawpha Country*. New Haven, Conn.: Yale University Press, 1963.

Feldman, Robert L. "In Defense of Reverend Hightower: It Is Never Too Late." *College Language Association Journal* 29, no. 3 (March, 1986): 352-367.

Kazin, Alfred. "The Stillness of *Light in August*." In *Faulkner: A Collection of Critical Essays*, edited by Robert Penn Warren. Englewood Cliffs, N.J.: Prentice-Hall, 1966.

Vickery, Olga W. "The Shadow and the Mirror: *Light in August*." In *The Novels of William Faulkner: A Critical Interpretation*. Rev. ed. Baton Rouge: Louisiana State University Press, 1964.

—Joanne McCarthy

See also *Absalom, Absalom!*; American identity: South; Faulkner, William; *Intruder in the Dust*; Mixed race and identity; Puritan and Protestant tradition; Racism and ethnocentrism; *Sound and the Fury, The*

Literary standards

DEFINITION: Literary standards are the norms by which literature is judged.

What is literature, what is not literature, and who decides are hard to define. Few critics make serious attempts at defining what literature is; few, however, have resisted the temptation of constructing a set of standards by which literature may be judged as superior or inferior; in fact, whole academic disciplines and degrees are based on the study of literary theory and criticism. The study of literature entails examination of a recognized body of "literary" works not only in their historical context but also as successful or unsuccessful works of art in themselves. One may therefore argue that standards for literature exist not only to define what literature is—and what good literature is—but also to exclude forms of literature that the critic deems unworthy. Such judgments are likely to generate controversy. Moreover, literary standards shift with the times;

many works have risen and fallen in critical estimation, sometimes being considered nonliterary during periods in which critics do not favor the works, and sometimes being "rediscovered" long after they were written when social and political attitudes favor them.

History

Historically, literature has been defined and judged from two perspectives: *formally*, that is, in regard to how the work adheres to a recognized set of standards for its genre (such as drama, novel, epic poem), and *substantively*, insofar as its subject matter and themes are deemed acceptable and worthy of literary focus. It is the latter that has been the source of most controversy. The Greek philosopher Aristotle was the first to propose standards for both: In his *Poetics* (c. 334-323 B.C.) for example, he defines tragedy as "an imitation [*mimēsis*] of an action that is serious, complete, and of a certain magnitude . . . through pity and fear effecting the proper purgation [*catharsis*] of these emotions"; formally, he defined the structure of tragedy and recommended it have unity of time, place, and action. The Roman poet Horace, in his *Ars poetica* (c. 17 B.C.), insists on decorum and states that poetry should instruct and please its audience. These and other "rules" of literature had a significant influence on writers, poets, and dramatists through the Renaissance and into the eighteenth century.

The rise of the novel and the Industrial Revolution in the nineteenth century brought other standards to bear as social concerns and the common individual began to dominate the subject matter of literature. Romantics such as Samuel Taylor Coleridge and William Wordsworth, for example, believed in the prominence of the human will and the individual's subjective experience of the world; naturalists such as Émile Zola and Theodore Dreiser emphasized those forces of society that shape the common individual's fate; writers as diverse as James Joyce and T. S. Eliot have been applauded for the epic scope of their works' concerns; and in the late twentieth century, as the world became smaller with increased telecommunications and interchange among diverse peoples, a multicultural ethic arose to accommodate and celebrate the literary expression of a plurality of cultures learning to coexist within the walls of the global village. Formal, as well as substantive, standards for literature have likewise shifted with the times; some even argue that written or printed literature and genres such as the novel will eventually die, to be replaced by multimedia works of art. The varied forces that shape literature, then, also influence what is called "good" literature.

The canon

Among academics, literary criticism emerged at the forefront of the debate with arguments about the "canon"—that is, the official list of great works that students study. Publications such as Mortimer J. Adler's *The Great Ideas: A Syntopicon of the Great Books of the Western World* (1952), coupled with a lack of access to the literatures of other cultures, have given the impression that "greatness" is restricted to a limited number of works judged by Eurocentric standards. The authors of the canon, as set forth in the twentieth century, are overwhelmingly white and male—a fact that implicitly devalues works by women and people of color. Henry Louis Gates, Jr., of Harvard University, argues that a truly adequate liberal education requires reckoning the "comparable eloquence of the African, the Asian and the Middle Eastern traditions." Students need a global perspective and a critical understanding of their total culture, he argues.

On the other hand, defenders of the canon, such as Irving Howe and John Searles, argue that reduced emphasis on the great ideas of Western civilization results in, and is partly responsible for, the crisis that already exists in the American educational system. According to this view, declining test scores and rising dropout rates are the outgrowth of too much curricular experimentation in the 1960's and 1970's. Education based on a disciplined, acknowledged "common core" of knowledge is needed to reverse these trends. Similar ideas are echoed in books by E. D. Hirsch (*Cultural Literacy*, 1987), Allan Bloom (*The Closing of the American Mind*, 1987), and Harold Bloom (*The Western Canon*, 1994).

Multicultural standards

In the 1980's and 1990's, the concept of multiculturalism was developed by activist members of cultural minorities to redress what was seen as a continuing pattern of unjust exclusion in a number of areas, including publication of marginalized groups' literary works and, by implication, their self-expression. Proponents take a broad approach to inclusiveness that embraces members of various marginalized groups, such as African Americans, Asian Americans, Latinos, women, gays, and people with disabilities.

In literature, the multicultural movement has resulted in two significant trends in the dissemination of ideas, both at the educational level and, through publishing, at the consumer level. First, public schools—previously seen as agents of Americanization (especially when confronted with the huge immigrant influx of the late 1800's and early 1900's)—have had to meet the educational needs of desegregated African Americans and, more recently, of new immigrants from Latin America and Asia. In the 1960's and 1970's, colleges and universities established ethnic studies and women's studies programs, inspiring the public school system to follow suit. A broad range of writings were suddenly legitimated as objects of scholarly inquiry, including slave narratives, autobiographies, and women's journals. Works formerly considered minor or obscure—such as Phillis Wheatley's *Poems on Various Subjects, Religious and Moral* (1773, condemned by Thomas Jefferson as beneath the dignity of criticism), James Weldon Johnson's *Autobiography of an Ex-Coloured Man* (1912), José Antonio Villarreal's *Pocho* (1959), the works of Sarah Orne Jewett, Black Elk, Zora Neale Hurston, and a host of others—were recognized as offering insights into the history and values of a particular people or group.

The second effect of the shift in literary standards was a steady rise in the popularity of works by newer authors giving voice to their cultural or other identities: N. Scott Momaday's *House Made of Dawn* (1968), Rudolfo Anaya's *Bless Me, Ultima* (1972), Frank Chin's *The Chickencoop Chinaman* (1972), Toni Morrison's *Sula* (1973), Alex Haley's *Roots: The Saga of an American Family* (1976), Maxine Hong Kingston's *The Woman Warrior: Memoirs of a Girlhood Among Ghosts* (1976), the "boom" in translations of Latin American literature such as Gabriel García Márquez's *Cien años de soledad* (1967; *One Hundred Years of Solitude*, 1970), Edmund White's *The Beautiful Room Is Empty* (1988)—the list has mushroomed since the 1960's. A concomitant boom in literature written expressly for young adults began to address such issues as divorce, sexual orientation, and ethnicity.

The history of literature, in its formal development and in the evolution and variety of its subject matter, goes hand in hand with the history of literary standards. Works that are critical of established social institutions or that emanate from oppressed groups are often denied, at least initially, the status of literature. Before Wheatley's poems could be published, for example, she had to be "examined" by eighteen of Boston's most prestigious male minds, who signed a document attesting the authenticity of her work—so doubtful were her "patrons" that she had been capable of producing the neoclassical verses in the collection. Other works, such as Harriet Beecher Stowe's *Uncle Tom's Cabin: Or, Life Among the Lowly* (1852), undergo radical shifts in assessment. Appearing at the height of abolitionist fervor, *Uncle Tom's Cabin* was widely read and, in the eyes of its author and others, successful in upholding the literary standards of its day: It was accurate in factual detail, appealed to the emotions, and moved the public to activism. By the standard of the 1960's generation, however, Stowe's novel was attacked for its sentimentality. James Baldwin also criticized the character Uncle Tom as a symbol of the submissiveness whites expect of blacks, coining a hateful epithet. Still other works have undergone the opposite shift in critical assessment. For example, the heroine of Kate Chopin's *The Awakening*, who in 1899 was reviled by editors and critics for her independence and sexual assertiveness, was hailed in the 1970's as a prototype of the liberated woman.

It seems evident from these and other examples that literary standards will continue to be promulgated for both good and bad reasons, and will continue to evolve with time. Whether such standards are allowed to threaten self-expression and therefore the preservation and celebration of diverse identities remains a question. Censorship has often reared its head in the past: James Joyce's *Ulysses* (1922), Vladimir Nabokov's *Lolita* (1955), William S. Burroughs' *The Naked Lunch* (1959), Philip Roth's *Portnoy's Complaint* (1969), and Andrea Dworkin's *Ice and Fire* (1987) have all been criticized and sometimes banned for their sexual content. Even Mark Twain's *Adventures of Huckleberry Finn* (1884) has been criticized, both for its celebration of interracial

Implications for identity

friendships and, retroactively, for its politically incorrect language. Many readers consider such works pornographic or deeply offensive and would like to see them regulated, whereas others counter that censorship only limits freedom of expression and replaces individual responsibility with tyrannical authority.

Henry Miller's works, including *Tropic of Capricorn* (1939), were not allowed to circulate freely in the United States until after a landmark decision by the Supreme Court in 1964 which came to be known as the Brennan doctrine. The Brennan doctrine removed the courts from the business of deciding literary standards by granting that obscenity is too subjective a matter, in most cases, for legal review. The trend since that time has been to relegate literary standards to the province of academic debate, where they will be able to make their greatest contribution to the evolution of self-expression.

SUGGESTED READINGS

Aristotle. *The "Poetics" of Aristotle*. Translated by Preston H. Epps. Chapel Hill: University of North Carolina Press, 1967. An excellent starting place, setting the pattern for attempts by critics to establish literary standards.

Bloom, Harold. *The Western Canon: The Books and Schools of the Ages*. New York: Harcourt Brace Jovanovich, 1994. Revisits and supports the theory of literary standards and of the canon, with appendices providing Bloom's own list, organized by four great ages of Western literature.

Booth, Wayne C. *The Rhetoric of Fiction*. 2d ed. Chicago: University of Chicago Press, 1961. A landmark work of the so-called Chicago School or of Neo-Aristotelian criticism, which seeks to establish systematic study of literature at the level of genre rather than exclusively at the level of the individual work.

Brooks, Cleanth, and Robert Penn Warren. *The Well-Wrought Urn: Studies in the Structure of Poetry*. New York: Harcourt Brace Jovanovich, 1947. A definitive example of the New Criticism, concentrating on the text of the work and avoiding discussion of such contextual issues as social history and the author's life.

Eliot, T. S. *What Is a Classic?* New York: Haskell House, 1944. An attempt to define a classic work.

Frye, Northrop. *Anatomy of Criticism: Four Essays*. Princeton, N.J.: Princeton University Press, 1957. Attempts definitions of various genres of literature—a key work of Neo-Aristotelian criticism.

Showalter, Elaine, ed., *The New Feminist Criticism: Essays on Women, Literature, and Theory*. New York: Pantheon Books, 1985. An excellent starting place in the study of feminist literary theory.

Tompkins, Jane, ed. *Reader-Response Criticism*. New York: Pantheon Books, 1980. Presents reader-response theory, which argues for the subjectivity of textual interpretation, and, by extension, the subjectivity of the literary standards.

Wellek, René, and Austin Warren. *Theory of Literature*. New York: Harcourt Brace Jovanovich, 1949. Attempts to define the difference between literature and nonliterature, arguing that literature is what defeats habits of thought and feeling, reawakening one's perception.

—*Christina J. Moose*

See also Canon; Censorship of literature; Fatwā; Multiculturalism; Stereotypes and identity

Little Foxes, The

AUTHOR: Lillian Hellman (1905-1984)
FIRST PRODUCED: 1939; first published, 1939
IDENTITIES: European American; South; women

The Little Foxes, Lillian Hellman's most well-known play, is a moralistic drama about changing values in the post-Civil War South. The play chronicles the rise of a materialistic and greedy new generation of Southerners at the expense of the former antebellum aristocracy. Hellman presents neither group with much sympathy, instead painting a negative portrait of society in conflict, motivated by money on one hand and outdated ideals on the other.

The siblings, Ben and Oscar Hubbard and Regina Giddens, are the representatives of new Southern immoral capitalism. Together, they attempt to form an enriching alliance with a Northern manufacturer, but in order to raise the necessary capital, Ben, Oscar, and Oscar's son Leo "borrow" bonds worth $88,000 from Regina's ailing husband, Horace Giddens, without his knowledge. Although the three siblings prefer to keep all the funds in the family, they are quite willing to take advantage of one another as they plan their transactions. In particular, the brothers want to profit more by lowering or eliminating Regina's percentage of the deal.

Regina, however, is a strong, clever, and self-reliant woman who is quite willing to go to any lengths in order to break out of her Southern, secluded lifestyle and head north to conquer Chicago society. She no longer loves her ailing husband, Horace, and blames her brothers for arranging her marriage. In the play's crucial scene, she refuses to bring Horace his heart medicine in the midst of an attack, knowing that if he dies she can manipulate the brothers into allowing her a 75 percent share of the financial deal. After Horace's death, she replaces the oldest brother, Ben, as the chief figure in the Hubbards' financial empire. Although alone at the end of the play, perhaps facing the future without a close relationship with her daughter, Alexandra, she has clearly dominated her brothers and achieved her goals.

Representing the Old South in the play are Birdie Hubbard, Oscar's flighty, alcoholic wife, and Horace Giddens, Regina's ailing husband. Although both are victims of the Hubbard greed, neither character has strength enough to stave off the sometimes cruel treatment they receive from their Hubbard spouses. Their ineffectuality and weakness underscores the inevitability of change in the Southern setting.

Perhaps the most winning character in the play is Alexandra Giddens, the daughter of Horace and Regina. She senses the values of Birdie and Horace and recognizes the maliciousness of Regina, Oscar, and Ben. She is no weakling. At the play's end she determines to separate herself from the Hubbard clan and strike out on her own. Her characterization presents hope for the future beyond the destructive Hubbards. The title of the play is an echo from the Bible, which tells of those "little foxes" who "spoil the vines" and the "tender grapes" (Song of Solomon 2:15).

SUGGESTED READINGS

Falk, Doris. *Lillian Hellman*. New York: Frederick Ungar, 1978.

Lederer, Katherine. *Lillian Hellman*. Boston: Twayne, 1979.

Rollyson, Carl. *Lillian Hellman: Her Legend and Her Life*. New York: St. Martin's Press, 1988.

—Delmer Davis

See also American identity: South; *Children's Hour, The*; Feminism; Hellman, Lillian

London, Jack

BORN: San Francisco, California; January 12, 1876

DIED: Glen Ellen, California; November 22, 1916

PRINCIPAL WORKS: *The Call of the Wild*, 1903; *The Sea-Wolf*, 1904; *White Fang*, 1906; *The Iron Heel*, 1907; *Martin Eden*, 1909; *South Sea Tales*, 1911; *The House of Pride and Other Tales of Hawaii*, 1912; *John Barleycorn*, 1913 (*John Barleycorn: Or, Alcoholic Memoirs*, 1914); *The Mutiny of the Elsinore*, 1914

IDENTITIES: European American; West and Southwest

SIGNIFICANT ACHIEVEMENT: Born into poverty and shaped by his experiences on America's westernmost lands and waters, London incorporated the latest European intellectual concepts into his fiction.

Four factors dominated Jack London's attitudes and writings: the hard circumstances of his childhood in California, his early discovery of the great nineteenth century scientists and philosophers, his adventures at sea, and his experiences in Alaska and the Yukon.

London was the illegitimate son of a spiritualist who subsequently made a marriage of convenience to a widower. While the union provided a home for two families, it seems to have involved little affection. London's stepfather was an unsuccessful provider, and London began work as a child to help support the family. Central California was still a rough region at the end of the nineteenth century, and the jobs the boy found included sweeping saloons and setting bowling pins. To escape the drudgery of such work, he borrowed enough money to buy a small boat and set himself up as an oyster pirate; later he switched sides to guard the same waters.

In 1893, London shipped aboard a sealing schooner bound for the Bering Sea. Out of this experience grew *The Sea-Wolf*, now recognized as one of the most important works of American sea fiction. Four years later London took part in another intensely masculine adventure, the Klondike gold rush, absorbing raw material for such sagas of the North as *The Call of the Wild*.

London's works were much more than transcriptions of actual experience. In a prodigious period of self-education as a young man, he absorbed an enormous body of literature, science, and philosophy. Thus *The Sea-Wolf* dramatizes the concept of the superman, developed by the German philosopher Friedrich Nietzsche. *The Call of the Wild* explores the concept of the survival of the fittest, pioneered by the philosopher Herbert Spencer, interpreter of scientist Charles Darwin. London led a robust and extraordinarily active life, and fancied himself a Nietzschian superman transposed to the American West, but his fiction makes clear his ambivalence at such a role.

London married in 1900 and divorced in 1904. He remarried a year later. By 1914, London's health was failing, due largely to chronic alcoholism, which he portrays in the memoir *John Barleycorn*. He died in 1916 at the age of forty, having written twenty novels and hundreds of short stories and articles.

SUGGESTED READINGS

Kingman, Russ. *A Pictorial Life of Jack London*. New York: Crown, 1979.

Labor, Earle. *Jack London*. New York: Twayne, 1974.

Lundquist, James. *Jack London: Adventures, Ideas, and Fiction*. New York: Frederick Ungar, 1987.

Nuernberg, Susan M., ed. *The Critical Response to Jack London*. Westport, Conn.: Greenwood Press, 1995.

Tavernier-Courbin, Jacqueline, ed. *Critical Essays on Jack London*. Boston: G. K. Hall, 1983.

—*Grove Koger*

See also Alcoholism; American identity: life on the sea; American identity: West and the frontier; *Sea-Wolf, The*

Lone Ranger and Tonto Fistfight in Heaven, The

AUTHOR: Sherman Alexie (1966-   )

FIRST PUBLISHED: 1993

IDENTITIES: Native American; West and Southwest

Sherman Alexie's initial foray into fiction (except for a few stories sprinkled among his poems), *The Lone Ranger and Tonto Fistfight in Heaven* appeared before his twenty-seventh birthday and was awarded a citation from the PEN/Hemingway Award committee for best first book of fiction in 1993. Praising his "live and unremitting lyric energy," one reviewer suggested that three of the twenty-two stories in the book "could stand in any collection of excellence."

Alexie grew up in Wellpinit, Washington, on the Spokane Indian Reservation; he is Spokane-Coeur d'Alene. Critics have noted that the pain and anger of the stories is balanced by his keen sense of humor and satiric wit. Alexie's readers will notice certain recurring characters, including Victor Joseph, who often appears as the narrator, Lester FallsApart, the pompous tribal police chief, David WalsAlong, Junior Polatkin, and Thomas Builds-the-Fire, the storyteller to whom no one listens. These characters also appear in Alexie's first novel, *Reservation Blues* (1995), so the effect is of a community; in this respect, Alexie's writings are similar to the fiction of William Faulkner. One reviewer has suggested that *The Lone Ranger and Tonto Fistfight in Heaven* is almost a novel, despite the fact that Alexie rarely relies on plot development in the stories and does not flesh out his characters. It might more aptly be said that the stories come close to poetry, just as Alexie's poems verge on fiction. The stories range in length from less than three to about twenty pages, and some of the best, like "The First Annual All-Indian Horseshoe Pitch and Barbecue," leap from moment to moment, from one-liner to quickly narrated episode, much like a poem.

That story begins, "Someone forgot the charcoal; blame the BIA." The next sentence concerns Victor playing the piano just before the barbecue: "after the beautiful dissonance and implied survival, the Spokane Indians wept, stunned by this strange and familiar music." Survival is a repeated theme in Alexie's work. The story then jumps to a series of four short paragraphs, each beginning "There is something beautiful about." Then we are told that Simon won at horseshoes, and he "won the coyote contest when he told us that basketball should be our new religion." A paragraph near the end is composed of a series of questions, each beginning "Can you hear the dreams." The last paragraph features a child born of a white mother and an Indian father, with the mother proclaiming: "Both sides of this baby are beautiful."

Beneath the anger, pain, and satiric edge of his stories, often haunted by the mythic figure of Crazy Horse and tinged with fantasy, Alexie offers hope for survival and reconciliation.

SUGGESTED READINGS

Bellante, John, and Carl Bellante. "Sherman Alexie, Literary Rebel." *Bloomsbury Review* 14 (May-June, 1994): 14-15, 26.

Kincaid, James R. "Who Gets to Tell Their Stories?" *The New York Times Book Review* 97 (May 3, 1992): 1, 24-29.

Price, Reynolds. "One Indian Doesn't Tell Another." *The New York Times Book Review* 98 (October 17, 1993): 15-16.

Silko, Leslie Marmon. "Big Bingo." *Nation* 260 (June 12, 1995): 856-858, 860.

—*Ron McFarland*

See also Alexie, Sherman; Native American identity; *Reservation Blues*

Long and Happy Life, A

AUTHOR: Reynolds Price (1933-   )

FIRST PUBLISHED: 1962

IDENTITIES: European American; South

A Long and Happy Life, Reynolds Price's debut novel, chronicles the struggles of a young woman to assume her place in the community as a wife and mother. Reviewers welcomed this novel about a believable, vulnerable young woman as a relief from contemporary fiction and its academic experiments in self-consciousness.

Unwed and surrounded by fecundity, Rosacoke Mustian feels marginalized from her rural Southern community. Abandoned by the young man she desires—Wesley Beavers—because she will not have sex with him, Rosacoke becomes desperate. Rather than suffer social ostracization, she decides to try to arrest Wesley's flight from the community and to bind him to her by giving him what he wants. In doing so, she mediates the tension between the demands of the community and the desires of the self. Her plan backfires as Wesley acknowledges her gift to him by calling her by another woman's name during the act. To him, Rosacoke is simply another woman with whom he is sexual. Rather than gratifying her, her plan hurts her.

As a result of their one act of lovemaking, Rosacoke becomes pregnant. Repenting her selfishness in having set out to trap Wesley into a marriage that he did not want, she decides to assume sole responsibility for her predicament. Wesley accepts his duty, however, and proposes to her, a proposal that she accepts as a duty to her unborn child. He rescues her from the plight of being an unwed mother and thereby being ostracized from the community, as happened to her friend Mildred. Through the examples of her parents and her brother, she recognizes that married life may be a grim disappointment to her romantic expectations. Even so, the marriage is derived from her love for Wesley, and it allows her and him to assume their places in the community.

Rosacoke's narrative reveals a design underlying her and Wesley's personal stories that suggests that their coupling was destined. The nature imagery in the novel invests narrative with a mythic significance that emphasizes regeneration. Rosacoke and Wesley, for example, make love in a broomstraw field after following a buck and his two does to the spring. A Christmas pageant, in which Rosacoke plays the Virgin Mary, at the novel's conclusion, implies that Rosacoke has been granted forgiveness. The novel satisfies what Price identifies as the audience's need for consolation. The novel implies that people's lives proceed in order, that God has not abandoned them.

SUGGESTED READINGS

Kreyling, Michael. "Motion and Rest in the Novels of Reynolds Price." *The Southern Review* 16 (Autumn, 1980): 853-868.

Rooke, Constance. *Reynolds Price*. Boston: Twayne, 1983.

Shepherd, Allen. "Love (and Marriage) in *A Long and Happy Life*." *Twentieth Century Literature* 17 (January, 1971): 29-35.

—Mara Lynn McFadden

See also American identity: South; Price, Reynolds

Long Day's Journey into Night

AUTHOR: Eugene O'Neill (1888-1953)

FIRST PRODUCED: 1956; first published, 1956

IDENTITIES: European American; family

Some have called *Long Day's Journey into Night* not only Eugene O'Neill's greatest play but also one of the finest American plays of the twentieth century. More courageously than any American play before, this powerful drama chronicles the ways in which people's identities emerge, for better or worse, from the family unit and develop through the choices they make as adults. "The past is the present. It's the future too," says Mary Tyrone, the mother in this family tragedy.

"Written in tears and blood," the play is based on O'Neill's own dysfunctional family, stricken by narcotic addiction, bitter recriminations, alienation, and the seductive lure of the American Dream. Despite the family's undeniable love for one another, this play is about the paralyzing and heartbreaking way in which each member yearns to escape from, but is forever tied to, painful regrets and one another. The predominant image of the play is a blanket of fog that cushions and isolates the family from themselves and each other and is occasionally pierced by the foghorn, summoning the characters to confront their pain, loss, and denial.

Set in 1912 Connecticut during eighteen hours, the play has four main characters: father James Tyrone, a semiretired actor whose insensitive, compulsive cheapness torments his family; mother Mary, denying yet succumbing to morphine addiction (caused by James's hiring of an incompetent doctor when Edmund was born); thirty-three-year-old son Jamie, whose alcoholism and dissolute life mask a lost, alienated soul; and twenty-three-year-old Edmund, a sensitive, dreamy writer afflicted with tuberculosis, who yearns to be a seaman.

James and Jamie's alcoholism (Edmund is no teetotaler, either) and Mary's drug addiction form their identities. James denies his alcoholism but drinks to forget past career mistakes and guilt over the desperate illness and unhappiness in his family. Mary's identity comes from her constant lying, hiding, and denial of her morphine addiction, blaming James's cheapness, herself for marrying him, and even Edmund for being born.

Jamie's alcoholism is part of his total alienation. He drinks to forget his personal and professional failure, jealousy of his brother, and James's constant reminders of his worthlessness. Consumed by past regrets, Mary, too, is alienated because of her addiction and because of her loss of faith in religion, her husband, and herself.

Addicted to the materialism of the American Dream, James is a rich landowner who is so miserly that he sends Edmund to cheap, incompetent doctors. Since neither Jamie nor Edmund has succeeded in a career, the American Dream's assumption that "you are what you do" confuses their identities.

Late in the play, as these tortured characters strive to exorcise their inner demons, O'Neill clearly shows the ways in which early family experience irrevocably forges adult identity. This scathingly honest portrait of the haunted and stricken Tyrones—their mistakes, guilt, blame, denial, love, and redemption—moves audiences and readers deeply, for in O'Neill's family identity they see something of their own.

SUGGESTED READINGS

Barlow, Judith E. *Final Acts: The Creation of Three Late O'Neill Plays.* Athens: University of Georgia Press, 1985.

Carpenter, Frederic. *Eugene O'Neill.* Boston: Twayne, 1979.

Gassner, John, ed. *O'Neill: A Collection of Critical Essays.* Englewood Cliffs, N.J.: Prentice-Hall, 1964.

—Howard A. Kerner

See also Addiction; Alcoholism; American Dream; O'Neill, Eugene

Looking for Mr. Goodbar

AUTHOR: Judith Rossner (1935-   )
FIRST PUBLISHED: 1975
IDENTITIES: European American; family; women

Looking for Mr. Goodbar, Judith Rossner's best-known novel, is a *roman à clef* about a young, convent-schooled, lower middle-class but respectable, Irish Catholic woman from the Bronx, New York City. Her body and psyche are scarred by a childhood, polio-induced curvature of the spine, which has been physically corrected by surgery. The twenty-eight-year-old woman has also suffered from an ugly-duckling complex as a result of having a supposedly more glamorous older sister. Theresa Dunn has little empathy, however, for a younger sibling, a conventional housewife who is perennially (and to Theresa, distastefully) pregnant.

Theresa's lack of self-worth, despite a degree from the City College of New York and a job as a first-grade schoolteacher, takes her down a bleak and ultimately violent path. That road begins with her first affair with a married English professor in college. He is depicted as a self-serving creep who cynically exploits her before leaving her.

Her subsequent means of escape from her feelings of rejection and loneliness are casual affairs, interspersed at one point by a relationship with a Jesuit-trained Irish Catholic lawyer whose lovemaking she finds anesthetic. Theresa comes to dread "the quicksand of Irish Catholic life in the Bronx" when James Morrisey becomes serious about her.

Rossner's story, based on the real New York murder case of Katherine Cleary by Joe Willie Simpson on New Year's Day of 1973, reaches a denouement when Theresa, temporarily estranged from James, meets Gary Cooper White in one of the singles bars, Mr. Goodbar's, that she regularly patronizes. This psychopathic drifter picks up Theresa, who needs little encouragement. Back in Theresa's Upper West Side apartment, Gary is offended when, after sex, Theresa tells him to leave. He stabs her to death.

The heroine has two identities. One is Theresa, the clever, attractive, capable, and popular schoolteacher; the other is Terry, the maimed self-hater, addicted to sex, filled with fear and shame, who feels that being degraded by men using her body is becoming to her. This dismal tale is told in the context of the destructive and joyless hedonism of New York in the 1960's and epitomized by the dialogue, which is studded with four-letter words. Rossner is ambivalent, however, about the extent to which blame should be placed on the sexually liberated schoolteacher or her brutal pickup. The author is more interested in portraying the particulars of a time and place and in raising questions than she is about providing answers.

SUGGESTED READINGS

Blackwood, Caroline. "Getting It All over With." *Times Literary Supplement*, September 12, 1975, 1012.

Fishbein, Leslie. "Looking for Mr. Goodbar: Murder for the Masses." *International Journal of Women's Studies* 3 (1980): 173-182.

Rinzler, Carol E. "Looking for Mr. Goodbar." *The New York Times Book Review*, June 8, 1975, 24-25.

—*Peter B. Heller*

See also Addiction; Adultery; Erotic identity; Violence; Women and identity

Lorde, Audre

BORN: New York, New York; February 18, 1934

DIED: Christiansted, St. Croix, United States Virgin Islands; November 17, 1992

PRINCIPAL WORKS: *Cables to Rage*, 1970; *New York Head Shop and Museum*, 1974; *Coal*, 1976; *The Black Unicorn*, 1978; *The Cancer Journals,* 1980; *Chosen Poems, Old and New*, 1982 (revised edition, *Undersong: Chosen Poems, Old and New*, 1992); *Zami: A New Spelling of My Name*, 1982; *Sister Outsider: Essays and Speeches*, 1984; *The Marvelous Arithmetics of Distance: Poems 1987-1992*, 1993

IDENTITIES: African American; disease; gay, lesbian, and bisexual; women

SIGNIFICANT ACHIEVEMENT: Lorde's poetry, essays, and autobiographical fiction are among the best American black lesbian feminist writings.

Audre Lorde began writing poems at an early age, as a child of West Indian heritage growing up in New York City's Harlem. Her early work progressed from personal consciousness to encompass a radical critique of her society. Lorde was graduated from Hunter College in New York, then went on to study for a year at the National University of Mexico. She obtained a library science degree from Columbia University in 1961.

African American lesbian author Audre Lorde, who wrote about her experiences battling cancer. (Dagmar Schullz)

Lorde married attorney Edwin Ashley Rollins in 1962, had two children with him, and was divorced in 1970. From 1970 onward, there was a lesbian focus in her life as well as in her work. In *Zami*, Lorde examines the powerful erotic journey of a young black woman who comes to terms with her lesbian sexual orientation. Powerful, deeply erotic scenes based in New York City's gay-girl milieu of the 1950's reflect Lorde's efforts to grapple with her own personal, sexual, and racial identity.

A teacher of writing at New York City area colleges, Lorde was keenly aware of racism—a condition she experienced as a child in New York City. This awareness was reflected in a radicalism in her work, including *Coal* and *Sister Outsider: Essays and Speeches*.

SUGGESTED READINGS

Bloom, Harold, ed. *Black American Women Poets and Dramatists*. New York: Chelsea House, 1996.

Christian, Barbara, ed. *Black Feminist Criticism: Perspectives on Black Women Writers*. Elmsford, N.Y.: Pergamon Press, 1985.

Martin, Joan. "The Unicorn Is Black: Audre Lorde in Retrospect." In *Black Women Writers (1950-1980): A Critical Evaluation*, edited by Mari Evans. Garden City, N.Y.: Doubleday, 1984.

—*R. C. S.*

See also African American identity; *Cancer Journals, The*; *Coal*; Erotic identity; Feminism; Lesbian identity; *Zami*

Love Medicine

AUTHOR: Louise Erdrich (1954-   )

FIRST PUBLISHED: 1984

IDENTITIES: Family; Native American

A dazzling meld of Native American storytelling and postmodern literary craft, Louise Erdrich's first novel, *Love Medicine*, was an immediate success. It quickly made the best-seller lists and gathered an impressive group of awards, including the National Book Critics Circle Award for fiction, the American Academy and Institute of Arts and Letters Award for best first novel, the Virginia McCormack Scully Prize for best book of 1984 dealing with Indians or Chicanos, the American Book Award, and the *Los Angeles Times* award for best novel of the year.

Sad and funny, realistic and lyrical, mystical and down-to-earth, the novel tells the story of three generations of four Chippewa and mixed blood families—the Kashpaws, Morriseys, Lamartines, and Lazarres—from the 1930's to the 1980's. Seven separate narrators tell their own stories in a discontinuous time line, each a puzzle piece of its own, but by the novel's end there is one story, one jigsaw puzzle picture of lost identities and the often humorous but always meaningful efforts of a fragmented people to hold on to what is left to them.

The characters in *Love Medicine* experience individual forms of alienation caused by physical and emotional separation from the communal root of their existence. They contend with the United States government and its policies of allotment and commodities; the Catholic church, which makes no allowances for the Chippewas' traditional religion; and with the seductive pull of life off the reservation, a life that cuts them off from the community whose traditions keep them centered and give them a sense of their identities. These three factors place the characters under the constant threat of loss of their culture. Erdrich makes this clear, but she presents the lives of her Native American characters as human experiences that readers who have no background in Native American cultures can readily understand. The three generations of characters in *Love Medicine* surface as human beings who deal with an unfair world with strength, frailty, love, anger, and most of all, a sense of humor.

SUGGESTED READINGS

Bartlett, Mary, ed. *The New Native American Novel: Works in Progress*. Albuquerque: University of New Mexico Press, 1986.

Owens, Louis. *Other Destinies: Understanding the American Indian Novel*. Norman: University of Oklahoma Press, 1992.

—*Jacquelyn Kilpatrick*

See also Catholicism; Economics of identity; Mixed race and identity; Native American identity; Religion and identity

Love Song of J. Alfred Prufrock, The

AUTHOR: T. S. Eliot (1888-1965)

FIRST PUBLISHED: 1915

IDENTITIES: European American

"The Love Song of J. Alfred Prufrock" is a psychological profile of a white, middle-aged, middle-class, late Victorian man suffering from an acute spiritual malaise as a result of his boring, unimaginative, routine, repressed bourgeois existence. The poem, T. S. Eliot's first major publication, immediately established his reputation as an important poet. It also announced one of the themes that Eliot explored throughout his career: the emptiness of modern life, made tedious by habit, sterilized by convention, in which self-awareness does not lead to self-knowledge but only to existential paralysis.

Prufrock epitomizes a frustrated man hopelessly alienated from his imagination and yet desperate for imaginative salvation. His life is filled with meaningless gestures and predictable encounters; his seamy world is agonizingly uninspiring. Prufrock is an effigy representing the cultural decadence and moral degeneration that Eliot equates with the society of his time. He is the product of a world suffering from a break with its past cultural heritage, a loss of tradition, a failure of institutional authority, and an unhealthy emphasis on individualism.

Eliot incorporates hallucinatory imagery to create a lethargic world where "the evening is spread out against the sky/ Like a patient etherised upon a table." The women who "come and go/ Talking of Michelangelo" suggest the transience and shallowness of contemporary relationships while ironically reducing the work of an Italian Renaissance master. Prufrock is afraid to "force the moment to its crisis." The people in his world mask their emotions and "prepare a face to meet the faces that you meet." The streets are "insidious" and "half-deserted"; people spend "restless nights in one-night cheap hotels." Deadened by routine, he complains that he has "measured out my life in coffee spoons." The portrait of Prufrock is particularly unflattering, but more pathetic because he realizes the nature of his dilemma but is still incapable of rectifying it. His vision at the end of the poem is one of possible redemption, of "mermaids singing," but his resignation is complete; he does not think that they will sing to him.

His identity crisis is exacerbated by the historical, social, and political upheavals that ripped Europe apart in the early twentieth century. His passivity, his lack of self-confidence, and the cultural squalor created by mediocrity constitute a searing indictment of a man bewildered by a world seemingly beyond his control, who lacks the moral courage to confront the situation, to assert himself and to change it. Prufrock mirrors the hostility and contempt Eliot felt toward modern twentieth century culture; he also depicts the type of individual Eliot felt the modern culture would create. Prufrock is an ineffectual boor whose singular identity is being eroded by the instability of his society; he is a face prepared for other faces.

SUGGESTED READINGS

Ackroyd, Peter. *T. S. Eliot: A Life*. New York: Simon & Schuster, 1984.

Bush, Ronald. *T. S. Eliot: A Study in Character and Style*. New York: Oxford University Press, 1984.

Kenner, Hugh. *The Invisible Poet*. New York: McDowell, Obolensky, 1959.

Wagner, Linda W. *T. S. Eliot: A Collection of Criticism*. New York: McGraw-Hill, 1974.

—*Jeff Johnson*

See also Eliot, T. S.; Existentialism; *Waste Land, The*

Lowell, Robert

BORN: Boston, Massachusetts; March 1, 1917

DIED: New York, New York; September 12, 1977

PRINCIPAL WORKS: *Lord Weary's Castle*, 1946; *The Mills of the Kavanaughs*, 1951; *Life Studies*, 1959; *For the Union Dead*, 1964; *The Old Glory*, 1965, rev. 1968; *The Dolphin*, 1973

IDENTITIES: European American; Northeast; religion

SIGNIFICANT ACHIEVEMENT: Lowell was one of the most influential of the poets, teachers, and critics of his time.

Robert Lowell was born into an established family of influential but unhappy New England Protestants. His mother's neurotic personality and his father's professional failure gave rise to frequent family tensions that may account for Lowell's later depressions and his feelings of spiritual homelessness. Inspired by Allen Tate's idea that poetry expresses experienced revelations of larger, impersonal ideas, Lowell transferred from Harvard to Kenyon College, where John Crowe Ransom

Noted poet of the confessional school Robert Lowell. (Fay Godwin)

taught him to use poetry as a craft with which to structure experience. After graduation in 1940 and conversion to Roman Catholicism, Lowell opposed America's involvement in World War II. His refusal to be drafted into the army earned him a year's confinement in jail described in "Memories of West Street and Lepke" in *Life Studies*. In 1965, Lowell publicly rejected President Lyndon B. Johnson's invitation to the White House Festival of the Arts—to Lowell, the idea of Americans killing innocent Vietnamese civilians echoed the Indian wars of earlier American history. Lowell's political activism reached its peak when he accompanied Senator Eugene McCarthy during the Democratic primaries in 1968.

Later in Lowell's life, his depressions, which were serious to the point that he at times was hospitalized, began to recur annually. Lowell's poetry became increasingly personal, at the expense of religion and formal structure. Looking for a sense of home, for himself and for his history, Lowell wrote in depth about New England. The publication of *Life Studies*, a key work of what came to be called the confessional school, was the poetry event of the year in 1959. Unable to find a home in New England or in New York or in his second marriage, Lowell left for England in 1970, hoping to rediscover his personal and artistic freedom. He remarried and recorded his "story of changing marriages" in *The Dolphin*. In 1977, new marital problems returned Lowell to his second wife in Manhattan. Burnt out after a tour of the former Soviet Union and weakened by heart problems, he collapsed in the seat of a taxicab in New York. He died as he lived and wrote: moving toward an unreachable destination in a world of lost connections. Among his contemporaries, he stood out as one who kept alive the notion of the poet's public responsibility. Lowell, as Norman Mailer observed in 1967, during the famous march on the Pentagon against the Vietnam War, "gave off at times the unwilling haunted saintliness of a man who was repaying the moral debts of ten generations of ancestors."

SUGGESTED READINGS

Axelrod, Steven Gould. *Robert Lowell: Life and Art*. Princeton, N.J.: Princeton University Press, 1978.

Hamilton, Ian. *Robert Lowell: A Biography*. Winchester, Mass.: Faber & Faber, 1982.

Mariani, Paul. *Lost Puritan: A Life of Robert Lowell*. New York: W. W. Norton, 1994.

Williamson, Alan. *Pity the Monsters: The Political Vision of Robert Lowell*. New Haven, Conn.: Yale University Press, 1974.

—Sonja H. Streuber

See also American identity: Northeast; Lowell, Robert, poetry of; Mental disorders; Vietnam War; World War II

Lowell, Robert, poetry of

AUTHOR: Robert Lowell (1917-1977)

PRINCIPAL WORKS: *Lord Weary's Castle*, 1946; *Life Studies*, 1959; *For the Union Dead*, 1964; *Notebook 1967-68*, 1969

IDENTITIES: European American; family; Northeast; religion

In his first major collection, *Lord Weary's Castle*, Robert Lowell contextualizes his Catholicism, his aversion to World War II, and his antagonism to mercantile Boston with an Irish ballad about the little man's exploitation by an immoral, all-powerful country. With demanding, intricate metrical forms and artificially charged language, the poems display Lowell's characteristic themes of personal, national, and historical self-destruction in the face of eternal suffering. The poems unfold a "vision of destruction." A sense of despair flows into such apocalyptic conclusions as, "The Lord survives the rainbow of His will." In such poems as "Mr. Edwards and the Spider" and "A Quaker Graveyard in Nantucket," however, this despair provides the defiant, life-giving force for the believer's self-reliant intellect, which is unafraid to face its own paradoxes.

In *Life Studies*, Lowell's style becomes less "distant, symbol-ridden, and willfully difficult," and his subjects become more personal (family history, mental breakdowns, and marital difficulties). The poet feeds on his own psychology and history. "Beyond the Alps" recalls Lowell's sad departure from Catholicism; "Memories of West Street and Lepke" narrates Lowell's prison experience during World War II. *Life Studies* primarily records, in psychological portraits of his childhood, his parents, and his wives, his changed attitude toward Boston. He assumes the city's weakness and vulnerability for himself. He opens his tight metrical forms for the freer forms, the precise descriptions, and the conversational style he found in the work of Elizabeth Bishop, William Carlos Williams, and Allen Ginsberg. Lowell tried to recapture the immediate success of *Life Studies* in *Notebook*, a diary of his reading, his personal life, and his poetic condemnations of the Vietnam War. In focusing on "always the instant, something changing to the lost," however, he abandoned the powerful connection to the past.

For the Union Dead represents Lowell's third distinct manner of linking experience and identity. In this work, consciousness is subject matter itself. He records key images of past and present events in poems such as "Neo-Classical Urn" and "For the Union Dead." Integrating American history and his autobiography, Lowell explains the terrors of urban life. He describes technological advancement and spiritual emptiness, powerlessness, isolation and social antagonism, all perpetually threatened by nuclear annihilation. In such political poems as "July in Washington," for example, Lowell uses his sense of the United States' traditions to criticize the evasive politics of the Eisenhower years. The poet as historian aims to give readers essential knowledge of themselves; this was Lowell's primary, yet unattainable, goal. He sought to make the personal the political, and the political the personal, and to charge both with a productive despair.

SUGGESTED READINGS

Axelrod, Steven Gould. *Robert Lowell: Life and Art*. Princeton, N.J.: Princeton University Press, 1978.

Tillinghast, Richard. *Robert Lowell's Life and Work: Damaged Grandeur*. Ann Arbor: University of Michigan Press, 1995.

Williamson, Alan. *Pity the Monsters: The Political Vision of Robert Lowell*. New Haven, Conn.: Yale University Press, 1974.

—Sonja H. Streuber

See also American identity: Northeast; Lowell, Robert; Religion and identity; Vietnam War; World War II

M

M. Butterfly

AUTHOR: David Henry Hwang (1957-   )
FIRST PRODUCED: 1988; first published, 1988
IDENTITIES: Chinese American; gay, lesbian, and bisexual

M. Butterfly is David Henry Hwang's fictionalized account of a real French diplomat who carried on an affair with a Chinese opera singer for twenty years, only to discover she was actually a man. Hwang's compelling drama examines themes of sexual and racial stereotyping, Western imperialism, the role illusion plays in perceptions, and the ability for one person to truly know another.

M. Butterfly contrasts Rene Gallimard with Pinkerton in Giacomo Puccini's *Madama Butterfly* (produced, 1904; published, 1935). Gallimard sees himself as awkward, clumsy at love, but somehow being blessed with the utter devotion of Song Liling, a beautiful Oriental woman. Hwang uses the word "Oriental" to convey an exotic, imperialistic view of the East. Gallimard becomes so absorbed with his sexist perception of Asian women that it distorts his thinking. He tests Liling's devotion by neglecting and humiliating her, ultimately forcing her to admit she is his "Butterfly," a character she has publicly denounced.

Unknown to Gallimard, Liling is a Communist agent, manipulating him to extract information about the Vietnam War. At the embassy Gallimard finds increased status because of his Oriental affair. When his analysis of East-West relations, based entirely on his self delusions, prove wrong, Gallimard is demoted and returned to France. His usefulness spent, Liling is forced to endure hard labor, an official embarrassment because "there are no homosexuals in China." Eventually, the Communists send Liling to France to reestablish his affair with Gallimard. When Gallimard is caught and tried for espionage, it is publicly revealed that Liling is a man. Liling now changes to men's clothing, effecting a complete role-reversal between Liling and Gallimard. Liling becomes the dominant masculine figure while Gallimard becomes the submissive feminine figure. Preferring fantasy to reality, Gallimard becomes "Butterfly," donning Liling's wig and kimono, choosing an honorable death over a dishonorable life.

M. Butterfly demonstrates the dangers inherent in living a life satisfied with shallow stereotypes and misconceptions. Gallimard's singular desire for a submissive Oriental woman was fulfilled only in his mind. It blinded him to every truth about his mistress, refusing even to accept the truth about Liling until he stood naked before him. It first cost him his career, then his wife, then his dignity, then his lover, and finally his life. Even when he is confronted by the truth, Gallimard can only respond that he has "known, and been loved by, the perfect woman."

SUGGESTED READINGS

DiGaetani, John Lewis. "*M. Butterfly*: An Interview with David Henry Hwang." *The Drama Review: A Journal of Performance Studies* 33, no. 3 (Fall, 1989): 141-153.

Skloot, Robert. "Breaking the Butterfly: The Politics of David Henry Hwang." *Modern Drama* 33, no. 1 (March, 1990): 59-66.

Street, Douglas. *David Henry Hwang*. Boise, Idaho: Boise State University Press, 1989.

—*Gerald S. Argetsinger*

See also Appearance and identity; Asian American identity: China, Japan, and Korea; Bisexual identity; Hwang, David Henry

Ma Rainey's Black Bottom

AUTHOR: August Wilson (1945-   )
FIRST PRODUCED: 1984; first published, 1985
IDENTITIES: African American

Set in 1927 in a Chicago recording studio, August Wilson's play, *Ma Rainey's Black Bottom*, explores the values and attitudes toward life and music of the classic blues singer, Ma Rainey. Their economic exploitation as African American musicians in a white-controlled recording industry, as well as their inferior social status in the majority white culture, become evident in the play's dialogue and action. As Ma Rainey puts it: "If you colored and can make them some money, then you all right with them. Otherwise, you just a dog in the alley."

For Rainey, the blues is "a way of understanding life" that gives folks a sense they are not alone: "This be an empty world without the blues." As such, the blues has been a source of strength for African Americans, and performers like Ma Rainey have been bearers of cultural identity. A major theme of *Ma Rainey's Black Bottom* and of other plays by Wilson is the necessity of acknowledging one's past and connecting with one's culture.

African American identity, however, with its roots in Africa and the rural South, is at times rejected by the members of Ma Rainey's band. The pianist, Toledo, for example, points out the "ancestral retention" involved in the bass player's trying to get some marijuana from another band member by naming things they have done together—in effect, an African appeal to a bond of kinship. Toledo's observation is immediately rejected by the bass player, who replies: "I ain't no African!" and by Levee, the trumpet player, who remarks: "You don't see me running around in no jungle with no bone between my nose." Levee also has a loathing for the South, which he associates with sharecropping and general backwardness. Levee's disregard for African American heritage extends to Ma Rainey's style of blues, which he calls "old jug-band s**t." He resents her refusal to use his jazzed-up arrangements and, at the tragic end of the play, when his hopes for a recording contract of his own are dashed, his rage is misdirected at Toledo, who happens to step on his shoe, and whom he stabs with his knife.

SUGGESTED READINGS

Adell, Sandra. "Speaking of Ma Rainey / Talking about the Blues." In *May All Your Fences Have Gates: Essays on the Drama of August Wilson*, edited by Alan Nadel. Iowa City: University of Iowa Press, 1994.

Crawford, Eileen. "The B-flat Burden: The Invisibility of *Ma Rainey's Black Bottom*." In *August Wilson: A Casebook*, edited by Marilyn Elkins. New York: Garland, 1994.

Pereira, Kim. *August Wilson and the African-American Odyssey*. Champaign: University of Illinois Press, 1995.

Shannon, Sandra G. *The Dramatic Vision of August Wilson*. Washington, D.C.: Howard University Press, 1995.

—Jack Vincent Barbera

See also African American identity; *Fences*; *Two Trains Running*; Wilson, August

McCarthy, Cormac

BORN: Providence, Rhode Island; July 20, 1933

PRINCIPAL WORKS: *The Orchard Keeper*, 1965; *Outer Dark*, 1968; *Child of God*, 1973; *Suttree*, 1979; *Blood Meridian: Or, The Evening Redness in the West*, 1985; *All the Pretty Horses*, 1992; *The Crossing*, 1994

IDENTITIES: European American; West and Southwest

SIGNIFICANT ACHIEVEMENT: McCarthy's identity is that of a lone individualist whose novels, set in the South and Southwest, explore the dark side of American life.

Until the publication of *All the Pretty Horses*, which won national awards and recognition,

Cormac McCarthy
(David Styles)

Cormac McCarthy was something of a cult writer, kept alive by a devoted circle of critics and readers who appreciated his dark, brooding sensibility and poetic prose style. Although he is now a writer with a national reputation, McCarthy remains a mystery man. He eschews publicity and seldom grants interviews. Restless and elusive, he has divorced twice and has lived in Chicago, Las Vegas, New Orleans, London, Paris, and various border towns in Texas and Mexico.

McCarthy's fiction explores violence and evil as a countermyth to the more official and optimistic premises of American society. McCarthy's early novels are set in Tennessee, the state in which he grew up and in which he was largely educated. These novels are gothic and nihilistic, and they reflect in style and mood the influence of such Southern authors as William Faulkner and Flannery O'Connor. When McCarthy moved to Texas, his novels engaged with the tradition of the American Western. These meditative Westerns are his signature pieces, and the first of them, *Blood Meridian*, is the touchstone of the McCarthy canon. A gruesome historical novel set in the 1840's, *Blood Meridian* concerns the maraudings of a band of scalp hunters as they rape, murder, and plunder in the borderlands of the Southwest. His next two novels, *All the Pretty Horses* and *The Crossing*, are also stories of youthful initiation into evil and are the first two novels in a projected series. They are set in a postwar world of conflicting and competing cultures, economies, and systems of values, and significantly include the terrain and culture of Mexico as well as Texas. Although set in modern times, these novels follow *Blood Meridian* in seriously interpreting the genre of the American Western, adding a dark, mysterious dimension that sophisticates the form beyond its popular formulaic identity.

SUGGESTED READINGS

Arnold, Edin, and Diane C. Luce. *Perspectives on Cormac McCarthy.* Jackson: University Press of Mississippi, 1993.

Bell, Vereen M. *The Achievement of Cormac McCarthy.* Baton Rouge: Louisiana State University Press, 1988.

Young, Thomas Daniel. *Tennessee Writers.* Knoxville: University of Tennessee Press, 1981.

—Margaret Boe Birns

See also American identity: South; American identity: West and the frontier; Faulkner, William; O'Connor, Flannery; Violence

McCarthy, Mary

BORN: Seattle, Washington; June 21, 1912

DIED: New York, New York; October 25, 1989

PRINCIPAL WORKS: *The Oasis,* 1949; *Cast a Cold Eye,* 1950; *The Groves of Academe,* 1952; *Memories of a Catholic Girlhood,* 1957; *The Group,* 1963; *Vietnam,* 1967; *Hanoi,* 1968; *Birds of America,* 1971; *The Mask of State: Watergate Portraits,* 1974; *Cannibals and Missionaries,* 1979; *The Hounds of Summer and Other Stories,* 1981

IDENTITIES: Family; Northeast; women

SIGNIFICANT ACHIEVEMENT: McCarthy's insightful criticism dissected the artistic, political, and social attitudes prevalent in the United States from the 1930's to the 1980's.

Mary McCarthy was a gifted, controversial writer. Admired by many for her intellectual perception and blunt honesty, she also aroused intense dislike in those who felt the sting of her candor. She had been praised for her writing talent throughout school. After graduation from Vassar, she married Harold Johnsrud and moved to New York, where she began her career, writing reviews for magazines such as *The Nation* and *The New Republic*.

She was a demanding critic, analyzing each work without deference to the author's reputation. She first came to the attention of the literary world in 1935 with a series of essays for *The Nation*, criticizing some of the most prominent book reviewers in the country for ignorance about modern literature. McCarthy, used to the role of an outsider from childhood, had no qualms about challenging the establishment.

During the 1930's, McCarthy became increasingly involved in left-wing politics, eventually becoming an active Trotskyite. She became drama editor of *Partisan Review*, although she felt somewhat of an outsider in the male-dominated literary group involved with that magazine. After having divorced Johnsrud in 1936, she married Edmund Wilson, the critic. They had a tempestuous, even abusive, relationship; however, he encouraged her to write fiction, and her first story, "Cruel and Barbarous Treatment," was published in 1939. McCarthy's fiction makes use of her own experiences; she was often merciless in exposing the foibles and weaknesses of everyone, including herself. Throughout her career, she offended friends and acquaintances who saw themselves reflected, often unfavorably, in her stories. McCarthy and Wilson separated in 1945.

In 1946, she married Bowden Broadwater, who also encouraged her writing. Her final marriage, in 1961, was to James West, a career diplomat. This marriage suited her. McCarthy was an active critic of the Vietnam War, traveling to South Vietnam and Hanoi. Several of her books explored the political turmoil in the United States during the 1960's and 1970's. She continued to be active until the last year of her life.

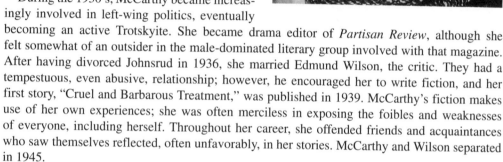

Mary McCarthy's The Group *(1963) created scandal for its honesty about women's lives; the author also embraced controversy in her politics. (Jerry Bauer)*

Suggested Readings

Brightman, Carol. *Writing Dangerously: Mary McCarthy and Her World*. New York: Clarkson N. Potter, 1992.

Gelderman, Carol. *Mary McCarthy: A Life*. New York: St. Martin's Press, 1988.

Hardy, Willene. *Mary McCarthy*. New York: Frederick Ungar, 1981.

McKenzie, Barbara. *Mary McCarthy*. New York: Twayne, 1967.

—*Mary Mahony*

See also Feminism; *Group, The*; *Memories of a Catholic Girlhood*; Vietnam War

McCullers, Carson (Lula Carson Smith)

Born: Columbus, Georgia; February 19, 1917
Died: Nyack, New York; September 29, 1967
Principal works: *The Heart Is a Lonely Hunter*, 1940; *Reflections in a Golden Eye*, 1941; *The Ballad of the Sad Café*, 1943; *The Member of the Wedding*, 1946
Identities: African American; European American; gay, lesbian, and bisexual; South

SIGNIFICANT ACHIEVEMENT: McCullers' Southern works represent initiation experiences and human isolation.

Carson McCullers was born Lula Carson Smith in Columbus, Georgia, a small town that resembles the setting of most of her works. As a child, McCullers studied the piano and was considered a prodigy, much like the main character in her critically acclaimed short story "Wunderkind" (1936), which is about fifteen-year-old Frances' aspirations to become a great pianist and her awakened sexuality. Like many of McCullers' short stories, "Wunderkind" is written in the *Bildungsroman* tradition, portraying adolescent initiation and search for identity. *The Heart Is a Lonely Hunter* and *The Member of the Wedding* also portray adolescent females searching for identity and struggling with complex internal questions. *Clock Without Hands* (1961) illustrates adolescent initiation experiences defined as a young mulatto man's search for knowledge of his birth parents and his African American heritage.

McCullers' portrayal of African American identities often demonstrates racial social injustices that occurred in America before the Civil Rights movement. Racial bias intensifies her African American characters' isolated feelings.

When she was seventeen, McCullers moved to New York, where she studied creative writing at Columbia University. Although she frequently returned to the South because of recurring illnesses, she felt ambivalent about her Southern heritage, saying her visits to the South brought about "a stirring up of love and antagonism."

McCullers experienced bisexual sexual identity throughout her early adulthood. In 1937, she married Reeves McCullers, and they lived in North Carolina until 1940, when they moved to the February House, where many well-known artists resided in New York. In 1940, McCullers fell in love with Annemarie Clarac-Schwarzenbach, to whom she dedicated her second novel, *Reflections in a Golden Eye*. In many of her works, McCullers depicts bisexual and androgynous characters.

In 1941, Carson divorced Reeves. She later remarried him, but because of declining health she frequently stayed with her mother and sister in Nyack, New York. She planned another divorce from Reeves in 1953, when he committed suicide. Although poor health affected her writing after 1947, her play *The Square Root of Wonderful* opened on Broadway in 1958. Her final novel, *Clock Without Hands*, presents issues related to McCullers' struggle with poor health. In the novel, J. T. Malone learns he has leukemia and faces death. McCullers died in 1967, having lived fifty years.

SUGGESTED READINGS

Carr, Virginia Spencer. *The Lonely Hunter: A Biography of Carson McCullers*. Garden City, N.Y.: Doubleday, 1975.

Cook, Richard. *Carson McCullers*. New York: Frederick Ungar, 1975.

Moore, Jack B. "Carson McCullers: The Heart Is a Timeless Hunter." *Twentieth Century Literature* 11 (July, 1965): 76-81.

—Laurie Champion

See also Adolescent identity; African American identity; American identity: South; *Ballad of the Sad Café, The*; *Bildungsroman* and *Künstlerroman*; *Reflections in a Golden Eye*

Macho!

AUTHOR: Victor Edmundo Villaseñor (1940-)

FIRST PUBLISHED: 1973

IDENTITIES: Latino; men

In this novel about a young Mexican who immigrates illegally into the United States, Victor Villaseñor suggests that the protagonist, Roberto, extracts his identity from the soil of the fields that he works. On the first and last pages of the novel, Villaseñor describes how volcanic ash has enriched the soil of a Mexican valley. At the end of the novel, Roberto has returned to this valley to work the land, applying what he has learned in the United States.

These homages to volcanic ash suggest that soil is not just the earth's outer covering but also its soul. Likewise, the soil is the soul of the people who work it. The novel refers to the Mexican Revolution of 1910, which was a popular movement to redistribute the ownership of land. In other words, land is fundamental to understanding not only the Mexican people but also the country's politics and history.

According to Villaseñor, Mexico's geography dictates the country's indigenous law. Mexico is mountainous, so villages are very isolated. As a result of their isolation, these villages develop their own systems of justice and never appeal to a higher authority. This law of the land is a violent code of honor, and the novel documents how this code places a premium on a woman's virginity and on a man's ability to fight. The definition of "macho" must necessarily emanate from an understanding of this law of the land.

The novel makes frequent references to César Chávez's movement in the 1960's to unionize agricultural workers in the United States. Villaseñor offers a complex portrait of Chávez, not allowing him to become a cardboard cutout representative of Mexicans who identify themselves with the soil. In the first place, one cannot make simplifications about Chávez because his movement distinguishes between the illegal Mexican immigrants, whom Chávez wants deported, and the Mexican Americans, whose rights Chávez seeks to protect through unionization. Furthermore, Chávez's identity is not simple because, while he is a hero to some, to others he is not macho because he is not a drinker or a womanizer.

Villaseñor concludes that Chávez is a "true-self hero," one who is not labeled readily as macho, but who trusts his own conscience and is not afraid to have enemies. In this respect, according to Villaseñor, Chávez is like Abraham Lincoln, Benito Juárez, John F. Kennedy, and Martin Luther King, Jr. On the novel's final page, Villaseñor qualifies Roberto also as a true-self hero when the protagonist returns to his native valley to work the fields.

Suggested readings

Lewis, Marvin A. *Introduction to the Chicano Novel*. Milwaukee: University of Wisconsin, Spanish Speaking Outreach Institute, 1982.

Shirley, Carl R., and Paula W. Shirley. *Understanding Chicano Literature*. Columbia: University of South Carolina Press, 1988.

Tatum, Charles M. *Chicano Literature*. Boston: Twayne, 1982.

—Douglas Edward LaPrade

See also Chicano identity; Civil Rights movement; Emigration and immigration; Latino American identity; Migratory workers

McKay, Claude

Born: Sunny Ville, Jamaica; September 15, 1889
Died: Chicago, Illinois; May 22, 1948
Principal works: *Constab Ballads*, 1912; *Songs of Jamaica*, 1912; *Spring in New Hampshire and Other Poems*, 1920; *Harlem Shadows*, 1922; *Home to Harlem*, 1928; *Banjo*, 1929; *Gingertown*, 1932; *Banana Bottom*, 1933; *A Long Way from Home*, 1937; *Harlem: Negro Metropolis*, 1940; *Selected Poems of Claude McKay*, 1953
Identities: African American; Caribbean
Significant achievement: McKay's writings capture the dialect of his native Jamaica, ushered in the Harlem Renaissance, and added a black voice to the early years of Soviet Communism.

Claude McKay was the youngest of eleven children in a rural Jamaican family. His parents instilled pride in an African heritage in their children. McKay's brother Uriah Theophilus and the English folklorist and linguist Walter Jekyll introduced McKay to philosophy and literature, notably to English poetry.

When he was nineteen McKay moved to Kingston and worked as a constable for almost a year. Encouraged by Jekyll, McKay published two volumes of poetry in Jamaican dialect in 1912, *Songs of Jamaica* and *Constab Ballads*. The first collection echoes McKay's love for the natural beauty of Jamaica while the second reflects his disenchantment with urban life in Kingston.

In 1912 McKay left Jamaica for the United States and studied at Tuskegee Institute in Alabama and at Kansas State College before moving to Harlem in 1914. His most famous poem, "If We Must Die," was published in 1919 and proved to be a harbinger of the Harlem Renaissance. The poem depicts violence as a dignified response to racial oppression.

Soon thereafter McKay published two other volumes of poetry, *Spring in New Hampshire and Other Poems* and *Harlem Shadows*, which portray the homesickness and racism that troubled McKay in the United States. Some of McKay's poems were anthologized in Alain Locke's *The New Negro* (1925), the bible of the Harlem Renaissance.

McKay also spent time in Europe and North Africa. In the Soviet Union in 1922 and 1923, he was lauded as a champion of the Communist movement and published a poem in *Pravda*. While in France in the 1920's, McKay preferred Marseilles over the white expatriate community in Paris.

McKay wrote three sociological novels about the attempts of black people to assimilate as outsiders in various places around the world: *Home to Harlem* is set in Harlem, *Banjo* in Marseilles, and *Banana Bottom* in Britain and Jamaica. The seamy realism of black urban life depicted in the first novel did not appeal to African American thinkers such as W. E. B. Du Bois, who preferred more uplifting and optimistic black art.

McKay continued to examine the place of black people in Western culture in his autobiography, *A Long Way from Home*, and in some of his posthumously published *Selected Poems of Claude McKay*. His conversion to Catholicism in his final years was the last step in his search for aesthetic, racial, and spiritual identity.

SUGGESTED READINGS

Cooper, Wayne F. *Claude McKay—Rebel Sojourner in the Harlem Renaissance: A Biography*. Baton Rouge: Louisiana State University Press, 1987.

Giles, James R. *Claude McKay*. Boston: Twayne, 1976.

Tillery, Tyrone. *Claude McKay: A Black Poet's Struggle for Identity*. Amherst: University of Massachusetts Press, 1992.

—*Douglas Edward LaPrade*

See also African American identity; Caribbean American literature; Du Bois, W. E. B.; Emigration and immigration; Harlem Renaissance

McMillan, Terry

BORN: Port Huron, Michigan; October 18, 1951

PRINCIPAL WORKS: *Mama*, 1987; *Disappearing Acts*, 1989; *Breaking Ice: An Anthology of Contemporary African-American Fiction*, 1990 (editor); *Waiting to Exhale*, 1992; *How Stella Got Her Groove Back*, 1996

IDENTITIES: African American; family; women

SIGNIFICANT ACHIEVEMENT: McMillan's novels and short stories explore the complex relationships among urban black women of the late twentieth century, their families, and the men in their lives.

Terry McMillan was reared near Detroit by working-class parents and later moved to Los Angeles, where she attended community college and read widely in the canon of African American literature. In 1979, at the age of twenty-eight, she received her bachelor of science degree from the University of California, Berkeley. In 1987, she began a three-year instructorship at the University of Wyoming, Laramie, and in 1988 received a coveted fellowship from the National Endowment for the Arts. After teaching in Tucson at the University of Arizona from 1990 to 1992, McMillan pursued writing as her full-time career.

The environment in which McMillan's views were formed prepared her for early marriage and a family, not the life of an intellectual and an artist. Her failure as an adult to meet the expectations of her culture and family created pressures that her work has consistently sought to address. Not surprisingly, her own struggle to adapt to cultural expectations resulted in an emphasis in her work on the tension in relationships between professional and blue-collar blacks, between women and men, and between members of the nuclear family. *Mama* depicts an acceptance by an intellectual daughter of her flawed mother. *Disappearing Acts* follows a love affair between a professional, responsible woman and an uneducated tradesman. *Waiting to Exhale* builds an ambitious collage of images from all three types of relationships.

McMillan's fiction addresses the archetypal dilemma of the disadvantaged—escaping the limitations imposed by one's culture and family while trying to preserve the advantages they inevitably offer. This dilemma leads her characters into conflicts of ideology; their struggle is the struggle for truth, their quest the search for meaning.

While some reviewers have attacked McMillan for her use of vulgar language, others have defended its realism and immediacy. The same is true of the explicit sexual references throughout her work, and indeed for her character portrayals themselves. Critics observe that MacMillan's characters all seem at times to have been exaggerated to achieve a calculated effect. McMillan's popularity, however, suggests that she understands her craft and that her audience approves her purpose.

Terry McMillan's books about African American women have been critical and commercial successes. (Marion Ettlinger)

SUGGESTED READINGS

Henderson, Mae Gwendolyn. "Speaking in Tongues: Dialogics, Dialectics, and the Black Woman Writer's Literary Tradition." In *Reading Black, Reading Feminist: A Critical Anthology*, edited by Henry Louis Gates, Jr. New York: Meridian, 1990.

Hernton, Calvin C. *The Sexual Mountain and Black Women Writers*. New York: Doubleday, 1987.

—Andrew B. Preslar

See also African American identity; Black English; Class and identity; Erotic identity

McMurtry, Larry

BORN: Wichita Falls, Texas; June 3, 1936

PRINCIPAL WORKS: *Horseman, Pass By*, 1961; *Leaving Cheyenne*, 1963; *The Last Picture Show*, 1966; *Moving On*, 1970; *All My Friends Are Going to Be Strangers*, 1972; *Terms of Endearment*, 1975; *Lonesome Dove*, 1985; *Streets of Laredo*, 1993; *Dead Man's Walk*, 1995

IDENTITIES: European American; family; West and Southwest

SIGNIFICANT ACHIEVEMENT: McMurtry's Southwestern novels portray the passing of the cowboy culture as social change brings death to old traditions.

Larry McMurtry has said that he grew up in a "bookless town" (Archer City, Texas) and compared his first stepping into a university library at age eighteen to the discovery of a literary landscape similar to the prairies on which his forebears settled. First at Rice University and then at the University of North Texas, he began serious reading and writing. His first novel, *Horseman, Pass By*, written in 1958, shortly after he was graduated from the University of North Texas, was published in 1961 after much polishing and revising. It tells the story of motherless young Lonnie

Bannon struggling to reconcile the noble tradition of cowboy honor and individualism represented by his grandfather, Homer, and the new opportunistic, exploitative attitude of his stepbrother, Hud. Made into a highly successful film, *Hud* (1963), this youthful book brought McMurtry to national attention, and he soon produced *Leaving Cheyenne* and *The Last Picture Show*, also set in the Texas ranching country surrounding the fictional Texas town of Thalia and tracing the passing of an old order as ranching gives way to oil.

After this Thalia trilogy, McMurtry turned to explore the urban side of the social transformation. His next three novels, known as the urban trilogy, represent a radical departure from the earlier books. Their recurring characters seem to have lost sight of a guiding past and to have no purposeful

Larry McMurtry achieved great success early in his career with his books about the American West. (Library of Congress)

future. McMurtry returned to the "horseman-god" for his Pulitzer Prize-winning *Lonesome Dove*. This epic story of former Texas Rangers Augustus McRae and Woodrow Call is set in the final years of the open range and great cattle drives. McMurtry's earlier themes—social change, the death of old traditions, the importance of the land, and the plight of a youth finding his way without familial or cultural stability—are revisited here with new depth and power. With this novel and *Streets of Laredo*, which completes Call's story after McRae's death, and *Dead Man's Walk*, which fills in the two men's early years as Texas Rangers, McMurtry taps the strength of his regional roots and achieves his full stature as a novelist.

SUGGESTED READINGS

Busby, Mark. *Larry McMurtry and the West: An Ambivalent Relationship.* Denton: University of North Texas Press, 1995.

Peavy, Charles D. *Larry McMurtry.* Boston: Twayne, 1977.

Reynolds, Clay, ed. *Taking Stock: A Larry McMurtry Casebook.* Dallas: Southern Methodist University Press, 1989.

Sewell, Ernestine P. "McMurtry's Cowboy-God in *Lonesome Dove*." *Western American Literature* 21 (November, 1986): 219-225.

—Jeff H. Campbell

See also Adolescent identity; American identity: West and the frontier; *Last Picture Show, The*; Rural life

McNickle, D'Arcy

BORN: St. Ignatius, Montana; January 18, 1904

DIED: Albuquerque, New Mexico; October 18, 1977

PRINCIPAL WORKS: *The Surrounded*, 1936; *La Política de los Estados Unidos sobre los gobiernos tribales y las empresas comunales de los Indios*, 1942 (with Joseph C. McCaskill); *They Came Here First: The Epic of the American Indian*, 1949, rev. 1975; *Runner in the Sun: A Story of Indian Maize*, 1954 (with Harold E. Fey); *Indians and Other Americans: Two Ways of Life Meet*, 1959, rev. ed. 1970; *Indian Man: A Life of Oliver La Farge*, 1971; *Native American Tribalism: Indian Survivals and Renewals*, 1973; *Wind from an Enemy Sky*, 1978; *The Hawk Is Hungry and Other Stories*, 1992

IDENTITIES: Native American

SIGNIFICANT ACHIEVEMENT: In novels, short stories, children's books, and scholarly works, McNickle focuses on communication problems between Native Americans and the dominant culture.

Born to a Scotch-Irish father and a French Canadian mother of Cree heritage, D'Arcy McNickle knew from an early age the problems of mixed identity that many Native Americans experience. Reared on a northwestern Montana ranch, McNickle, along with his family, was adopted into the Salish-Kootanai Indian tribe. Attending Oxford University and the University of Grenoble in France after completing his undergraduate education at the University of Montana, McNickle was as firmly grounded in Native American culture as he was in the white world.

Completing his formal education when the United States was gripped by the Depression, McNickle was among the writers who joined the Federal Writer's Project, with which he was associated from 1935 to 1936. His first novel, *The Surrounded*, was an outgrowth of this association. This book focuses on how an Indian tribe disintegrates as the United States government encroaches upon and ultimately grabs tribal lands and then sets out to educate the Native American children in such a way as to denigrate their culture and integrate them into the dominant society. Like McNickle, the protagonist of this novel, Archilde, has a mixed identity, being the offspring of a Spanish father and a Native American mother.

In his children's book, *Runner in the Sun*, McNickle deals with similar questions of identity centering on the inevitable conflicts between whites and Native Americans. The Native Americans strive in vain to preserve their culture and retain their grazing lands.

Such also is the focus of McNickle's posthumous novel, *Wind from an Enemy Sky*, in which tribal lands are condemned for the building of a dam and the sacred medicine bundle is given to a museum for display. McNickle also produced several works of nonfiction that grew out of his tenure with the Bureau of Indian Affairs and his directorship of the Bureau's division of American Indian development.

SUGGESTED READINGS

Parker, Dorothy R. *Singing an Indian Song: A Biography of D'Arcy McNickle*. Lincoln: University of Nebraska Press, 1992.

Ruppert, James. *D'Arcy McNickle*. Boise, Idaho: Boise State University Press, 1988.

_____. "Textual Perspectives and the Reader in *The Surrounded*." In *Narrative Chance: Postmodern Discourse on Native American Indian Literatures*, edited by Gerald Vizenor. Albuquerque: University of New Mexico Press, 1989.

—*R. Baird Shuman*

See also Acculturation; Mixed race and identity; Native American identity

Madwoman in the Attic: The Woman Writer and the Nineteenth-Century Literary Imagination, The

AUTHORS: Sandra M. Gilbert (1936-   ) and Susan Gubar (1944-   )
FIRST PUBLISHED: 1979
IDENTITIES: Women

The Madwoman in the Attic: The Woman Writer and the Nineteenth-Century Literary Imagination addresses the struggle that nineteenth century women writers underwent in order to determine their identities as writers. The work particularly analyzes the portrayal of women's identity in female authors' works of fiction and poetry. *The Madwoman in the Attic* quickly became a classic of feminist literary criticism. The book is notable for the incisiveness and for the clarity with which it recognizes a single theme in women's literature and for the encyclopedic breadth of information that it contains. The authors divided responsibility for drafting the chapters, and together wrote the introductory material.

Sandra Gilbert and Susan Gubar argue that nineteenth century women writers were faced with two debilitating stereotypical images of women; women were depicted in male writing as angels or as monsters. The pen in the male literary imagination was metaphorically seen as a penis, excluding women from the authority of authorship. Faced with such images, women writers suffered from an "anxiety of authorship," in contrast with the "anxiety of influence" Harold Bloom attributes to male authors. Their writings reveal this anxiety in the prevalence of submissive heroines and madwomen. These contrasting female types express the author's sense of division. The submissive heroine accepts cultural pressures to act as nineteenth century women were expected to act. The madwoman, on the other hand, vents the author's rage and her desire to reject the constraints her male-dominated culture places upon her. For example, in Charlotte Brontë's *Jane Eyre* (1847), the submissive Jane learns that Edward Rochester, whom she would have as her husband, already has a wife, the insane Bertha. Edward keeps Bertha locked upstairs in his mansion. Gilbert and Gubar see Jane's encounter with Bertha as a meeting with part of herself.

The majority of the works analyzed in *The Madwoman in the Attic* are by British authors: Jane Austen, Mary Shelley, Emily Brontë, Charlotte Brontë, and George Eliot receive chapter-length treatments. The poetry of American Emily Dickinson also is given substantial analysis. The vast range of references to major and minor works by women indicates that the struggle for identity and for authority of authorship is common to British and American women writers. These women writers, whether widely read or obscure and whether on one side of the Atlantic or the other, were exposed to literature written by the same male writers and to the same stereotypes and prevailing images of their cultures.

SUGGESTED READINGS

Bloom, Harold. *The Anxiety of Influence*. New York: Oxford University Press, 1973.

Heilbrun, Carolyn G. Review of *The Madwoman in the Attic*, by Sandra M. Gilbert and Susan Gubar. *The Washington Post Book World* 9 (November 25, 1979): 4.

Moi, Toril. *Sexual/Textual Politics: Feminist Literary Theory*. London: Routledge & Kegan Paul, 1985.

—*Joan Hope*

See also Feminism; Gilbert, Sandra M., and Susan Gubar; *No Man's Land*; Women and identity

Mailer, Norman

BORN: Long Branch, New Jersey; January 31, 1923

PRINCIPAL WORKS: *The Naked and the Dead*, 1948; *Barbary Shore*, 1951; *The Deer Park*, 1955; *Advertisements for Myself*, 1959; *The Presidential Papers*, 1963; *An American Dream*, 1965; *Cannibals and Christians*, 1966; *Why Are We in Vietnam?*, 1967; *The Armies of the Night: History as a Novel, the Novel as History*, 1968; *Miami and the Siege of Chicago*, 1968; *The Prisoner of Sex*, 1971; *The Executioner's Song*, 1979; *Ancient Evenings*, 1983; *Tough Guys Don't Dance*, 1984; *Oswald's Tale*, 1994

IDENTITIES: European American; Jewish; men

SIGNIFICANT ACHIEVEMENT: Mailer's nonfiction explores American and European cultural figures; his novels concentrate on heroes battling for their identities.

Norman Mailer attained fame in 1948 with his best-selling and critically acclaimed war novel, *The Naked and the Dead*. This work provides an encyclopedic view of Americans from all regions and ethnic identities going to war. Mailer's public celebrity forced upon him a keen consciousness of his own role in the culture. Repeatedly asked about his own opinions of politics and social issues, he began using fiction and nonfiction to explore his own identity—which was often in conflict with American values.

Whatever Mailer's subject—the Democratic convention that nominated John F. Kennedy in 1960 in *The Presidential Papers* or the protest against the Vietnam War in *The Armies of the Night*—he was concerned with how he could create an identity in the face of pressures to conform to society's dictates. *The Deer Park* and *An American Dream* feature heroes in conflict with American powers such as the Hollywood film industry and business tycoons.

Mailer made himself a controversial subject not only in his writing but in his life. He seemed to advocate a violent rejection of the status quo. "The White Negro" in *Advertisements for Myself* lauds the style of some African Americans and their white imitators who lived on the margins of society. His aggressive style was called into question when he stabbed his second wife and was briefly detained at Bellevue Hospital in 1960, shortly before he was to declare his candidacy for mayor of New York City.

In the late 1960's and 1970's Mailer came under increasing attack for his treatment of

Norman Mailer's fame began with The Naked and the Dead *(1948).* (Library of Congress)

women, with some critics becoming outraged that in his novel *An American Dream* the main character, Stephen Rojack, murders his wife and gets away with it. Mailer answers his critics in *The Prisoner of Sex* and made the issue of a woman's identity the crucial subject of his biography of Marilyn Monroe.

In the later stages of his career, Mailer has turned to issues of capital punishment, espionage, and assassination, probing, in *The Executioner's Song*, *Harlot's Ghost* (1991), and *Oswald's Tale*, the identities of murderer Gary Gilmore, of various spies in the Central Intelligence Agency, and of the assassin Lee Harvey Oswald in order to explore the shifting nature of American identity.

SUGGESTED READINGS

Lennon, J. Michael, ed. *Conversations with Norman Mailer.* Jackson: University Press of Mississippi, 1988.

Millett, Kate. *Sexual Politics.* New York: Doubleday, 1970.

Rollyson, Carl. *The Lives of Norman Mailer: A Biography.* New York: Paragon House, 1991.

—Carl Rollyson

See also American Dream; *American Dream, An*; *Naked and the Dead, The*; Vietnam War; World War II

Main Street: The Story of Carol Kennicott

AUTHOR: Sinclair Lewis (1885-1951)

FIRST PUBLISHED: 1920

IDENTITIES: European American; Midwest

Main Street: The Story of Carol Kennicott is a satiric attack on small-town life. In the 1920's, a large component of America's middle class sought a more liberal identity. The novel depicts the young, romantic Carol Kennicott's progressive disillusionment with life in a typical, old-fashioned American small town. Readers first see the bright, idealistic Carol alone on a hilltop, dreaming of the great things she will do in the future, feeling that she can conquer the world. She has an opportunity to realize one dream—to transform an ugly village into a thing of beauty—when she marries Dr. Will Kennicott and moves with him to the town of Gopher Prairie. Her attempts to bring liberal ideas to this philistine backwater prove futile; Gopher Prairie is not only resistant to her reforms but also suspicious of the reformer. She becomes a member of a group of socially prominent wives who call themselves the Jolly Seventeen, but they take umbrage at her sympathy for what was at that time a largely German and Scandinavian working class, instead defending their social and economic system against any thoughts of reform. Similarly, the literary Thanatopsis club rejects any efforts to improve their aesthetic sensibilities. Everywhere she sees a deep-rooted aversion to change. Carol's dreams are shattered by the dull reality of a narrow, petty, homogenous, white middle class bent on its own security and on the preservation of the status quo. When one of her friends tells her the townsfolk are criticizing her every movement, from her offbeat parties to her generous and egalitarian treatment of Bea, her Scandinavian housemaid, Carol is devastated and never quite recovers from the strong hostility she realizes that she has aroused.

The birth of a son brings some joy, but continuing tensions with the town and with her husband leave her restless and frustrated. Like the rest of Gopher Prairie, Will is suspicious of new ideas, harbors serious prejudices about class and nationality, and has little appreciation for his wife's aesthetic impulses. While Will finds consolation with a mistress, Carol flirts with a couple of like-minded free spirits but, continually discontent, leaves Will and escapes on her own to a job in Washington, D.C. She returns, however, two years later, deciding at last to compromise with Will and with the town. She has not, however, totally succumbed to "the village virus" that Sinclair Lewis suggests turns lively minds into dull and acquiescent ones. At the end of the novel, Carol confidently predicts that her new baby daughter will be "a bomb" that will eventually destroy the crushingly self-satisfied mediocrity of American small towns.

SUGGESTED READINGS
Bloom, Harold, ed. *Sinclair Lewis*. New York: Chelsea House, 1987.
Bucco, Martin. *Main Street: The Revolt of Carol Kennicott*. New York: Twayne, 1993.
Dooley, D. J. *The Art of Sinclair Lewis*. Lincoln: University of Nebraska Press, 1967.
Grebstein, Sheldon Norman. *Sinclair Lewis*. New York: Twayne, 1962.

—Margaret Boe Birns

See also American identity: Midwest; *Babbitt*; Lewis, Sinclair

Malamud, Bernard

BORN: Brooklyn, New York; April 26, 1914
DIED: New York, New York; March 18, 1986
PRINCIPAL WORKS: *The Natural*, 1952; *The Assistant*, 1957; *The Magic Barrel*, 1958; *A New Life*, 1961; *Idiots First*, 1963; *The Fixer*, 1966; *Pictures of Fidelman: An Exhibition*, 1969; *The Tenants*, 1971; *Rembrandt's Hat*, 1973; *Dubin's Lives*, 1979; *God's Grace*, 1982
IDENTITIES: Jewish
SIGNIFICANT ACHIEVEMENT: Malamud's works present the outsider, usually a Jew, who epitomizes the individual who must make moral choices.

Bernard Malamud's youth was spent in a setting much like that in *The Assistant*. His father was the owner of a small, struggling grocery store. His mother died when he was an adolescent. As a youth he had the freedom to wander around Brooklyn becoming intimately acquainted with the

Bernard Malamud, author of The Natural *(1952).* (Jerry Bauer)

neighborhood. It was not a Jewish neighborhood, but Malamud came to understand the Jewish experience through his hardworking parents, immigrants from Russia.

Malamud began writing stories in high school, and his writing career reflects the discipline and determination of many of his characters. After graduating from Erasmus High School, he earned a Bachelor's degree from City College of New York. He then attended Columbia University and earned the Master's degree that enabled him to teach. He taught immigrants in evening school in Brooklyn then in Harlem for eight years, while writing short stories, before getting a job at Oregon State College in Cascadia, Oregon. There he wrote four novels and a collection of short stories. Malamud received the National Book Award for the short-story collection, *The Magic Barrel*, in 1959. He also received the Pulitzer Prize in fiction and the National Book Award for *The Fixer* in 1967. He accepted a position at Bennington College in Vermont in 1961, where he spent the rest of his teaching career, except for two years as a visiting lecturer at Harvard.

Malamud's work has an allegorical quality like that of Nathaniel Hawthorne. His stories also reflect the Eastern European storytelling tradition. In this he is like such Yiddish writers as Sholom Aleichem and Isaac Leib Peretz. When Malamud describes, for example, a luckless character (called, in Jewish culture, a *schlemiel*) living in Brooklyn in the twentieth century, that person seems quite like someone living in the Jewish section of a Polish village. Malamud also captures in his works the sense of irony that pervades the folk stories of a people who recognize themselves as the chosen people and as the outcasts of society.

Malamud saw this paradoxical position as being the plight of all humanity, and he found in the Jew the ideal metaphor for the struggling human being. Acceptance of Jewish identity becomes, for his characters, acceptance of the human condition. Fusing this theme with a style that utilizes irony and parable, realism and symbolism, he presents the flourishing of the human spirit in an everyday reality of pressure and pain.

SUGGESTED READINGS

Hershinow, Sheldon J. *Bernard Malamud*. New York: Frederick Ungar, 1980.
Richman, Sydney. *Bernard Malamud*. New York: Twayne, 1966.
Solotaroff, Robert. *Bernard Malamud: A Study of the Short Fiction*. Boston: Twayne, 1989.

—Bernadette Flynn Low

See also *Assistant, The*; *Fixer, The*; Jewish American identity; *Natural, The*

Malcolm X

BORN: Omaha, Nebraska; May 19, 1925
DIED: New York, New York; February 21, 1965
PRINCIPAL WORKS: *The Autobiography of Malcolm X*, 1965 (with Alex Haley); *Malcolm X Speaks: Selected Speeches and Statements*, 1965; *By Any Means Necessary: Speeches, Interviews, and a Letter*, 1970
IDENTITIES: African American
SIGNIFICANT ACHIEVEMENT: Malcolm X went from being a street hustler to being a black leader and a symbol of fearless resistance against oppression.

Malcolm X's (born Malcolm Little) early years were marked by unsettling events: His family, threatened by the Ku Klux Klan in Omaha, moved to Lansing, Michigan, only to have their house burned down by a white hate group. Malcolm's father died in 1931 under mysterious circumstances, leaving his mother with the task of raising eight children. Malcolm eventually moved to Boston in 1941 and to New York in 1943, where he first experienced the street life of the African American urban poor. After becoming a burglar, he received a six-year prison term for armed robbery. In prison, he converted to the Nation of Islam and read voraciously on philosophy, theology, and history. The Nation of Islam helped him to acquire self-respect and gave him a new worldview, one that celebrated African American history and culture and in which whites were seen as forces of evil. Two years after his release, Malcolm—who by then had changed his last

Malcolm X recounted the evils of racism in the United States in his autobiography and speeches. (Library of Congress)

name to "X" in order to shed any links to a past in which white slave masters gave African American slaves their last names—became minister of the New York Temple Number Seven and the national spokesperson for the Nation of Islam. He brought unprecedented attention to the Nation: At a time when much of the United States was still segregated, Malcolm X voiced fearlessly what others only thought and denounced white racist practices.

Advocating strong moral codes and behaviors, Malcolm X became disenchanted with the Nation, suspecting the covert immorality of some leaders. After leaving the Nation of Islam, Malcolm X went on a pilgrimage to Mecca, where his warm reception by white Muslims (and his earlier contact in America with white students and journalists) led him to reject his earlier declarations that all whites were evil, and he accepted orthodox Islam as his faith. He adopted the name el-Hajj Malik el-Shabazz. Malcolm X traveled to Africa, meeting African leaders and recognizing the links between imperialist oppression of Africa and the situation of African Americans. Malcolm X was assassinated in New York after beginning to build Organization of Afro-American Unity, which featured cross-racial alliances and an international outlook.

SUGGESTED READINGS

Carson, Clayborne. *Malcolm X: The FBI File*. New York: Carroll & Graf, 1991.

Cone, James H. *Martin and Malcolm and America*. Maryknoll, N.Y.: Orbis Books, 1991.

Dyson, Michael Eric. *Making Malcolm: The Myth and Meaning of Malcolm X*. New York: Oxford University Press, 1995.

Malcolm X, with Alex Haley. *The Autobiography of Malcolm X*. New York: Grove Press, 1965.

Myers, Walter Dean. *Malcolm X: By Any Means Necessary*. New York: Scholastic, 1993.

—*Martin Japtok*

See also African American identity; *Autobiography of Malcolm X, The*; Nation of Islam

Mambo Kings Play Songs of Love, The

AUTHOR: Oscar Hijuelos (1951-   )

FIRST PUBLISHED: 1989

IDENTITIES: Family; Latino

Oscar Hijuelos' life in an advertising agency had little to do with his passion for writing. When he first began thinking of the story that would become *The Mambo Kings Play Songs of Love*, he knew that an uncle and an elevator operator would be his models. The uncle, a musician with Xavier Cugat in the 1930's and a building superintendent patterned after an elevator-operator-musician merged to become Cesar Castillo, the Mambo King. Cesar's brother, Nestor, laconic, retrospective, lamenting the loss of a lover he left behind in Cuba, writes the song in her memory that draws the attention of Ricky Ricardo. He hears "Beautiful María of my Soul" as he catches the Mambo Kings in a seedy nightclub where gigs are cheap but long. Ricky's interest changes their lives. The book altered Hijuelos' literary career by winning for him the Pulitzer Prize in fiction in 1990.

As the book opens, Cesar rots with his half-empty whiskey glass tipped at the TV beaming reruns. He seeks the *I Love Lucy* spot featuring Nestor and him as the Mambo Kings. Nestor has died. Cesar pathetically broods on the aging process, cirrhosis, and the loss of flamboyant times. Cesar's old, scratchy records—brittle and warped—resurrect his music stardom. He laments his brother's death by leafing through fading pictures.

In *The Mambo Kings Play Songs of Love*, Hijuelos presents pre-Castro Cubans, who, after World War II, streamed to New York. All communities may strive for the American Dream, but in Latino quarters, music, the mainstream of a culture, sought to free the oppressed. Hijuelos pursues thematic progression: The Castillo brothers become, for a moment, cultural icons by their appearance on *I Love Lucy*. Their fame does not last, however; Cesar comforts his ego with debauchery, and Nestor dies suddenly. The ironically named Hotel Splendour is where Cesar commits suicide.

SUGGESTED READINGS

Barbato, Joseph. "Latino Writers in the American Market." *Publishers Weekly* 238, no. 6 (February 1, 1991): 17-21.

Chávez, Lydia. "Cuban Riffs: Songs of Love." *Los Angeles Times Magazine*, April 18, 1993, 22-28.

Coffey, Michael. "Oscar Hijuelos." *Publishers Weekly* 236, no. 3 (July 21, 1989): 42-44.

Kamp, James, ed. *Reference Guide to American Literature*. 3d ed. Detroit, Mich.: St. James Press, 1994.

—*Craig Gilbert*

See also Hijuelos, Oscar; Latino American identity; *Mr. Ives' Christmas*; *Silent Dancing*

Man with Night Sweats, The

AUTHOR: Thom Gunn (1929-   )

FIRST PUBLISHED: 1992

IDENTITIES: Disease; gay, lesbian, and bisexual

The Man with Night Sweats is a collection of poems whose subject is the way people face death, particularly the way that gay men suffering from acquired immune deficiency syndrome (AIDS) have courageously fought that disease. Thom Gunn's book was praised by critics as a landmark, one of the first books of poetry about AIDS. Paul Monette's *Borrowed Time: An AIDS Memoir* (1988) was one of the first works of prose on this subject.

Born in England, Gunn has lived in San Francisco since 1960. Changing social attitudes and life in a more liberated sexual environment helped Gunn to express his sexual identity. He came out as a gay man in a 1976 book of poems called *Jack Straw's Castle*. The example of other gay writers, such as W. H. Auden, Christopher Isherwood, and Robert Duncan has also given Gunn the courage to write openly about homosexuality in his poetry.

Disliking obscure poetry, Gunn communicates in strong, simple words so that readers can understand his basic meaning on a first reading. The persons with AIDS in his poems work through feelings of fear, grief, rage, self-pity, and defeat in order to retain their courage and hope in the face of this disease. One long poem, "Lament," is written in heroic couplets emphasizing an AIDS sufferer's courageous effort to express himself despite the tube that doctors put down his throat, and how terribly difficult it is for him to reconcile himself to an early death, to die incomplete, before he has fulfilled his role in life. Many of the poems connect heroic poetry with the poetry of everyday life, showing the extraordinary bravery of persons struggling to live with AIDS.

"In Time of Plague" looks at how disease may change people's behavior and their sense of themselves. People who once defined themselves as risk-takers, daring to make emotional and sexual connections with other people, may have to reconsider how many risks are worth taking in a time when the exchange of bodily fluids could bring AIDS. If the message that taking certain kinds of risks could have mortal consequences sounds didactic, it should be noted that Gunn, while never preachy, does not hesitate to instruct people through his poems, for he believes that poetry should have moral import.

Gunn's book concludes on a note of hope, an optimistic poem called "The Blank" about a gay man who chooses to raise a child, helping the boy discover his own identity—whatever that identity turns out to be.

SUGGESTED READINGS

Gunn, Thom. *Collected Poems*. New York: Noonday Press, 1994.

_____. *Shelf Life: Essays, Memoirs, and an Interview*. Ann Arbor: University of Michigan Press, 1993.

Wilmer, Clive. "Thom Gunn: The Art of Poetry LXXII." *Paris Review* 37, no. 135 (Summer, 1995): 143-189.

—*Douglas Keesey*

See also AIDS; American identity: West and the frontier; Gay identity

Man with the Golden Arm, The

AUTHOR: Nelson Algren (Nelson Ahlgren Abraham, 1909-1981)

FIRST PUBLISHED: 1949

IDENTITIES: European American; Midwest

The Man with the Golden Arm was at first critically acclaimed, and it won the National Book Award in 1950. The protagonist, Frankie Machine (Majcinek), is also known as The Dealer. His metaphoric golden arm is a reference to his dice expertise at Zero Schwiefka's gambling parlor and to his injecting morphine to escape his problems. The novel is set in the somber buildings and dark alleys of Division Street in Chicago.

Often considered a naturalistic novel in the tradition of Stephen Crane, Frank Norris, and Theodore Dreiser, *The Man with the Golden Arm* presents morally bankrupt characters who cruelly exploit one another to survive. Violet Koskoska, for example, is a sexual predator who habitually locks her aged husband in a broom closet. Violet's lover, Sparrow Saltskin, a street thug, only wants Violet because she is easy sex. Sparrow even finishes eating a sausage sandwich while climbing into bed with Violet. It is during this grotesquely humorous scene that Violet states one of the novel's themes, that is, that any love is better than no love at all.

The self-destructive quest for love as a liberating force pervades the novel. Frankie's wife Sophie believes herself to be permanently crippled from a car accident caused by Frankie's drunk driving. Sophie keeps newspaper clippings of particularly freakish deaths and ridicules Frankie's dream of playing drums in a jazz band. A crutch is a symbol of her madness. Frankie, however, needs this sadistic behavior to justify his own inertia.

In contrast to the living death of Sophie, Molly-0 (Molly Novotny) represents vital love and passion. She stays with the brutal alcoholic Drunkie John because, like Sophie, Molly believes that even violent love is better than nothing. Molly comes to understand Frankie's desire for her equals her need for him. Casting Frankie as a rescuer from the sordid world of Division Street, however, is a tragic error for Molly. Frankie cannot cope with Sophie's madness, with Molly's idealism, and with morphine's control over him. He kills his dealer and finally commits suicide by hanging himself with the twine from a bundle of old newspapers. The environmental determinism pervading the novel is softened in the film version, which appeared in 1955, starring Frank Sinatra and Kim Novak. The film's changes contradict the novel's oppressive atmosphere and eliminates Nelson Algren's compassion for his marginalized characters.

The Man with the Golden Arm was harshly criticized during the 1960's for its perceived sentimentality. During the 1980's, however, writers defended the novel as having an existential theme written in a jazz lyrical style.

SUGGESTED READINGS

Gelfant, Blanche H. *The American City Novel.* Norman: University of Oklahoma Press, 1954.

Gilman, Sander L. *Difference and Pathology: Stereotypes of Sexuality, Race, and Madness.* Ithaca, N.Y.: Cornell University Press, 1985.

Tanner, Tony. *City of Words.* London: Jonathan Cape, 1971.

—*Helen O'Hara Connell*

See also Algren, Nelson; Erotic identity; Urban life

Management of Grief, The

AUTHOR: Bharati Mukherjee (1940-   )

FIRST PUBLISHED: 1988

IDENTITIES: Canada; family; religion; South Asian; women

Based on an actual event—the Sikh terrorist bombing of an Air India plane on June 23, 1985, which killed all 329 passengers and crew—"The Management of Grief" is Bharati Mukherjee's "tribute to all who forget enough of their roots to start over enthusiastically in a new land, but who also remember enough of their roots to survive fate's knockout punches." Mukherjee's story focuses on Shaila Bhave in the hours, days, and months following the deaths of her husband and two young sons. The story focuses on her forms of grief and guilt, which are specific to her culture. As an Indian wife, she never spoke her husband's name or told him she loved him—simple acts that Westerners take for granted. Her grief reveals who Shaila is, was, and will be. As do many of the characters in Mukherjee's stories and novels, she finds herself caught between cultures, countries, and existences. "At thirty-six," she considers, "I am too old to start over and too young to give up. Like my husband's spirit, I flutter between two worlds."

One of the worlds is Indian, including the highly supportive Hindu community in Toronto, from which she feels strangely detached. The Hindu community in Toronto is itself part of a larger Indian immigrant community that includes Muslims, Parsis, atheists, and even the Sikhs, tied by religion if not necessarily by politics to those responsible for the bombing, which is part of a struggle for autonomy being waged by Sikh extremists in India. Even within Toronto's Hindu community there are divided allegiances as parents "lose" their children to Western culture no less than to terrorist bombs. The other world, the "West," or more specifically Canada, is equally problematic, especially for Indian immigrants such as Mrs. Bhave, who are made to feel at best marginalized, at worst excluded altogether. She experiences the insensitivity of police investigators, the inadequacy of news coverage (the implicit message is that the victims and their families are not really Canadian), and finally the well-intentioned but ineffectual efforts of a government social worker's textbook approach to "grief management." The social worker enlists Mrs. Bhave's help in assisting those who have not been "coping so well."

The story's complex identity theme is reflected in its spatial diversity. It follows Mrs. Bhave from Toronto to Ireland (to identify remains) and then to India, where she believes she hears her husband's voice telling her: "You must finish alone what we started together." This seemingly irrational link to tradition, including her thinking that her husband and sons "surround her like creatures in epics," gives her the strength to leave India and return to Canada. Although she does not assume, as some of the older relatives do, that God will provide, she is provided for and in a way that precludes the reader's seeing her as entirely representative. Thanks to her husband's savings and the sale of their house, she is financially secure and so can afford to heed her dead husband's final admonition: "Go, be brave." Her future, including her future identity, may be uncertain, but in that uncertainty Shaila Bhave finds her freedom, one inextricably rooted in loss.

Suggested Readings

Carter-Sanborn, Kristin. "'We Murder Who We Were': *Jasmine* and the Violence of Identity." *American Literature* 66, no. 3 (September, 1994): 573-593.

Moyers, Bill. "An Interview with Bharati Mukherjee." In *Connections: A Multicultural Reader for Writers*, edited by Judith A. Stanford. Mountain View, Calif.: Mayfield, 1993.

Mukherjee, Bharati, and Clark Blaise. *The Sorrow and the Pity: The Haunting Legacy of the Air India Tragedy.* Markham, Ontario: Viking, 1987.

—*Robert A. Morace*

See also Acculturation; Asian American identity: India; Emigration and immigration; *Middleman and Other Stories, The*; Mukherjee, Bharati

Manchild in the Promised Land

Author: Claude Brown (1937-   )

First published: 1965

Identities: African American; Northeast

Claude Brown's classic autobiography *Manchild in the Promised Land* is a quintessentially American story of hardship and disadvantage overcome through determination and hard work, but with a critical difference. It became a best-seller when it was published in 1965 because of its startlingly realistic portrayal of growing up in Harlem. Without sermonizing or sentimentalizing, Brown manages to evoke a vivid sense of the day-to-day experience of the ghetto, which startled many readers and became required reading, along with *The Autobiography of Malcolm X* (1965), for many civil rights activists.

Manchild in the Promised Land describes Brown's resistance to a life path that seemed predetermined by the color of his skin and the place he was born. In the tradition of the slave narrative of the nineteenth century, Brown sets about to establish his personhood to a wide audience, many of whom would write him off as a hopeless case. The book opens with the scene of Brown being shot in the stomach at the age of thirteen after he and his gang are caught stealing bed sheets off a laundry line. What follows is the storyline most would expect of a ghetto child—low achievement in school, little parental supervision, and a sense of hopelessness about the future. There are crime, violence, and drugs lurking in every corner of Harlem, and young Sonny (Claude) falls prey to many temptations.

In spite of spending most of his early years committing various petty crimes, playing hooky from school, living in reform schools, and being the victim of assorted beatings and shootings, Brown manages to elude the destiny of so many of his boyhood friends—early death or successively longer incarcerations. Sensing that he would perish, literally or figuratively, if he remained on the path that seemed destined for him, he leaves Harlem for a few years and begins to chart a different outcome for his life, which includes night school, playing the piano, graduating from Howard University, and beginning law school.

Although Brown offers no formula for escaping the devastation that so often plagues ghetto life, he shows by example that it is possible to succeed in constructing, even in the ghetto, a positive identity.

SUGGESTED READINGS

Baker, Houston A., Jr. "The Environment as Enemy in a Black Autobiography: *Manchild in the Promised Land*." *Phylon* 32 (Spring-Summer, 1971): 53-59.

Hartshorne, Thomas L. "Horatio Alger in Harlem: *Manchild in the Promised Land*." *Journal of American Studies* 24, no. 2 (August, 1990): 243-251.

—*Christy Rishoi*

See also African American identity; American identity: Northeast; Brown, Claude; Slave narratives

Mansfield, Katherine (Katherine Mansfield Beauchamp)

BORN: Wellington, New Zealand; October 14, 1888
DIED: Fontainbleau, France; January 9, 1923
PRINCIPAL WORKS: *In a German Pension*, 1911; "Prelude," 1917; *Bliss and Other Stories*, 1920; *The Garden Party and Other Stories*, 1922
IDENTITIES: Women; world
SIGNIFICANT ACHIEVEMENT: Mansfield's stories revolutionized the art of short fiction.

For at least thirty years after her death, the public's interest in Katherine Mansfield's tragic, short life overshadowed what little critical attention her literary works attracted. Born to a large, upper-middle-class Wellington family, at age fourteen Mansfield traveled to England to attend Queen's College. In England, her contemporaries viewed her as a colonial, and as a result, as somewhat of an outsider. Upon graduating at age eighteen, she returned to New Zealand, only to find that she was equally out of place in what she now viewed as a provincial and cultureless New Zealand. Her two-year stay in New Zealand did prove fruitful, however: During this time she developed a taste for the writings of Oscar Wilde and the other aesthetes, and she began to experiment with a series of pseudonyms, identities, and sexualities. She also traveled around New Zealand, collecting impressions of colonial and family life that would surface in her some of her best stories.

After returning to England, getting pregnant, suffering a miscarriage, and marrying and leaving a man she hardly knew, Mansfield began her career as a writer, publishing her first collection of stories, *In a German Pension*. The same year she met John Middleton Murry and embarked on a tempestuous romantic and literary relationship that would continue until her death. With Murry, Mansfield wrote for and helped edit *Rhythm*, *The Signature*, and *The Athenaeum* magazines.

During the last years of her life Mansfield experienced serious health problems stemming from undiagnosed tuberculosis. In an effort to find a cure and a home, she traveled back and forth between England and the Continent. Not surprisingly, a sense of alienation and displacement colors her later, and perhaps most poignant works, such as "Miss Brill," "The Life of Ma Parker," and "The Doll's House." Her search for stability eventually led her to write stories about what she called "the undiscovered country," her native New Zealand. "The Woman at the Store" and "Ole Underwood" are local color stories, in the tradition of Kate Chopin and Sarah Orne Jewett, which draw upon dialect and customs to establish scenes and characters. Mansfield's ambivalent nostalgia for her New Zealand home and family also surfaces in her thinly veiled evocations of her childhood, "Prelude," "At the Bay," and "The Garden Party."

After her premature death at age thirty-four, her husband circulated a romanticized image of her life, and of his relationship with her, by publishing edited selections of her letters and diaries. These enjoyed great success, and it was not until the 1980's that a clear sense of their marital problems, numerous affairs, and health problems became public knowledge.

SUGGESTED READINGS
Alpers, Anthony. *Katherine Mansfield: A Biography*. New York: Alfred A. Knopf, 1954.
Baker, Ida. *Katherine Mansfield: The Memoirs of L. M.* London: Joseph, 1971.
Tomalin, Claire. *Katherine Mansfield: A Secret Life*. New York: Viking Press, 1987.

—*Geneviève Sanchis Morgan*

See also Erotic identity; Feminism; Mansfield, Katherine, short stories of

Mansfield, Katherine, short stories of

AUTHOR: Katherine Mansfield (1888-1923)

PRINCIPAL WORKS: *In a German Pension*, 1911; *Bliss and Other Stories*, 1920; *The Garden Party and Other Stories*, 1922; *The Doves' Nest and Other Stories*, 1923; *Something Childish and Other Stories*, 1924 (also known as *The Little Girl and Other Stories*, 1924)

IDENTITIES: Women; world

Influenced by Oscar Wilde and Anton Chekhov, Katherine Mansfield enjoyed a productive although short career as an essayist and short-story writer. Her first story, "The Tiredness of Rosabel," introduces many of the themes her later works explore—class difference, role playing, poverty, deception, and the solitary female. Almost all of her stories illustrate the fluid, relational, and fragile nature of personal identity.

Her first collection of stories, *In a German Pension* (1911), a satirical look at Germans' relationships to each other, their food, and their bodily functions, quickly went through three editions. Although she was later embarrassed by these stories, their success allowed her to place her later work in the better magazines of the day. Instead of the often comic nature of her first collection, her subsequent works became subtler, often abandoning traditional plot, and instead, substituting a momentary revelation. In such scenes, Mansfield manages to convey a character's history, personality, or dilemma in a brief flash of insight. An example of Mansfield's use of a momentary illumination is the twist at the end of "Bliss" (In *Bliss and Other Stories*, 1920), in which the reader and the main character, Bertha Young, find out about her husband's affair with her friend, Pearl Fulton. In typical Mansfield style, the main character learns little or nothing from such an epiphany; Bertha's glimpse of her husband's transgression tells the reader more about the delusional Bertha than she knows about herself.

"Prelude," published by Virginia Woolf and Leonard Woolf's Hogarth Press, earned for Mansfield a reputation as a serious, avant-garde writer. Perhaps her most well-loved story, "Prelude," is highly autobiographical, chronicling the development of the artist-child, Kezia Burnell, a thinly-veiled portrait of Mansfield as a child. Dealing with three generations of women, "Prelude" also examines the development of gender and sexual identities. Abandoning the traditional voice of an omniscient narrator, the narrative voice of "Prelude" emanates from the psyches of the many Burnell family members: Mrs. Fairfield, the kindly grandmother; Stanley Burnell, the overbearing patriarch; Linda Burnell, the unmaternal mother; Beryl Fairfield, the frustrated sister-in-law; and the children, Isabel, Kezia, and Lottie. For this story Mansfield developed a twelve-part montage of scenes, which, taken together, creates an implicit meaning. The sequel, "At the Bay," and another story, "The Daughters of the Late Colonel," also employ this montage style.

Another theme often explored in Mansfield's fiction is love, sex, and betrayal. Works such as "Frau Brechenmacher Attends a Wedding," "At Lehmann's," and "This Flower" chronicle the pain and violence associated with marriage, sexual awakening, and childbirth. Similarly, "The Little Governess" and "Pictures" focus on the tenuous position of the solitary female, who, with simply a misstep, may quickly cross the line between respectability and prostitution.

With their stylistic experimentation and frank exploration of class, gender, and identity, Mansfield's stories helped revolutionize the art of fiction. At her death, Virginia Woolf was to admit in her diary, "I was jealous of her writing—the only writing I have ever been jealous of." Although she died young, Mansfield produced an impressive array of stories, essays, and letters.

SUGGESTED READINGS

Fullbrook, Kate. *Katherine Mansfield*. Sussex, England: Harvester Press, 1986.

Kaplan, Sydney Janet. *Katherine Mansfield and the Origins of Modernist Fiction*. Ithaca, N.Y.: Cornell University Press, 1991.

Nathan, Rhoda. *Critical Essays on Katherine Mansfield*. New York: Continuum, 1988.

—Geneviève Sanchis Morgan

See also *Bildungsroman* and *Künstlerroman*; Class and identity; Colonialism; Mansfield, Katherine

Marble Faun, The

AUTHOR: Nathaniel Hawthorne (1804-1864)
FIRST PUBLISHED: 1860
IDENTITIES: European American; women

The Marble Faun, Nathaniel Hawthorne's final novel, examines two of the problems that interested its author late in his career: the complications of living abroad and the possible benefits of human suffering. Considered by some to be less successful than his earlier works, the novel nevertheless offers a unique picture of the effects of a foreign culture upon American lives and values.

The story follows the movements of a group of artists living in Rome in the 1850's. Miriam, a beautiful painter with a mysterious background, is haunted by a strange man from her past. In a moment of passion she allows Donatello, her Italian suitor, to murder the stranger by throwing him from the cliff once known as the Traitor's Leap. From this point Hawthorne's interest in the ability of guilt to bring about changes in identity guides the novel. Donatello, happy but shallow before the murder, soon develops a more profound understanding of human nature through the sympathy created by his feelings of remorse. His relationship with Miriam also deepens, though his shame at their mutual secret soon drives him into isolation at his family home in Tuscany. There Donatello finds himself unable to appreciate the natural beauty he loved as a boy. Having gained wisdom and experience, he has lost his youth and innocence. Donatello is guided through this difficult period by Kenyon, an American sculptor who acts as observer and partial spokesman for Hawthorne. Not only does Kenyon express many of his creator's ideas about Italian art and architecture but also he speculates about the effects of Italian life and culture on uprooted New Englanders such as Hilda, a young copyist he secretly loves. The depth of history, the power of Catholicism, and the overwhelming beauty of European art all pose threats to their Puritan heritage. Furthermore, Hilda, as a witness to the murder committed by Donatello and Miriam, faces the additional difficulty of keeping the crime a secret and so sharing in the guilt of the couple. Like Donatello, her remorse gradually changes her understanding of human nature, and by the book's end her harsh purity has softened into a greater sympathy for human weakness.

In his journals of the period Hawthorne speculates about the effects of living in a foreign country too long, and at the end of *The Marble Faun* he repeats his concerns. To live too long on a "foreign shore," the narrator notes, is to "defer the reality of life" until "between two countries, we have none at all." This desire to protect their American identity sends Kenyon and Hilda back to New England. Miriam and Donatello, forever linked by their experience, remain to suffer the punishment that their own guilt demands. Whether their fall, like that of Adam and Eve, was "fortunate" or not is one of the book's enduring questions.

SUGGESTED READINGS

Bell, Millicent. *Hawthorne's View of the Artist*. Albany: State University of New York Press, 1962.

Carton, Evan. *The Marble Faun: Hawthorne's Transformations*. Boston: Twayne, 1992.

Martin, Terence. *Nathaniel Hawthorne*. Boston: Twayne, 1983.

—Clark Davis

See also Expatriate identity; Hawthorne, Nathaniel; *Scarlet Letter, The*

Martín; &, Meditations on the South Valley

AUTHOR: Jimmy Santiago Baca (1952-   )

FIRST PUBLISHED: 1986

IDENTITIES: Adolescence and coming-of-age; Latino; Native American; West and Southwest

Told in the semiautobiographical voice of Martín, the two long poems "Martín" and "Meditations on the South Valley" offer the moving account of a young Chicano's difficult quest for self-definition amid the realities of the barrio and his dysfunctional family. Abandoned by his parents at a young age, Martín spends time with his Indio grandparents and in an orphanage before striking out on his own at the age of six. His early knowledge of his grandparents' heritage gives him the first indication that his quest for identity will involve the recovery of a sense of family and a strong connection with the earth.

As Martín grows older and is shuttled from the orphanage to his bourgeois uncle's home, he realizes that his life is of the barrio and the land and not the sterile world of the rich suburbs. Martín's quest eventually leads him on a journey throughout the United States in which he searches for himself amid the horrors of addiction and the troubled memories of his childhood. Realizing that he must restore his connection with his family and home, he returns to the South Valley by way of Aztec ruins, where he ritualistically establishes his connection with his Mother Earth and his Native American ancestry. "Martín" ends with the birth of his son and Martín's promise to never leave him. The cycle of abandonment and abuse seems to have ended, and Martín is on his way to becoming the good man he so strongly desires to be.

"Meditations on the South Valley" continues the story of Martín, reinforcing his newfound sense of identity. The poem begins with the burning of his house and the loss of ten years of writing. In the process of rebuilding his life, Martín and his family must live in the Heights, an antiseptic tract housing development that serves to reinforce his identification with the land of the South Valley. Told in brief sketches, the insights in "Meditations on the South Valley" encourage Martín to nurture the growing connections with his new family and his promise to his young son. The poem ends with the construction of his new home from the ruins of an abandoned flophouse in the South Valley. Martín's friends come together to construct the house, and, metaphorically, Martín and his life as a good Chicano man are reborn from the garbage piles and ashes of the house they reconstruct.

SUGGESTED READINGS

Levertov, Denise. Introduction to *Martín; & Meditations on the South Valley*, by Jimmy Santiago Baca. New York: New Directions, 1987.

Olivares, Julian. "Two Contemporary Chicano Verse Chronicles." *Americas Review* 16 (Fall-Winter, 1988): 214-231.

Rector, Liam. "The Documentary of What Is." *Hudson Review* 41 (Summer, 1989): 393-400.

—William Vaughn

See also American identity: West and the frontier; Baca, Jimmy Santiago; Chicano identity; Homelessness; Poverty

Masculinity and the masculine mystique

IDENTITIES: Men

At issue

Because literature has been a male-dominated field, many male writers have written about maleness. Such role development is apparent in American authors from the early nineteenth century onward. Washington Irving, Nathaniel Hawthorne, James Fenimore Cooper, and their contemporaries created a male role model who was intended to be contrasted to European models. A key facet of the American ideal of masculinity is self-reliance. The lone frontiersman, woodsman, cowboy, successful businessman, detective, or seaman populates American fiction.

History

In Irving's "The Legend of Sleepy Hollow" (1819), Ichabod Crane, a slightly effeminate schoolteacher, faces down Brom Van Brunt, a macho suitor of Katrina Van Tassel, a wealthy Dutch landowner's daughter. For Ichabod, masculinity is self-reliance based on reason and intellect. The American male in nineteenth century fiction, who may tend to violence, tempers himself by engaging in family matters and related virtues. Cooper's most famous hero, a "man's man," does not so temper—one might say degrade—himself. Natty Bumppo demonstrates great skills as a naturalist in *The Pioneers* (1823), as a fighter and tracker in *The Last of the Mohicans* (1826), and as an all-knowing sage in *The Pathfinder* (1840). Bumppo is an American Adam—resourceful, courageous, and self-reliant.

Realism　　During the American realism movement, which may be dated as occurring from 1865 to 1914, authors such as Stephen Crane, Mark Twain, and William Dean Howells explored a new concept of masculinity. In Crane's *The Red Badge of Courage* (1894), Henry is an innocent farm boy who becomes a man because of his Civil War experiences. Henry's bravery and cowardice are emphatically not mythic, as Natty Bumppo may be. Twain's *The Adventures of Tom Sawyer* (1876) and *Adventures of Huckleberry Finn* (1884) also show boys moving from innocence to experience. That movement is a highly moral one, and it reflects the hero's coming to rely upon himself.

Such concern for morality and self-reliance as masculine typifies William Dean Howells' *The Rise of Silas Lapham* (1885); the hero joins wealth with morality. The same morality is pervasive in Howells' *A Hazard of New Fortunes* (1890). Masculinity requires, in these works, morality. The hero is upright and sober; he can depend upon himself for correct judgment.

Modern period　　American writers began a tough guy school of writing that continued the tradition of self-reliance while discarding much of the primness of the late nineteenth century model. Such writers as Ernest Hemingway, Jack London, and John Steinbeck portrayed their heroes as strong, silent, and long-suffering. Often these heroes are beaten, physically and spiritually. They always rise above their situation by physical strength and self-reliance. After World War II, the fictional hero continued to be self-reliant in such manifestations as astronaut.

SUGGESTED READINGS

Berthoff, Warner. *The Ferment of Realism: American Literature, 1884-1919*. New York: Free Press, 1965.

Callow, James T. *Guide to American Literature from Its Beginnings Through Walt Whitman*. New York: Barnes & Noble Books, 1976.

Commager, Henry Steele. *The American Mind: An Interpretation of American Thought and Character Since the 1880's*. New Haven, Conn.: Yale University Press, 1959.

Deakin, Motley, and Peter Lisca, eds. *From Irving to Steinbeck: Studies of American Literature in Honor of Harry R. Warfel*. Gainesville: University of Florida Press, 1972.

Gross, Theodore L. *The Heroic Ideal in American Literature*. New York: Free Press, 1971.

Miller, Perry. *The New England Mind: The Seventeenth Century*. Cambridge: Harvard University Press, 1983.

—Dennis L. Weeks

See also Hawthorne, Nathaniel; Hemingway, Ernest; London, Jack; *Red Badge of Courage, The*; Steinbeck, John; Women and identity

Mass media stereotyping

The mass media (television, radio, films, large-circulation magazines, newspapers, large-scale advertising) have often relied on stereotypes. In the early 1990's, stereotypes still were common in the mass media, but progress had been made toward the eradication of stereotypes. Stereotypes contain assumptions that affect how society perceives a particular group; members of groups have protested, with varying degrees of success, stereotypical portrayals in the media. The number and varieties of stereotypes in the media is myriad and is not limited to stereotypes of ethnic or racial groups. Stereotypes may range from the perhaps merely annoying—the brainy boy in glasses (poor eyesight seems a requirement for intelligence in many forms of mass media)—to the most blatantly bigoted. One may argue that the mass media resists depicting life's complexities generally, and that stereotypes are a part of the general pattern in mass media of the reduction of experience to what is most readily understandable.

Minorities are underrepresented in the mass media, and when represented, they are often portrayed in stereotypical ways. The television show *Star Trek* (whose episodes were first telecast from 1966 to 1969), for example, was groundbreaking in its casting of actors of various ethnic and racial origins. An interracial kiss in one episode was censored.

Despite the increase in representation of various groups, some taboos have persisted. Homosexuals, for example, or interracial romantic relationships have continued to be almost invisible in the mass media. Models from all racial groups have been involved in commercials and newspaper advertisements, but Arab, Asian, Latino, Native American, and other groups' roles in the mass media have remained very limited. Stereotyping in the late twentieth century has persisted in other ways; for example, a police drama may feature partners who are white and black, but the black partner typically is not in the lead role.

Cursory research into the magazines, advertisements, radio shows, and films of the early twentieth century indicates that stereotyping was more prevalent and more virulent earlier in the century than it was later. The casual and prevalent presentation of stereotypes in the mass media of the early twentieth century, however, may concern those who look back upon it; they may ask themselves how their own time's products of mass culture may look to the future. The social movements that began in the 1960's, including the Civil Rights movement and the growth of feminism, and the awareness they generated among groups, are largely responsible for greater and less-stereotyped representation of different peoples in the media.

In television shows of the 1950's to the 1970's women were typically young, well-dressed, physically attractive, and submissive housewives. The career of television actress Mary Tyler Moore offers an example of how the mass media responded to social changes (critics and analysts generally agree that it took social changes to influence the media to discard stereotypes, rather than the other way around). *The Dick Van Dyke Show* first ran from 1961 to 1966; in it, Mary Tyler Moore played a timid young housewife. In 1970, *The Mary Tyler Moore Show* began to be broadcast, continuing until 1977. Mary Tyler Moore played a single working woman. Later television shows included such characters as Claire Huxtable, an outspoken wife, mother, and attorney. The character Murphy Brown, an extremely outspoken and respected professional, broke new ground in the media (after thousands of women had done so in life) by becoming a single working mother.

Historically, the mass media infrequently showcased older people. When older people were profiled, they were often sketched as weak, cranky, kind, senile, and old-fashioned. Late in the twentieth century, however, after prodding by organizations representing older people, the mass media began to focus more favorably on older people. Little progress has occurred, however, in ending stereotypes of the handicapped, of those with mental illness or retardation, and of the obese.

In the early 1990's, health and fitness occupied a substantial amount of space in the mass media. Obesity, a problem for many Americans, received some tolerance, but overweight people did not hold such positions as television news anchors or journalists, for example, and were seldom represented on television series except for the purpose of being the butt of jokes. Large-size clothing catalogs and advertisements, in another example, typically employed thin, small models to display their clothing.

Television and the movies have almost always shown characters living at a higher income than is reflected in reality. Viewers have often wondered how between-jobs actors, or police officers, or saxophone players, for example, could afford such photogenic housing as they have typically been seen inhabiting in the media. In addition, material items displayed in a character's abode have been more expensive than what that person could, in reality, normally afford. In the 1990's, police and law enforcement occupations comprised a large share of occupations on television; managers and other professional vocations occupied almost all the balance of positions represented. These occupations, although closer to the top than to the bottom of the economic ladder, still do not typically afford real people the kinds of lifestyles that they do for the characters of film and television. The lower middle class and the poor have been underrepresented in the media. Those who receive all their knowledge from the media might not be blamed for thinking that all the poor in the United States have Southern accents.

Radio   In radio in the 1980's and 1990's, various hosts of shows, including Rush Limbaugh and Howard Stern (both widely popular), jubilantly indulged in stereotyping, diminishing any sense that the displacement of stereotypes from the media is a matter of linear progress. These and other media figures have derided those who seek to end stereotyping, arguing that they are not obliged to follow the constricting rules of what is politically correct. That is, attempts to stop stereotyping may be viewed as acts of censorship, just as stereotyping may be viewed, because it denies people acknowledgement of their true experience, as a form of censorship. Strangely, then, those forms of communication that reach the most people are often involved in disputes about censorship.

SUGGESTED READINGS

Cantor, Muriel G., and Joel M. Cantor. *Prime-Time Television: Content and Control.* Newbury Park, Calif.: Sage, 1992.

Czarra, Fred, and Joseph Heaps. *Censorship and the Media: Mixed Blessing or Dangerous Threat?* Newton, Mass.: Allyn & Bacon, 1976.

Fowles, Jib. *Advertising and Popular Culture.* Newbury Park, Calif.: Sage, 1996.

Journal of American Culture, The.

Journal of Popular Culture, The.

Shohat, Ella, and Robert Stam. *Unthinking Eurocentrism: Multiculturalism and the Media.* New York: Routledge, 1994.

Smith, Anthony, ed. *Television: An International History.* New York: Oxford University Press, 1995.

Sochen, June. *Enduring Values: Women in Popular Culture.* New York: Praeger, 1987.

Sue, Jewell K. *From Mammy to Miss America and Beyond: Cultural Images and U.S. Social Policy.* New York: Routledge, 1993.

—Sharon Mikkelson

See also Appearance and identity; Demographics of identity; Multiculturalism; Pluralism versus assimilation; Popular culture; Racism and ethnocentrism

Maupin, Armistead

BORN: Washington, D.C.; May 13, 1944

PRINCIPAL WORKS: *Tales of the City*, 1978; *More Tales of the City*, 1980; *Further Tales of the City*, 1982; *Babycakes*, 1984; *Significant Others*, 1987; *Sure of You*, 1989; *28 Barbary Lane*, 1990 (compilation); *Back to Barbary Lane: The Final Tales of the City Omnibus*, 1991 (compilation); *Maybe the Moon*, 1992

IDENTITIES: Disease; European American; family; gay, lesbian, and bisexual

SIGNIFICANT ACHIEVEMENT: Documenting gay and lesbian life from the carefree 1970's to the 1980's, when acquired immune deficiency syndrome (AIDS), began to ravage the gay world, Maupin's novels attest the importance of chosen families, self-love, and acceptance of those who are different.

Armistead Maupin (pronounced "mop-pin") was born into a Southern, conservative household. He served a tour of duty in Vietnam, voted for Barry Goldwater for president, and worked in the office of ultraconservative newspaperman and later senator Jesse Helms. One of Maupin's earliest impressions of homosexuality came from the film *Advise and Consent* (1962), from which Maupin inferred that the only recourse available to the honorable homosexual was suicide.

Celebrity Anita Bryant's antigay campaign triggered Maupin's evolution from Southern conservative to gay liberal. Maupin moved to San Francisco, proclaimed his homosexuality, and discovered that concurrently he had found his authentic writing voice. In the mid-1970's, Maupin began writing a daily serial for the *San Francisco Chronicle* about life in San Francisco. Although the installments dealt with gay and straight characters, the most popular ones quickly became Anna Madrigal, a transsexual, and Michael Tolliver, her gay tenant.

Maupin repopularized the newspaper serial as a form of fiction, thus becoming known as the Charles Dickens of the twentieth century. Each installment had unity of time, place, and action and ended on a high point of drama or mystery. In his serials, Maupin followed the words of another nineteenth century writer, Wilkie Collins: "Make 'em cry, make 'em laugh, make 'em wait."

The readership of the daily 800-word installments burgeoned, and Maupin collected the writings into a series of three novels, beginning with *Tales of the City*. Moving the series to the San Francisco *Examiner*, Maupin created the installments that would later become *Babycakes* and *Significant Others*. *Sure of You*, the final novel about Anna, Michael, and their family of choice, was the only one not originally written in serial form.

The first three novels paint a gay community that, along with the straight community of the 1970's, revels in the freedom of sexual exploration and the use of recreational drugs. Between the third and fourth novels in the series, however, a main character dies of AIDS. The last three novels take on a more serious tone. Maupin's long-term domestic partnership with an HIV survivor and AIDS activist is reflected in the novels' sensitive depiction of a community coming together to live with the disease in love and dignity. Finding a national audience through the publication of these six popular novels, Maupin has since gone on to other media, including Broadway and television, to promulgate understanding of gay concerns and human rights issues.

SUGGESTED READINGS

Bass, Barbara Kaplan. "Armistead Maupin." In *Contemporary Gay American Novelists: A Bio-Bibliographical Critical Sourcebook*, edited by Emmanuel S. Nelson. Westport, Conn.: Greenwood Press, 1993.

FitzGerald, Francis. *Cities on a Hill: A Journey Through Contemporary American Cultures*. New York: Simon & Schuster, 1986.

Maupin, Armistead. "A Talk with Armistead Maupin." Interview by Tom Spain. *Publishers Weekly* 237 (March 20, 1987): 53-54.

—*Steven A. Katz*

See also AIDS; *Babycakes*; *Back to Barbary Lane*; Gay identity; Lesbian identity; Women and identity

Mehta, Ved

BORN: Lahore, British India (now Pakistan); March 21, 1934

PRINCIPAL WORKS: *Face to Face*, 1957; *Fly and the Fly Bottle*, 1962; *The New Theologian*, 1966; *Daddyji*, 1972; *Mahatma Ghandi and His Apostles*, 1977; *Mamaji*, 1979; *Vedi*, 1982; *The Ledge Between the Streams*, 1984; *Sound-Shadows of the New World*, 1985; *The Stolen Light*, 1989; *Up at Oxford*, 1993

IDENTITIES: Disability; family; South Asian

SIGNIFICANT ACHIEVEMENT: Mehta vividly describes the cultures in which he has lived and the experience of exile and blindness.

Ved Mehta has been telling the story of his own life for most of his career. This story includes the cultures in which he has lived. Mehta was born into a well-educated Hindu family in Lahore in 1934. At the age of three he lost his eyesight as a result of meningitis. Mehta's education took him away from his close-knit family and sent him to places that must have seemed like different worlds: Arkansas in the era of segregation, a college campus in suburban Southern California, and Oxford University. As a staff writer for *The New Yorker* and in his many books, Mehta makes those different worlds, including the world of blindness, come alive to the reader.

Mehta published his first book, *Face to Face*, when he was twenty-two. It is a highly readable account of his childhood, of his family's sufferings during the partition of India (they had to flee their native city when it became part of the new Muslim nation of Pakistan), and of his experiences as a student in America. The central subject, however, is Mehta's blindness and the ways in which he learns to be independent and successful despite his disability.

For many years after the appearance of *Face to Face*, Mehta allowed no hint of his disability to appear in his work, which he filled with visual descriptions. He published a novel and became a master of nonfiction. He wrote books introducing Indian culture and politics to Western readers; Mehta has also written a series of books on the excitement of intellectual life. In books on history and philosophy, theology, and linguistics, Mehta makes clashes of ideas vivid by describing intellectuals not only as thinkers but as people.

When Mehta returned to autobiography, beginning with *Daddyji*, he stopped suppressing the fact of his blindness. Instead, he tried to make the things that had formed his identity—his family, his disability, his experiences at schools for the blind, and the colleges and universities where he studied—as vivid as his other subjects. Beginning with biographies of his mother and father and working ahead through five more books to his graduation from Oxford, Mehta presents the story of his life, always as an exile seeking his place in the world, with eloquence and frankness.

SUGGESTED READINGS

Slatin, John M. "Blindness and Self-Perception: The Autobiographies of Ved Mehta." *Mosaic* 19, no. 4 (Fall, 1986): 173-193.

Sontag, Frederick. "The Self-Centered Author." *New Quest* 79 (July-August, 1989): 229-233.

—*Brian Abel Ragen*

See also Asian American identity: India; *Continents of Exile*

Melting pot

DEFINITION: The melting pot is a metaphor comparing a kettle in which ingredients are blended to the United States, where immigrants are assimilated into one society.

In the melting pot metaphor, melting diverse nationalities and races creates one entity, a new American identity. In 1782, French immigrant Michel-Guillaume-Jean de Crèvecœur, using the more American-sounding pen name J. Hector St. John, published a collection of essays entitled *Letters from an American Farmer*. These essays praised the quality of rural life in colonial America. In one essay entitled "What Is an American?" he wrote, "Here, individuals of all nations are melted into a new race of men." European immigrants left oppression, hunger, ignorance, and poverty behind to pursue life, liberty, and happiness in North America. From Crèvecœur's perspective, they blended their cultures into a new identity, dedicated to the goals of freedom and equality.

History

Crèvecœur came to Canada in 1754 during the French and Indian War as a soldier. After the war, he roamed the country and surveyed land around the Great Lakes. In 1765, he became a citizen of New York, married, and became a gentleman farmer. During the Revolution, he refused to take sides against British loyalists, so American patriots arrested and jailed him as a spy. When he was released, he fled, in fear for his life, to France, leaving his wife and children behind. French citizens found his essay collections interesting, and he became a minor celebrity. Benjamin Franklin helped Crèvecœur secure an appointment as French consul to New York. When he returned in 1783, he found his wife dead, his farmhouse burned, and his children living in foster homes.

In later essays, Crèvecœur revised his idealistic theory of a homogenous American society. He observed that the first wave of immigrants on the frontier lived in isolation with weak ties to government, religion, or morality. Their communities and farms symbolized hard work and self-reliance, and they were reluctant to make room for succeeding waves of immigrants. Some were assimilated, but debtors, speculators, traders, and castoffs of society moved on. Many of these people created problems with the Native American population.

In 1908, Israel Zangwill saw his Broadway play *The Melting Pot* performed. The four-act play dramatizes and resolves the conflict of Jewish separatism and Russian anti-Semitism. Walker Whiteside, star of the play, spoke the lines, "America is God's Crucible, the great Melting Pot where all the races are melting and reforming." Although critics gave the play bad reviews, audiences kept it running for 136 performances. The metaphor of the melting pot entered the American vocabulary.

Ironically, Zangwill became an ardent Zionist only eight years after the opening of *The Melting Pot* and repudiated the theme of his play. He declared that a character's statement that there should be neither Jew nor Greek was wrong. According to Zangwill, different races and religions could not mix, or at least not do so easily; a person's natural ethnicity would return.

The theory that American society is homogenous assumes that people from different ethnic backgrounds will resolve their differences in an environment of freedom and opportunity. The process of "melting" the origins, religions, languages, and traditions of Europeans, Asians, Africans, and Native Americans into a unique American identity is demonstrably incomplete. Whether the melting of various ethnicities into a new whole is a worthy or a possible goal is a source of controversy.

At issue

Many immigrants have been unwilling or unable to abandon their past identity for a new one. Strangers in a strange land naturally cling to what is familiar; assimilation has often been slow and difficult. Established groups, in turn, have set up legal, economic, and religious barriers to prevent assimilation of different races. In 1660, eighteen languages were spoken on Manhattan Island. In that heavily populated area in the 1990's, at least that many are spoken, probably many more. Those who criticize the metaphor of the melting pot point out that the United States has always been and continues to be multiethnic, multilingual, and multicultural, and that therefore the melting pot is more of a misguided ideal than an accurate representation of the acculturation process in the United States. The ideal, critics of the melting pot may argue, often covers morally questionable motives that are based on hatred of difference.

On the other hand, the melting pot metaphor still seems apt for Americans whose ancestors represent multiple ethnic groups, for example, someone with a German-Scotch-Cherokee heritage. To many others, however, the term "multicultural" applies to American society more realistically. Many Americans with distinct ethnicity like to use the metaphor of a bowl of tossed salad, in which each culture is represented as a separate entity.

SUGGESTED READINGS

Crèvecœur, Michel-Guillaume-Jean de. "What Is an American?" In *Letters from an American Farmer*. New York: Fox, Duffield, 1904.

Glazer, Nathan, and Daniel Patrick Moynihan. *Beyond the Melting Pot*. Cambridge, Mass.: MIT Press, 1963.

Hughes, Glenn. *A History of the American Theatre: 1700-1950*. New York: Samuel French, 1951.

—*Martha E. Rhynes*

See also Acculturation; Multiculturalism; Pluralism versus assimilation

Memoirs. *See* Autobiography of . . .

Memories of a Catholic Girlhood

AUTHOR: Mary McCarthy (1912-1989)

FIRST PUBLISHED: 1957

IDENTITIES: European American; family; religion; women

In *Memories of a Catholic Girlhood*, Mary McCarthy collected eight memoirs that she had previously published in magazines such as *The New Yorker* and *Harper's Bazaar*. Her introductory chapter, "To the Reader," describes her hope to create as accurate a record as possible of her role in her family's history, from early childhood until she attended Vassar. In fact, she frequently attempted to check the facts that appeared in the articles with another source. However, as an orphan "the chain of recollection—the collective memory of a family—has been broken." Thus, she compares herself and her brother, Kevin, to archaeologists who search for scraps of information to reconstruct events and discover motives to explain the events of their childhood.

McCarthy's parents, Roy McCarthy and Therese Preston, both came from wealthy families. Her father's family were Irish Catholics; she described the men as handsome, imagining they had once been "wreckers," plundering ships that foundered off the shore of Nova Scotia. Her mother's parents represented two separate cultural backgrounds. Harold Preston was a well-to-do Episcopalian; he worked as a lawyer. Augusta Morgenstern was a Jewish beauty. In *Memories of a Catholic Girlhood*, McCarthy seeks to find her place in this varied group.

She recalls her early childhood as idyllic. Although her father was at times irresponsible with money, the home was loving for Mary and her three younger brothers. Unfortunately, both parents died in the influenza epidemic of 1918. That marked the end of McCarthy's secure home environment. She was never to regain the tranquillity of her early childhood. Immediately after the children were orphaned, they were placed with a great-aunt and her abusive husband in a home only two blocks from the McCarthy mansion. Regular beatings and deprivation became the substitute for indulgence. After four years, her grandfather Preston rescued her, but her brothers remained behind.

Memories of a Catholic Girlhood records her attempts to find an identity in each new environment she faced. She discusses her desire to stand out in the convent school where she went for seventh and eighth grades. She was fascinated by the romantic names of the other girls at the school. She decided that names were the clue to everything. She spent successive years in a public school, then an Episcopal boarding school. Her life became a continual struggle to belong or to be noticed. Even in the Preston's home, she was aware of her isolation, describing it as a house of "shut doors and silences."

She explores all her different childhood locales, providing brilliant portraits: her Jewish aunts and the social sets in which they moved; the friends she visits in the West, where she finds a totally foreign culture; her family and herself, a girl searching for belonging.

SUGGESTED READINGS

Cully, Margo, ed. *American Women's Autobiography: Fea(s)ts of Memory*. Madison: University of Wisconsin Press, 1992.

Eakin, Paul. *Fictions in Autobiography: Studies in the Art of Self-Invention*. Princeton, N.J.: Princeton University Press, 1985.

Hardy, Willene. *Mary McCarthy*. New York: Frederick Ungar, 1981.

—*Mary Mahony*

See also American identity: Northeast; Catholicism; *Group, The*; McCarthy, Mary

Mennonites. *See* Religious minorities

Mental disorders

IDENTITIES: Disability; disease

Literature by and about the mentally ill aids understanding of the mind and society. Depictions of mental illness are like funhouse mirrors—scary, fascinating, and informative. One sees the normal psyche exaggerated and distorted, alien yet recognizable. This is one reason literature has always presented mental disorders. Moreover, some think that insanity and the genius that produces art are related; although this contention is debated, many great artists have had mental problems. What is rarer is people with mental problems who have also produced great art. Even inexperienced writers often produce powerful first-person accounts of mental disorders. Studying historical literature about mental disorders aids in understanding not only universals of the psyche but also specific societies' views of mental disorders.

In ancient Greek works, people are driven to madness by circumstances or the gods, but the inner processes of madness are unexamined. A true psychology began with later Greek philosophers. The biblical king Nebuchadnezzar, driven from his people, entered an animal-like state. Many of the cures by Jesus, seen as the casting out of demons, may have involved hysterical illnesses or mental disorders. In medieval Arthurian romances, Tristram and Lancelot have breaks with reason, distress, and guilt.

Until the eighteenth and nineteenth centuries in Europe, supernatural explanations for disordered behavior and thought predominated. Mentally disturbed and handicapped people were sometimes seen as touched by God, and other mental illnesses could be signs of demoniac activity. Most cultures also believed in natural explanations and medical cures, no matter how crude. Robert Burton's *Anatomy of Melancholy* (1621) discusses causes of melancholy (depression) such as stale air and too little sunlight.

Religion and mental problems, like madness and artistic genius, have long seemed linked. Indeed, in the eighteenth century, religious fervor was sometimes defined as insanity. Before then, religious ecstasies or fears were considered either as genuine contact with God, as deceptive acts of the devil, as natural healthy actions, or as nonsupernatural illness. The fifteenth century autobiography of Margery Kempe alternates religious passion with self-doubt; many of her contemporaries considered her mentally disordered. Thomas Hoccleve, also of the fifteenth century, was deeply aware of his own mental problems, which religion solved only temporarily. John Bunyan's *Grace Abounding to the Chief of Sinners* (1666), though cast in supernatural terms, may seem to twentieth century readers to depict bipolar (manic-depressive) illness.

Current writers see mental disorders in the lives of many artists, whether or not the artist was diagnosed and treated at the time. English Romantic poet William Blake, known for his poetry's elaborate personal mythology and for visions he claimed to literally see, has been called schizophrenic. Some identify bipolar disorder in the blisses and depressive depths that may be found in the poetry of Gerard Manley Hopkins.

Either schizophrenic or affective (mood) disorders have been ascribed in the twentieth century to many artists, including writers August Strindberg, Charles Baudelaire, Jonathan Swift, Samuel Johnson, Samuel Taylor Coleridge, Percy Bysshe Shelley, Joseph Conrad, and Franz Kafka. Many of these writers wrote about mental problems, as in Coleridge's depressed "Dejection, an Ode" or Kafka's dreamlike and paranoid works. Researchers have argued that mental disorders are much more common among artists than among the general population.

Others say such conclusions are overstated and caution about drawing conclusions regarding authors' lives from their work. Many artists, however, have recorded their own mental problems or time spent in asylums. The British poet Christopher Smart, after a fever, was in and out of madhouses and saw himself as excessive in "mirth and melancholy." William Cowper, another British poet of the eighteenth century, wrote about his difficult mood fluctuations. Nineteenth century British writer John Ruskin, whose grandfather had been psychotic, had a breakdown in 1861 and major depression through 1862.

In the twentieth century, Virginia Woolf suffered a major breakdown in 1904, refusing to eat and hearing voices, which she recorded in fictitious form (attributed to a tropical fever) in *The Voyage Out* (1915). Woolf experienced depression all of her life and ultimately killed herself. In the United States, a group of poets, called the confessional school, became famous for their mental disorders. Robert Lowell and members of his circle, including Theodore Roethke and John Berryman, all wrote poetry about the experience of mental illness. Although the image of the mad poet has captured the popular imagination, one may recall that such decidedly sane poets as William Carlos Williams and Wallace Stevens, to name two, were also active and influential in American poetry in the late twentieth century.

Literature is full of vivid images of mental disorders: the real melancholy and feigned madness of Hamlet, the delusions and obsessions of Miguel de Cervantes' *Don Quixote de la Mancha* (1605, 1615), Mrs. Rochester in *Jane Eyre: An Autobiography* (1847) by Charlotte Brontë, the obsessives, depressives, and neurasthenics in Edgar Allan Poe's fiction and poetry, and Boo Radley in Harper Lee's *To Kill a Mockingbird* (1960).

William Faulkner, Jerzy Kosinski, and John Barth have presented a number of figures with mood, thought, or character disorders. Faulkner's ability to present a disturbed inner life, as in *The Sound and the Fury* (1929), is impressive. Kosinski's hard, objective descriptions in *The Painted Bird* (1965) and *Steps* (1968) are chilling. Barth's *The Floating Opera* (1956) and *Lost in the Funhouse* (1968) mix humor and pathos. Peter Straub, also known for supernatural horror fiction, depicts real-life horrors such as sexual abuse, disassociation, and compulsive violence in fiction such as *Koko* (1988) and *The Throat* (1993).

Conrad Aiken's "Silent Snow, Secret Snow" uses snow as a metaphor for the self-enclosed world of the schizophrenic. "The Yellow Wallpaper" (1892), by Charlotte Perkins Gilman, shows a woman's descent into madness, with strongly feminist implications; Kate Chopin's *The Awakening* (1899) and Sue Kaufman's *Diary of a Mad Housewife* (1967) implicate the wife's social role as a cause of mental problems. Issues of the political power behind who gets to define madness also arise in *The Case History of Comrade V.* (1972), by James Park Sloan, which is written in the form of various psychiatric reports, each calling the facts of the others into question.

The mentally disordered killer is common in current fiction and film, perhaps best done by Straub, Robert Bloch (as in his 1959 novel *Psycho*), and Thomas Harris in *Red Dragon* (1981) and *The Silence of the Lambs* (1981).

Much current fantasy and science fiction depicts insane delusions and fears as literal truths. Robert A. Heinlein's "They" is a paranoid fantasy that turns out to be true. Sometimes the story can be interpreted as about either mental illness or a real event, as in John Wyndham's "Consider Her Ways" or in Marge Piercy's *Woman on the Edge of Time* (1976).

Philip K. Dick's science fiction depicts schizophrenic and paranoid realities. *Time out of Joint* (1959), *The Three Stigmata of Palmer Eldritch* (1965), and *Martian Time-Slip* (1976) are three examples. Dick writes about a world run under a caste system based on psychoses in *Clans of the Alphane Moon* (1975). Anna Kavan in *Ice* (1967) and William S. Burroughs in such novels as *Naked Lunch* (1959) and *The Soft Machine* (1961) mix science-fiction events or imagery with autobiographic elements of drug addiction and paranoia. Doris Lessing's fantastic fiction, including *The Golden Notebook* (1962) and *The Four-Gated City* (1969), often questions what madness is, seeing it as possibly a part of important personal transformation.

Nonfiction and fictionalized accounts

Some of the best and best-known fiction about mental illness is based on real experiences. Sylvia Plath's *The Bell Jar* (1963) depicts depression, institutionalization, and suicide. Plath was also associated with the confessional school. Mary Ward's *The Snake Pit* (1946) and Ken Kesey's *One Flew over the Cuckoo's Nest* (1962) focus on life in a mental hospital. Ward and Kesey are highly critical of the mental health care system. *I Never Promised You a Rose Garden* (1964), by Hannah Green (actually Joanna Greenberg), and *Lisa, Bright and Dark*, by John Neufeld (1969), depict the changes of thought and mood disorders. Robert Lindner's *The Fifty Minute Hour* (1955) contains fictionalized case histories from the therapist's viewpoint. *Lisa and David* (1961), by Theodore Isaac Rubin, and *The Three Faces of Eve* (1957), by Corbett H. Thigpen and Hervey M. Cleckley, are also fictionalized accounts by therapists. Chris Costner Sizemore wrote her own story in *I'm Eve* (1977).

In some of these, such as Kesey's book, the mental patients are seen more as political prisoners than as ill people in need of help, but the pain and isolation of a mental disorder are always clear. The female voices often indicate a connection between mental disorders and the position of a woman in society—something Plath makes explicit in *The Bell Jar* and implicit in much of her poetry. Fictionalized and nonfiction accounts of mental problems show that disordered behavior, thought, perceptions, and moods can coexist with genuine insight into one's own psyche and society.

Nonfiction first-person accounts of mental disorders often have the power and drama of fiction. The best is probably *Operators and Things: The Inner Life of a Schizophrenic* (1958), by Barbara O'Brien, with its elaborate visions of "hook operators" who control people, who are "things." Also noteworthy is Mark Vonnegut's *The Eden Express* (1975), concerning his schizophrenic episodes. Often careful self-observation and extreme introspection highlight these works, as in John Custance's *Wisdom, Madness, and Folly* (1952) and *Adventure into the Unconscious* (1954). Novelist William Styron's *Darkness Visible* (1990) is a moving memoir of depression.

The 1980's and 1990's saw many accounts of two kinds of mental problems. With growing social awareness of sexual abuse, many first-person accounts were published, including *My Father's House: A Memoir of Incest and Healing*, by Sylvia Fraser (1987), and *The Obsidian Mirror*, by Louise M. Wisechild (1988). Multiple personality disorder, often linked to childhood abuse, also is depicted in many excellent books. Such works include *Sybil* (1973), by Flora Rheta Schreiber, Daniel Keyes's *The Minds of Billy Milligan* (1981), *When Rabbit Howls*, by Truddi Chase (1987), and *Prism: Andrea's World* (1985), by Jonathan Bliss and Eugene Bliss.

SUGGESTED READINGS

Claridge, Gordon, et al. *Sounds from the Bell Jar: Ten Psychotic Authors*. New York: St. Martin's Press, 1990. Studies of important writers who battled mental illness.

Friedrich, Otto. *Going Crazy: An Inquiry into Madness in Our Time*. New York: Simon & Schuster, 1976. A study of what madness is and how it is defined, with examples from case studies, literary works, and authors' lives.

Glenn, Michael, ed. *Voices from the Asylum*. New York: Harper & Row, 1974. Concentrating on experiences within mental hospitals, this includes first-person accounts by staff and patients, poetry, and a short story by Poe.

Kaplan, Bert, ed. *The Inner World of Mental Illness*. New York: Harper & Row, 1964. An excellent selection of first-person accounts from published sources; some excerpts are brief or lack context, but are still effective and depict a wide range of illnesses.

Kaup, Monika. *Mad Intertextuality: Madness in Twentieth-Century Women's Writing*. Trier, Germany: Wissenschaftlicher Verlag Trier, 1993. Heavy on some literary terms, but useful study about cultural tendencies and lesser-known novels.

Peterson, Dale, ed. *A Mad People's History of Madness*. Pittsburgh: University of Pittsburgh Press, 1982. These first-person accounts go back to the fifteenth century. Excellent bibliography.

Porter, Roy. *A Social History of Madness: The World Through the Eyes of the Insane*. New York: Weidenfeld & Nicolson, 1987. A study of what madness is and how society defines it, including literary and first-person accounts.

Stanford, Gene, and Barbara Stanford, eds. *Strangers to Themselves*. New York: Bantam Books, 1973. First-person accounts, fiction about mental illness, and some clinical articles.

—Bernadette Lynn Bosky

See also *Awakening, The*; *Bell Jar, The*; *Darkness Visible*; Faulkner, William; Feminism; Incest; Kesey, Ken; Lowell, Robert; Piercy, Marge; *Yellow Wallpaper, The*

Metafiction

DEFINITION: A work of fiction concerned with the nature of fiction.

Metafiction is a running theme in much postmodern literature. Metafictional literature allows the artist to relinquish control of the narrative to chance configurations. In metafiction, the author grants higher privileges to ontology than to epistemology. The fictional world is constructed in a collaborative effort with the reader. All fictions do this, but in metafiction it is done consciously and with the reader's full knowledge. As the reader concentrates on the text, the world-making operation of the author is suspended. The author withdraws authority from the collaborative effort, leaving the reader to fill in the blank. A character's fictional world is constructed only to be deconstructed, dispersed among it various authorial inscriptions and reader inscriptions in the text. By exploring and exposing the postcognitive, ontological aspects of fictional world and character construction, the structure of fictional worlds and characters and their contents, and the problem of the author as part of the text, metafiction can be a kind of metaphysics of identity.

Ultimately, the most extreme manifestation of the metafictional tendency in literature is the *mise en abime*, in which a recognizable image of the primary text is embedded within that text. In short, there is a story that frames another story. The most widely recognized piece of contemporary metafiction is perhaps John Fowles's *The French Lieutenant's Woman* (1969).

Postmodern metafictional strategy emphasizes the reading rather than the writing of fiction. The distinction suggests a fundamentally altered view of the artist and of literary creation. Even when a protagonist is engaged in the production of a text, this writing is not represented as an original creation but as a kind of rereading. Metafiction dramatizes the process or product of reinscription and raises the mechanics and motivations of narrative to central importance. If to write is to invariably replicate what one has read and thus to reread, to read is also to rewrite.

For example, in Robert Coover's short story, "The Babysitter," only three facts can be ascertained. First, the babysitter arrives at the Tuckers' home. Second, the Tuckers leave for a party. Third, Jack and Mark play pinball. The rest of the story gives rise to an indefinite number of situations based on these givens. Based on these three facts alone, all of the situations described in the short story could be products of the babysitter's imaginings. Those imaginings (rape fantasy, the notion of being desired by more than one peer at the same time, or even being desired by the father of the children under her care) flow from the babysitter's mind, not a supposedly objective authorial voice. The babysitter's identity is affected greatly by this multiplicity of readings inherent in metafiction. Metafiction questions, even denies, the notion that a character's, and perhaps a person's, identity is a stable, unified, able-to-be quantified entity.

Characters are constantly faced with the question of whether they are reading or reenacting a historical script that preexists their critical endeavors or whether they have in important respects constructed this script through their desire to read it and their expectations that it will prove readable. In general, metafiction tends to emphasize plot over character, lending identity to character via the reader's embedding of his or her knowledge into the fiction. Metafictional plots tend to be paradoxical labyrinths, difficult (sometimes impossible) to follow, contrived, and often entrapping. Characters are more often than not stereotypes and can be drawn from other narratives (for example, the Cat in the Hat or Snow White). Metafictional characters may also be taken from the documents of history (often treated as just another unreliable text) as in the cases of Coover's Richard Nixon and Thomas Pynchon's Walter Rathenau and Mickey Rooney. At other times, the author breaks the narrative frame and becomes a character in the novel. Ultimately, metafiction becomes a testing of fiction itself.

To break narrative frames by allowing one level of the plot to intrude on another level is to introduce instability into a work of fiction, bringing the questions: What is the real story here? Who is this character? There is no single real world in the story, no sanctioned reality; there is no one real identity to a character. In Fowles's *The French Lieutenant's Woman*, the reader questions the character's identity: Is she an actress in a film or is she a historical figure?

Ultimately, characters in metafiction tend to be fragmented or multiple. They are authorial personas, and rarely agents of their own destinies. They are manipulated by plots they perceive as already inscribed. Their worlds resonate with the self-referential tendencies of a world that comes to acculturated subjects already textualized.

SUGGESTED READINGS

Elliot, Emory. *The Columbia History of the American Novel*. New York: Columbia University Press, 1991.

McHale, Brian. *Constructing Postmodernism*. New York: Routledge, 1992.

Petitjean, Tom. "Coover's 'The Babysitter.'" *Explicator* 54, no. 1 (Fall, 1995): 49-51.

—*Thomas D. Petitjean, Jr.*

See also Alienation; Barthelme, Donald; Literary standards; Pynchon, Thomas

Metamorphosis, The

AUTHOR: Franz Kafka (1883-1924)
FIRST PUBLISHED: "*Die Verwandlung*," 1915 (English translation, 1936)
IDENTITIES: Jewish; religion; world

Franz Kafka, who wrote relatively little in his short life and who published less, has been enormously influential on later writers, including writers in North America. He is considered an exponent of German expressionism—his work deals with a world that seems normal and recognizable but is also surreal, seemingly influenced by emotional and subconscious states, especially guilt.

Kafka has inspired a lengthy list of American writers. By creating a parallel between anguish and hope, employing a tightly controlled perspective, and adding a liberal sprinkling of black comedy, Kafka's work may be said to have influenced the works of writers as diverse as Edward Albee, Saul Bellow, Norman Mailer, Philip Roth, J. D. Salinger, and Walker Percy.

Kafka's frequently anthologized short story "The Metamorphosis" is the tale of a traveling salesman, Gregor Samsa, who awakens one morning to find he has become an enormous beetle. This transformation and estrangement reflects Kafka's view of the desperation connected with the human struggle for redemption. Gregor is killed as a result of his father's throwing an apple at him; the psychological and biblical symbolism of this act is clear but unstated. Kafka's emphasis on guilt and his technique of presenting the grotesque in bland, everyday language are perhaps most evident in the works of the Southern American writers in general and of Flannery O'Connor in particular. O'Connor recorded her observations about the story in her journal.

Kafka and O'Connor employ grotesque characters—physically or spiritually malformed—to demonstrate the human condition. Both writers are intrigued by a transcendent moment of grace, wherein a person can seek and be granted redemption. The two writers also share a biblical preoccupation with guilt and with parable. As does Kafka, O'Connor uses the world of the human spirit, the external world and the world within to demonstrate a collision of values. Gregor Samsa is destroyed by an apple, depicting the Fall; O'Connor's protagonists are often destroyed by the acknowledgement of their humanity. In the works of both writers there is often a veiled dialogue between the real and the symbolic. Many North American writers have incorporated Kafka's themes and techniques into their work, including his father-son confrontation, his disproportion between guilt and punishment, his emphasis on spiritual ambiguity, and his refined literary style.

SUGGESTED READINGS

Heller, Erich, ed. *The Basic Kafka*. New York: Simon & Schuster, 1958.

Kafka, Franz. *Letters to Friends, Family and Editors*. Translated by Richard Winston and Clara Winston. New York: Shocken Books, 1958.

Pawel, Ernst. *The Nightmare of Reason*. Toronto: Collins, 1984.

—*Joyce Duncan*

See also Appearance and identity; Existentialism; Psychological theories of identity

Mexican Americans. *See* Chicano identity; Latino American identity

Middle Passage

AUTHOR: Charles Johnson (1948-   )
FIRST PUBLISHED: 1990
IDENTITIES: African American

Middle Passage is the story of Rutherford Calhoun's life-changing journey aboard the slaver *Republic* in 1830. Like Charles Johnson's earlier *Oxherding Tale*, this book is narrated by a young black man born into slavery but with a superior education, whose story is rooted in nineteenth century history but whose savvy, humorous voice bespeaks a twentieth century intellectual consciousness.

Rutherford's adventures begin when he stows aboard a ship to escape a woman determined to bring him to the altar. The *Republic*, a slaver, ships out to Africa; there it picks up a special cargo—a hold full of men, women, and children of the mystical Allmuseri tribe. The *Republic*'s captain also secretly brings on board a crate containing the captured Allmuseri god.

Middle Passage blatantly evokes *Moby Dick: Or, The Whale* (1851), "Benito Cereno," and Homer's *Odyssey* (c. 800 B.C., English translation, 1616) among others. Johnson flaunts, mocks, and turns on end these similarities: His dwarfish Captain Falcon is a caricature of the crazed Ahab; the ringleaders of the revolting Allmuseri are Babo, Fernando, and Atufel; Isadora, Rutherford's intended, knits by day and unravels her work by night to forestall marriage to her new suitor. The *Republic*'s voyage is a darkly comic version of the *Pequod*'s, but one highlighting slavery's role in American history and economy. Whereas Herman Melville's Ishmael asks the philosophical question, "Who ain't a slave?" Johnson's Falcon educates Rutherford in the fundamentals of capitalism by pointing out, "Who ain't up for auction when it comes to it?"

Fittingly, then, Johnson's novel does not end when Falcon dies, the *Republic* sinks, and Rutherford is rescued. Rather, these events deliver Rutherford into the clutches of the *Republic*'s owners, come to check up on their investment. Also aboard the rescue ship is Isadora and her fiancé, wealthy black New Orleans mobster Papa Zeringue. Once Zeringue is exposed as a part owner of the *Republic*, Isadora is free to marry Rutherford, who joyfully embraces marriage as an emotional haven in a cannibalistic world.

Middle Passage charts Rutherford's growth from a self-serving opportunist to a responsible man who values the ties that link human beings. His passage from a worldview based on multiplicity, individualism, dualism, and linearity to acceptance of the Allmuseri concept of "unity of being" opens him up to love, compassion, and commitment.

Rutherford's growth into this new identity seems also to comment on Johnson's identity as a sophisticated black writer navigating his way through African American, American, Western, and Eastern traditions. Johnson calls *Middle Passage* his attempt to fill a literary void by producing "philosophical black literature." An admirer of writers such as Thomas Mann, Jean-Paul Sartre, Hermann Hesse, Herman Melville, and Ralph Ellison, who "understood instinctively that fiction and philosophy were sister disciplines," Johnson weds, in this work, his own interests in philosophy, African American history, and fiction.

In *Middle Passage*, Johnson reminds readers that the received American epic (literary and historical) has an African American counterpart, and he adds a new dimension to the slave narrative tradition by creating an African American narrator who speaks in a formidably intellectual voice. Johnson also insists that Rutherford be taken seriously simply as a human being engaged in exploring fundamental underpinnings of the human condition. Johnson won the 1990 National Book Award for *Middle Passage*.

Suggested readings

Johnson, Charles. "An Interview with Charles Johnson." Interview by Jonathan Little. *Contemporary Literature* 34, no. 12 (Summer, 1993): 158-182.

Keneally, Thomas. Review of *Middle Passage*, by Charles Johnson. *The New York Times Book Review*, July 1, 1990, 8.

Rushdy, Ashraf. "The Phenomenology of the Allmuseri." *African American Review* 26 (Fall, 1992): 373-394.

—Grace McEntee

See also African American identity; Johnson, Charles; Slave narratives; Slavery

Middleman and Other Stories, The

Author: Bharati Mukherjee (1940-   )
First published: 1988
Identities: Canada; family; religion; South Asian; women

The Middleman and Other Stories deals with the clash between Western and Third World cultures as technology and overpopulation join diverse peoples in tragicomic relationships. "A Wife's Story" is a good example of Bharati Mukherjee's storytelling technique. It is told in the present tense, begins abruptly, and has an interest, characteristic of literary minimalism, in brand names and consumerism. The narrator sees her Indian husband through American eyes when he visits her in New York City, where she is attending college. He is captivated by the meretricious glamour and abundance of consumer goods. The narrator realizes how Americanized she has become and how comically provincial her husband appears.

Alfred Judah in "The Middleman" is a man without a country, a Jew living in Central America and hoping to make his way to the United States. Some think he is an Arab and others think he is an Indian; he is despised by everyone. In "Orbiting," an American woman is living with an Afghan lover who is another man without a country, unable to obtain legal entry into any of the developed countries being flooded with immigrants.

In "Buried Lives," an Indian who is prospering in Sri Lanka abandons his responsibilities for a new life in America. After leading a terrifying underground existence, he finds himself engaged to be married in Germany. "Danny's Girls" is about immigrants who come to the United States for a better life and who become prostitutes. "Jasmine" has a similar theme.

"The Management of Grief," dealing with the 1985 bombing of an Air India jetliner, focuses on a specific incident but reveals a macrocosm. Through the eyes of one bereaved woman, the reader glimpses the diaspora that has scattered Indians across five continents, creating alienation and countless minor tragedies.

Mukherjee's experience as an upper-caste woman losing her tradition-bound, privileged identity was the turning point in her life. As an immigrant she was sometimes mistaken for a prostitute, a shoplifter, or a domestic servant. Her stories reflect her sympathy for the psychological traumas suffered by the Third World immigrants who have lost their old identities and who are trying to create new ones. Mukherjee is an Old World intellectual who has adopted New World values. The blending of old and new is another striking characteristic of her fiction. She dramatizes the cataclysmic changes taking place in human consciousness as cultures collide.

SUGGESTED READINGS

Chua, C. L. "Passages from India: Migrating to America in the Fiction of V. S. Naipaul and Bharati Mukherjee." In *Reworlding: The Literature of the Indian Diaspora*, edited by Emmanuel S. Nelson. Westport, Conn.: Greenwood Press, 1992.

Fakrul, Alam. *Bharati Mukherjee*. New York: Twayne, 1996.

Nelson, Emmanuel S., ed. *Bharati Mukherjee: Critical Perspectives*. New York: Garland, 1993.

—Bill Delaney

See also Asian American identity: India; Emigration and immigration; Feminism; "Management of Grief, The"; Multiculturalism; Religion; Women and identity

Midlife crisis. *See* Identity crisis

Midwest, the. *See* American identity: Midwest

Migratory workers

IDENTITIES: European American; Latino

In the Americas, migrant workers include farmworkers from the Caribbean, Mexico, and other countries of Latin America, blacks and whites from the Southern states, and Asians. John Steinbeck's works are notable in dealing with the depressed economic classes, especially migratory farmworkers. *The Grapes of Wrath* (1939) provides one example of proletarian literature, a sympathetic, perhaps even militant treatment of the working class.

History

Steinbeck's most notable work dealing with itinerant workers, *The Grapes of Wrath* relates the trials of a farm family, the Joads, who are driven from their home to California. There they seek work as migrant fruit pickers. Their journey and subsequent labor are marked by death and harassment. Despite the family's apparent defeat, Steinbeck portrays them as determined and dignified, a predominant theme in his work. *Of Mice and Men* (1937) was written first as a novel then produced as a play. It focuses on the friendship of two migrant workers and their ultimate defeat.

While the proletarian literature of Steinbeck and other writers of his time was grounded in the dignity and rights of the individual and his family, the explosion of Chicano literature was born in the rise of César Chávez's United Farm Workers of America in the 1960's. Chávez's movement gave voice to a long-silent and impotent minority, the migratory farmworkers living in squalid, inhumane conditions, working under life-threatening conditions, and earning a pittance for their labor.

Leading in development of Chicano literature was Luis Valdez with the Teatro Campesino. Chávez allowed Valdez to present his original drama to farmworkers as a means to strengthen his union. In contrast with Steinbeck, Valdez had been part of an itinerant farm family. Uncomfortable in middle-class city life, Valdez returned to his roots in the Salinas Valley. He sought to develop drama both reflective of and appealing to the farmworkers themselves.

The base of the teatro performance was the *acto*, Valdez's own creative approach to the one-act. Performed outdoors, *actos* included song and dance, use of masks, and few props. Initially, Valdez's concerns were solely with the farmworkers and the strike.

During the same era, Chicano fiction writers produced novels and short stories of the Chicano experience. These writers included José Antonio Villarreal, Tomás Rivera, and Miguel Méndez. Many Chicano poets dealt bitterly with the Mexican's experience in the Southwest, which was once part of Mexico.

Survey

In Chicano literature, Valdez credits such influences as Old Comedy, *commedia dell'arte*, Bertolt Brecht, Japanese theater, and the religious drama of the pre-Hispanic peoples of Latin America. His plays detail the farmworkers and their hardships in the fields. The characters, farmworker and owner, are more symbolic than realistic. The purpose of many of the *actos* is didactic—they teach while entertaining.

Rivera's *. . . y no se lo tragó la tierra* (1971; *And the Earth Did Not Part*, 1971) is a composite of stories and anecdotes. Some are socially or communally focused and some are individually focused. Chicano poets such as Tino Villanueva and others trace a cycle of the Anglos' being welcomed but rejecting the Mexicans' friendship, the prospering of the Anglos, the ruin of the land by the Anglos, the exile of the Mexicans into barrios, the seeking of work in the mines and the fields of the North, often with cultural alienation, and finally "an honest friend/ that by clear waters I await"—the friend being the United Farm Workers. As is the theater, Chicano poetry is strongly linked to the social struggles of the migrants. It affirms the Mexican American culture and maintains a flux between Spanish and English.

SUGGESTED READINGS

Bruce-Novoa. *Chicano Poetry: A Response to Chaos*. Austin: University of Texas Press, 1982.

Sommers, Joseph, and Tomas Ybarra-Frausto. *Modern Chicano Writers*. Englewood Cliffs, N.J.: Prentice-Hall, 1979.

—*Patricia J. Huhn*

See also Chicano identity; Chicano Renaissance; Class and identity; Economics of identity; Latino American identity; *Pocho*; Poverty; Rivera, Tomás; Steinbeck, John; Villarreal, José Antonio; *Zoot Suit*

Mile Zero

AUTHOR: Thomas Sanchez (1944-   )
FIRST PUBLISHED: 1989
IDENTITIES: Caribbean; South

Mile Zero, Thomas Sanchez's sweeping vision of Key West, Florida, brilliantly evokes the rich history and lyrical passion of the island. Key West is the southernmost point of the continental United States, where "Mile Zero," the last highway sign before the Atlantic Ocean, symbolizes the end of the American road. While Key West represents the end for the downtrodden Americans who gravitate there, the island promises hope for refugees fleeing Haiti's poverty across shark-ridden waters. Sanchez traces the island's shifting economy from a hub of the cigar industry to "a marijuana republic," then to "a mere cocaine principality." Sanchez laments how the drug trade has corrupted the American Dream.

Mile Zero's main character, St. Cloud, a former antiwar activist, drowns his self-doubt in Haitian rum and ponders his inability to sacrifice himself for his beliefs. He feels a strange kinship with MK, once a soldier in Vietnam and now a dangerous smuggler who has fled Key West for South America. MK's mysterious presence and the shadow of Vietnam permeate the book. St. Cloud imagines that his pacificism and MK's violence are two sides of the same coin. After Vietnam, returning soldiers and protesters both found themselves cast out of society.

When a Coast Guard cutter tows a refugee boat from Haiti into the harbor, Justo Tamarindo, a Cuban American police officer, drafts St. Cloud to help him prevent the deportation of the sole survivor, a boy named Voltaire. Voltaire's sad story reveals how America thrives at the expense of the Third World. Late in the novel, Voltaire escapes from the detention center where he is waiting to be deported. The young, malnourished boy dreams he has reached a heavenly land of plenty at a garish shopping mall before he dies a tragic death.

Meanwhile, Justo pursues Zobop, an enigmatic killer, who is roaming the island and leaving voodoo-inspired clues everywhere. After Zobop is killed, Justo learns that the murderer sought purification by destruction. Like El Finito, a powerful, apocalyptic hurricane that threatens to destroy the island, Zobop believes everything must be wiped out before it can be renewed.

In *Mile Zero*, Sanchez signals the necessity of cultural change. Vietnam is over, Justo thinks, but the bodies of the dead refugees augur the arrival of a new devil. America is doomed if it does not change. The novel's ambiguous ending, in which Justo, who may have contracted AIDS, pulls St. Cloud out of the ocean, brings its readers to mile zero, a place that can be either an ending or a beginning.

SUGGESTED READINGS

Abeel, Erica. "A Winning Sort of Loser." *The New York Times Book Review*, October 1, 1989, 7.
Bonetti, Kay. "An Interview with Thomas Sanchez." *Missouri Review* 14, no. 2 (1991): 76-95.
Rieff, David. "The Affirmative Action Novel." *The New Republic*, April, 1990, 31-34.

—Trey Strecker

See also American Dream; Sanchez, Thomas

Miller, Arthur

BORN: New York, New York; October 17, 1915

PRINCIPAL WORKS: *All My Sons*, pr., pb. 1947; *Death of a Salesman*, pr., pb. 1949; *The Crucible*, pr., pb. 1953; *A View from the Bridge*, pr. 1956, pb. 1957; *The Misfits*, 1961; *After the Fall*, pr., pb. 1964; *The Theater Essays of Arthur Miller*, 1978; *Timebends: A Life*, 1987

IDENTITIES: Family; Jewish

SIGNIFICANT ACHIEVEMENT: Miller's plays are widely regarded to be among the best plays ever written by an American.

Arthur Miller first achieved success as a dramatist with *All My Sons*. *Death of a Salesman*, widely regarded as Miller's most important play, contains many of the themes of identity that give distinction to Miller's plays: the tension between father and son, the dangerous material lure of the American Dream, the influence of memory on the formation of personality, and the common man in a tragic situation.

*Arthur Miller,
author of classic
American dramas
such as* The
Crucible *(1953)*.
(Inge Morath/
Magnum)

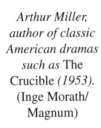

Partly in response to the anticommunist hysteria that was led by Senator Joseph McCarthy and the House Committee on Un-American Activities that swept the nation in the early 1950's, Miller wrote *The Crucible*. In 1955, Miller was denied a passport by the State Department, and in June, 1956, he was accused of left-wing activities and called before the committee. Unlike the girls in *The Crucible*, Miller refused to name others, and he was convicted of contempt of Congress in 1956, only to be fully exonerated by the United States Court of Appeals in 1958. During the turbulent summer of 1956 Miller also divorced his college sweetheart Mary Slattery and quickly married the famous actress Marilyn Monroe. Reflections of those two events recur throughout Miller's works and give shape to the identity of many of his major characters.

After completing the screenplay for *The Misfits*, which starred Monroe, Miller divorced the actress and married Inge Morath, events which may be reflected in *After the Fall*. Miller's later years saw the publication of his influential *The Theater Essays of Arthur Miller*, numerous revivals of his major plays, and his illuminating autobiography *Timebends: A Life*.

SUGGESTED READINGS

Ferres, John H. *Arthur Miller: A Reference Guide*. Boston: G. K. Hall, 1979.

Nelson, Benjamin. *Arthur Miller: Portrait of a Playwright*. New York: McKay, 1970.

Schlueter, June, and James K. Flanagan. *Arthur Miller*. New York: Frederick Ungar, 1987.

—Gregory W. Lanier

See also American Dream; Censorship of literature; *Crucible, The*; *Death of a Salesman*; Jewish American identity; Puritan and Protestant tradition; Religion and identity

Miller, Henry

BORN: New York, New York; December 26, 1891

DIED: Pacific Palisades, California; June 7, 1980

PRINCIPAL WORKS: *Tropic of Cancer*, 1934; *Black Spring*, 1936; *Tropic of Capricorn*, 1939; *The Rosy Crucifixion*, 1965 (*Sexus*, 1949; *Plexus*, 1953; *Nexus*, 1960)

IDENTITIES: European American

SIGNIFICANT ACHIEVEMENT: Publication of *Tropic of Cancer* in the United States signaled the end of major efforts to ban works of literature.

The three decades marking the most productive period in Henry Miller's life as a writer coincided with the period in which the legal community in the United States confronted the issues of publishing and distributing literary works that some people deem obscene or pornographic. The number of court cases on this issue reached an all-time high from the mid-1950's to the early 1960's. Famous trials considered such literary masterpieces as Vladimir Nabokov's *Lolita* (1955), William S. Burroughs' *Naked Lunch* (1959), Edmund Wilson's *Memoirs of Hecate County* (1949), and D. H. Lawrence's *Lady Chatterley's Lover* (1928). Some of these works were unavailable in the United States for many years as court cases dragged on or settled against publication.

The greatest number of trials involved *Tropic of Cancer*, first published by the Obelisk Press in Paris in 1934. In 1961, Grove Press published the book in the United States. Reviewers were mixed in their assessment, but tended to be sympathetic, perhaps because they realized that the publication involved a major censorship issue. Grove Press anticipated only minor opposition to the distribution of *Tropic of Cancer* since they had successfully defended the case for the U.S. publication of *Lady Chatterley's Lover* in 1959. Within a short period, however, some sixty court actions developed in all parts of the United States, requiring Grove Press, numerous booksellers, various library associations, and other groups to mount extensive defenses. Although each case differed in some details, the major question to be resolved was whether the book had any social value.

Witnesses from the scholarly and artistic communities were often as divided in their opinions as the reviewers had been. Consequently, in Connecticut and Pennsylvania the book was held to be obscene, while Massachusetts, Wisconsin, and Illinois ruled it not obscene. The most complex trial was held in Los Angeles in 1962, with many distinguished witnesses appearing for both sides.

Henry Miller
(Larry Colwell)

Initially the jury ruled *Tropic of Cancer* to be obscene; a decision eventually overturned. In July, 1964, the U.S. Supreme Court ruled in favor of Miller's book, giving it constitutional protection everywhere in the United States. With the case against *Tropic of Cancer* resolved, subsequent publications of Henry Miller's books, as well as most other books that censors wanted to ban, went unchallenged in almost all communities.

Tropic of Cancer, like most of Miller's writings, is best described as autobiographical fiction. He offers readers a complex artistic experience, demonstrated by an incredibly extensive and convoluted use of words, a sense of humor ranging from the bawdy to the most elevated and sophisticated, and narratives that often reach great heights of the imagination.

SUGGESTED READINGS

Martin, Jay. *Always Merry and Bright: The Life of Henry Miller*. Santa Barbara, Calif.: Capra Press, 1978.
Widmer, Kingsley. *Henry Miller*. New York: Twayne, 1963.
Winslow, Kathryn. *Henry Miller: Full of Life*. New York: St. Martin's Press, 1986.

—Thomas H. Falk

See also Censorship of literature; Erotic identity; *Tropic of Cancer*

Min, Anchee

BORN: Shanghai, China; 1957

PRINCIPAL WORKS: *Red Azalea*, 1994; *Katherine*, 1995
IDENTITIES: Chinese American; gay, lesbian, and bisexual; women
SIGNIFICANT ACHIEVEMENT: Min's powerful story of the Cultural Revolution is about rebellion against political and sexual repression.

Born in Shanghai, Anchee Min experienced political turmoil from an early age. During her childhood, Min's family was forced to move into a series of shabby apartments while her parents were demoted from their teaching positions to become factory workers. Min joined the Red Guards in elementary school and underwent a wrenching introduction to political survival when she was forced to denounce her favorite teacher as a Western spy.

Min's major experience with the clash between personal and political needs came at seventeen when she was assigned to an enormous collective farm. Forced to become a peasant in order to become a "true" revolutionary, Min witnessed the destruction of a friend whose relationship with a man led to her madness and his death. Min therefore knew the danger she faced when she fell in love with the leader of her work force, the charismatic Yan. The two eventually began a sexual relationship that violated the strictures against premarital sex and committed the "counterrevolutionary crime" of lesbianism.

Fighting to maintain her relationship with Yan and to survive the brutal life on the farm, Min received an unexpected respite when she was chosen to audition for the lead in a propaganda film, by Jiang Qing, wife of Mao Tse-tung, the Communist dictator of China. Min's return to Shanghai thrust her into an even more ruthless environment than the collective farm—the Shanghai film industry. Min was rescued finally through her relationship with the enigmatic "Supervisor," the film's producer, who became Min's lover and protector. Min's deliverance, however, was short-lived. Qing's fall from power in 1976 brought about the political destruction of those associated with her. The Supervisor was able to save Min from return to the collective farm, but he was unable to keep her from being demoted to a menial position within the film studio.

Faced with an uncertain future and continued repression, Min accepted an offer from the actress Joan Chen, a fellow film student in Shanghai, to emigrate to the United States, arriving in 1984. While learning English, she worked at a variety of jobs and received a Master of Fine Arts degree from the Art Institute of Chicago in 1990.

The great strength of Min's autobiography, *Red Azalea*, is its combination of frank narrative and lyrical description. Linking the personal and the political, Min uses sexuality as a metaphor for the individual's hunger for connection; sexual freedom thus indicates political freedom, and sexual expression becomes a revolutionary act.

SUGGESTED READINGS

Chang, Jung. *Wild Swans: Three Daughters of China*. Garden City, N.J.: Anchor Press, 1992.
Liang, Heng, and Judith Shapiro. *After the Nightmare*. New York: Alfred A. Knopf, 1986.
_____. *Son of the Revolution*. New York: Alfred A. Knopf, 1983.
Viviano, Frank. *Dispatches from the Pacific Century*. Reading, Mass.: Addison-Wesley, 1992.

—Margaret W. Batschelet

See also Asian American identity: China, Japan, and Korea; Erotic identity; Lesbian identity

Miracle Worker, The

AUTHOR: William Gibson (1914-   )
FIRST PERFORMED: 1957; first published, 1957
IDENTITIES: Disability; European American; family; South; women

The Miracle Worker recounts Helen Keller's discovery of language, through the teaching of Annie Sullivan, after losing her sight and hearing in early childhood. It was produced as a television play in 1957, was published in 1957, was produced as a stage play in 1960 and as a movie in 1962.

The story is set in the Keller family home in Tuscumbia, Alabama. In the opening scene, the family learns that baby Helen will survive a life-threatening fever. Her mother Kate, however, discovers the terrible price of Helen's survival when she realizes that the baby cannot see or hear. When Helen is six, her father is inclined to institutionalize her, but Kate wishes to search for better medical care. Alexander Graham Bell considers Helen's case but cannot help. Finally, the Kellers contact the Perkins Institute for the Blind in Boston; the director sends Annie to them.

When Annie first encounters Helen, the child has never been disciplined. Isolated in silence and darkness, Helen wanders the house and is prone to tantrums. Annie has herself been institutionalized, so she sympathizes with the urgency Kate feels about Helen. Annie is also blind, so she knows partly what Helen's world is like. She knows that the key to Helen's transformation is language. Annie succeeds in teaching Helen to finger-spell several words, realizing that her pupil understands this activity only as a memorization game—Helen does not understand that the sequences of letters have meaning. Meanwhile, Annie begins the task of teaching Helen manners. Lacking words, Helen expresses her emotions through actions, smashing objects when she is angry and striking people when frustrated. Annie responds with patience and determination.

The Keller family must also be taught to help Helen. Out of pity and guilt, they have allowed the child to rule the household, as Annie observes. To avoid enraged outbursts, family members indulge Helen's misbehavior. With difficulty, Annie persuades the Kellers to give her two weeks of isolation with Helen in the garden house. During this time, she makes progress only to see it erode upon returning to the main house; family members are unwilling to enforce the new rules.

In a crucial encounter, Helen pours out a pitcher of water in rage; Annie takes her forcibly to the pump to refill it and out of habit finger-spells "water" as Helen feels liquid gush over her hand. Suddenly, Helen understands that things have names, and that she can learn them through this new game and communicate her inner world to others. In the closing scene, Kate, Helen, and Annie go to the Perkins Institute. Helen is no longer isolated.

SUGGESTED READINGS

Balch, Jack. "A Miracle Named Patty." *Theater Arts* 44 (January, 1960): 26-29.
Gibson, William. "Second Wind." *Theater Arts* 43 (October, 1959): 17-20.

—Victoria Gaydosik

See also American identity: South; Intelligence; Keller, Helen; Physical disabilities and identity; School

Miscegenation. *See* Racism and ethnocentrism

Miss Lonelyhearts

AUTHOR: Nathanael West (Nathan Weinstein, 1903-1940)
FIRST PUBLISHED: 1933
IDENTITIES: Disability; Jewish

Generally considered Nathanael West's masterpiece, *Miss Lonelyhearts* is an intense indictment of the false promises of twentieth century America. Originally, West had envisioned writing a novel in the form of a comic strip, and this idea is evident in the use of brief chapters with illustrative titles. The novel, as with all West's novels, is concerned with identity through dreams. The Christ dream is a key theme in *Miss Lonelyhearts.*

As the novel opens, Miss Lonelyhearts, the young male writer of a newspaper advice column, can no longer ignore the misery of his correspondents and obsessively pursues some sort of control or order in life. The fraudulent guarantees and false dreams offered by religion, by nature, and by the media only lead to terrible destruction. Miss Lonelyhearts dies locked in an embrace with the disabled and impotent Doyle, one of his correspondents.

The grotesque characters in the novel are represented as nonhuman symbols. The editor Shrike's name is that of the bird that kills its victims by spearing them on thorns. His name is also similar to the word "shriek." Shrike's endless caustic speeches impale Miss Lonelyhearts in his quest for Christ-like compassion. Shrike's wife Mary is represented by breasts, but rather than nurturing, the breasts are teasing. Mary hides a medal in her cleavage and flaunts her breasts as she discusses her mother's terrible death from breast cancer. Betty, Miss Lonelyhearts' fiancée, is likened to nature and to a serene Buddha, but her calm innocence seems to invite violence. West writes that Betty is "like a kitten whose soft helplessness makes one ache to hurt it."

The Doyles' identity seems almost subhuman. Although Fay Doyle is associated with ocean imagery, she is more like some terrible beast from the sea. Her sexuality is terrifying; her thighs are likened to "two enormous grindstones." Her destructive powers are further illustrated when she hits her husband, who is disabled, with a rolled-up newspaper as he is pretending to be a dog. Ultimately Fay drives Peter Doyle to murder in his attempt to regain his degraded masculinity.

Images of sensory deadness pervade the novel. This deadness defines the sickness of modern times. *Miss Lonelyhearts* takes place in a world where all suffer from the awareness that consciousness cannot convert wishes into desires. Mastery over chaotic life forces has been achieved through assault upon and inhibition of the senses. *Miss Lonelyhearts* shows how resistance to and self-defense against the absurd lead only to violence.

SUGGESTED READINGS

Frank, Mike. "The Passion of Miss Lonelyhearts according to Nathanael West." *Studies in Short Fiction* 10, no. 1 (Winter, 1973): 67-73.

Jackson, Thomas H., ed. *Twentieth Century Interpretations of "Miss Lonelyhearts."* Englewood Cliffs, N.J.: Prentice-Hall, 1971.

Light, James F. "Violence, Dreams, and Dostoevski: The Art of Nathanael West." *College English*, 19, no. 5 (February, 1958): 208-213.

Long, Robert Emmet. *Nathanael West*. New York: Frederick Ungar, 1985.

—*Helen O'Hara Connell*

See also *Day of the Locust, The*; Violence; West, Nathanael

Mixed race and identity

IDENTITIES: Multiracial

Early depictions of mixed race assert the absolute difference of racial heritage. James Fenimore Cooper's *The Last of the Mohicans: A Narrative of 1757* (1826) features Cora Munro, the child of a slave and a British officer. Cora wavers between marrying an Indian or a British officer. Cooper uses Cora to imagine the possibility of a mixed racial identity, but ultimately has her die rather than allow her to commit miscegenation. In contrast, Lydia Maria Child's *Hobomok* (1824) features a white heroine who has a child with a Native American. The child of this union looks like his father, but his racial features "disappear" as he develops an identity as a white person.

Abolition and passing

Antislavery agitation in the mid-nineteenth century brought with it an increase in the depiction of people of black and white parentage. Authors used characters with a mixed race to dramatize the debate over national political identity. George Harris of Harriet Beecher Stowe's *Uncle Tom's Cabin: Or, Life Among the Lowly* (1852) is the son of a black mother and her white master. Harris becomes a strong spokesman in the novel for abolition, arguing that because black and white blood exist equally within him, they must enjoy equality in American social and political life. Frederick Douglass, in his *Narrative of the Life of Frederick Douglass: An American Slave* (1845) also argues that the existence of a class of slaves who are black and white destroys any theoretical justification for slavery, and that all individuals must be accorded the right of self-definition.

Given the many people of mixed race, the possibility of passing as white was real. Some racist novelists treated the issue hysterically, but many novels were written exposing how passing undermines any attempt to define people by racist precepts. William Wells Brown's *Clotel: Or, The President's Daughter* (1853), the first novel published by an African American, tells the story of a mulatto woman who adopts a white identity, marrying a white man in the North. *The House Behind the Cedars* (1900) by Charles W. Chesnutt, who was himself of mixed race, is another novel treating the question of individual identity that passing poses. Two works by white authors that use passing to satirize American racial attitudes are Kate Chopin's "Desiree's Baby," which concerns a man who rejects his wife and child due to the mistaken belief she is a mulatto, only to have his sense of identity disrupted when he discovers his own mother was black, and Mark Twain's *The Tragedy of Pudd'nhead Wilson* (1894) which features two infants, one of whom has a small amount of "black blood." Tom Driscoll discovers his heritage after decades of believing in his superiority, the result of his whiteness. Twain's character can no longer identify with blacks or whites and almost ceases to have any identity at all. Similarly, James Weldon Johnson's *Autobiography of an Ex-Coloured Man* (1912), an important novel about passing, features a mixed-race protagonist in a first-person narrative. The nameless narrator decides to embrace a white identity and marries a white woman and has children with her. The novel ends, however, with his realization that he has lost a full sense of his identity. The novels of passing use the problematic identities of individual characters to discuss a problematic national identity.

The novel of passing continued to be prominent in the early part of the twentieth century, but with a slightly different focus. The condition of a mixed-race person, in addition to a denunciation of racism, became a metaphor for the alienating condition of modern life. Novels such as Jessie Redmon Fauset's *There Is Confusion* (1924), Jean Toomer's *Cane* (1923), and Zora Neale Hurston's *Their Eyes Were Watching God* (1937) feature protagonists who vigorously assert individual identity even as society attempts alternately to impose or deny identity for them. Joe Christmas in William Faulkner's *Light in August* (1932) is an orphan who may or may not have a black father; even the hint that he may be part black grows into an obsession about his identity.

Edith Maud Eaton, known by the pen name Sui Sin Far, wrote autobiographical fiction and nonfiction about her experiences in the United States as the daughter of a Chinese woman and an Englishman. Experiencing extreme racism, Eaton embraced her Chinese identity in order to make a critique of American society. She was, in the early 1900's, the first Chinese American feminist writer. Gertrude Bonnin (Zitkala-Sa) similarly wrote of her experiences in her largely autobiographical fiction, collected in *American Indian Stories* (1921). N. Scott Momaday's *The Way to Rainy Mountain* (1969) charts his personal story as he tries to reclaim the Native American identity that had been overwhelmed by his European American cultural background. Gloria Anzaldúa, in her largely autobiographical *Borderlands: The New Mestiza-La Frontera* (1987) asserts her own mixed background and lesbianism to make multiracial identity a source of strength.

SUGGESTED READINGS

Berzon, Judith. *Neither White nor Black: The Mulatto Character in American Fiction.* New York: New York University Press, 1978.

Frederickson, George M. *The Black Image in the White Mind: The Debate on Afro-American Character and Destiny, 1817-1914.* New York: Harper & Row, 1971.

Jordan, Winthrop. *White over Black: American Attitudes Toward the Negro, 1550-1812.* Baltimore: Penguin Books, 1969.

Sundquist, Eric. *To Wake the Nations: Race in the Making of American Literature.* Cambridge, Mass.: Harvard University Press, 1993.

—Joe Boyd Fulton

See also Acculturation; African American identity; Ai; Asian American identity: China, Japan, and Korea; Bilingualism; Brown, William Wells; Chicano identity; Fauset, Jessie Redmon; Feminism; Identity crisis; Latino American identity; Lesbian identity; Multiculturalism; *Narrative of the Life of Frederick Douglass*; Native American identity; *Uncle Tom's Cabin*; Women and identity

The twentieth century

Mo, Timothy

BORN: Hong Kong; 1950

PRINCIPAL WORKS: *The Monkey King*, 1978; *Sour Sweet*, 1982; *An Insular Possession*, 1986; *The Redundancy of Courage*, 1991; *Brownout on Breadfruit Boulevard*, 1995

IDENTITIES: Asian; family; world

SIGNIFICANT ACHIEVEMENT: Exploring the colonial legacy in Hong Kong, Mo depicts individuals caught between Asian and Western traditions.

Two cultures meet in Timothy Mo's life. He was born in Hong Kong—his mother English, his father Chinese. When he was ten, the family moved to England, where he undertook a British preparatory schooling, then attended Oxford University to study history. Following graduation, he wrote reviews for *The Times Educational Supplement* and *New Statesman*. A bantamweight boxer, he also worked as a freelance journalist for *Boxing News*. He published his first novel at age twenty-eight.

Childhood in the British colony and frequent visits there after settling in England provided material for that novel, *The Monkey King*. Set in Hong Kong and nearby Macao during the 1950's, the narrative focuses on Wallace Nolasco, a Chinese Portuguese man from Macao. A former Portuguese colony, the area shares mixed traditions from its Chinese citizenry and its European colonizers. Like his father, Wallace denies his Asian ancestry, considers himself Portuguese, and holds everything Asian in contempt. In Hong Kong, he identifies more with the British than the Chinese. There, he marries a Chinese woman from a prominent and extremely traditional family. At first he rebels against the household's strict adherence to Asian customs, but after a prolonged struggle he accepts his dual heritage. In this novel and Mo's second work, *Sour Sweet*, the cultural conflicts are tempered with humor. In *Sour Sweet*, Mo enlarges his scrutiny of opposing traditions and their effects by recounting the trials of a Hong Kong immigrant family in London.

Mo's most ambitious book, *An Insular Possession*, returns to the early nineteenth century and the British establishment of Hong Kong after the First Opium War (1839-1842). The result of Mo's research in the region, the long novel not only provides a detailed historical account of this stormy era but also an incisive exploration of the era's cultural clashes as well. The postmodern narrative examines both the Chinese and British sides through a variety of techniques, but the book condemns neither. As does Mo's earlier work, *An Insular Possession* concludes that such distinctions as "British" and "Chinese" will fade once people understand their common humanity. A character observes that under "the different veneers of varying laws, institutions and civilisations . . . the Old Adam is the same. His nature contains the same admixture of bad and good."

Mo's fourth novel, *The Redundancy of Courage*, is a political fantasy. He has written and published steadily since his first novel's publication, contributing a body of fiction that looks beyond the different veneers.

SUGGESTED READINGS

Ramraj, Victor. "The Interstices and Overlaps of Cultures." In *International Literature in English*. New York: Garland, 1991.

Rothfork, John. "Confucianism in Timothy Mo's *Sour Sweet*." *Journal of Commonwealth Literature* 24, no. 1 (1989): 49-64.

—*Robert L. Ross*

See also Acculturation; Asian American identity: China, Japan, and Korea; Colonialism

Moccasin Telegraph and Other Indian Tales, The

AUTHOR: W. P. Kinsella (1935-   )

FIRST PUBLISHED: 1983

IDENTITIES: Canada; Native American

When William Patrick Kinsella began writing stories about the Ermineskin Reserve in Alberta, Canada, he knew little about Cree culture, but he did research, collected news about Native American activities, and incorporated that knowledge into later stories. He also made narrator Silas Ermineskin a little older and wiser, and leavened his poignancy with increasing humor. As a result, the fourth book of Ermineskin stories, *The Moccasin Telegraph and Other Indian Tales*, seems richer than previous volumes.

Kinsella's characters convey various aspects of Native American identity. Playfulness is conveyed by Frank Fence-post, who loves playing tricks on gullible white men. Respect for Native American heritage is embodied in Mad Etta, the wise old medicine woman, and Delores, who learns traditional Cree dances. Close connections to the land emerge in "The Ballad of the Public

Trustee," in which Silas sadly cannot prevent government seizure of an old friend's property, and family ties are central to "Pius Blindman Is Coming Home," in which an old woman stays alive hoping for her wayward son's return.

Kinsella does not romanticize or idealize Native Americans. Characters display no environmental wisdom, spiritual insights, or mystical powers. Several succumb to alcoholism, gambling, or crime, and Chief Tom is vilified as an "apple" (red on the outside, white on the inside) because he adopts western dress and acquiesces to every white man's wishes. Significantly, Kinsella does not cast these characters as victims of evil white influence but holds them accountable for their own weaknesses. This is one theme of "The Moccasin Telegraph," the title story, in which a drunken Native American wantonly kills a clerk during a robbery and is shot by the Royal Canadian Mounted Police while resisting arrest. When members of the American Indian Movement arrive to denounce the killing as racist police brutality, residents are irritated by the protests. To them, the dead man got what he deserved, and AIM means "A**holes in Moccasins." There are also admirable whites, like the fraudulent doctor who earns the affection of residents because of his sincere concern, and the head of a religious college, who treats Native American visitors with courtesy and understanding. Thus, while cultural backgrounds are important, individuals are still responsible for developing their own identities and must be judged individually.

Kinsella's portrayals of Native Americans sometimes seem harsh, but his respect and fondness for Native American culture and people nevertheless emerge. His balanced pictures of Native American life merit attention.

Suggested readings

Goldie, Terry. *Fear and Temptation: The Image of the Indigene in Canadian, Australian, and New Zealand Literature*. Montreal: McGill-Queen's University Press, 1989.

Johnston, Gordon. "An Intolerable Burden of Meaning: Native Peoples in White Fiction." In *The Native in Literature*, edited by Thomas King, Cheryl Calver, and Helen Hoy. Oakville, Ontario, Canada: ECW Press, 1987.

Murray, Don. *The Fiction of W. P. Kinsella: Tall Tales in Various Voices*. Fredericton, New Brunswick, Canada: York Press, 1987.

—*Gary Westfahl*

See also Canadian identity; Kinsella, W. P.; Native American identity

Mohr, Nicholasa

Born: New York, New York; November 1, 1935

Principal works: *Nilda*, 1973; *El Bronx Remembered: A Novella and Stories*, 1975; *In Nueva York*, 1977

Identities: Adolescence and coming-of-age; Latino; women

Significant achievement: Mohr writes of Puerto Ricans in New York, and her work features feminist characters.

The daughter of Puerto Rican immigrants, Nicholasa Mohr documents life in New York City's barrios. Mohr examines the Puerto Rican experience from the perspective of girls and young women. Her female characters face multiple social problems associated with the restrictions imposed upon women by Latino culture. The struggle for sexual equality makes Mohr's literature central to Latina feminism.

Mohr's characters are an integral part of her realistic portrayal of life in a barrio. The parallels between her characters and her experience are evident. Nilda Ramírez, for example, is a nine-year-old Puerto Rican girl who comes of age during World War II. She also becomes an orphan and is separated from her immediate family. There are close parallels between these events and those of Mohr's life. In other stories as well girls must face, alone, social adversity, racism, and chauvinistic attitudes. Gays also frequently appear in her work. Gays and girls or young women (especially those who have little or no family) have often been subjected to mistreatment in the male-dominated Puerto Rican culture.

Mohr, a graphic artist and painter, studied at the Brooklyn Museum Art School from 1955 to 1959. Her advocacy to the social underclass is visible in her visual art, which includes elements of graffiti. Her use of graffiti in her art attracted the attention of a publisher who had acquired several of her paintings. Believing that Mohr had a story to tell, the publisher convinced her to write a short autobiographical piece on growing up Puerto Rican in New York. Many changes later, that piece became *Nilda*, her first novel, which has earned several prizes. Mohr has also drawn pictures for some of her literary work.

New York City is as important to Mohr's writing as her Puerto Rican characters. The city, with its many barrios, provides a lively background to her stories. Her short-story collections *El Bronx Remembered* and *In Nueva York* stress the characters' relationship to New York. Mohr's work can be described as cross-cultural, being a careful and artistic portrait of Puerto Rican culture in New York City.

SUGGESTED READING

Mohr, Nicholasa. "An Interview with Author Nicholasa Mohr." Interview by Nyra Zarnowski. *The Reading Teacher* 45, no. 2 (October, 1991): 106.

—Rafael Ocasio

See also Acculturation; American identity: Northeast; *Bronx Remembered, El*; Catholicism; Economics of identity; Environment and identity; Feminism; Gay identity

Momaday, N. Scott

BORN: Lawton, Oklahoma; February 27, 1934

PRINCIPAL WORKS: *House Made of Dawn*, 1968; *The Way to Rainy Mountain*, 1969; *The Names*, 1976; *The Ancient Child*, 1989

IDENTITIES: Native American; West and Southwest

SIGNIFICANT ACHIEVEMENT: Momaday's works are poetically brilliant accounts of the landscape, the sacredness of language, and self-knowledge.

Among the most widely read and studied Native American authors, N. Scott Momaday manifests, in his writings, a keen awareness of the importance of self-definition in literature and life. From 1936 onward, his family moved from place to place in the Southwest, eventually settling in Albuquerque, where Momaday attended high school. He entered the University of New Mexico in 1954 and later studied poetry at Stanford University. In 1963, he received his doctorate in English and since then has held teaching jobs at various Southwestern universities.

In a semiautobiographical work, *The Way to Rainy Mountain*, Momaday writes that identity is "the history of an idea, man's idea of himself, and it has old and essential being in language." Momaday defines his characters in terms of their use or abuse of language; usually his characters find themselves relearning how to speak while they learn about themselves. Even the title of one of Momaday's essays, "The Man Made of Words," indicates his contention that identity is shaped by language. "Only when he is embodied in an idea," Momaday writes, "and the idea is realized in language, can man take possession of himself."

The forces that shape language—culture and landscape—are also crucial in Momaday's works. To Russell Martin, Western writing is concerned with the harsh realities of the frontier that "could carve lives that were as lean and straight as whittled sticks." This harsh landscape is present in Momaday's work also, but he has a heartfelt attachment to it. Having a spiritual investment in a place, in Momaday's writing, helps a person gain self-knowledge. To an extent, issues of identity were important to Momaday as well. Son of a Kiowa father and a Cherokee mother, Momaday belonged fully to neither culture. Furthermore, much of his early childhood was spent on a Navajo reservation, where his father worked, and he grew up consciously alienated from the surrounding culture.

To combat rootlessness, the imagination and its expression in language is essential. "What sustains" the artist, he writes in *The Ancient Child* "is the satisfaction . . . of having created a few incomparable things—landscapes, waters, birds, and beasts." Writing about the efforts of various people to maintain traditional culture in the face of the modern world, Momaday occupies a central place in the American literary landscape.

SUGGESTED READINGS

Martin, Russell, and Marc Barasch, eds. *Writers of the Purple Sage*. New York: Viking, 1984.

Ramsey, Jerold. *Reading the Fire*. Lincoln: University of Nebraska Press, 1982.

Velie, Alan R. *Four American Indian Literary Masters*. Norman: University of Oklahoma Press, 1982.

—Michael R. Meyers

See also American identity: West and the frontier; *Ancient Child, The*; *House Made of Dawn*; Native American identity

Monette, Paul

BORN: Lawrence, Massachusetts; October 16, 1945

DIED: West Hollywood, California; February 10, 1995

PRINCIPAL WORKS: *Borrowed Time: An AIDS Memoir*, 1988; *Love Alone: Eighteen Elegies for Rog*, 1988; *Becoming a Man: Half a Life Story*, 1992; *Last Watch of the Night: Essays Too Personal and Otherwise*, 1993

IDENTITIES: European American; gay, lesbian, and bisexual

SIGNIFICANT ACHIEVEMENT: Monette's fiction, poetry, and autobiographical writing constitute some of the most powerful explorations of gay experience in the age of acquired immune deficiency syndrome (AIDS).

When Paul Monette died he left a legacy of writing that spanned some twenty years, yet it seems clear that his enduring contribution to gay literature in general, and to the literature of AIDS in particular, will be the books he wrote during the last seven or eight years of his life. From 1987, when he lost his longtime partner Roger Horwitz, until his own death, Monette focused all of his creative energies on documenting the lives of gay men living with AIDS, on challenging homophobia in American culture, and on articulating a progressive vision for the gay community. He moved from provincial author of moderately amusing gay novels to national spokesman for gay people and passionate chronicler of the AIDS crisis.

In *Becoming a Man*, winner of the National Book Award for nonfiction, Monette reveals that he began writing at Philips Academy, Andover, turning to art as a way to escape the puritanical burden of his New England upbringing and the isolation he felt as a young gay student. The struggle to embrace his true identity lasted until his mid-twenties, when he met Horwitz. Only then did he leave the closet for the light of a satisfying life partnership and a career as a gay writer.

Monette's first critical recognition came for his volume of poems, *The Carpenter at the Asylum* (1975). His first novel, *Taking Care of Mrs. Carroll* (1978), is representative of the gay romances Monette wrote before AIDS upended his life in the mid-1980's. Monette called his romantic novels "glib and silly," but they consistently portray the reality of gay men loving each other and creating chosen families that support them. All of Monette's work is predicated on the assumption that gay love is natural, productive, and meaningfully integrated into the larger human community.

In 1985, however, Horwitz was diagnosed with AIDS, and Monette's writing took a clear turn, becoming far more personal and more resolutely political. *Borrowed Time* eloquently documents the couple's battle against AIDS during the early years of the epidemic. The book is a harrowing account of their personal suffering and a celebration of their courageous love. This fierce and passionate new voice is present in Monette's subsequent two novels, *Afterlife* (1990) and *Halfway*

Home (1991), each of which explores how gays have been devastated by AIDS and by the homophobic backlash it has generated. In his final volume of essays, *Last Watch of the Night*, Monette abandons imaginative literature to address more directly questions about the epidemic and the backlash. When he finally succumbed to AIDS, he had established himself for many gay men as the conscience of their community.

SUGGESTED READINGS

Clum, John. "'The Time Before the War': AIDS, Memory, and Desire." *American Literature* 62, no. 2 (1990): 648-667.

Roman, David. "Paul Monette." In *Contemporary Gay American Novelists*, edited by Emmanuel S. Nelson. Westport, Conn.: Greenwood Press, 1993.

—*Thomas J. Campbell*

See also AIDS; *Becoming a Man*; Gay identity

Moon Cakes

AUTHOR: Andrea Louie
FIRST PUBLISHED: 1995
IDENTITIES: Chinese American; family; women

Moon Cakes, Andrea Louie's first novel, builds upon the question: "What becomes of an eleven-year-old child whose father suddenly dies?" Suffering the pangs of increasing anger, alienation, and isolation, Maggie tries to restore balance and give meaning to her life as she searches for answers to this question. The transience, fragmentation, and truncation that dominate her narrative become a conceit for the emotional and social disruption characterizing her life since her father's death. The opening dream sequence, for example, introduces a little girl, wearing a "pint-size knapsack with an appliquéd penguin made of black and white felt" and pulling behind her a wagon. She is on an impossible quest to find what none have seen or heard of before, something called "moon cakes." This dream-quest impinges upon Maggie's life in the form of her journey into personal discovery and self-worth.

Born in a small town in the middle of Ohio, a place where "the land is very flat and well kept," Maggie has grown up with the stereotype of the all-American family, the embodiment of fantasy-like perfection, down to the last detail. Her father was a successful and altruistic physician. Her mother miraculously balances careers as a brilliant biochemist and university administrator. Her older sister juggles cheerleading and rigorous medical residencies, matriculation at an Ivy League university, and marriage as "a Chinese Martha Stewart." The second daughter of such a "model minority" family, Maggie, or "Xiao Li," as her father affectionately calls her, is from birth nurtured behind the veneer of assimilation. Her family heaps upon her the bountiful rewards of their American Dream. Innocent to the spiritual costs of their blind acquiescence and easy balance, she, too, embraces this world of mixed signals.

Her father's death removes this veil of innocence. The veneer that had stood between her and the world peeling away, Maggie finds a stuttering uncertainty, a void within herself. Those memories of her father—the cacophony of Cantonese opera as he calmly pressed his shirts, his childlike passion for ice cream and his stoicism when eating moon cakes once a year, for example—no longer seem "inner-resting," as her Ohio-bred neighbors once pronounced, but are inscribed with contradiction, opposition, and discord. The stability of his presence afforded no more than an illusion; she turns to the "seamlessly normal" world of sacrificing mothers with their outlandishly blond coiffures and blue-eyed lettermen sons to provide the yardstick by which she can measure herself. Such a yardstick seems ill-suited as she recognizes the depth of her differences. "I am," she laments, "a Chinese daughter born in the unlikely American landscape of farmers' sons." Whatever ties remained to this world are severed completely when these mothers and sons turn against her and spit curses from the sides of their mouths. In their expletives— Oriental, Japanese, Vietnamese, Korean—she loses any sense of who she is.

In the face of loss comes denial, as the narrator adopts a new name: "Maya, after some great ancient people I had read about in an encyclopedia," and begins whispering such words as *mi amor*, *la cucaracha*, and *quesadilla* for would-be lovers to hear. She meanders through a state university, bedecked head to toe in an all-purpose black wardrobe. Her destination invariably becomes "an empty study carrel in the deserted reaches of the Spanish literature section."

Maya next escapes to New York, resigned to lead her life as a Chinese bagel that "refuses to rise." Venturing away from the security of her sister's apartment, she wanders into the city and finds work with an upstart publishing house, all the while seeking a sense of the familiar in her surroundings: three abandoned cats, the savorlessness of instant noodles, and a plethora of empty boxes. Then, overwhelmed by the enormity and the unabashed ostentation of her sister's wedding plans, she suddenly books a ticket with a tour group bound for China. Unable to explain her impetuous behavior, even to herself, she knows only that she must search. As she boards the plane, there are only questions, no answers, only uncertainties, no absolutes.

In the tradition of the Chinese talk-story, given popular exposure by Maxine Hong Kingston and Amy Tan, Louie's narrative begins, "I want to tell you a love story," one that "has no beginning, no end," that "simply must start somewhere in the middle, which is now." The work eschews the comfort of this form in favor of uncertainty; following the death of the narrator's father, her encounters become increasingly brief, briskly alternating, nimbly evanescent. Life's capriciousness is reflected in the narrative, which ranges from her childhood schoolmate Beverly, born into an abusive family and victimized her whole life, who appears one day and who as suddenly disappears, to college soulmate Lance, who struts into Maya's life, who introduces her to one madcap platonic adventure after another, who grows silent, moves to California, and succumbs to acquired immune deficiency syndrome, to Alex, a student from Hong Kong who shares her love of food, Chinese mountains, and their futon, to their child, conceived in a moment of passion and miscarried in abandonment and despair. The people she meets and allows herself to care for appear at random out of nowhere and, without the slightest of transitions, pull away, quickly disappearing without a trace, the same way her father had done when she was eleven.

As a metaphor for the process by which Maya comes to terms with who and where she is in the world, the narrative pushes outward in all directions rather than flowing unidirectionally. Maya's search for a personal identity moves away from passive questioning and the rejection of her past toward an active redefinition. Those with whom she has formed any lasting bonds are ones who similarly have taken responsibility for their own self-definitions, their own self-worth. Candy, a gum-chewing bass player with no rhythm, lives a life with a cadence all its own. Renee, a bleached-blond pre-op transvestite whose elbows give him away, promises himself an operation. The child, Marcus, Korean by bloodline and vintage American in outlook and temperament, is precocious and self-assured, easily bored and increasingly weary for a place he knows to be home. Prior to leaving the Chinese mainland, Maya realizes, perhaps for the first time, that the pain and uncertainty characterizing her past, like the two stones she has collected somewhere along the way, bear upon her present but only as raw materials from which she must fashion her own future. The wholly personal nature of her voice becomes an expression of her emerging sense of power and authority and a celebration of her difference.

SUGGESTED READINGS

Awkward, Michael. *Negotiating Difference: Race, Gender, and the Politics of Personality.* Chicago: University of Chicago Press, 1995.

Brewer, María Minich. "A Loosening of Tongues: From Narrative Economy to Women Writing." *Comparative Literature* 99, no. 5 (1984): 1141-1161.

Cafarelli, Annette Wheeler. "Gender, Truncation and Ideology: Women and Autobiography." In *Literary History, Narrative, and Culture*, edited by Wimsal Dissanayake et al. Honolulu: The East-West Center, 1989.

Langbaum, Robert. *The Mysteries of Identity: A Theme in Modern Literature.* New York: Oxford University Press, 1977.

Smith, Sidonie. *A Poetics of Women's Autobiography: Marginality and the Fictions of Self-Representation*. Bloomington: Indiana University Press, 1987.

—*James A. Wren*

See also Asian American identity: China, Japan, and Korea; Kingston, Maxine Hong; Pluralism versus assimilation; Tan, Amy

Mori, Kyoko

BORN: Kobe, Japan; March 9, 1957

PRINCIPAL WORKS: *Shizuko's Daughter*, 1993; *Fallout*, 1994; *The Dream of Water: A Memoir*, 1995; *One Bird*, 1995

IDENTITIES: Family; Japanese American; women

SIGNIFICANT ACHIEVEMENT: Mori contributes to a growing body of literature that attempts to reconcile memories and experiences of a foreign country, in this case Japan, with life in the United States.

Encouraged by her mother, Kyoko Mori began writing at an early age, winning essay contests in grade school. Her grandfather taught writing, and her mother's family, reduced to near poverty after World War II as a result of their land having been redistributed, emphasized education, writing, and an appreciation of culture. Her mother fostered an appreciation of nature and art and encouraged her to apply to a nontraditional high school. In 1969, Mori was accepted and began classes one month after her mother's suicide.

Much of Mori's writing focuses on coming to terms with her mother's suicide. An appreciation of her mother's influence underlies these works, despite her discernible disquiet over the suicide. After her mother's death, Mori lived with her abusive father and manipulative stepmother until 1973, when she left Japan for the first time to attend a year of high school in Arizona. Mori then moved to the United States permanently to study writing, receiving her B.A. from Rockford College and her Ph.D. in creative writing from the University of Wisconsin at Milwaukee in 1984.

In 1990, Mori returned to Japan for the first time in thirteen years. This trip is the subject of *The Dream of Water*, which develops themes that appear throughout Mori's work: her mother's suicide, her relationship with her father, and the attempt to find a home between two cultures.

Mori feels somewhat out of place and a bit surprised to be living in the United States ("in a small Wisconsin town where the old women in diners don't look anything like my grandmother"). She also felt a "mixture of familiarity and strangeness," "fondness and regret" when she returned to Japan. "Home" is not a stable concept; she described the trip as "going from one foreign place to another."

Mori's writing can be seen as a way of establishing connections between these two cultures: "Most of my short stories are set in Japan, and my poems tend to juxtapose my memories of Japan with my life in the Midwest." Her work is also intended to give voice to her mother and to women in Japan, whose expression is restricted by a traditional, masculine culture. She perceives her identity "as a writer, not as a wife," unlike the women she describes in Japan.

SUGGESTED READINGS

Gillan, Maria Mazziotti, ed. *Unsettling America: An Anthology of Contemporary Multicultural Poetry*. New York: Viking, 1994.

Giovanni, Nikki, ed. *Grand Mothers: Poems, Reminiscences, and Short Stories About the Keepers of Our Tradition*. New York: Holt, 1994.

Lim, Shirley Geok-Lin, ed. *The Forbidden Stitch: An Asian-American Women's Anthology*. Corvallis, Oreg.: Calyx Press, 1988.

—*John Allen*

See also Acculturation; Adolescent identity; Asian American identity: China, Japan, and Korea

Mormons. *See* Religious minorities

Morrison, Toni

Born: Lorain, Ohio; February 18, 1931

Principal works: *The Bluest Eye*, 1970; *Sula*, 1973; *Song of Solomon*, 1977; *Tar Baby*, 1981;
Beloved, 1987; *Jazz*, 1992; *Playing in the Dark: Whiteness and the Literary Imagination*, 1992

Identities: African American; family; women

Significant achievement: Morrison is the first African American woman to receive the Nobel
Prize in Literature.

Toni Morrison was born Chloe Anthony Wofford; her family was blue-collar Midwestern. Her
parents had migrated from the South in search of a better life. From her parents and grandparents,
Morrison acquired a background in African American folklore; magic and the supernatural appear
with frequency in her work.

At Howard University, where she earned a bachelor's degree, she changed her name to Toni.
After receiving a master's degree in English from Cornell University, she taught at Texas Southern
University and then at Howard, where she met Jamaican architect Harold Morrison. Their marriage
ended after seven years. A single mother, Toni Morrison supported herself and two sons as a senior
editor at Random House, where she encouraged the publication of African American literature.
She has continued to teach at various universities, including Harvard, Yale, and Princeton.

Originally, Morrison did not intend to be a writer. She has said she began to write because she
could not find herself, a black woman, represented in American fiction. In a conversation with
novelist Gloria Naylor, published in *Southern Review*, Morrison speaks of reclaiming herself as a
woman and validating her life through the writing of her first book, *The Bluest Eye*, in which a
young black girl prays for the blue eyes that will bring her acceptance.

Morrison celebrates the culture of strong black women that she remembers from her childhood,
especially in *Sula*, *Song of Solomon*, and *Beloved*. She believes that being able to recognize the contribution and legacy of one's ancestors is essential to self-knowledge. Her characters are forced to
confront their personal and social histories and are often drawn back to their African heritage.

Some black male critics have challenged Morrison on the grounds that her male characters are
too negative, but the literary world has honored
her. In 1988, *Beloved* was awarded the Pulitzer
Prize for fiction. In 1993, Morrison became the
second American woman to receive the Nobel
Prize in Literature.

*Toni Morrison,
winner of the
Nobel Prize in
Literature in 1993.
(Maria Mulas)*

Suggested readings

Christian, Barbara T. "Layered Rhythms: Virginia Woolf and Toni Morrison." *Modern Fiction Studies* 39, nos. 3, 4 (Fall/Winter, 1993):
483-500.

Morrison, Toni. "An Interview with Toni Morrison." Interview by Nellie McKay. *Contemporary Literature* 24, no. 4 (Winter, 1983):
413-429.

Naylor, Gloria, and Toni Morrison. "A Conversation." *Southern Review* 21, no. 3 (July, 1985):
567-593.

Samuels, Wilfred D., and Clenora Hudson-
Weems. *Toni Morrison*. Boston: Twayne, 1990.

—*Joanne McCarthy*

See also African American identity; *Beloved*;
Feminism; Slavery; *Song of Solomon*

Moths and Other Stories, The

AUTHOR: Helena María Viramontes (1954-   )

FIRST PUBLISHED: 1985

IDENTITIES: Adolescence and coming-of-age; aging; Latino; women

The Moths and Other Stories focuses on the lives of Chicana women of various ages and backgrounds. The women in Helena María Viramontes' stories often face identity crises—they struggle with religion, adolescence, sexuality, family, and aging.

"The Moths" narrates the growth of a fourteen-year-old girl who cares for her grandmother. The grandmother's home is a refuge for the young woman, whose home is ruled by her father. When her grandmother dies, the girl laments the loss of a strong female figure who has helped shape her identity. "Growing" also focuses on a young Chicana woman who struggles with adolescence. Fifteen-year-old Naomi looks forward to her first date until her parents make her take along her little sister Lucia as a chaperone. Naomi insists that dating is "different" in America, but her parents insist on their own customs and Naomi wonders about the difficulties of growing up in a new country.

In the stories focusing on young women Viramontes raises the issues of religion, reproduction, and marriage. In "Birthday" a young, unmarried woman struggles over her decision to abort a child. "The Broken Web" focuses on a young woman and her struggles with repressed family memories. Martita learns that her father, Tomas, beat and cheated on her mother, and that her mother finally snapped and killed Tomas. "The Broken Web" shows a young woman dealing with the violence of her childhood. In "The Long Reconciliation" Amanda and Chato's marriage falls apart when Amanda refuses to bring children into their meager existence. After Amanda aborts their first child, Chato refuses all sexual contact with her and their marriage ends. "The Cariboo Cafe" focuses on the struggles of a young mother. Two children are kidnapped by a woman who has lost her own child in the political problems in Central America. Eventually the woman is discovered, and the children are taken away from her. She screams for her own son, Geraldo.

The final two stories focus on older women. In "Snapshots" Olga Ruiz, a middle-aged divorcée, attempts to come to terms with her past identities. As she sifts through family photographs, she realizes how little she has left of herself—she was too busy being a good wife and mother. "Neighbors" focuses on a lonely, elderly woman. Aura has nothing but her beautiful garden and her neighbor, Fierro. When a strange woman visits Fierro, Aura is upset by the change in their relationship. In her struggles with loneliness, Aura becomes fearful, and "Neighbors" examines the loneliness, isolation, and fear of being an old, solitary woman.

Women's issues are Viramontes' focus throughout *The Moths and Other Stories*, and her narratives focusing on the struggles of primarily Chicana women are tinged with the complexities of adolescence, sexuality, marriage, poverty, and family.

SUGGESTED READING

Yarbo-Bejarano, Yvonne. Introduction to *The Moths and Other Stories*, by Helena María Viramontes. Houston, Tex.: Arte Público Press, 1985.

—*Angela Athy*

See also Abortion and birth control; Adolescent identity; Chicano identity; Feminism; Religion and identity; Viramontes, Helena María

Motion of Light in Water: Sex and Science Fiction Writing in the East Village, 1957-1965, The

AUTHOR: Samuel R. Delany (1942-   )

FIRST PUBLISHED: 1988

IDENTITIES: African American; gay, lesbian, and bisexual

The Motion of Light in Water: Sex and Science Fiction Writing in the East Village, 1957-1965 is an account of the late adolescence and early adulthood of one of the finest science-fiction writers to emerge in the 1960's. Samuel Delany was the first black writer to rise to eminence in the genre and was one of the first writers to take advantage of the decline of censorship in the investigation of sexual identities. This memoir stops short of the period when he became a literary pioneer, but it examines in great detail the personal experiences that were later to feed that work. Its primary concern is the awakening of the author's homosexual identity, augmented—and slightly confused—by his early marriage to Marilyn Hacker, a white poet, and their setting up home on the Lower East Side of Manhattan.

The memoir describes—but not in strictly chronological order—Delany's unsteady emergence from the educational hothouse of the Bronx High School of Science into the "real world" of work and marriage. It contemplates, with slightly self-demeaning but sympathetic fascination, his early and precocious adventures in science-fiction writing and the gradual forging of his highly distinctive literary voice. It ends, after an astonishing profusion of erotic encounters, with his setting forth from the city of his birth to cross the Atlantic and explore the Old World, modestly recapitulating the kind of experiential quest pursued by all the heroes of his early novels.

The text of *The Motion of Light in Water* is broken up into brief numbered subchapters, some of which have further subchapters presumably introduced as elaborations and afterthoughts, emphasizing that it grew in a mosaic fashion rather than being written in a straightforward, linear manner. The second edition of the book is further augmented, offering additional testimony to the relentless curiosity with which the author has repeatedly worked through the catalog of his experiences.

The Motion of Light in Water is remarkable for its frankness and for its scrupulousness. It attains a paradoxical combination of warm intimacy and clinical objectivity that is unique. The analysis of actual experiences is combined with and subtly tempered by an extended reflection on the vagaries of memory. The metaphorical title refers to the essential elusiveness of the process by which the filtration of memory converts the raw material of incident and confrontation into the wealth of self-knowledge. There are very few works that capture the elusiveness of memory and celebrate its mercurial quality as well as Delany's.

SUGGESTED READINGS

Broderick, Damien. "The Multiplicity of Worlds, of Others." *Foundation* 55 (Summer, 1992): 66-81.
_____. *Reading by Starlight: Postmodern Science Fiction*. London: Routledge & Kegan Paul, 1995.

—*Brian Stableford*

See also African American identity; Delany, Samuel R.; Erotic identity; Gay identity

Moveable Feast, A

AUTHOR: Ernest Hemingway (1899-1961)
FIRST PUBLISHED: 1964
IDENTITIES: European American

"This is how Paris was in the early days when we were very poor and very happy," writes Ernest Hemingway of the years between 1921 and 1926 when, as a struggling young writer, he lived in Paris with his first wife, Hadley, and their son, Bumby. *A Moveable Feast*, a collection of twenty essays published after Hemingway's death, captures the moods of a city.

Having quit his job as a journalist, Hemingway lived in an apartment overlooking a sawmill. Selling only a few stories and living on very little money, he skimped on firewood, wore sweatshirts as underwear, and skipped more than a few meals. He borrowed books from Sylvia Beach's famous bookstore, where his credit was good and Sylvia herself could be counted on for small loans. Occasional windfalls came from lucky bets on the horses, but new clothes and dinners out were rare. The couple did not consider themselves poor. They found poverty ennobling and looked down on the rich.

The book offers without pardon or apology Hemingway's unvarnished opinions on the legendary writers and artists who worked in Paris at that time. He relished Gertrude Stein's food, liqueur, and encouragement but resented her treatment of him and his wife as "promising children." He judged the poet Ford Madox Ford foul-smelling, forgetful, and abusive and the painter Wyndham Lewis arrogant and cruel. Three essays reveal Hemingway's assessment of F. Scott Fitzgerald, whose talent, he writes, "was as natural as the pattern . . . on a butterfly's wings." For these accounts, Hemingway has been criticized by some for callously divulging Fitzgerald's most intimate personal confidences and lauded by others for his frank and affectionate disclosures. Hemingway depicts Fitzgerald as robbed of his art and his friends by alcohol and stripped of his dignity by a faithless and frivolous wife.

While offered as nonfiction, *A Moveable Feast* is as much a product of Hemingway's selective, often romanticized perception as it is an objective report. The book reveals more about its author than it does about Paris. Even warm in his bed with his wife sleeping beside him, he found little comfort for a troubled mind, lamenting that nothing is simple, "not even poverty, nor sudden money, nor the moonlight, nor right and wrong." Through all the essays runs this undercurrent of discontent, a gnawing hunger of the soul that plagued the writer and the fictional heroes he created.

SUGGESTED READINGS

Griffin, Peter. *Less than a Treason: Hemingway in Paris*. New York: Oxford University Press, 1990.
Rovit, Earl, and Gerry Brenner. *Ernest Hemingway*. Rev. ed. New York: Macmillan, 1986.
Tavernier-Courbin, Jacqueline. *Ernest Hemingway's Moveable Feast: The Making of Myth*. Boston: Northeastern University Press, 1991.
Weber, Ronald. *Hemingway's Art of Nonfiction*. New York: St. Martin's Press, 1990.

—*Faith Hickman Brynie*

See also Expatriate identity; Hemingway, Ernest; *Nick Adams Stories, The*; Stein, Gertrude

Moviegoer, The

AUTHOR: Walker Percy (1916-1990)
FIRST PUBLISHED: 1961
IDENTITIES: European American; religion; South

The Moviegoer was Walker Percy's first novel, and it won the National Book Award. The book did not, however, immediately attract a large number of readers. Its hero's quest for meaning includes some consideration of philosophical and religious issues about which Percy had read deeply for at least a decade before he wrote the novel. Many either did not see what Percy is conveying in the novel or they rejected the novel as too heavy-handed in its presentation of nonliterary matters. Others consider the novel Percy's finest work.

The quest takes place in perfectly ordinary settings. Binx Bolling, a successful realtor, lives in Gentilly, a middle-class suburb of the more colorful New Orleans, Louisiana. He has quietly disassociated himself from his genteel Southern background, which is exemplified in his Aunt Emily. His search for a new sense of self that does not depend on the imposing history of his Southern forebears generates the context of his searching. Instead of living up to his heritage, which he feels he cannot do, he immerses himself in the ordinary, looking for signals of meaning in his day-to-day life.

Moviegoing and affairs with successive secretaries give a refined hedonistic diversion to more important matters. Binx is a handsome man who finds it all too easy to be distracted from his quest and, instead, he avoids boredom as carefully as possible. As he becomes attached to his cousin, Kate, however, he changes because of the demands of her poor psychological health. Her previous attempts at suicide make her more than just another affair. His eventual marriage to her commits him to something that demands endurance; in fact, it leads him to the possibility of faith whereas for most of his life his family's Catholicism was meaningless.

Part of the strength of the novel lies in its evocation of place. Percy is a master at giving a sense of setting and character. The story, told from Binx's point of view, develops a rich sense of Southern personality based as much on gestures, speech patterns, and what is left unsaid as by what characters actually do say. The more subliminal levels of communication between people is captured precisely and with humor.

SUGGESTED READINGS

Hobbs, Janet. "Binx Bolling and the Stages on Life's Way." In *The Art of Walker Percy: Stratagems for Being*, edited by Panthea Reid Broughton. Baton Rouge: Louisiana State University Press, 1979.

Hobson, Linda Whitney. *Understanding Walker Percy*. Columbia: University of South Carolina Press, 1988.

Lawson, Lewis A. "Moviegoing in *The Moviegoer*." In *Walker Percy: Art and Ethics*, edited by Jac Tharpe. Jackson: University Press of Mississippi, 1980.

Tanner, Tony. "*The Moviegoer* and American Fiction: Wonder and Alienation." In *Walker Percy: Modern Critical Views*, edited by Harold Bloom. New York: Chelsea House, 1986.

—*Bill Jenkins*

See also Catholicism; Conversion, religious; Existentialism; Religion and identity

Mr. Ives' Christmas

AUTHOR: Oscar Hijuelos (1951-   )
FIRST PUBLISHED: 1995
IDENTITIES: Family; Latino

Oscar Hijuelos, who was awarded the Pulitzer Prize in fiction in 1990 for his splendid rendition of a life going sour, *The Mambo Kings Play Songs of Love* (1989), presents, in *Mr. Ives' Christmas*, the somber Mr. Ives. Mr. Ives sanely goes through his life with no malice toward fellow man or woman. He seeks the rewards of work and patience that he has become accustomed to earning, but one date, Christmas Eve, consistently seems to interfere with his life.

Hijuelos, born in New York City, grew up in a humble, immigrant Cuban family. At age four, he was exiled from the family by nephritis, a kidney inflammation that crippled his youth with a two-year quarantine from home and loved ones. Perhaps that near-orphan status inspired Hijuelos to develop the Edward Ives of this novel. A widowed printmaker visits the orphan Edward Ives on Christmas Eve, and, a few Christmases later, adopts him. His adoptive father idyllically rears the dark-skinned child, inspires him to pursue his love for drawing, and eventually guides him to the Arts Student League where he meets, on Christmas Eve, his future wife.

The picture postcard family image is shattered when, on Christmas Eve, the Ives's seventeen-year-old son is gunned down as he leaves church choir practice. A fourteen-year-old Puerto Rican kills the boy for ten dollars. Mr. Ives devotes his life to obsessive, unerring attempts to rehabilitate the murderer. Symbolically, Mr. Ives' favorite book is a signed copy of British novelist Charles Dickens' *A Christmas Carol* (1843). Hijuelos strongly relies on this book to link the two tales. The author emulates Dickens' populous canvases and uses his love of coincidence and contrivance as a metaphor for God's mysterious workings. The temperance of Mr. Ives allows him a longing for grace, a gift for contemplation, and a steady curiosity.

Hijuelos draws heavily on images from his New York neighborhood, his coterie of friends, and the milieu of gangs, muggers, and dope addicts at the end of his street. Differing from his other novels, *Mr Ives' Christmas* leaves no doubt that Hijuelos speaks of faith; a faith that mysteriously probes emotions, tested by death and the opportunity of forgiveness.

SUGGESTED READINGS

Chávez, Lydia. "Cuban Riffs: Songs of Love." *Los Angeles Times Magazine*, April 18, 1993, 22-28.

Coffey, Michael. "Oscar Hijuelos." *Publishers Weekly*, July 21, 1989, 42-44.

—*Craig Gilbert*

See also Hijuelos, Oscar; *Infinite Plan, The*; Latino American identity; *Mambo Kings Play Songs of Love, The*

Mukherjee, Bharati

BORN: Calcutta, India; July 27, 1940

PRINCIPAL WORKS: *The Tiger's Daughter*, 1971; *Wife*, 1975; *Darkness*, 1985; *The Middleman and Other Stories*, 1988; *Jasmine*, 1989; *The Holder of the World*, 1993

IDENTITIES: Canada; family; religion; South Asian; women

SIGNIFICANT ACHIEVEMENT: Mukherjee is perhaps the foremost fiction writer describing the experience of Third World immigrants to North America.

Bharati Mukherjee was born to an upper-caste Bengali family and received an English education. The most important event of her life occurred in her early twenties, when she received a scholarship to attend the University of Iowa's Writer's Workshop. Her fiction reflects the experimental techniques fostered at such influential creative writing schools.

At the University of Iowa, Mukherjee met Clark Blaise, a Canadian citizen and fellow student. When they moved to Canada she became painfully aware of her status as a nonwhite immigrant in a nation less tolerant of newcomers than the United States. The repeated humiliations she endured made her hypersensitive to the plight of immigrants from the Third World. She realized that immigrants may lose their old identities but not be able to find new identities as often unwelcome strangers.

Mukherjee, relying on her experience growing up, sought her salvation in education. She obtained a Ph.D. in English and Comparative Literature and moved up the career ladder at various colleges and universities in the East and Midwest until she became a professor at Berkeley in 1989. Her first novel, *The Tiger's Daughter*, was published in 1971. In common with all her fiction, it deals with the feelings of exile and identity confusion that are experienced by immigrants. Being female as well as an immigrant, Mukherjee noted that opportunities for women were so different in America that she was exhilarated and bewildered. Many of her best stories, dealing with women experiencing gender crises, have a strong autobiographical element.

Darkness, her first collection of stories, was well reviewed, but not until the publication of *The Middleman and Other Stories* did she become internationally prominent. Critics have recognized that she is dealing with perhaps the most important contemporary phenomenon, the population explosion and flood of immigrants from have-not nations. Mukherjee makes these newcomers understandable to themselves and to native citizens, while shedding light on the identity problems of all the anonymous, inarticulate immigrants of America's past.

Her protagonists are not the "huddled masses" of yesteryear; they are talented, multilingual, enterprising, often affluent men and women who are transforming American culture. Mukherjee's compassion for these newcomers has made her one of the most important writers of her time.

SUGGESTED READINGS

Chua, C. L. "Passages from India: Migrating to America in the Fiction of V. S. Naipaul and Bharati Mukherjee." In *Reworlding: The Literature of the Indian Diaspora*, edited by Emmanuel S. Nelson. Westport, Conn.: Greenwood Press, 1992.

Fakrul, Alam. *Bharati Mukherjee*. New York: Twayne, 1996.

Nelson, Emmanuel S., ed. *Bharati Mukherjee: Critical Perspectives*. New York: Garland, 1993.

—Bill Delaney

See also Asian American identity: India; Emigration and immigration; Ethnic composition of universities; "Management of Grief, The"; Melting pot; *Middleman and Other Stories, The*; Multiculturalism; Women and identity

Multiculturalism

Background   Sociologists first used the phrase "the melting pot" to describe the inclusion of many cultures in one homogeneous group. The melting pot theory, however, was soon challenged as incorrect as a description and as biased in its intent. Various groups decided that they wanted to maintain, rather than diminish, their cultural distinctions. African American and Native American writers in the 1960's and after especially rejected the idea that the United States and Canada were or should be melting-pot societies. Their rejection was reinforced by immigrants or children of immigrants in the 1980's and 1990's who produced literature that is critical of the theory. A major objection is that melting implies the merging of cultures and the loss of differences. Another objection is that the melting pot's idea of merging into one culture does not allow for the creation of new social systems to which all contribute. Instead, the melting-pot model continues the dominance of white, Anglo culture over smaller cultural groups, thus submerging differences. In the cases of distinct cultural groups and immigrant communities, merging into one culture means the loss of one's unique history, heritage, and cultural products.

A response to this concern has been pluralism. Pluralism is descriptive of differences but does not necessarily connote anything positive in difference. The word "multiculturalism" is often used by scholars and popular writers to indicate that a variety of cultures that maintain their differences within a social group is functional for the total group. More specifically, the maintaining of this variety is perceived as a counteraction to melting, merging, or dominance. Multiculturalism is considered a means by which differences can be appreciated, with each distinct culture contributing toward the whole. The concept of multiculturalism is adverse to the notion of a melting pot, and it is more positive about difference than pluralism. Multiculturalism values diverse identities of peoples and presumes the possibility that diverse groups can interact positively.

The United States and Canada are examples of multicultural societies. The two countries' multicultural status is explained in general literature such as Vincent Parrillo's *Diversity in America* (1996) and Stephen Castles and Mark Miller's *The Age of Migration* (1993). Neither country is unique in being multicultural. Nations such as Israel or Brazil or Jamaica all acknowledge how different cultural groups within them can be positive for the larger societies. American culture is dispersed globally, and with that dispersal there is recognition of the value of varieties of social groups, each with their own cultures, offering alternative cultural products within the same social order. Multiculturalism and its practical effects are the consequence of categories besides ethnicity. Multiculturalism allows for difference among such groups as age groups, sexual preference groups, class and economic stations, religious orientations, professional and work obligations, and educational statuses. Each group may develop a culture that offers unique values, lifestyles, and artifacts (material products). As Roosevelt Thomas argues in his book *Beyond Race and Gender* (1991), multiculturalism cannot be limited to the cultures that are produced by groups with different historical and geographical backgrounds.

Some groups in the United States and Canada do not value multiculturalism: Their ideologies **Multiculturalism** promote the alternative of one unified culture as the only means toward empowerment. All external **as a positive value** groups are considered alien to their values. Thus the controversy of whether a melting-pot model or a multicultural model is better for the health of a nation is extended to groups. Within groups the value of the multicultural model is debated. African Americans, for example, are faced with competing ideologies of integration and of separatism. In Canada, the province of Quebec has attempted to continue its French Canadian heritage, language, religion, and values partly through restricting the use of the other major language of the country, English, and partly through demanding that Quebec have a special political status within Canada. In Canada and the United States, Native American groups have sometimes rejected multiculturalism, especially through legal claims to ownership of lands that were taken by white settlers and national governments. Multiculturalism in North America, therefore, is one interpretation of the larger societies' cultural pluralism, but is not necessarily valued by parts of the populations of those societies.

In the book *Valuing Diversity: New Tools for a New Reality* (1995), authors Lewis Griggs and Lente-Louise Louw argue that there are very practical reasons for encouraging multicultural attitudes when pluralism is present. These include resolving conflicts in organizations as participants learn to appreciate cultural differences, the development of leadership that is open toward the varieties of persons and cultures present in groups and organizations led, the provision of a group environment that promotes sensitivity toward differences and results in better functionality, an acknowledgement of the reality of pluralisms through encouraging specific learning about what is different from each group participant's own culture, and the strengthening or empowering of groups and organizations by showing members the value of their diversity. Such policies allow each participant to feel positive about contributing from his or her cultural perspective.

Voices of Diversity (1994), by Sandra Slipp and Renee Blank, shows how a group's multicultural attitudes can positively affect specific life areas such as the workplace. Multiculturalism, therefore, is not only a theoretical perspective for scholars as they interpret groups and societies. Multiculturalism is a very practical attitude and approach that is encouraged by many economic, social, and political leaders seeking to increase the functionality of businesses, educational, social, and governmental groups.

SUGGESTED READINGS

Burkey, Richard. *Ethnic and Racial Groups: The Dynamics of Dominance*. Menlo Park, Calif.: Benjamin Cummings, 1978.

Henderson, Mae. *Borders, Boundaries, and Frames*. New York: Routledge, 1995.

Hollinger, David. *Postethnic America*. New York: Basic Books, 1995.

Leach, Joy. *A Practical Guide to Working with Diversity*. New York: AMACOM, 1995.

Slipp, Sandra, and Renee Blank. *Voices of Diversity*. New York: AMACOM, 1994.

—William Osborne
—Max Orezzoli

See also Acculturation; Melting pot; Multiculturalism, statistics of

Multiculturalism, statistics of

DEFINITION: Major cultural groups and large cultural communities form the populace of North America.

The United States and Canada are among the most important receiving nations in the world (along with Australia) of immigrating groups. Their constant, large immigration numbers have long added cultural groups to their societies, as incoming peoples attempt to maintain their heritages and continue producing their cultural artifacts. These include, most importantly, their religions and their languages. They also include their values, family styles, methods of doing business and practicing professions, specific interests in the arts, and whatever distinctive material they produce. Both countries tend to receive the immigrants they have historically welcomed: These immigrants have been, typically, people from nations in northwestern Europe. They are increasingly complemented, however, by immigrants from southeastern Europe, Asia, Africa, South America, and the Caribbean. Historically, there has been some shift away from using nationality as an exclusive criterion for immigration and toward favoring political refugees and persons from many nations who meet academic and professional criteria deemed useful to the host countries. The United States and Canada also include indigenous peoples among their cultural groups. These peoples were present before Europeans explored North America. These are generally categorized as Native Americans but have specific characteristics according to the nation or tribe or heritage to which they belong. The United States also has an important, large community of African American peoples, while Canada has a smaller proportion that is just as historic. There were blacks among Canada's seventeenth century settlements—before the largest numbers of slaves were brought to the United States.

There are distinctive differences, however, between the two countries both in their traditional ethnic makeup and in their latter twentieth century ethnic statistics. The most explicit are the proportions of French Canadians and the proportions of Hispanics or Latinos in the United States. In Canada, there are two national communities that are termed "charter groups." They originated in France or in Great Britain. They are dominant in their respective geographic areas. French Canadians are predominant in the province of Quebec, although they are widely scattered as well in Ontario and all provinces in the eastern part of the nation. Their importance has been recognized by the debate about the legal, political, and cultural status of Quebec. The United States, by contrast, has French-heritage residents mostly in the New England states and in Louisiana. Their social and economic power in the United States is not commensurate with that of French Canadians. The United States, in addition, has increasingly large Latino populations. The three largest and most politically influential communities of Latinos are Puerto Ricans, Mexican Americans, and Cuban Americans. New York and other northern cities have large Puerto Rican populations. South Florida has the largest Cuban American population. Southwestern states, including Texas, Arizona, New Mexico, and California have the largest Mexican American populations. Their large numbers, estimated to be more than thirty million, are augmented by immigrants from Central and South American nations. Canada, by contrast, has only small Latino communities mostly concentrated in Toronto, Ontario. Other statistical differences include the numbers of Inuit populations in Canada, which, along with Indians and Métis, are among the aboriginal Canadian groups. In the United States, indigenous groups do not include large populations of Eskimos. A further difference in ethnic composition has occurred because of differing immigration laws between Canada and the United States. Canada's eagerness to populate its large geographic area has tended to be reflected in immigration being more readily welcome than in the United States, especially after

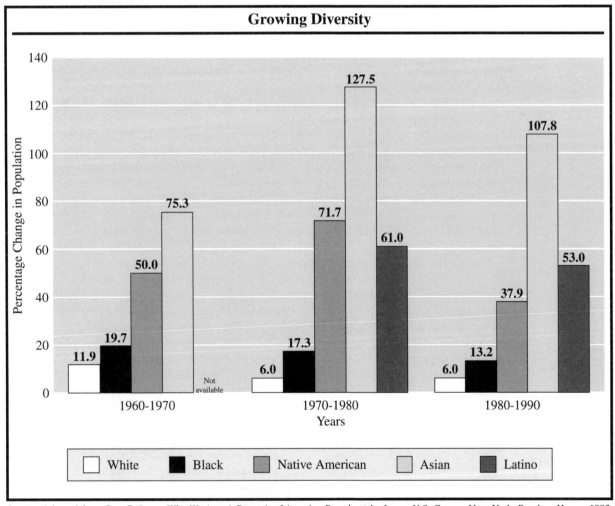

Source: Adapted from Sam Roberts, *Who We Are: A Portrait of America Based on the Latest U.S. Census.* New York: Random House, 1993. Page 67.

the settling of the western United States. Canada accepted larger proportions of World War II refugees, for example, and also welcomed U.S. citizens fleeing repression in the United States, for example, African Americans.

U.S. statistics   The growth of populations among multicultural groups in the United States can be assessed against the projected growth of populations worldwide. The Population Reference Bureau claimed that fertility rates were dropping globally in 1994; however, the world's population, expected to be approximately six billion in 1999, was estimated to be between eight and eleven billion by 2030. Southern Asia was expected to have the largest increases in population, adding approximately 1.2 billion additional persons to the planet, and developing countries generally were expected to at least double their populations by the year 2030. If this estimate is accurate, developing countries in Asia, Africa, and Latin America will account for between 85 and 87 percent of the world's total population by 2030. Africa will increase its percentage of world population most of all: from 12 to 19 percent. The industrialized countries, including the United States and Canada, will, by comparison, diminish from 22 to 14 percent of the world's population. This assessment is significant to the future of multiculturalism in the United States and Canada. When population pressures increase in the developing countries of other continents, pressures will be felt in developed countries to increase immigration. A major example directly affecting multiculturalism in the United States is Mexico. Mexico more than tripled its population between 1950 and 1990: The increase numerically was from twenty-seven million to eighty-five million people. Since Mexico is the country that sends the most emigrants to the United States, the statistics of the cultural composition of the United States are likely to continue to be dramatically affected by nations external to its borders. The Mexican example is a major reason why Latinos in the United States are expected to become a numerically larger group than African Americans by the year 2000. U.S. government demographers assume that the trends found in 1990 will continue, regarding the numbers of immigrants admitted to the country. In the 1990's, that number was slightly less than one million people per year.

In 1990, Latinos officially numbered 22.4 million people in the United States. This was approximately 9 percent of the total American population. It is believed by some analysts that this is an underestimate, especially because it is known that many Latino immigrants are illegal and are not counted. By the year 2050, the numbers of Latinos in the United States could be approximately eighty-one million persons. This means that they would have increased from 9 percent to roughly 21 percent of the total U.S. population. Significantly, they would become the largest ethnic minority group in the country and Latino culture would greatly affect non-Latino groups.

These estimates do not consider, however, the distinctions among the national groups that are labeled Latino. The label is broad and includes populations from distinct cultures. One example may be found in the political life of Latino communities. Cuban Americans are overwhelmingly Republican in registration and voting patterns, while Mexican Americans and Puerto Ricans tend to register and vote more heavily for Democratic Party candidates. Latinos also often continue their national preferences and biases when they live in the United States. A Chilean of European extraction, for example, and a Guatemalan Indian are both Latino; they otherwise may have little, including language, in common. It is simplistic to assume commonalities among the cultures of communities that are broadly labeled Latino. Although the growth of Latinos as a group is expected to be large in the United States, the fact that Latinos are many subgroups may become more apparent as this growth occurs.

African Americans numbered approximately 30.5 million persons in the United States in 1990. This was roughly 12.3 percent of the total population. By the year 2050, they may number over sixty million persons, doubling their total numbers and becoming 16 percent of the American populace. As with Latinos, the broad category of "African American" does not take cultural differences into account. Immigrating groups from the Caribbean may identify according to their national origins rather than as African Americans but, by the second generation, many people from

Ten Fastest Growing States: Population Increase, 1990 to 1995

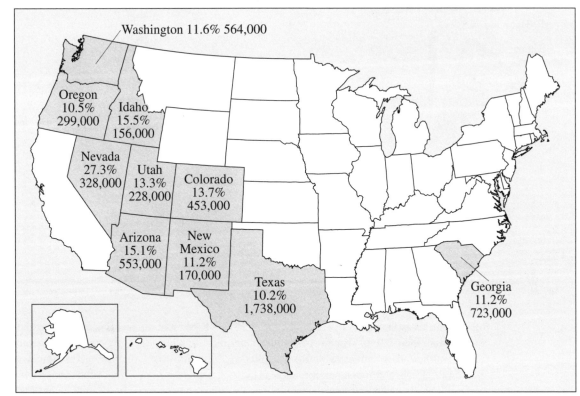

Washington 11.6% 564,000

Oregon 10.5% 299,000

Idaho 15.5% 156,000

Nevada 27.3% 328,000

Utah 13.3% 228,000

Colorado 13.7% 453,000

Arizona 15.1% 553,000

New Mexico 11.2% 170,000

Texas 10.2% 1,738,000

Georgia 11.2% 723,000

Source: U.S. Bureau of the Census.

Population of Selected States

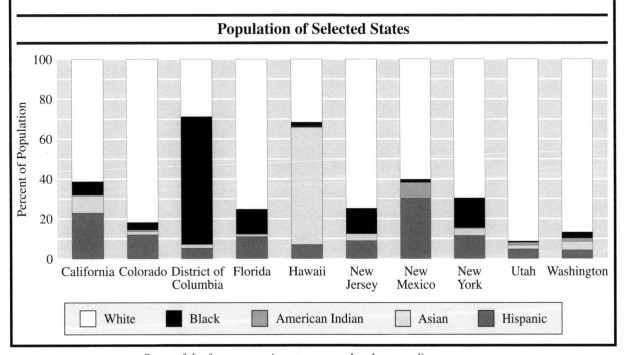

Percent of Population

California, Colorado, District of Columbia, Florida, Hawaii, New Jersey, New Mexico, New York, Utah, Washington

White ▢ Black ▮ American Indian ▮ Asian ▢ Hispanic ▮

Some of the fastest-growing states are also the most diverse states.

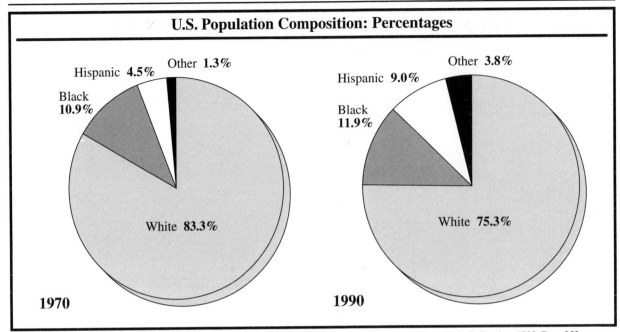

U.S. Population Composition: Percentages

1970

Other **1.3%**
Hispanic **4.5%**
Black **10.9%**
White **83.3%**

1990

Other **3.8%**
Hispanic **9.0%**
Black **11.9%**
White **75.3%**

Source: Adapted from Andrew Hacker, *Two Nations: Black and White, Separate, Hostile, Unequal.* New York: Ballantine, 1992. Page 252.

such countries as Jamaica, the Bahamas, Trinidad and Tobago, Haiti, and Barbados are considered and consider themselves African Americans. Culturally, however, they may maintain distinctions. These distinctions often have definite results in the workplace, religious affiliation, ways of speaking English, and social patterns such as marriage. One example is that educational levels and professional advancements tend to be higher among second-generation immigrant blacks than they are among African Americans with heritages of hundreds of years in the United States. Therefore, while African Americans will increase in numbers and in percentage of the U.S. population, the increases will not necessarily mean uniformity of culture.

In the 1990 census, there were nearly two million Native Americans designated. It is estimated that, by the year 2050, there will be approximately five million. This is an increase of 150 percent. The total U.S. population is projected to be about 380 million persons in 2050. The percentage (rather than the number) of Native Americans, if the estimates are correct, will remain about 1 percent of the population, the same as in 1990. As do Latinos and African Americans, Native Americans belong to distinctive subcultures: These are identified as continuing nations within the United States, each with a treaty or legal agreement with the U.S. government. By contrast, Asian Americans are expected to more than quintuple by 2050: In 1990, they numbered 7.5 million persons and were 3 percent of the U.S. population. By 2050, they may number more than forty million persons and be 11 percent of the population. All of the above groups show increases in estimates of number for the year 2050. One major cultural group, non-Latino white Americans, is not expected to increase its percentage of the U.S. population. The opposite is projected to be the case. Non-Latino whites represented 75 percent of the populace in 1990. It is estimated that they will represent only 53 percent by 2050. The cultural implications are significant. These include the diminution of non-Hispanic white political power, language, Protestant religion, and northwestern European values.

Canadian statistics

Canada, unlike the United States, has a legal framework for multiculturalism. In 1971, multiculturalism was proclaimed as the country's official policy. To attempt to put this into practice, a Minister of State for Multiculturalism was appointed. The purpose was to combat racism and to maintain ethnic cultures and their heritages.

In Canada at the end of the twentieth century, twenty-five million people may be categorized as approximately 35 percent British origin, 25 percent French origin, 5 percent combined British and French, and 35 percent "other," which means, for the most part, immigrant groups of other origins. Two percent are native peoples, and 1 percent is black. While the major factor in the growth of Canada's population was among existing populations, births being a far larger number than deaths, immigration in the early 1990's contributed to growth significantly. The immigrating groups, in terms of largest numbers of arrivals, were different from those of the United States. By 1992, immigration was largest from Asia and Africa. The largest numbers of arrivals came from Hong Kong, India, Ceylon, Poland, the Philippines, China, and Iran. Each of these countries sent more people to Canada than to the United States. Changes in Canada's immigration laws show a significant shift away from traditionally favored European and American immigrants.

SUGGESTED READINGS

Bogardus, Emory. *Immigration and Race Attitudes*. Lexington, Mass.: D.C. Heath, 1928. An excellent historic appraisal of the relation of racial feelings toward immigrating groups.

Castles, Stephen, and Mark Miller. *The Age of Migration*. New York: Guilford Press, 1993. Emphasizes a new world order, with global migrations affecting all nations.

Goldberg, David. *Multiculturalism*. New York: Basil Blackwell, 1994. A general reader that explains approaches to the subject and expresses the favorable and unfavorable feelings that social groups may have toward it.

Henderson, George. *Cultural Diversity in the Workplace*. Westport, Conn.: Quorum Books, 1944. A classic working guide to addressing multiculturalism in employment in the United States.

Henderson, Mae, ed. *Borders, Boundaries, and Frames*. New York: Routledge, 1995. Discusses how multiculturalism blurs ethnic and cultural boundaries.

Parrillo, Vincent. *Diversity in America*. Thousand Oaks, Calif.: Pine Forge Press, 1996. Discussion of diversity includes valuable statistical breakdowns of major ethnic groups.

Thomas, R. Roosevelt. *Beyond Race and Gender*. New York: AMACOM, 1991. Provides concepts for multiculturalism in the workplace and labor force statistics. Claims that multiculturalism is the end of assimilation.

—William Osborne
—Max Orezzoli

See also Acculturation; Melting pot; Pluralism versus assimilation

Munro, Alice

BORN: Wingham, Ontario, Canada; July 10, 1931

PRINCIPAL WORKS: *Dance of the Happy Shades*, 1968; *Lives of Girls and Women*, 1971; *Who Do You Think You Are?*, 1978 (U.S. title, *The Beggar Maid: Stories of Flo and Rosie*, 1979); *The Moons of Jupiter*, 1982; *The Progress of Love*, 1986; *Friend of My Youth: Stories*, 1990

IDENTITIES: Canada; women

SIGNIFICANT ACHIEVEMENT: Munro's short stories are among the finest of her generation.

Alice Munro grew up in a small rural community in western Ontario. Her father spent most of his life raising fox for the commercial fur market, which resulted in a life of poverty or abundance, depending on the changing conditions of the foxes and the market. Her childhood was filled with struggling to belong to her peer group and always excelling at academics. Her intelligence won for her scholarships to high school and college, and poverty made her drop out of college after her second year. Fear of poverty enticed her to marry Jim Munro when she was twenty.

Munro spent her entire childhood believing that she could and would write a great novel. She began writing poetry at age twelve and always kept her work hidden from her mother and family. After her marriage, she continued to write in secret, believing the cultural dictates of the times that women were either wives and mothers or artists, not both. Munro's work often deals, not surprisingly therefore, with the mother-child roles. Her parental characters are often composites

Canadian short-story writer Alice Munro. (Jerry Bauer)

of her own parents, grandparents, and other family members. Her descriptions of the town and countryside almost exactly recall the community of her youth.

Munro was able to publish several works a year while her children were growing up, and she became steadily more prolific. She uses the language of women talking about their lives. Munro's work is truly a matrilineal narrative in a literary world dominated by men's voice and realities.

SUGGESTED READINGS

Blodgett, E. D. *Alice Munro*. Boston: Twayne, 1988.

Redekop, Magdalene. *Mothers and Other Clowns: The Stories of Alice Munro*. New York: Routledge, 1992

Ross, Catherine Sheldrick. *Alice Munro: A Double Life*. Toronto: ECW Press, 1992

—*Sandra J. Parsons*

See also Canadian identity; Feminism

Mura, David

BORN: Great Lakes, Illinois; June 17, 1952

PRINCIPAL WORKS: *A Male Grief: Notes on Pornography and Addiction*, 1987; *After We Lost Our Way*, 1989; *Turning Japanese: Memoirs of a Sansei*, 1991; *Listening*, 1992; *The Colors of Desire*, 1995; *Where the Body Meets Memory: An Odyssey of Race, Sexuality, and Identity*, 1996

IDENTITIES: Japanese American

SIGNIFICANT ACHIEVEMENT: Mura's essays and poetry explore and affirm the ethnic identity that was denied to him in childhood and early adulthood.

In his writing, Mura processes a private and a public pain with which Asian Americans can readily identify. A third-generation Japanese American, or Sansei, Mura grew up on baseball and apple pie in a Chicago suburb where he heard more Yiddish than Japanese. He avidly read white male writers, cheered for the John Wayne-led actor soldiers against the Japanese in war films, and identified with European culture at the expense of his Japanese heritage. His parents never mentioned their years in the Japanese relocation camps during World War II. Obliterating their ethnicity became a way of claiming the American "good life" for themselves and their son.

In adulthood Mura came to realize the devastation that such denial of identity had brought to his own life. He began an addictive cycle of drug abuse and sexual promiscuity that led to difficult self-interrogation and a painful passage to awareness and self-esteem. In *A Male Grief*, Mura powerfully examines child abuse, addictive family systems, and the adult male's consumption of pornography as a way of coming to terms with his own destructive sexual behavior. When he began to feel shame about racist images such as submissive houseboys and geishas, he realized that it was himself of which he was really ashamed.

Mura's embrace of his ethnicity is a major theme of his work. His Japanese ancestors play an important role in the poems in his early collection, *After We Lost Our Way*. A part of his claiming Japan entailed a prolonged visit to the country, made possible for Mura when he was awarded a U.S./Japan Creative Artist Exchange Fellowship for 1984-1985. A book of memoirs, *Turning Japanese*, resulted, which wrestles with the complexities of self, sexuality, politics, cultural mores, and literary criticism. *The Colors of Desire* lays bare his private infidelities and the more public wounds of racism. Mura's writing vigorously smashes stereotypes, honestly processes wrong behavior, and aggressively claims his identity.

SUGGESTED READINGS

Choy, Ken. "David Mura: A Portrait of . . . " *ex*plan*asian*, Spring, 1994, 3.

Gidmark, Jill B. "David Mura: Tearing Down the Door." *Asian America: Journal of Culture and the Arts* 2 (Winter, 1993): 120-129.

Rossi, Lee. "David Mura." *ONTHEBUS 2*, no. 2 (Summer-Fall, 1990): 263-273.

—*Jill B. Gidmark*

See also Acculturation; Asian American identity: China, Japan, and Korea; Erotic identity; Identity crisis; Japanese American internment

My Ántonia

AUTHOR: Willa Cather (1873-1947)

FIRST PUBLISHED: 1918

IDENTITIES: European American; Midwest; women

Willa Cather's ambivalent feelings about the Nebraska prairie in which she came to young adulthood are most evident in *My Ántonia*, her novel about the immigrants who settled there. While she fully understood the inability of some of the settlers to adjust to the harsh extremities of weather and bleak environment, she most admired those who survived, prevailed, and later prospered. The prairie was such a force in her life that it is no wonder that the setting of the novel is considered to have as great an impact on the characters as any other character could have.

My Ántonia is a novel of interaction between people and their environment. The prairie, cruel and lovely, is too palpable, too moving and changing, to evoke picture-postcard images. The seasons are distinct, the extremes great: "Burning summers when the world lies green and billowy beneath a brilliant sky, when one is fairly stifled in vegetation, in the color and smell of strong weeds and heavy harvests; blustery winters with little snow, when the whole country is stripped bare and gray as sheet iron." The elements are a constant companion. Every day calls for interaction. The sun can be "blinding," the thaw can be a "broth of grey slush," the wind can have the "burning taste of fresh snow." This land is, at times, "impulsive and playful," able to moan, howl, and sing. The elements are punishing, kind and caressing, acting willfully, just as people might.

Into this comes a train from the east, carrying ten-year-old orphaned Jim Burden, the narrator, and Bohemian immigrants, the Shimerdas. The eldest daughter of the Shimerdas is Ántonia, the subject of the narration. Jim is going to live with his grandparents; the family is seeking a new life in farming. At first the new arrivals are overwhelmed with what they see: the inhospitable landscape, the sod huts, the abject poverty. The Shimerdas, however, do what is required and set about establishing a home. Ántonia throws herself into a full embrace of the land. She is suited to the challenge: strong, industrious, self-sufficient. Jim also comes to love the prairie, but he determines that he must seek friendlier climes, eventually becoming a New York lawyer.

When he returns to his once-loved prairie twenty years later, he finds Ántonia has changed. Although she is still life-affirming and still has the power to charm, she is slightly bedraggled, slightly mannish, surrounded by equally bedraggled, but happy, children and a childlike husband.

Willa Cather's prairie is hard and cruel, beautiful and vibrant. The land and the weather provide a setting that is as multidimensional, as complex, as any fictional character might be. Her novel is a tribute to the land and the pioneering spirit of those who tamed it.

SUGGESTED READINGS

Brown, E. K. *Willa Cather*. New York: Alfred A. Knopf, 1953.

Gilbert, Sandra M., and Susan Gubar. *Sexchanges*. Vol. 2. in *No Man's Land: The Place of the Woman Writer in the Twentieth Century*. New Haven, Conn.: Yale University Press, 1989.

Woodress, James. *Willa Cather: A Literary Life*. Lincoln: University of Nebraska Press, 1987.

—*Gay Zieger*

See also American identity: West and the frontier; Cather, Willa; *Death Comes for the Archbishop*; "Paul's Case"

My Days of Anger

AUTHOR: James T. Farrell (1904-1979)

FIRST PUBLISHED: 1943

IDENTITIES: European American; family; religion

My Days of Anger, one of the five novels in James T. Farrell's O'Neill-O'Flaherty series, chronicles the lives of two Chicago Irish-Catholic families with young Danny O'Neill as the central character. Published fourth but coming last in the chronology of Danny's life, *My Days of Anger* is a *Künstlerroman*; that is, a novel of a young protagonist's developing an identity as an artist. Set on Chicago's South Side from 1924 to 1927, the novel opens with Danny working nights and attending the University of Chicago days while initially aspiring to become a lawyer. As the novel closes, Danny has rejected this goal, the middle-class values of his family, his Catholicism, and the prejudices of his neighborhood, leaving Chicago for New York to become a writer.

As he develops, Danny undergoes numerous emotional and intellectual changes. Having grown up in the O'Flaherty household with a doting uncle and grandmother because his immediate family is too poor to keep him, Danny wrestles with the guilt of having enjoyed more advantages than his numerous siblings and learns to appreciate the struggles of his parents. He sees beyond the business ethics of his Uncle Al, a traveling salesman and his surrogate father, who, though meaning well, is pretentious and shallow. At the university, reading philosophy along with much Romantic poetry, he finds that Catholicism fails to explain a world he views as brutal and unjust. In the name of gaining experience, he drinks and carouses with prostitutes but soon realizes his immaturity, escaping the dissipation that plagues many of his friends. Farrell treats much of Danny's thought and behavior as the rebellion of an overly sensitive adolescent, but by the novel's end, Danny matures into an intellectual worthy of respect. Whereas he initially denounces and ridicules his family and friends, he comes to understand their difficulties and vows to redeem their meager lives through his art.

Danny O'Neill is very much an autobiographical character whose experience parallels the young James T. Farrell's. Danny's immigrant grandmother, his working-class parents, his deluded uncle, his fellow university students, and the young toughs on the streets all contribute to re-creating the Irish-Catholic Chicago neighborhood where Farrell grew up and that provides the setting for most of his work. As fiction, *My Days of Anger* exemplifies the artist's dilemma in an urban America where money and practicality are valued over sensitivity, imagination, and intellectual endeavor.

SUGGESTED READINGS

Branch, Edgar M. *James T. Farrell*. New York: Twayne, 1971.

Butler, Robert. "The Christian Roots of Farrell's O'Neill and Carr Novels." *Renascence: Essays on Value in Literature* 34, no. 2 (Winter, 1982): 81-98.

Fanning, Charles. "Death and Revery in James T. Farrell's O'Neill-O'Flaherty Novels." In *The Incarnate Imagination: Essays in Theology, the Arts, and Social Sciences*, edited by Ray B. Brown. Bowling Green, Ohio: Bowling Green State University Popular Press, 1988.

—Peter A. Carino

See also American identity: Midwest; *Bildungsroman* and *Künstlerroman*; Catholicism; Environment and identity; Urban life

My Name Is Aram

AUTHOR: William Saroyan (1908-1981)

FIRST PUBLISHED: 1940

IDENTITIES: Adolescence and coming-of-age; European American; family; West and Southwest

My Name Is Aram, one of William Saroyan's major works, is a collection of short stories that explores conflict between the personal and the official. Aram tells the stories as an adult remembering his boyhood in an Armenian American family.

In the first story, "The Summer of the Beautiful White Horse," readers meet Aram's magical cousin Mourad, who can steal a horse without penalty and without doing harm. In "The Journey to Hanford" the magical one is Uncle Jorgi, who pretends subservience to the official world, but plays his music anyway, instead of working in the fields. In "The Pomegranate Trees" Uncle Melik, lover of beauty, fails at his dream of growing pomegranates, but recognizes that the essence of beauty comes from within and is indestructible. In "One of Our Future Poets, You Might Say" Aram understands that a future poet does not have the approval of officialdom.

"The Fifty-Yard Dash" shows the folly of depending on the inner way without making a corresponding effort in the outer. In "A Nice Old-Fashioned Romance, with Lyrics and Everything," Aram's teacher, Miss Daffney, chooses official rules over personal affection. In "My Cousin Dikran, the Orator" a second-generation Armenian boy goes all the way over to officialdom, giving a prizewinning oration that is logical but wrongheaded.

In "The Presbyterian Church Choir Singers" Aram is paid by an elderly Christian lady to sing in a church choir. Here, a talent that should express the personal is hired to perform without joy. In "The Circus" Aram and a friend choose the personal—the circus—over the official—the school—and receive milder punishment than they expected. In "The Three Swimmers and the Grocer from Yale" three boys find that they prefer the more personal, eccentric grocer to his more normal replacement.

"Locomotive Thirty-Eight, the Ojibway" gives Aram the backing of a rich adult ethnic—an Ojibway Indian—who pays him to drive his Packard and have fun, encouraging the personal, while saying that Aram is naturally mechanical—official—because he's American. "Old Country Advice to the American Traveler" and "The Poor and Burning Arab" show immigrant Armenian adults who have lost their old-country authority, and the second-generation boys who have to adjust to allow for the personal. When "A Word to Scoffers" says that all people have to do is believe everything, suddenly personal and official worlds can coexist in humor and surprise.

SUGGESTED READINGS

Calonne, David Stephen. *William Saroyan: My Real Work Is Being*. Chapel Hill: University of North Carolina Press, 1983.

Floan, Howard R. *William Saroyan*. New York: Twayne, 1966.

Shear, Walter. "Saroyan's Study of Ethnicity." *MELUS: The Journal of the Society for the Study of the Multi-Ethnic Literature of the United States* 13, nos. 1-2 (Spring-Summer, 1986): 45-55.

—*Helen Shanley*

See also Saroyan, William; School; *Summer Life, A*

My Name Is Asher Lev

AUTHOR: Chaim Potok (1929-   )

FIRST PUBLISHED: 1972

IDENTITIES: Family; Jewish; religion

My Name Is Asher Lev, perhaps Chaim Potok's greatest novel, is an excellent example of the *Künstlerroman*, which is a novel about an artist's development. It confronts issues of Jewish and family identity in the post-Holocaust world. Asher Lev is a child prodigy artist, the only child of a Hasidic Jewish couple that lives in the Crown Heights section of Brooklyn. Aryeh Lev, Asher's father, serves as a personal emissary for the *rebbe* or tzaddik, the "righteous one" or religious leader of the Hasidic community.

The orthodox Hasidic Jewish culture into which Asher is born approves of creativity only in the context of interpretation of Talmudic passages. Asher finds it difficult, and at times embarrassing, to follow his muse; he finds it natural to draw and to create pictures. Rivkeh Lev, Aryeh's mother, initially supports Asher's desire to draw, but she soon sides with her husband, who believes that drawing and the fine arts are products of a gentile culture. In the years during and immediately following World War II, Aryeh Lev travels the world to minister to Hasidic Jews who have been displaced by the Nazi Holocaust. Since Hasids believe that the Jewish state will be re-created in Israel only with the coming of the Messiah, who has not yet arrived, Hasidic Jews generally did not support the creation of the state of Israel in 1948. Aryeh travels about the world for the tzaddik, defending himself and his spiritual leader from the arguments of Zionist Jews and gentiles and attempting to do good works. He returns to a household in Brooklyn where his son is neglecting study of the Talmud because of his personal obsession with art and aesthetics.

The tzaddik, however, is wise enough to allow Asher to follow his destiny and to mediate between his conflicting identities. The tzaddik arranges for Jacob Kahn, an expatriate from the Hasidic community and a world-renowned sculptor, to serve as Asher's artistic mentor. Asher's apprenticeship as an artist culminates with a midtown New York showing of his work. Central to the showing is a pair of paintings, *Brooklyn Crucifixion I* and *Brooklyn Crucifixion II*, which show his mother, crucified in the venetian blinds of their apartment, her face split into "Picassoid" thirds, looking to the father, the son, and the street. The works assure Asher's reputation as a great artist but also assure, because of their religious content, that he will have to leave his Hasidic community in Brooklyn, as he does at the end of the novel. With the tzaddik's blessing, he goes to Paris to board with a Hasidic family and to continue to worship and define himself as a Hasidic Jew artist.

SUGGESTED READINGS

Buber, Martin. *Hasidism and Modern Man.* New York: Humanities Press International, 1988.

Davenport, Guy. "Collision with the Outside World." *The New York Times Book Review*, April 16, 1972, 5, 18.

Idel, Moshe. *Hasidism: Between Ecstasy and Magic.* Albany: State University of New York Press, 1995.

Safran, Bezalel. *Hasidism: Continuity or Innovation?* Cambridge, Mass.: Harvard University Press, 1988.

—*Richard Sax*

See also Anti-Semitism; Holocaust; Jewish American identity; Potok, Chaim

N

Naipaul, V. S.

BORN: Chaguanas, Trinidad, West Indies; August 17, 1932

PRINCIPAL WORKS: *The Mystic Masseur*, 1957; *The Suffrage of Elvira*, 1958; *Miguel Street*, 1959; *A House for Mr. Biswas*, 1961; *Mr. Stone and the Knights Companion*, 1963; *An Area of Darkness*, 1964; *A Flag on the Island*, 1967; *The Mimic Men*, 1967; *In a Free State*, 1971; *Guerrillas*, 1975; *India: A Wounded Civilization*, 1977; *A Bend in the River*, 1979; *Among the Believers*, 1981; *Finding the Center*, 1986; *The Enigma of Arrival*, 1987; *A Turn in the South*, 1989; *India: A Million Mutinies Now*, 1990; *A Way in the World: A Sequence*, 1994

IDENTITIES: Caribbean; world

SIGNIFICANT ACHIEVEMENT: Naipaul has explored identity problems in the postcolonial world.

Viewing V. S. Naipaul's writing retrospectively, one can find in it a three-part pattern that suggests an orderly, seemingly calculated development, although the author did not plan this

V. S. Naipaul, author of the novel A Way in the World: A Sequence *(1994)* (Jerry Bauer)

development in advance. Naipaul's first three novels deal in ironic ways with the struggles of a Trinidad adjusting to its newly achieved independent status. These novels portray the foolishness and absurdity of Trinidad society as Naipaul, the observer, perceives it.

In *A House for Mr. Biswas*, the fourth book, Naipaul becomes more psychological in his approach and develops the novel by focusing on character rather than on external political events. Mr. Biswas yearns, in his desire to build a house, to make visible a personal identity that he must, for his own security, establish. Finally, in his later work, such as *India: A Wounded Civilization* and *Among the Believers*, Naipaul deals with the world outside Trinidad, exploring quests for identity by people who, like Naipaul himself, have left the island and ventured into other parts of the world.

Naipaul's personal and artistic quest has been to discover his lost identity and the identities of the countries and people about whom he writes. Born in the West Indies to Hindu parents newly arrived from northern India, a teenage Naipaul left Trinidad for postwar Britain, where he was awarded a bachelor's degree at University College, Oxford, in 1954.

Throughout his life, Naipaul, driven by the sense of his own rootlessness, has sought to discover where he belongs. Indian by ancestry, he is by no means Indian. He has asserted the impossibility of reclaiming his Indian roots in such books as his nonfiction *India: A Wounded Civilization* and *India: A Million Mutinies Now. Among the Believers* is Naipaul's nonfiction account of the life, culture, and affairs of the world of Islam. Naipaul writes of his travels to the nations of Iran, Pakistan, Malaysia, and Indonesia, countries whose effects, through immigration and political struggle, on North America have markedly increased in the late twentieth century.

Being of Indian ancestry yet being a Trinidadian, Naipaul never considered himself an integral part of Trinidad society. Finding no identity during his years in England or in his other ventures abroad, he continues to pursue his own identity. His body of work is a testimony to that effort.

SUGGESTED READINGS

Kelly, Richard. *V. S. Naipaul*. New York: Continuum, 1989.

King, Bruce. *V. S. Naipaul*. New York: Macmillan, 1993.

Mustafa, Fawzia. *V. S. Naipaul*. Cambridge, England: Cambridge University Press, 1995.

Weiss, Timothy. *On the Margins: The Art of Exile in V. S. Naipaul*. Amherst: University of Massachusetts Press, 1992.

—*R. Baird Shuman*

See also Alienation; Caribbean American literature; Islamic literature

Naked and the Dead, The

AUTHOR: Norman Mailer (1923-   )

FIRST PUBLISHED: 1948

IDENTITIES: European American; Jewish; Latino

The Naked and the Dead centers on a platoon of soldiers on the Asian island of Anopopei sent on a mission behind enemy lines. As the platoon advances, the novel flashes back to the soldiers' lives at home, showing how their identities have been shaped by their ethnic, racial, and regional cultures.

There is, for example, Wilson, an easygoing Texan, who favors strong drink and women. Joey Goldstein is self-consciously Jewish but good with his hands. Roth, another Jew, dislikes dwelling on his Jewishness and is bitter about his inability to get a job during the Depression, despite his being a graduate of City College in New York. He is countered by the anti-Semitic Gallagher, a Boston Irishman, and Sergeant Croft, another Texan, brutal and intolerant. Croft clashes with Lieutenant Hearn, a Harvard graduate who takes over leadership of the platoon. Croft is responsible for leading Hearn into an ambush that costs his life. Mexican and Italian characters round out Mailer's impressive geographical and ethnic study of American identity.

The main conflict in the novel is the debate between Lieutenant Hearn and General Cummings. Hearn is a liberal who resists the authoritarian nature of the Army. He wants to lead men because they voluntarily acknowledge his right to rule. Cummings disdains what he considers Hearn's sentimental view of human nature and government. To the general, it is discipline, force, and imagination that win wars and that govern life. He forces Hearn to lead the platoon patrol in order to learn a lesson about what it takes to drive men to a goal.

The Naked and the Dead is a novel about what the shape of the post-World War II world would be like. The novel projects the possibility that fascists such as Cummings may dominate American politics even as the fascists of Asia, Germany, and Italy are defeated. The individuals in the platoon are largely seen as powerless to change this fate, for they are too tied to the circumstances of their upbringing and education, and to their ethnic and regional identities. Liberals such as Hearn, who might prove worthy opponents in argument, are subverted not only by those like Cummings but also by people like Croft, a lowlier sort who parallels in the trenches Cummings' tactics in the strategy room.

Yet the novel does not suggest that fascism will ultimately triumph. Cummings' military plans become obsolete as the Japanese surrender. Much of the history that Cummings thinks he controls by manipulation and power actually occurs by accident.

SUGGESTED READINGS

Lennon, J. Michael, ed. *Conversations with Norman Mailer*. Jackson: University Press of Mississippi, 1988.

Lucid, Robert, comp. *Norman Mailer: The Man and His Work*. Boston: Little, Brown, 1971.

Poirier, Richard. *Norman Mailer*. New York: Viking, 1972.

Rollyson, Carl. *The Lives of Norman Mailer: A Biography*. New York: Paragon House, 1991.

—*Carl Rollyson*

See also *American Dream, An*; Anti-Semitism; Jewish American identity; Mailer, Norman; Stereotypes and identity; Violence; World War II

Naked Ladies

AUTHOR: Alma Luz Villanueva (1944-   )

FIRST PUBLISHED: 1994

IDENTITIES: Latino; women

Naked Ladies, Alma Luz Villanueva's second novel, explores four women's struggle for identity and survival within the confines of their racially biased and male dominated culture. The novel's title, taken from the name of a Northern California wildflower, symbolizes these four women's exuberant spirit of resilience and their unwavering determination to defy all threats of domination and destruction.

Alta, the novel's main character, and her friends, Katie, Rita, and Jackie, live in the San Francisco Bay Area. Despite differences in ethnic and class backgrounds, their lives have in common the struggles of child-rearing, homemaking, working, and obtaining an education. Their struggles are often aggravated by an array of problems, such as alcoholism, violence, infidelity, rape, incest, cancer, and acquired immune deficiency syndrome (AIDS). To prevent her family from falling apart, Alta tries everything she can to endure and change the abusive behavior of her husband, Hugh, to whom she was married at the age of fifteen. She blames herself for all the miseries and pains in her life because she feels inferior and ashamed of being a Mexican American woman. What devastates her most is Hugh's confession that he has contracted AIDS from an old man with whom he has been having a homosexual affair since the age of seventeen.

Like Alta, her friends have serious battles to wage. In their persistent struggle to survive, Alta and her friends realize that they can depend on one another for understanding and support. They also learn that they must stand up for their rights, pursuing the freedom and fulfillment of which they have long been dreaming.

The second part of the novel takes place in 1999. Alta has recovered from her sorrow over the death of Hugh, who died of AIDS, and the deaths of Katie and Rita, who died of cancer. She has managed to rear her two children, finish her college education, and start her career as a counselor. Alta falls in love with Michael, her African American colleague, has another baby, and becomes a grandmother. The ending thus brings hope of a better future for those who have survived.

The novel has received mixed reviews since its publication. Some praised the freshness and creativity in its narrative structure. The novel also has been praised for its portrayals of the complexities of interracial relationships. Others have criticized the novel's candid description of violence and sex. *Naked Ladies* has been highly regarded for its provoking but compelling presentation of women's search for self-realization.

SUGGESTED READING

Wheatwind, Marie-Elise. "Naked Ladies" Review of *Naked Ladies*, by Alma Luz Villanueva. *The Women's Review of Books* 11, no. 8 (May, 1994): 25.

—Aiping Zhang

See also Chicano identity; Feminism; Latino identity; Women and identity

Naming and identity

Names provide the primary means by which persons are known. The importance attached to naming a child varies among cultures. In some, naming is a ritual carried out with great ceremony; in others, the pleasing sound of a name or names of favorite book characters may be sources. In the United States, criteria for naming a child span the entire range from highly informal, even whimsical ones, to those based on considerable reflection.

Sometimes nicknames are temporary; others stick for a lifetime. Some nicknames are complimentary; others are neutral or derogatory. In any case, they are used when some characteristic is so marked that the nickname seems to identify the person more suitably than the actual name does. Furthermore, a person may acquire a name completely different from that given at birth. Some are adopted to hide one's identity or to show significant behavioral change, for example. In literature as in life, nicknames fall into several categories such as those associated with ethnicity or race, status or position, regional practices or customs, geographical location, and identification with religious or classical figures.

A character in Robert Bird's *Nick of the Woods* (1837) is Nathan Slaughter, suggesting possible character trait identity. This is confirmed when Nathan, also known as "Nick," ("nick" seems an appropriate verb) gains the name "Bloody Nathan." The apparently gentle Quaker turns out to be a violent man. Several characters in James Fenimore Cooper's Leatherstocking Tales (1823-1841) are named or undergo name changes that describe behavior. One is Hurry Harry March in *The Deerslayer* (1841). His shooting an Indian girl impulsively and endangering his companions demonstrates the behavior that his name suggests. The identity of the title character in Nathaniel Hawthorne's "Young Goodman Brown" is revealed in his name. He represents Everyman, capable of yielding to temptation and desire as all humans are. His wife's allegorical name, Faith, identifies her with the force of goodness in the world. Harriet Beecher Stowe's character Evangeline St. Clare, nicknamed Little Eva, in *Uncle Tom's Cabin* (1852) has a name that fits this angelic, blond, blue-eyed maiden who dresses in pure white and embodies the Christian virtue of charity.

Behavior or character traits

In twentieth century literature, the inherently royal aspect of Uncle Caesar in O. Henry's "A Municipal Report" is emphasized in "King Cettiwayo," a nickname given at first in jest. Upon finding that Uncle Caesar (also suggesting royalty) is descended from African nobility, the narrator better understands the depth of his loyalty. The name of Sinclair Lewis' Martin Arrowsmith in *Arrowsmith* (1925) suggests "straight as an arrow," or steadfast, which is appropriate for this humanitarian scientist. Arrowsmith is an idealist who fights the temptation to compromise his integrity. The name Burden identifies characters in William Faulkner's *Light in August* (1932) and Faulkner's Joanna Burden is obsessed with the issue of slavery; her "burden" is to fight for equality to the end. Ellen Glasgow's Mrs. Burden, in *They Stooped to Folly* (1929), is unable to free herself from the burden that her conscience imposes on her. The nickname "Haze" aptly describes the character Hazel Motes, a preacher with a flawed vision in Flannery O'Connor's *Wise Blood* (1952). With a figurative "mote," or particle, in his eye, his judgment is "hazy," and he preaches an antireligious doctrine rather than Christian love. In another O'Connor story, "A Good Man Is Hard to Find" (1953), the nickname the Misfit establishes the identity of a notorious escaped murderer. The African American writer Toni Morrison creates the character Dead Macon in *Song of Solomon* (1977). Because he is "dead" to human feeling as he relentlessly pursues material success, the name is a suitable one for this wealthy black businessman. The Native American writer James Welch nicknames the Blackfeet tribesman Fools Crow "White Man's Dog" in *Fools Crow* (1986). Whatever his virtues are, Fools Crow is identified as being weak and overly subservient to whites.

Ethnicity or race   Names or name changes that identify a character's ethnic group or race abound in North American literature. The African American writer, Harriet E. Wilson, published *Our Nig* (1859), in which Frado, a mulatto, is called "Our Nig" by her white masters. The subtitle, *Sketches from the Life of a Free Black, in a Two-Story White House, North, Showing that Slavery's Shadows Fall Even There*, explains the irony of the nickname. Willa Cather is representative of American writers who have focused on the experience of immigrants in the United States. Her use of noticeably Old World names establishes that identity. Among these works is *O Pioneers!* (1913) which tells of the experiences of the Swedish immigrants in the Bergson family on the Nebraska frontier. In *The Song of the Lark* (1915), the Swedish immigrant is Thea Kronborg, daughter of a Methodist minister in Colorado. *My Ántonia* (1918) returns to the Nebraska prairie in the story of Ántonia Shimerda, daughter of Bohemian immigrants. The mixture of Anglo-American and Asian names in such novels as Yoshiko Uchida's *The Best Bad Thing* (1983) demonstrates the family's sense of being torn between tradition and the desire to become more American.

The World War II era produced a number of works in which names identify ethnicity. For example, in 1941, Thomas Bell (originally Belejcak) published *Out of This Furnace*, in which John Dobrejcak is given two nicknames: "Dobie," reflecting a shortened name, and "Hunky" to indicate his Bohemian background. Tennessee Williams, in *The Glass Menagerie* (1944), deliberately uses the Irish name Jim O'Connor for the "gentleman caller"; because of his Irish name, Laura's mother automatically assumes that he surely must like to drink, a behavior that she rejects. Norman Mailer, in the World War II novel *The Naked and the Dead* (1948), uses names to highlight racial diversity. Julio Martinez is a Latino from San Antonio, Texas; Roy Gallagher has an Irish background; Joey Goldstein is stereotypically New York Jewish; "Polack" Czienwiez's name and nickname reflect his Polish-American ethnicity; Steve Minetta is Italian American; and William Brown represents the "all-round American," the "typical" white Protestant American.

Social status labels   Names or nicknames can also indicate social standing, or lack of it, as representative examples indicate. Thomas N. Page is only one writer who names a character Mammy to designate a black slave in his *Red Rock* (1898). At the other end of the social scale, Williams, in *Cat on a Hot Tin Roof* (1955), nicknames a wealthy plantation owner and his wife Big Daddy and Big Mama Pollitt. Rather than size, the nicknames identify them as the "bosses" on the plantation. Ralph Ellison's character of the Invisible Man emphasizes a total lack of identity, for in a racist society, he feels invisible, without an identity.

Skills or talents   Another name source identifies some skill or inherent gift. One early example is Hawkeye in Cooper's *The Last of the Mohicans* (1826). Nathaniel "Natty" Bumppo is called Hawkeye because of his precise marksmanship. In the later novel *The Pathfinder* (1840), he is called Pathfinder because of his extraordinary ability in the forest. Although the infant could not know of the "gift" he was credited with having, Tommy Luck in Bret Harte's "The Luck of Roaring Camp" is so named because, when he is born into a rough, untamed work camp community, he has an amazing softening effect on the profane, tough men. In a later novel, *Lady Oracle* (1976) by the Canadian novelist Margaret Atwood, Joan Foster first adopts her late aunt's name, Louisa K. Delacourt, and later develops an alter ego, Lady Oracle, because of her success as a mystic poet. Claude McKay, in *Banjo: A Story Without a Plot* (1929), gives the nickname "Banjo" to the character Lincoln Agrippa Daily because of his identity as a banjo player.

Some characters are associated with physical characteristics. For example, in Horatio Alger's *Ragged Dick* (1867), the title character is never identified by any other name in this "rags to riches" story. John Steinbeck's adolescent character Edward Carson in *The Wayward Bus* (1947) is nicknamed "Pimples" because of his skin condition. Similarly, in James Jones's World War II novel *From Here to Eternity* (1951) Judson is known as "Fatso" because of his size. The title character Little Big Man in Thomas Berger's 1964 novel serves a double purpose: to identify him with his short stature and to become his Indian name as a brave. The "Big" is indicative of his bravery and worthiness, since the lad is described as slender.

Appearance

Especially in literature of the American South, although not exclusively, a number of novels and stories contain characters who are identifiable largely by nicknames that reflect regional practices or geographic location. In the works of many Southern writers, use of the title "Miss" plus the first name (Miss Sallie, for example) identifies the character with the South. In some cases, the reader is never told the complete name. In the case of Kentuck in Harte's "The Luck of Roaring Camp," the miner who carries this nickname is identified with a place of geographical origin.

Regional

In the case of characters who are given names of figures in classical or biblical literature or with religious associations, their identity is dependent on the reader's knowing what the intended symbolic association is. For example, Pauline Cambron, who takes the name Sister Dolorosa in James L. Allen's story "Sister Dolorosa," illustrates a double intention. Her identity as a Roman Catholic nun is straightforward; however, the name "Dolorosa" further establishes an identity with suffering (*dolorosa* means "painful" or "suffering pain"). This is in character with the nun, for although she is attracted to a man, she keeps her vows and consigns herself to lifelong penance for having entertained thoughts of sexual attraction. Whereas one would expect Satan to be a nickname, it is otherwise in Mark Twain's novella *The Mysterious Stranger* (1916). Satan takes the human name Philip Traum, appearing as a handsome young man to whom people are drawn in spite of his misanthropic philosophy. Some other works have a character named Devil, thus identifying the character clearly. The identity of Lazarus, a character in William Faulkner's *Pylon* (1935), is dependent on a reader's recognizing that the tall, pale, gaunt, specter-like man who looks as if he could have returned from the dead, has the name of a biblical character who dies and is brought back to life by Jesus. A representative example of a classical figure used in naming a modern character is seen in Dion Anthony, a major character in Eugene O'Neill's play *The Great God Brown* (1926). Here, Dion is a nickname for the classical Dionysus, who represents, in classical literature and in O'Neill's character, creativity and imaginative power.

Allusions

SUGGESTED READINGS

Blicksilver, Edith, ed. *The Ethnic American Woman: Problems, Protests, Lifestyle*. Dubuque, Iowa: Kendall/Hunt, 1978. While naming is not the focus of this work, it provides the background out of which stereotyping of minority groups can occur.

Butcher, Philip, ed. *The Minority Presence in American Literature: 1600-1900*. 2 vols. Washington, D.C.: Howard University Press, 1977. Excerpts from more than thirty writers whose work contains ethnic minority characters.

Kim, Elaine H. *Asian American Literature*. Philadelphia: Temple University Press, 1982. An insightful introduction to the images of various Asian American groups in literature.

Nelson, Gerald B. *Ten Versions of America*. New York: Alfred A. Knopf, 1972. Provides a kaleidoscope of American characters that collectively make up a literary description of Americans.

Watkins, Floyd C. *In Time and Place*. Athens: University of Georgia Press, 1977. Discusses cultural changes, diversity, and the mobility of Americans, which influence and result in regional literature.

—Victoria Price

See also Atwood, Margaret; Cather, Willa; Faulkner, William; Hawthorne, Nathaniel; Lewis, Sinclair; McKay, Claude; Mailer, Norman; Morrison, Toni; O'Connor, Flannery; O'Neill, Eugene; Stereotypes and identity; Welch, James; Williams, Tennesse

Naming Our Destiny: New and Selected Poems

AUTHOR: June Jordan (1936-   )
FIRST PUBLISHED: 1989
IDENTITIES: African American; women

Naming Our Destiny: New and Selected Poems, June Jordan's most monumental volume of poetry, is a collection that covers a wide range of topics. The poems in the collection span more than thirty years; fifty pieces never published previously are also included in this volume. In *Naming Our Destiny*, Jordan demonstrates that it is her mission as an artist to change the world, and with the poems in this collection, Jordan takes a stance against oppression as she explores the black experience in America.

Jordan's volume begins with "Poem from Taped Testimony in the Tradition of Bernard Goetz." The poem, which starts, "This was not I repeat this was not a racial incident," reflects Jordan's willingness to include contemporary affairs that have political and historical significance in her poetry. With the verses of this poem, Jordan tries to show the reader, from a black woman's perspective, just what might pass through a mind like that of Bernard Goetz—a white man who shot black youths in a New York City subway in the early 1980's. Jordan looks unflinchingly at the reality of this event and states it in the simplest language. This poem also displays the power of idiomatic and colloquial language.

Another example of Jordan's devotion to exploiting instances of human oppression can be found in "The Female and the Silence of a Man." The poem, situated in the middle of the collection, is a response to Irish poet William Butler Yeats's "Leda and the Swan." Yeats's poem retells the myth of the rape of Leda by the god Zeus, who takes, for the act, the form of a swan. In her feminist revision of Yeats's classic, Jordan calls attention to women's plight as victims of male oppression. She does not perpetuate, however, Leda's victimization. She destroys the legacy of victimization by showing a woman becoming strong enough to silence her oppressor. The poem, while not technically complex, is as puissant as any written by those who adhere to a formalist credo.

Jordan's commitment to a search for justice is evident in her closing autobiographical poem, "War and Memory." The poem summarizes Jordan's life. Relating her own experiences to cultural and historical events, such as the Vietnam War and the War on Poverty, Jordan is able to speak on behalf of the world's oppressed, dispossessed, and disfranchised. Throughout *Naming Our Destiny*, Jordan appeals to the decency and humanity of her audience. Each poem is a plea for all to exercise compassion toward others. In *Naming Our Destiny* Jordan makes artful use of meter and rhyme to protest the everyday human oppression that might otherwise go unrecognized.

SUGGESTED READINGS

Erickson, Peter. "After Identity: A Conversation with June Jordan." *Transition* 63 (Winter, 1994): 132-149.

Hamill, Sam. "A Fool's Paradise." *American Poetry Review* 20 (March-April, 1991): 33-40.

Harjo, Joy. "An Interview with June Jordan." *High Plains Literary Review* 32 (Fall, 1988): 60-78.

—*Traci S. Smrcka*

See also African American identity; Black English; Feminism; Jordan, June; Racism and ethnocentrism

Narrative of the Life of Frederick Douglass: An American Slave

AUTHOR: Frederick Douglass (Frederick Augustus Washington Bailey, 1817?-1895)
FIRST PUBLISHED: 1845
IDENTITIES: African American

Frederick Douglass' *Narrative of the Life of Frederick Douglass: An American Slave*, one of the finest nineteenth century slave narratives, is the autobiography of the most well-known African

American of his time. The narrative chronicles Douglass' early life, ending soon after his escape from slavery when he was approximately twenty. It focuses on formative experiences that stand out in his life for their demonstration of the cruelty of slavery and of his ability to endure and transcend such conditions with his humanity intact.

Douglass' work follows the formula of many slave narratives of his day. He structures his story in a linear fashion, beginning with what little information he knew about his origins and progressing episodically through to his escape North. His recurring theme is the brutal nature of slavery, with an emphasis on the persevering humanity of the slaves despite unspeakable trials and the inhumanity of slave owners. Other themes common to Douglass' and other slave narratives are the hypocrisy of white Christianity, the linkage of literacy to the desire for and attainment of freedom, and the assurance that with liberty the former slave achieved not only a new sense of self-worth but also an economic self-sufficiency. Douglass' work is characteristic of the nineteenth century in that it is melodramatic and at times didactic.

Despite its conventional traits, however, Douglass' work transcends formulaic writing. The author's astute analyses of the psychology of slavery, his eloquent assertions of self, and his striking command of rhetoric lift this work above others in its genre. Particularly memorable scenes include young Frederick's teaching himself to read, the fight with the slave breaker Covey, the author's apostrophe to freedom as he watches sailboats on Chesapeake Bay, and his interpretation of slave songs as songs of sorrow.

When Douglass wrote this work in 1845, he had already earned a reputation as one of the most eloquent speakers for the Massachusetts Anti-Slavery Society. The *Narrative of the Life of Frederick Douglass* was published with a preface written by William Lloyd Garrison, which was followed by a letter by Wendell Phillips. An immediate success, the *Narrative of the Life of Frederick Douglass* soon went through five American and three European editions.

Douglass revised and enlarged the autobiography with later expansions, *My Bondage and My Freedom* (1855) and *The Life and Times of Frederick Douglass* (1881, 1892). Although these later versions are of historical value for their extension of Douglass' life story and for their expansion on matters—such as his method of escape—that Douglass purposefully avoided in his first publication, critics generally agree that the spareness and immediacy of the original *Narrative of the Life of Frederick Douglass* renders it the most artistically appealing of the autobiographies.

Today Douglass' book has become canonical as one of the best of the slave narratives, as an eloquent rendering of the American self-made success story, as a finely crafted example of protest literature, and for its influence on two important genres of African American literature—the autobiography and the literary treatment of slavery.

SUGGESTED READINGS

Dexter, Fisher, and Robert B. Stepto, eds. *Afro-American Literature*. New York: Modern Language Association of America, 1979.

Jackson, Blyden. *A History of Afro-American Literature*. Baton Rouge: Louisiana State University Press, 1989.

Smith, Valorie. "Form and Ideology in Three Slave Narratives." In *Self-Discovery and Authority in Afro-American Narrative*. Cambridge, Mass.: Harvard University Press, 1987.

—Grace McEntee

See also African American identity; Slave narratives; Slavery

Narrative of William W. Brown, a Fugitive Slave, Written by Himself

AUTHOR: William Wells Brown (1815-1884)
FIRST PUBLISHED: 1847
IDENTITIES: African American

In his slave narrative, William Wells Brown assailed the prevailing notion of his time that slaves lacked legal or historical selfhood. His autobiography asserts that he has an autonomous identity. *The Narrative of William W. Brown, a Fugitive Slave, Written by Himself*, like many of the stories written by former slaves, does more than chronicle a journey from bondage to freedom. The work also reveals the ways in which the former slave author writes a sense of self, denied by the South's peculiar institution, into existence.

So great was slavery's disregard of black personhood that William, as a boy on a Kentucky plantation, is forced to change his name when his master's nephew, also named William, comes to live as part of the white household. Brown never forgets this insult. He writes of his flight across the Mason-Dixon line: "So I was not only hunting for my liberty, but also hunting for a name." He finds a name by accepting as his surname that of an Ohio Quaker, Wells Brown, who gives him food and shelter during his escape. He also insists on retaining his first name, showing that his conception of freedom includes the ability to define, shape, and control one's own identity.

Brown is careful to record that his achievement of an unfettered identity is not without its tragic consequences. His personal freedom is undercut by reminders that his mother and siblings remain enslaved. When an escape undertaken in 1833 with his mother fails, his mother is sent to the Deep South, and Brown temporarily gives up his plans of liberty. His repeated sorrowful musings about his mother and sister suggest that Brown's freedom and self-definition are processes infused not only with hope and triumph but also with alienation and loss. His statement that "the fact that I was a freeman . . . made me feel that I was not myself" registers his ambivalence at forever leaving his family to find liberty.

Although his purpose is at times weakened by a tragic family history that includes memories of his sister's sale and visions of his mother performing hard labor on a cotton plantation, his understanding of national history lends resolve and determination to his quest. His thoughts of "democratic whips" and "republican chains" work to expose the severe contradictions that haunt the United States and reinforce his decision to risk becoming a fugitive once again in an attempt to reach Canada. In this way, Brown's personal narrative functions as national criticism. His narrative is an American autobiography and an unflinching examination of America.

SUGGESTED READINGS

Andrews, William L. *To Tell a Free Story: The First Century of Afro-American Autobiography, 1760-1865*. Champaign: University of Illinois Press, 1986.

Davis, Charles T., and Henry Louis Gates, Jr. *The Slave's Narrative*. New York: Oxford University Press, 1985.

Farrison, William Edward. *William Wells Brown: Author and Reformer*. Chicago: University of Chicago Press, 1969.

—*Russ Castronovo*

See also African American identity; Brown, William Wells; Slave narratives; Slavery

Nation of Islam

IDENTITIES: Religion

In 1930, Wallace D. Fard (also known as Walli Farrad or Farrad Muhammad) began spreading what would become the central precepts of the Nation of Islam. Tenets of the Nation of Islam include: Whites are devils and use Christianity to subjugate blacks, history should be retold so that blacks may be given the regal spot they deserve as original agents of civilization, and blacks should strive for independence and sociopolitical separation from whites. After Fard's disappearance in 1934, Elijah Muhammad, who had become acquainted with Fard in the early 1930's, succeeded him. The Nation of Islam generally adheres to tenets of the Islamic faith. The Nation of Islam sanctions the Koran and the worship of Allah. A central departure that the Nation of Islam makes from orthodox Islam is that Black Muslims do not necessarily have to make a pilgrimage to Mecca. Black Muslims also rigorously confront the conditions of African Americans in racist America. Despite internal crises within the Nation over the years, it continues to thrive and maintain high standards of cleanliness, discipline, and hard work. Strict codes of conduct regarding tobacco, dress, drugs, sex, and marriage are adhered to by its members. Malcolm X was chosen by Elijah Muhammad to expand the Nation of Islam; differences of opinion led to Malcolm X's breaking with the Nation of Islam in the early 1960's. Malcolm X was assassinated in 1965. After Elijah Muhammad's death in 1975, the Nation passed through a time of crisis in leadership. Louis Farrakhan became the leader; as his stature in the organization rose, so did membership—to approximately 100,000 in the mid-1990's. Farrakhan has been the subject of writings such as Jabril Muhammad's *A Special Spokesman* (1984) and *Farrakhan the Traveler* (1984).

Black Muslim doctrines have greatly affected African American literature. During the 1960's, the Black Arts movement, with such spokesmen as Amiri Baraka and Larry Neal, affiliated itself with major tenets of the Nation of Islam. The movement fostered a spirit recognizable in black American writing. Black Muslim and pro-Black Muslim writers created writings that were explicitly political, confrontational, and prescriptive, insisting on rigorous solutions to racism and inequality. Baraka's 1965 Black Revolutionary Theater manifesto, an antiwhite, antibourgeois, antiblack middle class, combative, and pro-Islamic assault on racism, stands as one of the clearest examples of the Nation's philosophy on black writing.

Another literary work influenced by the Nation of Islam is Malcolm X's *The Autobiography of Malcolm X* (1964), completed with the assistance of Alex Haley. Chronicling the life of Malcolm X, his conversion to and subsequent disputes with and breakaway from the Nation, the autobiography highlights the reasons for the Nation's beliefs and aspirations.

Several African American writings address the Nation of Islam in political, documentary fashion. Aside from the autobiography, a number of texts also recount Malcolm X's life and ideologies. These texts include: *Malcolm X Speaks* (1965), *Malcolm X Talks to Young People* (1965), *The End of White World Supremacy: Four Speeches* (1971), and *Malcolm X: The Last Speeches* (1989), edited by Bruce Perry and Betty Shabazz. The books feature famous speeches by Malcolm X. Other books by or about Malcolm X include George Breitman's *The Last Year of Malcolm X: The Evolution of a Revolutionary* (1967), Malcolm X's *By Any Means Necessary* (1970), and Peter Louis Goldman's *The Death of Malcolm X* (1973).

The Nation of Islam has also influenced African American literature in terms of writers' identities. Many African American writers have changed their names, dropping their Christian, slave names and adopting African or Muslim names. In addition to Baraka and Malcolm X, such writers as Katibu (Ron Milner) and Askia Muhammad Toure (Rolland Snellings) have changed their names. Elijah Muhammad, former leader of the Nation, has produced literature and advanced the principles and goals of the Black Muslims. His practical Islamic proposal for healthy eating in *How to Eat to Live* (1967), departs from the rebelliousness of his *Message to the Blackman in America* (1965) and *The Fall of America* (1973). James Baldwin's *The Fire Next Time* (1963) is a collection of two major essays, one of which, "Down at the Cross," compares the Nation of Islam favorably to Christianity.

SUGGESTED READINGS

Allport, Gordon W. *The Black Muslims in America*. Boston: Beacon Press, 1961.

Baraka, Amiri, and Larry Neal, eds. *Black Fire: An Anthology of Afro-American Writing*. New York: William Morrow, 1968.

Lincoln, C. Eric. *The Black Muslims in America*. 3d ed. Grand Rapids, Mich.: Wm. B. Eerdmans, 1994.

Lomax, Louis E. *The Negro Revolt*. New York: Harper & Row, 1962.

—Philip Uko Effiong

See also African American identity; *Autobiography of Malcolm X, The*; Baldwin, James; Baraka, Amiri; Black church; Civil Rights movement; Naming and identity

Native American identity

IDENTITIES: Native American

Early encounters by Westerners with Indian cultures led to numerous misconceptions about Native American oral traditions. Most Native American literatures, before European contact, belonged to the oral tradition. Works were originally conceived for dramatic presentation, often with music and dance, and as lyrics to songs, rather than as texts for the printed page. Some tribes made pictographic records, but this was not typical. Western readers, with the expectations of readers of printed works, erroneously concluded that Indian literature, which featured the repetition and strong parallelism of song and oratory, was primitive. Native American literature was also, understandably, pagan. Beginning with Spanish explorers, Europeans suppressed and destroyed Indian cultural creations. The great variety of Native American cultural life was largely replaced with European languages and culture and with a few stereotypes. Stereotypes about Indians have proved remarkably durable.

Western interpretations

Early European writings were historical accounts of first encounters with Indians, for example those described in John Smith's *The General History of Virginia, New England, and the Summer Isles* (1624), William Bradford's *History Of Plymouth Plantation* (1856), John Eliot and Roger Williams' studies of native languages, and descriptions by Captain Edward Johnson and Daniel

---

Native American Identity Milestones

prehistory onward	North America's first literature originates in the oral tradition of its native peoples. Common themes are respect for the physical and spiritual universe, use and appreciation of the power of words, and the need for tribal sharing and cooperation. Some tribes invent pictographs. Stories range from the sacred and ceremonial to the humorous to the mythological to the frightening. Perhaps the figure with the greatest literary legacy is the trickster.
1624	John Smith's *The General History of Virginia, New England, and the Summer Isles*.
1682	The captivity narrative becomes a literary staple with Mary Rowlandson's best-selling nonfiction story of her captivity. The full title of her work is *The Soveraignty and Goodness of God: Together with the Faithfulness of His Promises Displayed: Being a Narrative of the Captivity and Restauration of Mrs. Mary Rowlandson*.
1754	Benjamin Franklin advises the Albany Congress to study the principles of the Iroquois Confederacy and the oral tradition epic from which they came.
1772	Samsom Occom publishes the first literary work in English by a Native American, *A Sermon Preached at the Execution of Moses Paul, an Indian*. The execution sermon becomes a staple.
1784	Thomas Jefferson's *Notes on the State of Virginia* praises Indian oratory.
1808	*The Indian Princess*, by James Barker, the first American play on an Indian theme.
1819	John Gottlieb Heckewelder's *Account of the History, Manners, and Customs of the Indian Nations of Pennsylvania and the Neighboring States*.
1823-1841	James Fenimore Cooper's Leatherstocking Tales, adventure stories based on Indian warfare. Cooper's stoic Indian characters Chingachgook, Uncas, and Magua quickly become the most famous Indians in literature.
1829	William Apes, an Indian author and missionary of the early nineteenth century, publishes his autobiography, *A Son of the Forest*.
1833	The Walam Olum chronicles of the Leni-Lenape or Delaware tribe, once recorded as pictographs on birch bark, are translated into English.
1834	*Life of Ma-ka-tai-me-she-kia-kiak or Black Hawk*, by Black Hawk.
1835	William Gilmore Simms's *The Yemassee*.
1839	Henry R. Schoolcraft's *Algic Researches: Comprising Inquiries Respecting the Mental Characteristics of the North American Indians*.
1854	John Rollin Ridge's *The Life and Adventures of Joaquín Murieta* is the first novel by a Native American.

Gookin. Smith's account of Pocahontas became an American myth, for example, retold in *The Indian Princess* (1808) by James Barker, the first American play on an Indian theme.

After historical accounts came personal ones, the captivity narrative being central. Mary Rowlandson's best-selling nonfiction story of her captivity, published in 1682, established the genre of factual and fictional Indian captivity narratives. The full title of her work is *The Soveraignty and Goodness of God: Together with the Faithfulness of His Promises Displayed: Being a Narrative of the Captivity and Restauration of Mrs. Mary Rowlandson.* Some narratives were reasonably accurate; others were sensational. The captivity narrative endured into the twentieth century, Thomas Berger's *Little Big Man* (1964) being an example.

Thomas Jefferson and Benjamin Franklin wrote of their interest in Indian government, which was based largely on oral tradition. Jefferson's *Notes on the State of Virginia* (1784) praises Indian oratory, and Franklin advised the Albany Congress of 1754 to study the principles of the Iroquois Confederacy and oral tradition epic from which it came. The principles of the Iroquois Confederacy subsequently influenced the United States Articles of Confederation and the United States Constitution. Other oral tradition epics included the Walam Olum chronicles of the Leni-Lenape or Delaware tribe, which were recorded as pictographs on birch bark and later translated into English in 1833.

Oral tradition was also the source for the stories collected by ethnologist Henry R. Schoolcraft

Native American Identity Milestones — CONTINUED

1855	Walt Whitman demonstrates a fascination with Indian words in his *Leaves of Grass*.
1855	Henry Wadsworth Longfellow's *The Song of Hiawatha*, a grossly inaccurate and sentimentalized portrayal of Indian life and mythology.
1870	Bret Harte's *The Luck of Roaring Camp and Other Sketches*.
1883	Sarah Winnemucca's *Life Among the Paiutes*.
1890	Adolph Bandelier's *The Delight Makers*.
1891	*Sitting Bull's Message from the Spirit Life*, by Sitting Bull.
1891	Sophia Alice Callahan's novel *Wynema, a Child of the Forest* is perhaps the first by a Native American woman.
1910	*The Poems of Alexander Lawrence Posey*, by Alexander Lawrence Posey.
1912	Emily Pauline Johnson's *Flint and Feather*, poems.
1913	Emily Pauline Johnson's *Moccasin Maker*, short fiction.
1929	Oliver La Farge's *Laughing Boy*.
1932	John G. Neihardt's edition of *Black Elk Speaks* first appears in 1932 but is not widely read until the 1962 edition.
1935	John Oskison's *Brothers Three*.
1936	D'Arcy McNickle's *The Surrounded*.
1947	A. B. Guthrie's *The Big Sky*.
1953	*The Sacred Pipe* is transcribed by John Epes Brown.
1964	Thomas Berger's *Little Big Man*.
1968	N. Scott Momaday's Pulitzer Prize-winning *House Made of Dawn*.
1971	James Welch's *Riding the Earth Boy Forty: Poems*.
1974	James Welch's *Winter in the Blood*.
1976	Simon Ortiz's *From Sand Creek*.
1977	Leslie Marmon Silko's *Ceremony*.
1979	*The Best of Will Rogers*, by Will Rogers.
1984	*Coyote Stories*, by Mourning Dove, also known as Cristal Quintasket.
1986	*Fools Crow*, by James Welch.
1990	Gerald Vizenor's *Interior Landscapes: Autobiographical Myths and Metaphors*.
1990	*Mourning Dove: A Salishan Autobiography*, by Mourning Dove, also known as Cristal Quintasket.
1991	Gerald Vizenor's *The Heirs of Columbus*.
1991	*Grandmothers of the Light: A Medicine Woman's Sourcebook*, by Paula Gunn Allen.
1993	Lame Deer's *The Lakota Sweat Lodge Cards: Spiritual Teachings of the Sioux*.
1994	*Dry Lips Oughta Move to Kapuskasing*, by Highway Tomson.

in *Algic Researches: Comprising Inquiries Respecting the Mental Characteristics of the North American Indians* (1839). This and other volumes by Schoolcraft and others (for example, John Gottlieb Heckewelder's *Account of the History, Manners, and Customs of the Indian Nations of Pennsylvania and the Neighboring States*, 1819) who had conducted research among Indian tribes were among the sources used by poets and fiction writers who, with little personal experience of their own with Indians, wrote about Indian characters. The poet Henry Wadsworth Longfellow's *The Song of Hiawatha* (1855) was intended to help supply the United States with a legendary past; it makes highly, even grossly, inaccurate use of the legends and customs recounted by the researchers. Longfellow created a romantic, sentimentalized myth of Indian life that continues in American popular culture. Portrayals of Indians in early American literature appear in poems by Sarah Wentworth Morton, James W. Eastburn, Robert C. Sands, William Cullen Bryant, John Greenleaf Whittier, and Philip Freneau ("The Indian Burying Ground" and "The Indian Student"). Walt Whitman demonstrates a fascination with Indian words in his *Leaves of Grass* (1855). Whitman's poems include Indians in the national identity. His understanding that Indian culture preceded white colonization and his cataloging of Indian names would be later repeated in the twentieth century, in Maya Angelou's poem "On the Pulse of Morning."

Indian characters appear in the novels of Hugh Henry Brackenridge, Charles Brockden Brown, and Gilbert Imlay. Indian characters came to prominence in works by Lydia Maria Child, James Kirke Paulding, and Robert Montgomery Bird. Novelist William Gilmore Simms's *The Yemassee* (1835) makes a sympathetic portrayal of Indians who defend their land and culture. James Fenimore Cooper's Leatherstocking Tales (1823-1841) are adventure stories based on Indian warfare, and Cooper's stoic characters Chingachgook, Uncas, and Magua quickly became the most famous Indians in literature. Cooper's emphasis on Indian stoicism remained a theme in historical and fictional accounts. Such accounts were written by John C. Fremont, Lewis Garrad, and George Frederick Ruxton. Later writers who championed Indians in the West include Bret Harte, Helen Hunt Jackson, Adolph Bandelier (*The Delight Makers*, 1890), Mary Austin, Hamlin Garland, Oliver La Farge, A. B. Guthrie (*The Big Sky*, 1947), Stewart White, and Zane Grey.

Native responses   With the arrival of Europeans came missionary work, and the first Native American efforts at Western-style literary production typically involved the publication of the Bible in Indian languages. Syllabic and pictographic versions were produced. Samsom Occom published the first literary work in English by a Native American, *A Sermon Preached at the Execution of Moses Paul, an Indian*, in 1772. The execution sermon became a staple. William Apes, an Indian author and missionary of the early nineteenth century, probably wrote the first Native American autobiography, *A Son of the Forest* (1829). Sarah Winnemucca published *Life Among the Paiutes* in 1883; it is an autobiographical work that attempts to change white attitudes toward Indians. Native American works often express anger and sadness over the displacement, decimation, and the forced assimilation of Indians into white culture.

John Rollin Ridge, a Cherokee, wrote essays, fiction, and poetry in the nineteenth century. His *Poems* are perhaps the only book of poetry published by a Native American in the nineteenth century; his famous *The Life and Adventures of Joaquín Murieta* (1854) is the first novel by a Native American. Sophia Alice Callahan's novel *Wynema, a Child of the Forest* (1891) is perhaps the first novel by a Native American woman.

The words of Sitting Bull, Pontiac, Black Hawk, Lame Dear, and Lakota holy man Black Elk were translated into English but found little public interest until the late twentieth century. Transcriber John G. Neihardt's edition of *Black Elk Speaks* first appeared in 1932 but was not widely read until the 1962 edition. Other transcriptions of Black Elk's words were published in *The Sacred Pipe* (1953), transcribed by John Epes Brown. Black Elk intended his story to be told communally, with the stories of other members of his tribe, and not chronologically but thematically, a non-Western approach that may be confusing to many students of Indian literature. "As-told-to" autobiographies are considered a distinct literary subgenre of Native American literature.

A sit-in at the Bureau of Indian Affairs, 1972. (Library of Congress)

Emily Pauline Johnson achieved fame with her poems (*Flint and Feather*, 1912) and short fiction (*Moccasin Maker*, 1913). Two other novelists of the early twentieth century are Mourning Dove (Cristal Quintasket) and John Joseph Mathews. John Oskison's *Brothers Three* (1935) depicts Oklahoma memorably. Salish Indian D'Arcy McNickle published *The Surrounded* in 1936; the novel is based on life on a Montana reservation. Humorists Alexander Posey and Will Rogers satirized politics local and international. New Mexico Kiowa writer N. Scott Momaday's Pulitzer Prize-winning *House Made of Dawn* (1968) is often cited as the work that transformed Indian literature. In this novel and in autobiographical fiction and verse, Momaday's explorations of the themes of personal identity, of feelings of alienation, of the blending of cultures, of a sense of place, of the sacred nature of words, and of the complexities of ethnic identity became central issues among Native American writers of the later twentieth century, including Paula Gunn Allen, Peter Blue Cloud, Simon Ortiz, Lynn Riggs, Leslie Marmon Silko, Highway Tomson, Gerald Vizenor, Frank Waters, and James Welch, among others.

A key theme of the late twentieth century Indian literary renaissance is that language is an affirmation of survival. For example, Welch's use of existential and surrealistic imagery explores the absurdity of reservation life and the importance of context for establishing identity. These ideas are explored in Welch's *Riding the Earth Boy Forty: Poems* (1971) and *Winter in the Blood* (1974). Silko and Allen explore multiculturalism in Indian life as a source of pain and of strength; Silko's

The twentieth century

705

Ceremony (1977) is an example. Vizenor's work offers his call for a "literature of survivance" to counter what he calls "manifest manners." He points to the modern complications of national, tribal, and multicultural ways of reading Native American literature.

Much debate concerns Native American writing that seeks to express an unromanticized affinity for cherished traditions. Some Native American writers seek to bring Native American traditions into the broader American consciousness; other writers advocate separation from the dominant culture, wishing to keep Indian traditions private and isolated. Separatists strongly criticize white authors who write about Indian values, rituals, and religious symbols. For some Indian poets, the clash over the forced use of English and cultural imperialism is not resolvable. White authors who deal with Indian subjects, notably Tony Hillerman, Barbara Kingsolver, and Michael Dorris, receive varying degrees of acceptance by Indian readers.

SUGGESTED READINGS

Bruchac, Joseph. *Survival This Way: Interviews with American Indian Poets*. Tucson: University of Arizona Press, 1987. Interviews with a number of Indian poets, emphasizing questions of identity, influence, and multiculturalism.

Hill Witt, Shirley, and Stan Stener, eds. *The Way: An Anthology of American Indian Literature*. Alfred A. Knopf, 1974. Essays, poetry, and fiction about Indian life from European contact to the twentieth century.

Katz, William Loren. *Black Indians: A Hidden Heritage*. New York: Atheneum, 1986. Escaped slaves and other blacks became part of Indian tribes beginning with the first arrivals of Africans to the American continent; this book tells their story.

Vizenor, Gerald, ed. *Narrative Chance: Post Modern Discourse on the American Indian Literatures*. Norman: University of Oklahoma Press, 1989. Late twentieth century critical interpretations of Indian writings.

—*Wesley Britton*

See also Acculturation; Allen, Paula Gunn; American identity: Northeast; American identity: West and the frontier; Kingsolver, Barbara; Momaday, N. Scott; Multiculturalism; Pluralism versus assimilation; Silko, Leslie Marmon; Stereotypes and identity; Vizenor, Gerald; Welch, James

Native Speaker

AUTHOR: Chang-rae Lee (1966?-   )
FIRST PUBLISHED: 1995
IDENTITIES: Korean American

Native Speaker is a Korean American narrator's probe into who he is. The probe is begun when the narrator's Caucasian wife leaves him. *Native Speaker* takes place in New York City during a time when Korean markets are being boycotted by black customers, and a Korean American councilman, John Kwang, is a possible candidate for mayor. The narrator, Henry Park, works for a private, CIA-style agency. Henry's current assignment is to investigate John. Park does not know the purpose of the investigation or who is paying for it; he imagines the client to be a xenophobe.

Henry was close to his father, who is dead. Henry's father was an immigrant who did well with a chain of produce markets and believed above all in family. John, onto whose staff Henry insinuates himself as a volunteer, sees his staff as a family. Henry finally betrays John, who feels close to him because he is Korean. John urges him to yell at him, to be disrespectful, to not treat him as a revered father figure. When they are sharing a drink, Henry almost forgets the reason he is with John.

The narrator's child, before his death, was being reared American-style, "untethered," allowed to walk all over Korean customs. Henry wanted his child to have "the authority and confidence that his broad half-yellow face could not." In a sense, Henry was rearing his child to have the confidence he does not have. Henry is devastated by the child's death, but he acts "serene as Siberia" after it happens. That is part of why his wife has left him. She wants him to acknowledge that having the child and having him die is the worst thing that has happened to them.

He has the impression at times that the politician, John, is not really speaking English but is being dubbed. Henry had had this same impression of himself as a child. He describes himself as "the obedient soft-spoken son" and asks himself whether being an invisible employee at the firm is the assimilation he craves. He has no control over the information he brings in about John. It is used for the detaining, by the Immigration and Naturalization Service (INS), of several dozen

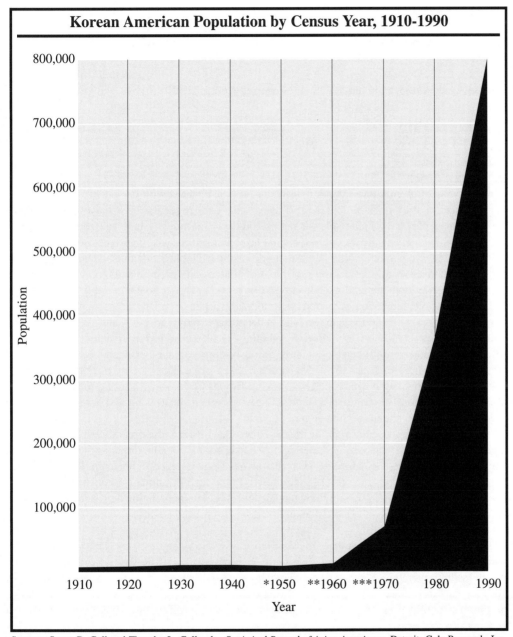

Korean American Population by Census Year, 1910-1990

Sources: Susan B. Gall and Timothy L. Gall, eds., *Statistical Record of Asian Americans.* Detroit: Gale Research, Inc., 1993. Ong Bill Hing, *Making and Remaking Asian America Through Immigration Policy, 1850-1990.* Stanford, Calif.: Stanford University Press, 1993.

* Data for Hawaii only.

** Foreign-born Koreans only.

*** Does not include Alaska.

immigrants. This INS raid in turn plays a role in the politician's downfall. The politician's American Dream ends.

Henry reflects that he has exploited his own and calls that his "ugly immigrant's truth." He thinks about his father and decides that his father would choose to see his deceptive behavior toward John "in a rigidly practical light," that is, as part of the struggle to survive in America. Henry leaves the firm, reconciles with his wife, and joins her in teaching English to non-native speakers.

SUGGESTED READINGS

Goldberg, Jeffrey. "The Overachievers." *New York* 28, no. 15 (April 10, 1995): 42-51.

Klinkenborg, Verlyn. "Witness to Strangeness—*Native Speaker* by Chang-rae Lee." *The New Yorker*, July 10, 1995, 76-77.

—Jennifer Westmoreland

See also Asian American identity: China, Japan, and Korea; Identity crisis

Natural, The

AUTHOR: Bernard Malamud (1914-1986)
FIRST PUBLISHED: 1952
IDENTITIES: Jewish

In *The Natural*, Bernard Malamud indicates his artistic concern with personality development in an allegorical story utilizing baseball to present the challenges the hero must undergo. Roy Hobbs, the new player on the last-place Knights, has the opportunity to help gain the pennant and discover his own identity. Roy, however, cannot bring himself to make the right choices.

Structured in two parallel stories, the novel presents Roy Hobbs's attempts to succeed. In both stories, Roy undergoes allegorical trials of initiation that test his strength and moral fiber. In both he fails by placing immediate, personal satisfaction ahead of larger goals. In the first story, Roy, a nineteen-year-old, has been discovered by the alcoholic, spent-out Sam Simpson, who hopes the presentation of Roy to Sam's manager will redeem Sam. Roy can pitch and hit, armed with Wonderboy, a bat crafted for him from a lightning-felled oak tree. His first test comes when traveling to training camp. When the train mysteriously stops, a challenge match between Roy and the current superhero of baseball, the Whammer, takes place. Roy strikes out the Whammer, making it seem Roy may indeed replace him. After Roy passes the test of strength, his values are tested by a mysterious woman to whom he is attracted. When she asks him what he wants to be, his selfish response, "the best in the game," is unworthy.

In the second story, a decade after the major setback that his response precipitated, Roy is trying to get back on track. He arrives at the Knights's locker room and announces to the beleaguered manager, another father figure, Pop Fisher, that he has been assigned to his team. Roy shows he can save the Knights and draw the lagging crowd. Pitted against another hero, Bump, he again defeats his rival on the field. Honored by the fans on a special appreciation day, he again fails the humility test when he repeats his selfish intention to be the best and neglects to credit his teammates and manager.

His dealing with women parallels the first story also. He is attracted to glamorous, ruthless women who manipulate him to their selfish goals. He is presented with an alternative in Iris Lemon, who helps him overcome a slump. A woman who has experienced life's difficulties herself, she tells him that "suffering teaches us to want the right things." He nevertheless chooses all the wrong things when he rejects her, his team, his manager, and his best self by throwing the final game.

SUGGESTED READINGS

Astro, Richard, and Jackson J. Benson, eds. *The Fiction of Bernard Malamud*. Corvallis: Oregon State University Press, 1977.

Field, Leslie, and Joyce Field, eds. *Bernard Malamud: A Collection of Critical Essays*. Englewood Cliffs, N.J.: Prentice-Hall, 1975.

Hershinow, Sheldon J. *Bernard Malamud*. New York: Frederick Ungar, 1980.
Richman, Sydney. *Bernard Malamud*. New York: Twayne, 1966.

—Bernadette Flynn Low

See also *Assistant, The*; *Fixer, The*; Identity crisis; Kinsella, W. P.; Malamud, Bernard

Naylor, Gloria
BORN: New York, New York; January 25, 1950

PRINCIPAL WORKS: *The Women of Brewster Place*, 1982; *Linden Hills*, 1985; *Mama Day*, 1988; *Bailey's Cafe*, 1992

IDENTITIES: African American; women

SIGNIFICANT ACHIEVEMENT: Naylor's exploration of black communities stresses the relationship between identity and place.

When she gave her introverted daughter a journal from Woolworth's, Gloria Naylor's mother opened the door to writing. In high school, two experiences shaped Naylor's emerging identity: nineteenth century English literature taught her that language can be a powerful tool, and Martin Luther King, Jr.'s 1968 assassination turned her to missionary work. Instead of going to college, for the next seven years she traveled as a Jehovah's Witness, abandoning the work in 1975, when she began to feel constrained by the lifestyle.

At Brooklyn College, her introduction to black history and the discovery of such literary foremothers as Zora Neale Hurston and Toni Morrison gave her the inspiration to try writing herself. Completing her first novel, the best-seller *The Women of Brewster Place*, signified, she has indicated, her taking hold of herself and attempting to take her destiny into her own hands. After winning a scholarship to Yale University, Naylor discovered that, for her, graduate training was incompatible with writing fiction. She nevertheless completed a master's degree in 1983, when the Afro-American Studies department allowed her second novel, *Linden Hills,* to fulfill the thesis requirement. *Linden Hills* illustrates the effects of materialism on an elite all-black community that lacks a spiritual center.

The central feature of all of Naylor's novels is an enclosed black community where characters learn to embrace their identities in the context of place. Naylor's powerful settings combine elements of the ordinary with the otherworldly, allowing for magical events and mythic resolutions. For example, *Mama Day* takes place on the imaginary island of Willow Springs and weaves the history of the Day family from the point of view of the powerful matriarch Mama Day, a conjure woman. Naylor's own family history provides her with a rich sense of community, but she paradoxically treasures solitude. Married briefly, she refuses to remarry or have children and teaches writing to keep from being too much of a recluse. Naylor's strength is portraying convincing multigenerational characters in specific settings.

SUGGESTED READINGS

Naylor, Gloria. "Love and Sex in the Afro-American Novel." *The Yale Review* 78, no. 1 (1989): 19-31.
Puhr, Kathleen M. "Healers in Gloria Naylor's Fiction." *Twentieth Century Literature* 40, no. 4 (1994): 518-527.

—Christine H. King

See also African American identity; *Bailey's Cafe*; *Women of Brewster Place, The*

Neruda, Pablo (Neftalí Ricardo Reyes Basoalto)
BORN: Parral, Chile; July 12, 1904
DIED: Santiago, Chile; September 23, 1973
PRINCIPAL WORKS: *Veinte poemas de amor y una canción desesperada*, 1924 (*Twenty Love Poems and a Song of Despair*, 1969, 1976); *Residencia en la tierra*, 1933, 1935, 1947 (*Residence on*

Earth, 1946, 1973); *Canto general*, 1950 (English translation, 1991); *Los versos del capitán*, 1952 (*The Captain's Verses*, 1972); *Odas elementales*, 1954 (*Elementary Odes*, 1961); *Cien sonetos de amor*, 1959 (*One Hundred Love Sonnets*, 1986); *La espada encendida*, 1970 (the flaming sword)

IDENTITIES: Latino; world

SIGNIFICANT ACHIEVEMENT: Neruda's bold imagery has been influential around the world; he was awarded the Nobel Prize in Literature in 1971.

Pablo Neruda was one of the greatest poets of the Spanish American avant-garde, sharing its many poetic heights and political lows. His Stalinism in (bad) verse never completely drowned the powerful poet in him; particularly the erotic strand in his work proved to be quite resilient and accounted for his resurrections. Neruda's type of poetic Marxism was typical of the Latin American artistic appropriation of leftist revolutionary ideologies in the twentieth century.

He began writing poetry when he was ten years old. In 1920, he adopted the name Pablo Neruda. In 1924, when he was twenty years old, he published his most widely read book of romantic love poems. In 1927, he was named an honorary consul; it was in isolation and desperation in Ceylon that he wrote his most powerful avant-garde work, *Residence on Earth*. In the 1930's he moved to Spain. He was particularly close to Federico García Lorca, whose murder at the hands of fascists came as a great shock.

Neruda reacted to the betrayal of the Spanish Republic by democratic nations—who refused to aid Spain—by embracing communism. During the war, he returned to Chile to start a long political career, which followed all the ups and downs of the Communist Party politics in his country and in Latin America. In 1948, he had to flee to exile, where he completed his grand epic song of Latin American geography, history, and politics, *Canto general*. The United States gets its due share of invectives in this book. Aside from the artistically embarrassing Stalinist hyperbole, Neruda in *Canto general* speaks on behalf of a contemporary Latin America injured periodically by U.S. imperial interests. Since his erotic poetry had no place in the party line at that time, he published *The Captain's Verses* anonymously in Italy, pretending that it was a work of a captain in the Spanish Republican army. After Joseph Stalin's influence waned, Neruda's political stance softened, and he rediscovered poetry through odes on simple things and through erotic love sonnets. In the 1960's, he welcomed the Cuban Revolution, but his love remained unrequited as the Cubans had their own ideas about the uses of Marxism. In *La espada encendida*, Neruda returned somewhat to his avant-garde visionary poetry of the 1930's. He died of cancer during the first days of the Augusto Pinochet coup against the government of Salvador Allende in 1973.

SUGGESTED READINGS

De Costa, René. *The Poetry of Pablo Neruda*. Cambridge, Mass.: Harvard University Press, 1979.

Santí, Enrico M. *Pablo Neruda: The Poetics of Prophecy*. Ithaca, N.Y.: Cornell University Press, 1982.

—*Emil Volek*

See also Spanish Civil War

New and Collected Poems

AUTHOR: Ishmael Reed (1938-   )

FIRST PUBLISHED: 1988

IDENTITIES: African American; European American; Native American; religion

Ishmael Reed is primarily known as a novelist. Most critical works about him deal with his fiction, and the leading books about contemporary African American poetry mention him only in passing. His poetry, however, repays reading and study—for the light it casts on his novels, for its treatment of the Hoodoo religion, and for the same verbal facility and breadth of reference that is praised in his fiction.

New and Collected Poems includes the earlier works *Conjure* (1972), *Chattanooga* (1973), and *A Secretary to the Spirits* (1977). *Conjure*, Reed's first and longest book of poems, is a mixed bag. Filled with typographical tricks that Reed later all but abandoned, it also has moments of striking wit, like the comparison of the poet to a fading city in "Man or Butterfly" or the two views of "history" in "Dualism: In Ralph Ellison's *Invisible Man*."

Conjure largely deals with the Hoodoo religion, Reed's idiosyncratic combination of ancient Egyptian and contemporary North American elements with the Caribbean religion of vodun, or voodoo, itself a mix of Yoruba and Christian elements. In "The Neo-HooDoo Manifesto," Reed invokes American musicians, from jazz and blues greats to white rock and rollers, as exemplars of a religious approach based on creativity and bodily pleasure. Hoodoo is polytheistic, excluding only those gods who claim hegemony over the others. Reed's main disagreement with vodun springs from its acceptance of the "dangerous paranoid pain in the neck . . . cop-god from the git-go, Jeho-vah." The history of Hoodoo is outlined in Reed's novel *Mumbo-Jumbo* (1972). Its view of all time as synchronous informs the setting of *Flight to Canada* (1976), in which airplanes coexist with plantation slavery, but the fullest expression of Hoodoo's spirit and aesthetic is given in *Conjure*.

Chattanooga is named for Reed's home town, and the title poem is a paean to the area where Reed grew up and its multicultural heritage. "Railroad Bill, a Conjure Man" is a charming account of how the hero of an old-fashioned trickster tale deals with Hollywood. *A Secretary to the Spirits* is a short book with a few impressive works in it, notably, the first poem, "Pocodonia," expanding what seems to have been a traditional blues song into something far more complex and strange.

The work since *A Secretary to the Spirits* appears in the last section of *New and Collected Poems*, "Points of View." The quality is mixed, but the outrage and the wit that characterize so much of Reed's work can be found in this last section, as in "I'm Running for the Office of Love."

SUGGESTED READING

Martin, Reginald. *Ishmael Reed and the New Black Aesthetic Critics*. New York: St. Martin's Press, 1988.

—*Arthur D. Hlavaty*

See also African American identity; Reed, Ishmael; Religion and identity

Ng, Fae Myenne

BORN: San Francisco, California; 1956

PRINCIPAL WORK: *Bone*, 1993

IDENTITIES: Chinese American

SIGNIFICANT ACHIEVEMENT: Ng brings the perspective of an Asian American to the American experience of immigration and assimilation.

Fae Myenne Ng's writing depicts a cultural divide between her assimilated generation and that of her Chinese parents. Reared in San Francisco's Chinatown by working-class parents who immigrated from China, Ng acquired an excellent education, receiving degrees from the University of California at Berkeley and an M.F.A. from Columbia University. *Bone*, her first novel, took her ten years to write, during which time she supported herself as a waitress and temporary worker, as well as by a grant from the National Foundation for the Arts. As does Leila, the narrator of the novel, Ng is an educated woman who understood her parents' working-class world. In the novel, the Chinese mother is a poorly paid, overworked garment worker. The father holds down a series of dead-end jobs that include janitor, dishwasher, houseboy, and laundry worker. The couple have worked their fingers to the bone to provide for their daughters. *Bone* is a tribute to the family's father, who represents a generation of Chinese men who sacrificed their personal happiness for the sake of their families. Ng's inspiration was the old Chinese men living alone and impoverished in single room occupancy hotels in Chinatown. Chinese America's bachelor society came to America to work the gold mines, to build the railroads, and to develop California agriculturally. These immigrants became men without roots.

The novel also depicts the conflicts of the family's three daughters with their old-fashioned parents. There is the middle daughter Ona, whose suicide suggests she could not adjust to American society and maintain her identity as a dutiful Chinese daughter. Nina, the youngest daughter, affirms a modern identity and escapes to New York City. Leila, the eldest daughter, is a complicated combination of the old Chinese ways and new American cultural patterns. As does Nina, the rebellious daughter, Ng moved to New York City. Leila, with her ability to assimilate the new while keeping faith with the past, is the daughter who most mirrors Ng's identity as an Asian American. Ng's work adds to the tradition of the immigrant novel.

SUGGESTED READINGS

Stetson, Nancy. "Honoring Her Forebears." *Chicago Tribune*, April 4, 1993, C12.

Wong, Sau-Ling Cynthia. *Reading Asian-American Voices: From Necessity to Extravagance.* Princeton, N.J.: Princeton University Press, 1993.

—Margaret Boe Birns

See also Asian American identity: China, Japan, and Korea; *Bone*; Emigration and immigration

Nick Adams Stories, The

AUTHOR: Ernest Hemingway (1899-1961)

FIRST PUBLISHED: 1972 (in book form)

IDENTITIES: European American; Midwest

Between 1925 and 1933, Ernest Hemingway published sixteen stories about a character he called Nick Adams. Appearing in various collections and arranged in no particular time sequence, the narratives appeared disconnected and incomplete. In 1972, after Hemingway's death, the stories were collected, arranged in the chronological order of Adams' life, and augmented with eight unpublished fragments found after Hemingway's death. From this reorganization emerged a coherent picture of Nick's life from his boyhood in upper Michigan through his adult experiences. Nick Adams' life runs parallel to Hemingway's life.

Nick's formative years bring him face-to-face with meaningless suffering, violence, death, and what Hemingway depicts as the futility of human existence. For example, in "Indian Camp," the boy accompanies his father, a doctor, to deliver an Indian woman's baby. His father uses a jackknife to perform a Cesarean section without anesthetic. The baby is delivered successfully, but the woman's husband is so ravaged by his wife's suffering that he commits suicide.

Later, as an adolescent runaway riding the rails, Nick meets a brain-damaged former prizefighter in "The Battler." The fighter, Ad Francis, is prone to violent outbursts and is kept in check by his companion, Bugs, who subdues him with a blackjack. In "The Killers," Nick is working in a small-town diner when gangsters from Chicago come to murder a local man. The man is resigned to his fate and neither fights nor flees when Nick warns him of danger.

Years later, Nick fights in Italy as a soldier in World War I and is wounded. In "Now I Lay Me" he resists sleep, convinced that if he ever closes his eyes, his soul will leave his body. In "Big Two-Hearted River," Nick returns from the war physically healed but wounded in soul; he searches for solace and deliverance in the rituals of camping and fishing.

Nick Adams is a prototypic Hemingway hero: concerned, reflective, an outwardly impassive soldier and sportsman ravaged in mind and spirit by terrors against which he can mount no defense. He must face evil, futility, and the nothingness of existence alone and unaided. Defeat is inevitable and unavoidable; only defeat with dignity offers hope of redemption. From the character of Nick Adams arise the protagonists of Hemingway's most famous novels. Nick is similar to Jake Barnes in *The Sun Also Rises* (1926), Robert Jordan in *For Whom the Bell Tolls* (1940), and Frederic Henry in *A Farewell to Arms* (1929).

SUGGESTED READINGS

Benson, Jackson J., ed. *New Critical Approaches to the Short Stories of Ernest Hemingway.* Durham, N.C.: Duke University Press, 1991.

Gurko, Leo. *Ernest Hemingway and the Pursuit of Heroism.* New York: Thomas Y. Crowell, 1968.

Young, Philip. *Ernest Hemingway.* New York: Holt, Rinehart and Winston, 1952.

—Faith Hickman Brynie

See also American identity: Midwest; Hemingway, Ernest; *Moveable Feast, A*; *That Summer in Paris*; World War I

Night

AUTHOR: Elie Wiesel (1928-   )
FIRST PUBLISHED: *Un di Velt hot geshvign*, 1956; *La Nuit*, 1958 (English translation, 1960)
IDENTITIES: Family; Jewish; world

Night, Elie Wiesel's memoir of the Holocaust, tells of his concentration camp experience. Encompassing events from the end of 1941 to 1945, the book ponders a series of questions, whose answers, Moché the Beadle, who was miraculously saved from an early German massacre, reminds the boy, lie "only within yourself."

Moché, who teaches the boy the beauty of biblical studies, is a strange character with a clownish awkwardness, more God's madman than mentally ill; he is also a recurring figure in later Wiesel works. After Moché returns to town to describe the horrible scenes he has witnessed, no one listens to this apparently insane rambler who, like Cassandra, repeats his warnings in vain. The clown, a moving and tragic fool, is unable to convince the Jewish community of its impending doom. Despite arrests, ghettoizations, and mass deportations, the Jews still cannot believe him, even as they embark for Auschwitz.

In 1944, the young narrator is initiated into the horrors of the archipelago of Nazi death camps. There he becomes A-7713, deprived of name, self-esteem, identity. He observes and undergoes hunger, exhaustion, cold, suffering, brutality, executions, cruelty, breakdown in personal relationships, and flames and smoke coming from crematories in the German death factories. In the barracks of terror, where he sees the death of his mother and seven-year-old sister, his religious faith is corroded. The world no longer represents God's mind. Comparing himself to Job, he bitterly asks God for an explanation of such evil. The boy violently rejects God's presence and God's justice, love, and mercy: "I was alone—terribly alone in a world without God and without man."

After a death march and brutally cruel train ride, young Wiesel and his father arrive at Buchenwald, where his father soon dies of malnutrition and dysentery. As in a daze, the son waits to be killed by fleeing German soldiers. Instead, he coolly notes, on April 11, 1945, "at about six o'clock in the evening, the first American tank stood at the gates of Buchenwald."

In addition to wanting to elucidate the unfathomable secret of death and theodicy, the narrator lived a monstrous, stunted, and isolated existence as an adult. He saw himself as victim, executioner, and spectator. By affirming that he was not divided among the three but was in fact all of them at once, he was able to resolve his identity problem. The autobiography's last image shows Wiesel looking at himself in a mirror: The body and soul are wounded, but the night and its nightmares are finally over.

SUGGESTED READINGS

Rittner, Carol, ed. *Elie Wiesel: Between Memory and Hope.* New York: New York University Press, 1990.

Rosenfeld, Alvin H., and Irving Greenberg, eds. *Confronting the Holocaust: The Impact of Elie Wiesel.* Bloomington: Indiana University Press, 1978.

Sibelman, Simon P. *Silence in the Novels of Elie Wiesel.* New York: St. Martin's Press, 1995.

—Pierre L. Horn

See also *All Rivers Run to the Sea*; Anti-Semitism; Holocaust; Wiesel, Elie

'night, Mother

AUTHOR: Marsha Norman (1947-   )
FIRST PRODUCED: 1982; first published, 1983
IDENTITIES: European American; family; women

"The things we as women know best," Norman has explained, "have not been perceived to be of critical value to society." The mother-daughter relationship is a "perfect example of that." At the play's outset, the middle-aged Jessie announces to her mother, Thelma, that she is going to kill herself. Norman has described the ninety minutes that follow as "the fight of their lives." Thelma exhorts, cajoles, and pleads with Jessie to abandon her plan. Jessie remains implacable. She feels trapped in the house she and Thelma share. Her husband has abandoned her; her son is a delinquent. She blames her epileptic fits for her failings as a wife and mother and for her inability to hold a job. She also blames the epilepsy—considered emblematic by critics of the plight as a woman in society—for rendering her unconscious and out of control, to be handled and observed by others.

Jessie has not felt in charge of her life, but she takes charge of her death. At the play's opening, she is collecting old pillows and towels to minimize the mess when she shoots herself. Such meticulousness indicates Jessie's need for control, and is ironic in view of the violence of the act she is planning.

Not until Norman heard an audience laugh at its dark humor during a reading of the play did she have confidence of its acceptance. Her husband at the time, Dann Byck, Jr., produced *'night, Mother* for its Broadway run, the personal nature of the project causing Norman to want to keep it in the family. The play won four Tony nominations, including best play, and a Pulitzer Prize in 1983. A film version, scripted by Norman, appeared in 1986.

Critical discussion has focused on the issue of suicide in the play, but its feminism has also been debated. Some feminists condemn *'night, Mother* for perpetuating the stereotype of the self-destructive woman. Others praise it for highlighting the struggle of women like Thelma to relinquish their hold on adult children. "We all lose our children," Norman, a mother of two, has remarked: "You think for a lifetime they belong to you, but they are only on loan." Regarding the violence in the play, Norman has commented that women "are not afraid to look under the bed, or to wash the sheets; we know that life is messy."

SUGGESTED READINGS

Betsko, Kathleen, and Rachel Koenig. *Interviews with Contemporary Women Playwrights.* New York: William Morrow, 1987.

Harriott, Esther. *American Voices: Five Contemporary Playwrights in Essays and Interviews.* Jefferson, N.C.: McFarland, 1988.

Hart, Lynda, ed. *Making a Spectacle: Feminist Essays on Contemporary Woman's Theatre.* Ann Arbor: University of Michigan Press, 1989.

Savran, David. *In Their Own Words: Contemporary American Playwrights.* New York: Theatre Communications Group, 1988.

—*Amy Allison*

See also Feminism

No Man's Land: The Place of the Woman Writer in the Twentieth Century

AUTHORS: Sandra M. Gilbert (1936-   ) and Susan Gubar (1944-   )
FIRST PUBLISHED: *The War of the Words*, 1988 (vol. 1); *Sexchanges*, 1989 (volume 2); *Letters from the Front*, 1994 (vol. 3)
IDENTITIES: Women

No Man's Land: The Place of the Woman Writer in the Twentieth Century, an ambitious three-volume series by the most influential feminist literary critics of their generation, addresses the changing identities of female and male writers of the twentieth century. In particular, Sandra M. Gilbert and Susan Gubar analyze the literature and literary movements of the century as products of a war between the sexes. As the series title suggests, as women gained power, beginning in the late nineteenth century, through the women's movement, and as women discovered new identities for themselves, men experienced a corresponding sense of emasculation, perceiving themselves as "no-men."

In volume 1, *The War of the Words*, Gilbert and Gubar describe the ways that literary modernism, the prevailing style of the 1920's and 1930's, differs in the works of male and female writers, grounding their arguments in analysis of social and cultural events. They conclude that modernism and avant-garde writing are the result of a sexual battle between men and women. Modernism has traditionally been considered largely a male movement; Gilbert and Gubar credit women writers with a greater role in its development than most previous critics do.

Volume 2, *Sexchanges*, argues that, as sex roles change, the sexes battle, resulting in changes in what is perceived as erotic. Definitions of sex and sex roles evolved through three phases: rejection and revision of Victorian feminine ideals; antiutopian skepticism about the feminization of women; and "the virtually apocalyptic engendering of the new," perhaps most strongly influenced by the realization that while sex is biological, gender is an artifice, not a natural condition.

Volume 3, *Letters from the Front* analyzes works by women that seem particularly to express the psychological effect of social change. The discussions focus on the notion of the "family plot," referring to the changing structure of the family, the changing notion of narrative, and burial of the idea that the family has a single or static structure.

The three monumental volumes discuss works by numerous major and minor women writers. Americans receiving especially in-depth treatment include Kate Chopin, Edith Wharton, Willa Cather, Marianne Moore, and Sylvia Plath. Gilbert and Gubar also trace ongoing traditions of black and lesbian women's writing. The analyses consistently focus on the social and historical forces that shape identity and self-perception.

Suggested readings

Blankley, Elyse. Review of *Sexchanges*, by Sandra M. Gilbert and Susan Gubar. *Women's Review of Books* 6 (September, 1989): 24-25.

Froula, Christine. Review of *The War of the Words*, by Sandra M. Gilbert and Susan Gubar. *The New York Times Book Review*, February 7, 1988, 12-13.

Showalter, Elaine. Review of *Letters from the Front*, by Sandra M. Gilbert and Susan Gubar. *London Review of Books*, October 20, 1994, 36-37.

—Joan Hope

See also Canon; Feminism; Gilbert, Sandra M., and Susan Gubar; Literary standards; *Madwoman in the Attic, The*; Women and identity

No-No Boy

Author: John Okada (1923-1971)
First published: 1957
Identities: Japanese American; West and Southwest

No-No Boy depicts a second generation Japanese American's struggle to balance his loyalty to the Japanese culture, to his parents, and to his country, the United States. Ichiro Yamada is interned during World War II. He is put in jail for answering no to the two critical questions on the allegiance questionnaire. His two negative answers are his refusal to serve in the American armed forces and his refusal to forswear allegiance to Japan and pledge loyalty to the United States. After he is released from prison, Ichiro moves back to Seattle and is caught between two seemingly irreconcilable worlds. On one side, there are his parents, who are very proud of being Japanese. On the other side, there is the United States, a country to which he still feels he belongs.

During his search for his identity, Ichiro meets several people who help shape his perspective on himself and on his relationship with America. One of his close friends, Kenji, joins the military during the war. He loses a leg and has only two years to live. What Kenji physically goes through, Ichiro experiences emotionally. Being a no-no boy, Ichiro is looked down upon by his brother and other Japanese Americans who believe he has betrayed the country. During one of their conversations, Kenji and Ichiro jokingly discuss whether they want to trade places. The fact that both of them are willing to do it comments on the kind of social environment they have to deal with and on the choices they have made.

Kenji also introduces Ichiro to Emi, a person who can empathize with Ichiro's experience. Emi's husband has left her because he is ashamed of his brother Mike and of Emi's father, who elect to be repatriated back to Japan. Mike is a World War I veteran. He is incensed by how Japanese Americans are treated by their own government during World War II and eventually decides to go back to a country he does not know or love. Emi saves Ichiro from plunging into an emotional abyss. They find a friend and companion in each other. After witnessing the death of his friend, Freddie, who is also a no-no boy, Ichiro starts to think about his own future. In "the darkness of the alley of the community" that is "a tiny bit of America," he starts to chase that faint and elusive insinuation of promise as it continues "to take shape in mind and in heart."

SUGGESTED READINGS

Chin, Frank. "Come All Ye Asian American Writers of the Real and the Fake." In *The Big Aiiieeeee! An Anthology of Chinese and Japanese American Literature*, edited by Frank Chin et al. New York: Meridian, 1991.

Kim, Elaine H. *Asian American Literature*. Philadelphia: Temple University Press, 1982.

—*Qun Wang*

See also Acculturation; Asian American identity: China, Japan, and Korea; Identity crisis; Japanese American internment; Okada, John

Nontraditional family

IDENTITIES: Adolescence and coming-of-age; family; men; women

DEFINITION: Nontraditional families vary from the "nuclear family," which is a family of a husband, wife, and their shared biological children.

At issue

Through the presentation of families other than the nuclear family, which is assumed to be the norm, literature shows how nontraditional families fulfill, or fail to fulfill, the functions of nurturing, teaching, protecting, and providing, which are the family's main purposes for existing. Nontraditional families include single-parent households, stepfamilies, adoptive families, grandparents or other nonparent relatives raising children, and homosexual couples with or without children. Large extended families living together might also be considered to be nontraditional (although this kind of family is traditional) because it is relatively rare in North America in the late twentieth century.

The traditional nuclear family is actually a relatively new family unit. In many cultures and throughout much of human history, families included many more people: grandparents, aunts, uncles, cousins, and various in-laws. Families have also historically included fewer members than the nuclear family does. Death from childbirth, wars, diseases, and desertion have long removed members of families. Literature shows that stepparents, stepsiblings, half-siblings, and in-laws are not modern inventions. The ways in which these variant families are accepted or not accepted by their communities can inform the reader about the culture and time period being discussed and about the culture and time period that produced the story.

Governments and religions have refused to acknowledge certain groups as families. Mothers and their out-of-wedlock children have often been refused the status granted other families. Stepchildren and stepparents have often had trouble coming to an understanding with one another. Gay and lesbian couples have almost always been denied the right to live together and the right to raise children.

Historically, the family has provided a rich ground for the telling of stories. Stories about perfectly happy, perfectly normal families teach few lessons, however, and would provide little information, and would, in fact, be boring. Two sources, the Bible and Greek mythology, are at the root of much of Western literature and cultural thought about families. Actually reading about families in these two sources is often hair-raising. In the Bible one finds examples of polygamous marriage, half-siblings, patriarchal families (wherein grown sons and their families live under the authority of their father), and other nontraditional families (such as Ruth and her mother-in-law Naomi, or Mordechai and his foster daughter, Esther). Greek mythology abounds with tales of nontraditional families wherein parents, siblings, and cousins are related in intricate marriages, and stepparents and stepchildren do not get along. The male gods engender many children out of wedlock, a situation that often makes the mortal women outcast—along with their children—despite the women's helplessness to prevent their rapes.

Fairy tales, another mainstay of literature, often involve step-relatives, who are usually cruel. Snow White is threatened repeatedly by her stepmother, Hansel's and Gretel's stepmother convinces their father to abandon them in the woods, and Cinderella is a slave to her stepmother and stepsisters, having only a godmother to care about her. The loving sister in "The Seven Swans" must sacrifice herself to save her brothers from their stepmother's curse. In short, the nontraditional family, including many family problems, is as old as Western literature.

Because family is so important to younger children and identity to older ones, the literature directed at these audiences deals extensively with these issues. Younger children need stories that show that their parents love them and will protect them, and younger children need stories that show that it is natural for families to have occasional strife. Teenagers need stories that show them other teenagers facing the same problems that they or their peers face, including family problems.

Traditional families are often shown in this literature, but, increasingly, so are other types of families. Controversy has surrounded many of these texts, in particular those that address the most nontraditional family, the gay or lesbian couple. Leslea Newman's *Heather Has Two Mommies* (1989) and Michael Willhoite's *Daddy's Roommate* (1990) are two of the better-known works that address this issue. Written for younger readers, these books are meant to show that there is nothing wrong or abhorrent about these families, families which children may experience. Some claim, however, that there is something wrong or abhorrent about gay or lesbian families, and that children should be so told.

Examples of how adolescents struggle to find their identities can be found in Cynthia Voigt's novels about the Tillerman family and their friends. The father of the four Tillerman children—Dicey, James, Maybeth, and Sammy—never married their mother, and deserted her before the birth of Sammy. When their mother suffers a nervous breakdown, thirteen-year-old Dicey, assuming the role of guardian and parent, manages in *Homecoming* (1981) to bring her siblings first to an aunt's house and then to a home with their grandmother. In *Dicey's Song* (1982), all of the children must learn to live by a new set of rules, with a new set of assumptions, and so must the old woman. To form a family, Dicey and her grandmother must re-evaluate what it is that they expect from family. In *Sons from Afar* (1987), James, the older brother, is seeking to understand why he is the person he is. He convinces Sammy, the more confident younger brother, to accompany him on a journey that teaches them more about each other than about their father. *A Solitary Blue* (1983) is the story of Jeff, Dicey's friend, who is the son of a professor who is at first almost completely oblivious to his latchkey son. The boy's mother abandons them to go back to her spoiled life with her wealthy grandmother. The story demonstrates that sometimes one must let go of family and that sometimes children of divorced parents must choose between their mothers and fathers.

Other examples of adolescent literature that focuses on nontraditional families, and the place of children within those families, can be found in Harper Lee's *To Kill a Mockingbird* (1960), a novel filled with nontraditional families. S. E. Hinton's *The Outsiders* (1967) is a tale of three brothers living on their own following the death of their parents. Judy Blume's *Are You There God? It's Me, Margaret* (1970) is the story of a girl entering puberty and struggling with her parents' interfaith marriage. *I Know Why the Caged Bird Sings* (1970) is Maya Angelou's examination of a lost childhood and survival. Patricia MacLachlan's *Sarah, Plain and Tall* (1985) is a story of a widower, his children and the woman who joins them as wife and new mother.

Contemporary adult literature   Literature for adults also addresses nontraditional families, but it is rarer that the search for identity within the family is a major element of the work. Alice Walker's *The Color Purple* (1982) examines one woman's escape from the bondage of a traditional marriage. Anne Tyler's *The Accidental Tourist* (1985), details a broken marriage and a close relationship between adult siblings. Barbara Kingsolver's *Pigs in Heaven* (1993) explores the issues of adoption and the desire of Native Americans to keep their children within their heritage. Dorothy Alison's *Bastard out of Carolina* (1993) is a disturbing look at how an illegitimate child's extended family tries to protect her when her mother chooses to stay with a boyfriend even after watching him rape the girl. In adult fiction, the traditional family is often portrayed in a critical light.

Margaret Atwood's dystopian novel *The Handmaid's Tale* (1985) contains a particularly disturbing depiction of women who have had their identities stripped away. Their society calls them, and treats them as, Wives, Aunts, Marthas, Econowives, Handmaids, Jezebels, or Unwomen. No room for individuality is left to them in the patriarchal, almost polygamous, society of the novel. Ursula K. Le Guin's *The Left Hand of Darkness* (1969) details how society and family might look if every person had the ability to be either a father or a mother. Marge Piercy's *Woman on the Edge of Time* (1976) shows the trials of an older Hispanic woman in late twentieth century America, where she has been declared insane and lost custody of her child. John Varley's *Steel Beach* (1992) examines questions of identity, with a particular emphasis on gender.

Two canonical novels that address the issue of nontraditional families include Nathaniel Hawthorne's *The Scarlet Letter* (1850), which explores the relationship between a single mother and her child and the mother's relationship with the father of that child and with her husband. Harriet Beecher Stowe's *Uncle Tom's Cabin: Or, Life Among the Lowly* (1852) addresses the breakup of slave families in the service of economics. The novels of William Faulkner, including *The Sound and the Fury* (1929), examine the pain that families can cause when different family members have different expectations regarding the importance of pride and honor.

SUGGESTED READINGS

Beer, William R., ed. *Relative Strangers: Studies of Stepfamily Process*. Totowa, N.J.: Rowman & Littlefield, 1988. An examination of the dynamics of stepfamilies, discussing stepparent-stepchild relationships, blended families, and half-siblings.

Bettleheim, Bruno. *The Uses of Enchantment: The Meaning and Importance of Fairy Tales*. New York: Random House, 1975. Examines what fairy tales teach and how fairy tales may affect children. Family interactions receive a great deal of attention.

Coontz, Stephanie. "The American Family and the Nostalgia Trap (Attributing Americans' Social Problems to the Breakdown of the Traditional Family)." *Phi Delta Kappan*. 76, no. 7 (March, 1995): 1-20. This article discusses the myths that surround the debate over traditional and nontraditional families in American society.

Washington, Mary Helen, ed. *Memory of Kin: Stories About Family by Black Writers*. New York: Doubleday, 1991. This is a collection of stories and poems about families, traditional and nontraditional. Of particular note are the stories and poems about slaves and the problems they had keeping their families together.

—*Susan Jaye Dauer*

See also Adolescent identity; Divorce; Gay identity; Lesbian identity

Normal Heart, The

AUTHOR: Larry Kramer (1935-   )
FIRST PRODUCED: 1985; first published, 1985
IDENTITIES: Disease; European American; gay, lesbian, and bisexual

Larry Kramer's landmark play, *The Normal Heart*, chronicles major events in the early years of the acquired immune deficiency syndrome (AIDS) epidemic in New York City. The play's 1985 production at the Public Theatre riveted the attention of diverse audiences to the devastation of the new disease. As an instrument of political rhetoric and as a classically structured drama, *The Normal Heart* has power to move emotions and change minds.

In the summer of 1981, Ned Weeks visits Dr. Emma Brookner, who is treating virtually all the gay men in New York afflicted with rare, immune system-related diseases. Brookner has heard of Ned—and his "big mouth." She is looking for a gay man to lead in this new crisis; she urges him to express his anger toward those in power who are apathetic and to convince gay men to stop engaging in sexual activity. She believes the disease is spread through sex.

Ned begins to act, exploring the failure of *The New York Times* to cover the epidemic adequately. In so doing, he meets a gay reporter, Felix Turner, to whom he is immediately attracted. A key relationship in the play is between Ned and his brother Ben, a lawyer. Although Ned is impatient with his brother's reluctance to help the organization Ned has formed in response to the epidemic, it is clear that what Ned wants most from Ben is unconditional acceptance and love.

As Ned and Felix grow closer, Ned's organization of gay men confronting the health crisis struggles with an unresponsive mayor's staff on the outside, while battling ego clashes and differences in style within. Bruce Niles, a banker, attractive and cautious, is elected president of the group instead of Ned. Ned's anger—and his commitment—increase dramatically when Felix becomes ill. Although the organization wins some victories in terms of fundraising and media exposure, Ned and Bruce fight continually; Ned is finally removed from the board of directors.

In the play's poignant finale, Ned and Felix are married by Dr. Brookner in the hospital. Felix dies, and Ned remembers he meant to tell his lover about a recent trip to Yale, where he met many young gay people at a dance "just across the campus from that tiny freshman room where I wanted to kill myself because I thought I was the only gay man in the world." Kramer's play was one of the first in what has been an eloquent response from the artists of the theater to AIDS. As a result of Kramer's anger, daring, and artistry, this disease is better understood.

SUGGESTED READINGS

Hoffman, William M. *As Is*. New York: Random House, 1985.

Kaufman, David. "The Creative Response—Art Born of Anguish: Creative Expression of the AIDS Epidemic." *Horizon*, November, 1987, 13-20.

Kimmelman, Michael. "Bitter Harvest: AIDS and the Arts." *The New York Times*, March 19, 1989, 2-6.

Shewey, Don, ed. *Out Front: Contemporary Gay and Lesbian Plays*. New York: Grove Press, 1988.

—James B. Graves

See also AIDS; *Angels in America*; Coming out; Kramer, Larry

Norris, Frank

BORN: Chicago, Illinois; March 5, 1870

DIED: San Francisco, California; October 25, 1902

PRINCIPAL WORKS: *McTeague*, 1899; *The Octopus*, 1901; *The Pit*, 1903; *A Deal in Wheat and Other Stories of the New and Old West*, 1903; *The Responsibilities of the Novelist and Other Literary Essays*, 1903; *The Third Circle*, 1909; *Vandover and the Brute*, 1914

IDENTITIES: European American; West and Southwest

SIGNIFICANT ACHIEVEMENT: Norris is one of the first writers in the United States to express class conflict in a manner greatly influenced by naturalism.

Frank Norris' creativity first showed itself in his ability to paint. His family moved from San Francisco to Europe, first London, then Paris in 1887, so that he could study art. His career as a painter was short and the family returned to San Francisco.

American naturalist writer Frank Norris. (Library of Congress)

Travel was a significant part of Norris' life. In addition to Europe, during his short life he made trips to South Africa and Cuba. In the United States, he lived on both coasts for long periods of time. Despite his travels, Norris is primarily a novelist of the American West. His novels and short stories are about poor, hardworking people who must struggle not only with nature and the disasters it can deliver to them but also with rich and powerful men and corporations, who can be equally brutal.

An author who influenced Norris was Émile Zola, a French novelist of the late nineteenth century who created the literary school of naturalism. Norris was introduced to Zola's works when Norris studied for a year at Harvard University. In Zola and Norris, naturalism was a literary technique for the representation of social and economic class differences and class warfare. Particularly in Norris' work, laboring classes are symbolic of victimized good and upper classes are symbolic of tyrannical evil. For example, in *The Octopus* the central conflict is between some California farmers and the Southern Pacific Railroad.

Norris did not write with the scientific objectivity that was part of the intellectual foundation of naturalism. His works often contain romantic idealism and even melodrama. Norris defends this practice in an essay titled "A Plea for Romantic Fiction." In this essay he describes realism as "harsh, loveless, colorless, and blunt," whereas romanticism can get at the colorful, "living heart of things."

The Octopus and *The Pit* were to be the first two books in a trilogy about wheat. The books illustrate Norris' observations and ideas about economics and social forces. He was planning a trip to India to get information for the third book when he died of complications from appendicitis. He was living in San Francisco and was thirty-two years old.

SUGGESTED READINGS

Hochman, Barbara. *The Art of Frank Norris.* Columbia: University of Missouri Press, 1988.

McElrath, J. *Frank Norris Revisited.* New York: Twayne, 1992.

Marchand, Ernest. *Frank Norris: A Study.* New York: Hippocrene Books, 1964.

—*Judith L. Steininger*

See also American identity: West and the frontier; Dreiser, Theodore; Economics of identity

Northeast, the. *See* American identity: Northeast

Notes from the Underground

AUTHOR: Fyodor Dostoevski (1821-1881)

FIRST PUBLISHED: *Zapiski iz podpolya,* 1864 (English translation, 1913)

IDENTITIES: Religion; world

Fyodor Dostoevski's *Notes from the Underground* has two sections, which at first reading are only obliquely related. Part 1 begins: "I am a sick man. . . . I am a spiteful man. I am a most unpleasant man," with the narrator, the underground man, then proceeding to demonstrate this negative self appraisal to a hostile, imaginary audience, whom he periodically addresses as "gentlemen." Part 1 relates the underground man's cynical views of human nature, especially the human nature of "modern man." In a sometimes rambling, often cogent monologue, the underground man assaults the constructs of societies founded upon the ideals of rationalism, the philosophy that humans are logical creatures capable of solving any problem, thereby developing the perfect utopian society. The underground man hates such a society since it leaves little room for choice. Making a rational decision, the underground man argues, involves very little of what is at the core of humanity—free will. Giving examples of people in history choosing the irrational over the rational, the underground man demonstrates the contradiction of identity: Making the logical choice brings happiness, yet it does not express freedom. The expression of freedom and of individual identity is bound to the irrational, to do intentionally what is not right. The wrong choice brings suffering. This "negative freedom," which defines personality and produces suffering, is the paradox of the soul. The underground man is condemned to brood upon this dilemma.

Beginning with the poem "Apropos of Wet Snow," part 2 illustrates the underground man's ideas expressed in part 1. The underground man relates a series of incidents from sixteen years before, when he was twenty-four. The incidents occurred because of his desire for self-humiliation. After an officer brushes the underground man aside in order to break up a fight, the underground man gains his "revenge" by bumping into him one day on a bridge—after two years of planning. Thrown into a lonely three-month depression because of this demeaning episode (the underground man is aware of the absurdity of his petty revenge), the underground man eventually craves companionship and reestablishes communication with four former schoolmates whom he loathes. Inviting himself to a farewell party for one of the group, the underground man insults the men and acts atrociously but begs to be included when they decide to go to a brothel. The four, however, abandon the underground man, who sleeps with a young prostitute named Liza. Enamored by the power he holds over her, the underground man delights in humiliating her, but when she unexpectedly confesses her sins and renounces prostitution, thanking him for his kindness, he is shocked and leaves. Weeks later, when the underground man is involved in a ludicrous argument about wages with his servant, Liza appears to thank him for prompting her to engage a more wholesome life. Devastated that she should see him so petty, he forces himself upon her and spitefully casts money at her afterward. As she runs off, the underground man feels some guilt but only halfheartedly pursues, soon giving up. The novel ends with the comment that although the underground man has written more, "we might as well stop here."

SUGGESTED READINGS

Mochulsky, Konstantin. *Dostoevski: His Life and Work*. Translated by Michael Minihan. Princeton, N.J.: Princeton University Press, 1967.
Wasiolek, Edward. *Dostoevsky: The Major Fiction*. Cambridge, Mass.: The MIT Press, 1964.
Wellek, Rene, ed. *Dostoevsky: A Collection of Critical Essays*. Englewood Cliffs, N.J.: Prentice-Hall, 1963.

—*Dana Anthony Grove*

See also Dostoevski, Fyodor; Existentialism; Underground man: a literary archetype

Notes of a Native Son

AUTHOR: James Baldwin (1924-1987)
FIRST PUBLISHED: 1955
IDENTITIES: African American

James Baldwin is a fine novelist, as such works as *Go Tell It on the Mountain* (1953) and *Giovanni's Room* (1956) prove. Many readers consider his nonfiction to be even finer than his fiction. His essays, which may be found in collections such as *Notes of a Native Son* (1955) and *Nobody Knows My Name: More Notes of a Native Son* (1972), are passionate and often scathing.

His personal feelings and experiences are freely expressed in his essays. His anger at black-white relations in America, his ambivalence toward his father, and his thoughts on such writers as Truman Capote, Norman Mailer, and William Faulkner are displayed openly. He is honest, and made enemies for it. On the other hand, he has many readers' respect for saying what he thinks.

Notes of a Native Son was Baldwin's first nonfiction collection, and it contains his "Autobiographical Notes" and three sections totaling ten essays. In "Autobiographical Notes," Baldwin sketches his early career—his Harlem birth, his childhood interest in writing, his journey to France. "Autobiographical Notes" and various essays describe the difficult process of Baldwin's establishment of his identity. Part 1 of *Notes of a Native Son* includes three essays. "Everybody's Protest Novel" examines *Uncle Tom's Cabin: Or, Life Among the Lowly* (1852), which Baldwin considers self-righteous and so sentimental as to be dishonest. "Many Thousands Gone" examines Richard Wright's *Native Son* (1940), which Baldwin describes as badly flawed. "*Carmen Jones*: The Dark Is Light Enough" is another biting review, of the Hollywood motion picture musical *Carmen Jones* (1955). Baldwin says that the film lacks imagination and is condescending to blacks. Part 2 contains three essays. "The Harlem Ghetto" is one of the most powerful, digging into the physical and emotional turmoil of Harlem, including problems between blacks and Jews. "Journey to Atlanta" looks at an African American singing group's first trip to the South. It is a humorous, cynical, look at the treatment that the group, which included two of Baldwin's brothers, received. "Notes of a Native Son" examines Baldwin's anger and despair after his father's death.

Part 3 contains four essays. "Encounter on the Seine: Black Meets Brown" and "A Question of Identity" are about the feelings and attitudes of Americans in Paris in the 1940's and 1950's. "Equal in Paris" is Baldwin's account of being arrested and jailed, temporarily, in a case involving some stolen sheets that he did not steal. Baldwin describes the insight he had while in the hands of the French police: that they, in dealing with him, were not engaging in the racist cat-and-mouse game used by police in the United States. Finally, "Stranger in the Village" discusses Baldwin's time in a Swiss village and the astonished curiosity of people who had never seen a black person before. In all these essays, Baldwin explores his world and himself.

SUGGESTED READINGS

Leeming, David. *James Baldwin*. New York: Alfred A. Knopf, 1994.

Rosset, Lisa. *James Baldwin*. New York: Chelsea House, 1989.

—*Charles A. Gramlich*

See also African American identity; Baldwin, James; Civil Rights movement

Novel Without a Name

AUTHOR: Duong Thu Huong (1947-   ); translators Phan Huy Duong and Nina McPherson

FIRST PUBLISHED: *Tiêu thuyêt vô ðê*, 1990 (English translation, 1995)

IDENTITIES: Vietnamese American; world

Novel Without a Name is the story of a young platoon commander, Quan, who struggles to find his identity in the confusion of the last days of the Vietnam War. Ten years before the novel opens, Quan joins the army with his boyhood friends, Bien and Luong. Each represents a different response to the search for identity in the chaos of war. By the time of the novel's opening, Luong has risen in the ranks of the army; he is an officer at division headquarters and deputy to the commander. He accepts and disseminates Party ideology, finding a space for himself in the bureaucracy of war. Bien, on the other hand, never rises above sergeant. The deprivations of the war lead him to mental illness, and he is imprisoned as a lunatic. Quan's struggle for identity is the most complicated.

At the heart of the book is Quan's journey, taken under Luong's orders, into the interior of Vietnam to free Bien from his imprisonment. As Quan travels, he reflects, dreams, and hallucinates about the horrors of the war. Quan recalls the glory showered on the three friends when they joined the army, contrasting it to the death and destruction around him. He strives to find meaning in his encounters with an old man and child, with a woman whose job it is to bury the dead, and with a skeleton he finds hanging in a hammock. When he encounters Party officials on a train and hears their cynical assessment of the Vietnamese people, he begins to suspect that his only identity is as a puppet, as someone who follows orders from above and enforces those orders on those below.

In the final pages of the novel, a confrontation with one of his privates who has destroyed a cache of American medicine startles Quan into the realization that all the death and loss has been meaningless. This bleak epiphany is underscored when Quan sees his first American, a prisoner, and realizes that he no longer hates Americans. He sees the American as a pawn of another government, just as Quan himself is the pawn of his own government.

Although North Americans have had ample opportunity to consider the American experience in Vietnam, they have had little chance to view the war from a North Vietnamese perspective. *Novel Without a Name* demonstrates the futility of war from the point of view of the common soldier.

SUGGESTED READINGS
Allen, Douglas, and Ngo Vinh Ling, eds. *Coming to Terms: Indochina, the United States, and the War.* Boulder, Colo.: Westview Press, 1991.
Bao Ninh. *The Sorrow of War: A Novel of North Vietnam.* Translated by Phan Than Hao and edited by Frank Palmos. New York: Pantheon Books, 1995.
Huynh, Jade Ngoc Quang. *South Wind Changing.* St. Paul, Minn.: Graywolf Press, 1994.
—Diane Andrews Henningfeld
See also Hayslip, Le Ly; Vietnam War; *When Heaven and Earth Changed Places*

O

Oates, Joyce Carol
BORN: Lockport, New York; June 16, 1938

PRINCIPAL WORKS: *A Garden of Earthly Delights*, 1967; *them*, 1969; *Bellefleur*, 1980; *Marya: A Life*, 1986; *You Must Remember This*, 1987; *Where Are You Going, Where Have You Been? Selected Early Stories*, 1993; *Will You Always Love Me? and Other Stories*, 1996

IDENTITIES: European American; family; religion; women

SIGNIFICANT ACHIEVEMENT: Oates's fiction describes the psychological conflicts of American society.

Joyce Carol Oates was reared in New York. She was graduated from Syracuse University and earned a master's degree from the University of Wisconsin. In 1962, Oates and her husband Raymond J. Smith settled in Detroit. The poverty, industry, social turmoil, and riots of the inner city provided fodder for Oates's creative imagination. Consequently she utilized the setting in several works, including the novel *them* and the story "How I Contemplated the World from the Detroit House of Correction and Began My Life Over Again."

During the 1970's, Oates and her husband lived in Canada, teaching English at the University of Windsor in Ontario. While in Canada, the couple also began publication of a literary magazine, *The Ontario Review*. Since 1978, Oates has taught writing at Princeton University in Princeton, New Jersey. To describe Oates' writing career as prolific seems an understatement. She admits to writing more than four hundred stories. She has published more than eighteen short-story collections, several volumes of poetry, and more than nineteen novels. In addition, she writes book reviews, plays, and literary essays. Several of her works, including "Where Are You Going, Where Have You Been?" have been adapted to film. Oates describes her writing as "realistic allegory." Her fiction explores the conflict inherent in the attempt to define oneself in a turbulent society.

Prolific author Joyce Carol Oates (Norman Seeff)

Oates's skills as an artist excel in form as well as theme. For example, her series of novels *Bellefleur*, *A Bloodsmoor Romance* (1982), and *Mysteries of Winterthurn* (1984) combine American history with elements of gothic romance, horror, and detective fiction. In addition, she has written several suspense novels under the pseudonym Rosamond Smith. Thus, Oates uses a variety of styles to portray social dilemmas.

Oates, as have other twentieth century writers, uses violence in her fiction to depict the chaotic, unsettled aspects of twentieth century American life. The violent situations in Oates's fiction often include incidents of rape, incest, murder, or suicide. These violent conflicts drive many of her characters to the edge of madness. Hence, Oates portrays the reality of the American experience and its complexities.

SUGGESTED READINGS

Bloom, Harold. *Joyce Carol Oates*. New York: Chelsea House, 1981.

Friedman, Ellen G. "Joyce Carol Oates." In *Modern American Women Writers*, edited by Elaine Showalter. New York: Macmillan, 1991.

Johnson, Greg. *Understanding Joyce Carol Oates*. Columbia: University of South Carolina Press, 1987.

Waller, G. F. *Dreaming American: Obsession and Transcendence in the Fiction of Joyce Carol Oates*. Baton Rouge: Louisiana State University Press, 1979.

—*Paula M. Miller*

See also American Dream; American identity: Northeast; Class and identity; Erotic identity; Rape; Violence; *Where Are You Going, Where Have You Been?*

Obasan

AUTHOR: Joy Kogawa (Joy Nozomi Goichi, 1935-   )
FIRST PUBLISHED: 1981
IDENTITIES: Canada; Japanese American; women

Joy Kogawa's *Obasan* has forced critics to include Asian Canadians in their study of ethnic literature; it is such a fine work no critic can ignore it. Kogawa has defined political and cultural connections between the Japanese immigrants of Canada and America. Both groups were held in internment camps during World War II. Their property was seized, and their families were often separated. In Canada and the United States the men of the families fought for their new countries while their wives, children, and siblings remained interred. Arguably one of the finest literary renderings of this experience, *Obasan* investigates what happened as a result of these practices.

Naomi Nakane, the protagonist of *Obasan*, appears emotionally paralyzed at the beginning of the novel. Unable to move beyond her own past in the camps and unable to reconcile the loss of her parents, Naomi has retreated into silence and isolation. Canada has essentially told Japanese Canadians that they are untrustworthy, second-class citizens at best, so Naomi retreats from her ethnic identity as well. Her Aunt Emily, however, is articulate, learned, professional, and politically active. Aunt Emily encourages Naomi to learn about the terrible things done to Japanese Canadians and to act on her anger. Naomi gains the impetus for change.

Shortly before the family's relocation to the internment camps (when Naomi is a child), Mrs. Nakane leaves to visit family in Japan. She never returns and the family carefully guards the secret of her fate. It is only as a thirty-six-year-old adult that Naomi is given the letters that reveal her mother's story of disfigurement and subsequent death as a result of the atomic bombing. The mother, herself, has imposed silence on the other family members. Naomi tries to engage her mother's presence, to heal the rift between them, although her mother is not physically there. In writing the novel Kogawa has constructed an elaborate attempt to embrace the absent voice, to contain the mother in some manner useful to Naomi's own construction of identity.

Poetic passages describe this imagined reunion. Dream sequences also punctuate the narrative, providing the touching lyricism that moves the novel beyond most of the literature written around the internment camp experience. Bound with the sociopolitical analysis provided by Aunt Emily and Naomi's personal history, the novel sets high standards for literature on ethnic identity.

SUGGESTED READINGS

Cheung, King-Kok. *Articulate Silences: Hisaye Yamamoto, Maxine Hong Kingston, Joy Kogawa*. Ithaca, N.Y.: Cornell University Press, 1993.

Davidson, Arnold E. *Writing Against the Silence: Joy Kogawa's "Obasan."* Toronto: ECW Press, 1993.

Lim, Shirley Geok-Lin. "Japanese American Women's Life Stories: Maternality in Monica Sone's *Nisei Daughter* and Joy Kogawa's *Obasan*." *Feminist Studies* 16, no. 2 (Summer, 1990): 289-312.

Wong, Sau-ling Cynthia. *Reading Asian American Literature: From Necessity to Extravagance.* Princeton, N.J.: Princeton University Press, 1993.

—Julie Tharp

See also Asian American identity: China, Japan, and Korea; Japanese American internment; Kogawa, Joy

O'Connor, Flannery

BORN: Savannah, Georgia; March 25, 1925

DIED: Milledgeville, Georgia; August 3, 1964

PRINCIPAL WORKS: *Wise Blood*, 1952; *A Good Man Is Hard to Find*, 1955; *The Violent Bear It Away*, 1960; *Everything That Rises Must Converge*, 1965

IDENTITIES: European American; religion; South; women

SIGNIFICANT ACHIEVEMENT: O'Connor's short stories and novels combine tragic and comic visions, showing the surprising possibilities of God's grace in a world darkened by sin.

Flannery O'Connor summed up her identity in a threefold characterization, calling herself "a Catholic, and a Southerner, and a writer." Her Catholicism is evident in every story, though few seem to be overtly religious in the conventional sense. Similarly, the South is an element in every story, even those few not set in the South. Finally, as a writer, she experienced the ironic detachment that came from being unusual; her fiction is peopled with misfits and with "normal" Southerners.

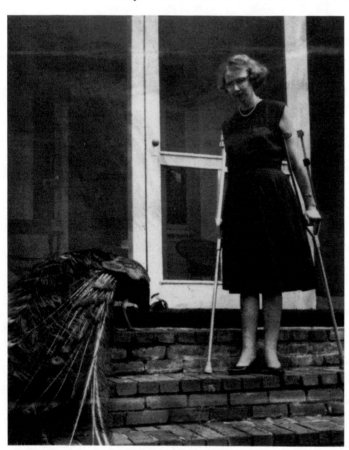

Flannery O'Connor's short stories often examine religious issues. (Joe McTyre)

Her Catholicism and her Southern identity provided a sense of rootedness for O'Connor. Milledgeville, Georgia, an ancestral home to which the O'Connors moved when Flannery was thirteen, had been the state capital before the Civil War. The Catholic church there was built on land donated by one of O'Connor's ancestors. O'Connor's fiction is peopled by familiar Southern types—the itinerant preacher, the illiterate field hand, the former or would-be aristocrat. Such types O'Connor found not in books but in her home town.

Her Catholicism made O'Connor not so much an outsider as a member of a minority culture within an overwhelmingly Protestant South. At Peabody High School in Milledgeville, O'Connor earned a reputation not as a writer but as a cartoonist. She did not continue cartooning beyond college, but O'Connor is often thought to show the cartoonist's touch in her characterizations. Her characters are drawn in bold, exaggerated strokes that rather than distort nature, reveal a hidden truth.

O'Connor remained in Milledgeville during college, receiving her B.A. in 1945 from the Georgia State College for Women. By then she had already been writing short fiction, samples of which brought her acceptance into the Master of

Fine Arts program at the University of Iowa. A portion of her master's thesis was published as a short story the following year, and she earned her M.F.A. in 1947. A series of short story publications followed in such prestigious magazines as *Mademoiselle*, *Sewanee Review*, and *Partisan Review*. Having become an established professional, O'Connor, like so many young American writers, moved to New York in 1949.

By the end of 1950, however, O'Connor was diagnosed with disseminated lupus, the disease that would claim her life. In 1951, she moved back to her mother's farm near Milledgeville, where she remained until her death in 1964. In the years between, O'Connor produced most of the fiction for which she is best known. These works received critical and popular approval, winning five O. Henry Awards, two major grants, and two honorary doctorates.

SUGGESTED READINGS

Asals, Frederick. *Flannery O'Connor: The Imagination of Extremity*. Athens: University of Georgia Press, 1982.

Bloom, Harold. *Flannery O'Connor*. New York: Chelsea House, 1986.

Shloss, Carol. *Flannery O'Connor's Dark Comedies: The Limits of Inference*. Baton Rouge: Louisiana State University Press, 1980.

Walters, Dorothy. *Flannery O'Connor*. Boston: Twayne, 1973.

—John R. Holmes

See also American identity: South; Catholicism; "Good Country People"; "Good Man Is Hard To Find, A"; "Revelation"

Okada, John

BORN: Seattle, Washington; September, 1923
DIED: Seattle, Washington; February, 1971
PRINCIPAL WORK: *No-No Boy*, 1957
IDENTITIES: Japanese American; West and Southwest
SIGNIFICANT ACHIEVEMENT: Okada introduced Japanese American literature to the United States.

John Okada was a Nisei, or second-generation Japanese American. He grew up in the Pacific Northwest and witnessed the internment of 120,000 Japanese Americans during World War II. Unlike the character Ichiro in *No-No Boy*, however, Okada was not a no-no boy (a person who answered no to two critical questions on the loyalty questionnaire—refusing to serve in the American armed forces and refusing to forswear allegiance to Japan and pledge loyalty to the United States). He volunteered for military service and was sent to Japanese held islands to exhort Japanese soldiers to surrender. The experience helped him shape his perspective on the war.

After he was discharged from the military in 1946, Okada went to the University of Washington and Columbia University. He earned two B.A. degrees and an M.A. degree studying, in his own words, "narrative and dramatic writing, history, sociology." He started working on *No-No Boy* while he was an assistant in the Business Reference Department of the Seattle Public Library and at the Detroit Public Library. After a stint as a technical writer for Chrysler Missile Operations of Sterling Township, Michigan, he and his wife Dorothy moved back to Seattle. *No-No Boy* was completed in 1957. Okada had a hard time trying to find publishers who were interested in his work. *No-No Boy* was first published by Charles Tuttle of Tokyo. After Okada died, his wife offered all of his manuscripts, including the one of his second novel, to the Japanese American Research Project at the University of California at Los Angeles. They were rejected. Dorothy burned them shortly after, when she was preparing to move.

Okada was proud to be a Japanese American. He examined the double consciousness of the Japanese American community. *No-No Boy* portrays the psychological confusion and distress experienced by many Japanese Americans, especially second generation Japanese Americans (U.S. citizens by birth, culturally Japanese) during and after World War II. *No-No Boy* portrays the struggle of those who are caught between two worlds at war.

SUGGESTED READINGS

Chin, Frank. Afterword to *No-No Boy*, by John Okada. Seattle: University of Washington Press, 1976.

Kim, Elaine H. *Asian American Literature*. Philadelphia: Temple University Press, 1982.

—*Qun Wang*

See also Acculturation; Asian American identity: China, Japan, and Korea; Identity crisis; Japanese American internment

Older Americans. *See* Aging

Olsen, Tillie

BORN: Omaha, Nebraska; January 14, 1913

PRINCIPAL WORKS: *Tell Me a Riddle*, 1961; *Yonnondio: From the Thirties*, 1974; *Silences*, 1978

IDENTITIES: European American; Jewish; women

SIGNIFICANT ACHIEVEMENT: Olsen has given voice to the voiceless, capturing their point of view and helping them resist those who are more powerful.

Tillie Olsen began writing early in life. Circumstances, however, silenced her pen for decades. While rearing four children and working at a variety of jobs, she was only able to write fragments. Throughout her life, however, she has remained active and involved, helping laborers organize, giving encouragement to fledgling writers, and chronicling the life of the working class.

Olsen, who left school after the eleventh grade, has worked on behalf of laborers, including the packing house workers in Kansas City and the dock workers in San Francisco. She has acted on her belief that by working together, people can have a significant impact. She is sensitive, however, to those who must struggle alone and has paid them tribute in her short fiction, lectures, and essays. *Silences*, for example, includes references to a multitude of little-known writers, and chronicles many of the circumstances that may have contributed to their obscurity.

Olsen refuses to allow circumstances to dictate the literary canon. Instead, she is intent upon

Tillie Olsen, author of Tell Me a Riddle *(1961).* (Leonda Fiske)

rediscovering lost classics, such as Rebecca Harding Davis' "Life in the Iron Mills" (1861), and upon encouraging academics to reconsider their reading lists. From her point of view, many deserving authors, along with their visions, have been overlooked as a result of groundless aesthetic and cultural biases.

Olsen might have been among the unheralded but, in her case, the social climate of the 1960's and 1970's afforded her a wide hearing. Since that time, each of her published works has been eagerly awaited and greeted with enthusiasm in the literary world. In recognition of her talent and her achievements, she has secured numerous fellowships, grants, and honorary degrees. She has served as a writer-in-residence and visiting lecturer throughout the United States. She has also won numerous awards. These awards are a testimony to Olsen's importance as a writer who has given others not only memorable portraits but also a fresh context in which to approach literature and life.

SUGGESTED READINGS

Coiner, Constance. *Better Red: The Writing and*

Resistance of Tillie Olsen and Meridel Le Sueur. New York: Oxford University Press, 1995.

Faulkner, Mara. *Protest and Possibility in the Writing of Tillie Olsen*. Charlottesville: University Press of Virginia, 1993.

Nelson, Kay Hoyle, and Nancy Huse, eds. *The Critical Response to Tillie Olsen*. Westport, Conn.: Greenwood Press, 1994.

Orr, Elaine Neil. *Tillie Olsen and a Feminist Spiritual Vision*. Jackson: University Press of Mississippi, 1987.

Pearlman, Mickey, and Abby H. P. Werlock. *Tillie Olsen*. Boston: Twayne, 1991.

—*C. Lynn Munro*

See also Canon; Economics of identity; *Silences*; *Tell Me a Riddle*

On the Road

Author: Jack Kerouac (1922-1969)
First published: 1957
Identities: European American

Jack Kerouac spontaneously wrote the unedited bulk of *On the Road* on a 120-foot roll of teletype paper in 1951. There is some disagreement about how much editing was required of him before it was finally accepted for publication, by which time he considered the novel somewhat passé. His *Visions of Cody* (1972) treats approximately the same period as is covered in *On the Road* from a variant and more positive perspective while delving into the narrator's chronic identity split. *On the Road* became the bible of the Beat generation and Kerouac's most famous work, a vital contribution to his life story as told in his Legend of Duluoz novels.

On the Road's cross-continental journeys are based on Kerouac's trips, mostly by car and bus and often accompanied by his friend Neal Cassady, the frenetic, charismatic, independent scholar from the West. Cassady's name in the novel is Dean Moriarty. The novel begins with Dean and Sal Paradise (Kerouac) meeting in New York City and progresses through four mostly fast-paced trips, back and forth between New York and California, up and down the Eastern Seaboard, along the Gulf Coast, and down into Mexico, with notable stopovers in Denver and New Orleans, the latter to visit Old Bull Lee (William S. Burroughs). The open road, poverty, drugs, alcohol, jazz, hunger, sex, speed, and characters met along the way create intense situations that allow the travelers to observe, react, and consider while becoming more familiar with their own identities.

Narrated in Kerouac's rhythmic first-person stream-of-consciousness style and in the vernacular of his subculture, *On the Road* carries on the literary tradition that travel imparts knowledge. In this American novel, outward movement is initiated in part by Paradise's confusion and Moriarty's exuberance. Travel and motion trigger inward exploration for Paradise the introvert and Moriarty the extrovert. Insights are often traumatic, as Paradise discovers when he wakens in a Des Moines YMCA not knowing who he is. This frightening reduction to blank-slate status returns him to his beginnings and readies him for the lessons to follow. Ed Dunkel's comment that Dunkel is in fact a ghost when he walks familiar Times Square sidewalks brings to Paradise the sobering realization that he too is no more nor less than an embodied spirit with an expiration date. Driving toward a Mexican pueblo, Paradise feels that he is driving "across the world and into the places where we would finally learn ourselves," but despite the camaraderie and reverie of the road, Paradise's view is much the same at journey's end as at its beginning, when he likens Moriarty and Carlo Marx (Allen Ginsberg) to "the man with the dungeon stone and the gloom, rising from the underground, the sordid hipsters of America, a new beat generation that I was slowly joining," and of which at the close Paradise is an initiate.

Suggested readings

French, Warren. *Jack Kerouac*. Boston: Twayne, 1986.

Gaffié, Luc. *Jack Kerouac: The New Picaroon*. New York: Postillion Press, 1977.

Kerouac, Jack. *On the Road*, edited by Scott Donaldson. New York: Penguin Books, 1979.

Hipkiss, Robert. *Jack Kerouac: Prophet of the New Romanticism*. Lawrence: Regents Press of Kansas, 1976.

—*Mary L. Otto Lang*

See also Countercultures; *Dharma Bums, The*; Drugs; Ginsberg, Allen; *Howl*; Kerouac, Jack; Popular culture

On These I Stand: An Anthology of the Best Poems of Countée Cullen

AUTHOR: Countée Cullen (1903-1946)
FIRST PUBLISHED: 1947
IDENTITIES: African American; religion

On These I Stand: An Anthology of the Best Poems of Countée Cullen is a collection of the formerly published poems for which Countée Cullen wanted to be remembered. Written during the 1920's and 1930's, these poems are from such works as *Color* (1925), *Copper Sun* (1927), *The Ballad of the Brown Girl* (1928), *The Black Christ and Other Poems* (1929), and *The Medea and Some Poems* (1935). Cullen also includes six new poems on subjects ranging from a tribute to John Brown ("A Negro Mother's Lullaby") to the evolution from birth to death ("Dear Friends and Gentle Hearts"). Cullen maintains the style of classical lyricists such as British poet John Keats in this collection, using rhymed couplets, ballads, or sonnet forms.

Color emphasizes racial themes and shows the influence of ideas associated with the Harlem Renaissance. There are religious overtones in some of the poems about the burden of racial oppression. The speaker recognizes a loss of faith but laments the racial prejudice against more religious blacks in "Pagan Prayer." Cullen's Simon the Cyrenian transcends his race by helping Christ bear the cross in "Simon the Cyrenian Speaks." The poem for which Cullen is widely known, "Yet Do I Marvel," questions the value of God's decision to give creative talent to a black person, whose talents are ignored.

Cullen joined other Harlem Renaissance writers in using African motifs. In "Heritage," one of the longer poems in *Color*, the speaker asks the question, What is Africa to me? An exotic and stereotyped image of Africa emerges, and the question is unanswered.

The selections from *Copper Sun* and *The Black Christ and Other Poems* show that gradually Cullen moved away from ideas about racial identity to those that preoccupy a Romantic mind influenced by Keats, Percy Bysshe Shelley, or Edna St. Vincent Millay. There are numerous poems on love, death, and the difficulties of the creative spirit in overcoming the burdens of the physical self.

"The Black Christ" is an extended narrative poem that demonstrates Cullen's love of the Romantic or transcendent, his interest in religious themes, and his concern about the plight of African Americans. The narrator, a black Southerner, witnesses the lynching of his brother, Jim. As Jim is enjoying a spring day with a white woman, a white man insults the woman and attacks Jim, who responds by killing him. Jim's lynching tests the narrator's faith in God. As the narrator berates his mother for her faith, Jim appears, resurrected, helping the narrator reclaim his faith. To complete *On These I Stand*, Cullen chose examples from *The Lost Zoo* (1940), his book of poems for children. "The Wakeupworld" and "The-Snake-That-Walked-Upon-His-Tail" instruct and delight. The collection *On These I Stand* attests Cullen's Romantic vision, his attraction to Harlem Renaissance themes, and his depiction of the African American experience.

SUGGESTED READINGS

Baker, Houston A. *Afro-American Poetics: Revisions of Harlem and the Black Aesthetic*. Madison: University of Wisconsin Press, 1988.

Huggins, Nathan. *Harlem Renaissance*. New York: Oxford University Press, 1971.

Turner, Darwin T. *In a Minor Chord: Three Afro-American Writers and Their Search for Identity*. Carbondale: Southern Illinois University Press, 1971.

—*Australia Tarver*

See also African American identity; Cullen, Countée; Harlem Renaissance; Religion and identity